Las 8 Leyes d

Libro de actividades para colorear

Este sorprendente tesoro de salud es de:

____

Las citas de las Escrituras están tomadas de la versión de King James de la Santa Biblia.

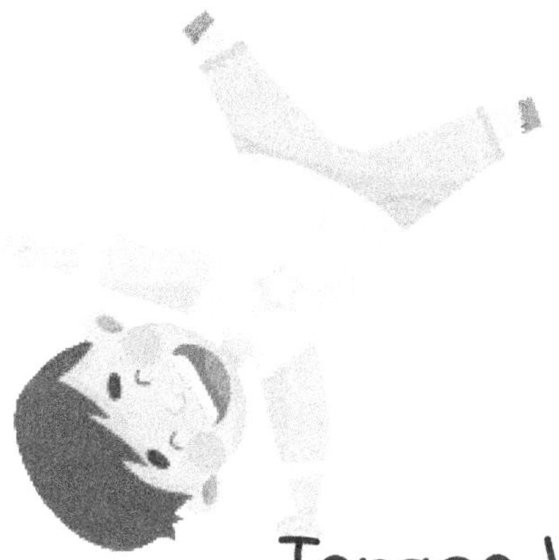

Terase Wallace, RN

Portada diseñada por Rocel Hernandez
Ilustraciones interiores de Rocel Hernandez

Earnest Ink Publications
www.earnestink.net
reader@earnestink.net

Acompañanos en este apasionante viaje a través de las 8 Leyes de la Salud!

¡Nutrición!

¡Ejercicio!

¡Agua!

¡Luz Solar!

¡Templanza!

¡Aire!

¡Descanso!

¡Confianza en DIOS!

Las 8 Leyes de la Salud, forman un acrónimo:

N - Nutrition

E - Exercise

W - Water

S - Sunlight

T - Temperance

A - Air

R - Rest

T - Trust in God

"Todo lo puedo en
Cristo que me
fortalece"
Filipenses 4:13

NEWSTART

NEWSTART es una marca registrada de
la Universidad de Weimar. Uso permitido.

Nuestros hermosos cuerpos
fueron creados por Dios..

¿Puedes nombrar las
partes del cuerpo?

"Te alabaré, porque asombrosa y
maravillosamente he sido hecho;maravillosas
son tus obras,y mi alma lo sabe muy bien"
Salmos 139.14

¿Te falta alguno?
Aquí tienes algunas pistas.

Cabeza
Ceja
Ojo
Nariz
Boca
Barbilla
Pecho
Estómago
Pierna
Rodilla
Pie
Dedo del pie

Frente
Mejilla
Diente
Lengua
Labios
Hombro
Espalda
Cintura
Cadera
Muslo
Tobillo

Rizos
Cabello
Oreja
Cuello
Brazo
Codo
Mano
Dedo
Nalga
Talón

NUTRICIÓN

"Si, pues, coméis o bebéis, o hacéis otra cosa,
hacedlo todo para la gloria de Dios"
I Corintios 10:31

¿Por qué es importante para nosotros consumir frutas y vegetales?

Porque tienen vitamina C que fortalecen nuestros huesos y dientes ¡y nos ayudan a correr, saltar y jugar!

Comer distintos tipos de frutas y verduras y de diversos colores nos protege de enfermedades.

Las frutas nos dan la energía que necesitamos para jugar, aprender y explorar.

Tienen muchos nutrientes que ayudan a nuestro cuerpo a crecer fuertes y sanos.

Ellos ayudan a que nuestro cerebro funcione mejor para hacernos más inteligentes.

¿Cúal es tu favorita?

____

¡Comer muchas frutas, vegetales, frutos secos, legumbres y semillas nos mantiene sanos y fuertes!

¡Come sano; sé feliz!

Dato Curioso:

¿Sabías que las hojas de las piñas son utilizadas para hacer ropa?

¡La tela se llama fibra de hoja de piña!

¡¡Vaya!!
¡Es genial!

¡¡La comida que comemos puede cambiar como se sienten nuestro cuerpo y nuestro cerebro!!

Consumir frutas, vegetales, frutos secos, legumbres y semillas nos ayuda a resolver problemas de manera rápida y correcta.

Dato Curioso:

¿Sabias que las zanahorias están compuestase en un 88 % de agua?

También vienen en distintos colores como naranja, morado, rojo, banco amarillo y negro. ¡Disfrútalas todas!

Encuentra y colorea las frutas y vegetales.

Aquí tienes algunas pistas: nabo, manzana, brócoli, zanahoria, coliflor, berenjena, maíz, calabaza, guisantes y lechuga.

Ayuda a Carson a encontrar su camino a través del laberinto. ¡Necesita tomar la manzana para llevarla a la escuela!

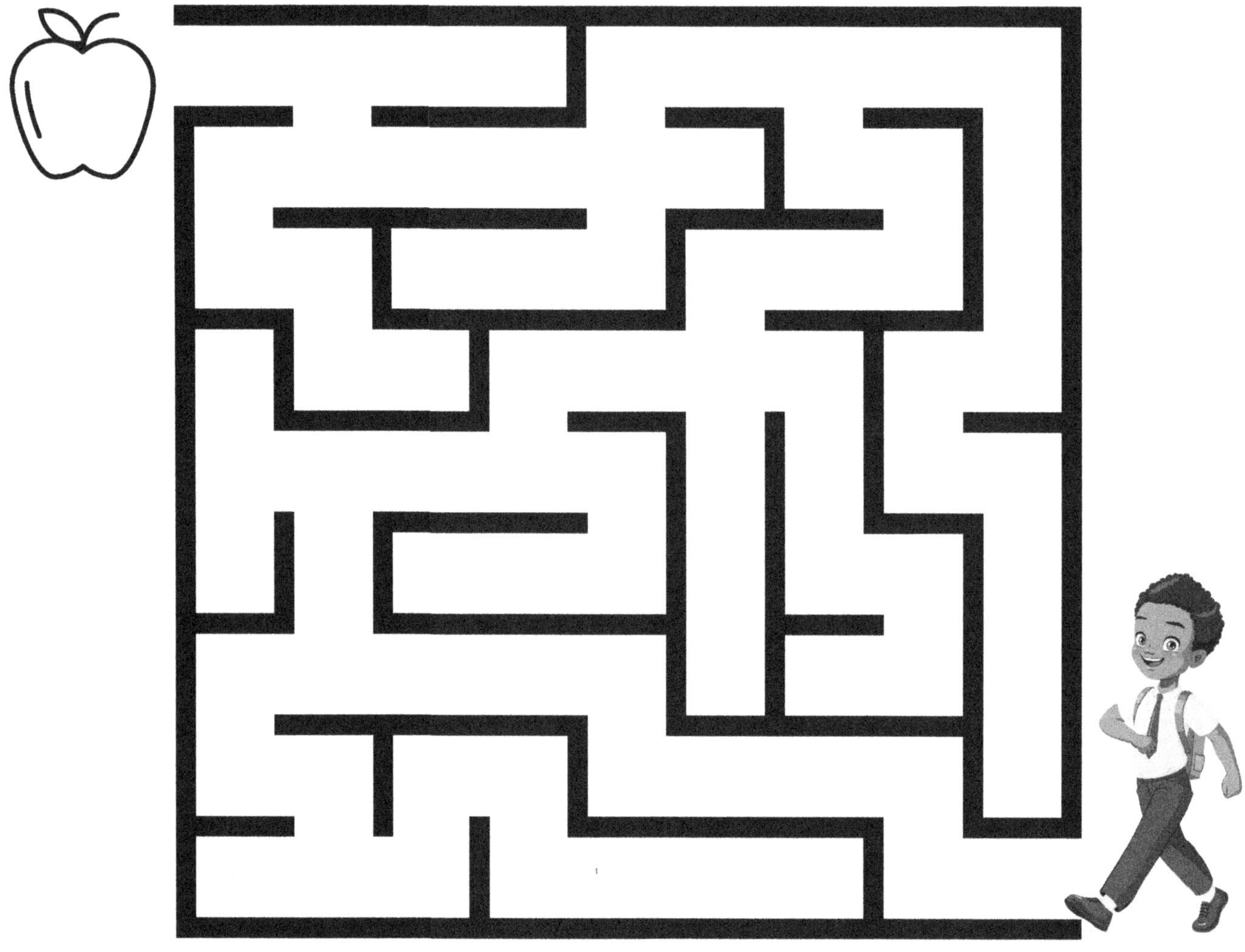

¡Una manzana al día mantiene alejado al doctor!

¡Es muy importante elegir comer alimentos saludables!

Alimentos Saludables | Alimentos no Saludables

¿Cuáles son las decisiones correctas que debo tomar?

Yo elijo comidas saludables para mantenerme lo más sano posible.

Los alimentos saludables son aquellos que vienen de una planta.

Dibuja líneas para conectar los alimentos saludables al círculo del centro.

Aquí hay algunas pistas:
Los alimentos saludables son las frutas, vegetales y frutos secos.

¡Asegúrate que tu comida contenga una gran parte de frutas o vegetales, como zanahorias, manzanas y brócoli. Luego agrega algunos frutos secos, granos, semillas y legumbres para hacerlas más deliciosas!

Cocinar en conjunto hace que la hora de comer sea más divertida y entrañable.

Comer juntos en familia hace que la hora de la comida sea muy especial.

Saborea los colores.
Siente el brillo.

Colorea el arcoíris
de buenos alimentos.

EJERCICIO

"Y anduvo Enoc con Dios, y
desapareció, porque le llevó Dios"
Genesis 5:24

Hacer ejercicios nos
hace más fuertes, más
inteligentes y más felices

Nos encanta caminar
a la escuela y en los
parques naturales.

Me gusta hacer
ejercicio en el parque.
¡Woohoo!

El ejercicio nos ayuda a mejorar el movimiento de nuestro cuerpo de distintas maneras y a ganar confianza en nosotros mismos..

Caminar después de comer ayuda a nuestro estómago a digerir mejor la comida. ¡Ayúdanos a encontrar a nuestro amigo Alex!

¡Guau!

Nosotros hacemos ejercicio jugando a la pelota.

Yo hago ejercicio saltando la cuerda.

¿De que otras maneras podemos hacer ejercicio?

Respuesta:_____________________

¿Puedes encontrar las palabras ocultas que muestran las distintas formas en que podemos hacer ejercicio?

D	E	A	E	X	C	O	R	R	E	R	B
C	O	N	F	U	S	E	D	Y	B	D	I
S	A	L	T	A	R	V	S	Z	N	F	C
U	F	R	U	S	T	J	A	T	E	D	I
P	G	Y	H	C	I	U	D	I	R	H	C
S	K	O	L	A	S	G	V	R	V	A	L
E	P	E	L	O	T	A	I	E	O	P	E
T	N	Q	R	E	W	R	Y	D	U	P	T
C	A	M	I	N	A	R	E	D	S	Y	A

Pelota
Jugar
Saltar
Correr
Bicicleta
Caminar

AGUA

"Mas el que bebiere del agua que yo le daré, no tendrá sed jamás; sino que el agua que yo le daré será en él una fuente de agua que salte para vida eterna."

Juan 4:14

Dato Curioso:

¿Sabías qué?
¿Nuestro cerebro tiene cerca de 75 % de agua?
¿El 90 % de nuestros pulmones son de agua?
¿El 85 % de nuestra sangre es agua?
¿Los músculos tienen 75 % de agua?
¿Sabías que la mayor parte de nuestro cuerpo, cerca del 70 %, está compuesto de agua?
¡Interesante, el 70 % de la tierra también es de agua!

¡Vaya!
¡¡Servimos a un gran y maravilloso Dios!!

¡Los niños de menos de ocho años necesitan al menos 4 tazas de agua al día!

Agua:

¡La elección cristalina para nosotros!

Prefiere el agua, en lugar de la soda, bebidas energéticas, bebidas altas en azúcar, jugos, o leche.
¡Tu cuerpo la necesita!

Es importante tomar
la decisión correcta.

Bebidas como la soda, el
café o el té, no nos da lo
que el cuerpo necesita.

Tomar agua en ayunas
durante la mañana es una
práctica saludable para todos..

¡Tomar agua nos
da energía!

¡Tomar agua nos
hace felices!

¡Tomar agua previene los
dolores de cabeza y
ayuda a la memoria!

¡Tomar agua nos ayuda a estar
sanos, ayuda al cuerpo a
sentirse mejor y fortalece
nuestro corazón!

LUZ DEL SOL

"La luz es agradable; qué hermoso es ver
el amanecer de un nuevo día."
Eclesiastés 11:7

La luz del sol elimina los gérmenes y nos mantiene sanos.

¡La luz solar aporta vitamina D, que fortalece nuestros huesos y dientes!

¡La luz del sol ayuda a mejorar nuestro estado de ánimo, nos ayuda a ser felices!

¡Tomar sol durante el día nos ayuda a dormir mejor durante la noche!

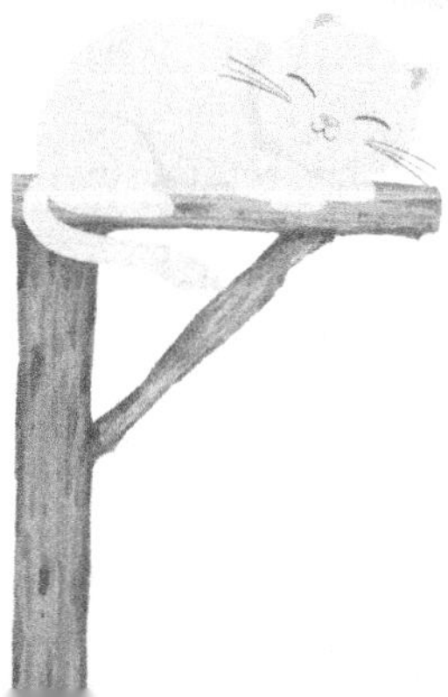

Trabaja al aire libre en las mañanas
y las primeras horas de la tarde
para recibir la mejor luz solar.

¡Nos encanta ir a la playa en verano, donde tomamos mucha luz solar. Pero recuerda proteger tu piel del sol directo!

Nos encanta hacer muchas actividades al aire libre. ¡Eso nos hace felices!

¡Me encanta explorar al aire libre!

Me encanta jugar al aire libre con mi mascota. ¡Es muy divertido!

Plantamos flores y vegetales para tener otra razón para estar al aire libre.

La luz solar nos aporta vitamina D natural que nos ayuda a crecer sanos y fuertes.

Dato curioso:

Si no fuera por el sol no habría vida en la tierra. El sol provoca las diferentes estaciones, las mareas en los oceanos, el tiempo y el clima.

TEMPLANZA

La templanza es el autocontrol.

"Así que, hermanos, os ruego por las misericordias de Dios, que presentéis vuestros cuerpos en sacrificio vivo, santo, agradable a Dios, que es vuestro culto racional"

Romanos 12:1

Practicamos el autocontrol cuando podemos controlar nuestras emociones.

La mejor manera de practicar el autocontrol es PARAR, PENSAR, REZAR y luego ELEGIR la opción correcta.

A veces, hacer una pausa en las actividades puede ayudarnos a mejorar el autocontrol.

El autocontrol es saber que puedes hacer algo y decidir que no lo harás!

Demostramos autocontrol cuando decimos no a las cosas malas y elegimos las buenas.

Las cosas que decimos o hacemos pueden hacer que los demás se sientan bien o mal.

El autocontrol también es aprender qué decir y qué no.

Marca con una ✓ cuáles debes decir en voz alta y con una X cuáles debes guárdate para ti.

✓ = Decirlo X = No Decirlo

- ☐ Hoy estas muy linda.
- ☐ Lo compartiré contigo.
- ☐ ¡Qué malo eres!
- ☐ Jesús te quiere.
- ☐ Todo es culpa tuya.
- ☐ Te ayudaré.
- ☐ Eres fea.
- ☐ ¿Puedo sentarme contigo?
- ☐ No me gustas.
- ☐ Soy mejor que tú.
- ☐ Me encantaría jugar contigo.
- ☐ Nunca hablaré contigo, jamás.

AUTO-CONTROL

Cuanto más conozcamos a Jesús,
más autocontrol tendremos.

Rellena los espacios en blanco para deletrear la guía del autocontrol.

P_R_R

PE_SA_

RE___

E__GIR

Las respuestas están en la página 42

Tener auto-control es tomar la mejor decisión.

Por favor, guía a Kasey a llegar a la mejor opción para la cena.

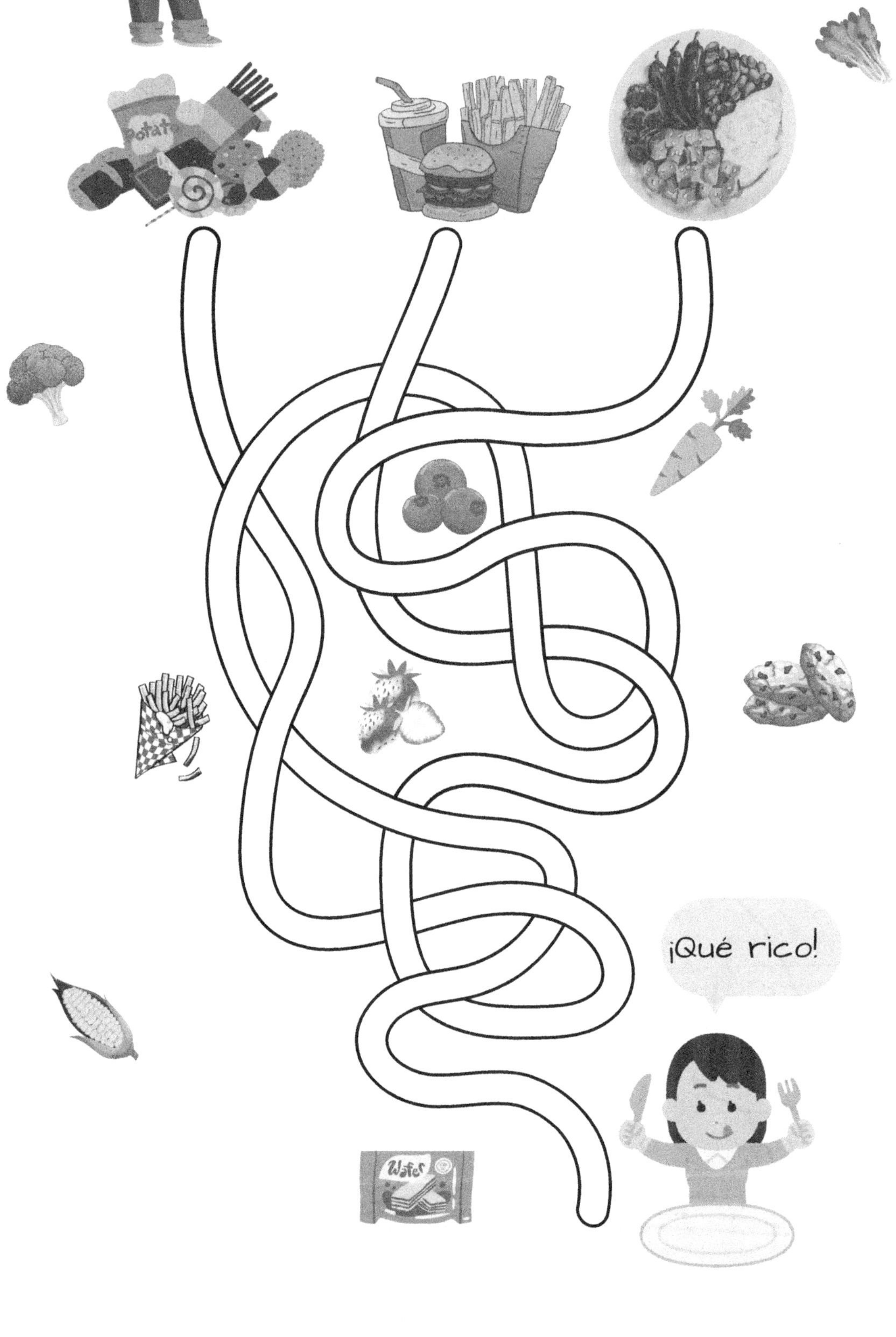

AIRE

"Formó, pues, Jehová Dios al hombre del polvo de la tierra y sopló en su nariz el aliento de vida; y fue el hombre alma viviente"

Genesis 2:7

¿Por qué el aire fresco nos hace bien?

El aire fresco nos hace más felices.

El aire fresco limpia nuestros pulmones.

El aire fresco fortalece nuestro sistema inmunológico, y nos mantiene sanos.

El aire fresco nos da más energía y nos ayuda a enfocarnos mejor.

El aire fresco nos ayuda a dormir mejor en las noches.

¡El aire fresco nos ayuda a estar tranquilos, relajados y felices!

Respira profundo; es gratis.

¿Cuáles son algunas formas de tomar aire fresco?

Tomamos aire fresco cuando realizamos actividades al aire libre, como jugar, hacer ejercicio, caminar, hacer senderismo y acampar.

Recibimos aire fresco cuando abrimos las ventanas.

Tomamos aire fresco plantando flores y árboles y teniendo algunas plantas en casa como calas o malamadres que ayudan a limpiar el aire.

Obtenemos aire fresco cuando respirasmos profundamente en lugares que tienen buena circulación de aire.

Me gusta hacer senderismo en parques naturales con mis padres, donde el aire es freco y limpio.

¡El aire también puede ser nocivo para nuestro cuerpo!

El aire que respiramos está contaminado cuando está sucio con gases o químicos.

Aléjate del aire sucio como el humo, químicos, olores a gas, humo fuerte, moho y basura apestosa.

Aquí hay un sencillo ejercicio de respiración para relajar la mente y el cuerpo:

¡Comienza!

Inhala a través de tu nariz mientras cuentas hasta 4.

Aguanta la respiración miestras cuentas hasta 4,

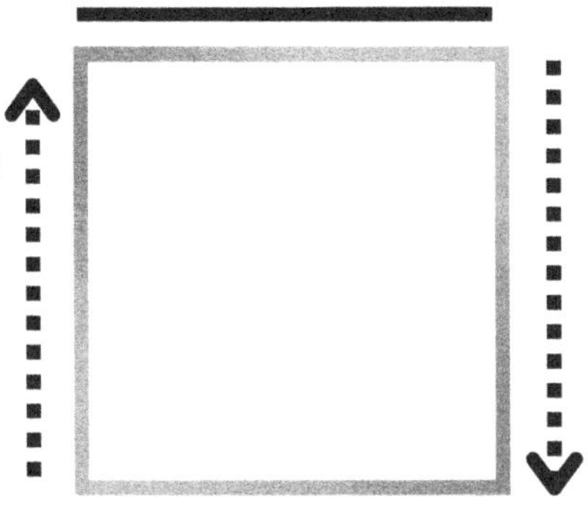

Exhala mientras cuentas hasta 4.

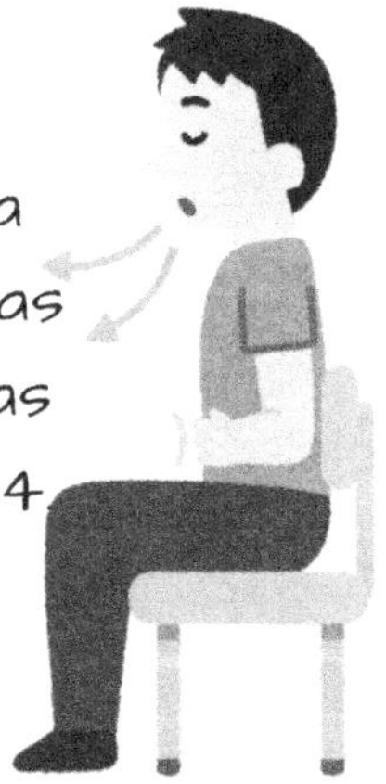

Relájate y luego repite.

Descansar

"Venid a mí todos los que estáis trabajados y cargados, y yo os haré descansar. 29 Llevad mi yugo sobre vosotros, y aprended de mí, que soy manso y humilde de corazón; y hallaréis descanso para vuestras almas; 30 porque mi yugo es fácil, y ligera mi carga."

Mateo 11:28-30

¿Por qué necesitamos descansar apropiadamente?

Descansar apropiadamente nos ayuda a comportarnos mejor y a disminuir la ansiedad.

Dormir lo suficiente nos ayuda a sentirnos más felices, recordar mejor las cosas, mantenernos enfocados, prestar atención y aprender cosas nuevas más fácilmente.

Un adecuado descanso ayuda a fortalecer nuestro cuerpo y estar más sanos, haciéndonos menos propensos a enfermarnos.

Descansar adecuadamente ayuda a nuestro cuerpo a trabajar y a recordar mejor lo que aprendemos.

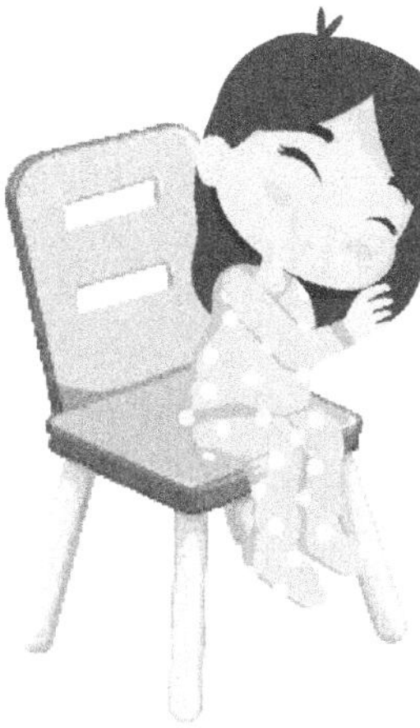

Nuestro cuerpo y mente, necesitan descansar para recargarse, repararse y mantenerse sanos.

Estas son algunas formas de mejorar el descanso naturalmente.

Tener buenos hábitos de descanso nos ayudan a dormir mejor por las noches.

Planifica tiempos de juego al aire libre con pausas de descanso y tranquilidad.

Asegúrate de dar tiempo a tu cerebro para que descanse y se calme antes de ir a la cama.

Tomar una siesta durante el día nos ayuda a mejorar nuestro estado de ánimo.

Apaga la computadora, el televisor, los videojuegos y demás equipos electrónicos cuando vayas a dormir.

Limitar la cantidad de tiempo que pasamos con estos dispositivos durante el día nos ayudará a dormir mejor por las noches.

Establece una rutina regular para acostarte cada noche.

Come saludablemente y no consumas grandes comidas, cafeína o azúcares antes de irte a la cama.

No comas muy tarde o cerca de la hora de irte a dormir.

¡Descansar correctamente durante la noche nos ayuda a sentirnos despiertos y enfocados en la escuela y mejorar el aprendizaje!

¿Puedes encontrar las palabras ocultas en la siguiente sopa de letras?

QUE TENGAS DULCES SUEÑOS

D	E	S	C	A	N	S	O	Z	C	S	X
O	T	E	I	K	I	U	L	O	W	I	R
R	E	N	O	C	H	E	Y	A	M	E	L
M	M	A	I	S	F	Ñ	O	N	P	S	S
I	M	L	G	K	R	O	Q	C	L	T	E
R	O	I	L	I	N	O	N	I	A	A	E
D	N	S	H	O	O	H	A	B	I	T	O
E	G	A	P	R	E	N	D	E	R	G	N
S	A	L	U	D	A	B	L	E	I	F	E

DORMIR
APRENDER
HABITO
SALUDABLE

SIESTA
NOCHE
DESCANSO
SUEÑO

Dato Curioso:

¿Sabías que los niños necesitan cerca de 10 horas de sueño cada noche?
Dormir adecuadamente nos ayuda a comportarnos mejor, aprender mejor y a tener cuerpos, cerebros y mentes más saludables.

CONFIANZA EN DIOS

"Confía en el Señor de todo corazón y no te apoyes en tu propia inteligencia. Reconócelo en todos tus caminos y él enderezará tus sendas"
Proverbios 3:5-6

Dios nos ayuda a tomar las decisiones correctas.

La Biblia contiene historias asombrosas sobre cómo Dios ayuda a su pueblo a sentirse valiente y fuerte para que pueda tomar buenas decisiones.

Jesús sabe los que nos hace felices, sanos y fuertes. Él nos dará la fortaleza para seguir lo que es correcto.

Si cometemos un error, Jesús nos perdonará cuando se lo pidamos. Él nos ayuda a dejar de hacer cosas malas y a comenzar a hacer cosas buenas.

Las familias que leen la Biblia y
rezan unidas son más felices.

La Biblia es una carta de amor de Dios hacia nosotros, está llena de hermosas promesas que nos hacen sentir felices, seguros y animados.

Reza y lee La Biblia y haz que alguien sepa lo maravilloso que es Dios.

Dios nos ama tanto que creó este hermoso mundo y nos proporcionó las cosas de la naturaleza para nuestra salud, sanación y felicidad.

Padre Celestial, por favor ayúdame a
seguir las 8 leyes de la salud para que
pueda ser feliz, saludable y fuerte.
En el nombre de Jesús, te lo ruego. Amén.

"Todo lo puedo en Cristo
que me fortalece"
Filipenses 4:13

Padre Celestial, gracias por
ayudarme a estar sano y fuerte.
Ayúdame a seguir estos 8 pasos
para ser más feliz y más saludable
y ayúdame a compartirlo con otros.
En el nombre de Jesús, Amén.

"Amado, yo deseo que tú seas prosperado en todas las cosas, y que tengas salud, así como prospera tu alma."
3 Juan 2

¡Tu pedido nos alegró el día, y esperamos haber hecho lo mismo contigo! Nos emociona compartir esta experiencia y estamos seguros de que a tu hijo le encantará. No dudes en explorar más de nuestra colección-siempre hay algo nuevo por descubrir.

Si tienes alguna pregunta o simplemente quieres saludarnos, nos encantaría saber de ti.

Contáctanos en cualquier momento al correo:
reader@earnestink.net
¡Gracias por ser parte de nuestra aventura!

Earnest Ink
Publications
earnestink.net

Made in the USA
Las Vegas, NV
20 February 2026

42319782R10039

FISH MIC —
GREAT LAKES

The most comprehensive guide ever written on fishing in the Great Lakes from Michigan. Loaded with information and practical advice for those who fish — or want to fish — the Great Lakes from Michigan ports and rivermouths.

by Tom Huggler

Cover Photos: Lower Peninsula by Randy Carrels

Upper Peninsula by Tom Huggler

All black and white photos are by the author unless otherwise noted.

Friede Publications

For

JOE ZIKEWICH

a good friend and one helluva fisherman.

Friede Publications
2339 Venezia Drive
Davison, Michigan 48423

Printed in the United States of America

ISBN 0-9608588-5-7

— Michigan DNR photo —

1
2
3
4
5
6
7
8
9
10
11
12
13
14
15
16
17
18
19
20
21
22
23
24
25
26
27
28
29
30
31
32
33
34
35
36
37
38
39
40
41
42
43
44
45
46
47
48
49
50
51
52
53
54
55
56
57
58
59
60
61
62
63
64
65
66
67
68
69
70
71
72
73
74
75
76
77
78
79
80
81
82
83

CONTENTS

NOTE: Maps included with each chapter are not to be used for navigational purposes.

Lower Peninsula

Upper Peninsula

INTRODUCTION

To the reader: Please indulge me while I sort through the answers to three questions that might just explain what this book is all about.

"*Why fish?*" is one of those simple questions that defy a simple answer. It would be much easier to write about why Lake St. Clair muskies attack prey half their own size or why chrome No. 88 Sutton Spoons, pattern-fished in the fall at Harrisville, are hot tickets for king salmon. I am often asked questions like that, and you can find those answers and others elsewhere in this book.

But no one has ever asked me, "Why fish?" The question, as you might have guessed, demands an uncompromising answer. Here it is: I fish because I am selfish. Fishing is the ultimate in self-indulgence. Although habit forming, it is a good habit, causing neither blindness nor senility, neither obesity nor drunkenness. On the contrary, I often see things with the clarity of a crackling white wine by the time I step off a trolling boat, shuck my chest waders or tuck away my tip-up flags.

There is something about fishing—which does not always entail catching—that reduces a world of call-forwarding and four-laned hyperactivity to one of reason and order.

Ishmael went to sea, in *Moby Dick*, when he realized he was bringing up the rear of funerals and fantasizing about knocking people's hats from their heads. Likewise, some time passes after getting off a trolling boat before I again make monster faces at people who pass me on the expressway.

Jim Harrison, a writer and sportsman from northern Michigan, says fishing has kept him sane since age five, that it is "the most wonderful thing I do in my life, barring some equally delightful unmentionables, and not disregarding gluttony and booze. It's in the top five." I agree.

My earliest fishing recollection is of Dad running down the bank of the Thunder Bay River near Alpena, drawn to my screams and the lunker bass that had busted my line as I struggled to pull the fish from the river. I guess I was about five. Then, at 10 or so, I remember Dad and me hauling 10-quart pails of perch, in shiny yellow and green, up the driveway home. We caught the jumbos, two and three at a time, at Quanicassee on Saginaw Bay.

That was 30 years ago. Since then, I have stood alone for hours, wrestling with silver salmon on an Alaskan stream that ox-bowed through tundra to the sea. Fresh-run, the silvers contained sea lice clinging to their backs. And many nights I have slept alone on solid ground, yet felt the earth heave to and fro with Lake Michigan rollers and heard the sound of downrigger cables whining in my ears.

It is entirely possible that my present near-sightedness is due as much to watching monofilament disappear into the opaqueness of stream and lake as it is to reading *Walt Disney Comics & Stories*.

"*Why fish the Great Lakes*?" Because they are a wonderful place, not only to catch a tremendous variety of gamefish, but also to lose yourself in order to find yourself. So vast they contain 99 percent of America's fresh water, the Five Sisters are at once mysterious, moody, sublime. Stare over the side of your boat—bobber-watching or not—for an hour, then tell me your thoughts. I will likely understand, no matter how silly they may sound.

Fishing in the Great Lakes has never been better than it is now. Don't seriously listen to those stories about the "good old days." The truth is, sport fishermen never had it so good, and in some areas it is going to get even better.

"*Why this book*?" Because today's discriminating Great Lakes fisherman demands it. He or she is not just a boat fisherman. He is also a pier fisherman, a surf fisherman, a river fisherman. He wants detailed maps to tell him where to go to catch fish. He wants easy-to-understand copy that tells him when to fish at all seasons, what local lures and specialized tactics are productive at different times of year, and how to get additional information. He wants to know where to launch his boat, where to buy bait and tackle, and who to hire in case he needs a guide. He wants to know how many fish the department of natural resources has stocked and where they were released.

For all these reasons, now comes *Fish Michigan—Great Lakes*. I hope this new book is everything you expect it to be. Countless hours went into its research and its preparation, and there are literally hundreds of key fishermen I could thank—if room existed—for so freely telling me about their methods, lures and hotspots. It is true: Great Lakes fishermen are among the friendliest and most helpful of all anglers. Perhaps they know that giving out the reasons for their full fish box today will help ensure that tomorrow—when others are netting fish and the only thing in their coolers is melted ice—the favor may be returned.

At any rate, I thank them all because, simply put, the book would not be possible without their unselfish help. No one person can fish all 3,000 shoreline miles of Michigan's real estate on the Great Lakes. It is likewise impossible for one person to know everything there is to know about catching fish at every location. I have never claimed to be an expert on anything, and, after having written this book, I am more convinced than ever that I was right.

Every effort has been made to make *Fish Michigan—Great Lakes* an honest, accurate and most useful book. Whether or not it is will depend upon where it is found. If dust gathers on its uncracked spine while it roosts, untouched, on the top shelf of your bookcase, then I suppose the project will have failed. Instead, I hope it finds its dog-eared way to your car dashboard, your stack of often-read outdoor magazines, even your already-bulging tackle box.

If you find errors or misleading information, I'd welcome hearing from you. You can contact me at P.O. Box 98, Otisville MI 48463.

Tight lines and good fishing to you.

Tom Huggler
Otisville, Michigan
January 8, 1986

HOW TO FISH THE GREAT LAKES

FLATLINE TROLLING for TROUT and SALMON

If you've ever wanted to give Great Lakes trout and salmon trolling a go, now is the right time. First, there are plenty of opportunities for a large variety of gamefish. Second, fishermen have developed surefire methods for taking fish. And third, equipment and electronics are highly developed.

Yet you, like many other fishermen, might be afraid to try the Great Lakes trolling game because (1) you don't think you can afford it and (2) you can't understand it. I remember the first time I stepped aboard a Great Lakes trolling boat. That was a dozen years ago, when downriggers and electronics were pretty basic and when a lure was either a Rapala or a Dardevle. Even so, it was still a heady experience trying to figure out how to raise cannonballs, attach monofilament to releases, and read the bottom on a graph.

Much more faces today's beginner. We've come a long way with our sophisticated trolling equipment and tactics in the past 12 years. So how can he expect to break into the excitement with any chance of success? And will he have to hock the family burial plots to do it? Trolling certainly has grown more complex, perhaps even incomprehensible, at times, to today's beginner.

I know the feeling. I've been checking out portable word processors lately, and the experience is intimidating. I don't understand the operating systems of these new computers. I can't fathom their language codes. I can't even read the keyboards of some models. The main difficulty, it seems, is that the more advanced and experienced we grow, the more specialized becomes our language in explaining it to others.

Taking temperature is a critical part of Great Lakes trolling.

The problem, then, lies in reducing all the specialized information to readable English, and that's the purpose of this section. I hope to replace the mystery and reduce the complexity of Great Lakes trolling with easy-to-understand explanations so that a first-time fisherman can do it successfully.

I'll start with inexpensive trolling methods, then cover downrigger tactics from *A* to *Z*. Finally, I'll show you how to fine-tune your fishing program with add-on considerations. And I'll make every effort to key this information to the various trout and salmon species so that you can apply it immediately. Don't own a boat? We'll cover shore-fishing tactics, too. I'll also give some tips on how to catch the other main species of fish, a veritable smorgasbord, available to anglers in Michigan's Great Lakes.

First off, why troll at all? Because trolling allows you to cover more area than you could by merely casting or drifting (although those tactics will take salmon and trout, as well as other fish). And there's a lot of area to cover. Lake Superior is the second-largest lake in the world. And, collectively, the Great Lakes contain 99 percent of America's fresh surface water.

To troll successfully you have to narrow that area down. Although lake trout have been taken in Lake Superior to 300 feet deep, and even though Manistee anglers catch steelhead on the surface over nearly 300 feet of water, most action occurs in water less than 150 feet deep. Except for offshore reefs, this limits the sport to shoreline areas. In northern Lake Huron, you can find water that is 150 feet deep within a quarter-mile of shore. In Saginaw Bay you will never find it. The point here is to learn to think in terms of where fish are found.

Where are fish generally found? For spring fishing think in terms of shallow water. However, keep in mind that offshore winds that blow warm water out will help to send fish to deeper habitat. Pressure from too many boats will do the same, as will a bright sun at mid-day—especially in the case of king salmon.

From ice-out until mid or late May, trout and salmon invade shallows in search of spawning smelt, alewives and other baitfish. Most trollers begin setting lines in the upper 25 feet of water, but there are times when browns, steelhead, salmon and even lake trout will cruise wave troughs and rivermouths in water as shallow as six feet.

As the Great Lakes continue to "turn over" from winter to summer temperatures, a thermocline begins to form. The thermocline is a horizontal band or layer of water of a certain temperature that has water of a different temperature above and below. Quite often baitfish and the predator species will be found in this preferred zone of water or along its edge—that is, just above or just below. It helps to have a temperature probe aboard your boat to find out where the thermocline is. Also, remember that wind, in particular, can alter its shape, depth and temperature from day to day.

A temperature probe is also valuable because different fish prefer different optimum temperatures. Lake trout, for example, prefer 48-52 degrees F., especially when it is found on or near an irregular bottom of cobblestone, hardpan or gravel. On-feed lakers will leave this environment to feed and are then sometimes taken near schools of baitfish far from bottom. An old-time tactic, still in vogue on Lake Superior and select places on the other Great Lakes, is to fish for lakers with wire line and attractors ahead of big spoons.

Salmon like 54- to 56-degree-F. water. Both cohos and kings readily suspend, that is, hold at a depth somewhere between the surface and bottom, usually in the thermocline or near it. You should keep in mind, though, that kings are more structure-oriented and/or more light-sensitive than cohos. It is not uncommon to catch the bigger kings on deep-running lures while those near the surface trigger strikes from cohos. Like cohos, pink salmon, which are especially abundant in Lake Huron, prefer the upper layer of water.

I think of browns and steelhead/rainbows as I do kings and cohos. Although the two trout species can tolerate warmer water (60-70 degrees F.), browns appear to like structure whereas steelhead—at least in the Great Lakes—like to cruise near the surface. Those previously mentioned Manistee trollers, for example, made excellent catches of steelhead in summer 1985 on surface-running crankbaits. Brown trout have a strange habit of liking to porpoise in small schools. It is not uncommon to see them rolling and cavorting (they often look like yellow-bellied carp) on the surface on warm summer afternoons.

In fall, schooling salmon appear offshore from natal release sites, then move to the shallows in stages. One week may find them in 80 feet of water two miles offshore. The following week they could be within a mile and in 50 feet of water. Ten days later, they might be at harbor mouths or within the harbor itself. This staging activity begins with king salmon as early as late July or as late as mid-August. By Labor Day, fish are normally in the shallows. Cohos follow kings within two to four weeks. Lake trout are generally next to spawn, with early October normally prime time (fishermen in Michigan waters of lakes Huron and Michigan, however, are not allowed to keep lake trout caught after August 15). Brown trout and steelhead are next, invading streams as late as Thanksgiving.

Knowing how to rig for these species requires some understanding of their preferred habitat—including depth, structure and temperature. The differences determine how fast, or how slow, you should troll, and that determines what lures and how to rig them for best results. In early spring, for instance, when fish are sluggish, a slow trolling speed (1.0-2.0 mph) is best. By mid-May, when temperatures are 50 degrees F. and rising, you can kick trolling speed to 3.0 or even 4.0. mph. During the dog days of summer, some fishermen slow down again and concentrate on putting lures right on target. Again in fall, when water temperatures are cool, a slower speed is often the ticket.

How, then, does one rig for Great Lakes fishing? To begin, if you have ever trolled for northern pike or walleyes, you can use the same method for trout and salmon. The tactic is called "flatlining," and it is nothing more than a lure pulled behind the boat while the motor is running There is no simpler, inexpensive—nor sometimes more effective—way to catch them. The method is especially productive in spring and fall, when fish are in the shallows. But it is a rare trolling boat that, even in summer, does not run a flatline or two.

One advantage to flatlining is that a small boat can be a plus

Heavy-duty level-wind reels and medium-action rods in seven to nine feet are standard. Note straight butt section for placing in tube holders.

and, although helpful, electronics are not a must. Sure, you should have some heavy-duty rods and reels and specialized lures, but if you are an active boat fisherman now, chances are you already own the basic equipment to get started. In fact, many a small-boat angler has used spring close-to-shore trolling experiences as a springboard for jumping with both feet into the Great Lakes trolling game.

Depending upon boat size and number of anglers aboard, you can usually run from two to four flatlines. A two-rod setup works best if one lure is pulled down the center. There, churning action from the propeller often stirs up schooling baitfish, which draw hungry predators. Fifty to 100 feet behind the boat is a good rule for length, but the distance will vary according to the digging ability of the lure, the angle of your rod, the pound test of your fishing line, and what the fish seem to prefer on a given day. Brown trout, in particular, are easily spooked, so most flatliners after browns run lures back as far as 400 feet. Cohos, on the other hand, are sometimes drawn to commotion and will hit lures flatlined 25 feet behind the boat.

If you add a third rod, keep the corner lines shorter than the center line (sometimes called a "highline" because the rod may be run straight up). On turns, the outside lines will run under the center rig and thus avoid tangles. If you add a fourth rod, run it down the middle, but at the same distance as the corner lines.

I like two-piece medium-action rods from eight to nine feet long for flatlining. I prefer a straight butt section (for ease in extracting from tube-type rod holders) and plenty of guides. My 8-1/2 foot Daiwa's Strike series is a good rod for all but the biggest king salmon, but there are many good rods, including some by Shakespeare, Eagle Claw and Berkley, on the market. Ryobi baitcasters, Shakespeare Sigma, Garcia Ambassadeur 5500, Penn 209 or 210 and Daiwa 27H or 47H reels are all good choices in reels for flatlining. And they are not overly expensive. Some stores run rod-and-reel specials for as low as $29.95. Twelve-pound test is fine overall, but if water is especially clear or fish (such as brown trout) are spooky, lighten up to six- or eight-pound test. If targeting king salmon, beef up your line to 17- or even 30-pound test.

What lures should you run off flatlines? Spoons weighing from 2/5 ounce to one ounce are good choices. Consider Kastmasters, K.O. Wobblers, Little Jewels, Locos, Mainliners, Cobras, Devle Dogs, Cop-E-Cats, Krocodiles, Little Cleos and Dazzlers. Silver is an all-around good color, especially in combination with orange, red, green, blue, yellow or chartreuse. Crankbaits are also effective when flatlined. Good ones are Hot 'N Tots, Hot Shots, Willy's Worms, Bug Plugs, Wiggle Warts, Fat Raps, Shad Raps, and Tadpollies in similar colors. Flatfish, J-Plugs, Ping-A-Ts, and Countdown Rapalas are other effective plugs. There are dozens of others.

Most lures have a maximum depth that they dig, depending upon many variables—rod angle, boat speed, type of line, to name just a few. Remember to mate choices that are compatible with each other. Flatfish and Rapalas, for instance, don't pull at the same speed. Test lures over the boat side before releasing. Remember, too, that the further back you spot your lures, the greater the opportunity for tangle, especially when lures run out of whack with each other. To keep lures tracking straight, some flatline trollers place small bobbers about 50 feet ahead of their offerings.

Another consideration is hook set. Monofilament stretches, so a fish drilling a lure at 400 feet behind the boat is not likely to be as well hooked as one striking at 40 feet. A solution to this problem is to use manufactured pinch-pad releases or homemade alligator clips with electricians's tape or rubber tubing over the teeth. Some trollers attach the release to the boat transom or stern-end hook by way of a 12- to 24-inch piece of wire cable (a long leader used for pike fishing works well), then pinch the monofilament and bend the rod into a *C* shape. A strike snaps the rod straight up, thus helping set the hook.

A second advantage to using pinch-type releases is that lures will enter the water sooner, thus allowing them to find maximum depth much quicker. This can be helpful in tight-traffic situations or if you plan to run several lines and want to avoid tangles.

Rubber-core sinkers are another way to get lures deeper with less line required. Attach them from two to six feet ahead of lures, but then be sure to test the lure over the side to see if action is severely dampened. It is also a good idea to know the distance behind the boat that your lures are running. Strikes mean that the action is good and that the length from the boat is just right. Some trollers mark the distance with a piece of bright thread or a rubber band on the line. Other methods involve counting the travels across your level-wind reel or counting the pulls as you strip line out.

Some flatlined lures give the best action when tied with swivels, especially ball-bearing swivels. Others require direct tying with improved clinch knots. Some body baits, such as floating Rapalas, work best behind a loop knot. Always experiment to find out what is ideal.

To my thinking, the most important consideration for successful Great Lakes trolling is to fish with a determined program. The guy who sends down whatever happens to catch his eye, without regard to where it is going or for what species of fish, is going to end his troll with clean lures and little more.

Good casting or flatline spoons include (left to right) Little Cleo, Kastmaster, Little Jewel, K.O. Wobbler, Loco, Krocodile.

DOWNRIGGER TROLLING for TROUT and SALMON

Assuming you have a flatlining operation down pat, it is now time to consider downriggers. Whoever coined that word was, no doubt, a no-frills kind of thinker. What more direct way to name a fishing tool that sends lures to whatever depth the troller desires? "Downrigger" says it better than anything I could write.

Downriggers are simple devices, yet a lot of people don't completely understand how they work and how they can enhance a trolling operation for Great Lakes trout and salmon. One reason is because the evolution of the downrigger has gone hand in hand with the increasing sophistication of electronics. People often confuse the two. Understandable, especially when you consider that some downriggers have now been linked with electronics. For example, today you can buy computerized downriggers that oscillate (raise and lower lures) on timed cycles and that measure temperature and boat speed versus lure speed.

To the uninitiated, the new fishing aids can be mighty intimidating, in terms of both cost and operation. But sophisticated aids—Loran C, RFD radios and ProCombinators, for example—though all helpful to downrigger trolling, are not necessary to catch fish.

Neither are downriggers. But the truth is, they have become as basic to the sport as toothpaste is to brushing teeth. And they are just about as simple to use.

Let's start there—how downriggers work and why they can make you a better fisherman.

Today, about 10 American manufacturers make downriggers, which all work on the same basic principle and even look somewhat alike. Each features a reel and an arm. The reel, which looks like a pulley, can be as small as five inches in diameter to as large as 12 inches. It holds 150-200 feet of 150-pound-test cable, usually made of seven-strand stainless steel. The arm will extend from 12 inches to eight feet and is designed to carry the cable over the boat side or stern. A small reel at the end of the arm guides the cable along its length and into the water. The cable is lowered and raised through a simple gear system, operated either electrically or by a hand crank.

Downriggers allow a weight—either a cannonball or a torpedo-shaped piece of lead—weighing from three to 15 pounds—and a fishing lure to be lowered to any depth desired. Most downriggers contain a counter device that measures, in feet, the amount of cable released. On the weight itself or somewhere on the cable is a release device that holds the angler's monofilament. It may be a tube-shaped pressure release, pinch-pad type, doughnut-shaped type, or simply a size-16 rubber band secured with a half-hitch. Lures are sent back from two feet to 200 feet behind this release. Then the weight and lure are lowered to the desired depth and the downrigger reel locked in place. The angler shoves his rod into a nearby holder, cranks up all slack to make a good arc in his rod, and waits for a strike.

A striking fish breaks the release far below the surface, and the rod snaps to, hooking the fish and allowing the angler to play it on a free line. As he fights the fish, he or someone else brings up the downrigger weight, and if the fish is a good one—such as a slugfest king salmon—all other lines are pulled so that the angler has a wide-open field of battle.

Downriggers give trollers the advantage of being able to pinpoint lures at certain depths, then keep them there. Prescribed depths depend upon water temperature, availability of structure, or presence of baitfish—sometimes all three. Further, downriggers allow trollers to run several lines without fear of tangle. And they can be quickly and efficiently set.

Downriggers can be mounted two ways: either permanently by drilling holes and using bolts, or temporarily by tightening C-clamps, to the transom or sides of a boat. Those that go over the sides are called out-downs and usually feature long arms. On larger boats it is possible to mount six (or more) downriggers—two out-downs, two stern-end models (to either side of an outboard or exhaust ports of an inboard engine), and two corner setups. Most serious Great Lakes fishermen run four downriggers—two out-downs and two stern-end units. Those with only two downriggers usually place them to either side of the boat or off the back.

You can buy downriggers for as little as $40 each or as much as $500 each. The downrigger market is highly competitive, meaning that fishermen have plenty of options and prices from which to choose. And because many fishermen, after a few years of trolling with their starter (usually manual) units, trade up for electric and otherwise sophisticated models, there is a good market for used downriggers.

Now that you have mounted downriggers to your boat, how do you fish with them? The answer depends upon how many you own, what type of fish you are seeking, and what time of year you are trolling.

Most trollers complement their downrigger arsenal with flatlines. Two out-down or corner-set downriggers with a flatline run down the middle is a good basic operation. But you can mix as many as three flatlines with two or more downriggers, too. And on bigger boats, it is not uncommon to see the aft end bristle with a dozen or more rods.

The first time I fished with downriggers on my 16-foot boat was nearly the last time. I was trolling off Grindstone City in Lake Huron, which is notorious for its crosswinds. The lake was kicking up three- and four-footers that spring day. A partner and I ran four lines that constantly tangled. We spent more time sorting out our fouled lines than we did fishing. It was very frustrating, because I knew I was doing things wrong but didn't know how to correct the problem.

You too will have to experiment with fine-tuning your own operation, but there are some things to keep in mind. Remember, for example, that waves and sharp turns tend to lift and drop lures. This causes them to flutter, and sometimes they can run afoul of each other. Long leads (the distance from release to lure) can cause a set of fits, too, as can your choice of lures. Since each lure has an optimum trolling speed at which it imparts the best action, running too slow or too fast can cause it to wander. As suggested in "Flatline Trolling for Trout and Salmon," page 4, until you know what your lures will do, test them over the boat side at various distances, then temporarily set aside those that go belly-up or that run off from side to side on their own adventures.

If rigging four or more downriggers, think in terms of patterning them in a *V* shape. That is, set inside (stern-end) lines deeper and outside (corner or out-down) lines shallower. Why? Because on turns, outside lures will ride up, inside lures will dig down, and those out the back will stay reasonably straight if you have not made leads too long. That's another important point: Outside lines can sport longer leads than inside lines. And if you are running attractors (dodgers or cowbells—"junk lines" as some call them), the place to rig them is off the stern. When thus patterned, downrigger lines will pass under flatlines on slow turns.

But take these as just suggestions because, again, rigging depends upon conditions. On calm seas, for example, you can get away with different rigging tactics; indeed, sometimes you may want to reverse the idea completely. For example, Mike McKee, a highly touted charterboat captain out of Michigan City, Indiana, nearly always rigs lines in an inverted *V*—outside lines deep with short leads, inside lines shallow with longer leads. The reason? Inside lines are now in the prop wash. Coho salmon (the principal predator species in southern Lake Michigan) are attracted to propeller action and the flash of lures and attractors and brightly painted cannonballs.

But under most conditions (and especially if you are new at the sport), *V*-shaped rigging pays the best dividends. Howard Mills, a veteran Lake Huron sport fisherman who recently earned his captain's license, puts it this way: "I wouldn't think of setting up a trolling operation without knowing exactly where all the lures are and what they are doing." Mills is a proponent of *V*-shaped rigging, but he takes the system one step further. He staggers leads as well as depths. The reason is to cover as much productive water as possible, especially on slow turns, which produce about half the strikes aboard his boat, the *Paramour*.

Here is an example. Assume that salmon are peppering the graph from 25-50 feet deep. Two out-downs are set at 20 and 22 feet respectively. Corresponding release lengths are 75 and 85 feet. Corner-set riggers are 25 and 30 feet deep with release lengths of 40 and 50 feet. A single stern-end downrigger is locked at 45 feet deep and features a shorter release of only 30 feet. All the productive depths, therefore, are covered with varying lead lengths (sometimes salmon and trout hit lures with short leads, sometimes long leads). Slow turns pose no tangles because, again, outside lines ride up and inside lines dig down.

Time of year and the species of fish you are after also dictate set-up tactics for downriggers. In early spring, for example, trout and salmon invade shallows for warm water and baitfish. As detailed in "Flatline Trolling for Trout and Salmon (page 2), most trollers scour the upper 25 feet of water and will often venture into water as shallow as five feet deep.

A good trick is to drop downrigger weights just under the surface and pull floating body baits such as Bagley Bang-O-Lures, J-11 Rapalas, Rebel Fastracs and Long A Bombers. As depths increase, try lures that dig down a little—crankbaits such as Willy's Worms, Bug Plugs, Shad Raps, Wee Warts. You can mix in spoons, too, either heavier hardware like Krocodiles and Cobras or flake-thin choices like Flutter Chucks and Andy Reekers.

Generally, spring fish are hungry and if you can find them (warm-water areas such as factory and power-plant outflows, rivermouths, and thermal bars are the places to look), you can usually entice them to strike.

But sometimes worked-over fish develop lockjaw. Then you may find that the size of lures makes as much difference as color preferences. Sometimes salmon will pound large lures, then snub them for smaller ones the following day. Release lengths and trolling speed are two other variables that you should experiment with if marked fish won't hit.

In summer, trolling pastures increase in size as the thermocline forms and fish move offshore. Anglers now have to hunt fish with both electronics and an increased arsenal of lures. Once again, downriggers do the job. Besides kicking up boat speed, fishermen begin to stack lures, a practice which involves adding lures and/or rods to already-set lines.

In its simplest form, stacking is merely adding slider rigs. To an eight-foot strip (not more than the length of the rod) of monofilament, the fisherman adds a swivel and snap to each end. A flutter-type spoon goes on one end; the other is secured to the monofilament of the line already in place. The angler then tosses the lure overboard and it "slides" roughly halfway to bottom, where line-bow from the boat's forward movement holds it in place. A strike further slides the lure to bottom. Sometimes anglers have to pop releases clean—that is, manually release their lures—when using sliders.

More sophisticated stacking methods involve the use of rubber bands or manufactured stacking devices to add lines and/or rods at prescribed depths. Thus, it is possible to send an original setup down 15 feet, then add a second line and lower it, say 25 feet. Two lures now are working, one at 25 feet and one at 40 feet. Depending upon depth, it is possible to add (stack) up to three lines to one already in place.

Most trollers run heavy spoons (big Cop-E-Cats, Locos, Mainliners), plugs (J-Plugs, Canadian Plugs, Gold Stars), or attractors (dodgers, cowbells) with flies or spoons on bottom and thin hardware above.

Besides increasing the amount of water trolled, another advantage to stacking is that the practice may produce two species of fish. Deep-running lures often trigger strikes from lake trout, brown trout and Chinook salmon (all of which prefer structure), while top-set lines may pick up steelhead and coho salmon (which often cruise close to the surface).

In the fall, when salmon and trout approach the shallows, downriggers do a big job toward putting them in your cooler. If trolling traffic is not too thick, many fishermen lengthen leads with the shallow-set downriggers. Trolling speeds decrease, and big spoons and wobbling plugs (Tadpollies, Flatfish, Kwikfish) get the nod. As in spring, flatlines and downriggers nicely complement each other.

Some anglers have found a new use for downriggers when salmon are at rivermouths and in the rivers themselves in late fall, winter and spring. The fishermen use small boats or special driftboats to hover above holding spots. Then, with the aid of downriggers, they drop crankbaits from one to five feet under the surface. Male fish, which are especially territorial during the spawning period, rush at lures repeatedly danced before their noses. Spawn bags rolled downstream along bottom is another rated tactic just now coming on with downrigger fishermen in rivers.

I'll further detail the habits and preferred habitats of Great Lakes trout and salmon (see page 14). But first, now that you have considered downriggers, it's time to complete your trolling program by thinking about specialty techniques.

Double-header. One fish struck an out-down rod and is being netted while a second strike occurred off a stern-end rigger.

SPECIALIZED TROLLING TACTICS for TROUT and SALMON

In the summer of 1985, when sport-fisherman Randy Espinon returned to the dock at Manistee (13) with a 31-pound Lake Michigan Chinook, a small crowd gathered around.

"What'd he hit?" "How did you catch him?" were questions asked most often.

"I had just switched baits," Randy answered. "He hit a green Sparkle Fly behind a chrome fluted dodger at 32 feet down in 85 feet of water."

That specific, detailed information satisfied most of the onlookers. But whether or not they, or even Espinon (who is a good fisherman—his king was no fluke), knew it, that particular lure in that particular color at that certain depth tells only a small part of why the salmon struck.

There are many more pieces to the puzzle. What was Randy's trolling speed, for instance? What colors were his other lures, and how close were they to the hot one? What size dodger did he use, and how long was the lead? Did he use a swivel or did he tie the lure directly? What pound test was his line? The day had shifted between clouds and sunshine. What was the available light when the fish struck? What was the water temperature, the wind direction, the wave action? Then, why did the salmon strike? Was hunger the reason? Simple aggression? Finally, did it attack on its own or through a predator-pack action?

This is a planer board ("ski") with two boards. Note tether rope and rod/reel combo.

Mind-boggling questions, these, but important to consider. There is a saying, "Ten percent of the fishermen catch 90 percent of the fish." There is some truth to it, and you can bet that most of those 10 percent rely on fine-tuned trolling tactics. From reading this section, this book, you will be able to duplicate successful tactics, though never completely. Why not?

Because advanced rigging is as much an attitude as it is a technique. You have to fish often and with intensity, clearing your mind of the car payment almost due or the leaking faucet in the basement. Trolling for trout and salmon is serious business. This is especially true among the boat-for-hire skippers, who have to produce if they want to pay the bills. Not surprisingly, then, they are among the best fishermen. And nearly to a man they say to me: "Tell your readers it's the little things that count. You have to know where every lure is and what it's doing. Then you'll catch fish." If you are on the big water just for a boat ride and have adopted the habit of merely dropping lures whenever and wherever the mood strikes, then you shouldn't wonder why hours later your cooler contains only melted ice.

Washing lures for hours without strikes is frustrating and boring. Your time might be better spent sitting at home and watching new paint dry on the living-room walls. One time I took my two kids, who were then about seven and 12, aboard a charterboat. We pulled 13 lines for eight straight hours and never had a knock-off, didn't even mark a fish. The kids never asked to go salmon trolling again. Our skipper didn't do anything wrong, as far as I knew. It was just an off day. Even the best fishermen suffer through such days.

But most of the time, if you go at your fishing like it's your last chance to catch anything, you'll adopt a serious, determined attitude, and you will begin to apply specialty tactics. Here are the ones to consider:

Planer Boards. A planer board is a one- to six-foot-long ski-shaped board that is keel-weighted and angle-cut to run on its edge. One or more of these boards can be attached to either or both boat sides with tether ropes. Pinch-pad releases are used off the board itself or are mounted to slider rings (shower-curtain rings or large paper clips soldered to alligator clips work nicely) on the tether rope. Using rings, it is possible to stack a single board with four lines, the position of each ring on the rope being controlled by the amount of line released. Planer boards nicely complement downriggers and outriggers to increase the width of the trolling lane. They do take up a lot of room, however, so it is inconsiderate to use them on crowded seas.

Planer boards are especially effective on spooky fish like brown trout and sometimes king salmon. The boards are particularly useful in spring and fall shallows. Rapalas, Flatfish and small crankbaits work well with planer boards. So do small spoons, especially heavy hardware like Krocodiles and Little Cleos.

Outriggers. These are 12- to 24-foot-long wooden or fiberglass poles that lean to either or both sides of larger boats (usually 22 feet or longer). A pulley at each end of the pole holds a tether rope, which allows the angler to hand-over-hand his lure to the end of the pole. Monofilament to the lure is held by a release, usually a spring-loaded Black's Release or a clothespin-type release.

For lures, most anglers rely upon heavy spoons and big-lipped crankbaits that wiggle down to depths of several feet. Some anglers use lead-core line to get floating plugs and flutter-type spoons under the surface. A few prefer to accomplish the same goal with one-pound smooth-cast lead balls. Pressure-snap sinker releases then drop the weight when a fish strikes. Outriggers nicely complement a downrigger arsenal, and a decided advantage is that they can easily be stacked by simply adding an extra release or two to the tether rope.

Trip Divers. These are saucer- or delta-shaped devices that attach a few feet ahead of lures, which they spear to depths in a ratio to the amount of line released. By either setting a dial or releasing a preset amount of line, the fisherman can prescribe the depth of his lure, even thin flutter-type spoons and floating plugs. A strike "trips" the diver (also called a "planer"), which allows the angler to either play the fish without excess drag or to easily retrieve his lure and diver if the strike is missed. Some divers reset themselves after strikes. Trip divers allow fishermen to run an extra line or two close to the boat and are useful either in place of out-downriggers or when positioned between the out-downs and corner-set or stern-end downriggers. Popular models include Pink Ladies, Dipsy-Divers and Jon's Divers.

Oscillating Downriggers. This type of downrigger is so new and so innovative that I decided to include it in this section rather than the one on downriggers. This specialty aid is a computerized downrigger with a built-in memory that allows a fisherman, merely by pushing a button, to return lures automatically to a preset strike zone. An even bigger advantage, however, is that it also raises and lowers cannonballs and lures five feet at 15- to 90-second intervals. An even more sophisticated model, which oscillates at five-second intervals, will appear on the market soon,

But do they work? I'll admit I was pretty skeptical of Cannon's Digi-Troll downrigger when it first appeared in 1984. But, says sport-troller Al Spiers of Michigan City (2), Indiana, "My two Digi-Troll downriggers outfish my other units (also two downriggers) by a margin of two to one." So after you've added everything else to your arsenal, you might want to consider this space-age aid. But know that an oscillating downrigger can bust a $500 bill, and they are so new that there are no used ones to consider buying.

One further note about downriggers, outriggers, planer boards, and trip divers. Use the same general rod and reel suggestions as recommended in the earlier discussion on flatlining (page 2). Give additional consideration to reel choices, however, as your

A well-rigged Great Lakes trolling boat with downriggers and outriggers (long poles straight up — unset — to either side).

trolling program becomes more sophisticated. Personally, I like level-wind reels with star drags, anti-reverse features and big spools capable of holding up to 300 yards of 14-, 17- or even 20-pound test line.

Downrigger Releases. As mentioned on page 5, a release device holds the angler's monofilament to the downrigger cable or weight. When a fish strikes, the monofilament is "released" from the downrigger. There are many types (pinch-pad, tube-shaped, doughnut-shaped) and brands on the market, and all do a reasonably good job. The Offshore Release is probably the most popular of the pinch-pad types. Many fishermen continue to rely on the bullet-shaped Walker Release, a spring-loaded release that has been around nearly as long as downriggers themselves. Black's Releases and Roemer Releases are pressure-type releases that are simple to use and very effective. Even simpler are rubber bands secured with half-hitches to monofilament and downrigger cables. Remember, though, that all releases lose effectiveness as leads are lengthened. Some models, however, are adjustable and allow you to compensate somewhat.

Release Length (also called *Lead*). Release length—the distance from the release device or weight to the lure—is important for several reasons. Two of the most important are to get the maximum action from the lure and to be able to run several lures near each other without fear of tangle.

Release lengths depend on several factors. But there are no hard-and-fast rules, so experiment. Just be sure to check lures periodically to make sure that they are tracking straight. Release lengths depend, for example, on the type of fish you are seeking. Brown trout, for instance, seem to prefer lures some distance from the boat (although I have also seen them caught in the engine wake itself.) That is why many fishermen run flatlines as far back as 300 feet and spot downrigger-trolled lures as far as 100 feet behind cannonballs. At times, king salmon won't drill lures that are run tight to weights or that are too close to the boat. At other times, it makes little difference. Cohos actually seem to prefer lures in the prop boil, as well as those run right behind brightly painted weights. Lake trout don't mind short leads either and, for the most part, neither do steelhead.

Release lengths also vary with the time of year. As a general rule (and I emphasize "general"), lengthen cannonball leads to 50-75 feet in spring and fall when fish are in shallow water. In summer, when you are trolling deep water, tighter leads from 10-30 feet may trip a salmon's trigger.

Lure Colors. The rule of "dark day/dark lures, bright day/ bright lures" is a good one—most of the time. But I am not at all sure why. Most lures, even dark-colored ones, have white-or chrome-colored undersides, anyway. And it would seem to me that on a dark day a light-colored lure would show up better than a dark one. You would also think the reverse is true, but that is often not the case. I have noticed, for example, that Chinooks will often paste black lures in the inky darkness before dawn, then, as day progresses, they gradually prefer lighter lures—first khaki, dull orange or brown, then blues and greens, and finally silver or bone.

I spent some time in the summer of 1985 testing the new Color-C-Lector on Lake Michigan salmon and Skamania steelhead. This probe told me what color(s) fish could most readily see at certain depths, depending upon the amount of light penetration at the time of testing. But I could draw no conclusions as to its effectiveness. Sometimes fish hit the lures we were told would work; most often they did not.

What does this mean? I have long assumed, and it is only an assumption—hardly even a theory really—that fish readily see most lures pulled through the area where the fish happen to be, at least in the mostly clear waters of the Great Lakes. Color probably plays a role of some sort, but I suspect that of far more importance are lure action, time of day, and the behavior of other nearby fish. It is the combination of these and other stimuli that most likely cause a fish to hit.

Why do fish strike? Out of hunger, to be sure. But being predators, trout and salmon also appear to attack from simple aggression. Why else do some brown trout, already fat as footballs and gorged to the gullet with baitfish, try to find room for one more morsel? I have seen them spit out a half-dozen smelt or alewives, mostly undigested, when their bellies were already crammed with food. Predator pack behavior is another consideration, although that is probably another facet of simple aggression.

Most salmonids travel and feed in schools, and when one hits a

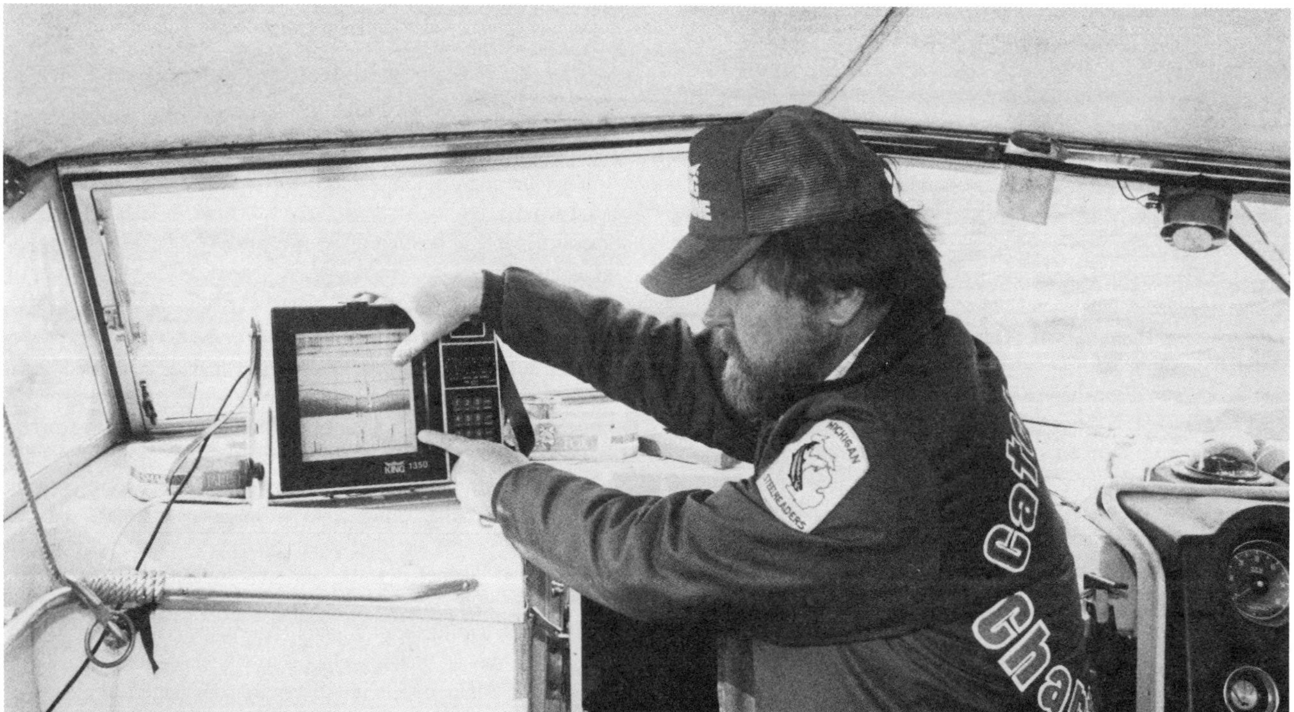

Graphs and various other depth-finding electronics are important if you want fish in the box.

lure, others often do, too. George Richey, an Honor, Michigan, lure maker and veteran sport troller, once caught two seven-pound cohos at the same time on the same two-hook fly (see "Two-For-One Salmon," page 84). And any lake-trout fisherman knows that a pass over reef structure loaded with lakers rarely produces only a single fish.

In the summer of 1985, five of us trolled Lake Huron's Thunder Bay (33) for brown trout. Finally, after three hours, a rod popped. I grabbed it and had fun playing with a three-pounder that leaped a half-dozen times. His actions must have spurred others into striking because suddenly three more rods went off together. Ten minutes later, we had four browns, from three to seven pounds each, in the box. But that was it—four hours of trolling condensed into that single flurry.

Running a trim trolling operation with specialized tactics will certainly increase your chances for strikes. But what extra things can you do to up your scores even more? Here are several considerations:

Trolling Speed. Vary it occasionally. Momentarily speeding up, then slowing down, can produce strikes. Trolling in an *S* pattern or a loose figure-eight helps vary lure speed, too. Sometimes trout and salmon will chase lures burned by; other times they want them tantalizingly slow and on target. Water temperature and atmospheric pressure likely have much to do with fish preferences and, as a result, trolling speed. Below 45 degrees F. and above 65 degrees F., for example, most trollers keep lures under 2.5 mph. In between those marks, they may run as fast as five mph.

Electrical storms can scatter trout and salmon and send them deep, and resulting high-pressure systems can keep them there for awhile. This situation may force anglers to search for days until they find regrouped fish. When forced to hunt salmon, most trollers kick up boat speed and opt for lures that can be pulled fast.

Add or Take Away Flash. Lake-trout trollers know that the more flash they can present, the better the chances are that fish will be attracted. This is especially true in the murky depths near bottom structure, where lakers are usually found.

Dodgers and cowbells effectively do the job. For example, Captain Norm McComb of Onekama (14) trolls for Lake Michigan lake trout with two strings of Les Davis Odd Ball cowbells hooked together to make a six-foot line of flash with huge blades. He drags them and cannonballs along bottom. Skipper Jim Maki of Marquette (74) runs cowbell strings behind 0-sized dodgers to wake up Lake Superior lakers as deep as 300 feet. Captain Larry Hartwick of Harbor Beach (50) has perfected a tactic called "skipping" for Lake Huron forktails. He puts an angler on each downrigger, then tells him to raise and lower weights gently, just so they bump bottom every few feet. This stirs up mud, which, coupled with the steady flash of turning chrome, prods lakers into a feeding fenzy.

Sometimes just a hint of flash or color ahead of lures will produce strikes. Some anglers, for example, remove the hooks from a Williams Wabler spoon, turn it around, and use it as a flasher. A large Flatfish, again with hooks removed, will also work to attract trout and salmon.

But too much flash, particularly in clear, shallow water, may turn off fish, especially king salmon. Then it is best to run a couple of lines with attractors, along with some offerings pulled clean. (As noted on page 6, in deeper water many fishermen stack their attractor rigs with small flutter-type spoons). You can subdue flash, too, by downsizing attractors. That is, opt for small delta-shaped blades rather than big clam-shaped ones on cowbells, or choose 00 or even 000 dodgers instead of the 0-sized eight- or 10-inchers.

Cowbell with various Wobble-Glos.

Pattern Fishing. I first learned about this tactic from Bob Stone, a Lake Michigan charterboat skipper from Wisconsin. The idea is to simulate a school of baitfish by running identical lures closely together.

It works. One September morning, a partner and I were fishing for kings out of Harrisville (37) on Lake Huron. A radio report tipped us off about schooling fish nearby that were hitting chrome J-Plugs halfway to bottom in 30 feet of water. We didn't have any chrome Js, but Joe found a fistful of No. 88 silver Sutton Spoons. We put them on our four downriggers, which we locked in at 18, 20, 22 and 24 feet, after staggering leads from 20-30 feet. Over the next 90 minutes, we caught five kings to 23 pounds each, lost a pair, and had a couple of more knock-offs.

Monochromatic Fishing. This is a variation of pattern fishing, and again the purpose is to imitate a school of baitfish. Monochromatic fishing, however, involves running the same lure *colors*, but not necessarily the same type. Further, the lures are not placed unusually close to each other. Skip Stafford, a charterboat captain out of New Buffalo (1), was the first to use the term, "monochromatic" fishing, and probably discovered the method. Another skipper, Bill Muirhead of Milford, Michigan, has experienced success by using the monochromatic method on one side of his boat while choosing a variety of color for lures on the other side. That way, if a certain color suddenly becomes productive, Muirhead can switch to the monochromatic method on either or both sides of his boat.

Other Tactics. Fine-tuned trolling methods bring to mind several other ideas, which, according to their originators, work. Captain Howard Mills of Algonac, Michigan, for example, releases lures, then allows them to wobble to the surface while he holds the rod or watches it in a holder—a practice called *fluttering*. *Rattle-producing plugs*, such as jointed J-Plugs and Clatter Tads, have produced for some in stained or dirty water, most notably in harbors. In spring, savvy skippers like Frank Arleth of Roscommon, Michigan, tie *loop knots* to their Rapalas and other body baits to give the lures proper up-and-down and left-and-right action.

Much of the fun involved with trolling the Great Lakes is coming up with such advanced rigging tactics. Their use makes better fishermen out of those that are already pretty good.

SHORE- and PIER-FISHING TACTICS

Not everyone owns a boat or can afford to hire a charterboat skipper to take him fishing. Fortunately, there are many publicly owned places along the 3,000 miles of Michigan's Great Lakes coastline where shore anglers can follow their sport. These public access sites include piers, breakwalls, harbors and rivermouths—all places where fishermen and other recreationists congregate. Other spots include lonely beach strands far from a dwelling or road.

To the shore-bound fisherman, pastures often seem greener in the trolling lanes far out into the lake. But sometimes the fishing is better close to shore, occasionally in water so shallow that boat anglers can't reach it. This is especially true in early spring and again in fall, when trout and salmon cruise shoreward to feed or to spawn.

In summer, Chinook salmon and sometimes Skamania steelhead make commando-like raids on rivermouths, where they seek food sluicing along with the current. Pier and breakwall anglers catch them in the inky darkness before dawn. Even during daylight hours, fishing here can be phenomenal. That is because trout and salmon are often attracted to the river's changing water temperature—warmer than the lake in spring or cooler than the lake in fall.

Also, fish may suddenly appear when a shift in wind direction sends a plume of discolored river water into the cleaner lake at a different angle than usual. At times this milky water, also called the "color line," even washes back toward shore along the edges of the structure. Because the darker water helps to camouflage their approach, predators are often found in the area. So boat fishermen stitch an invisible seam along the inside edge of the color line, and pier and breakwall anglers cast their lures and bait into it.

In spring, trout and salmon can be caught in wave troughs, depressions which have been scooped out by pounding waves over a period of time. These six- to 12-foot-wide and three- to eight-foot-deep troughs are usually found in sandy bottoms close to and parallel to shore. All salmonid species like to cruise these troughs in search of spawning smelt or alewives.

Landed anglers, then, not only have opportunity but bonus chances as well to catch Great Lakes trout and salmon (and, as we shall see, many other species). Those who fish from the shorelines are called "surf fishermen."

Most shore fishermen either spincast 2/5- to one-ounce spoons and spinners or stillfish nightcrawlers, wigglers, (larvae of the mayfly), spawn bags, minnows or cut bait such as frozen smelt or alewives. Spincasters wade into the surf or river or stand on the piers or breakwalls. They use the fancast method, making perhaps 15-20 casts in a left-to-right or right-to-left sequence until all available water has been covered. They vary the speed of retrieve and the color, shape and size of lures until a fish strikes. Open- or closed-faced spinning reels or baitcasting reels mated to one- or two-piece medium-action rods from five to eight feet long and featuring a pistol grip work well.

Bait fishermen, on the other hand, usually opt for noodlestick rods from nine to 14 feet long. These buggy-whip rods, usually made of graphite, help anglers to both feel the soft tap of an interested salmon or trout and to set hooks. Many veterans spool their open- or closed-faced reels with monofilament as delicate as one- or two-pound test.

Most pin spawn bags under the knot or thread chunks of dried steelhead spawn still in the skein onto small treble hooks. Then—with the aid of a small sinker 12-24 inches above the bait—they toss the offering into the lake. A good trick is to add a small chip of styrofoam or miniature marshmallow to a spawn bag to help keep it just off bottom. For the same reason, some use bobbers with spawn and other bait, and still others rely upon wave action to lift the bait to and fro along bottom.

No matter what bait you use, once you have cast it out, reel in all slack and slide the rod butt into a rod holder—usually a piece of two-inch PVC pipe. Set the drag for slight tension, then sit back and wait for a strike. Some fishermen leave the bail open on open-faced reels so that a thieving trout or salmon can run with the bait for a few feet. Then the angler sets his hook with a hard snap of the wrist. Another tip is to add a bell or a small bobber to the monofilament near the rod tip to register strikes while you spincast with another outfit.

Likely spots to cast to from piers and breakwalls are in the "chute" between the structures (especially before boat traffic chases any fish out), at the ends, and along the outside edges. At rivermouths, toss lures and bait by quartering across the flow after first choosing a spot upstream as a casting target. The object is to let your offering tumble along near bottom with the current while you spool with a steady retrieve. Strike zones are nearly always just outside of the main current, near structures such as rocks or logs, or in holes just before they lip out into the open lake. Along the shore, target your offerings in wave troughs and near any structure (boulders, logs, dropoffs) that is available.

GREAT FISH OF THE GREAT LAKES

Following is a brief description of each of the gamefish species that anglers will find in the Great Lakes plus some general catching tips. Detailed catching information, including local lures and tactics, is included, when applicable, in each port and rivermouth description throughout the book.

Chinook Salmon

Planted out as spring fingerlings by the DNR, Chinook salmon spawn and die in the fall as four-year-old adults (these are mostly females; many of the males spawn and die in the fall as three-year-olds). Chinooks are the largest of the Pacific Ocean imports, often attaining weights of 30 or more pounds.

Identifying characteristics, besides their great size, include a gray/black mouth and gray gums, 15-17 rays on the anal fin, and a nearly squared tail. Dime-bright in spring and early summer, adult fish turn a light olive, then a khaki color, as they begin to school off natal release sites in late summer, preparatory to spawning.

Chinooks (or "kings" as they are commonly called) prefer 54-degree-F. water, usually near structure, although they will sometimes suspend between top and bottom when food (mostly smelt, alewives and other minnows) is nearby. They are often spooky in clear, shallow water and are intolerant of racket from churning props and flashing lures all around them.

Chinooks are good fighters that will thoroughly test tackle. They willingly strike body baits in spring shallows, spoons and flies at all depths in summer, and large wobbling plugs and big spoons in fall shallows. Nearly all colors attract them at one time or another.

Coho Salmon

Cohos (they are occasionally called "silvers," too) spawn and die as three-year-old adults, a year and one-half after being planted in the Great Lakes as 18-month-old smolts. Average size of spawners is about eight pounds; however, they may grow as large as 20 pounds.

The inside of the mouth is usually black, with teeth set in gray/white gums. The anal fin contains 13-15 rays, and the tail is slightly forked. Like kings, cohos are bright silver in spring and summer and turn darker as spawning time nears. Male cohos develop a pronounced hook jaw by the time they enter rivers, normally in September or October.

Cohos—another West Coast immigrant—are generally found closer to the surface than kings; consequently, most are taken on shallow setups. You'll want to pull planer boards and run outriggers, especially in spring and fall, and it's always a good idea to flatline at least one outfit right in the prop wash itself, 25-50 feet behind the boat. When summer fishing, cover all the depths where 52- to 56-degree-F. water is observed. Even then, a line within 10 feet of the surface will often take cruising cohos. They like small plugs and spoons in hot colors—fluorescent red, chartreuse, yellow, and orange are preferred. In late summer and fall, they will nail bright-colored dodgers ahead of trolling flies or squids.

Atlantic Salmon

"Atlantics," as these scrappy East Coast salmon are usually called, are often confused with brown trout. One difference is the tongue, which on the Atlantic salmon is narrow, pointed, and tipped with four to six small teeth. (The tongue of the brown trout is broad, square, and tipped with 11-12 large teeth). On an Atlantic, the upper jaw barely reaches the rear of the eye; on a brown, it extends beyond the eye. If you still can't tell the two species apart, try "tailing," (holding the fish by gripping its girth ahead of the tail) the fish. A brown trout will not slip from your grasp; an Atlantic probably will.

Atlantics spawn in fall but do not necessarily die after completing reproductive chores. The average weight of an adult is eight to 10 pounds, and they are excellent fighters, often leaving the water several times before yielding to the net.

They are caught mostly in Lake Michigan, where they have been released in small numbers since 1972, and are taken incidentally to other species.

Pink Salmon

Pink or hump-backed salmon are the smallest of the Pacific Coast salmonids, averaging 1-1/2 to two pounds each. Also called "pinks" or "humpies" (males develop a pronounced hump on their backs when they enter rivers with females to spawn), they were accidentally released into Lake Superior by Canadian fisheries biologists in 1955 and are now found in all five Great Lakes. Lake Huron is especially abundant with these natural-spawning pinks, and some anglers view them as a nuisance there.

Actually, they are sporting fun on light line, both in the open lake through trolling tactics and in rivers where they spawn every two years. Until recently, it was thought that the little salmon preyed on zooplankton and other small organisms. Now biologists and fishermen alike realize that pinks are voracious feeders of small minnows and that they will willingly strike lures, especially those trolled in the upper 50 feet of the Great Lakes.

When caught in the lake, the silvery fish are easily confused with young cohos or Chinooks. A closer look will reveal that the caudal fin (tail) contains large, oval black blotches called "parr marks." Other features include small scales (170-229 in the row above the lateral line) and 24-35 rakers in the first gill arch. In September, as spawning time nears, their dark-green backs and upper sides descend to white bellies, and parr marks are elongated dark spots with doughnut-like holes.

Lake Trout

With the exception of coaster brook trout, the lake trout is the only salmonid native to the Great Lakes. In cleaner waters, such as portions of Lake Superior, lake trout (also called "lakers" or "forktails") sustain populations through natural reproduction. Even so, federal and state hatcheries throughout the Great Lakes region continue to raise them.

Average weight of an adult laker is about eight pounds, but huge fish of 50 or more pounds have been caught. Besides a characteristic forked tail, lake trout sport lower fins edged with white, 11 rays on the anal fin, creamy bellies, and upper sides and backs of light spots on a darker gray/green background.

They do not die after spawning in lake-shoal waters during October. Lake trout prefer 46- to 50-degree-F. temperatures and also like structure. In summer they are caught as deep as 300 feet but in spring and fall enter shallows to feed and spawn respectively. They are bottom-oriented fish and only occasionally suspend to seek food.

Jig fishermen catch them year-round (in Michigan waters of Lake Huron and Michigan the season is May 1-August 15) with silver spoons and bright-colored jigs tipped with cut bait. Trollers use wire line or downriggers to spear big flashing spoons, dodgers and flies, or cowbells and small plugs and spoons, along bottom.

Brown Trout

Brown trout grow to 30 pounds in the Great Lakes but typically weigh in at four to eight pounds. They are exciting fish to catch because they give a strong accounting of themselves and also like to leap. Browns are also shy, moody fish, sometimes difficult to entice into striking.

As noted in "Atlantic Salmon" (page 16), brown trout have broad, square tongues tipped with 11-12 large teeth in mouths that are whitish in appearance. The anal fin contains 12 or less rays, and the tail is squared. Lake-caught browns are silver in appearance, with upper sides sprinkled with check marks that resemble small *X*s (unlike river browns which usually are a brown/yellow in color and sport red dots on their sides).

They like water temperatures of 60-70 degrees F. and are often found near bottom among boulder fields and jagged structure. On calm summer days of heat and humidity, however, they can sometimes be seen porpoising in small schools that resemble frolicking carp.

Trollers take them from spring through fall on small spoons and plugs in silver, white, chartreuse, copper, dull-orange or gold colors. Tactics include longlining with light line or spincasting with spoons in the shallows when browns move homeward to spawn in fall.

Steelhead

Steelhead are a surf- and pier-fisherman's dream come true. Although most spawn in Great Lakes tributaries in spring, plenty show up at rivermouths in fall, too, mainly to feed upon the eggs of other spawners, namely brown trout, lake trout and salmon. In the river, steelhead readily hit spawn or bright-colored flies rolled along bottom, and in the lake, trollers catch them incidentally to other trout and salmon.

Also called "steelies," steelhead are actually lake-run rainbow trout. Many races are now planted in the Great Lakes by the eight states and one Canadian province that own bordering real estate. Some of the governments release rainbows in harbors, where they stay put to provide year-round sport. Steelhead, on the other hand, may travel great distances in the Great Lakes before returning each year to spawn.

Skamania, Rogue, Siletz and Umpqua river strains—all summer-run steelhead recently imported from the West Coast—are already serving up June and July sport for shallow-water trollers. They promise to provide action in streams from August until March.

Steelhead/rainbows have mouths and gums that are white in appearance, and their anal fins contain 10-12 rays. Average weight is about seven pounds although 20- to 25-pounders are caught each year. Steelhead do not die after spawning; however, few live beyond six years.

Spring trollers catch them in the shallows with other salmonids. Summer-caught fish usually come off outriggers and flatlines. Like cohos, steelhead like silver and hot colors in lures.

Splake

Splake are a hatchery-bred hybrid cross between brook trout and lake trout, with some characteristics of both parents. They are sometimes planted in harbors and bays to provide a year-round fishery for jig and spincast fishermen, although they can also be caught with trolling methods. They average three to five pounds.

The tail is less forked than a lake trout but not as square as a brook trout. The anal fin contains 10 rays, and the sides and upper backs most generally are spotted, resembling lake trout rather than the wormy pattern of the brook trout.

Brook Trout

Brook trout, often called "brookies" or "squaretails," are also called "coasters" when they live in the Great Lakes. Along Lake Superior and in Grand Traverse Bay (where they are infrequently caught by spincasters after steelhead or trollers after salmon or lake trout), coasters may grow to five pounds each. Recently, the DNR has begun planting fingerling brookies in selected locations such as Eagle Bay and Presque Isle Harbor in Lake Huron, Bowers Harbor in Lake Michigan, and the Little Huron River and Copper Harbor in Lake Superior.

Great Lakes brookies usually lack the pronounced red dots circled by blue haloes that are characteristic of stream brook trout. However, they are easily identified by the square tail and lower fins edged in white with a black border. Usually the back contains a wormlike pattern of black over olive or blue/black.

Besides salmon and trout,

here are four other cold-water gamefish species:

Lake Herring

Lake herring, also called "ciscoes," usually run about 12-15 inches in length and weigh from 1/2 to 3/4 pound. Normally bottom feeders like their larger cousins, the lake whitefish, herring are most abundant from the Straits area east to Canada. They are caught in midsummer during the annual mayfly hatch and also in late November and early December when they move into Great Lakes shoal waters to spawn. Like whitefish, ciscoes are delicious to eat.

Lake Whitefish

A main target of commercial fishermen but also actively sought by a growing number of sport anglers, whitefish are abundant in many portions of the Great Lakes. Whitefish are often found to depths of 200 and even 300 feet, except in late fall when schools of the three- to eight-pounders move into hard-bottom areas of 15-25 feet deep to spawn.

Whitefish are a delicacy when baked, pan-fried or smoked, but they are not always easy to catch. Their tiny mouths are soft, making hook set and retrieve difficult, especially at great depths. Still, jig fishermen catch them on single salmon eggs, freshwater shrimp, tiny minnows and insects such as Canadian soldiers and mayflies. In addition to the spawning period, best times are winter (through the ice) or in June or July.

Menominees

—Photo by Richard Smith—

Also called "round whitefish," menominees are mostly bottom feeders that are targets of commercial fishermen. However, in spring and fall, they move into shallow waters near rivermouths of the northern portions of the Great Lakes to feed and to spawn respectively. That is when pier and shore fishermen catch them with single salmon eggs and small worms. The rest of the year, menominees are difficult to find.

Round whitefish can grow to four or five pounds, but most are caught as 12- to 15-inch fish that weigh one or two pounds each. In recent years, anglers have been taking them from the Au Sable River mouth north in Lake Huron and from the Manistee River mouth north in Lake Michigan. In Lake Superior, the eastern Upper Peninsula, especially Alger County stream mouths and the Grand Marais pier, is another popular area.

Smelt

Dipping for spawning smelt in April and May is how many winter-weary anglers herald the coming spring. Prospects vary from year to year along Lake Michigan and Lake Huron tributaries, but there are usually enough smelt to provide a determined angler with a meal or two.

These good-to-eat silvery slivers (they average seven or eight inches in length) are also available in Lake Superior, although populations have tumbled in recent years. Native to the northern Atlantic Coast, smelt made their way up the St. Lawrence River to the Great Lakes. Their introduction to Lake Michigan was assured when they were planted in Crystal Lake in 1912.

Some anglers catch the biggest ones—up to a foot long—by jigging through the ice in deep arms of the Great Lakes such as Grand Traverse Bay. You sure can't accuse smelt fishermen of being dull. A few shanty anglers, for example, rely on lanterns to cause plankton, a principle food, to rise near the surface, then catch the smelt on single salmon eggs or freshwater shrimp. Others use bicycle wheels mounted to the ceiling of the shanty to act as fishing reels and to help them quickly send lures to bottom and retrieve fish before the school moves on.

The following descriptions are for warm-water species of fish in the Great Lakes.

Walleyes

The largest member of the perch family, walleyes are caught in selected bays throughout the Great Lakes from the statewide opener on May 15 until its close on February 28. (Certain areas are open year-round, too; check the *Michigan Fishing Guide* for details.)

Walleyes like structure that is not too deep. Look for rocky ledges, reefs, contour breaks, river-channel inclines, sand bars and drowned timber from 10-50 feet deep. They prefer water temperatures from 55-65 degrees F. and, because they are primarily night-feeders, are often taken during low-light conditions and after dark.

To catch them, most anglers either troll or driftfish with live bait such as minnows, nightcrawlers or leeches. Other fishermen have developed specialized tactics such as "counting down" while spincasting with weight-forward spinners or trolling with downriggers and planer boards and small lures.

Many claim that the walleye is the Great Lakes finest table delicacy because the flesh is firm and white and has a mild flavor. The best eaters are one- and two-pound fish, the typical size, although walleyes may grow to 15 pounds or more. They are not noted as aggressive fighters.

Largemouth Bass

—Photo by Randy Carrels—

Shallow, sandy Great Lakes bays containing lily pads, cattails or bulrushes are usually home to largemouth bass, also called "bigmouths." Here, they share home turf with northern pike, muskies and panfish.

Unlike smallmouths, largemouth bass can tolerate warmer temperatures—to 80 degrees F.—but they are similar to smallmouths in that they spawn in late spring or early summer and that the males are especially protective of nests.

A decent bigmouth from the Great Lakes is four pounds, although they grow much larger in inland lakes.

Spincasting with spoons, plugs, spinnerbaits, buzzbaits, and surface poppers is the rated method for catching them, no matter where they are found. Along the Great Lakes, many fishermen wade the shallows for bass or cruise shoreline areas in small boats pushed by a quiet outboard or electric motor.

Smallmouth Bass

Also called "bronzebacks" or "smallies," smallmouth bass furnish some of the best fighting action among all Great Lakes species. Some anglers claim that, ounce-for-ounce, a smallmouth can outduel a Skamania steelhead, Chinook or Atlantic salmon or brown trout. Twelve to 15 inches is average size, although some smallmouths grow to 20-23 inches and will plunge a butcher's scale beyond five pounds.

In the Great Lakes, bronzebacks are most often found off points, around islands, and over shallow-water reefs—especially when the water is not too deep (three to 25 feet) and where a hard bottom of cobblestone, gravel or rock is found. Don't overlook areas of current, too, such as wind-swept points and rivermouths. Smallies like 65- to 70-degree-F. water and are most easily caught when they invade shallow water to spawn. This normally occurs from late June through mid-July.

The males, especially protective of spawning beds, will drill spinnerbaits, spinners, and small spoons cast nearby. Live bait is also a solid producer in spring, summer and fall. Try wigglers, hellgrammites, leeches, worms, and minnows, either pinned to skirted jigs or fished clean. Smallmouths will also hit streamers, dry flies and small poppers when flyfished by wading anglers.

Muskellunge

—Ontario MNR photo—

There are three kinds of muskellunge, or "muskies" as they are usually called, in certain waters of the Great Lakes. *Great Lakes* muskies have a color pattern of dark spots over a light background. *Northern* or *purebred* muskies, on the other hand, are sometimes difficult to distinguish from northern pike, unless you look carefully at gill covers and cheeks. (The northern pike's cheeks are fully scaled; the northern muskie's cheeks, along with its gill covers, are half-scaled.) *Tiger* muskies are hatchery-bred crosses of northern-pike and northern-muskie parents. Sterile hybrids, tigers feature the head-scale pattern of the pike with the color pattern of the muskie—longitudinal bars on their sides over a light background (except that the bars are darker than on a purebred muskie)

Most muskies caught in Great Lakes bays, Lake St. Clair and the St. Mary's River are the spotted Great Lakes strain fish. However, tigers are caught in some drowned rivermouths where they have been released, and northern muskies often live in rivers, such as the Manistee, that flow into the Great Lakes.

Habits, habitat and catching tactics approximate those for northern pike, except that muskie veterans beef up their equipment with heavy-duty rods and reels and huge plugs, spoons, and bucktail spinners.

Northern Pike

Northern pike to nearly 40 pounds have been taken from the Great Lakes, although most average five to eight pounds. They are caught in shallow, weedy bays and in drowned rivermouths—actually inland lakes—such as Hamlin, Manistee, Macatawa and Pentwater, along Lake Michigan. Fearless as well as fearsome, pike are efficient predators with large teeth and the willingness to attack prey half their own size.

Northerns are brown/yellow or green/yellow in appearance with white undersides and reddish fins when the light shines through them. Their upper flanks exhibit a pattern of yellow/white blotches that vary in color, depending upon the bottom composition where they are found.

Soon after ice-out, pike spawn in marshy areas. Beginning on the May 15 opener, anglers catch them by trolling or spincasting spoons and plugs along weed lines and over dropoffs. Bobber fishing with two- to eight-inch suckers, smelt or shiners is also productive. In winter, tip-ups replace bobbers, and many pike are also speared by anglers who wait patiently in shanties (also called "ice shacks" or "darkhouses") while jigging a decoy minnow in the murky depths below the ice.

Contrary to what some people believe, northerns are very good to eat, especially in winter, when the meat is firm.

Yellow Perch

Perch fishing is one of the few really good angling bargains left to just about everybody. You don't need a boat and motor since many "yellow-bellies," as perch are often called, are taken from piers, breakwalls, boat docks and shore itself.

The prolific yellow-belly is plentiful; well distributed in lakes Michigan, Huron, Erie and St. Clair; and fairly easy to catch. If you can find perch, they can usually be coaxed into biting small jigs, spoons, and Russian Hooks tipped with a minnow, wax-worm, mousie or redworm.

The goal of most serious perchers is to catch a 50-fish limit of jumbos—those ruler-long slabs that each weighs a pound or more. This can be done in early spring at ice-out, when perch invade Great Lakes tributaries and shoreline shallows to spawn and again in fall when they return to feed. In summer and winter, yellow-bellies move about in hungry schools, according to age class (five- to 10-inchers are the most common), in water that is 10-50 feet deep. Nearly always they are found over hard-bottom areas (cobble, sand, gravel) near weed beds.

Yellow perch are among our best-eating Great Lakes fish.

Bluegills and Pumpkinseeds.

Bluegills and pumpkinseeds (the pumpkinseed is also called "sunfish," but both species are members of the sunfish family) provide fun sport through the ice and in May over spawning beds. Most fishing activity occurs on inland lakes, although anglers who seek them in certain Great Lakes shallow-water bays—especially in Lake St. Clair—are often rewarded.

In order to catch the big ones—the snub-nosed one-pounders that stretch from the tip of your middle finger to your watch band—you must use one- or two-pound-test line and the tiniest spoons or ice flies you can find. Take special pains to cover the hook barb completely. Careful, determined jigging, an inch or so at a time, will produce strikes that are notoriously soft.

Crappies

Crappies are caught in shallow bays of the Great Lakes and at rivermouths on early and late ice when they enter shallows to feed and in April and May when they return to these areas to spawn. Often called "papermouths" because of the thin membrane that covers their soft mouths, crappies can tolerate fairly warm water (to 80 degrees F.) that is cloudy.

Average size is eight or nine inches, although two-pound slabs nearly as round as dinner plates and measuring 15-17 inches also appear. Anglers that get into such jumbos rarely catch only one since crappies move around in age-class groups, much like back-alley thugs looking for a mugging victim. In this case, the victim will likely be small minnows or emerging insects.

When fished through the ice, crappies willingly strike small spoons and jigs sweetened with a minnow, piece of worm or larval form such as a mealworm or waxworm. In open water, anglers catch them on spinners, small spinnerbaits, and skirted jigs with or without meat. Papermouths will also hit live bait fished halfway to bottom with the aid of a bobber. Night fishing with lighted bobbers is especially effective in the shallows in spring and fall.

White Bass

Also called "silver bass" or "silvers," white bass look like large members of the sunfish family but actually belong to the sea bass family, which contains striped bass or stripers. Most silvers weigh about a pound and average 10-12 inches in length.

White bass live in shallow, clear waters of Lake St. Clair and Lake Erie and certain warm-water bays like Saginaw Bay. They travel in schools, which sometimes number several hundred fish, and may move several miles in a day while looking for food or suitable places to spawn (normally hard-bottom shoal water).

When white bass go on a feeding spree, usually early or late in the day, they often send panicked minnows flying from the water. Feeding silvers are easy to catch with any kind of small lure if you can get close enough to cast to them. The school will quickly move on, but if you can stay with them, it does not take long to fill a 25-fish limit.

Channel Catfish

Probably the most underharvested gamefish in the Great Lakes, channel catfish, or "channel cats" as they are usually called, are quite prolific in shallow warm-water bays such as Green Bay, Saginaw Bay and Little and Big Bays de Noc. They also live in many Great Lakes tributaries—the St. Mary's, Cheboygan, Grand, Muskegon, St. Clair and Detroit rivers, to name just a few—and they inhabit Lake St. Clair and Lake Erie.

Channel cats grow to 10 pounds or more and are good to eat if skinned and dressed for the table soon after catching them. Most anglers hook them by bottomfishing worms or various blood and stink baits, but catfish will also hit driftfished lures and baits as well as downrigger-trolled plugs and spoons.

Night fishing from an anchored boat or while sitting on a pier is the best time to catch them. Yet catfish have a pretty good appetite during daylight hours, too.

Rock Bass

The same southernmost shallow-water regions of the Great Lakes that produce bluegills and pumpkinseeds also produce another member of the sunfish family, the rock bass. These fish, like bluegills, travel in schools but are much easier to catch. Ten or 12 inches is a good-sized fish.

Rock bass hit small spinners and just about any live bait when jigged or retrieved slowly along bottom, especially in areas where there are drowned brush piles, rock piles, gravel bars and timber.

Other Warm-Water Species

Carp, buffalofish, freshwater drum (sheepshead), bullheads, mooneyes, suckers, carpsuckers, longnose gar and bowfin (dogfish) are other warm-water species that inhabit shallow, warm areas of the Great Lakes. But since most fishermen consider them rough species and because they are usually caught incidentally to other fish, I have not given them special consideration.

Channel catfish.

Carp shot with a bow.

Sea-Horse

LOWER PENINSULA

Note: Maps included with each chapter are not to be used for navigational purposes.

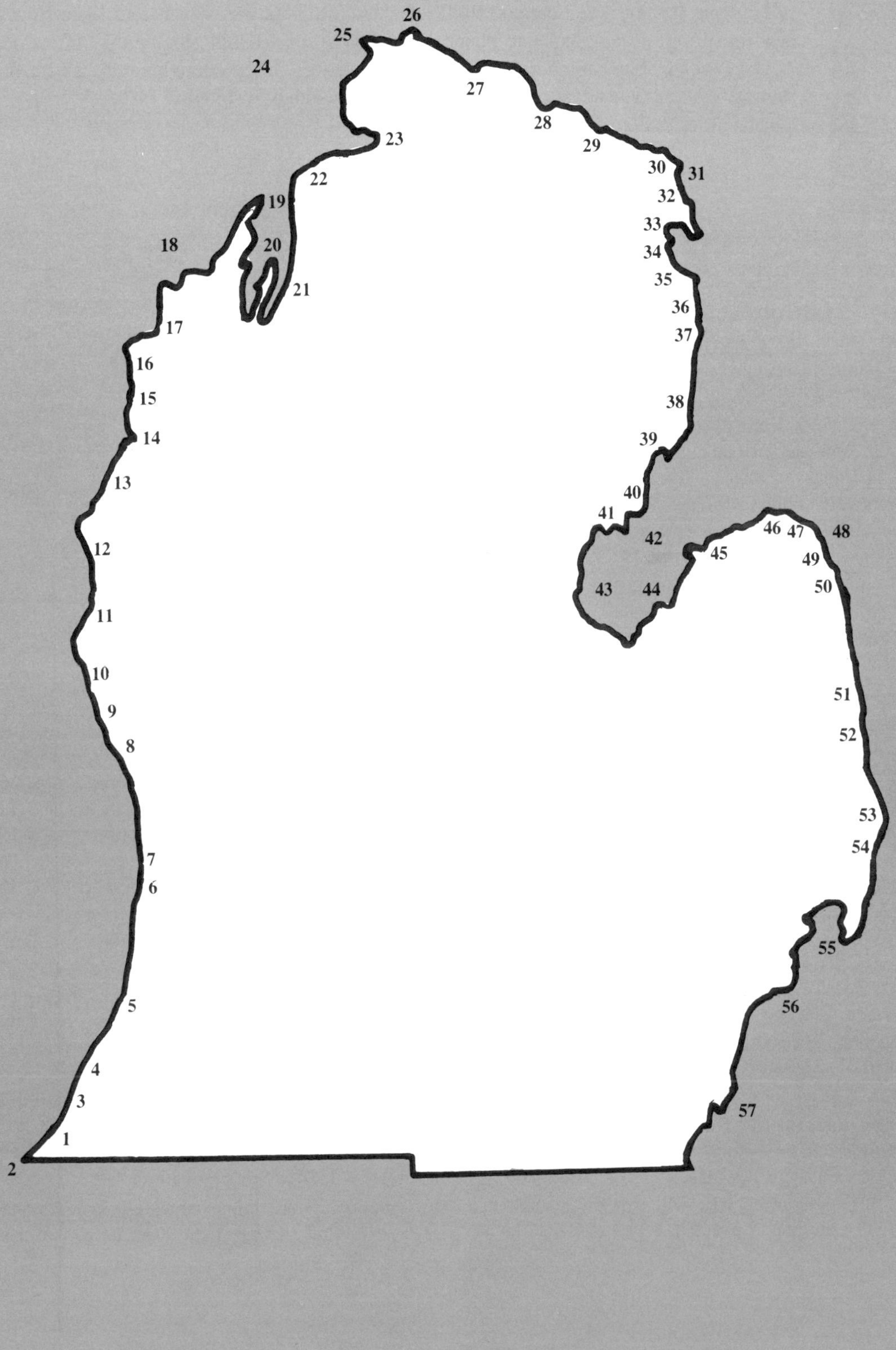

1
NEW BUFFALO

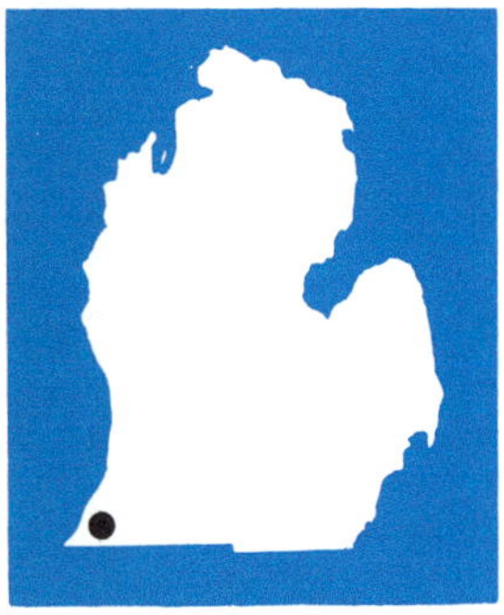

Michigan's southernmost Lake Michigan port, New Buffalo serves up outstanding sport for spring salmon and summer (Skamania) steelhead. Also available are brown trout, lake trout and Michigan steelhead in spring, as well as some phenomenal July-August fishing for jumbo yellow perch.

The area has long been popular with tourists, as well. They come here to visit the dunes, stay in modern state parks, and take advantage of southeastern Michigan hospitality. Fishermen, too, can enjoy the excellent facilities and accommodations.

Fishing Schedule

It is no secret that salmon congregate in southern Lake Michigan shallows off Michigan City, Indiana, and New Buffalo and Benton Harbor/St. Joseph, Michigan. Plenty of thermal gush from the factory belt from East Chicago west to Michigan City, spring rains, the sun, and tributary runoff all add up to early warm water. Michigan-, Indiana-, Illinois-, and Wisconsin-planted fish mix freely in the region as they feast on the hordes of smelt, shiners and alewives that make spawning appearances each *spring*.

Ice-out, depending upon temperatures as well as wind direction and velocity, can occur by late March or early April. Fishermen off the Cook Nuclear Plant at Bridgman (3), just a few miles north, jig for cohos and browns as early as February.

New Buffalo spring breakwall anglers take fish by flinging spawn bags, nightcrawler gobs, and frozen two-inch alewives into lake shallows, then allowing the bait to settle to bottom on a tight line. Spincasters can also score by tossing K.O. Wobblers, Little Jewels, Kastmasters, Devle Dogs, and other heavy spoons. Try silver color, alone or in combination with blue, hot green, chartreuse or blaze orange. Blue Fox, Rooster Tails, and Mepps spinners also rate when spincast in spring.

One of the most successful trollers out of New Buffalo is Captain Skip Stafford, who ramrods a fleet of boats for hire collectively called Skipper's Charters. Typical spring rigging on *Skipper III*, a 32-foot Trojan Sportfisherman, includes four stern-end Cannon downriggers with four-foot arms and two out-downs with five-foot booms. The six riggers are set up in a standard *V*—that is out-downs are high and back-end models are set deeper, with the center unit going down the furthest.

When fishing is slow, Captain Skip won't hesitate to stack extra spoons via Offshore Releases or rubber bands to already-set downriggers. Release lengths vary, but stacked offerings are kept within 10 feet of the parent line. He will typically swing out a pair of outriggers featuring 17-pound-test lead-core line, sometimes stacking with rubber bands attached to free-sliding coil-spring releases. Yellow Bird side planers are hauled out for brown trout and Skamanias if fish are in shallow and are spooking from engine rumble or boat shadow.

When I fished with Stafford on April 22, 1985, (see "How to *Buffalo* Spring Salmon," page 29) we deep-sixed J-Plugs and lookalike Lucky Louies and Canadian Plugs in white with red cheeks, banana with brown stripes on back, silver bullets, white with chartruese back, hot green with white belly, and lemon with black ladderback. We also pulled hot lemon-with-silver-belly Fat Raps. These plugs were all downrigger-trolled. We sent out silver-with-red-prism Williams Wablers on the outriggers and did not use planers. Other lures reportedly hot in spring at New Buffalo include J-11 Rapalas in just about any color, hammered-silver and lime-and-chartruese Flutter Chucks, Lindy-Little Joe Shadlings and Pop Tails, Lucky Lures, and Northport Nailers.

Skip also practices something he calls "monochromatic" fishing. The word means "one color," and to achieve it he simply runs several different lures at the same time—all of the same color. There are many variations to the method, but the goal is to simulate a school of baitfish. The key, however (as with any lure choice), is to mate lures that are compatible. Otherwise, some offerings won't run in harness with others, and you'll be wasting time washing ineffective baits or, worse yet, having to perform time-consuming surgery on fouled lines.

So it is not uncommon to see a dozen rods bristle from the aft of a Skipper charter, and monochromatic fishing is a major reason that Stafford and the three or four other captains that work for him cooler upwards of 2,000 trout and salmon each trolling season. Typical coolers yield 25 percent cohos from April 1 to May 15 and about 40 percent king salmon from April 15 to June 15. Skamanias contribute at least one-fourth of all catches in July and the first half of August. Michigan steelhead, browns and lake trout also figure in the season-long tally .

In early spring, trollers target the warmest water possible, such as at the flow of Galien River discharge into the lake. (Also in

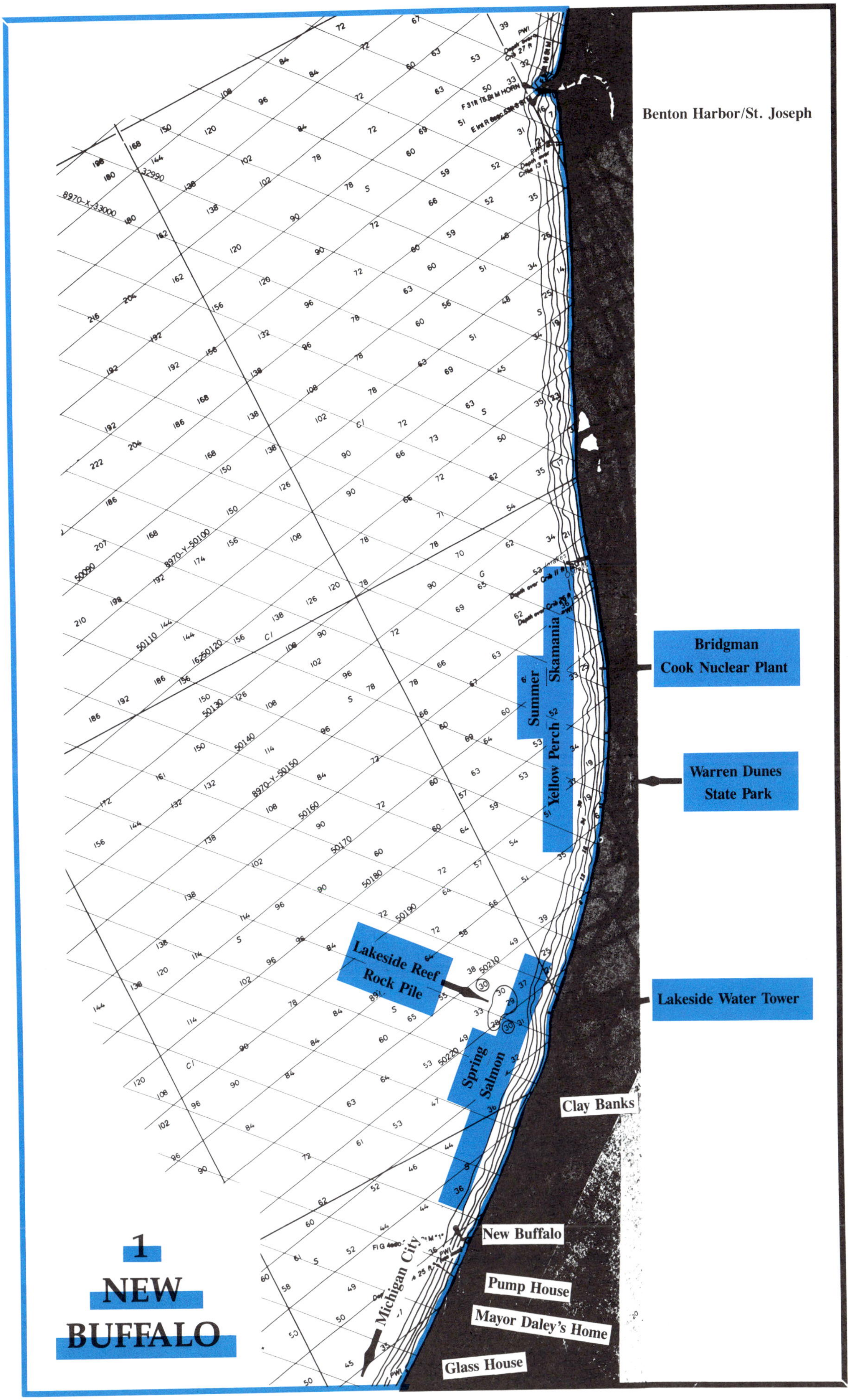
Benton Harbor/St. Joseph
Bridgman
Cook Nuclear Plant
Warren Dunes
State Park
Lakeside Water Tower
Summer
Skamania
Yellow Perch
Lakeside Reef
Rock Pile
Spring
Salmon
Clay Banks
New Buffalo
Pump House
Mayor Daley's Home
Glass House
Michigan City
1
NEW
BUFFALO

Jim Ford of Otisville (left) caught this 17-pound Skamania out of Michigan City (2) while fishing with Captain Jon Belliveau (right).

NEW BUFFALO (cont.)

early spring, the Galien River produces some nice steelhead throughout its length.) Other spots include the Cook Plant at Bridgman and several nameless creeks. Warm-water areas can also be found in the wave-scooped trough paralleling shore, the upper 10-20 feet of water throughout the lake, and vertical bars that create an edge effect—caused from the lake turning over prior to establishing its thermocline. Many spring fishermen have installed surface thermometers, which allow them to constantly monitor lake-top temperatures.

By June most of the salmon have headed for deeper water, and trollers have to probe depths to 150 feet to find them. They also bump into lake trout, especially if they target 48- to 52-degree-F. water on or near bottom and run dodgers or cowbells with plenty of flash ahead of small plugs and spoons.

SUMMER

By mid-June, reports of *summer* steelhead are coming in to New Buffalo and to Michigan City, where they were released by the Indiana DNR. With hefty releases also going into the St. Joseph River a few miles north, New Buffalo's reputation as a producer of big Skamanias will only be enhanced.

Male fish enter the fishery first and seem to take delight in trouncing lures in solid silver or those containing hot red or hot orange. The 20-pound-plus male steelhead—torpedo-shaped and built to smash tackle—do much of their fighting out of water and are enormous fun on light line. Trollers catch the exciting Skamanias in the upper 25 or so feet of water, and many report good catches during the heat of the day—from about 10 a.m. until 2 p.m.

July also sees the return of jumbo yellow perch that flock to the breakwall and offshore structure to 60 feet deep. A popular spot is the Rock Pile (also called Lakeside Reef) in 25-30 feet of water, surrounded by depths to 44 feet. Perch stack up at the structure, located about a mile offshore from the Lakeside Water Tank, to nail emerging newly hatched crayfish.

If you can find live "craws" in area tackle shops, guard the bait with your life and thread only half at a time (the smallest crayfish are the most effective) onto small hooks. Then toss to bottom with the help of a bell or slip sinker and hang on for strikes. Catches of perch to ruler length and beyond occur each summer.

FALL

Fall should see the return of browns and a few steelhead. Salmon drift through the area, too, en route to natal spawning streams such as the St. Joseph River. For those who don't want to add winter preservative to their outboards just yet, southern Lake Michigan receives the following spring's vanguard of small coho, released only a few months earlier as smolts (18-month-old fish). This can be an exciting fishery in November for the small, yet fiesty salmon.

But spring is catching time in southern Lake Michigan, with the months of April through July serving up fully 90 percent of the season-long action.

Landmarks south of the harbor include the Pump House (one mile), former Chicago Mayor Daley's house (three miles), an unnamed creek (3-1/2 miles), and the Glass House (five miles—just over the Indiana line). To the north is the Clay Banks (two miles), the Lakeside Water Tank (four miles), Warren Dunes (seven miles) and the Cook Nuclear Plant at Bridgman (nine miles).

Planting Records

The Michigan DNR has not released salmon here in recent memory. Coho and Chinook salmon that show up off New Buffalo are from Michigan plants further north or from Indiana and Illinois releases. A DNR release of 30,000 lake trout did, however, go over the Rock Pile off Lakeside Water Tower and will be repeated annually for the next five years.

Also, the DNR plans to stock structure off New Buffalo with 30,000 fish each year. New Buffalo has a long history of 10,000-15,000 annual Michigan steelhead releases. These will be continued along with 15,000 brown-trout (mostly yearlings) plants, a program begun in 1982.

Facilities

The DNR operates a boat launch two miles northeast of New Buffalo on the Galien River. Access is also available at the New Buffalo Township and New Buffalo City parks. Those with state park stickers affixed to their windshields can launch at no charge

Lake Michigan

Length—307 miles

Breadth—118 miles

Length of coastline (including islands)—2,730 miles

Total water surface—22,300 square miles

Drainage basin—45,600 square miles

Maximum depth—1,333 feet

Average depth—489 feet

Volume of water—1,180 cubic miles

at Warren Dunes State Park. Though the DNR operates no harbor of refuge, overnight boaters can use facilities at Oselka's Snug Harbor Marina, 514 Oselka Dr., New Buffalo. Call (616) 469-2600. New Buffalo, a community of nearly 3,000, has plenty of accommodations.

Further Information

Chambers of Commerce:

1. Harbor Country Chamber of Commerce, P.O. Box 212, New Buffalo 49117; (616) 469-5409.
2. West Michigan Tourist Association, 136 Fulton St. E., Grand Rapids 49503; (616) 456-8557.

Bait & Tackle Shops:

Impatient II, 135 E. Buffalo St., New Buffalo 49117; (616) 469-5570.

Charter Fishing:

1. Captain Skip Stafford, Skipper's Charter Service, 1296 Linden, St. Joseph 49085; (616) 429-4040. 32-foot Trojan, *Skipper III*, plus other boats.
2. Captain Don Cook, New Buffalo Charter Services, 125 N. Whittaker St., New Buffalo 49117; (616) 469-4510. 31-foot Bertram, *NBC II*.

Department of Natural Resources:

Two fisheries biologists work out of District Headquarters at 621 N. 10th St., Plainwell 49080; (616) 685-6851.

Coast Guard:

Michigan City, Indiana, Station, (219) 879-8371.

How to *Buffalo* Spring Salmon

The sun this April 22 had already heated the earth to 70 degrees as we snaked our way down the Galien River to where it squirts out the New Buffalo breakwall chute into Lake Michigan. Small rafts of half-tame mallards—the drakes sporting heads of polished green—paddled out of our way. Reports of hot salmon action from Michigan City north to South Haven (5) had me aboard the *Skipper III*, a 32-foot Trojan Sportfisherman run by Captain Skip Stafford. I would be stripped to a polo shirt by noon, when temperatures would creep into the mid-80s. The year before, when I fished Lake Michigan on May 9, I wore a snowmobile suit. What a difference a year makes!

With a roar of the twin 233-cubic-inch Mercruiser inboards, we cleared pierheads. After running a mile north, we shut down to a crawl, and First Mate George Pope began trimming lines—six downriggers, a pair of stacked outriggers, and a flatline—with J-Plug-type lures.

I keep records of trolling trips, and my notes tell me that at 8:25 a port-side out-down rod jumped to like a fencing sword. Tim Matheson, a Shakespeare rep aboard the boat, swapped muscle power with that spirited fish, a 14-pound king. At 9:20 we hit a double-header (nine and 14-pound Chinooks), farmered a king at 9:40, and slid an eight-pounder into the box at 9:50.

We were nicely cracking toward a full cooler when we began losing fish. By 11 o'clock we had missed strikes or fumbled away hooked fish a half-dozen times. These strange things happen on trolling boats—kind of like a baseball hitter's batting slump, I suppose. But the slump lasted only a short time, and soon we were back in the plus column again.

Over two days, we handled 32 fish, coolering about a dozen and a half. Not bad for shirtsleeve weather in April at one of Michigan's finest early spring hotspots for trout and salmon.

Tom Huggler
Otisville

2

MICHIGAN CITY

What's an Indiana port doing in a book titled, *Fish Michigan*? For one reason, because so many Michigan fishermen—who can buy a special one-day license for only $3—travel the short distance from Michigan's border after gamefish that don't understand state boundary lines.

Another reason is that there are some unique fishing opportunities here. Though Indiana controls only one percent of the surface area of Lake Michigan, for three or four weeks in midsummer, she has a corner on what some claim is the most electrifying fishery the moody monster has ever served up. In a word this exciting angling is called *Skamania*. Skamanias, the newest addition to a long history of salmonid plants by the Indiana DNR, are torpedo-shaped steelhead imported from the Skamania River in Washington State.

Besides the new-breed steelhead and Chinook and coho salmon, Michigan City also serves up brown trout, winter-run steelhead, lake trout and yellow perch.

All this in a beautiful environment of sand dunes and beaches. All this is why I decided to include the port of Michigan City, Indiana, in *Fish Michigan*.

Fishing Schedule

Shore fishermen begin slinging frozen alewives, spawn, nightcrawlers, and silver-plated spoons off Northern Indiana Public Service Commission's (NIPSCO) warm-water discharge as early as February. Most of the catch is small brown trout, but sometimes cohos and usually yellow perch are also available.

SPRING

As *spring* approaches and the ice goes out, fishing continues to improve off the J-shaped pier and the mouth of Trail Creek, where a new 15-acre park has added some 2,000 feet of fishable shoreline. Called Hoosier Slide for the sand dune that once stood there, the park begins on the west side of Trail Creek and runs west from Goerg Marina at the Franklin Street bridge, around the Cargill grain elevator to the pier opposite the marina opening and lighthouse, then west along along the beach past the company's warm-water discharge. The creation of the park on property donated by NIPSCO means that shore anglers no longer have to check through the company gate.

By early April, boats begin to make their appearance both in the harbor and outside breakwalls. Weekend days may see hundreds of perchers working the pier with wigglers, crayfish, minnows and worms. At night, smelt fishermen and dippers take over. Thus, for a period in April each year, the piers serve up 24-hour sport.

Over the winter and early spring, coho and Chinook salmon have concentrated in shallow southern Lake Michigan because it warms first. Also, the combination of factory thermal discharge, spring rains, and spring sun draws spawning smelt and alewives, which, in turn, act as magnets for the predator species. Boaters and pier fishermen alike report hot action in April and May to depths of 60 feet.

Planer boards, outriggers, flatlines and shallow-set downriggers account for most catches. Countdown and jointed Rapalas, Bagley Shadlings, Hot 'N Tots, Thinfins, and Wee Warts are small plugs to try for cohos. Hot spoons include Dardevle Imp Klickers, Thindevles, Lucky Lures, small Northport Nailers and Killer Spoons. Canadian Plugs, J-Plugs, Rebel Spoonbills, and Long A Bombers are deadly on spring kings. So are magnum Nailers, KC Spoons, and Big Ed Flutter Chucks. Cohos like silver and the hot colors: red, orange, and yellow. Kings go for those colors plus green, blue, khaki, and white.

Anglers stalking the pier area stringer their share of spring salmon, too. Hot casting spoons include Cobras, K.O. Wobblers, Kastmasters, Little Jewels, and Krocodiles. Try pure silver or any of the previously mentioned colors. Roostertails, Mepps No. 5 Aglia spinners, Mepps Syclops spoons, and Blue Fox Vibrax spinners also score. Spawn is a further hot spring ticket off the pier.

SUMMER

But most of the talk at Michigan City these days is about the Skamanias that begin showing up in early *summer*, around mid-June. Skamanias, summer-run steelhead, enter natal rivers in late July or early August instead of in spring. There, they stay until late winter when they drop eggs. Then the spawned-out adults drift back to Lake Michigan, where they belly-up to a table loaded with smelt, alewives and other forage species. Strengths restored, these chrome-bright fighters prepare to do it all over again. Because of this unique timing, Skamanias are proving to be the ideal drawing card to bridge the span from early summer, when salmon flee warming southern Lake Michigan shallows, until fall, when the salmon return to spawn.

Indiana was the first state to rear and release Skamanias in the Great Lakes and, at this writing, is the only state with adult fish returning to native release sites in rivers. Eventually, Michigan anglers will catch them at other locations as well.

The Indiana DNR first released Skamanias about eight years ago. Their goal, to produce summer Lake Michigan sport, for Hoosier anglers, has been realized.

The first perch fishing rod to go overboard announces the Skamanias' arrival. By July 15, they are usually caught in the upper 25 feet of water over depths to 60 feet. That means you are likely to see acrobats before realizing they are hooked. It also means that Skamanias are accessible to trollers working out of boats as small as 16 feet.

Shore-bounders, too, can take the steelhead in summer. Some pier anglers toss nightcrawler gobs pinned to hooks and suspended three or four feet below a bobber. Others fling 2/5- to 3/4-ounce spoons in plain silver or silver with combinations of red, orange, blue, yellow or green. Skamanias often move close to piers and breakwalls in loose schools, so action can be frantic one hour, then go flat as day-old beer the next.

Rumor had it that Skamanias freight-trained lures, scrapped like back-alley thugs and tugged butcher scales to 20-pounds-plus. Indiana weight records fell six times in three years with 24- to 25-pound fish. "Salmon don't hold a candle to these guys," more than one veteran fisherman told me. Supposedly, you couldn't buy red fluorescent paint in Michigan City stores after the word went out along the piers and throughout the trolling fleet that Skamanias attacked red-colored lures like provoked bulls.

I had to find out first hand if the stories were truth or fiction. So I spent three days in July 1984 in the Michigan City area trying my hand at the Great Lakes' newest game. My conclusion? ***Those aren't just "stories"***. I have fished throughout much of the Great Lakes, and nowhere have I gotten more bang for my buck than with Skamanias (see "Super Steelhead," page 32).

Silver-colored lures, especially those sporting hot red or hot orange, get first nod for the summer steelhead. On another 1984 trip with Jon and Debi Belliveau, skippers of the *Grande Dame*, we caught Skamanias on white-with-orange-stripe Stainless Steelers, silver-with-red prism Marek-L-Lures, and silver J-Plugs. The Belliveaus used to charter for Lake Erie walleyes. But they caught Skamania mania, and now they spend summers in Michigan City. Their *Grand Dame* outriggers typically receive small crankbaits such as Hot 'N Tots and Wiggle Warts. Again, silver or white with hot prism is the password.

Other good Skamania plugs are J-11 orange-and-gold Rapalas, orange Fat Raps, orange-with-black-dot magnum Tadpollies, and shad-colored Bagley Magnum Small Fries. Rated hardware includes silver and silver-and-fluorescent Lucky Lures, Flutter Chucks, Evil Eyes, and Silver Strike-ER Lures. A medium to brisk troll works best (2.5-4.0 mph if you have a speedometer), but you may have to experiment. On strikeless days, vary lure offerings, lure sizes and release lengths. Sometimes highlines outproduce downriggers.

Although heavy boat traffic will spook these steelhead, it is also true that mid-day is often the best time to try for them. One key is to work untrolled water away from the boat pack. Hotspots alternate among where Trail Creek spews into the big lake, off the NIPSCO cooling towers, in front of Mt. Baldy (a mile west of town), along the Indiana Dunes National Lakeshore, and off Burns Ditch west of Michigan City at Burns Harbor.

FALL

Skamania action is over by mid-August, but perch fishing remains good into the *fall*. So does lake-trout action up to 15 miles from shore in August and in shoreline shallows in September and October. Michigan City also gets a modest return of salmon. Those willing to hold off winterizing their boats can pick up small cohos—the vanguard of next spring's trolling targets—as late as Thanksgiving.

With the exception of the warm-water discharge at the power plant, there are no *winter* fishing opportunities to speak of.

Planting Records

The Indiana DNR has released an average of 300,000 king fingerlings, 130,000 coho smolts, 150,000 yearling lake trout, and 125,000 winter-run steelhead each spring over the past several years. The DNR terminated brown-trout releases in 1981.

After a virulent virus shut down the Skamania River in Washington State a few years ago, Indiana nurtured the world's only supply of disease-free Skamania eggs. The DNR has been releasing close to 200,000 yearlings annually at Trail Creek and the Little Calumet River. In a joint venture with the Michigan DNR, Indiana plans to stock the St. Joseph River (see 4, St. Joseph/ Benton Harbor) with both Chinooks and Skamanias. Fishing opportunities are therefore expected to improve.

Facilities

You can trailer your boat to Michigan City, which has good ramp and dockage facilities at city-owned Washington Park Marina. Space, however, is at a premium during the height of Skamania frenzy. Call (219) 874-6221 for details. Michigan City, a city of 36,000, offers plenty of accommodations in all price ranges. Indiana Dunes State Park has camping facilities amid spectacular surroundings.

Further Information

Chambers of Commerce:

1. Michigan City Area Chamber of Commerce, 719 Franklin Square, Michigan City IN 46360; (219) 874-6221.
2. LaPorte County Convention & Visitors Bureau, 1503 S. Meer Rd., Michigan City IN 46360; (219) 872-5055. For fishing information call the hotline number at (219) 872-0031.

Bait & Tackle Shops:

1. Lake Michigan Tackle Shop, 1315 Franklin St., Michigan City IN 46360; (219) 872-*FISH*.

Charter Fishing:

1. Captain Charlie Enyeart, King Charters, 3223 S. Franklin St., Michigan City IN 46360; (219) 879-6962. 32-foot Trojan Express, *Quik-Draw*.
2. Jon and Debi Belliveau, Custom Charters by Belliveau, P.O. Box 714, Michigan City IN 46360; (219) 879-4800. 34-foot Silverton, *Grande Dame*.

Department of Natural Resources:

A DNR fisheries biologist is stationed at the Naval Armory Building in Michigan City. Call (219) 874-6824.

Coast Guard:

Michigan City Station, (219) 879-8371.

Super Steelhead

Captain Charlie Enyeart wheeled his 32-foot Trojan Express, *Quick-Draw*, past Michigan City's hook-shaped pier and headed for Mt. Baldy, a big sand dune west of town. It was already noon, and the blazing Indiana sun had us reaching for the sunscreen lotion and sunglasses. In our party of four, only Darrell had caught a Skamania, and when we asked him what they were like, he simply smiled and said, "You'll see."

Charlie was setting a third downrigger when a center stern rod suddenly snapped to. False alarm:The fish turned out to be a 4-1/2 pound coho that had drilled a silver-with-orange ladderback No. 4 J-Plug. Charlie coolered the little salmon, then reset his lure 45 feet behind the ball and sent it down 18 feet.

An hour later, I saw a huge silvery bullet tailwalking on Lake Michigan. Tarpon-like, it tried to shake hooks. By the time someone got to the popped rod, the Skamania, about a 12-pounder, was gone. Twenty minutes later, the same thing happened, and then a quarter-hour after that, a third Skamania pirouetted once in a dramatic 10-foot leap before spitting a No. 88 Sutton Spoon at the boat.

"How *do* you catch them?" I wondered.

After a fourth kiss-off, Charlie shortened release lengths. Moments later, while watching the Lowrance graph, I saw what appeared to be a big fish bird-dogging one of our lures. "Gray-liner," I yelled, and just then an out-down rod sprang into life. Again, no Skamania, but rather a 16-pound Chinook. Charlie scooped him aboard, and a Silver Horde with red skeletal design popped from his lower jaw.

Charlie reset the rigger; then all hell broke loose. A nine-pound steelhead pasted it before Charlie could turn his back. What seemed like a long time later, while our skipper netted my first Skamania, another rod went off, and this time a 12-pounder detonated from Lake Michigan.

Over the next two hours we boxed 14 fish, including three doubles and 11 Skamanias to 14 pounds each. The last time I saw fish jump like that was at Sea World's porpoise show.

At day's end my stomach ached from rod butts being jammed into it, and I had trouble sleeping that night.

I had caught Skamania Mania.

Tom Huggler
Otisville

Shallow-water trolling in late June and July produces Skamanias off Michigan City. These fishermen are using both outriggers and downriggers.

2 MICHIGAN CITY

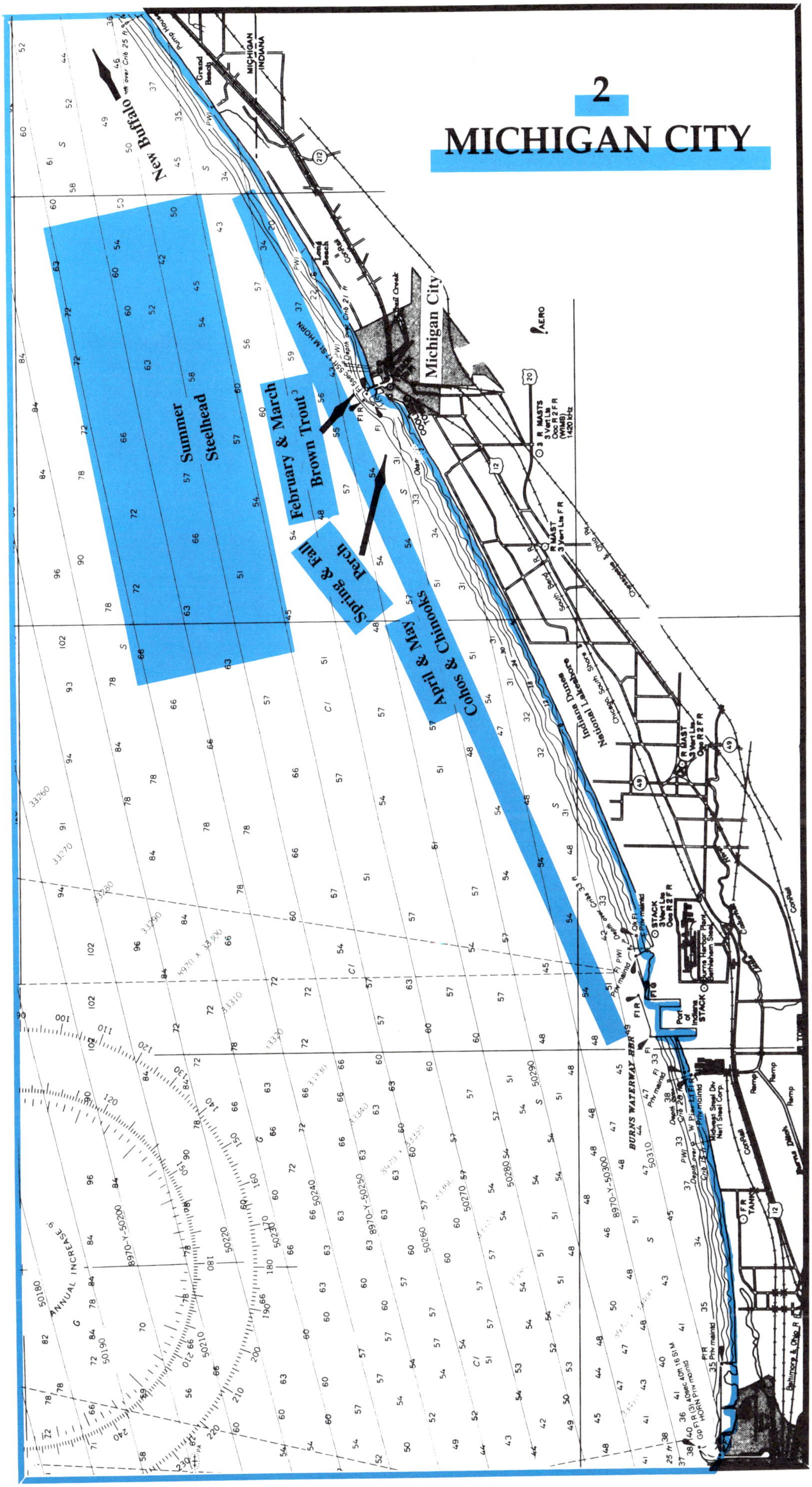

3
BRIDGMAN

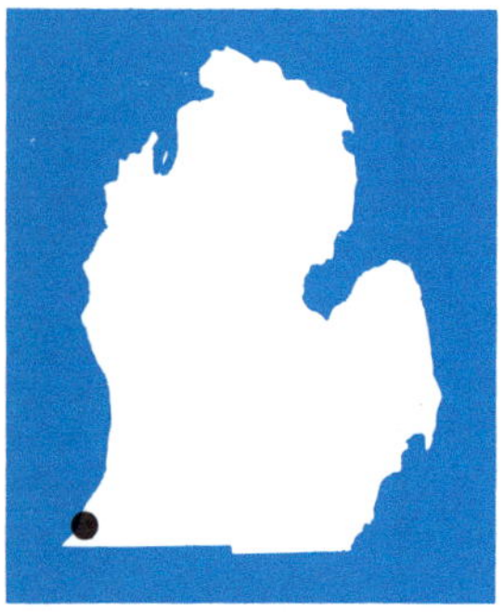

Southern Lake Michigan holds vast schools of coho and Chinook salmon each spring. Why? The shallow dish-pan basin warms more quickly than elsewhere, plus warm-water effluent from factories, power plants and streams hasten ice-out. The warming waters attract schools of smelt and, later, alewives along shoreline shallows. Hordes of salmon—wolf-pack coho from one to three pounds and cliques of five- to 25-pound thuggish kings—are right on their tails. After winter's torpor, the salmon are hungry.

Flurries of spring action occur throughout the region but especially at Bridgman, where anglers are able to fish the warm-water discharge off the Cook Nuclear Plant as early as March.

Besides outstanding spring salmon action, the Bridgman area also serves up spring brown trout as well as some opportunities for other gamefish throughout the long fishing season.

Fishing Schedule

Ice-out anglers go after salmon and trout as early as March, when ice floes bob throughout the area. Fishermen at this time should exercise great care, however, (see “Close Call,” page 36) and should stay off the icebergs when jigging. Those with boats dance Jigging Rapalas or Swedish Pimples off bottom, while others spincast with spoons and spinners. Action can fairly sizzle from browns to five pounds and cohos to three pounds.

Keep lures on the small side for cohos. Consider flatlining Little Cleos, Imp Klickers, K.O. Wobblers, Tiny Tads, Hot Shots and small Fire Plugs. Number 7 Rapalas, Hot 'N Tots, Wiggle Warts, and Fat Raps are good plugs to pull off outriggers and planers.

SPRING

The Bridgman area also sees Chinook salmon in *spring*. You'll score best on the big kings with body baits, especially those resembling minnows. Try straight and jointed Rapalas from size 7 through 13, Rapalas, Bang-O-Lures, Long A Bombers, and Rebel Spoonbills.

Experiment with both size and color. Inexplicably, salmon one day want big plugs, then wrinkle lips at everything but down-sized offerings the next. You will rarely go wrong with silver color, but also send down combinations of chartreuse, hot orange, green, and blue. If I'm not getting hits within 30 minutes, I start changing lures. I won't even wait 30 minutes if I know that salmon are present and other guys have the nets out.

SUMMER

Spring action generally shuts down by Memorial Day, when, as *summer* nears, trout and salmon flee the shallows and head for deeper water.

But then in June and sometimes even into the heat of summer, yellow perch become available over rocky shoals. They are there after a favorite food, crayfish, which are hatching off the reefs. Anglers pinch the tails of the small crabs and thread them to small hooks. Many fish with a two-hook spreader rig and use a bell sinker to spear the offering (shiner minnows and worms will also produce) to bottom. Keep a tight line and jiggle the bait every now and then. And remember, a run of big yellow-bellies can flush you out of bait in a hurry.

This area also produces summer lake trout to depths of 150 feet. Once you've located the big lakers, slow troll small plugs and spoons mated with attractors such as cowbells or dodgers. Best trolling speed is the 2.0- to 3.0-mph range. Because lakers are bottom-oriented fish, they don't always shape up on graphs, and that is why some Bridgman-area trollers drop cannonballs in the mud, lift them a crank or two, then crawl along until those rods start popping. Some laker anglers drag weights right in the mud, claiming that the stirred-up action can trigger forktails to feed.

FALL

Fall sees a modest return of salmon, mostly fish cruising up or down the lake to natal release sites.

WINTER

Winter fishing activity is limited to bait and spincast anglers working the warm-water discharge from shore or small boats on days when they can get out.

Planting Records

The DNR has not released fish at Bridgman. For area planting records, see 1 (New Buffalo) and 4 (Benton Harbor/St. Joseph).

Facilities

A shallow-water boat launch is available at the small public park in Bridgman. However, it is very difficult to launch or trailer a boat there in rough water (winds prevail from the west). As a result, many anglers, especially those with big boats, launch from New Buffalo (1) , nine miles south, or Benton Harbor/St. Joseph (4) , a few miles north. Also, there are no pier or breakwall fishing opportunities at Bridgman.

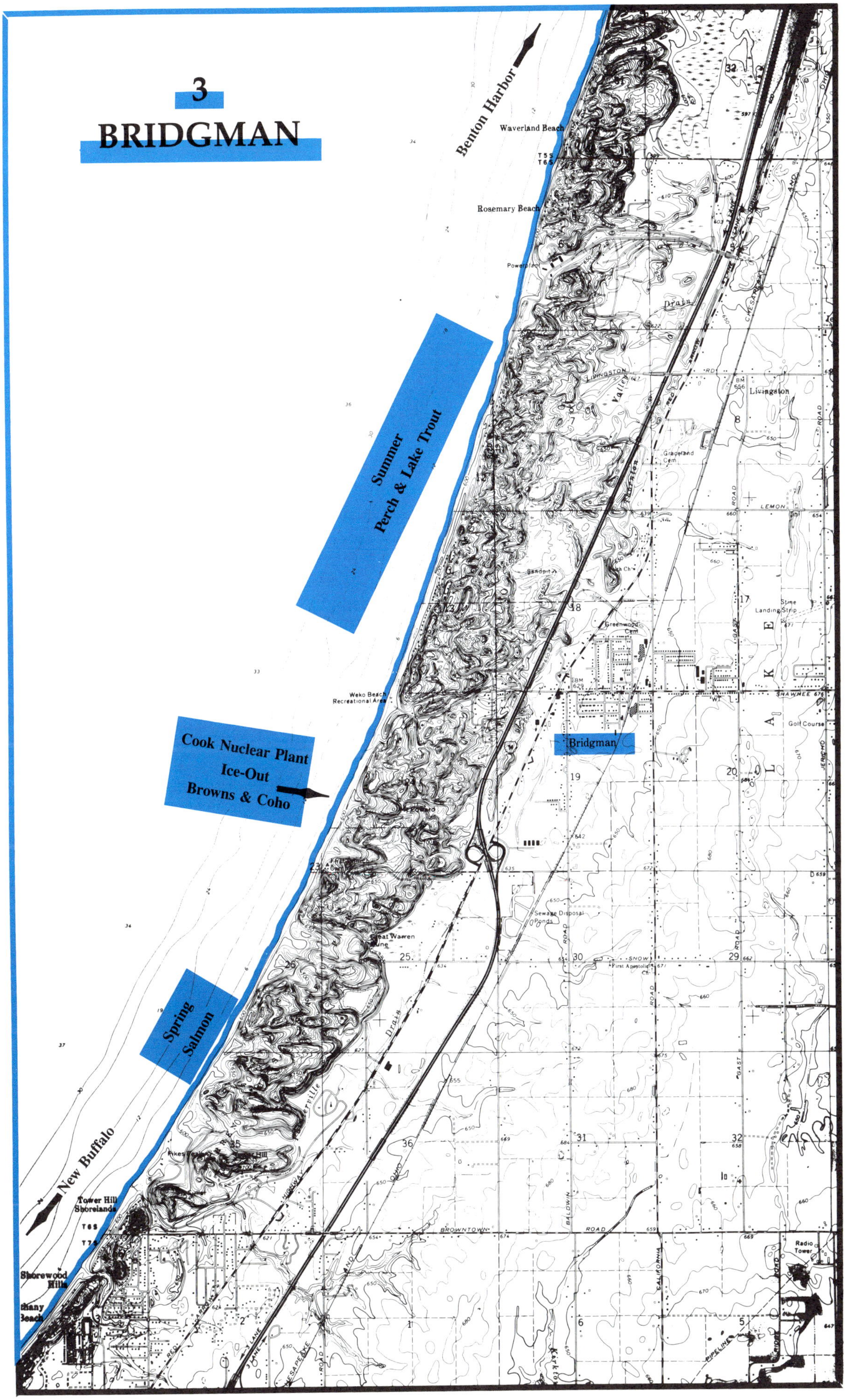
3
BRIDGMAN
Benton Harbor
Waverland Beach
Rosemary Beach
Summer
Perch & Lake Trout
Livingston
Graceland Cem
Greenwood Cem
Weko Beach Recreational Area
Cook Nuclear Plant
Ice-Out
Browns & Coho
Bridgman
Golf Course
Sewage Disposal Ponds
Spring
Salmon
New Buffalo
Tower Hill Shorelands
Shorewood Hills
Radio Tower

Close Call

Dangerous icebergs were out in full force on March 3, 1985, as Rick Dunlap of Lansing and I were fishing in 30 feet of Lake Michigan water a quarter-mile offshore from the Cook Nuclear Plant at Bridgman. Thanks to warm-water discharge from the plant, this is a hotspot for ice-out brown trout and coho. But some fair-sized 'bergs also ply the region in late winter/early spring. On that day, an offshore (east) wind moved the ice masses along, so Rick and I kept a wary eye out while jigging from my 14-foot aluminum boat.

Suddenly an iceberg half the size of a school bus (the part I could see) moved too close for comfort. Before I could push off with an oar, the 'berg tangled in our anchor rope. Instantly it began to pull the boat under.

I was in the bow, so Rick quickly tossed me our fillet knife so that I might cut the anchor rope free. But when I lunged for the rope, the knife point stuck in the ice, my hand slipped along the handle, and the blade slashed open my palm (which later took 17 stitches to close). Meanwhile, my partner and gear went into Lake Michigan, as our boat slipped from sight. Foolishly, we had earlier removed our life jackets to use as cushions.

I climbed to safety on the iceberg, then managed to help Rick also clamber aboard. A nearby party of fishermen, for some reason, ignored our cries for help. Luckily another boat soon chanced by to rescue us. My own boat—minus $300 worth of tackle and equipment—resurfaced five minutes later.

I'll probably fish the nuclear power plant again for spring trout and salmon. But you can bet there won't be any icebergs in sight.

Doug Twichell
Dimondale

Further Information

Chambers of Commerce:

1. Southwest Michigan Tourist Council, 151 E. Napier Ave., Benton Harbor 49022; (616) 983-1529.
2. Harbor Country Chamber of Commerce, P.O. Box 212, New Buffalo 49117; (616) 469-5409.3. West Michigan Tourist Association, 136 Fulton St. E., Grand Rapids 49503; (616) 456-8557.

Bait & Tackle Shops:

Linn's Landing, 4445 Lake St., Bridgman 49106; (616) 465-6209.

Charter Fishing:

1. Captain Rick LaCourse, 2002 Lakeview, Oregon OH 43618; (419) 255-3385. 28-foot Baja, *Formula I.*
2. Captain Casey Clark, 6889 Curtis Dr., Coloma 49038; (616) 468-4717. 24-foot Sea Star, *K-C Spooner.*
3. Captain Al Laaksonen, 6070 W. Main, Kalamazoo 49009; (616) 375-6305. 30-foot Chris Craft Tournament Fisherman, *Finlander.*
4. Captain Skip Stafford, Skipper's Charter Service, 1296 Linden, St. Joseph 49085; (616) 429-4040. 32-foot Trojan, *Skipper III*, plus other boats.

Department of Natural Resources:

Two fisheries biologists work out of District Headquarters at 621 N. 10th St., Plainwell 49080; (616) 685-6851.

Coast Guard:

Benton Harbor/St. Joseph Station, (616) 983-6114.

Small-boat trollers such as these get ice-out salmon and trout off the Cook Nuclear Plant at Bridgman.

4

ST. JOSEPH/ BENTON HARBOR

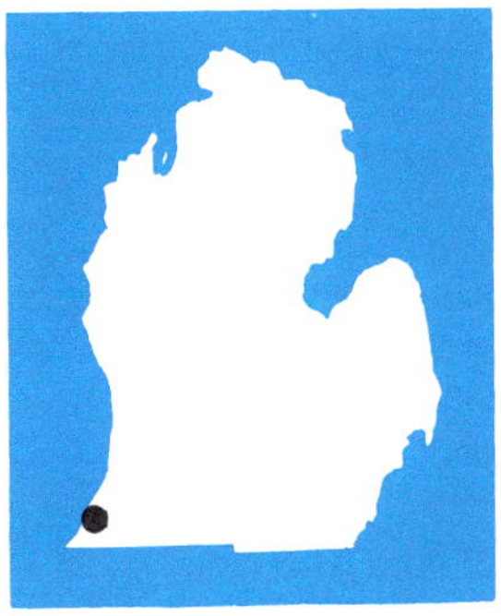

Tucked away in southern Lake Michigan, the twin cities of St. Joseph/Benton Harbor share a common harbor and piers.

The area serves up outstanding spring coho and Chinook salmon fishing, along with periodic good brown-trout, steelhead and lake-trout action. These same species are caught throughout the summer and become plentiful once again in fall, especially powerful king salmon, which poise in the big-lake shallows while anticipating their annual spawning run up the St. Joseph River.

Excellent summer fishing exists for yellow perch off the piers and within a mile of shore. The area also serves up Skamania (summer-run) steelhead from releases made in the Michigan City, Indiana, (2) area.

Fishing Schedule

Southern Lake Michigan is the first to warm, so salmon migrate here in late fall and throughout the winter. As the ice goes, they feed upon spawning smelt and alewives in the shallow areas and at the mouths of streams.

SPRING

Spring activity begins soon after ice-out, usually in early April, but as early as late March or as late as mid-April. Area anglers usually key first off the Cook Nuclear Plant, about nine miles to the south at Bridgman (3), or at the Palisades Nuclear Plant, to the north at South Haven (5).

In early May 1985, I fished St. Joseph/Benton Harbor with Captain Rick LaCourse and First Mate Dave Yeager aboard LaCourse's 28-foot Baja, *Formula I*. Cohos, followed by browns and kings, are usually the first fish to arrive here, but an overall poor coho return had LaCourse and most other trollers in deep water hunting lake trout instead. We roared straight out 7.3 miles to 140 feet of water.

LaCourse, who has been fishing St. Joseph/Benton Harbor for 15 years, set up five Big Jon downriggers, a pair of Dipsy-Divers, and two flatlines. Release lengths off the downriggers were all eight or nine feet. The outdowns were set at 33 and 35 feet respectively. Stern-end setups went down 45, 25, and 66 feet. For lures Rick opted for yellow-and-silver and green-and-silver Fin-Weaver spoons and a lemon/lime Flutter Chuck. Using rubber bands, he control-stacked both outdowns and the starboard-corner downrigger with similar hardware about 10 feet above. Rick prefers 210 Penn level-wind reels and 8-1/2 foot Eagle Claw downrigger rods.

He rigged the Dipsy-Divers to special Eagle Claw 10-foot rods. To one diver he attached a green-and-silver Fin-Weaver, setting it back 60 feet. A J-11 orange Rapala 90 feet back went on the other. He spotted the highlines, armed with white-and-bone crawdad Wiggle Warts, behind the boat about 100 feet.

Our skipper then locked in trolling speed at 1.8-1.9 knots on his Ensign trolling-speed indicator. We were fishing slow rollers on a bright, sunny day with five-mph winds from the west. The low chop made it easy to pick out temperature differences in the thermal bar, a spring phenomenon — caused from the lake turning over — that creates a vertical wall of differing water density and temperature.

We began setting lines at 8:00 a.m. and at 8:25 took our first fish, an unclipped eight-pound lake trout, on a green-and-silver Fin-Weaver attached to a Dipsy-Diver (with ring on) at 33 feet deep. When we pulled lines at 3:30 p.m., six other lakers (including another uncut fish, a possible sign of natural reproduction) from six to 11 pounds each had found their way into the cooler. So had a four-pound Skamania steelhead and a pair of eight-pound king salmon. We caught most of our fish in the 47-degree-F. water that lay next to water only a degree or two colder. Our take for five fishermen was on the poor side of average for a spring trip from this port.

When cohos are available, trollers take them in relatively shallow water (20-40 feet deep) within a mile or two of shore. Planer boards and outriggers are popular, along with shallow-set downriggers and flatlines. Troll from the pierheads south toward the Cook Plant. Key landmarks on shore include the Junked Cars, at three miles south, and the Chalets (A-frame cabins), at 7-1/2 miles down the lake. An excellent spring trolling spot is a steep ledge 20-30 feet deep that runs for about 3/4 mile offshore from the Chalets.

Best king-salmon fishing occurs north of the pierheads. Local landmarks include the Clay Banks (two miles north), White House (four miles north), and Rocky Gap (seven miles north).

Finlander charterboat-skipper Al Laaksonen also spring fishes St.Joseph/Benton Harbor along with Michigan City (2) and Ludington (12). Laaksonen is a meticulous record keeper who can tell you where and when he has caught every fish since 1977, as well as how deep and what lure was used. That's a lot of bookkeeping, especially when you consider that in 1984 alone Laaksonen boxed over 1,500 trout and salmon.

Much of his spring data pertains directly to St. Joseph/Benton Harbor, and his concise one-page annual reports are revealing. In 1985 the *Finlander* saw 130 April fish (62 kings, 63 cohos, and five fish of other species) and 460 May fish (228 kings, 106 cohos, 107 lakers, 17 steelhead, and two browns) come over the transom. The average catch per trip was 22 fish in April and 20 in May. During April, 23 fish were caught in the upper 10 feet, 40 were taken from 11-29 feet deep, and 49 came from depths of 30-49 feet. During May these respective catches were 23, 157, and 160. Another 62 fish were caught from 50-69 feet deep.

Fin-Weavers were hot lures, especially those in green and yellow with silver. Also productive were silver and green J-Plugs and gold, silver, and yellow Wiggle Warts and Hot 'N Tots.

SUMMER

Salmon fishing remains good until June, although fish can be taken throughout the *summer*, especially in early morning, by casting off pierheads or trolling near them. Summer lake-trout trollers score by running Wobble-Glos behind cowbells and dodgers close to bottom in depths from 100-150 feet. Trollers pulling plugs and spoons in plain silver or silver with hot-orange or hot-red designs can pick up Skamania steelhead by washing lures in the upper 30-40 feet of water. Best times are late June through mid-July.

During especially hot periods in July and August, yellow perch flock to hard-bottom areas of rubble and gravel. They are there to eat hatching crayfish and are available from the piers and in offshore depths to 60 feet. Live crayfish, if available in bait and tackle shops, are the best bait, but wigglers, worms, and inch-long shiner minnows also produce.

FALL

Fall fishing centers around returning Chinook salmon. The big, mature spawners can be taken in shallows and in the harbor itself as early as late August and as late as the end of September. Big, wobbling plugs, such as J-Plugs, Tadpollies, and Flatfish, are good lures, especially in hot colors.

The piers also get a run of steelhead, beginning in October and lasting until early December. Try spawn or nightcrawlers fished off bottom, or fancast heavy spoons or spinners. Orange or silver are rated colors.

WINTER

Several guides work the St. Joseph River in fall and *winter* for salmon and steelhead. The river also contains northern pike and smallmouth bass.

Planting Records

This port has a long history of Chinook salmon, steelhead and lake-trout releases. Every year since 1980, from 48,000-90,000 lake trout have gone into Lake Michigan at offshore reefs. An average of 300,000 Chinooks, planted yearly also since 1980, was cut back to 100,000 in 1984. Steelhead releases averaged 40,000 yearlings and 300,000 fall fingerlings until 1984, when the fingerling release program was discontinued. Look for future releases of Skamania steelhead as well as continued hefty plants of lake trout and king salmon.

Facilities

Benton Harbor, with 16,450 people, and St. Joseph, with more than 11,000 residents, offer plenty of restaurants and lodging facilities. A good place to launch your boat and rent a slip is LaSalle's Landing Marina, 143 Industrial in St. Joseph. Call (616) 982-0812. Services at the DNR-run harbor here include gasoline, water, electricity, restrooms, haul-out facilities and a holding-tank pump-out. The telephone number of the dock attendant is (616) 983-5432.

Campgrounds abound in the area. Public parks include Van Buren State Park (616-637-2788), to the north, and Warren Dunes State Park (616-426-4013), to the south. Private campgrounds include a KOA in Benton Harbor at 3527 Coloma Rd., (616) 849-3333, and a travel-trailer park, the House of David, located at the corner of M-139 and Empire Avenue in Benton Harbor, (616) 927-3302.

Further Information

Chambers of Commerce:

1. Southwest Michigan Tourist Council, 151 E. Napier Ave., Benton Harbor 49022; (616) 983-1529.2. Twin Cities Area Chamber of Commerce, P.O. Box 1208, Benton Harbor 49022; (616) 925-0044.

Bait & Tackle Shops:

1. Tackle Haven, 741 Riverview Rd., Benton Harbor (616) 925-0341.
2. Mollhagen's, 600 Fisherman Rd., St. Joseph, (616) 983-3851.

Charter Fishing:

1. Captain Rick LaCourse, 2002 Lakeview, Oregon OH 43618; (419) 255-3385. 28-foot Baja, *Formula I.*
2. Casey Clark, 6889 Curtis Dr., Coloma 49038; (616) 468-4717. 24-foot Sea Star, *K-C Spooner.*
3. Al Laaksonen, 6070 W. Main, Kalamazoo 49009; (616) 375-6305. 30-foot Chris Craft Tournament Fisherman, *Finlander.*

Department of Natural Resources:

Two fisheries biologists work out of District Headquarters at 621 N. 10th St., Plainwell 49080; (616) 685-6851.

Coast Guard:

Benton Harbor/St. Joseph Station, (616) 983-6114.

5 For 5

One Saturday morning in late April, I ran a charter of four customers four miles north of Benton Harbor. We set down in 40 feet of water off the White House and began setting lines at 20-35 feet deep. We had a half-dozen rigged when two of the fellows pounced on the No. 2 and No. 4 rods, which had gone off together.

Suddenly the No. 5 rod popped. Three of my customers now had fish on. The fourth customer was holding the net, trying to figure out which fish to scoop up first. When the high diver (another rod attached to a Dipsy-Diver) went off, he grabbed it and tossed the net down.

I was trying to figure out how I was going to handle netting chores, plus steer the boat, when a fifth rod sprang to. "Get it!" I yelled.

"There's nobody left," somebody said.

One of the fishermen swung aboard an eight-pound lake trout, then grabbed the other rod, now thumping as though alive with, as we found out later, a 13-pound laker on the other end. The other three fishermen each caught 15-pound king salmon.

That was the only time in 15 years of experience that I have ever gone five for five on my boat.

Captain Rick LaCourse
Benton Harbor, *Formula I*

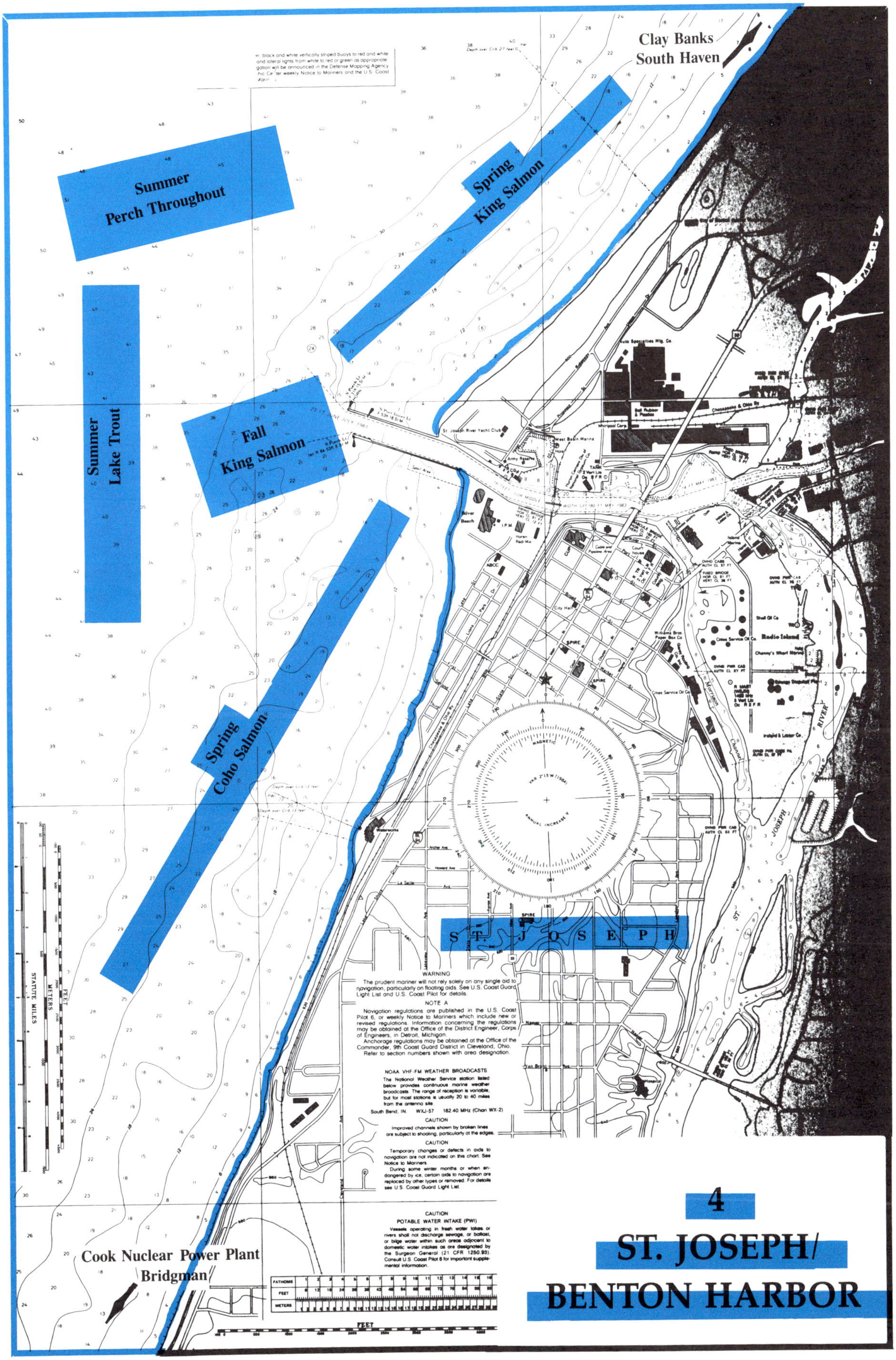
Clay Banks
South Haven
Summer
Perch Throughout
Spring
King Salmon
Summer
Lake Trout
Fall
King Salmon
Spring
Coho Salmon
ST. JOSEPH
Cook Nuclear Power Plant
Bridgman
WARNING
NOTE A
CAUTION
4
ST. JOSEPH/
BENTON HARBOR

5

SOUTH HAVEN

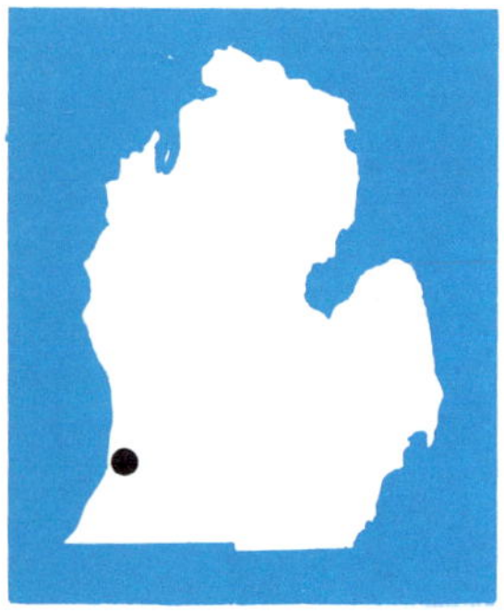

Nestled among the southern Lake Michigan sand dunes, South Haven offers good to excellent fishing for spring salmon and summer yellow perch. Because deep water is found fairly close to shore, the region marks the beginning of lake-trout country. Facilities for fisherman and tourist alike are excellent in the town of 6,500. Many charterboat captains work the area in the spring, then leave for ports further north as summer deepens and fishing opportunities improve.

Fishing Schedule

Few events in the outdoors create as much stir as a horde of smelt prowling big-lake shallows for a place to spawn. These silver slivers are to blame for a whole new definition of fun.

Here is what happens. From mid-March to late April, warming weather conditions force spring run-off into bank-full rivers heading for the Great Lakes. Sun, wind, rain and factory/power-plant effluent combine to weaken pack ice in harbors and along shorelines. Soon the ice breaks up, melting as it drifts out to sea. Water temperatures creep toward 40 degrees F., schools of smelt appear along shoreline shallows, and anglers in the know turn out in force throughout the Great Lakes.

SPRING

Spawning smelt have been turning on winter-weary South Haven anglers every *spring* for decades. Using lanterns, dipnetters attract the fish close to the South Haven pier at night, then scoop them aboard the slabs. Area streams also get smelt runs.

In the South Haven area, when the ice goes out early, usually by April 1 or soon thereafter, spring fishing for coho and Chinook salmon, along with brown trout and some steelhead, begins. Action centers around the Palisades Nuclear Power Plant thermal discharge, located 6-1/2 miles south of the pierheads, and at the Black River outflow at South Haven.

Because of southern Lake Michigan fish surging north, spring salmon activity remains good until about Memorial Day. That is not to say that it dries up in summer. On the contrary, there is some fair to good salmon fishing over deep water all summer long and into the fall. But many anglers in summer go after lakers and perch. More in a moment.

Tactics for early season salmon include using outriggers and planer boards in the shallows. Since no thermocline has formed, the salmon may be just about anywhere from 25 to 150 feet of water. Al Laaksonen, captain of the *Finlander*, spring fishes out of South Haven, in addition to several other southern Lake Michigan ports. His meticulous records show that lures run from the surface to 50 feet deep produce the best April and May catches. Trollers target the warmest water they can find. Not surprisingly, best catches occur where there are concentrations of baitfish.

Body plugs such as J-7 to J-11 Rapalas, Rebel Fastracs, and Bang-O-Lures are good choices. So are Fin-Weavers, Fub Wobblers, Northport Nailers, Lucky Lures, and Flutter Chucks. Start with green and silver colors, then mix in yellow, gold, and white.

Overall, the best fishing occurs from April 15 until July 1, says Captain Donald Buckberry, who with his wife Sis has been chartering out of South Haven for 12 years. Spring rigging on their *Early Bird* calls for spoons set three to 90 feet behind cannonballs on four stern-end and two out-down Walker downriggers. Don opts for greens on white, orange on white, or plain silver as lure choices. If hunting fish, he will vary trolling speeds, scatter his hardware spread, and stack with rubber bands and add-a-lines. When the thermocline develops, usually by early June, trollers begin looking for the 54-degree-F. mark that salmon like.

Then, too, is when lake-trout season swings into high gear. Dodgers mated to "haircut" (small) flies, Bead flies and squids score. Spin-N-Glos, P-Nuts, Clatter Tads and Fire Plugs are other good laker lures behind dodgers or cowbells. Others pull wire line and pound big flashing spoons in and out of the mud. Best summer lake-trout trolling depths appear to be 100-150 feet down in 48- to 52-degree-F. water.

SUMMER

The South Haven area has long been popular with perchers. Captain Don Nichols has been running party-boat charters from Nichols Landing for many years, and it is plenty of fun on a summer morning if the perch are in. Perch fishing is good at this port all *summer* but really kicks off when midsummer doldrums of heat and humidity warm the water. Then, crayfish begin hatching on reefs, and these, in turn, draw hordes of hungry perch. Thus, small crabs are the best bait, although minnows work, too. The Rock Pile, a mile south of the piers in about 40 feet of water, is a popular hotspot for yellow-bellies.

FALL

Fall fishing for perch remains good, as does trolling for trout and salmon. The piers stay active all fishing season with bait and spincast fishermen who take a smorgasbord of game fish from yellow perch to Chinook salmon.

Winter opportunities are limited to stretches of open water in the river, and there is little fishing activity.

5
SOUTH HAVEN

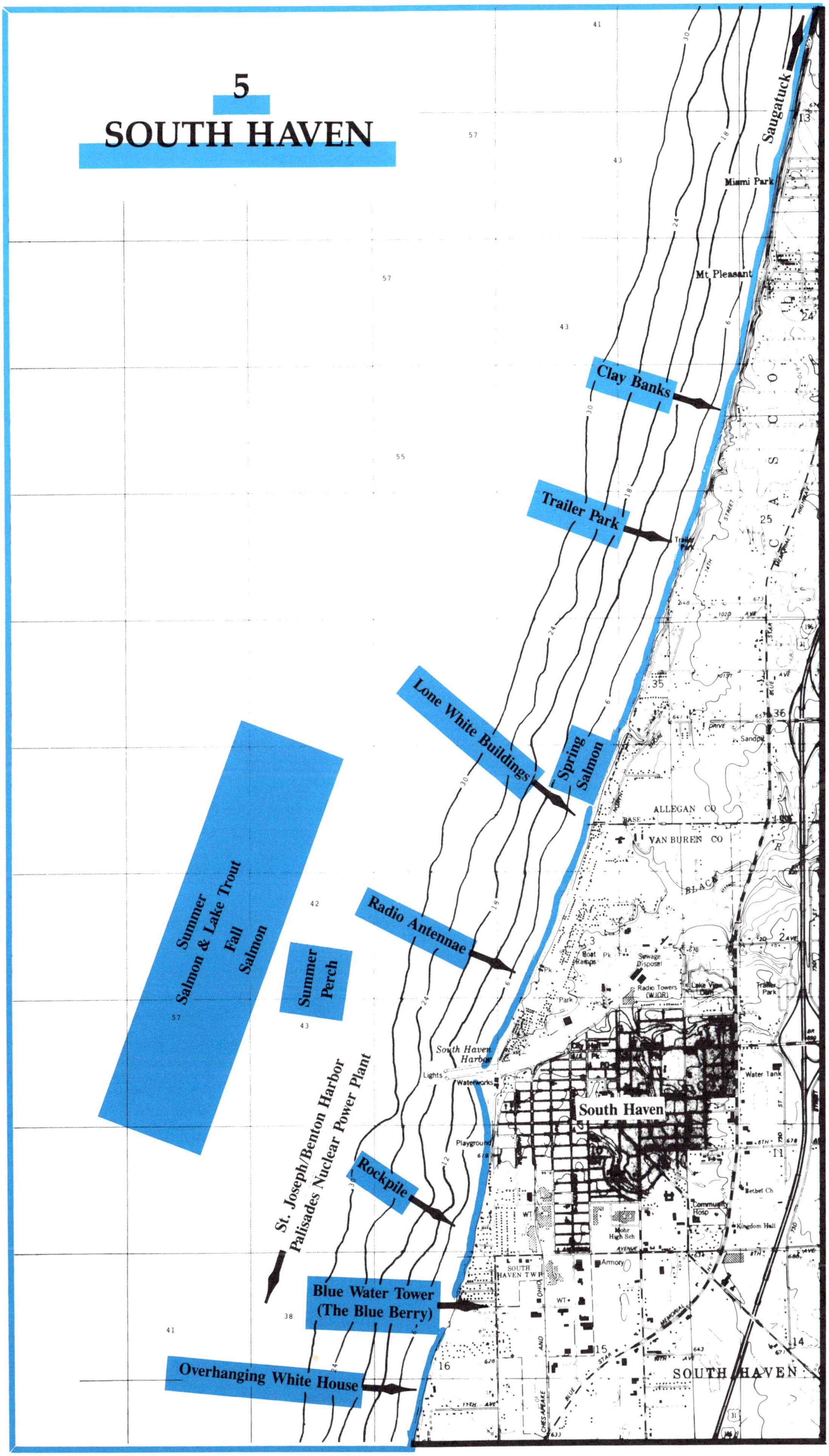

The pier at South Haven serves up angling action during the open-water fishing season.

SOUTH HAVEN (cont.)

Landmarks to about seven miles south out of the pierheads include the Drain Tube, tall Blue Water Tower, White Overhanging House (perhaps fallen into the lake as you read this), the Green Fence, Deer Lick Creek, Doctors' Row Cottages, the Sand Dunes, Palisades Nuclear Plant, and Brandywine Creek. Landmarks to 4-1/2 miles north are the Radio Antennae; long White Buildings at Sleepy Hollow; the Trailer Park, and the Clay Banks.

Planting Records

South Haven and the Black River have had a long history of DNR plants for trout and salmon, with annual releases in the early 1980s including up to 100,000 lakers and 125,000 kings. Through at least 1990, the DNR plans average annual releases of 60,000 lake trout, 75,000 Chinooks, 10,000 steelhead, 10,000 rainbows and 15,000 brown trout.

Facilities

A public boat launch and several private ramps await boaters. A state-run harbor of refuge has water, electricity, restrooms, shower facilities and a holding-tank pump-out. The dock attendant's number is (616) 637-3171. Although there is no boat launch at Van Buren State Park, just south of town, there are some shoreline or cartopper fishing opportunities. A total of 205 campsites are available.

Further Information

Chambers of Commerce:

1. West Michigan Tourist Association, 136 Fulton E., Grand Rapids 49503; (616) 456-8557.
2. Greater South Haven Chamber of Commerce, 535 Quaker, South Haven 49090; (616) 637-1450.

Bait & Tackle Shops:

1. J.C. Bait & Tackle, 141 Dunckley Ave., South Haven 49090; (616) 637-1849.
2. Ward's Baits, 282 Dyckman Ave., South Haven 49090; (616) 637-2745.

Charter Fishing:

1. Captain Donald Buckberry, Early Bird Charters, 2177 66th St., Fennville 49408; (616) 543-4540. 27-foot Sportcraft "C" Eagle, *Early Bird*.
2. Captain Al Holmes, 726 Francis St., South Haven 49090; (616) 637-1643. 25-foot *Two Bits*.
3. Captain Jim Vander West, Blue Chip Charters, P.O. Drawer 8333, Holland 49422; (616) 392-9687. 31-foot Sport Fisherman Cruiser, *Blue Chip* (April and May only).
4. Captain Don Nichols, Nichols Landing, South Haven 49090; (616) 637-8193. Large-party boat, *Captain Nichols* (perch fishing only).

Department of Natural Resources:

Two fisheries biologists work out of District Headquarters at 621 N. 10th St., Plainwell 49080; (616) 685-6851.

Coast Guard:

South Haven Station, (616) 637-2208.

Double Strike

My first trout and salmon trolling trip on the Great Lakes certainly was a memorable one. It was May 1974 when freelance-outdoor-writer David Richey (now outdoor writer for the *Detroit News*) invited me along on Captain Emil Dean's boat, the *Mary E.* Captain Dean, one of the pioneers of downrigger trolling (he helped invent an early model, long before they were manufactured), was already becoming a legend. Mort Neff, the long-time host of TV's *Michigan Outdoors*, was aboard, too. We were going to fish South Haven that weekend, and I would get to babysit a couple of rods.

Getting to meet these famous people and learn something about the exciting sport itself was quite a thrill for a young writer just getting into the business.

But I guess the biggest kick was catching my first Great Lakes salmonid. The fish banged a corner out-down rod, and, per instructions from Emil about holding the rod high and not horsing the fish, I was able to lead a 12-pound, six-ounce lake trout into the net. Quite a thrill indeed.

Another incident that occurred that day I'll also not soon forget. Two poles went off three seconds apart, and, figuring we had on a double-header, two anglers pounced on the sprung rods. Come to find out, one eight-pound lake trout had drilled both lures, clown-colored Flutter Spoons Emil had set about 15 feet apart. That was one hungry laker.

Although others claim that double strikes are not so unusual, it has never occurred again over the many years that I have trolled the Great Lakes.

Tom Huggler
Otisville

6
SAUGATUCK

'00 people. Anglers flock here
rch, and fall kings and cohos.
uck charterboat skipper.

SPRING

in
in
B
ki
st
tw
gc

in
sa
wa

O
sta
a s
the
mi
fee
sho
tro
op
cra
tio

out
sal
nin
ger
ind
Ch
pou
Ho
and

can still be caught by using specialized tactics. Lake trout, for

SUMMER

ble-Glos, Fire Plugs, Tiny
Chargers, Spring Spoons)
ien the strings of flash are
ver, green, blue, and char-

ınd trout many miles from
unning lures in the thermo-
:p-set lines often take Chi-
and side-rigged offerings
lhead and the occasional
eyed trollers are always on
ooth water surrounded by
-bombing seagulls. These
ersion, pasture of baitfish,
hore trout and salmon.

ting salmon is to be on the
re dawn. Many times, in
ong with occasional steel-
luice of food-rich Kalama-
an. Spawn bags fished on
pe LumaLures or fluores-
arious speeds triggers the

for its outstanding perch
ef area of rock and gravel
sts large clusters of boats
gy weather by mid to late
r structure, and yellow-
s that everyone likes to
me bait and tackle shops
ny fishermen either catch
re they will have enough
s, then pin them to No. 2
ig or jigging off bottom
ien use pyramid- or bell-
ı spreader eight inches
, claiming that the bigger
perch must be fished ever so carefully if you hope to catch any.

Inch-long shiner minnows are a second choice, followed by wigglers and worms.

FALL

As summer wanes, king salmon begin massing offshore for their annual *fall* assault on the Kalamazoo River, plus there are plenty of other salmon coursing to natal release sites up and down the lake. Once more, trollers lengthen leads as salmon approach the shallows. The boat fishermen break out big plugs and spoons in riot colors—bright red, fluorescent orange, hot yellow and combinations of those colors with silver, black, pearl and chartreuse. Good plugs include J-Plugs, Lucky Louies, Dandy-Glos, Tadpollies and Flatfish. Productive spoons are Big Ed Flutter Chucks, magnum Northport Nailers and Lucky Lures.

Perching from the piers is good again in October, and spawn and spincast fishermen can take steelhead and brown trout until Thanksgiving.

WINTER

Winter fishing activities are limited to panfishing and spearing northern pike from shanties or setting tip-ups for them. Best catches come from bayous of the Kalamazoo River.

Color-Line Steelhead

For many years, Great Lakes trollers and pier fishermen have known that the color line is a good place to catch steelhead. The color line, also known as the "mud line" or "scum line," is the discharge of dirty water from rivermouths into the Great Lakes. Depending upon currents and wind direction, this discolored flow of water may seep into the lake for several miles. Predatory species, like trout and salmon, often cruise inside the color line, where they attack baitfish and other prey coming down the flow.

Savvy trollers stitch an invisible seam as they zig-zag troll along the edge of color lines. Pier and breakwall anglers have learned to take advantage of a wind shift that may send discolored water along an outside wall. By dunking spawn bags or casting spoons into the color line, they often get fast action from steelhead, browns and salmon.

The color lines are especially productive in spring due to the presence of spawning smelt in the shallows. Fall is another good time when the salmonids themselves enter natal streams to spawn. Most fishermen forget about the color lines in summer. They shouldn't.

Recently, boat fishermen have learned that color lines often develop miles offshore and can be hotspots for coho salmon and steelhead, in particular, as these topwater-oriented fish cruise in the protective dark water. Longlining with Rapalas or Tadpollies in plugs or heavy spoons like Krocodiles or Mainliners can produce fast action from steelhead. Short-set surface lines will take cohos. Both species are attracted to planer boards and outriggers as well.

Color-line trollers off Manistee (13), in particular, have had good success as far offshore as 12 or 15 miles over depths of 400 or more feet. Color lines this far out are generally pockets of discolored water (sometimes containing leaves or other bits of debris) and are caused by currents or winds. Sometimes the temperature will be different in a color line than in surrounding water, too, and this may well attract both baitfish and trout and salmon.

Color lines are a strange phenomenon of the Great Lakes, and trollers are just now beginning to learn how productive they can be.

Jumbo yellow perch like this one are caught each summer during hot-weather periods at Saugatuck and other southern Lake Michigan ports.

Planting Records

The Saugatuck Reefs currently receive 60,000 lake-trout fingerlings, and the Kalamazoo River gets 100,000 spring fingerling Chinooks, 15,000 brown-trout yearlings, and 15,000 steelhead yearlings. These annual DNR stockings of hatchery-reared fish will continue through at least 1990.

Facilities

The DNR does not maintain a harbor of refuge at Saugatuck. There are launch facilities, however, all along the Saugatuck waterfront on the Kalamazoo River.

Further Information

Chambers of Commerce:

West Michigan Tourist Association, 136 Fulton E., Grand Rapids 49503; (616) 456-8557.

Bait & Tackle Shops:

1. Schippa Marine, 726 Water St., Saugatuck 49453; (616) 857-4558.
2. Tony's Tackle, 726 Water St.,. Saugatuck 49453; (616) 857-4664.

Charter Fishing:

Captains Kevin, Fred and Lyle Schippa, Schippa's Charter Service, P.O. Box 385, Douglas 49406; (616) 857-4558.

Department of Natural Resources:

Two fisheries biologists work out of District Headquarters at 621 North 10th St., Plainwell 49080; (616) 685-6851.

Coast Guard:

Holland Station, (616) 399-9330 or 399-9331 or South Haven Station, (616) 637-2208 or 637-4661.

6 SAUGATUCK

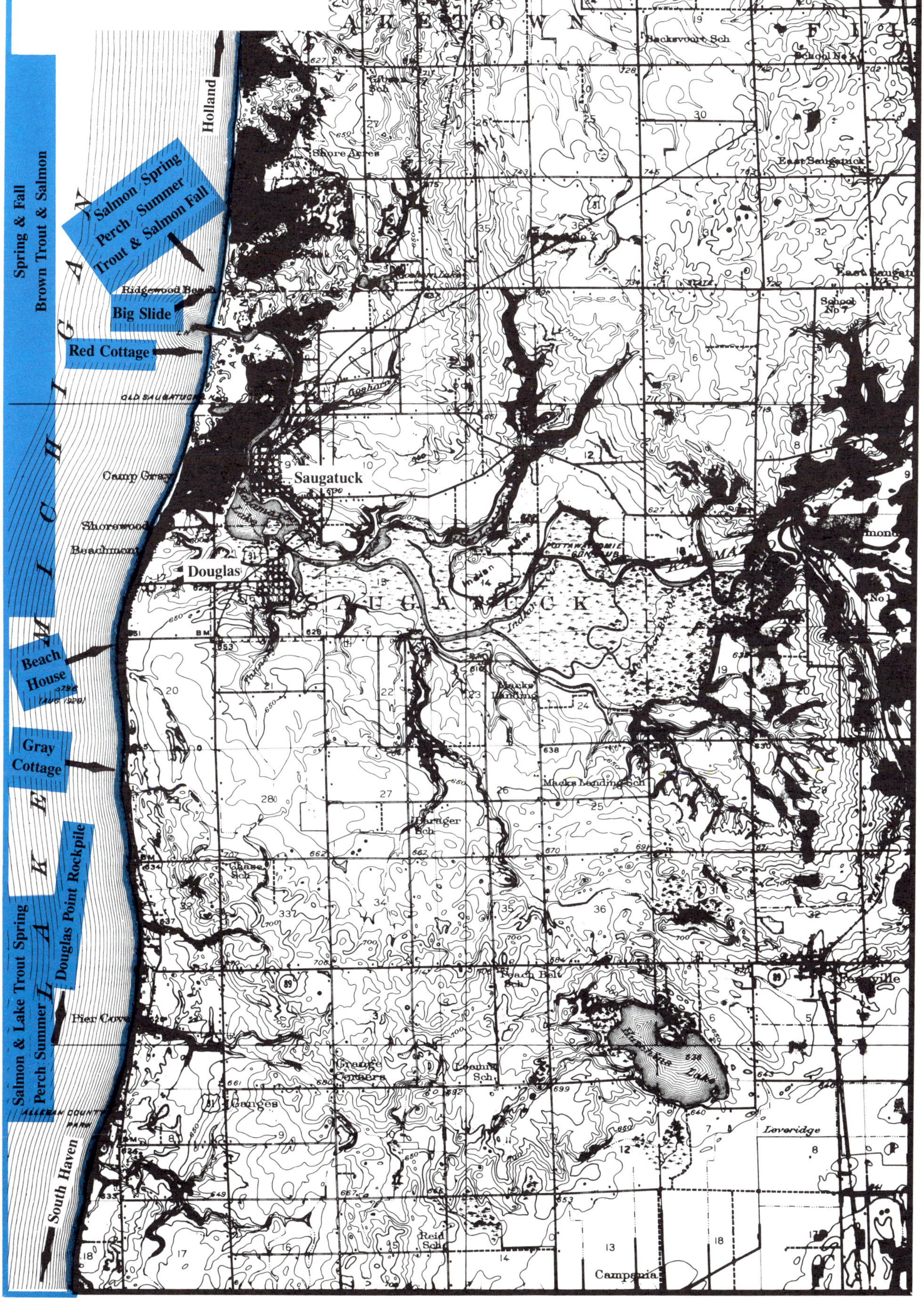

Holland
Salmon Spring
Perch Summer
Trout & Salmon Fall
Spring & Fall
Brown Trout & Salmon
Ridgewood Beach
Big Slide
Red Cottage
LAKE MICHIGAN
Camp Gray
Shorewood
Beachmont
Saugatuck
Douglas
Shore Acres
Backsvoort Sch
East Saugatuck
Beach House
Gray Cottage
Douglas Point Rockpile
Salmon & Lake Trout Spring
Perch Summer
Pier Cove
Ganges
South Haven
Macks Landing Sch
Leveridge
Campania

7
HOLLAND

Holland, a city of 25,000, is located on Lake Macatawa (Mack Lake, as it is called locally), a drowned rivermouth of the Macatawa River.

The DNR has discontinued lake-trout and brown-trout stockings at this port, but there is still good fishing for these species and other salmonids, especially in spring when southern Lake Michigan fish surge north. Another problem is that the Holland area lacks structure, and those two reasons are why most of the dozen or so charterboat skippers, including long-time-pro Jack Nagelkirk, fish the Holland area in spring and early summer, then head for Ludington (12) or other ports to the north for late-summer and fall salmon action.

Fishing Schedule

SPRING

According to Nagelkirk, the best *spring* fishing is due west of the Holland channel in 60-90 feet of water. When viewed from the water, the channel is the smallest land point. It is far easier to locate the large sand dune (part of Holland State Park) on the north side of the channel. The diamond-shaped dune has one apex pointing to the channel and is visible from a 14-foot boat as far offshore as 120-foot-deep water.

Elsewhere, spring trollers target 10-50 feet of water. Landmarks north of pierheads include a series of hills that begins with the diamond-shaped dune and continues for 12 miles to Port Sheldon. Other landmarks are the Spy Glass (also called the Condos), Tunnel Park (which features some ripple structure in 40-60 feet of water), and the Pigeon Lake outlet off Port Sheldon. Grand Haven (8) is north of Port Sheldon.

A 30-foot-deep hole 100 yards southwest of the southern pierhead generally serves up a few fish to early hour trollers. Southbound landmarks include Point West, Mac Hills, Castle Park (at 1-1/2 miles), Halfway Creek, and the Three Sliders (three sand dunes). The port of Saugatuck (6) lies further south.

Spring trollers seek Chinook and coho salmon as well as brown trout and steelhead. According to Captain Nagelkirk, who averages better than 12 fish per charter, best catches occur from late April through mid-June, with kings and cohos accounting for 55 percent and 35 percent respectively of the total take. Nagelkirk runs five to eight rods off downriggers and three to five rods off highlines and trip divers. The exact number depends upon what the fish seem to prefer from day to day and how many customers are aboard his boat.

Most king salmon are taken in early summer off long-released J-Plugs or dodgers and squids run tight to cannonballs. Cohos hit the attractor rigs, too, along with Lucky Lures and Northport Nailers. Primary colors at Holland are silver, chartreuse, and green, with white, black, and gold the second set of choices. Productive trolling speed varies from 2.4-2.6 mph.

The piers produce sporadic spring action for trout and salmon

Jennifer Huggler, the author's daughter, caught this five-pound Chinook salmon in southern Lake Michigan on a summer morning.

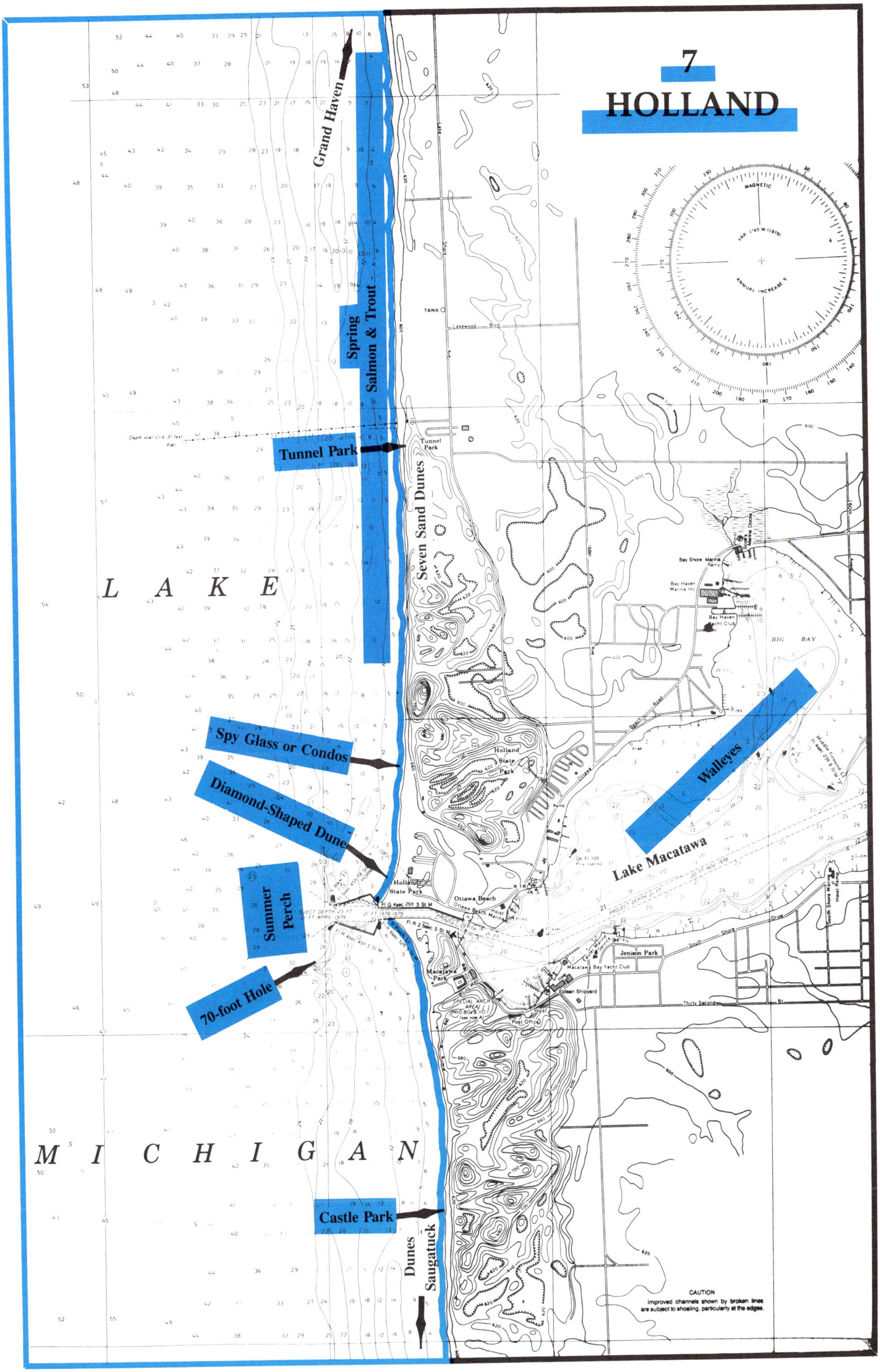
7
HOLLAND
Grand Haven
Spring Salmon & Trout
Tunnel Park
Seven Sand Dunes
LAKE
Spy Glass or Condos
Diamond-Shaped Dune
Summer Perch
70-foot Hole
Walleyes
Lake Macatawa
Holland State Park
Ottawa Beach
Jenison Park
Macatawa Park
Eldean Shipyard
Bay Shore Marina
Bay Haven Marina Inc
Bay Haven Yacht Club
BIG BAY
MICHIGAN
Castle Park
Saugatuck Dunes
CAUTION
Improved channels shown by broken lines are subject to shoaling, particularly at the edges.

fishermen who cast spoons and dunk spawn bags or nightcrawlers. Good perch fishing occurs off and on throughout the *summer*, with minnows and worms the primary baits.

Those who continue to troll the Holland area in late summer and early *fall* generally target water from 80-200 feet deep. Action at this time from pier and shoreline is hit and miss for salmon and trout, but there is, again, some perching worthy of mention. It is also important to note that Lake Macatawa has an outstanding population of three- to six-pound walleyes. This is a shallow lake that is dark-stained with tannic acid, however, and therefore it is not easy to fish.

Winter fishing opportunities are limited to Lake Macatawa, with panfish, walleyes and northern pike the targeted species.

Planting Records

The DNR makes no current and has no planned stocking of hatchery-reared fish for the immediate Holland area. For area planting details see 8 (Grand Haven) and 6 (Saugatuck).

Facilities

The DNR does not maintain a harbor of refuge at Holland. There is a state-operated boat launch, however, located between Anchorage and Bay Haven marinas, on the northwest side of Lake Macatawa. Holland State Park features a launching ramp for small boats (14 feet or under.)

Further Information

Chambers of Commerce:

1. Holland Area Chamber of Commerce, 7 East 8th St., Holland 49423; (616) 392-2389.
2. West Michigan Tourist Association, 136 Fulton E., Grand Rapids 49503; (616) 456-8557.

Bait & Tackle Shops:

1. American Tackle, 152 Douglas Ave., Holland 49423; (616) 392-6688.
2. Main Sport & Marine, 60 E. 8th St., Holland 49423; (616) 392-1871.

Charter Fishing:

1. Captain Jack Nagelkirk, 512 W. 21st St., Holland 49423; (616) 392-3376. 26-foot Chris-Craft, *Micky-J II.*
2. Captain George Pierson, 315 N. 145th Ave., Holland 49423; (616) 396-3918 or 396-8827. 25-foot boat, *Arkie III.*

Department of Natural Resources:

Two fisheries biologists work out of District Headquarters at 621 North 10th St., Plainwell 49080; (616) 685-6851.

Coast Guard:

Holland Station, (616) 399-9330 or 399-9331

Thunder Mountain Lakers

People can say what they want to about lake trout being second-class citizens—how they're easy to catch, don't scrap like salmon, taste greasy and so forth. If they ever bang a triple on these fork-tailed gamesters, they might sing a different tune. I did and I do.

It happened out of South Haven (5) one June morning when Carl Freeman took a southwest heading past Palisades Nuclear Power Plant, then grabbed a handful of rpms to push his 27-foot Sportcraft, *Miss T Morning*, through rolling seas. Minutes later, when Thunder Mountain, a big sand dune and local landmark, lay dead off our port side, I flipped on the graph. A jagged bottom shaped up 120 feet below. "No marks," I said after studying it a minute or two. Freeman was eyeing his digital depth marker.

"They're there," he said. "Probably in the mud. Send 'em down while I fine-tune our location.

I stripped off five pulls of mono on the starboard level-wind, twirled the 20-pound-test mono into a loop before tucking it into a pressure release, then hit the button on a Cannon downrigger. Down went the silver-and-green Lucky Lure to 120 feet on the counter. Next, the port-side ball sucked a chartreuse K.C. Spoon out of sight in the cobalt water. I locked that rig in at 115 feet. Carl was backing down on the throttle even more while angling the *Miss T Morning* toward Thunder Mountain.

I dropped the two stern-end downriggers. Each speared a bright-silver cowbell string into the blueness below. A hot-green Fire Plug followed the other. I locked in each at 125 feet so they would just miss bottom. Then I turned to tell Carl that everything was set. He was waving his arms.

"Fish on!" he blurted. "Number two rigger."

I reached for the port-corner rod, already straight up and bucking. Ripping it from the holder, I power-cranked it into a tight *C*. A weighty fish twisted below while snitching a couple of pulls of mono off the reel. Carl suddenly yelped again and sprang for the starboard out-down rod, jumping now like someone stabbing an accusatory finger. When he lifted the pole, line squealed off.

"This one's a hog!" Carl said. "Can you back up and put it in neutral?"

Fumbling behind my back, I found and then jerked the throttle stick into "neutral". On the way back to my corner, rod bowed in my hands, the port-side out-down pole suddenly leaped. Quickly reeling in a few feet of line, I jammed the first rod back into its tube holder, then grabbed the out-down rig. Typical of lakers, this fish was heading down and out, no sizzling power run, like a salmon, just determined bullheadedness to stay stuck to the reef. I pumped the rod a couple of times, and the fish cut left to right.

"One more for a full house," I said to Carl, my eye on the still-set fourth downrigger.

Had we left the boat running, we might well have caught four at once.

Jack Warner
Genesee

8
GRAND HAVEN

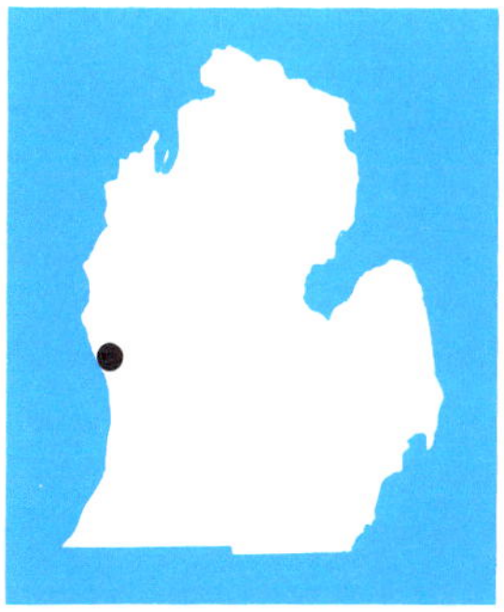

"Most people think of the Grand River as just a big, lazy river. They have no idea of the tremendous fishery here and in Lake Michigan." So says Grand Haven charterboat-captain Ken Whitney. Hefty stockings of cohos, Chinooks and steelhead, along with lake trout, contribute to good fishing, plus the Grand Haven area gets plenty of other salmon migrating north and south to native streams where they were released.

North-shore landmarks which aid fishermen include the Stack (at one-quarter mile), the County Park (at one mile), the Last Cottage North (at two miles), and Hoffmaster State Park (at four miles). South-bound landmarks are the Picture Screen (a white hilltop cottage framed with a white wooden fence—at one mile), Brucker Street (at 1-1/2 miles), Rosy Mound (a one-time sand dune, now leveled—at three miles), Twin Sisters (two sand dunes—at four miles), and the Pumping Station (at seven miles).

Fishing Schedule

SPRING

Good spots to fish vary with the season. In *spring*, one of the best places is a half-mile south of the piers along a narrow ditch that runs perpendicular to shore in 30-75 feet of water. Off the County Park, down 50-75 feet over water that is 100 feet deep is also good for brown trout and salmon, as is a small creek that outlets at Hoffmaster State Park.

Whitney's catch records show about 60 percent king salmon, 25 percent lake trout, 10 percent cohos, and five percent steelhead and browns. To catch spring kings, Ken longlines on the surface with Tadpollies and Wee Warts and runs five electric Proos downriggers. Out-downs are typically rigged shallow, with releases set at 30-60 feet. Stern-end downriggers get scattered depths and varying release lengths. Good lures are body baits and Northport Nailers, and a favorite startup color in spring is bright green on silver.

A charter in May 1984 had five businessmen aboard Whitney's 30-foot boat, the *TeraKen*. The first 45 minutes of the troll saw several strikes, but no one was quick enough to snatch rods from holders in time to catch any fish. Then, over the next 20 minutes, the men caught the next eight fish without a loss, clearing every line set. The salmon continued to hit steadily until 11:30, with many doubles and triples keeping everyone's hands full. Someone counted the damage—22 kings from eight to 22 pounds each in the fish boxes. The *TeraKen* needed three fish for limits, but the salmon turned off until 12:45. That's when three decided to hit all at once, and by one o'clock the *TeraKen* headed for port with five happy fishermen on deck and one pleased captain at the wheel.

SUMMER

Summer tactics for trout and salmon call for fast trolling lures that are scattered throughout the thermocline to 15 feet above and 15 feet below. Ken runs slider rigs on all downriggers, usually J-Plugs below and Northport Nailers above. Good color combos are white with red, white and black, white and blue, and silver and green. A decided problem in the Grand Haven area is the lack of deep-water structure. The trench off the Picture Screen holds fish when temperatures are right. For example, a turnover of water from heavy winds may bring trout and salmon in close for a brief period. But most summertime trollers target the water from Rosy Mound to the Pumping Station, where a contoured bottom runs

Salmon-fishing fever starts off Grand Haven by late July or early August most years.

from shore to about 80 feet deep. This is often the best spot for salmon in August and early September.

The Grand Haven piers furnish perch-fishing action off and on throughout the summer, plus spoon tossers can often catch kings during the hour before sunrise.

Fall offshore tactics call for slow speeds, shallow-set downriggers and longlines, and leads from 30-60 feet. Plugs in bright and dark green on silver, yellow, and pearl and green get priority. During late fall, Whitney opts for bright-red or bright-yellow Tadpollies and Wee Warts and runs other plugs in white-and-red and green-and-silver colors.

Winter fishing activities are limited to the Grand River bayou system, where ice fishermen catch panfish and spear northern pike.

Spring Kings

Although I feel like a fool later, I do it every year anyway. "*Yahhhhooo!*"

"What the hell was that for?" wonders a shocked fellow-angler, usually a newcomer to the spring trolling game.

"That was a lot of pent-up emotion from a long, boring winter."

"Well, warn me before you do it again."

"I won't do it again," I explain. I only do it once or twice each spring, usually when I hook into the first fish."

"Good. Thanks."

Regulars who pound the Great Lakes in search of salmon soon after ice-out know the joy that a spring-charged king or coho can bring. You can just feel a salmon swapping ends—through 100 yards of 12-pound-test line and eight feet of graphite rod. You can see the sun bounce off chrome-bright sides that hint of purple. You can hear waves cuff the boat bow and the siren-like sound of wind in downrigger wires.

Along about March or April, I used to do my best to put high-school English students to sleep with John Masefield's poem, "Sea Fever." The lines, "And all I ask is a windy day with the white clouds flying/ And the flung spray and the blown spume, and the sea gulls crying" always made me think of trolling for spring salmon.

Now that I no longer teach school, I'm on the water more than ever. It's strange how I think of "Sea Fever" when setting the season's first trolling lines.

Spring salmon fishing can get a funny kind of full nelson on a guy. And one of the nice plusses of this sport is that it happens in several places around the state.

***Yahhhhooo!* for that.**

Jack Warner
Genesee

Planting Records

Grand Haven is receiving 30,000 fall fingerling lake trout, and the Grand River watershed gets 400,000 each of coho smolts and king-salmon fingerlings, along with 20,000 steelhead yearlings. These annual DNR stockings are expected to continue through at least 1990.

Facilities

The DNR maintains a harbor of refuge with the following services: transient accommodations, gasoline, water, electricity, restrooms, shower facilities and holding-tank pump-out. The telephone number of the dock attendant is (616) 846-5590.

Further Information

Chambers of Commerce:

West Michigan Tourist Association, 136 Fulton E., Grand Rapids 49503; (616) 456-8557.

Bait & Tackle Shops:

1. Grand Sport Center, 317 N. Beacon Blvd., Grand Haven 49417; (616) 842-4420.
2. Woods & Waters Sports, 128 Columbus, Grand Haven 49417; (616) 842-8244.
3. American Tackle Outfitters, 8470 W. Olive Rd., West Olive 49460; (616) 399-5650.

Charter Fishing:

1. Captain Ken Whitney, 15170 155th Ave., Grand Haven 49417; (616) 846-1539. 30-foot Pacemaker, *TeraKen.*
2. Captains Bill and Judy Draper, 17660 168th Ave., Spring Lake 49456; (616) 842-2054. 30-foot Chris-Craft, *Red Boat.*

Department of Natural Resources:

Two fisheries biologists work out of District Headquarters at State Office Building, 350 Ottawa NW, Grand Rapids 49503; (616) 456-5071.

Coast Guard:

Grand Haven Station, (616) 842-2510 or 842-2511.

8 GRAND HAVEN

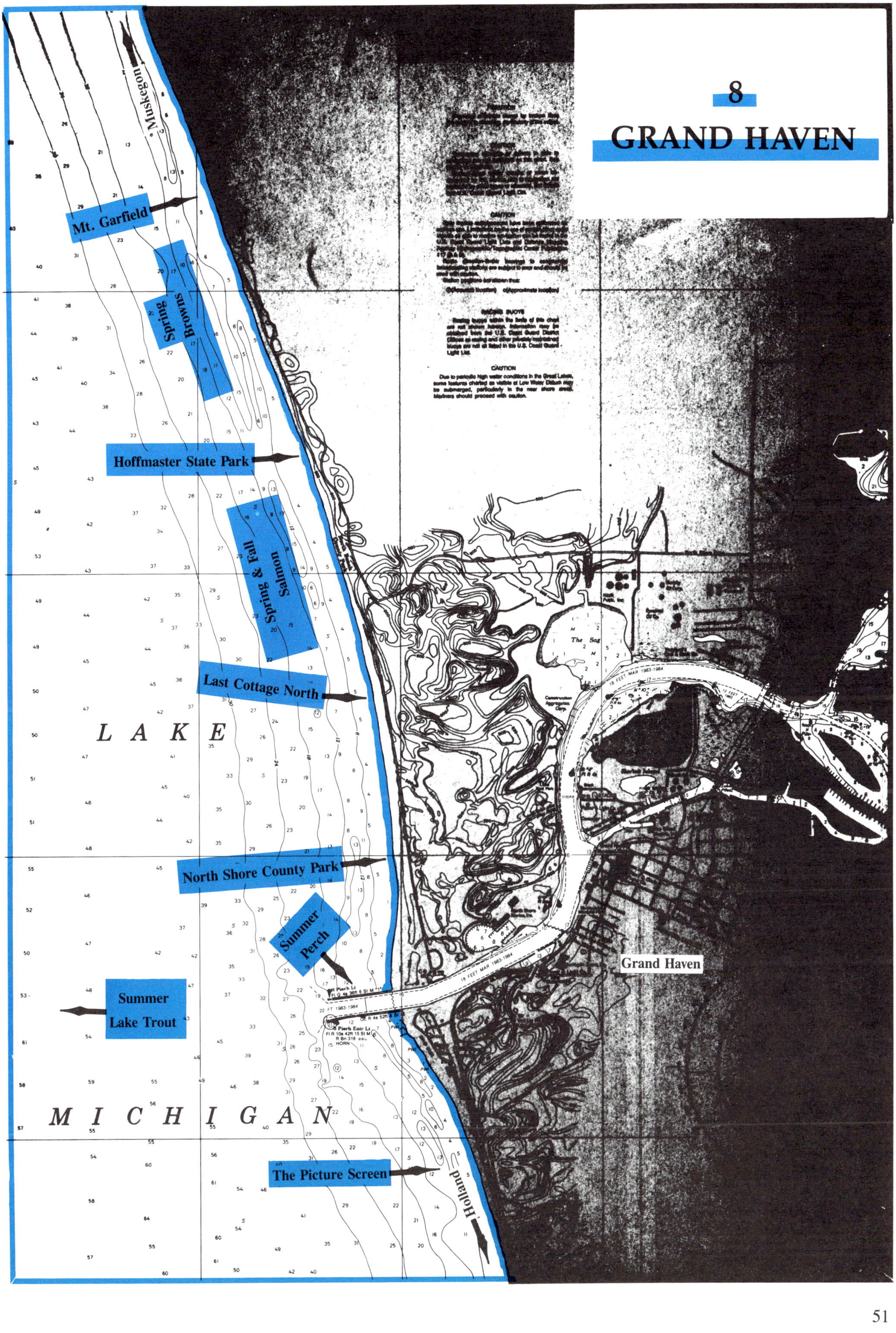

9
MUSKEGON

There are several reasons why Muskegon is a major draw for Lake Michigan fishermen. One is hefty plants of Chinook salmon, steelhead, brown trout and lake trout. Another is the exciting return of the walleye fishery to Muskegon Lake and the Muskegon River. Third, there is space aplenty on the piers, where anglers get good in-season action for trout and salmon as well as yellow perch. And 4,000 tons of rock that went into making the artificial Muskegon Reef, just south of the piers, have been attracting fish for happy anglers.

Another plus is that Muskegon Lake furnishes blow-day sport when trollers can't get onto the big lake.

Fishing Schedule

South of the piers, trollers hunt trout and salmon in the area off Mono Lake where some uneven lake bottom is available. Water depths vary from 100-190 feet, with trolling lures presented from 30-100 feet down, both there and farther south off Mt. Garfield. Best spot north is two miles from the channel in 90 feet of water off a fort structure, locally called the Block House, in the state park. The Muskegon Reef should become increasingly popular as lake-trout fingerlings released by the DNR grow into catching size. At the present time the reef acts as a magnet for spring salmon and browns, summer yellow perch, and staging salmon in late summer. In spring there is also trout and salmon activity along the entire shoreline in shallow water to 50 feet deep.

SPRING

The port of Muskegon is synonymous with Captain Bernie Halverson, its best-known fisherman and one of the Great Lakes most innovative skippers. In *spring*, Halverson pays particular attention to what he calls the "plume," the flow of dark-stained water from the Muskegon River into Lake Michigan. In the absence of wind, this flow seeps out a mile or more, and Bernie says salmon often seek it in order to stalk river-flow food.

"For a salmon, it's like walking up to the refrigerator," he says, "especially when you can find 50-degree-F. water right next to the plume. A north or south wind in summer, though, often blows the plume right out of the temperature range."

Another condition Bernie looks for in spring is what is known as an "interface," warm shoreline water that butts up to cold water. "An interface is different from the horizontal thermocline," he explains, "because it makes for a vertical wall of water at two temperatures." He locates such a phenomenon by looking for surface trash (leaves, dead alewives, etc.), a difference in water color, or a ripple effect next to calm water. He fishes the interface by zig-zagging in and out along it—"stitching the seam," he calls it—for two or three miles. Then he'll turn around and troll back through it again.

Start-up lures for Muskegon-area trollers are mostly body baits (Bombers, Rapalas, Rebels) in black and silver, silver, and blue and silver. These lures are either flatlined or run off shallow-set downriggers. Many boat fishermen break out planer boards and outriggers in spring, too, and run Countdown Rapalas or small lures such as Krocodiles from them.

Pier fishermen get in their licks by balling spawn or worms to shankless hooks and fishing the natural baits off bottom. Others spincast spoons under one ounce in plain silver or mated with other colors.

SUMMER

By *summer*, when trollers have to hunt fish, tactics involve kicking up boat speed, as well as finding the thermocline and running lures both above and below as well as through it. Most fishermen also stack their lure offerings with add-a-lines or slider rigs. Fast-trolled lures include J-Plugs, Cop-E-Cat spoons or Krocodile spoons. When fish show up on graphs, Halverson and others slow down and switch to medium-speed lures such as Chargers, Manistee Wobblers, Dardevle Imp Klickers, and even Tadpollies. Blue-and-white, green-and-silver and various combinations of yellow, chartreuse, pearl, and black are favorite summer-hunting colors.

Salmon that are schooled and readily striking often get to taste silver-with-red-spots Lucky Lures, chrome-and-brass or yellow-with-red-dots Flutter Spoons, and white-and-blue or black-and-gold Northport Nailers.

Summer perching from the piers and over the Muskegon Reef is usually good. Both ends of the quarter-mile-long by 300- to 400-yard-wide reef are marked with buoys. The exact location is about a half-mile south of the piers in 25 feet of water. There, algae forms on the rocks (some as big as small cars) and produces food for plankton and other micro-organisms. The food chain then continues through larvae and crayfish, which ultimately attract predator species such as yellow perch and salmon. Minnows, worms or wigglers pinned to two-hook perch spreaders and lightly jigged off bottom can result in a fine mess of yellow-bellies for the table.

Walleye fishing in Muskegon Lake is good all summer, with both trollers and jig or drift fishermen reporting success in the river channel and along its inclines. The waters of Muskegon Lake, however, are dark-colored, and, therefore, dark lures

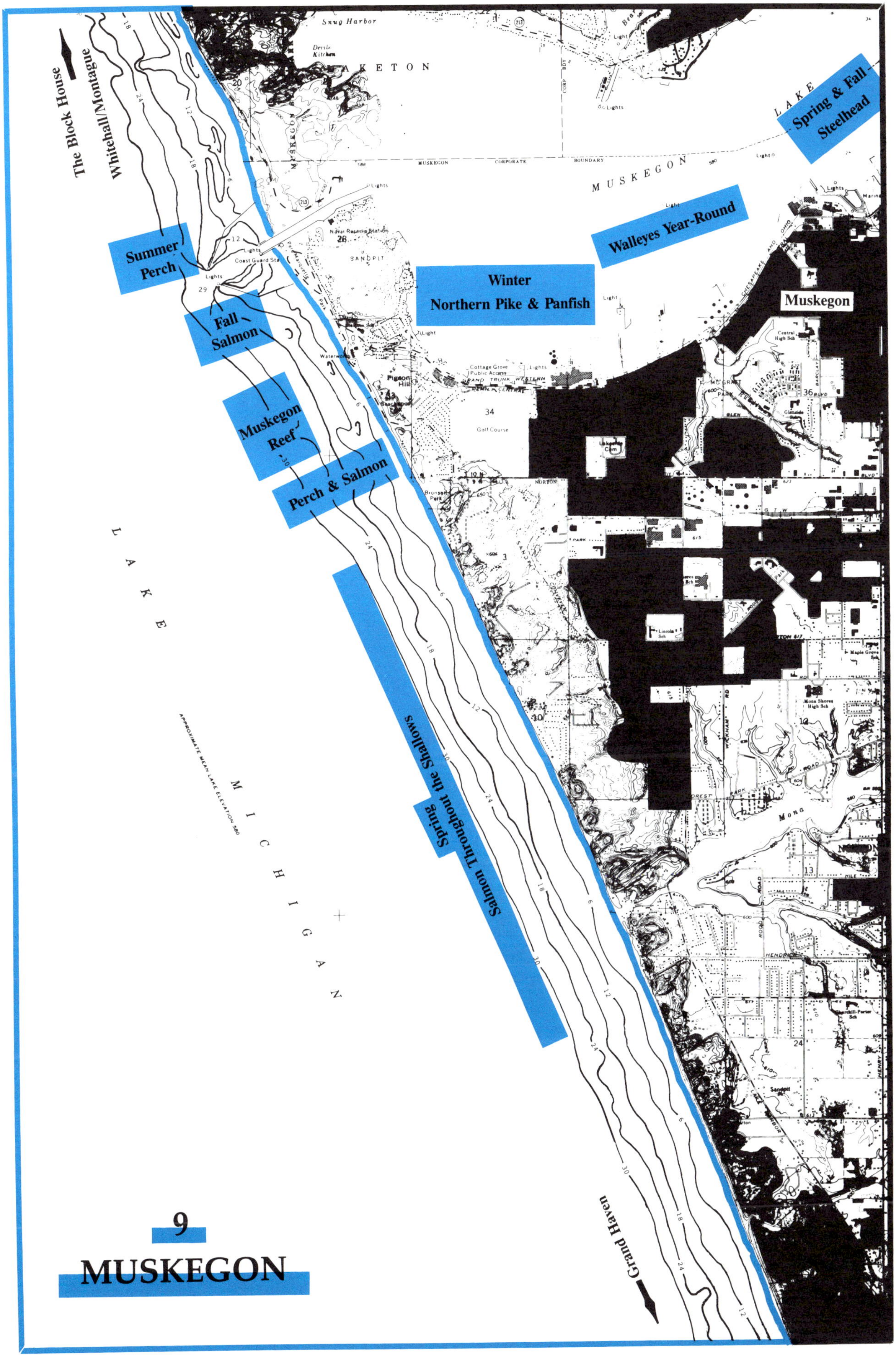
The Block House
Whitehall/Montague
Summer Perch
Fall Salmon
Muskegon Reef
Perch & Salmon
Winter Northern Pike & Panfish
Walleyes Year-Round
Spring & Fall Steelhead
Muskegon
Spring Salmon Throughout the Shallows
LAKE MICHIGAN
Grand Haven
9
MUSKEGON

Muskegon Lake produces largemouth bass for anglers who seek them. The happy angler is the author's best-known fishing partner, Joe Zikewich of Lake Orion.

MUSKEGON (cont.)

(brown, gold, dull orange, black) are most productive.

FALL

Fall sport improves for salmon as the soon-to-spawn battlers mass in the shallows. Trollers now opt for big wobbling plugs and large spoons in bright colors, and they lengthen leads to these lures. Muskegon Lake gets plenty of attention from trollers when the big fish enter. (The DNR currently allows a snagging fishery from September 10 to October 25 between Croton Dam and the access site located at Pine Avenue in Newaygo County.) Shallow-set downrigger or flatline fishermen, who troll slowly or simply row small boats in Muskegon Lake, get smashing strikes from both Chinooks and steelhead. The Muskegon River hosts drift-boat fishermen as late as Christmas or until freeze-up. In addition, the piers remain productive from late August through November, when steelhead enter the river system in preparation for spring spawning.

WINTER

Winter fishing activities on Muskegon Lake are usually productive for northern pike, walleyes, yellow perch and crappies. Sometimes a big steelhead or brown trout will cruise under shanties and nail lures jigged for panfish.

Planting Records

The Muskegon Reef receives 30,000 fall fingerling lake trout, the Muskegon River gets 100,000 spring fingerling Chinooks and 50,000 yearling steelhead, and Muskegon Lake outlet receives 15,000 brown-trout yearlings. These annual DNR stockings will continue through at least 1990.

Facilities

The DNR maintains a harbor of refuge with the following services: transient accommodations, gasoline, water, electricity, restrooms, shower facilities, holding-tank pump-out and VHF-FM radio. The telephone number of the dock attendant is (616) 722-3361. There is an excellent launch facility here, and several others are located at commercial marinas around Muskegon Lake.

Further Information

Chambers of Commerce:

1. Muskegon Area Chamber of Commerce, 1065 Fourth St., Muskegon 49441; (616) 722-3751.
2. West Michigan Tourist Association, 136 Fulton E., Grand Rapids 49503; (616) 456-8557.

Bait & Tackle Shops:

1. Larry's Bait & Tackle, 190 Laketon Ave., Muskegon 49441; (616) 722-6824.
2. Angler-Archer Sporting Goods, 2008 Lake Ave., North Muskegon 49445; (616) 744-5992.
3. Shoreline Service, 1080 Lakeshore Dr., Muskegon 49441; (616) 759-7254.
4. Springs Sporting Goods, 280 Ottawa, Muskegon 49441; (616) 722-7107.

Charter Fishing:

1. Captain Bernie Halverson, 607 W. Sunset Dr., North Muskegon 49445; (616) 744-4493. 24-foot Lone Star, *Chinook*.
2. Captain Bob Reineke, Lake Michigan Sport Fishing, 918 Central Ave., North Muskegon 49445; (616) 744-3691.

Department of Natural Resources:

Two fisheries biologists work out of District Headquarters at State Office Building, 350 Ottawa NW, Grand Rapids 49503; (616) 456-5071.

Coast Guard:

Muskegon Station, (616) 759-8581 or 759-8582.

Capture the King

In the Great Lakes he can grow to nearly 50 pounds. Sleek-muscled and strong, he tackles lures with the tenacity of a nose guard. He snaps tough fishing line as though it were kite string, runs figure-eights around cannonball cables, busts open knuckles of anglers who forget to grip reel handles. He can make your arms ache from cranking, your stomach sore from a rod butt jammed too hard, too long. He can cause you to lose sleep, both before and after your encounter.

To rephrase a line from an Elton John song: "I guess that's why they call him the *king*."

King salmon have captivated me for as long as they have been in the Great Lakes, and that is nearly 20 years now. I well remember the first time I met a king at close range. It occurred one dark night many years ago while wader fishing at Harrisville Harbor (37). A large fish the size of a rubber torpedo nearly knocked me over. I've had a healthy respect for kings ever since.

Over the years, these brutish salmon have provided many thrills. With the exception of Skamania steelhead, no open-lake gamefish is as pulse-maddening to catch. With the exception of brown trout, no other cold-water species is as mysterious or moody.

Readers who have caught them know the kind of bear hug that the Chinook, as he is called, can get on a fisherman. Those who have yet to catch a king, also must wait to be captured by kings. One fish can do it.

Jack Warner
Genesee

10

WHITEHALL/MONTAGUE

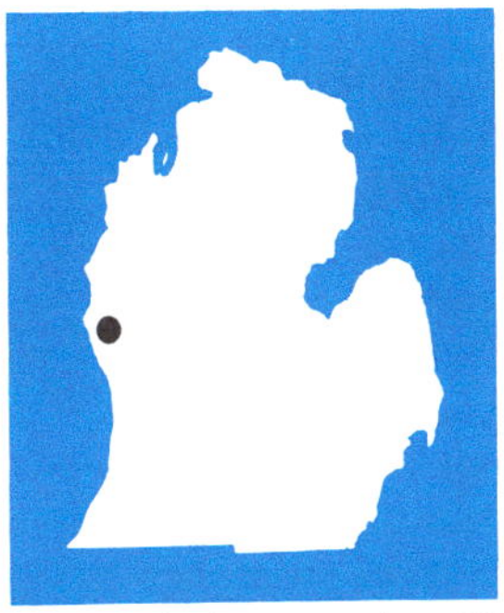

A secret is anything "kept from the knowledge of any but the initiated." The White Lake area at Whitehall and Montague, north of Muskegon is definitely a secret. Nestled among huge shoreline sand dunes, 2,571-acre White Lake has long been a popular resort spot for downstate and Chicago-area vacationers. But you rarely heard much about Lake Michigan fishing in the region. Instead, the fisheries at Muskegon (9), to the south, and Pentwater (11) and Ludington (12), to the north, got the headlines.

Anglers might want to take another look. Area reefs receive lake trout. And steelhead (including 20,000 summer-run strain) and brown trout have been stocked in the White River. Salmon heading north and south to natal release sites are fair pickings for local trollers, plus browns are available in spring. The piers serve up solid perching in spring, summer and fall. White Lake itself, which is actually a five- to six-mile-long drowned rivermouth, affords excellent fishing for several species (see "White Lake Bonus, page 56) and is an ace in the hole for Lake Michigan blow days.

What more could a fisherman want? No wonder the local chamber of commerce calls the White Lake area "Michigan's best-kept secret."

Fishing Schedule

Because of this bounty of good fishing, more and more charter-boat operators are setting up to do business here. One is Captain Bob Price, who began hiring out his 28-foot Carver Santa Cruz, the *Millie Ann*, six years ago.

SPRING

Price's fish box contains a mixed bag in *spring*. Chinooks of five to 15 pounds are the mainstay, but he also brings in brown trout, steelhead, lake trout and coho salmon. He runs five downriggers—two out-downs, a pair of stern-corner models, and one across the center stern. Corner rigs are set first and run down the deepest; then Price establishes a pattern of deep to shallow at three- to five-foot intervals. Spring and early summer lures include Hot 'N Tots, Rapalas, Fat Raps, Northport Nailers and small J-Plugs. Best colors are black, silver, orange, green, alone or in combination with each other.

Price cites trolling speed as critical to impart proper action to his lures. Sometimes he runs the same lure types and colors but staggers them as previously described. Other times he will stack his offerings, spotting plugs deep and metal lures above. Most spring fish hit in 10-50 feet of water, but a bright sun can move the fish—kings especially—to deeper water.

A plus of fishing the Whitehall/Montague area is that there is little competition from other trollers. Even the piers are strangely bare in spring. Anglers that do appear sling marble-sized spawn bags into the open lake. Most use a barrel sinker stopped 15 inches above the hook with a snap swivel or small split shot. Others toss 2/5- to 3/4-ounce spoons in bright colors such as red, orange, yellow, hot green or chartreuse. Use the fan-cast method and vary retrieves until you get an arm-shocking strike from a trout or salmon.

According to Dick Sturgis, another good skipper in the area, key landmarks to the north include the Three Sisters (a series of high sand dunes), the Golf Course, the Red Cottage, the Scallops, and Little Point Sable Lighthouse. South-bound trollers key in the shallows off the Duck Lake outflow in spring, then head offshore for 60-130 feet of water in *summer*.

SUMMER

Sturgis, who is from Flint, says that king salmon make up probably 50 percent of his season-long catch at this port. Coho (25 percent), lake trout (15 percent), and brown trout (10 percent) constitute the other half. April and May are the best months for browns, with May being ideal for lake trout and salmon. The area is also productive for salmon from early July until Labor Day. Steelheading is traditionally good from mid-September until November, but it should also be worth trying in July and August as summer-run steelies, released in 1984, enter White Lake.

FALL

The piers produce sporadic salmon throughout the summer and become productive again in *fall*. As mentioned, perch are a season-long staple, plus, at times, walleyes and northerns can be taken from these slabs as Lake Michigan fish enter White Lake. Beginning in early August, most trollers change their lures to bigger plugs and spoons, and a few add dodgers and flies. There are no specific local colors or hot lures to report, and that is partly because more experimenting anglers are needed.

WINTER

Winter fishing activities are limited to White Lake, where anglers catch crappies, perch, northern pike, bluegills and a few walleyes.

The White Lake Area Sportfishing Association is attempting to improve the fishing quality of the area. For details and membership application, contact the group at P.O. Box 157, Montague 49437 or call (616) 894-6336.

Planting Records

The White Lake North and South reefs are each slated to receive 60,000 fall fingerling lake trout each year through at least 1990. Although these fish won't be catching size for five or six years, the DNR has historically released lakers at these reefs for

White Lake Bonus

White Lake-area anglers don't complain too much about Lake Michigan blow days that chase them from the big water. There is always White Lake to fish. The five- to six-mile-long drowned rivermouth at Whitehall/Montague has some outstanding fishing opportunities for smallmouth bass and northern pike plus good numbers of yellow perch, crappies, walleyes and largemouth bass. A run of Lake Michigan white bass, wiped out years ago with the demise of their principal forage—the grayback minnow—may be re-established, thanks to a big influx of gizzard shad. About 2,000 Indiana white bass have been caught, brought back from that state, and—with the DNR's approval—released by sportsmen in White Lake.

The lake also serves up Chinook salmon in fall; brown trout in spring, summer and fall; and steelhead in spring. In some ways White Lake could be Michigan's best-kept fishing secret.

September is the best month for the smallmouths due to the abundance of young-of-the-year gizzard shad upon which they feed. But fishing is good from the May opener (usually the Saturday before Memorial Day) until November. Usually every summer, smallmouth-ace Ray Capek—part owner of Lake Land Outfitters, a bait and tackle shop in Whitehall—tosses back about 200 bronzebacks from two to 4-1/2 pounds each.

Capek fishes for smallmouths at drowned lumber piles off Cook Point, the east side of Long Point, east of Scenic Drive on the south side, and the narrows on the south side of the lake. He also targets the weed line, which extends as far offshore as 200 yards.

In spring he vertical-jigs with Hopkins Spoons and bucktails and in summer switches to rubber crayfish, four-inch fake salamanders, and plastic worms. He rigs these artificials Texas-style (sink the barb into your lure, turn and bring out the barb again). Hot colors are brown, black or dark green.

A good spot for largemouth bass is uplake from the bathing beach along weedbeds on the Montague side (south side) of the lake. Try buzzbaits, spinnerbaits and rubber worms on warm, muggy evenings.

Ray caught a fine seven-pound northern the day I fished with him in the summer of 1984. We were casting yellow spinnerbaits around boat docks on the southeast shore. Other good pike haunts include weedbeds off Dowie Point, in 10-20 feet of water just up the lake from the yacht club near Scenic Drive, and weed beds along South Shore Drive.

I caught a slab-sided 14-inch black crappie on a Mepps Comet spinner slowly pulled through weeds. According to Ray, White Lake contains both white and black crappies. Good spots are southeast-side points off the Mill Pond Road, the east side of Long Point, and both sides of Cook Point. These are summertime spots; for winter action, try 300 yards offshore from White Lake Drive. You will likely catch bluegills and a few sunfish here at this spot, too. Deep-water contours off Indian Point and Murray Road are excellent winter fishing grounds for yellow perch that will hit Russian Spoons tipped with a flap of perch belly, perch eye or small minnow.

White Lake gets a small run of Lake Michigan walleyes, and there are resident fish in White Lake to seven or eight pounds each. A good early season tactic is to drift or back-troll Lindy Rigs with air-injected nightcrawlers off weedline shelves. Add a bullet sinker 18 inches above the crawler. During active feeding periods of July, August and early September, Bomber crankbaits work well if retrieved tight to the weeds. The 20-foot contour off Long Point and the 40-foot contour off Indian Point are good spots to try.

White Lake has something for everyone, and fishing pressure is only medium at best.

Tom Huggler
Otisville

many years, so adult fish are available now. The last stocking of yearling fish was made in 1984.

Also, the White River in Oceana County is currently getting 15,000 steelhead yearlings, and the White Lake Channel receives 7,500 fall fingerling brown trout. These annual stockings will continue through at least 1990.

Facilities

The DNR maintains a harbor of refuge with the following services: transient accommodations, gasoline, water, electricity, restrooms, shower facilities, holding-tank pump-out and VHF-FM radio. The telephone number of the dock attendant is (616) 722-3361. A public boat launch is located just south of Montague on the northwest shore.

Montague and Whitehall, with populations of 2,400 and 3,000 respectively, offer plenty of accommodations for visiting fishermen.

Further Information

Chambers of Commerce:

1. White Lake Area Chamber of Commerce, 124 Hanson, Whitehall 49461; (616) 893-4585.
2. West Michigan Tourist Association, 136 Fulton E., Grand Rapids 49503; (616) 456-8557.

Bait & Tackle Shops:

1. Lake Land Outfitters in Whitehall, (616) 894-4670.
2. Armstrong's Bait & Tackle, 200 Lake St., Whitehall 49461; (616) 894-6753.
3. Skipper's Landing, 4464 Dowling, Montague 49437; (616) 893-4525.

Charter Fishing:

1. Captain Bob Price, 1165 Scenic Drive, Muskegon 49441; (616) 744-4138. 28-foot Carver Santa Cruz, *Millie Ann*.
2. Captain Dick Sturgis, 3348 Ridgecliffe Dr., Flint 48504; (313) 232-5439.
3. Captain Bob Kimble, Long Point Charter Service, 6265 Old Channel Trail, Montague 49437; (616) 894-6038. 22-foot boat, *Ol Ugly*.

Department of Natural Resources:

Two fisheries biologists work out of District Headquarters at the State Office Building, 350 Ottawa NW, Grand Rapids 49503; (616) 456-5071.

Coast Guard:

Muskegon Station, (616) 759-8581 or 759-8582.

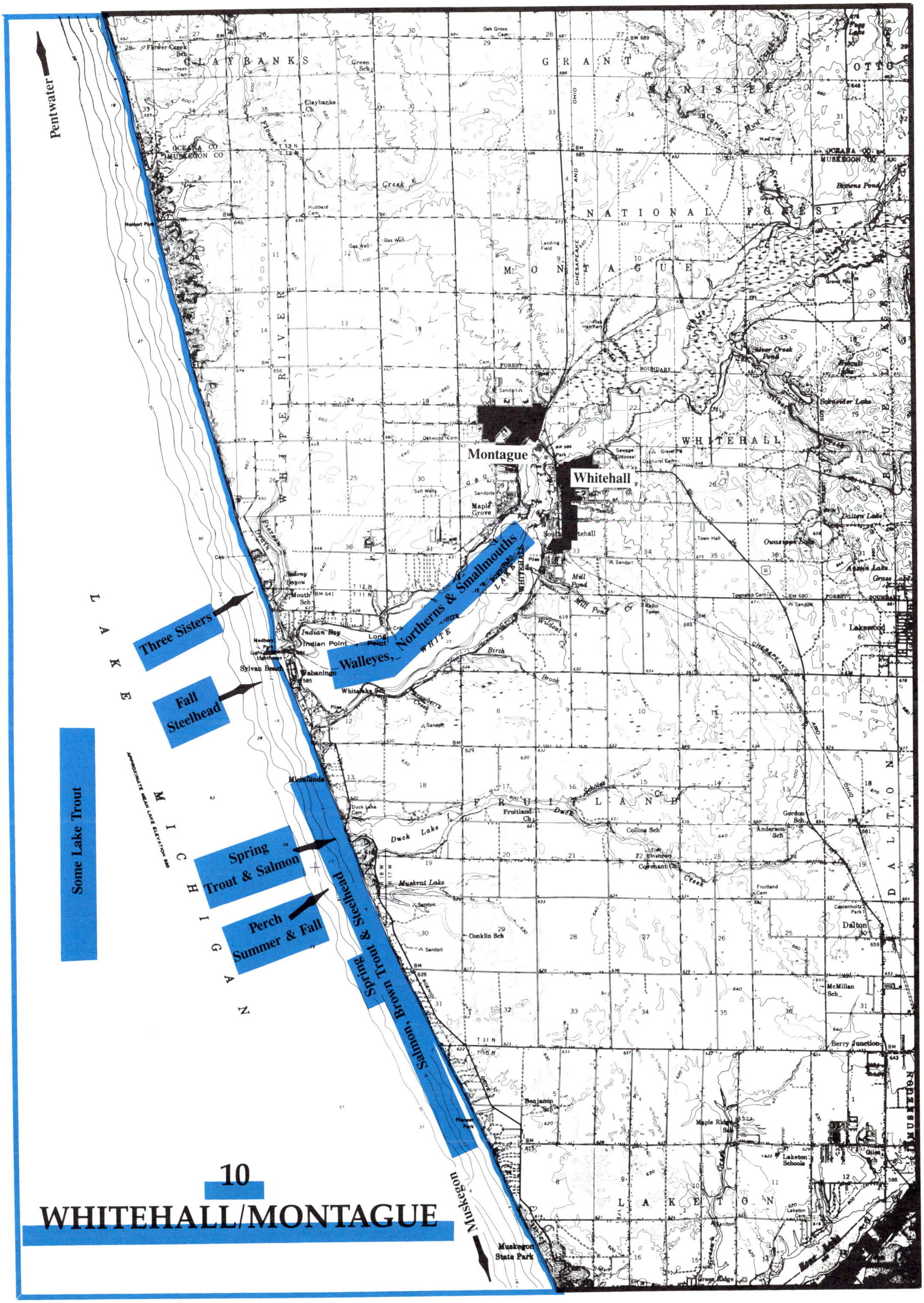

Pentwater
Montague
Whitehall
Three Sisters
Fall Steelhead
Walleyes, Northerns & Smallmouths
Some Lake Trout
Spring Trout & Salmon
Perch Summer & Fall
Spring Salmon, Brown Trout & Steelhead
LAKE MICHIGAN
Muskegon
Muskegon State Park
WHITE RIVER
CLAYBANKS
GRANT
MANISTEE NATIONAL FOREST
MONTAGUE
WHITEHALL
FRUITLAND
LAKETON
DALTON
10
WHITEHALL/MONTAGUE

Crappies like this dandy stringer held by Richard Egner of Downers Grove, Illinois, are available in White Lake.

Tom Richards (left) of Mt. Morris, Michigan, knows that certain drowned rivermouths, like Pentwater Lake, are good spots to try for muskies.

11
PENTWATER

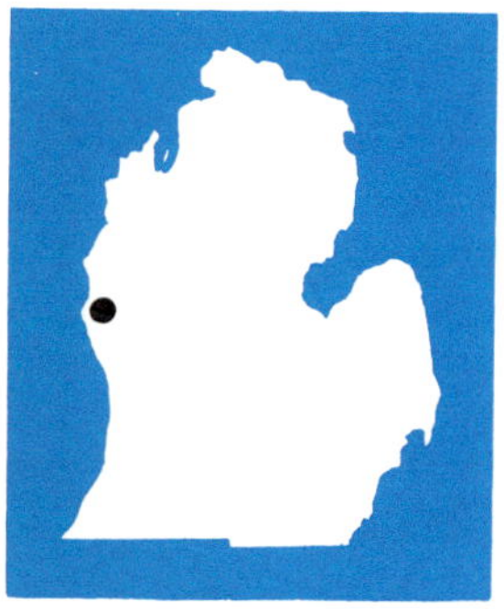

Pentwater, a small town of about 1,100 people, lies 10 miles south of Ludington (12) on Lake Michigan. A resort community, Pentwater attracts both tourists and fishermen. Anglers catch plenty of salmon coursing north to Ludington in late summer, plus the Pentwater region serves up good lake-trout and steelhead fishing from resident plants of those species.

Pierheads flanking the Pentwater River mouth provide shorebound action, and Pentwater Lake itself serves up blow-day trolling sport for trout and salmon as well as warm-water species such as northern pike, smallmouth and largemouth bass, yellow perch, crappies and occasional walleyes.

Just south of the piers is a residence known locally as the Glass House, and a little further south and just offshore is the wreck of the *Anna Minch*. Still moving south, at a mile below the piers is the former site of three sand dunes, now called the Three Bares. Further yet down the shoreline are the Dead Hole area off Cedar Point Park; Juniper Beach (at seven miles); the wreck of the *Novadock*, marked by a black buoy; the Silver Lake Sand dunes (at nine miles); Pine Island (a stand of tall pine trees on the beach); and the lighthouse at Little Point Sable (11 miles).

North-bound landmarks include the Duna Vista Resort, the Three Sisters (three high sand dunes), Bass Lake outlet, Summit Point, and the Rock Pile, near the Consumers Power Company "Project" a couple of miles below Ludington.

Throughout most of the trolling season, the best fishing occurs from Juniper Beach to the lighthouse, with the most popular spot being the front of the biggest sand dune where bottom drops from 40 to 100 feet. Another area of sharp structure breaks is found just north of the lighthouse at Pine Island.

Fishing Schedule

SPRING

"Coho" Bob Maynard, who books charters out of his bait and tackle shop in Pentwater, says that spring fishing activity kicks off with smelt dippers scoring from the piers. Action begins about April 10 and usually lasts through the month. Pier fishermen in spring also catch menominees, brown trout, steelhead, yellow perch and some salmon. Spawn bags fished below slip sinkers or bobbers produce well on trout and salmon. For the soft-striking menominees, try single salmon eggs or red worms on small shankless hooks weighted with one or more BB-sized shot.

Narrow spoons, such as Krocodiles or Kastmasters in 2/5- to 3/4-ounce, work well for trout and salmon. Good spring colors are fluorescent orange and silver or glow-green and silver. Blue-and-silver Little Cleos doctored with paint-on orange spots are sometimes hot, too.

Offshore spring fishing is good for kings, cohos, steelhead and browns, with laker fishing coming on after the May 1 opener. According to skilled charterboat-captain Bill Muirhead, who lives in Milford but also owns a house on Pentwater Lake, from ice-out to about May 10 is ideal for shallow-water trolling for browns. Muirhead runs three- to five-inch minnow-imitating plugs (Rebels, Rapalas) with chrome sides to resemble smelt. Longlining with a bit of lead or attaching these lures to outriggers or planer boards is the rated method for browns. They typically make up about 10 percent of Muirhead's spring bag.

Bill pulls out all the stops to catch spring and *summer* salmon, which he says constitute about 50-60 percent and 10-20 percent respectively of his overall catch through Labor Day. From May 1 (when he usually begins fishing the Pentwater area) until Memorial Day, he sends down small spoons—Northport Nailers, Flutter Chucks, Locos, Westport Wobblers, and Doctor Spoons—relying on silver as the primary color. At various times, he runs downriggers, outriggers, planer boards and trip divers and even weights some side-rigged or flatlined offerings with up to 10 ounces of lead. These decisions are based upon weather and temperature variables, but Muirhead also plays the hunch game and listens carefully to his marine radio for daily catching clues.

SUMMER

Summer also serves up good lake-trout trolling near bottom in depths from 85-140 feet. Slowly trolling cowbells to which green or chartruese P-Nuts have been added is the local catching method. A few fishermen pull wire line and big spoons of silver.

Beginning in late July, when kings and cohos are massing offshore preparatory to making spawning runs, Muirhead switches to magnum-sized spoons and begins to add fluorescent colors to the mix of silver choices. By August 10, he has begun to switch his trolling arsenal to Silver Hordes, J-Plugs, Salmon Spots, and dodger/fly combinations. Fluorescent or silver colors in plugs work best at Pentwater, with silver dodgers and black trolling flies and squids also getting the nod.

FALL

Cohos figure as high as 30 percent in Bill's *fall* catch. Keeping similar lures in a close group (sometimes called "pattern fishing" or "monochromatic fishing") is a little-known tactic that helps Muirhead to full coolers at this time. Since cohos don't mind close leads and plenty of flash, Muirhead bloodknots 30 feet of

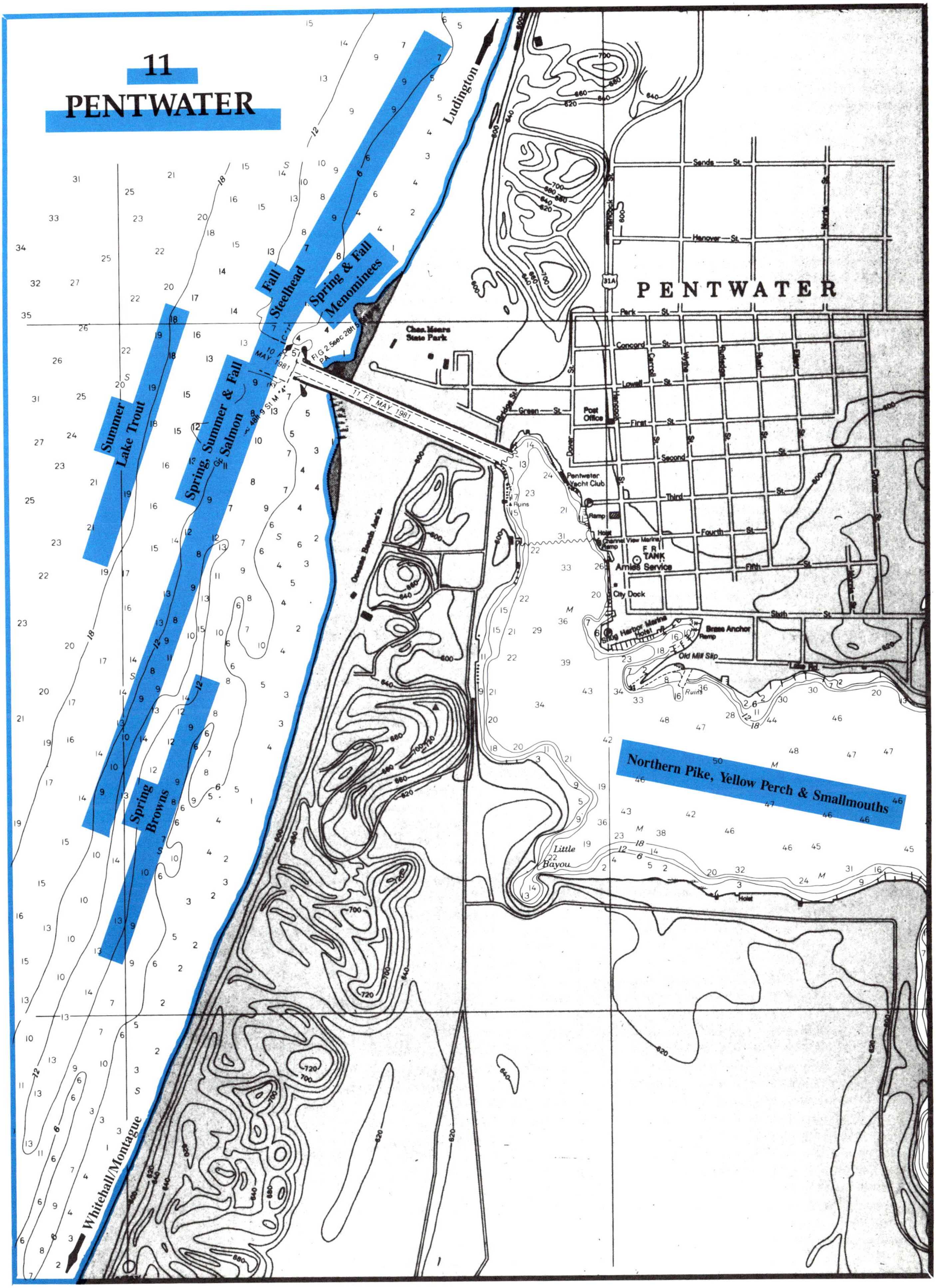
11
PENTWATER
Ludington
Whitehall/Montague
Fall Steelhead
Spring & Fall Menominees
Summer Lake Trout
Spring, Summer & Fall Salmon
Spring Browns
Northern Pike, Yellow Perch & Smallmouths
PENTWATER
Chas. Mears State Park
Post Office
Pentwater Yacht Club
City Dock
Little Bayou
Old Mill Slip
Brass Anchor
Sands St.
Hanover St.
Park St.
Concord St.
Lowell St.
Green St.
First St.
Second St.
Third St.
Fourth St.
Fifth St.
Sixth St.
11 FT MAY 1981

20-pound-test *clear* Stren line to his usual trolling line of 20-pound-test *gold* Stren. Then, he adds a rubber band just below the knot and hooks the rubber band to his cannonball. Thus, he runs five downrigger-trolled lures—usually the same size and color—all at 30 feet behind the boat.

Other Pentwater-based trollers report summer-end catches of salmon off Pine Island and the Silver Lake Sand dunes in 25-35 feet of water. Hot lures are silver or blue J-Plugs, green-with-black ladderback Canadian Plugs, silver or blue Mac Squids, and black-and-silver or black-and-gold Northport Nailers.

Steelhead catches in Lake Michigan shallows and in Pentwater Lake improve dramatically by late October and last through Thanksgiving. Most steelies are caught on surface-run plugs set 60-150 feet behind the boat, depending upon wave chop (the calmer the day, the longer the lead). Tadpollies, Hot 'N Tots, Red Fins, and No. 4 Silver Hordes are the rated lures, with silver or green the best colors.

Besides trout and salmon, the piers in fall also yield excellent catches of whitefish and menominees. Red worms pinned to No. 10 or No. 12 hooks, then run to bottom with small split shots and slowly jigged, produce best. The key catching period is November 1 through December 10 most years.

Winter fishing activities are good on Pentwater Lake for northern pike, crappies and yellow perch. These species, along with two- to five-pound smallmouth bass, are taken year-round and serve as an ace in the hole on days when Lake Michigan is blown over.

Planting Records

The Pentwater area is receiving 70,000 lake-trout and 5,000 steelhead yearlings annually through at least 1990. Salmon and brown trout caught in the region are from plants elsewhere, except that there may be some natural reproduction in the Pentwater River, too.

Facilities

The DNR maintains a harbor of refuge with the following services: transient accommodations, gasoline and diesel fuel, water, electricity, restrooms, shower facilities and holding-tank pump-out. The telephone number of the dock attendant is (616) 869-8301. Boat launches on Pentwater Lake are located at the city docks on the northeast side, at Snug Harbor Marine Center, and two blocks below Sixth Street.

Further Information

Chambers of Commerce:

1. Pentwater Area Chamber of Commerce, P.O. Box 614, Pentwater 49449; (616) 869-4150.
2. West Michigan Tourist Association, 136 Fulton E., Grand Rapids 49503; (616) 456-8557.

Bait & Tackle shops:

1. Coho Bob's Gun and Coho Shop, 484 Wythe St., Pentwater 49449; (616) 869-7751.
2. Hart True Value Hardware, 112 E. Main St., Hart 49420; (616) 873-3807.

Charter Fishing:

1. Captain Bill Muirhead, 634 Union St., Milford 48042; (313) 685-3041. 24-foot Slickcraft, *Spider*.
2. Captain Ralph Fairbanks, Rte. 1, Box 24-A, Irons 49644; (616) 266-5111 or 869-5032. 31-foot Chris-Craft, *The Hunter*.
3. Captain Whitey Vermeulen, P.O. Box 143, Brethren 49619; (616) 477-5676 or 869-7441. 38-foot boat, *The Sportsman*.

Department of Natural Resources:

Two fisheries biologists work out of District Headquarters at 8015 S. US-131, Cadillac 49601; (616) 775-9727.

Coast Guard:

Ludington Station, (616) 843-9088 or 843-2447.

Pent-Up Action at Pentwater

Pentwater is an excellent port because it is protected from both north and south winds by Big and Little Sable points. Also, these points at certain times hold cooler water closer to shore than most ports—an important consideraton as salmon migrate toward shore in late summer/early fall.

I well remember a charter here in late August one year when, typically, we ran south to Juniper Beach at daylight to set lines. Following normal procedure, I began setting highlines in 25 feet of water, then planned to angle into deeper water while rigging downriggers. Before I could turn to the downriggers, however, we boxed three fine kings—one off a flatline and Rapala and two off No. 5 chrome Silver Hordes off outriggers.

Since action was so good in water less than 40 feet deep, I turned back toward shore and headed for sand dunes there. By nine o'clock we had four kings, a brown trout and four cohos. Again, the Silver Hordes off outriggers produced, as did chrome-and-white Northport Nailers shallow-set to downriggers at five to 15 feet deep.

Then, everything suddenly went flat as pear juice on a plate. Radio traffic was uncommonly slow, suggesting that other trollers had hit the skids, too. On a hunch, I moved into shallow water—10-15 feet deep—where the water was about five degrees cooler, then turned and headed back north. We had three hits at once, all from five- to eight-pound cohos, that helped fatten the cooler. Action continued steadily until eleven o'clock, with Doctor Spoons run 60 feet back and close to bottom the hot lure. I remember that the trolling speed on my E.M.S. Hawk was 3.75.

We needed two fish for a four-man limit of 20, but after a mile and one-half of fruitless trolling, we decided to reef lines and run for port. Suddenly, everyone yelled "Fish on!" as both outside downriggers went off. Those two small cohos nicely filled us out, and we were dockside in time for lunch.

Captain Bill Muirhead
Milford

12
LUDINGTON

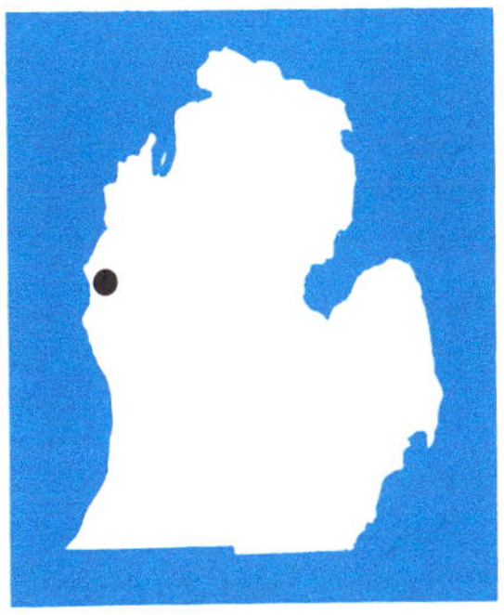

Located in the central portion of the Lake Michigan shoreline, Ludington produces outstanding fishing for boat and shore anglers. After a spring flurry of fishing activity, later warming trends cause the lake to stratify, and excellent summer fishing for salmon and trout begins in June and runs into the fall. Limit catches of Chinook salmon, coho salmon and lake trout are common, with an occasional steelhead or brown trout snapping the rod into action.

Besides fall salmon, rivermouth fishermen experience solid runs of steelhead in spring and fall on the Pere Marquette River, which empties into Lake Michigan here. Trolling boats criss-cross this discharge in view of surf fishermen on shore and along the pier. Eight miles north, the Sable River at Big Sable Point gets similar attention.

Ludington, with plenty of access onto the lake, is a popular port among anglers and tourists alike. Weekends in summer and early fall host an armada of fishing craft, but, fortunately, there is plenty of room to roam. The trolling fleet, therefore, will be strung out for miles up and down the coast.

Fishing Schedule

SPRING

Spring fishing kicks off soon after ice-out when smelt and alewives make a spawning appearance in area shallows. Hungry salmon—both kings and cohos—are close behind, although the hottest spring action occurs further south in the big lake. In fact, many Ludington-area charterboat skippers opt for the ports of Michigan City (2) New Buffalo (1) Benton Harbor/St.Joseph (4) and others.

But you can take salmon, along with occasional steelhead and lake and brown trout, at Ludington by running small spoons and plugs in the top 25-50 feet of water. Do this by rigging shallow-set downriggers or breaking out planer boards and outriggers. High-line setups will also trigger strikes.

SUMMER

Summer fishing starts in June, when the lake begins to stratify, and improves throughout the months of July, August and September. Anglers key from the "project" (Consumers Power Company's man-made lake, located about four miles south of Ludington), to as far north as Manistee (13).

Ludington is an excellent summer lake-trout port. To catch the five- to 15-pounders, motor straight out from the harbor three to five miles to depths up to 150 feet. Find 48- to 52-degree-F. water near bottom, then run baits either on bottom or close to it. Good lure choices include cowbells with P-Nuts or Sutton Spoons, along with combinations of dodgers with flies or Jon Squids. Best color choices are yellow, green, black, and silver.

Groups of boats can usually be found two miles offshore at Big Sable Point, where the trollers are after not only lake trout, but salmon as well. Structure, with drops from 70 to 150 feet, begins there and continues southwest about four miles before leveling out. Underwater currents that run northerly create an upswelling, which moves a steady flow of baitfish for predator species lying along structure breaks. Big dividends are often waiting for anglers who will take the time to troll this area. A key landmark is the bath house, six miles north of the harbor at Ludington State Park.

Typical rigging on the charterboat *Finlander*, captained by the highly respected Al Laaksonen, includes six Big Jon downriggers—four E 1000 units across the back and a pair of corner out-downs. Laaksonen normally runs short leads of four to 10 feet on downrigger-trolled lures. In spring and fall, he'll send crankbaits out 100-350 feet on port and starboard sides via outriggers and lead-core line. Occasionally Deep Sixes (trip divers) are spotted on each side close to the boat. He will also run drop leads—small sinkers attached to pressure releases—out from 100-350 feet. Flatlines passed down the boat wake follow from 150-200 feet.

Lure picks should include spoons such as Northport Nailers and Fin-Weavers, along with body baits like J-Plugs, Gold Stars, and Tiger Plugs. Silver, green, and pearl are the hit colors, but keep a few others ready because on some days fish are finicky.

Ludington marks the beginning of dodger/fly country. A large percentage of both cohos and kings are taken with 00- or 0-sized dodgers pulling Sparkle Flies, Jon Flies, Crinkle Flies, and Michigan Squids. Chrome, white, red, green, and 50/50 banana and key-lime dodgers are hot numbers when rigged 10-15 inches ahead of trolling flies in similar colors along with black.

Because the bright sunlight of a summer mid-day can force salmon to move into deeper waters, early morning and late evening are best trolling hours in the shallows. As Labor Day approaches and the spawning urge quickens, salmon move into shallow water to stay. Then, most trollers set downriggers shallow again, sometimes only 10-15 feet.

According to Laaksonen, who keeps meticulous records of his charters, June finds best catches in the 50- to 99-foot depths, which in 1985 produced 54 fish. The 100-foot-plus mark served up 33 fish. Laaksonen's records further show 35 fish caught with lures set from 11-29 feet, 23 fish taken on lures at 30-49 feet, and 27 from lures washed at 70 feet-plus.

In July the 50- to 99-foot mark produced 208 salmonids, with

100-foot depths and beyond netting 152 fish. Best level to troll lures appeared to be 70 feet or more, where 218 fish were caught. Second best was the 50- to 69-foot range, which produced 51 fish.

August fishing improves for both salmon and trout, with shallower water depths rating highest of all. For best results, run the previously mentioned lures down 30-70 feet.

Ludington is not just a big-fish port. Truth is, from May through October the piers and offshore structure to 70 feet deep serve up good numbers of yellow perch. Midsummer is an especially good time to dunk minnows, crayfish or worms from the pier or from anchored boat. A summer hotspot is the Rock Pile, about three miles south of the harbor in 25 feet of water.

FALL

Fall sees many anglers fishing closer to shore, including trollers with smaller boats, who are now able to fish the harbor. As salmon begin their quest for spawning grounds, action can be fierce, with many larger fish hitting body baits and spoons. Labor Day weekend is often the peak period, although the date can vary by two or more weeks either way. But when salmon are porpoising in the shallows, pier fishermen have best results tossing heavy spoons or bait fishing with fresh spawn. Although many good-sized Chinooks are caught throughout the summer, weights will usually run higher in fall, with hang-belly kings ranging in the upper 20s to 30-pounds-plus. Cohos average six to nine pounds, and anglers catch fair numbers of husky steelhead and browns, too.

Not So Calm Before the Storm

I'll never forget that August morning. When I met my three clients at the Ludington dock, they were anxious to hit the water and get after those big king salmon. I was excited, too, but kept an eye on the weather, as skies were cloudy and rain was being forecast to the south and west. Even though the water was calm, most of the smaller boats decided to stay dockside and wait for the storm to pass through.

But I put my 30-foot boat, the *Finlander*, on a 320-degree heading, and we roared out into Lake Michigan seven miles. Once there, we shut down, and I set the first line with a spoon known as a Fin-Weaver. As soon as I reached for a second outfit, the first rod jumped to life. Fish on! While one of the customers battled what I knew was a dandy king salmon, I dropped the second line. Pow! It, too, went off with a bang. Ten minutes later, we slid twin fat kings into the cooler. We reset the lines and put out the rest of the *Finlander*'s arsenal.

Maybe it was the impending storm—I don't know—but everything seemed to take fish that morning. By 9:30 a limit catch filled the box. Our 16 kings checked in between 10 and 25 pounds each, and the four cohos we managed to put on ice averaged seven pounds each.

By 10:30 the *Finlander* was back in the harbor. As I tied up the boat, the storm began.

Captain Al Laaksonen
Ludington, *Finlander*

Planting Records

Ludington has had a steady record of lake-trout and brown-trout releases. An average of 60,000 yearling lake trout have been released at Ludington Reef annually since 1980. Future stockings will depend on inventory, but the 1985-1990 annual target includes 70,000 lakers. Brown-trout plants will continue at the annual rate of 15,000.

Sable River releases have averaged 200,000 Chinook fingerlings for each of the past several years, and the five-year plan calls for equal numbers. Coho releases were discontinued after 1982.

Facilities

Public facilities, which include gasoline and diesel fuel, water, electricity, restrooms and holding-tank pump-out, are available in Ludington at the state-run harbor. The telephone number for the dock attendant is (616) 843-9611.

Several launch ramps in the harbor await boaters, including a pay public launch located at the end of Ludington Avenue past the Coast Guard station; a free city ramp located below Washington St. bridge across from the charterboat docks; and on the same side, a pay ramp located up the channel from the bridge.

Campgrounds are available throughout the Ludington area, including Ludington State Park (616) 843-8671, north of the harbor; Crystal Lake Campground & Resort, (616) 757-4510, near Scottville on Hansen Rd.; Kibby Creek Travel Park, (616) 843-3995, south of Ludington off US-31 on Deren Rd.; and Lakeview Campsite on Peterson Rd., (616) 843-3702.

Further Information

Chambers of Commerce:

1. Ludington Area Chamber of Commerce, 102 Ludington Ave., Ludington 49431; (616) 843-2506.
2. West Michigan Tourist Association, 136 Fulton St. E., Grand Rapids 49503; (616) 456-8557.

Bait & Tackle Shops:

1. Abrahamson Sport and Marine, 5485 East Ludington, Ludington 49431; (616) 843-2990.
2. Pere Marquette Port Center, 214 W. Ludington Ave., Ludington 49431; (616) 843-8676.

Charter Fishing:

1. Captain Al Laaksonen, 6070 W. Main, Kalamazoo 49009; (616) 375-6305. 30-foot Chris Craft Tournament Fisherman, *Finlander*.
2. Captain Dick Swan, 3230 Oakland Dr., Clare 48617; (517) 386-3220. 25-foot *Lite Liner*.
3. Captain Pete Ruboyianes, 1195 S. Delaney Rd., Owosso 48867; (517) 725-9842. 30-foot Sea Ray, *Dreamweaver II*.

Department of Natural Resources:

A fisheries biologist works out of District Headquarters at 8015 S. 131 Rd., Cadillac 49601; (616) 775-9727.

Coast Guard:

Ludington Station, (616) 843-9088.

12 LUDINGTON

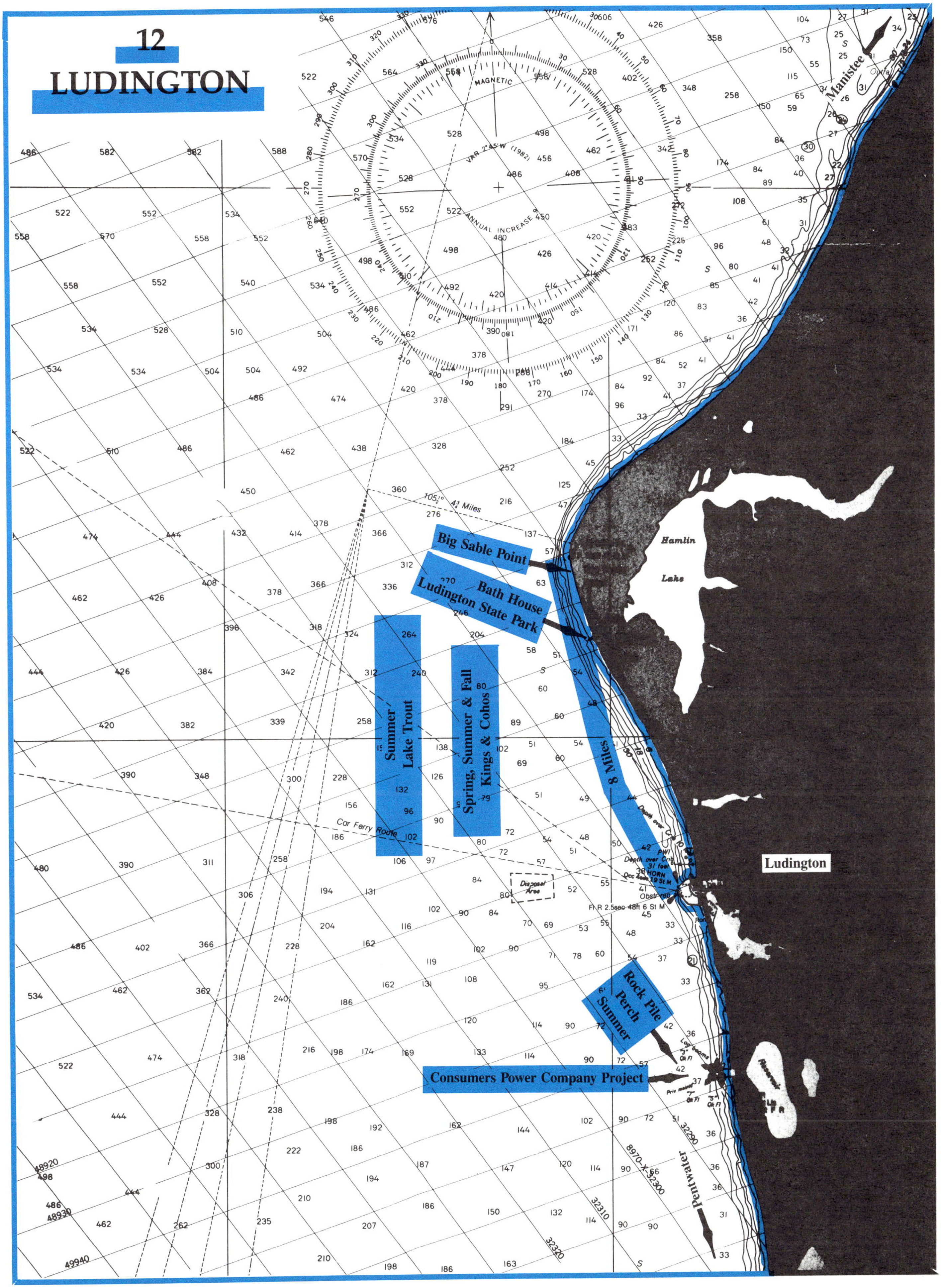

13
MANISTEE

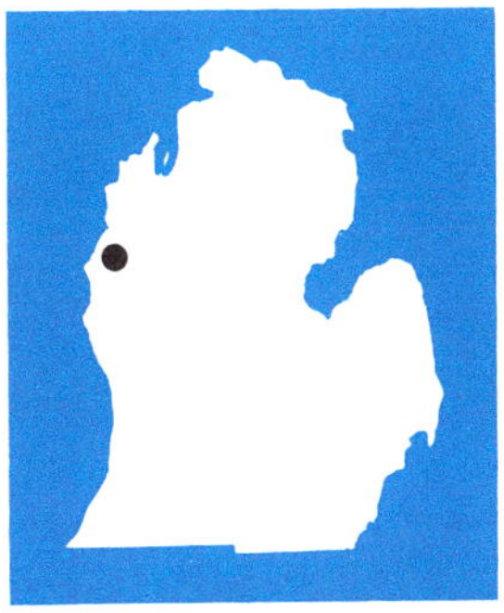

Without a doubt, Manistee is the most popular port on Lake Michigan. Excellent fishing facilities and accommodations go hand-in-hand with hefty stockings of hatchery-reared trout and salmon to draw anglers from throughout the Midwest. In August and September, they sometimes jam the piers and jockey for valuable casting space. At this time, close-to-shore trollers, rods bristling from boat ends, criss-cross pierheads and look like giant water spiders skating over the surface.

Hotspots north of the piers include the Green Onion (the lime-green water tower in Manistee) in 50 feet of water, among rocks off the state park, and off the Five Cottages. South-bound trollers key at the Clay Banks (three miles below piers), the golf course, and eventually at Gurney Creek (eight miles south). Others target the dropoff that begins some 2-1/2 miles straight out from pierheads then gradually swings closer to shore. At Gurney Creek, for example, the dropoff is only three-quarters mile off shore.

In short, there is plenty of trolling water off Manistee.

Fishing Schedule

SPRING

Spring activity begins at ice-out in early to mid-April, with brown trout and Chinook and coho salmon the trump cards. Actually, browns begin showing up in the harbor in winter, when some ice anglers get them by jigging and fishing tip-ups, both here and in inland Manistee Lake. As ice unplugs the harbor and disappears from the Lake Michigan shoreline, the browns show up in force. Spawning smelt keep them close in until May, then alewives hold them until about Memorial Day.

Many of the browns taken here are actually Wisconsin fish that have romped across the lake. Jack Stauff, a charterboat captain from Jackson, works the Manistee area each spring and summer. "I know we're catching a lot of Wisconsin fish," he claims, "because of their different fin clips. Some days half our catch are what we figure are Wisconsin browns."

The shallow-water fishery for both browns and salmon, with incidental catches of lakers (which must be returned if caught before May 1) and steelhead, appeals to small-boat fishermen because they can easily work in close to shore. Some browns are caught in water that is only two or three feet deep, a fact that makes them a popular target for surf fishermen and pier anglers, too.

Fresh brown-trout or steelhead spawn tied up in bags the size of small olives are murder on browns and salmon. The key is to use fresh spawn and to keep it off bottom with the aid of a piece of marshmallow. Most shore fishermen use a perch spreader to fish two spawn bags, rigging their outfits with a barrel-type slip sinker or bell-shaped sinker. Casting far from piers or shore, they slide rod butts into portable holders, crank in the slack, then wait for hits.

Some wave action is desirable, as it keeps the spawn swaying back and forth and dribbles scent with the to-and-fro motion. Plus, it helps roil the water, which encourages trout and salmon to cruise close. Manistee pier anglers always take advantage of a wind change that may blow the color line in along the slabs. Baitfish move in with the protective conditions, and the predators are usually right behind.

Other shore and pier anglers fish gobs of nightcrawlers, and a few rely upon frozen two-inch alewives or small smelt. Spincasters toss Little Cleos, Kastmasters, K.O. Wobblers, small Locos and even Mepps Spinners and Roostertails. Hot colors vary from day to day, but hardware casters can hardly go wrong with silver alone or in combination with other colors.

Most boat anglers, like trolling-ace Joe Zikewich of Lake Orion, rely on longlining techniques and light line to fill a cooler of spring browns and salmon. Many will highline outfits stocked with four-pound test, running lures back 100-150 feet. Even those that use downriggers often run a leader of four- or six-pound test behind 10- or 12-pound-test backing. They drop their cannonballs just below the surface, and, depending upon water clarity, may spot lures from 25-75 feet behind the balls.

Joe has registered solid success with black-and-white (hand-painted), black-and-gold, and orange-and-gold Rapalas fished with the above method (except that he reaches for two-pound cannonballs) or off planer boards. Small Fire Plugs in blue and chrome, orange and yellow or plain chrome are good producers as are yellow-with-red dots, chrome-and-blue and chrome-and-yellow Flutter Spoons. Also, try red-and-yellow Andy Reekers and lime-and-pearl or black-and-yellow Wiggle Warts.

Depending upon schooling action and trollers' ability to find the fish—then make them hit—spring coolers may contain 50-75 percent browns. Another savvy skipper, who works Manistee from April through September, is Dave Greshem. Typical rigging aboard Greshem's 26-foot *Tackle Buster* includes three stern-end downriggers and two out-downriggers, along with a pair of outriggers.

"Slow trolling—depending, of course, on the lures we're using—is important when spring fishing at Manistee," says Greshem's driver, Carl Christie. "Dave will change props in spring just for Manistee browns, and we also use a trolling plate to slow us down. Sometimes I'll run at only 450 rpms."

Productive lures aboard the *Tackle Buster* include Countdown Rapalas, small Flatfish, Hot 'N Tots, Tiny Tads and Hot Shots in plugs—Chargers, Flutter Spoons, Cop-E-Cats, Devle Dogs and Cleos in spoons. Rated colors are silver combinations with orange, blue or green; copper with brown; yellows; pearl; greens; and chartreuse.

It pays to experiment. Slow, wide *S*-turns and speeding up and slowing down often trigger strikes. One trick that Jack Stauff employs when all else fails is to run a set of small home-made cowbells fashioned from Junebug Spinners. Removing the hooks from a Flatfish, then running it as an attractor ahead of a Countdown Rapala, can give the lure just enough extra kick to interest a brown trout.

In addition to the color line—usually good early and late in the day—trollers target the chute between piers, parallel to the south wall in 10-12 feet of water, and up tight to shore. Wave action causes a series of troughs along the sandy bottom close to and parallel to shore, and brown trout love to hide in these troughs. An especially good one during most spring trolling seasons is located just offshore from the Green Onion.

SUMMER

To catch kings and cohos in spring and *summer*, Joe Zikewich relies upon dodger/fly matchups on his two out-downriggers and J-Plugs, Flutter Spoons or Northport Nailers run clean on stern-end rigs. Inside lures are thus extended out further in the pattern. To illustrate, here is a typical setup aboard Joe's 16-foot Sea Nymph, the *Shelldrake*: (1) a chrome dodger/blue-and-silver Sparkle Fly at starboard-side out-down and set at 20 feet, (2) a yellow-with-red-dots Flutter Spoon on left stern-end rigger and set at 30 feet, (3) blue-on-white Northport Nailer at 40 feet on right-side stern-end downrigger, (4) white dodger/black Michigan Squid on port-side downrigger and set at 50 feet.

Manistee serves up fair to good lake-trout fishing in June and July to trollers who target hard-bottom areas from 120-180 feet deep. One of the best laker takers at this port is legendary charterboat-captain Emil Dean, who has nearly 20 years of day-after-day experience on the big water here. Emil relies on various types of cowbell strings attached to downrigger balls with hefty rubber bands, then run on or near bottom. Hot lures are traditionally Clatter Tads, Tiny Tads, Fire Plugs, P-Nuts and L'il Guys in various combinations of chartreuse, green, yellow, blue, and pearl.

Early morning pier fishermen can nail foraging king salmon on spincast spoons and bottomfished spawn bags during the summer. As the month of August closes out, the slabs become highly active with salmon fishermen. Also, in July and August, the Manistee piers will produce good catches of yellow perch on minnows and worms.

FALL

Outriggers and flatlines trolled far from shore pick up steelhead and cohos near the surface all summer long and into the *fall*. Small spoons and plugs in hot colors are most effective, especially when trolled in and out of offshore slicks—color lines, smooth-water patches (indicating surface temperature differences), and floating pastures of debris. The piers are solid producers of Chinook salmon, steelhead and menominees in fall, too, with incidental catches of brown trout also reported.

Steelhead fishing in October and November is superb on Manistee Lake, with small-boat fishermen either rowing or slowly putting along with small outboards to keep big wobbling plugs (Flatfish, Kwikfish, Ping-A-Ts, Tadpollies) at a crawl. Silver, with or without warm colors, rates best. Trollers work both sides of the river channel and target areas of pilings and other structure.

WINTER

Winter fishing activities are limited to spearing, tip-up fishing or open-air jigging on Manistee Lake. Northern pike, muskellunge, walleyes, yellow perch, crappies, bluegills, steelhead and brown trout are the catchable species.

Planting Records

The Manistee area has traditionally received hefty DNR Lake Michigan stockings. Through at least 1990, these are the planned releases: Manistee River—100,000 fingerling kings, 50,000 steelhead yearlings and 15,000 brown-trout yearlings; Little Manistee River—375,000 coho smolts and 500,000 Chinook fingerlings; Manistee Reef—60,000 lake-trout yearlings.

Facilities

The DNR maintains a harbor of refuge with the following services: transient accommodations, gasoline, water, electricity, restrooms, shower facilities, holding-tank pump-out and VHF-FM radio. The telephone number of the dock attendant is (616) 723-6491. There are commercial boat launches found along the river and around Manistee Lake as well as at Manistee Harbor. The best one is a city-owned, modern six-lane facility, on the southeast side of the harbor, with lots of parking space. Expect to pay a nominal fee.

Further Information

Chambers of Commerce:

1. Manistee Area Chamber of Commerce, Mason St. at US-31, Manistee 49660; (616) 723-2575.
2. West Michigan Tourist Association, 136 Fulton E., Grand Rapids 49503; (616) 456-8557.

Bait & Tackle Shops:

1. Fisherman's Center, 263 Arthur St., Manistee 49660; (616) 723-7718.
2. Insta-Launch, 20 Park Ave., Manistee; (616) 723-3901.
3. Riley's Tackle Shop, 289 River St., Manistee 49660; (616) 723-3354.

Charter Fishing:

1. Captain Emil Dean, Route 1 Box 21, Bear Lake 49614; (616) 362-3760. 32-foot Luhrs, *Mary-E.*
2. Captain Dave Greshem, 3856 Iris, Waterford 48095; (313) 623-2828. 26-foot boat, *Tackle Buster*.
3. Captain Bud Raskey, 2380 Main, RR 3, Manistee 49660; (616) 723-9414. 31-foot boat, *Michelle*.

Department of Natural Resources:

Two fisheries biologists work out of District Headquarters at 8015 S. US-131, Cadillac 49601; (616) 775-9717.

Coast Guard:

Manistee Station, (616) 723-7412 or 723-5561.

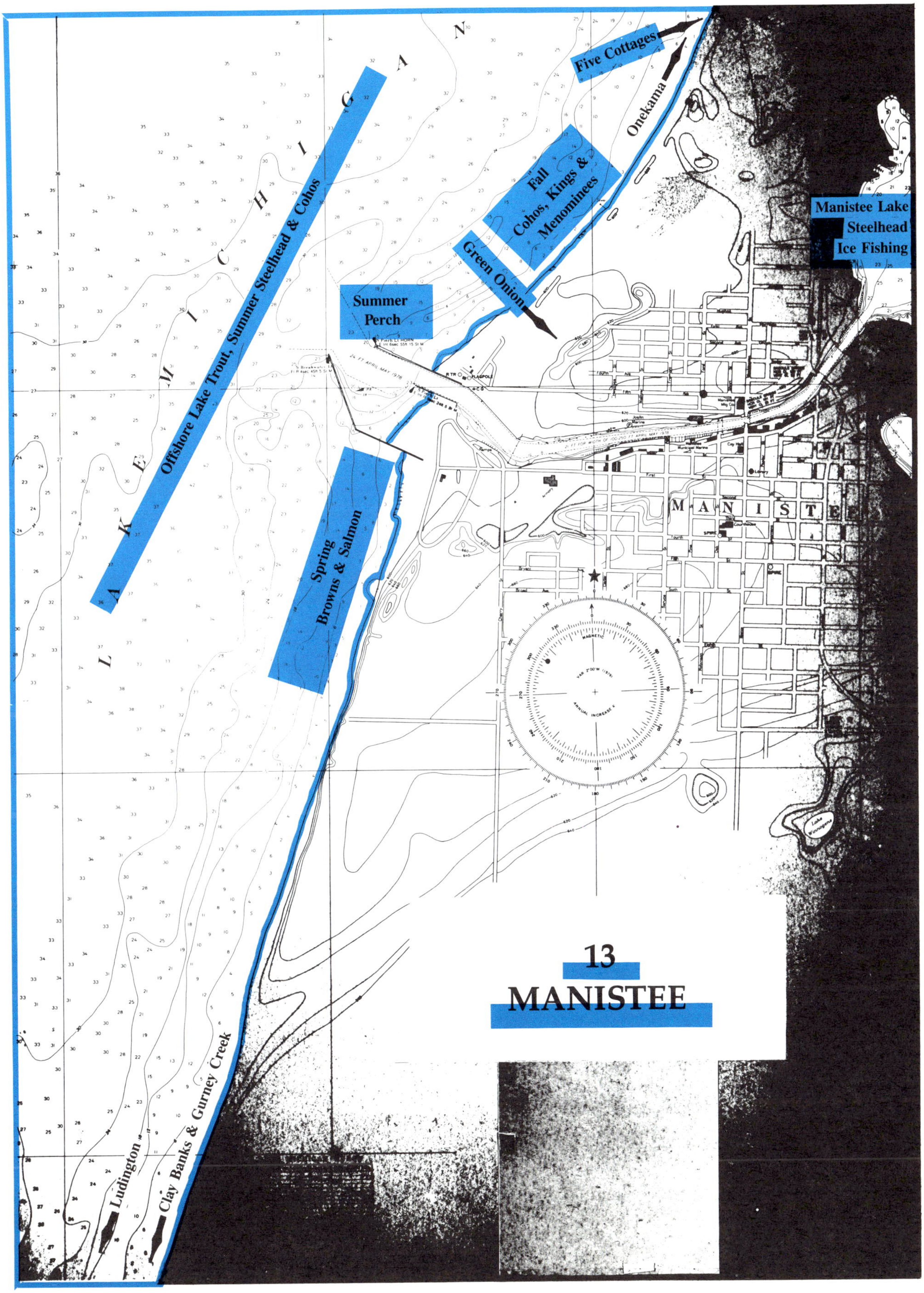
Five Cottages
Onekama
Manistee Lake
Steelhead
Ice Fishing
Fall
Cohos, Kings &
Menominees
Green Onion
Summer
Perch
Offshore Lake Trout, Summer Steelhead & Cohos
L A K E M I C H I G A N
Spring
Browns & Salmon
M A N I S T E E
Lake Winnogene
Ludington
Clay Banks & Gurney Creek
13
MANISTEE

Spring Browns at Manistee

Spring blow days on Lake Michigan can come with the regularity of Tiger baseball rainouts, so my buddy Eldon Thomas of Flint and I were really excited to note a flat calm on Lakc Michigan at Manistee when we arrived. It was early morning on a cold day in April. A heavy cloud cover suggested snow; we slid on coveralls and parkas. Steam curled from the harbor like camp smoke as I sliced my 16-foot boat, the *Shelldrake*, through the ditch between pierheads on a slow throttle.

We cleared the north light at exactly 8:00 a.m., found the color line that seeped into the lake from the Manistee River outflow, and slow-trolled on the inside dirty edge. Then, Eldon took over the wheel while I sent two out-downs halfway to bottom at 12-14 feet and passed a pair of flatlines down the center stern. One of these I hooked to a cannonball and locked at five feet.

At 8:05 the lines were just nicely set. At 8:06 the port-side out-down went off, and I lunged for the rod. I barely had it jerked clear of the holder when, 50 yards behind the *Shelldrake*, a cream-colored brown trout cleared Lake Michigan in a tremendous leap.

"Did you see that?" Eldon hollered with excitement. "This is going to be a repeat of last weekend."

"Take the rod," I offered.

"No way. You drew first blood."

I didn't argue and dug in instead. My fish ran up parallel to the boat, rolled once on the surface, and cut toward the boat. Eldon made a sharp inside turn while I passed my rod under the inside flatline. The brown fell in behind our wake, where I let him slug it out for awhile. Then I led him to the boat again so Eldon, who had put the boat in neutral, could slide a net under the fish. Just as the meshes closed over the brown's head, I got a good look at the yellow Flutter Spoon dangling from his lower jaw.

The eight-pound fish, as fat as a pregnant tuna—if there were such a thing—taped 21 inches. I had heard about these "football-shaped browns" and, like the saying goes, seeing is believing. This fish was built like an NFL nose guard.

"You're next," I said to Eldon as he slid the handsome fish into our magnum cooler.

Eldon Thomas' middle name must be Flutter Spoon; I swear he runs those thin lures more than any other type for just about all kinds of trout and salmon trolling. He is constantly tinkering with them—rebending them into shape, sharpening hooks, and doctoring them with punch-out prism tape.

At 9:30, Eldon swapped muscle with a nine-pounder, and by day's end we had coolered five more brown trout from three pounds to nine pounds. The fish hit hammered chrome-and-blue-striped Flutter Spoons, too, as well as Countdown Rapalas in silver and black. We thought it was an excellent trolling trip.

Then the following weekend we boxed 11 fish out of 22 hits. That's super brown-trout fishing in anybody's book.

Joe Zikewich
Lake Orion

These successful fishermen are trolling Manistee Lake in October for steelhead.

14
ONEKAMA

You have to look hard on a Michigan highway map to spot tiny Onekama, located on the northeast shore of Portage Lake. And you probably won't see the Onekama area mentioned in most magazine articles on Lake Michigan salmon fishing. Instead, the heralded ports of Manistee (13) and Ludington (12), to the south, and Frankfort (16) and Platte Bay (17), to the north, cop the headlines. Onekama is relegated to being Lake Michigan's unsung salmon port.

But from April through October, this friendly town caters to trollers and pier fishermen and offers salmon action that is difficult to beat. It all happens along majestic sand dunes and some of the finest beaches on Lake Michigan.

Fishing Schedule

SPRING

At ice-out, king salmon and brown trout move in close to shore among the sand dunes. The fish are searching for warm *spring* water that's spewing from Portage Lake and for easy pickings in the smelt-rich shallows. Anglers criss-cross troll the pierheads and work the 10- to 50-foot water in front of the Three Sisters (three sand dunes 1-1/2 miles north) and the Big Slide (a high bluff another mile north, just below Pierport). Landmarks to the south include the Saddle (a dip between two dunes), Bar Creek, and the Five Cottages (just north of Manistee, 13).

In addition, the Onekama area has two great trolling spots that, at times, serve up tremendous action. One is Portage Lake, which I'll discuss in a moment. The other is the Barrel, a deep four- to five-square-mile hole 1-1/2 miles offshore from the Three Sisters. The Barrel features 50 feet of water on the east side, 55 on the north end, 65 on the west side, and 60 feet on the south end. Depths within the Barrel range from 110-155 feet. In summer, lake trout like to stack up throughout the structure, and salmon stage here in preparation for their onshore onslaught.

Captain Kevin Hughes, who brings over 1,000 fish per season (an average of six to seven for a half-day charter) over the transom of the *Sandpiper*, his 28-foot charterboat, is one of the first boats out of Portage Lake in early spring. Chinooks and brown trout are the two species Hughes targets until summer.

When specifically fishing for kings, he prefers J-Plugs, Grizzly Plugs, Lightning Lures and Rapalas. Color selections depend upon cloud cover, depth fished, water clarity, and the forage base being fed upon by salmon. But a good general rule is to reach for chromes and other bright lures on bright days and darker colors (gold, black, dull orange, brown) on overcast ones. White combinations of Lightning Lures and various plugs work well in morning and evening.

When kings don't cooperate, Kevin "buzzes" them by trolling fast, even in spring, when most trollers let lures crawl by. Buzzing speed is 2.5-4.0 knots on the *Sandpiper*'s Datamarine knotmeter. Hughes varies release lengths with time of day, cloud cover, boat traffic and depth of water fished. In other words, he is constantly experimenting, although another general rule is the deeper he goes, the tighter to cannonballs he places releases. Also, slider rigs help increase the trolling arsenal on days when it is necessary to hunt kings.

Here is a typical example of what determined fishing and experimentation can do. On May 14, 1985, six of us climbed aboard the *Sandpiper* for an all-day charter. I was hoping that Lois Birchfield, an assistant editor at *Outdoor Life* magazine, and her friend Stacy Hanson would each catch a big king salmon on their first visit to Lake Michigan. Joining us that day were Tim Hughes—Kevin's brother and first mate—and Gene Stout, a professor of finance at Central Michigan University.

We began setting lines at seven o'clock in 40-50 feet of water north of the pierheads. There was an east/southeast wind at 10-15 mph and a hazy sun trying to peek through cloud cover. From the outriggers, Tim and Kevin sent out a No. 3 pearl-colored J-Plug on one side and a chartreuse-colored magnum Zipper Spoon with a rubber-core sinker ahead of it on the other side. The *Sandpiper* features six downriggers. Beginning with the starboard-side outdownrigger, here is the rigging pattern the brothers employed: (1) No. 4 J-Plug in green and yellow with black ladderback—32 feet down—and an orange-on-white Lightning Lure as a slider; (2) a white-and-green Lightning Lure down 15 feet; (3) a black-and-red Lightning Lure down 35 feet; (4) a white-and-orange Lightning Lure down 24 feet; (5) another Lightning Lure in white and robin-egg blue set at 14 feet; and (6) a similar spoon in white with dark-blue stripes set at 30 feet and a chrome E.T. Spoon as a slider.

Numbers *1*, *3* and *6* riggers all were deep-set lines with 30-foot release lengths. The shallow-depth offerings (numbers *2* and *5*) featured 120-foot releases, and No. *4*—a middle-depth setup—was run back 80 feet behind the cannonball.

We had a knock-off at 7:45 a.m., but when nothing else had happened by nine o'clock, we trolled in close to shore. At this time, Kevin stripped one outrigger, replacing it with a planer board and a silver-and-black Rapala. Still no strikes, so we headed for deeper water and kept changing colors and replaced a

This Indiana fisherman is happy he came to Onekama to troll for salmon.

couple of the Lightning Lures with J-Plugs. At ten o'clock, Lois hung a dandy 20-pound salmon that struck a white-and-blue Lightning Lure. The fish gave her the fight of her life, with a 200-yard sprint and bulldog fight at the boat. When he came to the net, only one hook of the treble was in his lip. One good shake of the head and it would have pulled out.

At noon we began trolling south of the pierheads where the water was 1.5 degrees F. warmer, thanks to the plume coming out of Portage Lake. In the next hour, we caught four carbon-copy kings of seven to eight pounds each. Blue-on-white Lightning Lures did the damage early, so Kevin and Tim sent down five of the hot lures. Besides the warm water, there was a concentrated slick of dead alewives in the area, plus no other boats were out to spook fish in the 38-42 feet of water. The kings were suspended at 18-28 feet over these depths in spite of the bright sun, which by now had burned away the morning haze.

We caught several more salmon that afternoon, including a dime-bright 13-pounder for Stacy. Then, to make sure that Lois would drive back to New York City with sore arms, we let her muscle down a 22-pound brute that drew circles around the boat like some freshwater shark.

Catching keys that day were (1) finding warm water, (2) discovering a hot lure, then running with it, (3) keeping a fast trolling speed (Lightning Lures can be bent to achieve good action—nervous rod tips are clues), and (4) Lady Luck.

Chinooks make up about 50 percent of the annual catch aboard the *Sandpiper*. Brown trout, normally taken from ice-out until June 1, constitute another 10 percent.

To catch browns, Hughes relies upon 20-pound-test line (unusually heavy for spring browns, but customers lose too many fish on light line), outriggers and two-edged planer boards, and a good assortment of Rapalas and Rebels in jointed, floating and sinking models. Solid spring colors include black and silver, blue and silver, crawdad, perch, and pearl. A hotspot is the vertical thermal bar at the pierheads where the warm Portage Lake outflow meets a cold Lake Michigan.

Lazy *S*-patterns on a troll of 2.5-3.0 knots produce best, especially when flatlined lures are run 120 or more feet behind the boat and planers are sent out 100 feet to the sides. Another catching key is to fine-tune baits. Both Hughes and another top-flight local skipper named Tom Van make sure hooks are not bent, bills are not cracked, and eyelets are secure. In addition, Van adds a small split ring to his Rapalas to give them good action.

SUMMER

Summer trolling continues to be good for king salmon at the Barrel and improves for lake trout. Lakers make up about 15 percent of Kevin's annual catch. The most productive lure is the cowbell or Whirl-A-Gig and Wobble-Glo or P-Nut combination. He runs different matchups and colors until finding the taste that lakers like for the day. Chartreuse, chrome, chrome and brass, green, and blue-prism tape on chrome blades are favorite colors in attractors. Good plug colors are white, green, and key lime.

Lakers are bottom-hugging fish, and that is why Kevin likes to work lures tight behind the cannonball, which he bounces or drags on bottom. A large dodger and fly sometimes helps to wake up sluggish forktails. To most bottom-running offerings, Hughes stacks Lightning Lures to interest suspended lakers and salmon. When all else fails, he drags along bottom Les Davis Odd Ball cowbells—a five-foot string of flash (two sets mated together) with palm-sized chrome blades. When fishing for lakers, Kevin always runs his lure very slowly (1.5-1.9 knots).

The Portage Lake piers also produce summer perch, and Portage Lake itself is good for a wide variety of gamefish species. Warm-water types include perch, smallmouth and largemouth bass, crappies, bluegills, northern pike and muskies. Brown trout and steelhead in spring and king salmon in fall are other draws. Portage Lake has depths to 60 feet and contains weedy areas, submerged wrecks, rock piles and drowned pilings—all of which attract fish.

Coho-salmon action improves as summer wears on, and these fiesty fish make up about 20 percent of Kevin's annual catch. Cohos hit the same basic lures as kings, but when targeting the smaller salmon, Hughes opts for smaller spoons and plugs in a variety of wild colors. Pinks, oranges, polka dots, and bright yellow are good choices. A No. 2 yellow-with-orange-tape Lightning Lure and a No. 3 J-Plug in green and blue-prism tape have been local favorites. Sparkle Flies, Crinkle Flies and Michigan Squids, all pulled behind dodgers, are rated, too. Good colors in attractors include white, key lime, kelly green, chartreuse, orange, fluorescent red, chrome and chrome-fluted. Best colors in flies are black, green, silver, and blue.

FALL

Fall fishing at Onekama is excellent for schooling kings and cohos and improves offshore and in Portage Lake for steelhead from October 1 until ice-in. Orange Rapalas and Lightning Lures with orange tape seem to be consistent color and lure choices, but don't overlook silver J-Plugs and silver-and-black Rapalas. Catching tactics include running outriggers, planer boards and flatlines in the upper 40 feet over water that is 100-400 feet deep. Best trolling speed is 2.5-2.9 knots. The piers are also productive in fall for salmon, trout and perch.

WINTER

Winter fishing is rated good at Portage Lake, with the shallows at the end of the lake producing good catches of bluegills, crappies and perch. Off the city park, many pike fishermen set tip-ups and wait in shanties with spear close by. Late-ice fishermen anxiously await jumbo yellow perch that enter Portage Lake from Lake Michigan at this time to spawn.

14 ONEKAMA

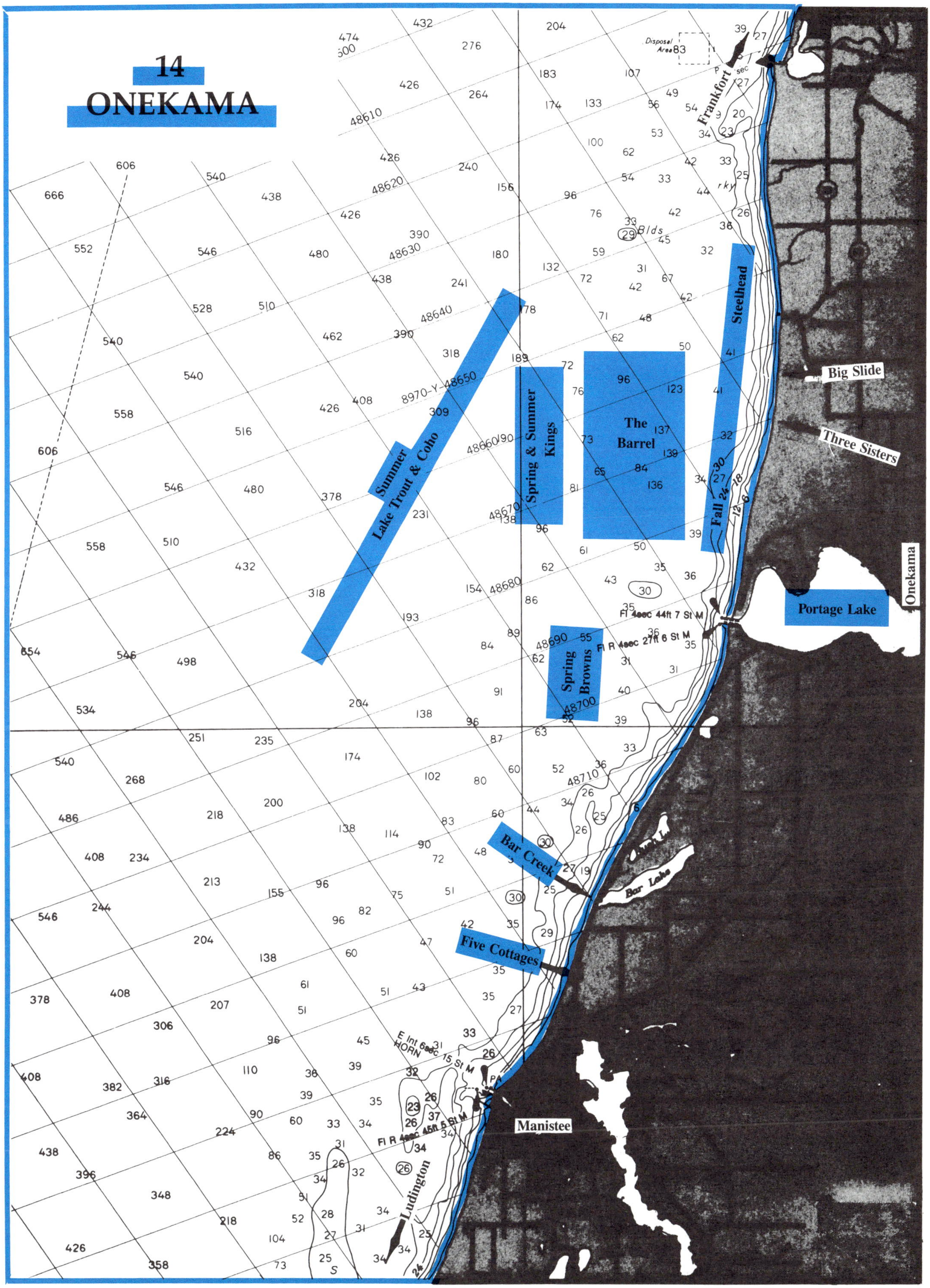
Frankfort
Disposal Area
Steelhead
Big Slide
Three Sisters
Fall
Onekama
Portage Lake
The Barrel
Spring & Summer Kings
Summer Lake Trout & Coho
Spring Browns
Bar Creek
Bar Lake
Five Cottages
Manistee
Ludington
Fl 4sec 44ft 7 St M
Fl R 4sec 27ft 6 St M
E Int 6sec 15 St M HORN
Fl R 4sec 45ft 5 St M
8970-Y-48650

Planting Records

The Onekama area is currently receiving 60,000 lake-trout yearlings, 75,000 spring fingerling Chinooks and 10,000 brown-trout yearlings. These annual plantings will continue through at least 1990. In addition, the area receives a large number of brown trout from Wisconsin waters and hosts passage cohos en route to Platte River and king salmon heading for Manistee.

Facilities

The DNR maintains harbors of refuge at Manistee (13) and Arcadia (15) At Portage Lake there are several privately owned marinas with rental slips and boat launches. The Onekama village maintains a free boat launch at the east end of Portage Lake.

Further Information

Chambers of Commerce:

1. Manistee County Chamber of Commerce, US-31 at Mason St., Manistee 49660; (616) 723-2575.
2. West Michigan Tourist Association, 136 Fulton E., Grand Rapids 49503; (616) 456-8557.

Bait & Tackle Shops:

1. Townline Home Center, 4855 Main St., Onekama 49675; (616) 889-4858 (open year-round).
2. The Boat House, M-22 on south side, Onekama 49675 (616) 889-3371.
3. C and T Marina, M-22 on north side, Onekama 49675; (616) 889-4671.

Charter Fishing:

1. Captain Kevin Hughes, Touch of Class Charter Service, (313) 733-8473. After April 1—P.O. Box 442, Onekama 49675; (616) 889-4342. 28-foot Bertram, *Sandpiper*.
2. Captain Tom Van, 5190 Main St., Onekama 49675; (616) 889-9679. 26-foot Stamas, *Beverly J.*

Department of Natural Resources:

Two fisheries biologists work out of District Headquarters at 8015 S. US-131, Cadillac 49601; (616) 775-9727.

Coast Guard:

Manistee Station, (616) 723-7412 or 723-5561.

The Kings of Spring

If anyone ever needed a big spring-charged Chinook salmon, it was Brian Gleeson.

The previous day, we had trolled Lake Huron during a snowstorm, boating only a pair of shakers for our efforts. Today, out of Onekama on Lake Michigan, the frigid west wind was getting to us, even through snowmobile suits. Only a brutish king could make Brian forget about the long drive from his home in Darien, Connecticut, and the fact that, so far, this trip, too, was turning into another bitterly cold boat ride. Usually a talkative fellow, Brian had become strangely quiet.

Skipper Kevin Hughes must have read my thoughts. Suddenly, he and first-mate Joe Zacharias began to reef downrigger lines. They changed lures and release lengths, then sent down new choices into the gray-green lake. Next, Hughes angled the *Sandpiper*, his plush trolling boat, northwest from the Portage Lake pierheads, where we had been fishing, toward the Barrel. This offshore scoopout had paid past ace-in-the-hole dividends.

We never got there. An out-down rod beside Brian suddenly sprang to, just missing his cap. He recovered quickly enough to snatch the thumping rod and speed-reel to tighten into the fish, his first salmon. Typical of big outlaw kings, this one sprinted up and away, parting the water in a spectacular leap. Then it deep-sixed again and headed for Wisconsin. We spectators roared our approval; Brian jammed the rod butt into his belly and clenched his teeth. His face registered either shock or fear—I'm not sure which.

Over the next quarter of an hour, the 20-pounder gave an excellent accounting: two more power runs that twice sizzled line from Brian's level-wind reel, a mad-dash figure-eight through the cannonballs—now swinging beneath the boat like pendulums—and head-shaking antics as Joe finally closed a net over it. The fish met the deck with a heavy thud. Sun flashed off its silverware-bright side, and its loose scales on the floor looked like someone had spilled a pocket of new dimes.

Brian remained animated for hours.

"They are *so* powerful," he repeated, "and my wrists ache. Unbelievable. I hope we catch some more."

He got his wish. We boxed 18 salmon during the rest of that day and the next morning.

Gerry Bethge
New York City

15 ARCADIA

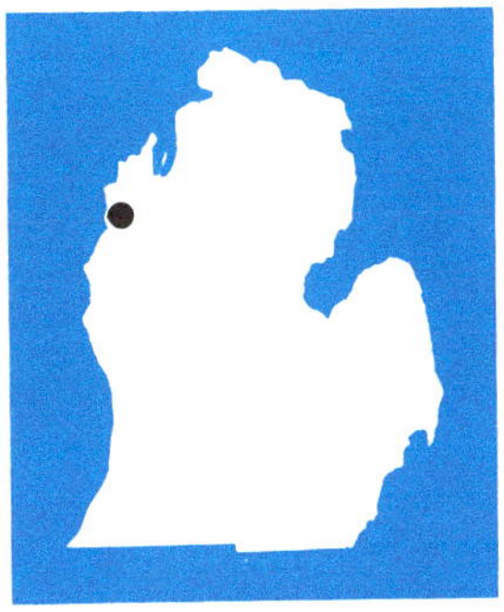

Arcadia is a small natural harbor nestled among towering sand dunes of the Lake Michigan shoreline. Pierpoint, Onekama (14) and Manistee (13) lie to the south, while Frankfort (16) Point Betsie and Platte Bay (17) dot the picturesque landscape to the north.

Few fishermen had heard of Arcadia until Robert Henderson of Vestaburg caught the state-record brown trout, a 34-pound, eight-ounce bruiser, here in May 1984. (Henderson's fish also held the world record for a short time). Besides brown trout, the Arcadia region produces Chinook and coho salmon, lake trout and a few steelhead.

If you want to enjoy good fishing opportunities with little competition from other trollers, then Arcadia is for you.

Fishing Schedule

Arcadia can produce fair to excellent brown-trout fishing in the shallows from ice-out until mid-May. Many of the browns are, no doubt, Wisconsin fish that have romped across Lake Michigan, but there are also Michigan DNR-released browns in this area. For best results, slow-troll with body baits or small spoons in water that is five to 25 feet deep. Landmarks to the north include a huge sandy bluff at two miles and the Herring Hole (popular with Frankfort-area trollers) at six miles.

SPRING

Most boat fishermen leaving Arcadia Harbor in *spring* target shoreline structure and creekmouths to the south. Landmarks include two large sand dunes (at 1-1/2 and three miles), a level shoreline area at Pierport, the Big Slide (at six miles), and the Barrel (at seven miles). The Barrel, a round-shaped piece of underwater structure that varies from 35-105 feet deep, is popular with Onekama trollers (see 14 for catching details).

Although few do it, fishermen can also catch brown trout, along with an occasional steelhead and Chinook, from the breakwalls—lines of large rocks that jut into Lake Michigan. The north breakwall is about half as long as the south-side structure.

On April 19, 1985, I and Dave Taylor, a friend of mine from Otisville, joined Captain Kevin Hughes aboard the *Sandpiper*, a charterboat that Hughes skippers out of Onekama (14). Kevin puts the *Sandpiper*, a 28-foot Bertram, in at Arcadia, and this was her maiden voyage of the long trolling season. Kevin's father, Howard, from Grand Blanc, was at the wheel, and Greg Gershon, a lure manufacturer from Clare, helped our captain tend lines.

In spite of all the fishing I had done in the Great Lakes over many years, I had never experienced a super day of brown-trout fishing. That would soon change.

Howard wheeled the *Sandpiper* through shallow Arcadia Lake and out the chute between the breakwalls into Lake Michigan. It was early morning, and the sky was a pewter color, promising a drizzly April day instead of the sunshine we had hoped for. Tendrils of fog hung over the sand dunes as Howard cut left and headed for the deep notch between hills. Although the air temperature was 53 degrees F., the water temperature was only 41 degrees. That meant that fish would likely be sluggish and keying on warm-water areas such as creekmouths and near the surface of the lake, now heaving slowly, as though it were a sleeping giant.

Spring browns can be difficult to find and equally hard to coax into striking, and that is why savvy trollers use minnow-imitating plugs and small lures with lots of action. Long leads and side rigging are two ways to improve your odds.

Here is how Hughes, who, in my opinion, is one of the best skippers on Lake Michigan, set up our trolling system for the day: two planer boards, two outriggers, two out-downriggers, one stern-end downrigger and one flatline. With Greg's help, Kevin armed the plancrs with a Long A Bomber in blue and black with a mirror finish and an H-13 Rapala in crawdad finish (orange belly and bronze tiger back). Releases were set at 140 and 130 feet respectively. Next, the two men set the outriggers with a Long A Bomber with black back and clear-plastic sides (120 feet back) and a Countdown Rapala in black and silver (120 feet back).

That left three downriggers. Gerson, who makes Lightning Lures, clipped a #2 model in copper color with fire tape (hot orange) to the port-side out-down and set it at eight feet, then added a #3 Lightning Lure in black and pearl to the starboard-side out-down. While he locked this setup at five feet deep, Kevin sent a chrome-and-green ET Spoon 50 feet back and six feet down off the port-side downrigger. The final offering was a center-stern flatline, a J-9 Countdown Rapala in silver and black at 150 feet.

We trolled these lures for 90 minutes without a strike, then suddenly it began to rain and the browns turned on. Taylor was the first to grab a sprung rod. His diligence paid off with a six-pound battler that hit the H-13 Rapala. Within five minutes that fish was joined in the cooler by a five-pound brown that struck the pearl-and-black Lightning Lure. While Greg fought him to the boat, I was trading muscle with a four-pound brown that hit one of the Bomber lures. For the next two hours, we had fairly steady action from four- to seven-pound brown trout, ending up with eight fish in the box and at least that many lost. Even Kevin, who takes this kind of action all in stride, admitted that it was a fine day of spring brown-trout trolling in Lake Michigan.

In addition, we caught and released two lake trout (the season is currently closed until May 1), including a fine 10-pound fish. "It is possible to target browns all spring long," says Captain Hughes, "but most of my customers want to catch salmon." Spring-charged Chinooks are a big draw in April and May in this area. For catching details, see 14 (Onekama).

The Browns of November

Some of the loneliest Michigan people in mid-November are sportsmen who opt for a fishing rod instead of a deer rifle. With some 750,000 of the boys in blaze-orange in the woods, there sure is plenty of standing room in the state's rivers, along the pounding Great Lakes surf, and on the piers that finger out into the big lakes.

"What's catchable in November, anyway?" you might ask.

Well, perch have been known to crowd Saginaw Bay (43 and 44) cuts then, spawning lake trout still stack up in shoal water (although they must be returned if caught from Lakes Huron and Michigan after August 15), schools of steelhead continue their stream assault, and menominees and whitefish enter lake shallows to spawn.

And, for the few that know about it, brown trout jam certain rivermouths as a preliminary to running these same streams. If balladeer Gordon Lightfoot was a trout fisherman, he might have sung about the browns of November instead of its gales.

I am one of a few fishermen who have been quietly singing the praises of late-fall brown trout for many years. October is often good for stream brownies. The firearm deer season (November 15-30) is an even better time, at least on certain rivers along Lake Michigan and Lake Huron. We catch them on spawn, spinners and flies.

I've seen browns in some rivers as early as the second week of October and as late as mid-December. During one period, I caught brown-trout limits on Thanksgiving Day four years in a row. On one of those holidays, instead of stuffing myself with turkey, I fished in a rainstorm and battled 25 browns to the net.

What's my secret? There is no secret. Like with any other river-run fish, timing is the whole thing. I watch the rivers like a baker babysits his ovens. Usually, brown trout and steelhead follow Chinook and coho salmon, and browns can offer the last solid run of the year.

Apparently, water temperature is not nearly as important as constant water level. Along Lake Michigan, a strong west wind will help; along Lake Huron, an east wind may do the job. Once browns make up their minds to penetrate rivers, they will do so in one or two big thrusts and will usually stay in the river for seven to 10 days. But I have also seen them in and out in just three days.

Not all of us sportsmen go deer hunting in November. Or if we do, we also make sure there are a pair of waders and a rod and reel in the trunk.

Ron Betz
Vassar

Summer produces fair to good trolling sport for lake trout to depths of 180 feet. Most fishermen run cowbells or dodgers ahead of small Fire Plugs, P-Nuts, Clatter Tads, and trolling flies. Many stack these bottom-running offerings with light spoons in the hopes of interesting a salmon or two. As summer progresses, the likelihood of that increases dramatically, especially from migrating coho returning to Platte Bay (17) and kings returning to Frankfort (16), their respective release sites.

Fishing in *fall* remains good for salmon and improves in October and November with steelhead and brown-trout catches (the lake-trout season currently closes on August 15). Breakwall fishermen at Arcadia report sporadic catches of yellow perch all season long, and there is some opportunity for perch and northern pike from Arcadia Lake itself.

Winter fishing opportunities are minimal and are limited to the small lake itself.

Planting Records

The DNR releases 60,000 yearling lake trout at Arcadia each year and will continue to do so through at least 1990. Other trout and salmon caught here are from releases at other ports. For detailed stocking information see 17 (Platte Bay), 16 (Frankfort), 14 (Onekama) and 13 (Manistee).

Facilities

The DNR maintains a harbor of refuge with the following services: transient accommodations, gasoline and diesel fuel, water, electricity, restrooms, shower facilities, holding-tank pump-out and VHF-FM radio. The telephone number of the dock attendant is (616) 889-9653. This harbor of refuge, called Veteran's Memorial Marina, contains two free boat-launching ramps. There is also a boat ramp and a few slips at Arcadia Marina, but expect to pay a nominal fee for usage. The telephone number is (616) 889-4559. Camping is also permitted at the marina.

Further Information

Chambers of Commerce:

1. Manistee Chamber of Commerce, US-31 at Mason St., Manistee 49660; (616) 723-2575.
2. West Michigan Tourist Association, 136 Fulton E., Grand Rapids 49503; (616) 456-8557.

Bait & Tackle Shops:

See 16 (Frankfort) and 14 (Onekama).

Charter Fishing:

1. Captain Kevin Hughes, Touch of Class Charter Service, P.O. Box 153, Corunna 48817; (517) 743-6269. 28-foot Bertram, *Sandpiper*.
2. Captain Earl Janssen, P.J. Charter Service, RR#1, Arcadia 49613; (616) 889-5950.

Department of Natural Resources:

Two fisheries biologists work out of District Headquarters at 8015 S. US-131, Cadillac 49601; (616) 775-9727.

Coast Guard:

Frankfort Station, (616) 352-4242 or 352-9151.

15
ARCADIA

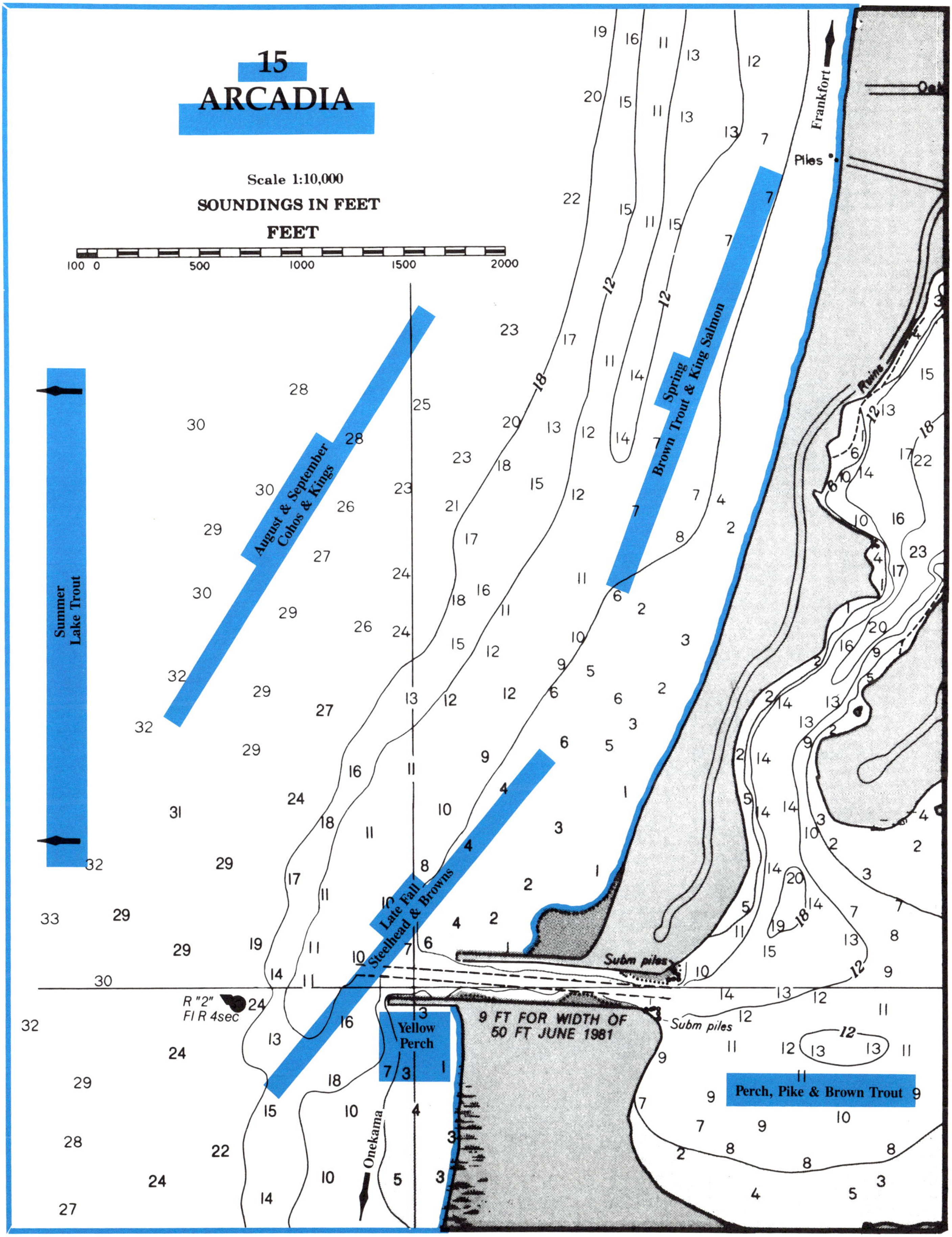

Scale 1:10,000
SOUNDINGS IN FEET
FEET
100 0 500 1000 1500 2000
Summer Lake Trout
August & September Cohos & Kings
Spring Brown Trout & King Salmon
Late Fall Steelhead & Browns
Yellow Perch
Perch, Pike & Brown Trout
Frankfort
Onekama
Piles
Ruins
Subm piles
Subm piles
9 FT FOR WIDTH OF 50 FT JUNE 1981
R "2" Fl R 4sec

The Arcadia area produced this fine catch of Lake Michigan brown trout. The happy fisherman is Dave Taylor of Otisville.

16
FRANKFORT

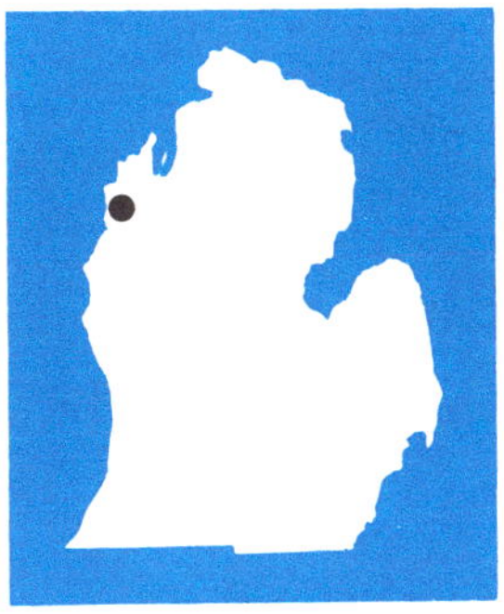

Frankfort is a scenic little town nestled in the northwestern Lower Peninsula among Lake Michigan sand dunes. If you are a fisherman, there are at least four reasons why you won't visit just once: (1) the Elberta and Frankfort piers serve up a smorgasbord of fishing fun from early spring until freeze-up. (2) the Betsie River hosts exciting runs of steelhead, (3) Betsie Lake affords trolling opportunities in a sheltered environment when the big lake is blown over, and (4) Lake Michigan itself features good structure and good trolling for all five major trout and salmon species.

Fishing Schedule

SPRING

I have fished the piers in early April, but sometimes it is possible to get on them in March. Use extreme caution, however, as they are usually ice-slicked this early in the *spring*, and that is why some pier anglers wear cleats—normally used for ice fishing—on their boots. Wind with a northern bent provides calm water off the Elberta (south-side) slab. Conversely, a wind with a southern edge helps make the Frankfort (north-side) structure more productive. Of course, some anglers fish the chute between the pierheads, too, especially if boat traffic is not too heavy.

We have caught steelhead to seven pounds each by bottomfishing spawn bags. Our technique calls for knotting up grape-sized bags of fresh steelhead roe to which a small chip of styrofoam has been added. The chip, or a miniature marshmallow helps to keep bait moving just off bottom, especially if you have added a small slip sinker stopped by a tiny split shot about 12 inches above your bait.

Other fishermen pin wigglers or nightcrawler gobs to shankless hooks and fish those baits in the same manner. A few float bobbers to keep bait just off bottom. These techniques produce brown trout in spring, too, as well as a few Chinooks and cohos.

Menominees are yet another spring (and fall) visitor to the Frankfort/Elberta piers. When anglers retrieve busted spawn bags, they know it is the work of menominees; therefore, many go after the slim fish with single salmon eggs or worm bits. Gale Van Alstine, a friend of mine from Drayton Plains, has caught menominees here by fishing two hooks above a slip sinker, another tactic that apparently works.

The Betsie River receives sporadic spurts of steelhead from mid-March through early May, with peak fishing normally occurring just as sucker runs are diminishing. Most steelheaders fish below Homestead Dam—in fact, competition is often shoulder to shoulder there—but there are also opportunities above the dam all the way to Kurick Road, the upstream limit for the year-round season.

Both charter fishermen and sport trollers appear in the shallows near Frankfort soon after ice leaves Betsie Lake, sometime in mid-April, occasionally sooner. The target species in early spring is brown trout and steelhead. Typical rigging involves shallow-set downriggers, long flatlines, planer boards and outriggers. Frank Arleth, a good charterboat captain who trolls the area beginning in May, reports success with those tactics, plus he will often add a pair of Dipsy-Divers to outriggers. Rapalas in orange, blue, black, and perch colors (in that order) score best. Other productive body baits include jointed and deep-diving Rebels, Red Fins and Bagley Bang-O-Lures. Best colors are orange-bellied lures with black, pearl or metallic-green tops.

Most trollers cruise shoreline shallows to 25 feet deep and cluster near pierheads and on the shallow side of the Herring Hole. This is a deep piece of structure off Lower Herring Lake, located five miles south of Frankfort.

Jon Nissen is another good charterboat skipper among the growing number working out of Frankfort. Nissen fishes from April through November, with spring and fall browns and steelhead constituting about 10 and 25 percent, respectively, of his season-long take. When targeting browns, Jon chooses black-and-silver or black-and-orange Rapalas, Rebels and Bombers, often adding red-sparkle prism tape to the sides of plugs. Small spoons such as Krocodiles, Little Cleos and Cobras also work well in silver alone or in combination with red, orange, blue or green.

Nissen reports most strikes occurring on planer boards, but flatlines and outriggers also produce. Lead lengths on side-rigged offerings are only 10-30 feet, but longlines are spotted from 100-180 feet behind the boat. Optimum trolling speed, according to an EMS Hawk, is 2-3/4 to 3-1/2 mph. Other catching keys involve trolling in areas of rocky shoreline, around pierheads and off stream mouths such as the Lower Herring Lake outlet. A zig-zag pattern works best.

When targeting steelhead in spring and fall, Jon relies on Rapalas in the previously mentioned colors, plus he adds pearl-and-white Bombers; nickel-and-blue or green Northport Nailers; and white-and-blue, green or orange Lightning Lures and Flutter Chucks. Release lengths are normally 80-150 feet off longlines, with trolling speed locked at 2-1/2 to 2-3/4 mph.

Summer produces good catches of lake trout and salmon. Until

SUMMER

a thermocline forms sometime in June, you can catch these fish in shallows from 15-60 feet deep. In fact, a 14-pound lake trout now on my den wall hit a Wobble-Glo pulled behind a chrome-fluted dodger on Memorial Day a couple of years ago. George Richey and I were trolling in 20 feet of water off sand dunes between Frankfort and the Herring Hole when the fish struck. Lakers, of course, are legal to keep if caught after May 1.

But Frankfort has a better reputation for its Chinooks and cohos, and by mid to late June, trollers generally report good catches. Besides Nissen and Arleth, other good local charterboat fishermen include John King of the *King Fish*, Casey Richey (George's son) of the *Luremaker* and Jim Mattis of the *Tam Boo*. These men target the following areas for summer salmon: (1) The Six-Mile Hole—located six miles off the lighthouse at Point Betsie on a 15-degree heading, (2) The Bank—a ledge that drops from 55 feet to 140 feet and is found offshore from Point Betsie to Frankfort, (3) The Flats—a relatively flat area below the southern edge of the bank and running south for about a mile, (4) The Herring Hole—already referred to.

Jon Nissen, the key contact for this chapter, reports that Chinook and coho salmon make up about 40 and 30 percent respectively of his season-long take at Frankfort. To catch the salmon, he relies upon plugs, spoons, and 0 or 00 dodgers with trolling flies, specifically Sparkle Flies or Michigan Squids. Good local color combinations in attractor/flies include chrome dodger with green, blue or black flies; green-and-yellow dodgers or chartreuse dodgers with green or blue flies; and red dodgers with blue or black flies. Release lengths are three to 10 feet, and optimum trolling speed is 2-1/2 to 3.0 mph.

With plugs and spoons (sometimes stacked above dodgers and flies, but more often flatlined or run off downriggers), Nissen lengthens leads from 20 to 80 feet and gooses boat speed as high as 3-3/4 mph (depending on lure action). Good plug choices are Gold Star, Grizzly or J-Plugs in pearl, pearl and green, pearl and black, green, green or blue prism, black, and chrome. Hot spoons have been Flutter Spoons, Lightning Lures and Eppinger Flutter Chucks in nickel and green or blue, white and green or blue, black and green or blue, and solid silver.

Nissen relies heavily upon Loran-C to both find microstructure in the trolling areas mentioned and then hold a course over it.

The piers continue to produce in summer, with early morning salmon a major draw. Most fishermen fling spoons in either silver alone or in combination with orange, blue, green or chartreuse. A few report catches from LumaLures and other glow-type hardware, especially in the black hour before dawn. Mid-day perching is good off the piers, too, off and on all summer. Worms or minnows are the best baits.

FALL

Fall fishing is excellent at Frankfort, with the piers once more becoming active as kings, cohos, brown trout and steelhead (usually in that order) approach shore. Trollers again rely on planer boards when boat traffic permits their use. There are generally two fall fishing peaks at Frankfort—Labor Day and again in late September or early October when coho have left the area for Platte Bay (17).

Die-hard pier fishermen and trollers alike can take steelhead through deer season if they can tough the cold weather. When steelhead are still in deeper water during this time, they will hit dodger/fly combinations usually run for cohos. Once the steelhead enter Betsie Lake, however, better lures are shallow-set J-Plugs or Gold Stars (when trolling fast) or Tadpollies, Kwikfish or Flatfish (when trolling slow). Best colors are fluorescent orange or red, run separately or in combination with silver, black or green. River fishermen also catch steelhead, although spring is a decidedly better time.

Planting Records

The Betsie River is currently receiving 15,000 brown trout and 15,000 steelhead, and reefs off Frankfort are getting 65,000 lake trout. These annual stockings of yearlings will run at least through 1990. Cohos caught off Frankfort are Platte River fish, and kings are likely from Manistee (13), although some of each are probably naturally reproduced in the Platte and Betsie rivers.

Facilities

The DNR maintains a harbor of refuge with the following services: transient accommodations, gasoline and diesel fuel, water, electricity, restrooms, shower facilities, haul-out facilities and holding-tank pump-out. The telephone number of the dock attendant is (616) 352-4391 or 352-9051.

There is a boat launch on Betsie Lake at Frankfort and another at Elberta.

Further Information

Chambers of Commerce:

1. Benzie County Chamber of Commerce, P.O. Box 505, Beulah 49617; (616) 882-5802.
2. West Michigan Tourist Association, 136 Fulton E., Grand Rapids 49503; (616) 456-8557.

Bait & Tackle Shops:

1. Elberta Sport Shop, 603 Frankfort Ave., Elberta 49628; (616) 352-4434.
2. Ted's Bait & Tackle, 787 Michigan Ave., Benzonia 49616; (616) 882-5361.
3. Frankfort Tackle Box, Frankfort 49635; (616) 352-7673.

Charter Fishing:

1. Captain Jon Nissen, 113 Amherst, Toledo OH 43614; (419) 385-8975. 27-foot Sportcraft, *E-Z Ketch*.
2. Captain Frank Arleth, 1499 W. Burdell, Roscommon 48653; (517) 275-5869. 26-foot Stamas, *Sally-E*.
3. Captain Casey Richey, RR #1 Box 280, Honor 49640; (616) 882-4571. 24-foot Starcraft, *Luremaker*.
4. Captain Jim Mattis, 2399 Dam Rd., Benzonia 49616; (616) 882-4163. 28-foot Bertram, *Tam Boo*.
5. Captain John King, 17181 Beech-Daly, Redford 48042; (313) 255-7877. 22-foot boat, *King Fish*.

Department of Natural Resources:

Two fisheries biologists work out of District Headquarters at 8015 S. US-131, Cadillac 49601; (616) 775-9727.

Coast Guard:

Frankfort Station, (616) 352-4242 or 352-9151.

GREAT LAKES TRIVIA

Michigan is sinking into the Great Lakes—as it has been for the past 500 million years—at the rate of one millimeter per year.

No matter where you stand in Michigan, you are never more than 85 miles from a Great Lake.

Approximately 38,459 square miles of Great Lakes water is included within Michigan's boundaries.

Lake Superior is the second-largest lake in the world; only the Caspian Sea is larger.

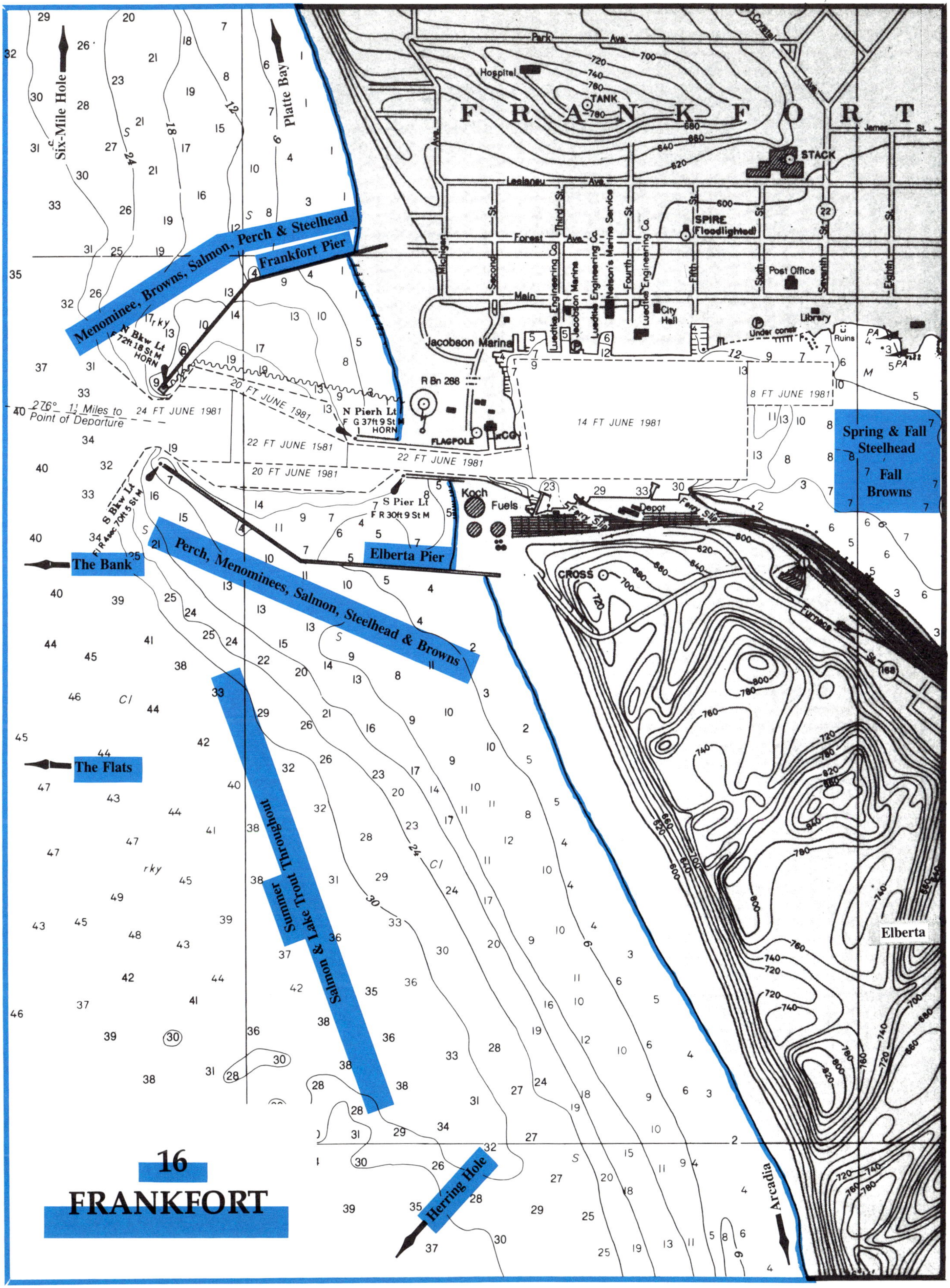
Menominee, Browns, Salmon, Perch & Steelhead
Frankfort Pier
Six-Mile Hole
Platte Bay
FRANKFORT
Spring & Fall Steelhead
Fall Browns
Jacobson Marina
The Bank
Perch, Menominees, Salmon, Steelhead & Browns
Elberta Pier
The Flats
Summer Salmon & Lake Trout Throughout
Elberta
Herring Hole
Arcadia
16
FRANKFORT

Pier Pressure Pays Off

Winds of the world go by different names. North Africa has its sirocco weather; southern Asia has its monsoons. East Coast cod men suffer nor'easters three days running.

Great Lakes anglers get high winds, too. The worst ones, in Lake Michigan where I fish, come in late fall and very early spring. In March, they slice through snowmobile suits and push hungry waves licking over breakwalls and piers, plastering them with treacherous ice. We shore-bound anglers who fish the piers have special names for these winds, too, but they can't be printed in this book. Let "cold," "nasty" and "miserable" suffice.

I was baby-sitting twin rods on the Frankfort pier one March day during such a howling wind. The sister slab at Elberta disappeared rhythmically under crashing sweeps. Earlier that morning I had planned to fish there, but those surly waves quickly changed my mind. Even on this north pier, things were looking grimmer as the wind increased in strength.

Tip-toeing around on ice cleats didn't do much to keep me warm. Neither did a generous slug of blackberry brandy that had hit my stomach like a linebacker blow and was likely on its way up. Only a strike would serve to take my mind off the discomfort.

But the strike never came, so 20 minutes later I cranked up my lines and headed for the truck camper.

Now I realize that's not an exciting action story. You were probably expecting something like, "The rod tip bucked like a rodeo bronc and the reel screamed in protest as the 10-pound steelhead smoked from the gray depths, tail-walked a dozen feet, and tried to spit the steel from his lower jaw!" Sorry to disappoint you, but I wanted to emphasize right off that the piers can be lonely and dangerous. And they do not always produce fish.

When they do, however, action can be fast and fun. I like to fish the Great Lakes slabs for a number of reasons—besides the smorgasbord of fish species they serve up. One reason is the long fishing season—about eight months in all. Second, piers are well distributed around the Great Lakes. Third, pier and breakwall fishing is inexpensive sport. Not everyone can afford downriggers and trolling graphs, let alone boats. Fourth, the piers are full of friendly people who share advice and fishing stories and will lend a net when you need it.

On slow fishing days, piers often take on a carnival-like atmosphere, with radios blaring, ships plying the harbor, and strollers everywhere. Finally, the piers offer a common denominator of sorts among anglers. One day you're rod-watching next to a retired millionaire, and the next day your neighbor is a laid-off Buick assembly-line worker whose benefits have run out and whose next meal is what he can clip to the stringer.

I have a hard time telling most folks apart on a pier. I suspect they do, too.

Tom Huggler
Otisville

Piers such as this one at Onekama serve up summer salmon to early morning and evening fishermen. The Frankfort and Elberta piers are highly productive, too. The angler is Ron Spomer who lives in Moscow, Idaho.

17
PLATTE BAY

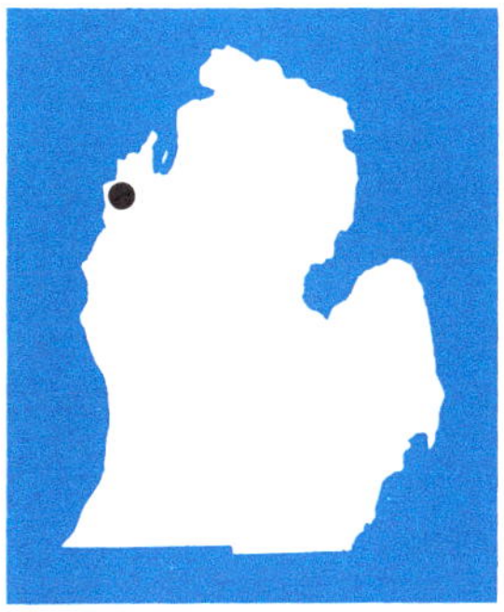

It's hard to imagine a Great Lakes angler alive today who has not heard of Platte Bay, site of the Great Lakes first coho-salmon returns in 1967. It is also the place where several people drowned Labor Day weekend that same year when "coho fever" prompted foolhardy fishermen to tackle Lake Michigan in anything that floated, including cartoppers and canoes.

Much has happened since. Coho fever still runs rampant here, but fishermen have learned to be cautious. A few miles upriver, the DNR has built a huge, modern hatchery which produces most of Michigan's salmon for Great Lakes plantout. And the DNR has fine-tuned its stocking program here as elsewhere.

Good fishing continues to draw anglers from throughout the state as well as the rest of the Midwest and Pennsylvania, New York and New Jersey. A million coho smolts, released each spring in the Platte River, have returned an excellent number of mature spawners 18 months later, in September and October. Fishing is good for spring and summer browns and Chinook salmon, too. The only place on the Great Lakes where I have ever experienced a Grand Slam—at least one coho, king, brown, steelhead and laker in a single day—occurred in Platte Bay. Depending upon the season and weather conditions, fishermen here can have it all: trolling, on Platte Bay and Loon Lake; surf fishing, at the rivermouth; and wading, in the clear stream itself.

Fishing Schedule

Hardly a day goes by from about March 1 until Memorial Day that some steelheader isn't tossing spawn bags or working small streamers in the Platte River. The rivermouth is especially popular in spring and again in fall from Labor Day until freeze-up. On New Year's Day 1983, Scott Kincaid of Flint and I braved zero temperatures to fish the available open water here and were rewarded with three steelhead, including a fine 12-pound male that drilled Scott's spawn bag.

SPRING

The soon-to-spawn steelhead move upriver in waves from Lake Michigan throughout *spring*. Many bait anglers fish the surf within a quarter-mile of where the quick-running Platte gushes into Lake Michigan between small sand dunes. Others roll spawn bags or wigglers through known steelhead lies all the way to the US-31 bridge east of Honor (the upstream limit for the extended season). Still others troll the shallows and pick up browns and an occasional lake trout and salmon, in addition to steelhead. With all these methods available, be advised that the Platte River and Platte Bay get plenty of attention from competing fishermen.

One of the best is a young man named Casey Richey, the son of trolling-fly-maker George Richey. Casey earned his stripes as a top-flight fisherman on Platte Bay brown trout. Only recently he scuttled his 14-foot aluminum boat and 7-1/2 hp outboard for a bigger boat and, since passing his captain's test, now runs charter trips in Platte Bay and out of nearby Frankfort (16).

In 1984, when Casey still had the small boat, he caught 389 fish, including 64 brown trout, while running only two lines and a pair of hand-cranked downriggers. Spring tactics involve trolling with No. 9 or No. 11 Rapalas in black and silver or fluorescent red and gold while paralleling shore in four to 12 feet of water. Casey uses six-pound-test line and spots his lures from 250-300 feet behind the boat—otherwise, the wary browns will snub his offerings.

As is often true with brown trout, success is a hit-or-miss affair, but when fish are in the shallows, there is no better sport. One of Casey's best days occurred April 13 a couple of years ago when he and a high-school chum named David ventured into Platte Bay in Casey's small boat. But I'll let Casey tell his own story:

"David had never landed a brown before, and within an hour we caught a two-man limit of 10 fish. David liked that so well, he asked if we could do it again the next day. I said 'Sure!' So we went out longlining the following morning and had on at least 25 brown trout. We landed 18 but returned eight to grow up. The 10 we kept averaged six pounds each, about the size of the fish we had taken the day before. One was a 12-pound dandy that David had mounted."

Most spring trollers target the five- to 25-foot-deep water while paralleling the shoreline in both West and East Platte Bay. Otter Creek, which sometimes hosts a good run of spawning smelt, is another good area to try besides the Platte River. As mentioned, brown trout and steelhead make up much of the spring bag, but most coolers will also contain a salmon or two (lake trout must be returned if caught before May 1).

SUMMER

Summer trollers head for the deeper water of both bays. There is plenty of jagged structure from 80-150 feet deep, and those that know how to stitch the seam—work lures along bottom without hanging up—will catch brown trout, Chinook salmon and lake trout. Cowbells with sewn minnows, P-Nuts or flutter-light spoons behind are favorites. Earl's Pearls and Whirl-A-Gigs are local cowbells that are popular. Many trollers that stack the bottom-running rigs with small J-Plugs or light spoons pick up king salmon. Longlines, outriggers and planer boards continue to take steelhead and cohos off and on all summer.

On humid, calm days when the sun is blazing, the flatlined and side-rigged offerings will also take brown trout, although catches are far from consistent. Slow trolling a zig-zag pattern and opting for silver- or pearl-colored X5 or U20 Flatfish is a popular technique. McMahon Spoons, Rattlespoons and Krocodiles, as well as Sugar Spoons, if you can find them, are good hardware choices. Try silver, copper and brass as basic colors, then mix and match with chartreuse, yellows and greens. Keep in mind, too, that browns will often hit lures doctored with prism tape. There are huge brown trout lurking in Platte Bay. A 31-1/2 pound monster caught here by Jack Duffy on a hot afternoon several summers ago held the state record for many years.

By late July or early August, trollers begin picking up cohos and kings in both West and East Platte Bay. That is when most make the switch to dodgers and flies.

FALL

The switch marks the beginning of *fall* fishing, and it is when trolling traffic thickens, peaking on Labor Day weekend. In a typical year, hot salmon action lasts for 10 days to two weeks, but this period can occur as early as late August and as late as the third week in October. Platte River water level and temperature are determining keys.

Casey Richey's 1984 catch record that I referred to earlier included 185 cohos and 140 kings. His lure choices for kings are Grizzly Plugs in pearl or green and yellow and Flutter Chucks in lemon/lime or chrome with blue or green tape. He usually stacks these above dodger/fly combinations for cohos. Leads vary from five to 15 feet and trolling speed from 1.5-3.0 mph. For cohos, he runs his father's Metallic or Sparkle Flies in these color combinations:

Black Sparkle Fly with white or red dodger
Blue Sparkle fly with yellow/white or chrome dodger
Green Sparkle fly with green/yellow or chrome dodger
Yellow Sparkle fly with green/yellow or chartreuse dodger
Blue/silver Metallic Fly with chrome or yellow/white dodger
Green/silver Metallic Fly with green/yellow or chrome dodger
Laser or silver Metallic Fly with chrome dodger

After cohos enter the river, they typically stage for a second time in Loon Lake. Trollers who run a circular pattern and work the 20- to 35-foot drop can take fish with the above color combinations in dodgers and flies. Dodgers and spoons also produce.

Over the years, king-salmon and brown-trout fall runs in the Platte River have diminished to the point where catches are purely incidental to spawning cohos and steelhead. Most steelhead that enter the river in September and October are opportunistic feeders of salmon eggs. By deer season, however, the steelhead may well be spring spawners that have arrived early and will now winter over.

WINTER

Other than the late-season steelheading mentioned, there are no *winter* fishing activities to report, at least at the rivermouth. Platte Lake, however, yields fair northern-pike catches to tip-up and spear fishermen.

Planting Records

The only hatchery-reared fish currently being stocked in the Platte River are coho smolts. After several years of releasing one million cohos, the DNR has trimmed plants to 750,000 annually through at least 1990. Many of the steelhead that run the river are naturally reproduced, plus some from other plants wander here. No doubt many of the brown trout caught in Platte Bay are Wisconsin fish.

Facilities

There is no harbor of refuge at Platte Bay. The DNR maintains a fairly good launching ramp, and there is plenty of parking space. Expect possible difficulty at the Platte River mouth, however, as a sand bar often obstructs boat passage.

Further Information

Chambers of Commerce:

1. Benzie County Chamber of Commerce, P.O. Box 505, Beulah 49617; (616) 882-5802.

2. West Michigan Tourist Association, 136 Fulton E., Grand Rapids 49503; (616) 456-8557.

Bait & Tackle Shops:

1. Casey's Corner, M-22 at the Platte River Bridge; (616) 325-3636.

2. Riverside Canoes, M-22 at the Platte River Bridge; (616) 325-5622.

Charter Fishing:

Captain Casey Richey, RR #1 Box 280, Honor 49640; (616) 882-4571. 24-foot Starcraft, *Luremaker*.

Department of Natural Resources:

Two fisheries biologists work out of District Headquarters at 8015 S. US-131, Cadillac 49601; (616) 775-9727.

Coast Guard:

Frankfort Station, (616) 352-4242 or 352-9151.

Two-For-One Salmon

One September afternoon a couple of years ago, Chris Nelson (from Honor) and I were trolling East Platte Bay for coho salmon. It was a beautiful fall day with plenty of bright sun and not much chop on the water. But the best part of all was that most boats had the net out and often.

Sharing the action, Chris and I were on our way to building a nice two-man limit of 10 salmon, from six to nine pounds each. Our good fortune was coming on fluted-chrome dodgers and trolling flies, 55 feet down over 90 feet of water. We took turns getting to the sprung rods.

About 7:00 p.m. a rod started bucking like crazy. My turn. When I put some muscle into the pole, it felt like a good king salmon of 12 or 15 pounds was on the other end. But after a wild 10-minute fight, imagine my surprise to see two coho salmon hooked to the same lure.

How was this possible?

Well, the lure, a green Sparkle Fly, had tandem hooks about two inches apart. Since cohos usually feed in schools, and then in a frenzied manner, two fish must have gone for the same lure at the same time.

I've spent much of my life trolling the Great Lakes, but never have I heard of this happening before. To my knowledge, the closest incident was a single fish that struck two separate lures trolled 10 yards apart (see "Double Strike," page 42).

But that day Chris and I got two cohos for the price of one.

George Richey
Honor

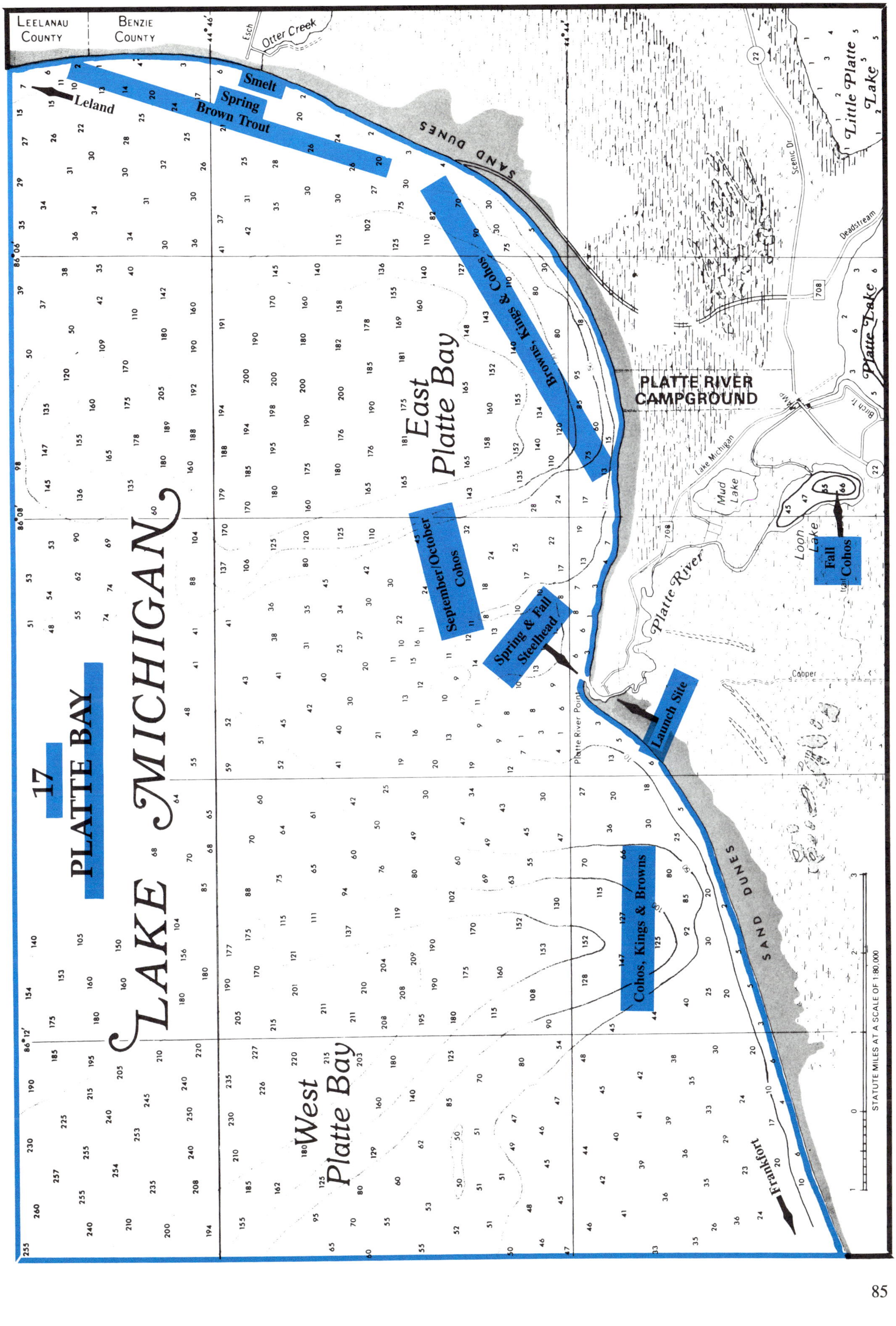
17
PLATTE BAY
LAKE MICHIGAN
West Platte Bay
East Platte Bay
Leelanau County
Benzie County
Leland
Smelt
Spring Brown Trout
Browns, Kings & Cohos
September/October Cohos
Spring & Fall Steelhead
Launch Site
Cohos, Kings & Browns
Fall Cohos
PLATTE RIVER CAMPGROUND
Platte River
Platte River Point
Otter Creek
Esch
SAND DUNES
Scenic Dr
Deadstream
Little Platte Lake
Platte Lake
Loon Lake
Mud Lake
Lake Michigan
Birch Tr.
Cooper
Frankfort
STATUTE MILES AT A SCALE OF 1:80,000

Smelt dipping can be very good some years in small streams emptying into Lake Michigan in the Platte Bay region.

The Leland area occasionally produces large lake trout like this 20-pounder held by Bruce Bosshart, who lives in Minnesota.

18

LELAND and the MANITOU ISLANDS

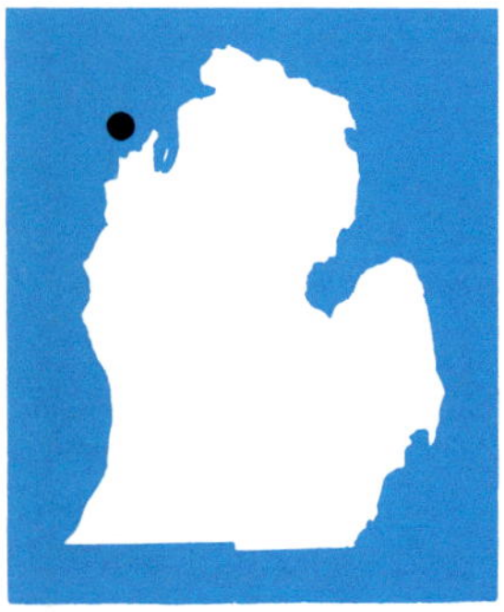

"The Manitou Islands have the best fishing in the Great Lakes." That's a pretty strong statement, considering the large number of ports and rivermouths around the state which serve up outstanding angling action. The assessment comes from Jack Duffy, one of Michigan's most respected fishermen and a charter-boat captain out of Leland, headquarters for trollers who fish the Manitous, about 10 miles offshore. Duffy caught the one-time state-record brown trout, a 31½ pound brute from Platte Bay (17). He has been fishing out of Leland since moving here from Midland about 10 years ago.

Jack claims that fishermen who know the tricky structure and currents of the Manitous can catch 20 and 40 kings a day. "Steve Otterbein (another veteran guide out of Leland) took 48 kings there one day last summer, 30 on an all-day charter and 18 more on an evening trip."

Fishing Schedule

SPRING

In spite of good salmon-catching opportunities, it is lake trout that draw most fishermen to the Leland area. *Spring* activity for lakers begins at the May 1 opener (and remains steady until the August 15 closure) at Good Harbor Bay, halfway between Leland and North Manitou Island, and one to two miles offshore between Blackledge's Point and the extreme north end of Lake Leelanau. These are the three best structure grids although there are plenty of others.

One reason the fishing is so good is because of dramatic depth changes, up to 300 feet within a quarter-mile. Most trollers target the bottom of such jagged structure, from 50-200 feet deep, especially when optimum temperatures of 48-52 degrees F. can be found. Depth, however, is a secondary consideration to temperature, and that is because the rich abundance of structure makes this region of Lake Michigan a lake-trout pastureland. Another reason for good fishing is a steady supply of smelt and alewives in the area.

If you are trailering your own boat to fish this port, however, you will not be able to depend upon other fishermen for much help. That is not because they are unfriendly, but is due to the vastness of the trolling grounds, which makes it hard to maintain communications with other anglers. Another reason for the lack of fishermen is that the Leland Harbor area is small, and dockage space is at a premium. For years, Otterbein and Duffy pretty much had the charter business here to themselves. Now there are 18 boats for hire working this area, and there is no room left for more. Sport trollers, however, can launch on a daily basis or spend the night in their boats anchored offshore in the outer harbor.

Another reason that Leland hosts few sport fishermen is that, although there are plenty of lake trout, in recent years they have been running small due to heavy Indian gillnetting in the region. Cowbells rigged to P-Nuts and other small plugs catch the smaller lakers. There are some fish here, however, to 30 pounds each; to catch them, most of the local fishermen and some of the charter-boat captains pull wire, opting for large silver spoons run clean or for chrome dodgers and trolling flies. Best attractor colors in either dodgers or cowbells include chrome, green or white with lures in silver, chartreuse or green. Tactics include fishing tight to bottom structure and occasionally bumping bottom with cannonballs, then swinging off.

Besides lake trout, spring trollers catch incidental brown trout and steelhead. According to Duffy, it is very possible to target these two species by running highlines for steelhead and longlining in spring shallows for browns. However, few do it because of high local interest in lakers and salmon.

SUMMER

King-salmon fishing kicks off in early *summer* and lasts until September. Action is far more spread out than it is for lake trout. Key areas include 1-1/2 miles in front of Leland, throughout Good Harbor Bay, the east and northeast shores of North Manitou Island (especially off the lighthouse in structure known locally as the Crib), the Peterson Park area north of Leland, and in the shoal waters off Pyramid Point. Trollers who hunt salmon may wander as far as 20 miles from Leland, all the way northeast to Cat Head and Lighthouse points. Incidentally, in addition to kings, coho salmon occasionally show up in midsummer in the Vessel Point area of northeast North Manitou Island.

Much remains to be learned about currents and winds in this area, but a definite advantage is that boat fishermen nearly always have a place to set lines. That is because there is a wide variety of temperatures and depths to consider, plus the lee sides of points and the island feature calm water on hard-blowing days from all directions except a due-north wind. Spoons such as Northport Nailers (white with green or blue tape and silver with blue tape), Fin-Weavers (chartreuse or silver) and Lucky Lures (orange and silver and blue and silver) are the mainstay, but J-Plugs, Canadian Plugs and Rapalas in various colors also produce.

In addition, Steve Otterbein relies heavily on Silver Strik-ERs and silver-plated No. 44 Flutter Spoons. An accountant in the off-season and meticulous record-keeper of his fishing success, Steve has caught between 1,271 and 1,954 fish out of Leland every year

18

LELAND and the MANITOU ISLANDS

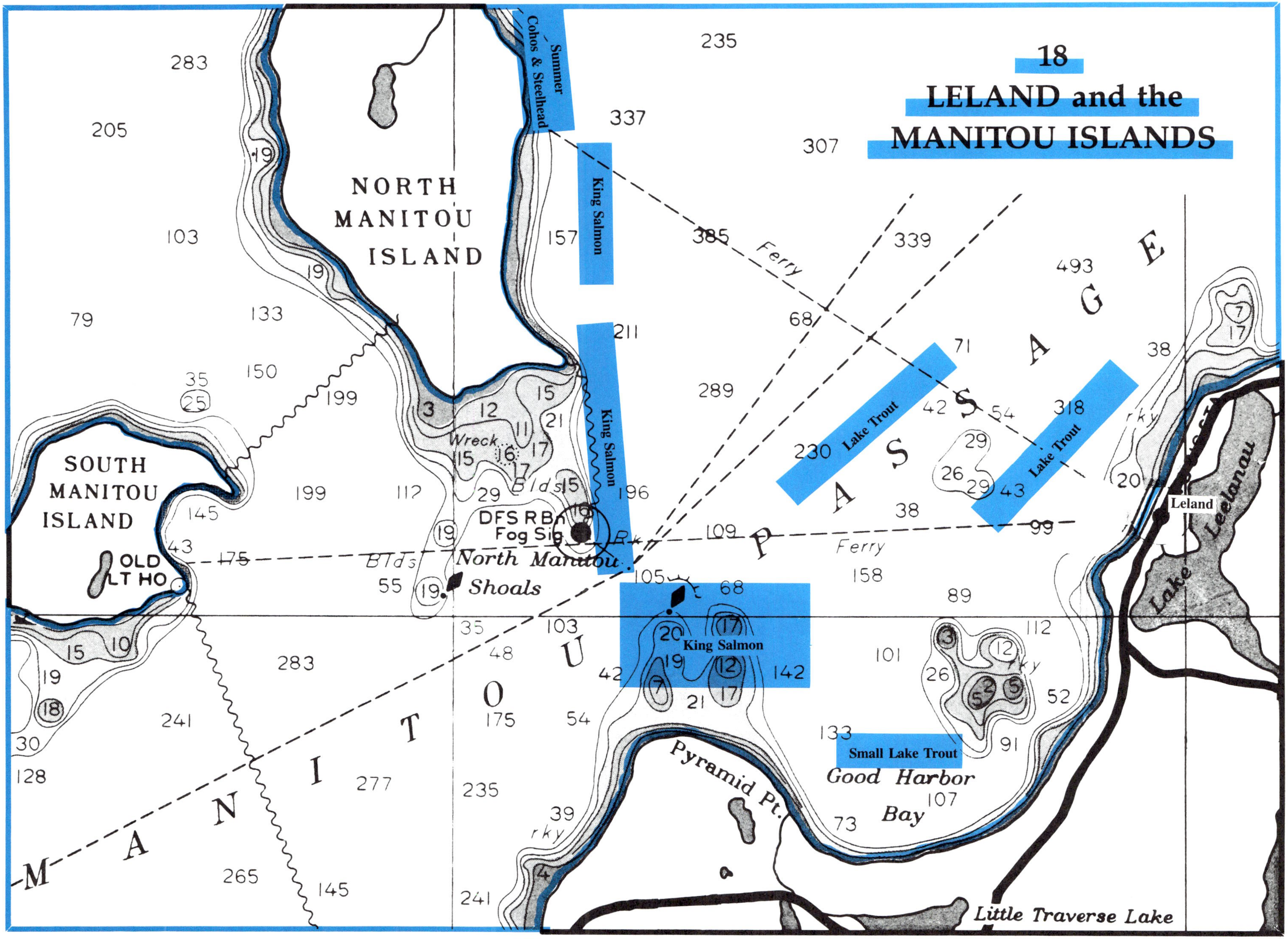

since 1979.

Besides salmon and lake trout, the short run of the Leland River from the manmade waterfall to Lake Michigan hosts a midsummer run of yellow perch. In fact, perch seem to be coming back in the area, with commercial netters (Duffy also works for Carlson's, the leading white commercial fishing enterprise in the area) taking them to depths of 300-400 feet. Most of the perch that enter the river—presumably to feed—are small, but jig fishermen can also catch a few jumbos. Some fish from their anchored boats, while others toss jigs and bottomfish with bait from piers.

The salmon fishery in the Leland area is mostly over by the end of August. Some kings are caught near the Leland Harbor entrance and in Good Harbor Bay in September, but the fishing is not consistent. The salmon apparently sustain themselves through natural reproduction in small area streams and perhaps in the Leland River itself, as no plants are made. Surf fishermen and close-to-shore trollers in *fall* also pick up brown trout and steelhead by longlining or side-rigging small spoons and plugs.

There is no *winter* fishery to speak of in the Leland area other than some incidental jigging for lake trout and whitefish in the bays of Lake Michigan when the ice is safe.

Planting Records

There are currently no releases of hatchery-reared fish, nor are there any plans to stock any.

Facilities

The DNR maintains a harbor of refuge with the following services: transient accommodations, gasoline and diesel fuel, water, electricity, restrooms, shower facilities, holding-tank pump-out, and VHF-FM radio. The telephone number of the dock attendant is (616) 256-9132. There is a modern boat-launch facility at Leland, and anglers with small boats can also put in at Glen Arbor.

Further Information

Chambers of Commerce:

West Michigan Tourist Association, 136 Fulton E., Grand Rapids 49503; (616) 456-8557.

Bait & Tackle Shops:

The Fish Hook, 110 W. River St., Leland 49654; (616) 256-9501.

Charter Fishing:

1. Captain Steve Otterbein, 7427 Pinewood Ct., Traverse City 49684; (616) 946-2204. 31-foot Chris-Craft, *Sea Dog*.
2. Captain Jack Duffy, 4027 Oxford Dr., Leland 49654; (616) 256-7457. 26-foot Stamas, *Whitecap*.

Department of Natural Resources:

Two fisheries biologists work out of District Headquarters at 8015 S. US-131, Cadillac 49601; (616) 775-9727.

Coast Guard:

Charlevoix Station, (616) 547-2541 or 547-2565.

A Day Meant for Sleeping In

I should have known it was going to be one of those days. Clue one was when we had to swipe the battery from George Richey's truck in order to get his boat started. The delay cost us the pole position at the Platte River launch ramp, so we had to get in line and wait 20 minutes to launch his boat, the *Luremaker*. The second clue occurred when George's long-shaft outboard hung up on the sand bar that often obstructs boat traffic at the entrance to Platte Bay. I can assure you that the waist-deep water of the Platte River will curl toes and tighten buttocks in September.

George and I soon forgot those minor obstacles as we began setting trolling lines for coho salmon in the west side of Platte Bay. An autumn sunrise promised a beautiful day of fishing, and already two or three other fishermen in nearby boats had their nets out and were swinging aboard salmon.

That's when George's graph decided to quit. While I steered for the A-frame cottages on shore, my friend, who has the mechanical ability of a zoo monkey with an arc-welding torch—and is equally as dangerous—began taking apart the graph. Soon, parts were strewn on the dash and front seat, but eventually George found the problem—a busted stylus. He hailed someone he knew in a passing boat who just happened to have a spare stylus. Incredible luck, we assured each other, until George's buddy ran over our port-side Yellow Bird planer.

Meanwhile, everyone else was catching fish.

And eventually we got a strike and even had the feisty salmon to the net, when he decided to power dive once more. Too bad he chose to do that under the propeller. The line parted, and off swam our would-be first fish with a $3.95 dodger and $2 Sparkle Fly. This kind of luck plagued us all day, and we never did catch a fish. When the blazing sun mercifully sank in the western sky, then finally snuffed itself out below the horizon, we headed for shore.

At least I knew what was facing me there, one more ice-water shock as I pulled George's boat—upriver now—over the sandbar. All in all, it hadn't been that bad a day, I decided. George's wife would have a cold beer and a hot supper waiting.

We got to eat it, too, about eleven that night. First we had to jump-start George's truck and fix the flat tire on his boat trailer.

Tom Huggler
Otisville

19
NORTHPORT

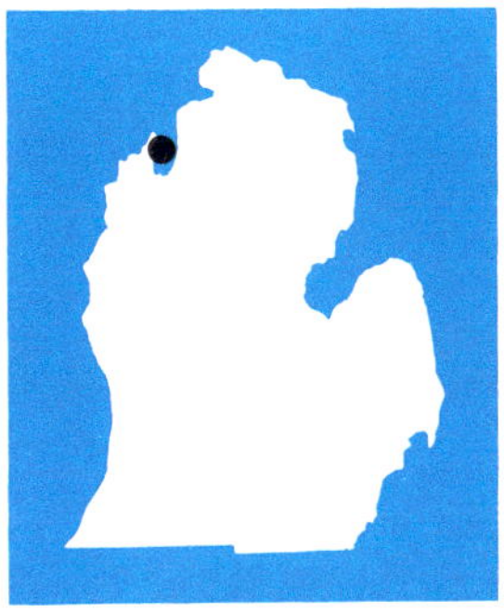

Northport is a picturesque harbor lying at the head of the West Arm of Grand Traverse Bay toward the end of the Leelanau Peninsula. Key gamefish species happen to also be targeted by commercial fishermen in the area and include both lake trout and whitefish. In fact, Indian gillnetters have impacted lake trout to the point where mostly small fish are the only ones taken by sport fishermen.

Besides these two species, however, there are some fair to excellent fishing opportunities for yellow perch, brook trout and smallmouth bass, in addition to incidental catches of brown trout and Chinook salmon.

Visitors will be treated to spectacular scenery of sand dunes and beautiful beaches. And, since the Leelanau Peninsula is a major tourist gathering point, fishermen will find good accommodations and friendly people.

Fishing Schedule

SPRING

Yellow-perch fishing kicks off *spring* angling activities in Northport Bay, with nice stringers of good-sized yellow-bellies common from ice-out until early June. The rated tactic is to fish with minnows or wigglers just off bottom with two-hook perch spreaders and small bell-shaped sinkers. Depths from 10-50 feet pay off for boat fishermen who either stillfish while anchored or driftfish with the prevailing west wind.

Chugging with Swedish Pimples and wigglers on bottom is a good spring technique for catching whitefish from one to four pounds each. Chugging is the practice of driftfishing or slow-trolling with short rods, light line and two- to six-ounce sinkers, necessary to put bait on bottom in depths to 100 feet. A sleeper activity in spring is to fish for brook trout off the Northport Creek mouth by casting small spoons and spinners or bottomfishing with nightcrawlers. This off-again on-again fishery produces most consistently in May.

SUMMER

Summer angling opportunities remain fair to good for yellow perch and improve for lake trout. For best results on lakers, troll silver spoons along the east-west reef at the head of Grand Traverse Bay. Summer is also the best time to catch smallmouth bass among rocks and boulders within the harbor, mostly in depths to 20 feet. This is a casting fishery from boat or shore, with most anglers tossing Burke's Wig Wag Minnows and similar jigs and action plastics. Other good lures include spinner and jig combinations, small-sized crankbaits, and weighted spinners. A few fishermen drift with Junebug Spinners or slow-troll with nightcrawler harnesses. Besides the harbor, many of the drowned points and boulder fields in the West Arm of Grand Traverse Bay produce smallmouth bass throughout the summer and into the fall.

FALL

In addition, *fall* yields good to excellent catches of menominees and whitefish within the Northport Harbor area. Again, chugging produces the most action from whitefish, whereas menominees readily strike single salmon eggs or small pieces of worms fished with small hooks near bottom. Perch also return to Northport Bay in fall, and there are increasing numbers of Chinook salmon that are returning to the foot of Grand Traverse Bay to spawn.

Although Indian gillnetting has impacted lake-trout populations in the Northport area, there are still opportunities for sport fishermen.

Winter opportunities are rated very good for whitefish and yellow perch, with most ice anglers jig-fishing spoons and larvae or cut bait in the harbor and off area points to depths of 100 feet.

All in all, Northport serves up good sport fishing without much competition.

Planting Records

There are no DNR releases of hatchery-reared fish at Northport. For full details on area plants, see 20 (Grand Traverse Bay).

Facilities

The Department of Natural Resources maintains a harbor of refuge at Northport with these services: transient accommodations, gasoline and diesel fuel, water, electricity, restrooms, shower facilities, holding-tank pump-out, launch ramp and VHF-FM radio. The telephone number of the dock attendant is (616) 386-5411 or 386-5461.

There are also boat launches at Omena Bay and Suttons Bay. Both are located south of Northport Bay.

The Bountiful Yellow Perch

Try this pop quiz: What fish species is the best eating, most abundant, easiest to catch, and enjoyed by hundreds of thousands of Great Lakes anglers? Largemouth bass? Nope. Bluegills? Wrong again.

The answer is *yellow perch*. Especially in the Great Lakes, perch fishing just keeps getting better and better.

Here is inexpensive family sport, close to home and fun. A perch rod and reel takes up about as much room in your car as another coat hanger in the closet. Perch fishing is one of the few really good angling bargains left. Basic equipment is all that is needed. Any kind of spinning or casting reel, a rod of any length, a bell-or pyramid-shaped sinker, a perch spreader (to allow two hooks), and size-4 hooks that are pin-prick sharp are the rule.

Perch are accessible, too. You will find them in bays, off piers, and in reasonably shallow water throughout the Great Lakes. Going after the yellow-bellies makes as much sense as remembering to sign your 1040 for "refund due." You can get skunked on perch, too, but it doesn't happen very often. They travel in schools and are usually on the move, so action stops and starts about as often as a ferris wheel. If you begin to nod off between strikes, it's time to haul anchor and try a new spot.

A hungry perch will hit most anything, but minnows—especially spot tails or emerald shiners—are the best bait. Wigglers (the larvae of the mayfly) and worms are old standbys. So are small crayfish if you can find them for sale or are able to catch your own. In fact, perch swarm to shallow-water reef areas in midsummer because crayfish are just hatching there. This occurs in southern Lake Michigan and Lake Huron at several ports.

Not all the catching fun in the Great Lakes belongs to the steelheaders and the run-and-gun salmon trollers. Yellow perch have a large and faithful following, too.

Further Information

Chambers of Commerce:

West Michigan Tourist Association, 136 Fulton E., Grand Rapids 49503; (616) 456-8557.

Bait & Tackle Shops:

Best Tackle Shop, Northport

Charter Fishing:

Captain Bill Crandell, P.O. Box 501, Suttons Bay 49682; (616) 271-3643. 22-foot boat, *Tuna Noodle*.

Department of Natural Resources:

Two fisheries biologists work out of District Headquarters at 8015 S. US-131, Cadillac 49601; (616) 775-9727.

Coast Guard:

Charlevoix Station, (616) 547-2541 or 547-2565.

Drift a River, Catch a Steelhead

Driftboat fishing has recently come into vogue in the Great Lakes region. What was considered a novelty five years ago is now becoming commonplace on the Au Sable, Manistee, St. Joseph and other wide-flowing Michigan steelhead streams.

Most of us guides use McKenzie River driftboats, a generic term nowadays for double-ended, rocker-bottomed boats about 16 feet long that resemble the seagoing New England dories used by Grand Banks cod fishermen. The center section rides in the water, and the prow and stern are turned up to crest out of the water. The oarsman sits in the middle and, using light oars (that usually turn over because they lack gunwale pins), holds the boat in a current by lightly backstroking. Once a driftboat is properly balanced and the oarsman has the hang of things, it is easy to propel and steer. A driftboat can turn on a dime, hold steady in a raging current and be easily maneuvered in white water.

These boats are important to the business of catching river steelhead because they allow the angler to get into the right position and stay there. We try to herd fish, literally, to the lower ends of holes, where they smash our lures out of simple aggression. Some of these fish, the feisty bucks in particular, can just about jerk your arm off. At least you think they can.

We use four rods to run digging plugs—Hot 'N Tots, Bug Plugs, Shad Raps, Deep-Diving River Runts and others—down through steelhead lies. For some reason, gold, metallic-green, chartreuse, and hot-orange lures work best. Sometimes red is good, too. Maybe steelhead are like bulls, easily provoked by red and other hot colors. I try to work my driftboat down and across the places where I know steelhead like to stack up, either to rest or to spawn. I work the water in sections, making sure that our lures cover every bit.

Working a driftboat properly, at least on the Michigan streams where I fish, is not unlike a well-played game of Pac-Man. There is only one difference—steelheading is more fun.

Dave Keene
Flint

19 NORTHPORT

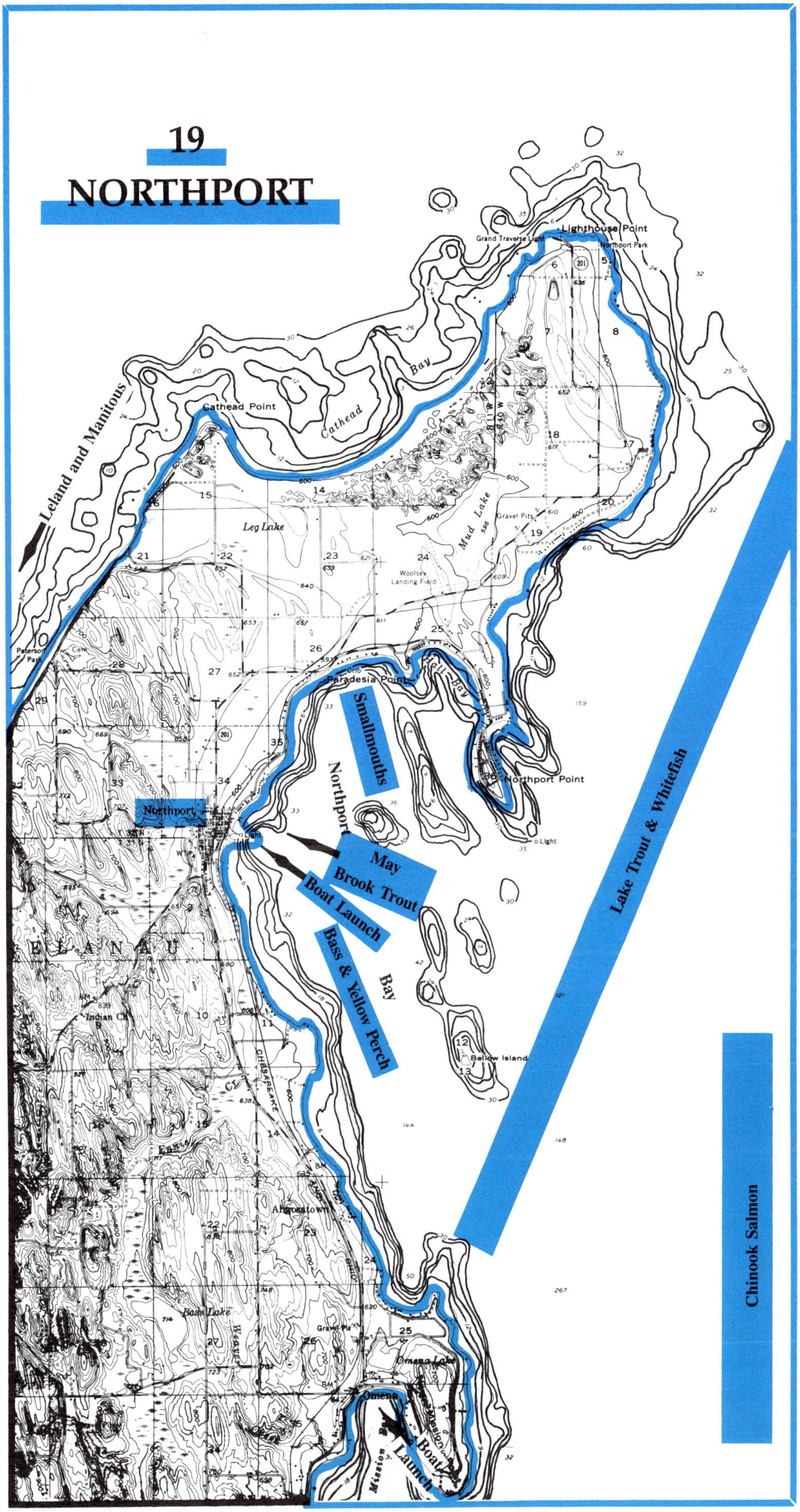

Grand Traverse Bay has fair to excellent fishing for a variety of species. — Michigan DNR photo —

20

GRAND TRAVERSE BAY

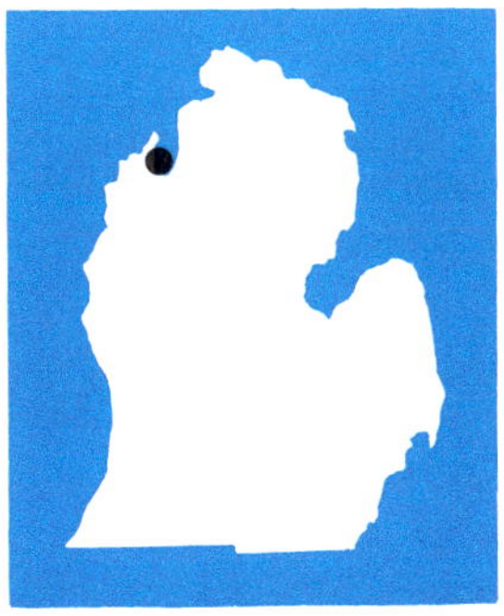

Although Grand Traverse Bay, in northwest Lower Michigan, has been hit hard by Indian gillnet fishermen, there remain good to excellent fishing opportunities for whitefish, yellow perch and brown trout. Sport anglers can also expect to catch smallmouth bass, northern pike, brook trout, steelhead, lake trout and Chinook salmon, with opportunities ranging from poor to very good depending upon time of year. The Grand Traverse Bay region is a major hub of the state's tourist industry, and visiting fishermen will find a host of accommodations. They will also discover some of Michigan's most scenic real estate—rolling wooded hills peppered with clean, clear lakes and a network of handsome streams, such as the Boardman River, that are tributary to Grand Traverse Bay.

The bay itself is split into two arms—both with good fishing opportunities—by the long finger-like Mission Peninsula. Traverse City proper and the inflowing Boardman River are located at the base of the West Arm, which also includes Greilickville, Suttons Bay and Northport (19). The East Arm, which contains depths to nearly 600 feet, features the small community of Acme at its lower end and Elk Rapids (21) about midway up the arm.

Fishing Schedule

SPRING

Ice, which usually doesn't form until February, often lingers until April. When it finally goes, many small-boat anglers gun the winter preservative from their outboards, break out planer boards, and sharpen hooks for brown trout. This *spring* breakup generally occurs first in the lower reaches of the East and West arms. Many of the small streams that freight spring runoff into Grand Traverse Bay host spawning smelt, and brown trout converge in shallow water off the tributaries to wax fat on the offerings. Most browns average 2-1/2 to four pounds, but there are six- and eight-pounders available, too.

Traverse City native Roy Olk is one of the best sport anglers on Grand Traverse Bay. For spring browns, Olk longlines a rod or two and also puts out a couple of planer boards. Hot lures are small Rebels or Rapalas in combinations of silver with black or blue. Roy targets 10-30 feet of water for a mile on each side of the Boardman River mouth in the West Arm and from Traverse City State Park to Deepwater Point in the East Arm.

The brown trout move offshore sometime in May when smelt complete spawning chores. Still available through summer and into the fall, browns, however, become an incidental species, and few anglers target them.

Spring steelheading centers at the Boardman River mouth (and upstream) and off Four Mile Road (just east of Traverse City State Park). Annual stockings of yearling fish occur at both locations. Shallow-water trollers rigged for brown trout and wading fishermen who cast spoons or roll spawn bags or wigglers in the river can get into steelhead to 10 pounds each.

May is also an excellent time to catch brook trout off the Boardman River and other creekmouths. Bowers Harbor, halfway up the Mission Peninsula on the West Arm side, is receiving annual stockings of brook trout and should grow into an exciting sport fishery. Best catching method is to spincast small spoons or spinners with gold or silver blades near structure. Brookies will also hit a wind-drifted or slow-trolled nightcrawler harness if the offering is small in size. Fish to four pounds each are available, but most will average one to two pounds and tape 15 to 18 inches in length.

The lake-trout opener on May 1 doesn't draw the interest of fishermen like it used to, but in spite of the heavy gillnetting that has occurred in recent years, there are sport-catching opportunities available. Lakers can be caught throughout the bay from depths of 50-150 feet through the combination of downrigger-trolled cowbells and P-Nuts or Wobble-Glos. Chartreuse, yellow, green and combinations of these three colors are productive. Another good spring tactic is to anchor and jig over a rocky bottom with a lead-head jig or a No. 5 or No. 7 Swedish Pimple and strip of sucker meat. This is the rated method for catching whitefish, too, which run from two to six pounds in size and which are widely sought by Grand Traverse Bay fishermen. Most boats with whitefish in the coolers also contain a lake trout or two (currently the limits are 12 and two respectively).

Perch are found throughout both arms and at all seasons. Two key locations include Bowers Harbor and along East Shore Road from its junction with M-72 to McKinley Road. In spring, try driftfishing or anchored jigging with wigglers, small minnows or worms pinned to bare hooks.

SUMMER

Summer sport remains consistent for lake trout and perch and improves tremendously for whitefish. By late June and throughout July, you can see flotillas of 30-50 boats each as jig fishermen concentrate over located schools of whitefish. Most rely upon light line (four- to eight-pound test) and jig Swedish Pimples with cut bait or wigglers pinned to a bare hook. They find bottom with the aid of a heavy slip sinker, then vigorously jig, occasionally lifting their bait a couple of feet and allowing it to flutter to bottom. Strikes usually occur on the drop.

In the West Arm, the best spots for whitefish are south of Lee Point, off the coal pile at Greilickville, 30-60 feet deep in front of the Boardman River (especially when mayflies are drifting down the river and into the bay), below Lookout Point off the Wysong Gravel Pit, at the entrance to Bowers Harbor, and between Neah-Ta-Wanta and Tucker points just outside the harbor.

East Arm whitefish hotspots in summer include 100-foot depths straight out from Acme, off Dock Road at Deepwater Point, and off Yuba.

Smallmouth-bass fishermen can get action in June, July and August by drifting nightcrawlers or two-inch shiners off drowned points and the rocky structure to 25 feet deep. Spawning smallies will also hit spinnerbaits, straight-line spinners and poppers in just about any color. Find rock-bottom areas from three to 12 feet deep, and either spincast from an anchored boat or wade from shore. A few northern pike are taken off the Boardman River mouth each summer by live-bait fishermen and trollers pulling red-and-white spoons or Flatfish in various colors.

Grand Traverse Bay has received experimental and sporadic salmon plants throughout the years. Coho stockings at Greilickville's Brewery Creek have been discontinued, but now it appears as though Chinooks will be released annually in the Boardman River. These fish should be available to West Arm trollers, beginning in July and lasting through September, as the fish move in stages to their natal release site (salmon are also caught in the East Arm. For catching details, see 21, Elk Rapids.). Dodgers and flies along with clean-running spoons and J-Plugs will interest kings cruising at 50-120 feet. Good colors to try on bright days are silver, alone or in combination with chartreuse, green, and blue. On darker days try dull orange, khaki, brown or black. When kings crowd the rivermouth in water under 50 feet, hot-fluorescent colors produce.

FALL

Fall fishing, therefore, is typically good for king salmon, and along with the shallow-water trollers, spoon tossers from the Traverse City pier can also score. Try 2/5- to 3/4-ounce K.O. Wobblers, Little Cleos and Krocodiles in combinations of silver with hot colors. Brown-trout and steelhead fishing also improve somewhat in fall shallows, and whitefish are again available, beginning in late October as they move to shoal-water areas under 50 feet deep to spawn. A good hotspot is the 35-foot-deep hole at the extreme southeast corner of the East Arm below Acme. Some fishermen also report catching ciscoes, or round whitefish, at this time, and perch become willing biters again.

WINTER

Winter anglers fish from open boats in December and most of January. When the arms freeze over, they then venture offshore up to several miles in search of whitefish (lake trout that are caught must be returned, as the season currently begins May 1 and ends August 15) and yellow perch. Winter perching is considered to be the best of the year by many Grand Traverse Bay anglers, who concentrate on 30-40 feet of water in the extreme southern portions of both arms. For whitefish, try any of the areas mentioned, but also keep an eye out for clusters of shanties and open-air fishermen as clues to local action. Ice fishermen also catch a few brown trout and steelhead.

Planting Records

Grand Traverse Bay is receiving ample stockings of hatchery-reared fish. West Arm releases include 300,000 spring fingerling Chinooks and 15,000 steelhead yearlings in the Boardman River, 60,000 lake-trout yearlings and 60,000 fall fingerling brown trout at Greilickville, and 10,000 brook-trout yearlings in Bowers Harbor. In the East Arm, the Elk River receives 10,000 steelhead yearlings, Cresswell gets 60,000 lake-trout yearlings, while Acme and Old Mission Harbor each receive 100,000 laker yearlings. Both steelhead (15,000 yearlings) and brown trout (54,000 fall fingerlings) are being planted off Four Mile Road between Traverse City and Acme.

All of the above figures are planned annual stockings by the DNR through at least 1990.

Facilities

The DNR maintains a harbor of refuge at Traverse City with the following services: transient accommodations, gasoline and diesel fuel, water, electricity, restrooms, shower facilities, holding-tank pump-out, night security and VHF-FM radio. The telephone number of the dock attendant is (616) 941-2317.

There is also a DNR harbor of refuge at Greilickville with seasonal accommodations only. Facilities include gasoline, pay-telephone station, water, electricity, restrooms, dock attendant, haul-out services and holding-tank pump-out. For Suttons Bay and Northport harbor facilities see 19 (Northport). Elk Rapids (21) lists harbor accommodations at that location.

There are several places to launch a boat in Grand Traverse Bay. In the West Arm, the DNR maintains a free, modern ramp at the end of Hill Top Rd. At Greilickville, the township of Elmwood charges a nominal fee for its excellent launch. Other free ramp facilities are located at Traverse City (city-owned) and Bowers Harbor (DNR-maintained).

East Arm launches include a couple of private ramps at Old Mission Harbor, a city-owned pad at Sunset Park, a municipal ramp in Acme, an Acme Township-owned ramp at Dock Road, and one at Yuba Road.

Further Information

Chambers of Commerce:

1. Traverse City Area Chamber of Commerce, 202 Grandview Parkway, Traverse City 49684; (616) 947-5075.
2. West Michigan Tourist Association, 136 Fulton E., Grand Rapids 49503; (616) 456-8557.

Bait & Tackle Shops:

1. Tackle Box, US-131 N., Acme 49610; (616) 938-1590.
2. Traverse Bay Tackle, 848 S. Memorial, Traverse City 49684; (616) 943-8380.

Charter Fishing:

1. Captain Kent Slaughter, c/o Scott Wills of Sail North, 13272 W. Bayshore Dr., Traverse City 49684; (616) 947-2260. 34-foot boat, *Aurora*.
2. Captain Bob Schlitts, 5277 Barney Rd., Traverse City 49684; (616) 947-7642 or 946-4949. 28-foot boat, *Beaker*.

Department of Natural Resources:

Two fisheries biologists work out of District Headquarters at 8015 S. US-131, Cadillac 49601; (616) 775-9727.

Coast Guard:

Charlevoix Station, (616) 547-2541 or 547-2565.

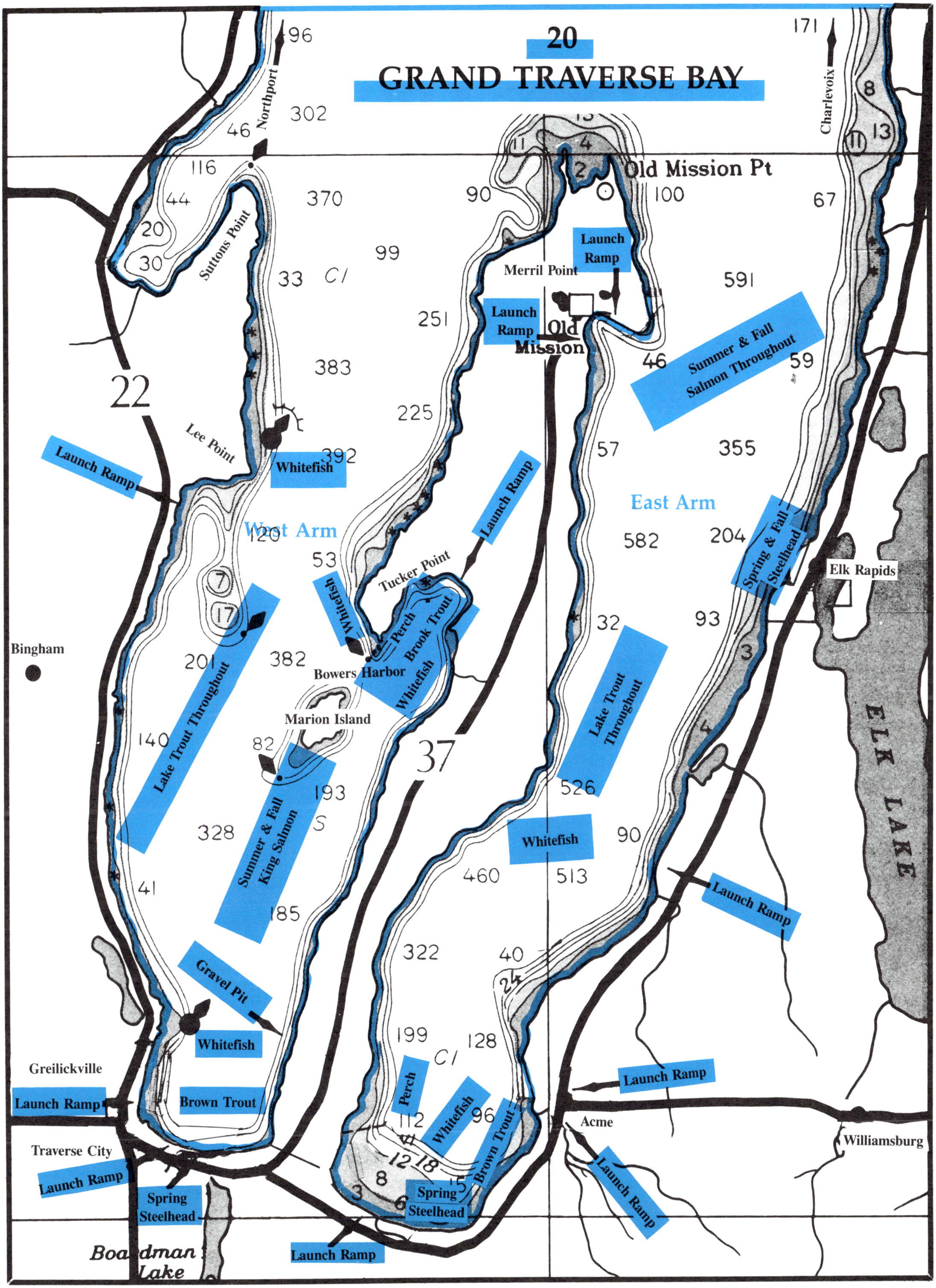
20
GRAND TRAVERSE BAY
Old Mission Pt
Northport
Suttons Point
Lee Point
Charlevoix
Launch Ramp
Merril Point
Old Mission
Summer & Fall Salmon Throughout
Whitefish
West Arm
East Arm
Tucker Point
Perch
Brook Trout
Bowers Harbor
Marion Island
Bingham
Lake Trout Throughout
Summer & Fall King Salmon
Spring & Fall Steelhead
Elk Rapids
ELK LAKE
Gravel Pit
Greilickville
Brown Trout
Traverse City
Spring Steelhead
Boardman Lake
Acme
Williamsburg
22
37

21
ELK RAPIDS

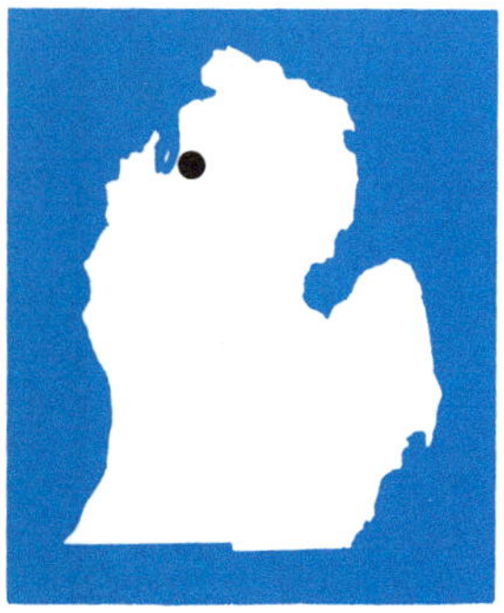

Elk Rapids, a resort community of 1,500 people, lies halfway along the East Arm of Grand Traverse Bay. This entire east shore of the bay is rocky and dangerous, a condition, however, that also makes for good fishing for lake trout and whitefish even though these species are targeted by commercial fishermen in Grand Traverse Bay. Breakwall and boat fishermen also catch good numbers of yellow perch and fair to good numbers of salmon, brown trout and steelhead.

Fishing Schedule

The earliest open-water fishing opportunities are for yellow perch, beginning each *spring* shortly after ice-out. Perch seem to be making a big comeback in Grand Traverse Bay, and by May 1, many anglers seek them in depths from 20-50 feet. Rated tactics include dunking worms and small minnows from the pier or lightly jigging minnows or wigglers pinned to two-hook perch spreaders off bottom in areas of strewn rock and other structure.

The trolling fleet typically takes to the East Arm on May 1, the lake-trout opener in Lake Michigan. According to charterboat-captain Bill Jarvis, lake-trout fishing remains good through the annual closure on August 15. Early spring trollers look for the warmest water possible (off the mouth of the Elk River and smaller streams flowing into the East Arm), then move to deep-water structure (from 50-150 feet deep), as spring merges into summer.

Jarvis runs Big Jon flashers ahead of P-Nuts in chartreuse, yellow or green. Spring rigging on Jarvis' 28-foot charterboat, the *Silver Hook*, includes four electric Big Jon downriggers and two outriggers with or without two planer boards. Side-rigged lures for steelhead and brown trout are blue-and-chrome Northport Nailers or small crankbaits in hot colors. About 75 percent of Jarvis' season-long catch is lake trout, with Chinook salmon, brown trout and steelhead constituting the remainder.

Summer fishing remains good for lake trout and improves for whitefish and Chinook salmon. In fact, the best time of year to catch the two- to five-pound whitefish is during the month of July. Then, drift fishermen and trollers chug Swedish Pimples, with or without cut bait or wigglers, in water that is 75-125 feet deep. The technique calls for using heavy sinkers and light line and being sure to work baits up and down off bottom. July and August is also the time that Chinook salmon, released at the Boardman River at Traverse City, begin staging in the bay preparatory to mounting spawning drives. Jarvis often replaces bottom-running cowbells/P-Nuts with Les Davis Herring Dodgers 14 inches ahead of trolling flies or silver squids.

Stacking of the attractor rigs with Northport Nailers or similar spoons run clean can often result in a mixed-bag catch. For example, last summer a father and his two sons, ages five and nine, went fishing with Jarvis and caught four lake trout, three kings that each weighed 20 or more pounds, and one brown trout. Bill said that experience was quite a thrill for the youngsters, who did all the catching.

In *fall*, fishing interest picks up again for yellow perch from the breakwalls and in the shallows and for steelhead and brown trout, also available to surf, pier and small-boat fishermen in the shallows. Spawn bags fished on bottom or small spoons and plugs trolled just under the surface produce the best action.

There are some excellent *winter* fishing opportunities in the East Arm for whitefish and yellow perch. Try hard-bottom areas in 50-75 feet of water for whitefish and 10- to 40-foot depths for yellow-bellies.

Planting Records

The DNR is currently stocking 10,000 Michigan steelhead yearlings in the Elk River and 60,000 lake-trout yearlings off Cresswell. Plans call for both releases to continue through at least 1990. For further information about Grand Traverse Bay plantings, see 20.

Facilities

The department of natural resources maintains a harbor of refuge with the following services: transient accommodations, gasoline, water, electricity, restrooms, shower facilities, holding-tank pump-out and VHF-FM radio. The telephone number of the dock attendant is (616) 264-9920. A modern boat-launch facility can accommodate all trailerable craft.

Further Information

Chambers of Commerce:

1. Elk Rapids Area Chamber of Commerce, P.O. Box 854, Elk Rapids 49629; (616) 264-8202.
2. West Michigan Tourist Association, 136 Fulton E., Grand Rapids 49503; (616) 456-8557.

21
ELK RAPIDS

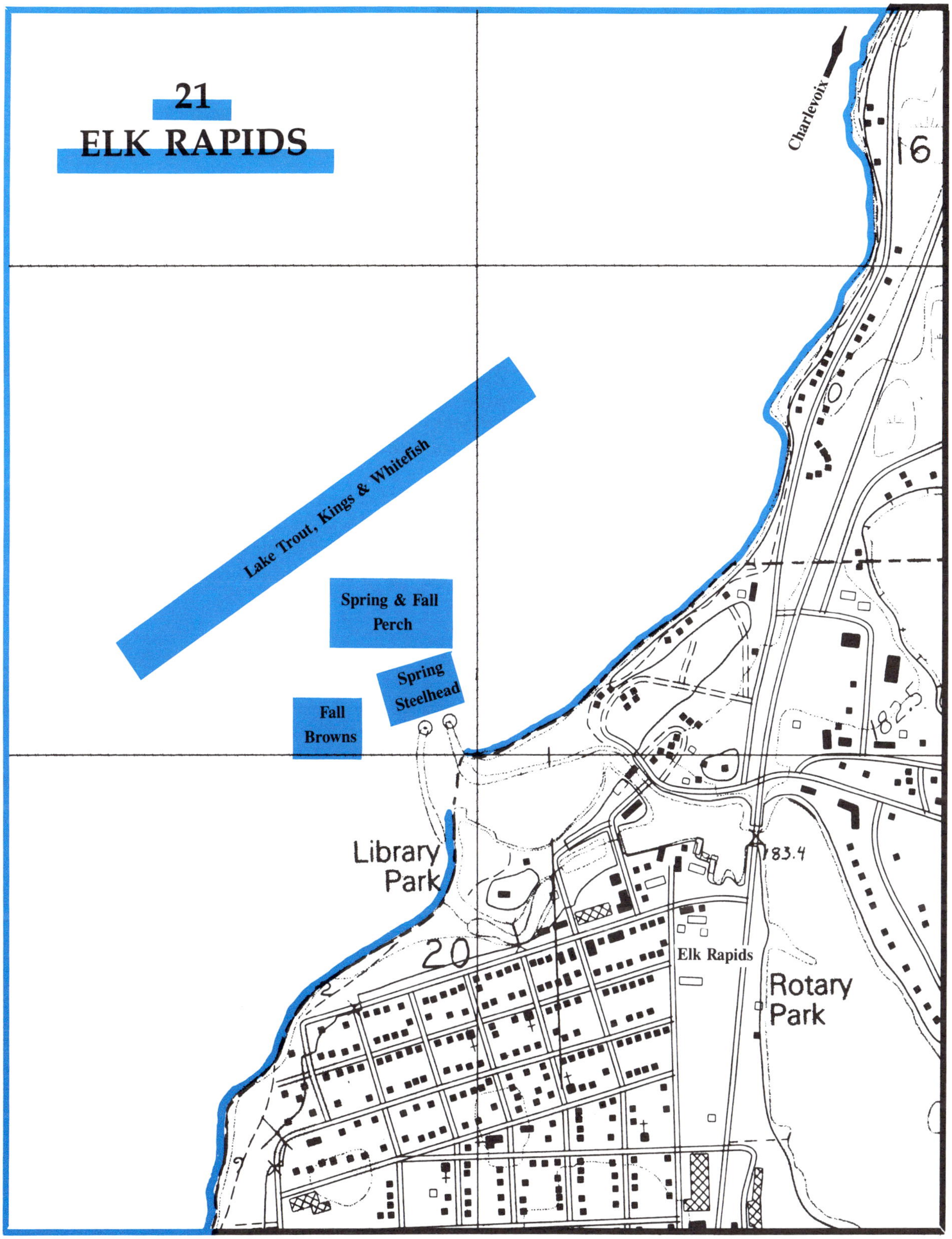

Bait & Tackle Shops:

Bait & Bobber, 111 Dexter, Elk Rapids 49629; (616) 264-4311.

Charter Fishing:

Captain Bill Jarvis, Pine Hollow Charters, 10354 S. Bayshore Dr., Elk Rapids 49629; (616) 264-9552. 28-foot Omega, *Silver Hook*.

Department of Natural Resources:

Two fisheries biologists work out of District Headquarters at 1732 W. M-32, Gaylord 49735; (517) 732-3541.

Coast Guard:

Charlevoix Station, (616) 547-2541 or 547-2565.

22
CHARLEVOIX

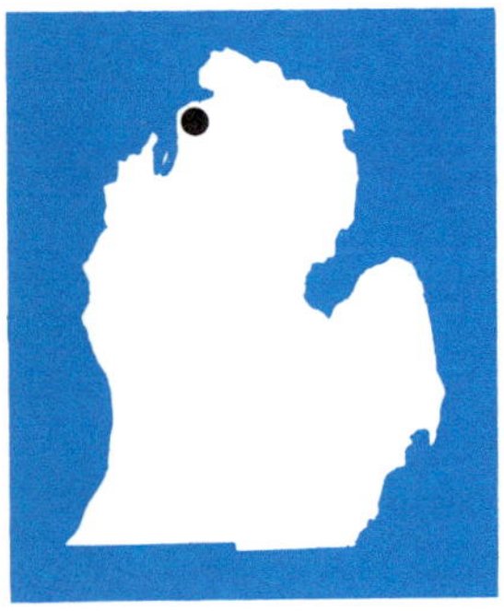

Although smelt numbers remain low in western Lake Superior, Lake Huron and Lake Michigan dippers report good spawning returns in recent springs. When smelt are running, fishermen get turned on for at least two reasons: (1) Many like to dip the good-eating silvery fish for the table and freezer. (2) Salmon and trout swarm to the shallows like barnyard pigeons to spilled grain.

Depending upon locale, spring smelt runs last from early April until early May, and in many spots the smelt are replaced by alewives, gizzard shad and lake emerald shiners that seek sandy-bottomed shallows to spawn. Salmon and trout don't discriminate—they move in an out of these shallows to scarf as many baitfish as their bellies can hold. In a single season between spring and fall, kings can add half their weight and cohos can double weights.

Many of the small streams in the Charlevoix area, namely from Nine Mile Point to Fisherman Island, receive smelt in spring. Trout and salmon that lurk in the shallows provide accessible sport for close-to-shore trollers and surf fishermen alike.

Fishing Schedule

After boating past the pierheads at Charlevoix, anglers will see these landmarks to the northeast: Big Rock Point, the Big Rock Nuclear Power Plant and Nine Mile Point. Soon after rounding the corner of Little Traverse Bay (23), they can see the cement plant stacks and the town of Petoskey, with Harbor Springs across the bay. The distance between Charlevoix and Petoskey is about 12 miles. To the southwest of the Charlevoix piers are the cement plant, South Point and Fisherman Island.

SPRING

Charlevoix trollers can target lake trout, salmon or brown trout from spring through fall or rig potluck and catch what they can. John Golomb, a brown-trout fishing ace from Saginaw, has been coming to Charlevoix in *spring* for many years. Ninety percent of his take is brown trout, with lake trout constituting the remainder. It is easy to see why Golomb catches very few salmon, upon considering his trolling methods. John slow-trolls ivory-colored Flatfish in early morning, switching to yellow Flatfish later in the day and sometimes to small spoons in evening. He also longlines Rapalas and runs homemade cowbells and sewn minnows behind dodgers when the artificials fail. The cowbells are 24- to 30-inch strings of three to five small clam-shaped blades in copper, brass or chrome. John prefers small gray shiners or smelt for bait in spring and lake emerald shiners in summer (see "How to Sew a Minnow," page 102, for sewing instructions.)

Golomb claims that the last week in April until the first week in June is prime time for catching browns. His 16-foot aluminum boat and 5-1/2 hp outboard allow him to slow-troll in the shallows where brown trout are apt to be feeding. Browns are super-wary fish, and that is why he patterns a zig-zag trolling course, no matter what lures he is pulling. Browns have a tendency to follow a straight-trolled lure but often will hit it when you "crack the whip." Not only do such sharp turns give a new action to lures, they also help eliminate boat shadow and disassociate lures with engine noise and prop chop.

"You have to know the area before you can expect to catch brown trout consistently," Golomb advises. He targets water from five feet to 40 feet deep and works areas of structure such as contour breaks near the cement plant and in the cove region where the short run of river from Lake Charlevoix comes gushing into the lake.

Spring trollers might also look to the Big Rock nuke plant for ice-out action for browns and salmon. Rapalas, Long A Bombers and Rebel Fastracs are good body baits to pull in spring from downriggers. Try brown-trout, chrome-and-green, black-and-silver, fire-tiger, and crawdad colors. Steelhead will hit these lures as well as hot-colored small crankbaits such as Fat Raps, Shad Raps, Willy's Worms and Hot Shots. Lakers and browns prefer the smaller cranks, too, along with small spoons (Krocodiles, Little Jewels, Dazzlers, Mainliners) and cowbells with P-Nuts, Spin-N-Glos, Tiny Tads or L'il Guys. Generally, best colors will be greens, yellows, chartreuse and combinations of those colors.

SUMMER

Summer sport can be fast for lake trout in depths of 50-feet-plus. Jack Duffy, a charterboat skipper out of Leland (18), makes an early summer run to the Charlevoix area each year to try for lake trout. "We fish tight to dropoffs between Charlevoix and Petoskey in 50-80 feet of water," Duffy says, "and run mostly chrome-bladed cowbells ahead of P-Nuts in chartreuse or green." Jack claims there are plenty of lakers from Fisherman Island to Petoskey but that the fish are small because Indian netters have picked off many of the bigger ones. "In a single pass one day here we took 12 lakers in 39 minutes," he said "but none was what you could call a lunker."

Many Charlevoix lake-trout trollers pull wire line with three-way swivels, cowbells and sewn minnows, too. Bluebacks (lake emerald shiners) are preferred bait for summertime lakers. Golomb remembers a summer day years ago when he caught a five-fish limit of lake trout (the limit is currently three) from 12 to 14 pounds each, using the wire-line tactic. His wife, meanwhile, was reading a book while she waited for John in their car. "I

22
CHARLEVOIX

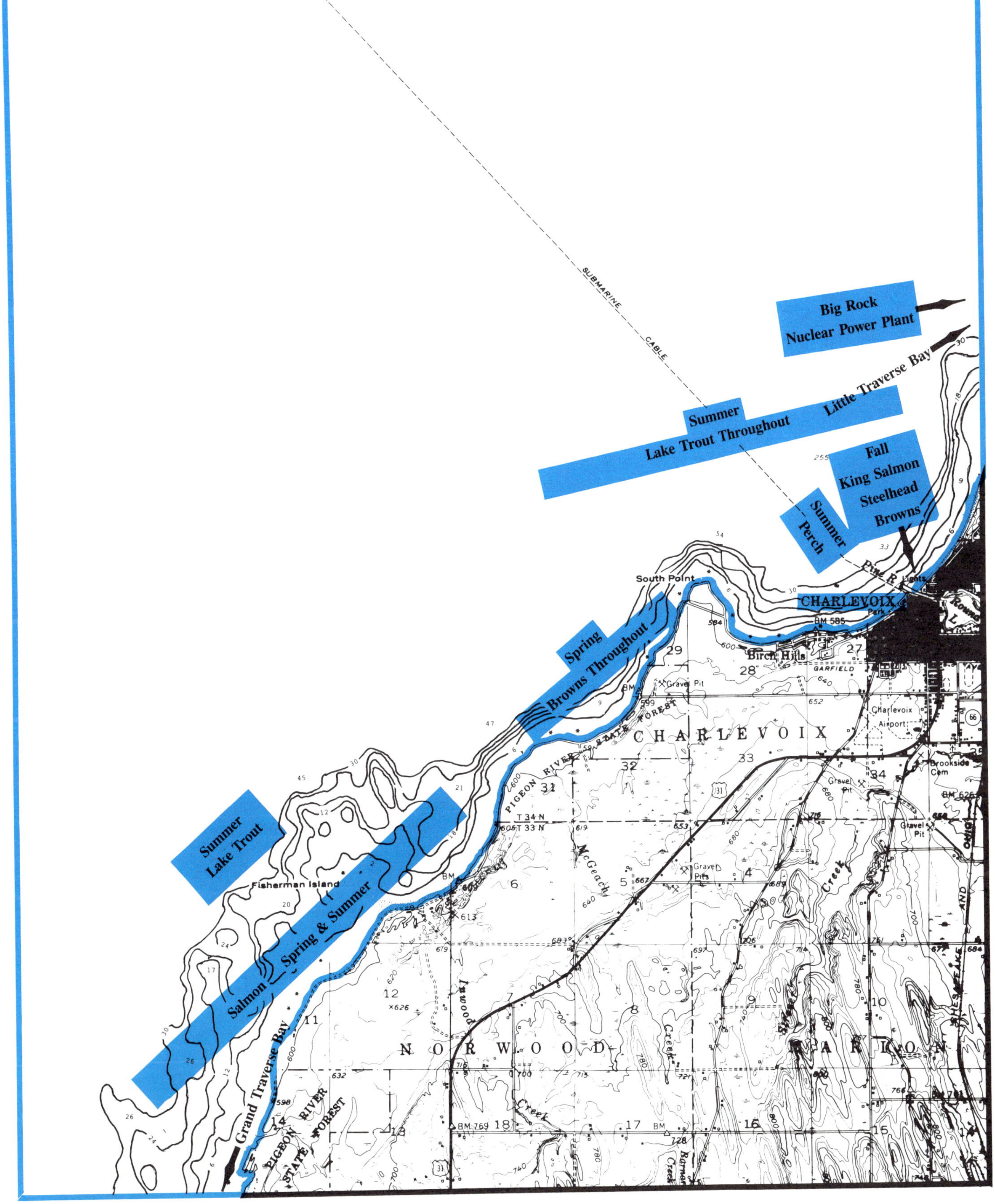

Lois Birchfield, left, came all the way from New York City to sample lake-trout fishing in Lake Michigan. She says she is coming back to try it again.

CHARLEVOIX (cont.)

came back and asked her to go back out with me so that we could catch five more," Golomb recalls. "We did, too."

The Charlevoix piers are popular with spoon-tossers and spawn-bag fishermen throughout the open-water fishing season. Anglers catch mostly brown trout and steelhead in spring, yellow perch in summer, and lake trout (which must be returned if caught after August 15) and salmon in early fall. In October and November, the piers serve up brown trout and steelhead.

Salmon fishing improves by late summer as kings begin schooling in preparation for September spawning drives. Fast-trolled J-Plugs or imitations of this popular lure are hot tickets in depths from 75 to 25 feet, depending on how close to shore the salmon are staging. In *fall* shallows, trollers switch over to Flatfish, Tadpollies and Ping-A-Ts and back off on trolling speed. Hot fluorescent colors in those plugs and big spoons get the nod, with trollers criss-crossing the pierheads and entering Lake Charlevoix itself. Brown-trout and steelhead fishing in fall is also good in the shallows, the lake, and the Boyne and Jordan rivers.

Winter fishing activities are limited to Lake Charlevoix, where ice anglers catch yellow perch, brown trout and lake trout as well as a few northern pike and steelhead.

Planting Records

The Charlevoix area has long received healthy stockings of hatchery-reared fish including lake trout, brown trout, steelhead and salmon. Annual DNR target releases through at least 1990 include 148,000 lake-trout yearlings at Charlevoix and 90,000 each at South Point and Fisherman Island, 300,000 Chinook fingerlings at Medusa Creek (location of cement plant), and 50,000 brown-trout fingerlings at Charlevoix. The Boyne and Jordan rivers will each receive 10,000 steelhead yearlings, and the Boyne River, which was stocked in 1984 with 9,000 Rogue River steelhead yearlings, will likely get additional summer-run steelhead as stocks become available.

Facilities

The DNR maintains a harbor of refuge with the following services: transient accommodations, gasoline and diesel fuel, water, electricity, restrooms, shower facilities and holding-tank pump-out. The telephone number of the harbor master is (616) 582-6597 (days) and 582-6611 (evenings and weekends).

There is a modern boat-launch facility here, too.

Further Information

Chambers of Commerce:

1. Charlevoix Chamber of Commerce, 408 Bridge St., Charlevoix 49720; (616) 547-2101.
2. West Michigan Tourist Association, 136 Fulton E., Grand Rapids 49503; (616) 456-8557.

Bait & Tackle Shops:

Ward Brothers Charter Boats, Inc., Foot of Antrim St., Charlevoix 49720; (616) 547-2371.

Charter Fishing:

1. Captain Mark White, Maple St., North Point, Charlevoix 49720; (616) 547-6618. 26-foot Stamos, *Eclipse*.
2. Captains Bernie Ward, Jr., Bernie Ward III, and Donald L. Ward, Ward Brothers Charter Boats, Inc., Foot of Antrim St., Charlevoix 49720; (616) 547-2371 or 547-2350. 31-foot Chris-Craft, *Sonny Don II*, 31-foot Bertram, *Russell Lyn*, 36-foot Chris-Craft, *My Fran II*.

Department of Natural Resources:

Two fisheries biologists work out of District Headquarters at 1732 W. M-32, Gaylord 49735; (517) 732-3541. The DNR also maintains the Charlevoix Fisheries Station, P.O. Box 205, Charlevoix 49720; (616) 547-2914.

Coast Guard:

Charlevoix Station, (616) 547-2541 or 547-2565.

How to Sew a Minnow

In spite of the huge array of Great Lakes trolling lures now on the market, natural bait remains a solid choice of many brown-trout and lake-trout fishermen. Rigging sewn minnows behind cowbells is a proven tactic that has worked for generations of fishermen. Here is how to do it:

Get a four- or five-inch suture needle from a local doctor, hospital or surgical supply house. Tie a small treble hook to one end of a 20-inch piece of 10- to 30-pound-test monofilament and pass the other end through the needle eye. Next, push the needle and mono into the side of the minnow just above and behind the anal vent. Bring the needle out the mouth and slide the shank of the treble hook into the fish through the entry hole. Draw tight and hook one barb of a second treble through the lower jaw of the minnow and out its mouth. Loop the mono a couple of times through the hook eye, draw tight, and tie it to the cowbell. That's all there is to it.

When trolled, the minnow will circle behind the cowbell to attract a hungry trout. Some anglers dampen the action of the bait by adding weight, such as a wrap sinker to the line just ahead of the bait.

You can sew just about any kind of minnow, but most fishermen who use the method prefer small smelt or grey shiners.

23

LITTLE TRAVERSE BAY

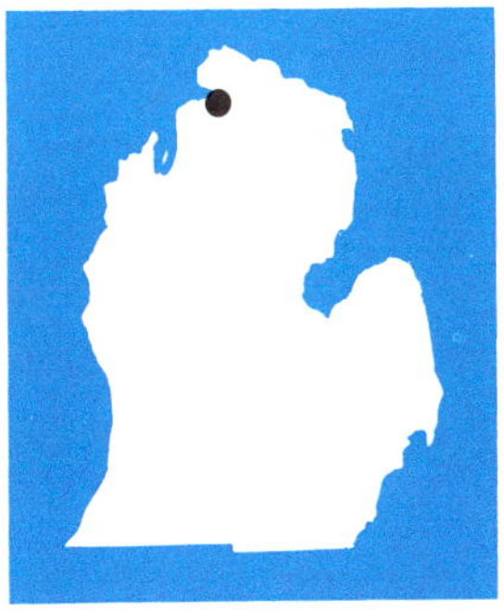

One of Michigan's most picturesque areas, the Little Traverse Bay region of northwest Lower Michigan beckons tourists from throughout the country. Many come to fish, as Ernest Hemingway no doubt did during his summer sojourns in Petoskey as a young man. And the fishing is good for several species, both in Little Traverse Bay—about six miles long by five miles wide, with a gradually sloping bottom that touches 190 feet deep—and at the mouth of the Bear River.

Another plus for fishermen: According to Reg Sharkey, a DNR retiree and area angler, "Local fishermen out of Petoskey are a friendly lot, willing to share their knowledge with visiting anglers."

Fishing Schedule

SPRING

SUMMER

In Little Traverse Bay there is something to catch year-round. In spring, surf anglers and river anglers cast spoons and spinners and stillfish spawn bags off creekmouths between Petoskey and Harbor Springs and in the Bear River outflow for steelhead and brown trout. Tannery Creek and other area freshets get a good smelt run most years and are also good areas for steelhead fishing. Rocky shoal waters near shore most likely host spawning smallmouth bass in late June and early July, although there are no reports of anyone fishing for bass. Winter fishermen catch lake trout, brown trout, steelhead/rainbows, ciscoes, northern pike and yellow perch. During the open-water season, trolling fishermen work the contour breaks and points for Chinook salmon and lake trout.

Here are how three of the best local anglers go after trout and salmon. Bobby Ryan of Conway scores on both Chinooks and lakers from early July through September but says that tricky currents in the area can make for tough trolling until anglers learn how to fish them. This is a developing fishery, with tactics and lures changing from season to season. For Ryan, best catching times for salmon are before daylight to 9 a.m. and from 6 p.m. until dark. Lakers are plentiful and fairly easy to catch, especially off Harbor Point as the (current) August 15 closure nears. Good lures for both salmon and trout are green Michigan Squids behind a dodger, as well as Northport Nailers and J-Plugs. Ryan relies on light-colored lures for rigs nearest the surface and darker choices for those that are deep.

Dick Seguin of Petoskey gets top king-salmon action for about six weeks after Labor Day. Best times are from early morning until 10 a.m. and from 4 p.m. until dark, with green P-Nuts in back of dodgers and long leads of 60-100 feet behind downrigger weights the payoff tactic. Lake trout love the combination, too. Seguin has learned that, in spring and early summer, lakers stack up along a reef off Nine Mile Point. Spring fishing with gold-and-white-belly No. 9 Rapalas will take brown trout on the Harbor Springs side of the bay,

Bud Knight, a retired DNR fisheries technician who lives north of Petoskey, likes matching wits with the wily brown trout in Little Traverse Bay. Best success occurs from ice-out until the shallows warm, usually in early June. Try the Harbor Springs side of the bay and run small light-colored Flatfish on a slow troll. Knight also reports success on kings with green-and-gold Northport Nailers, Finn Spoons and white Flatfish, usually by pulling these choices behind dodgers. Knight usually changes to darker baits in late afternoon as light intensity wanes and he also stresses the importance of trolling speed.

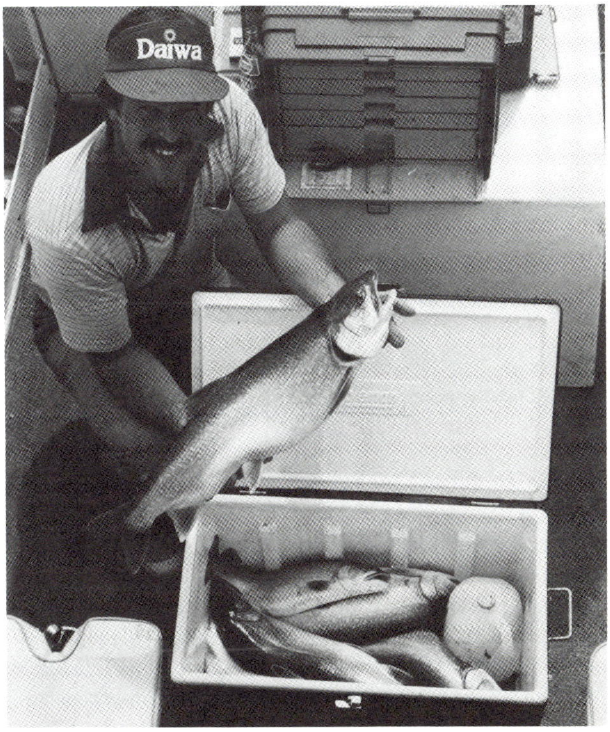

Lake trout, such as these fine specimens, are the mainstay of summer trolling in Little Traverse Bay. Chinooks, brown trout and steelhead/rainbows are also available.

Winter sport keys around good numbers of ciscoes in depths of 100 or more feet. Anglers catch these round whitefish on light tackle by jigging with Swedish Pimples or bait fishing with small minnows. Big fish of 17-18 inches and weighing two-pounds-plus are not uncommon. March is the best month to catch them. Cisco fishermen will also catch a few rainbows in the Harbor Springs harbor as well as brown trout and lake trout throughout the bay. Clusters of ice fishermen are often catching clues. There is some off- and on-again spearing sport for northern pike in shoal waters between Harbor Springs and Petoskey, plus, at times, portions of the bay serve up excellent catches of jumbo yellow perch. The water is clear and cold, however, and lacks any extensive areas of weed beds. Therefore, perch will likely be over structure.

Also in winter, the Bear River mouth and the Petoskey waterfront produce occasional hot action for brook trout. The DNR has released Assinica-strain brookies in the Bear during each of the past several years, and many of these fish drop back into Little Traverse Bay to provide a limited ice fishery. A bluegill rod rigged with light monofilament line, a bobber, and a waxworm or piece of nightcrawler will draw strikes.

Planting Records

In addition to brook trout, the Bear River is stocked with 10,000 steelhead yearlings each spring. Petoskey is getting 90,000 lake trout annually, a three-fold increase from planting rates of the early 1980s. Harbor Springs is the target for 15,000 rainbow-trout yearlings and 50,000 brown-trout fingerlings. All of these stockings are being made annually through at least 1990.

Facilities

The DNR maintains a harbor of refuge at Petoskey and another at Harbor Springs. Each has the following services: transient accommodations, gasoline, water, electricity, restrooms, shower facilites, holding-tank pump-out and VHF-FM radio. The telephone number of the Petoskey dock attendant is (616) 347-6691. For Harbor Springs information call (616) 526-5355.

A boat launch is located at Petoskey.

Further Information

Chambers of Commerce:

1. Petoskey Regional Chamber of Commerce, 401 E. Mitchell St., Petoskey 49770; (616) 347-4150.
2. West Michigan Tourist Association, 136 Fulton East, Grand Rapids 49503; (616) 456-8557.

Bait & Tackle Shops:

Young's Bait & Party Store, US-31 & M-68, Alanson; (616) 548-5286.

Charter Fishing:

None known. Refer to Charlevoix (22).

Department of Natural Resources:

Two fisheries biologists work out of District Headquarters at 1732 W. M-32, Gaylord 49735; (517) 732-3541.

Coast Guard:

Charlevoix Station, (616) 547-2541 or 547-2565.

Double Headers

Figuring the lake trout weighed only five pounds, I leaned over the side of our boat to let it go.

"Box him," Joe said.

"But he's number six, the limit fish."

"Box him," my partner said again. "Let's go try for salmon. Bet we can get some out there over those reefs in 80-100 feet of water."

I seriously doubted that. Everyone knows how salmon pull a Houdini in early summer and just plain disappear from their spring haunts near shore. Sure, they show up in those 10- to 100-foot depths again later in the summer. But in June and July, you'd have as much luck finding salmon as finding a bored kid at a Rolling Stones concert. Or so the big-lake trollers say.

But one thing I have learned in nearly 10 years of ramming around the Great Lakes while fishing with my buddy Joe is to trust his instincts. So we reefed lines and stripped them of cowbells and Wobble-Glos.

Then, while I wheeled Joe's boat due north from the entrance to White Lake in Lake Michigan, he began rigging for salmon action. A Silver Bullet (No. 5 silver J-Plug) went on the port out-down rod, and a No. 4 green ladderback J-Plug on the starboard pole. Next, Joe clipped a size-0 chrome-fluted Herring Dodger mated with a blue Sparkle Fly to one of the stern-end rods. The other got a big silver-and-green Loco spoon.

I cut back the throttle and watched while Joe's graph scratched out a bottom reading. The bottom was pancake-flat at 95 feet. Suddenly, it became slightly jagged, up and down between 92 and 100 feet. Structure.

"Crank 'er up just a scooch," he said, then, satisfied with boat speed, sent down his lure. I watched the cannonball's descent on the graph until it stopped at 90 feet. Next, my partner set the other out-down at 85 feet, the Dodger/Fly combo at 95 feet, and the clean-running Loco at 92 feet. Then he opened his box of Flutter Spoons—his favorite lure—and, choosing a clown-colored No. 44, clipped it to an eight-foot strip of mono. After adding a swivel-snap to the other end, he attached the offering to the mono on one of the stern setups, then flipped the potato-chip-thin spoon into our wake. It slid about halfway to the cannonball where a belly in the line held it. Rigging a second slider with a green Thumb King spoon, he sent that, too, over the side.

"Now, we wait," Joe said. "Any marks?" he asked.

But the lake seemed as sterile as an office watercooler. A half-hour passed, then an hour. I was growing sleepy from the monotonous whine of wind in our downrigger wires. Then a smudge mark like a dirty thumbprint shaped up at 65 feet. A dozen carets appeared around and below.

"There's our kings," I said. "Sixty-five down."

We caught three over the next hour, giving us double-headers on lakers and kings for the day. Many other Lake Michigan trollers do the same thing—go for lake trout in morning and kings in afternoon.

Eldon Thomas
Flint

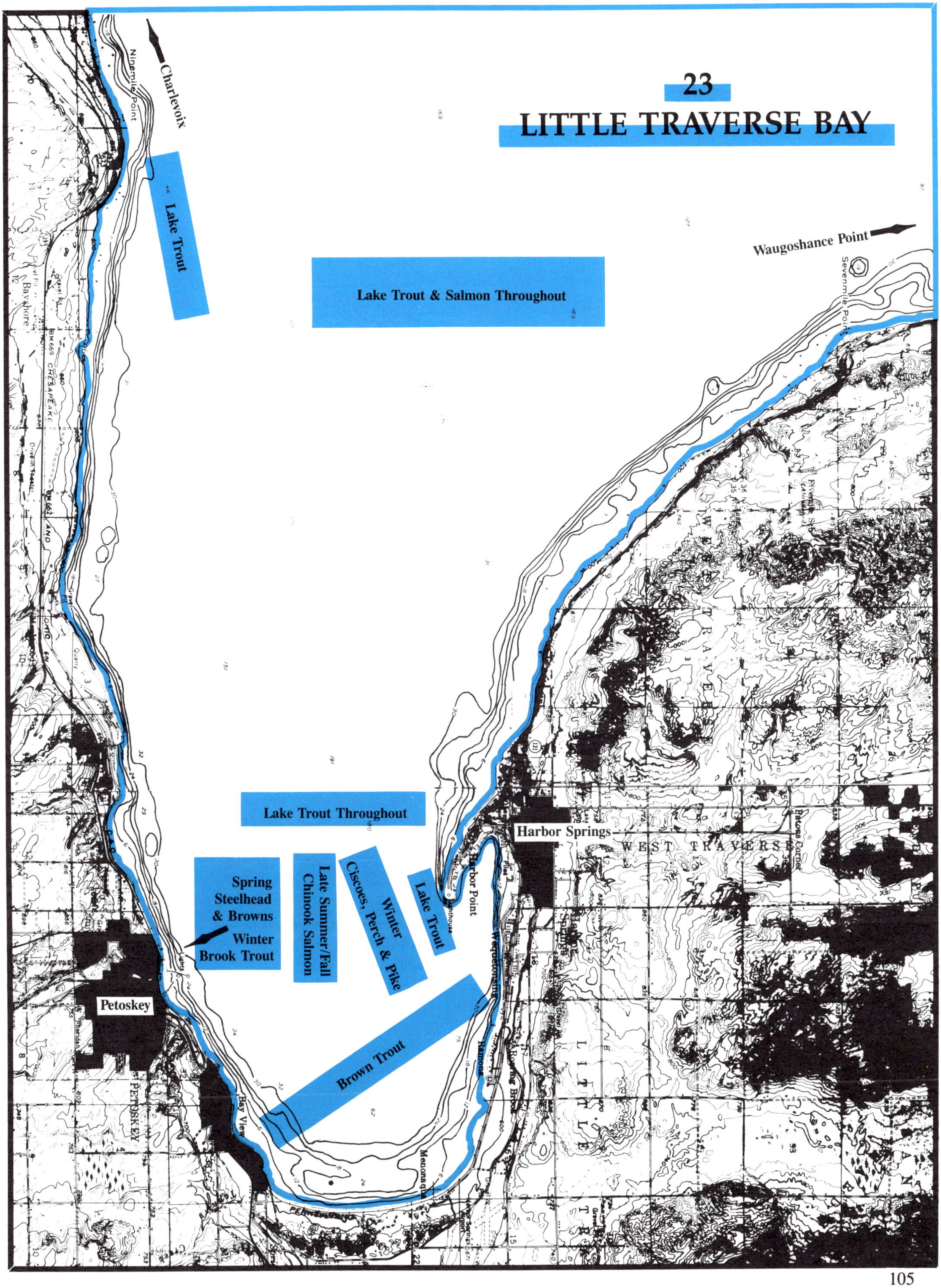
23
LITTLE TRAVERSE BAY
Charlevoix
Ninemile Point
Lake Trout
Lake Trout & Salmon Throughout
Waugoshance Point
Sevenmile Point
Bayshore
Lake Trout Throughout
Harbor Springs
WEST TRAVERSE
Harbor Point
Spring
Steelhead
& Browns
Winter
Brook Trout
Late Summer/Fall
Chinook Salmon
Winter
Ciscoes, Perch & Pike
Lake Trout
Petoskey
Brown Trout
Bay View
Menonaqua
Wequetonsing
Ramona
LITTLE

24
BEAVER ISLAND GROUP

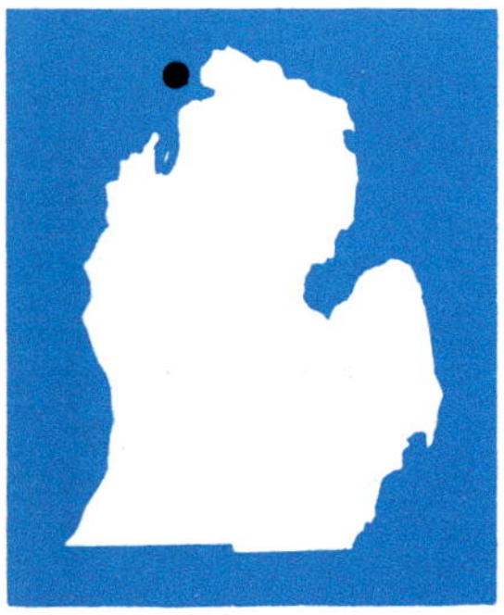

Located 32 miles from Charlevoix (22) in Lake Michigan, Beaver Island, along with Hog, High and Garden islands, offers some unusual fishing opportunities. Late spring, summer and early fall are the best times to come for smallmouth bass, northern pike, yellow perch and carp. (Yes, carp—and on a fly rod, no less!)

Some fishermen make the trek across always potentially dangerous Lake Michigan with a seaworthy boat and plenty of fuel. Others board the ferry that runs daily between Charlevoix and Beaver Island (contact the Beaver Island Navigation Company, 102 Bridge St., Charlevoix 49720; 616-547-2311.) There is also airplane service to the island from two Charlevoix carriers: Island Airways (616-547-2141 or 616-448-2458) and McPhillips Flying Service (616-547-2141). Those who fly generally hire a local fisherman to guide them or rent a boat on Beaver Island.

However you arrange your trip, it is best to go with at least one angler who is experienced with the area. According to Glen Sheppard, publisher of the *North Woods Call* and the key contact for this chapter, the shoal waters around the islands are extremely dangerous. An inexperienced navigator can easily take out the bottom of a boat. No craft less than 20 feet long should be considered, and it should be equipped with radio, depth sounder, charts, and have someone aboard who knows the area well. Sometimes certain bays can be entered only by wading and lining the boat over shoals. Unforecast storms and fog can hit in minutes, marooning anglers on these outer islands.

Fishing Schedule

Most people come here for smallmouth bass in late June and early July when smallies enter shoal waters to spawn. Most of the fishing activity centers along the western shore of Hog Island from Fisherman Bay to Baltimore Bay and on Garden Island in Jensen Harbor; Sturgeon, Manitou, and Northcutt bays; and Indian and Island harbors. There are many other areas along the rocky shorelines, in and among pencil reeds throughout, and pockets of spawning habitat near huge boulders and over drowned rock fields.

Rated fishing tactics include wading and spinfishing four- to six-pound-test line while casting crawdad-colored jigs, small Countdown Rapalas, Mister Twisters, Super Dupers, spinnerbaits and rubber worms. Fishing with jigs is especially effective when fishermen work them up and down over structure and in and out of weeds. Most bass hit as the lure drops and can be difficult to hook if your line is too slack or you are not sensitive to the strike.

Sheppard says that, in the late 1950s and through the mid-1960s, it was not uncommon to catch and release as many one- to three-pound smallmouths (and some to five pounds) as your arm could stand. But smallmouth bass are easily overfished when too many anglers target them, and that is what has occurred in the Beaver Island group. Publicity brought literally hundreds of fishermen each summer by the early 1970s. ("I counted at least 100 in one small Hog Island Bay about 10 years ago," Sheppard said.).

The smallmouth ecosytem is a fragile one, due to changing water temperatures and depths during spawning. Wind changes can alter water temperatures in the Great Lakes by five or 10 degrees in only a couple of hours. Sheppard, who has been fishing the area for some 30 years, theorizes that this condition sends bass off beds and, if the scenario repeats itself often enough, can ruin a year's entire hatch.

Although fishing here is still fair to good, most smallies now are barely legal or sub-legal in size. We'd like to be able to report fantastic catches of lunker bronzebacks, but facts are facts, and the truth is that smallmouth aficionados will catch larger fish, if not more fish, from nearby mainland waters like Lake Charlevoix and the Intermediate Lakes.

Spring fishing for yellow perch can be very good in the bays around Hog and Garden islands. Use wigglers, minnows or worms. Bigger fish will also hit small Mepps spinners slowly retrieved. A good place to troll for northerns is over shoal water between the two islands, in Island Harbor and Northcutt Bay, and in Beaver Island Harbor. Rapalas and spoons (Dardevles, Kush Spoons, Red Eyes) produce best, with red and white or jack of diamonds two solid color combinations to try.

Big spawning carp, which show up in the clear waters of Fisherman Bay and in Island Harbor, will take surface flies as well as bait fished along bottom.

Beaver Island Harbor used to support a well-known perch fishery, but nets and an alewife invasion dealt it a double blow years ago. It started to come back, but Indian gillnetters have been cutting into gains. The Indians have also been catching lake trout from reefs all around Beaver Island, and there is an undeveloped sport fishery for anyone wanting to try it.

Planting Records

There are no stockings of hatchery-reared fish in the Beaver Island group.

Facilities

The DNR maintains a harbor of refuge at the north end of

24
BEAVER ISLAND GROUP

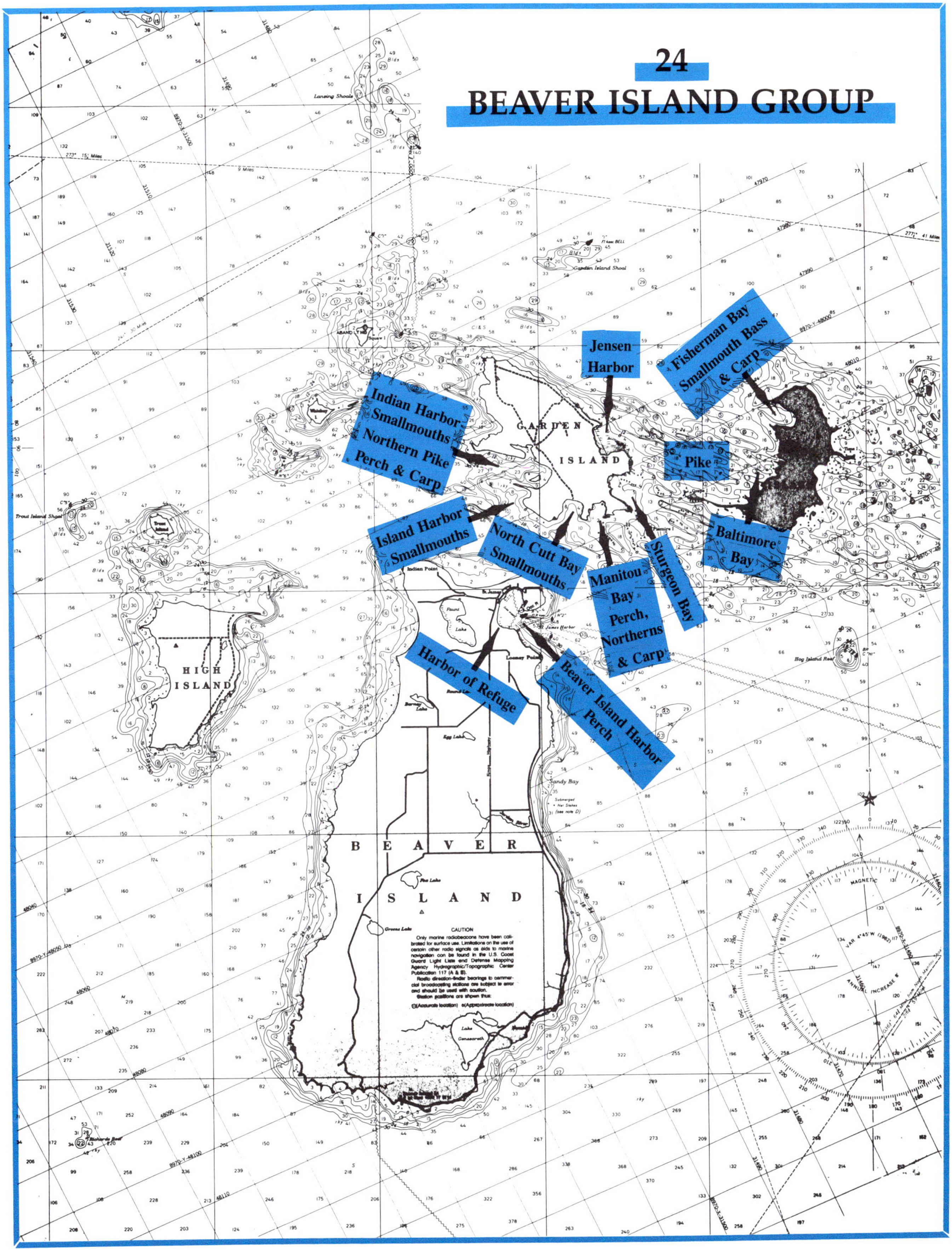

Beaver Island with the following services: transient accommodations, gasoline, water, electricity, restrooms, shower facilities, holding-tank pump-out and VHF-FM radio. The telephone number of the dock attendant is (616) 448-2252.

Further Information

Chambers of Commerce:

West Michigan Tourist Association, 136 Fulton East, Grand Rapids 49503; (616) 456-8557.

Bait & Tackle Shops:

None known. Refer to Charlevoix (22) and secure tackle needs before leaving the mainland.

Charter Fishing:

None known. For current information on possible guide service, contact Dan Higdon, Island Rentals, St. James 49782; (616) 448-2266. Another source is the Erin Motel in St. James, (616) 448-2240. Higdon has boats and motors for rent.

Bays in the Beaver Island group yield northern pike from small fish, like the one in this photo, to lunkers.

Department of Natural Resources:

Two fisheries biologists work out of District Headquarters at 1732 W. M-32, Gaylord 49735; (517) 732-3541.

Coast Guard:

Charlevoix Station, (616) 547-2541 or 547-2565.

Make Mine a Smallmouth

It was Roger Blankenship's turn to cast. I held the canoe steady with my wide stern-end paddle shoved into the gravel bottom, while the clear waters of the Jordan River gurgled around it.

"The bass splashed right next to that rock," Roger said, pointing with his baitcasting rod as he flung a small, brightly colored spinner on target. The gold-bladed lure sliced the surface, and instantly a hungry fish socked it.

"He's on!" my partner squealed and set the hooks with a deft snap of his wrist. "And he's a fighter, too!" The smallmouth jumped twice, spraying water as it tried to toss the hooks. Then it arrowed for the opposite bank, stripping line from Roger's ultralight reel with a whine. Roger kept his rod tip up so the bass could thrash against its strength. Twice more the fiesty battler broke water, then made short bids for freedom while a tight line creased the water surface. Roger wore down the scrapper in a couple of more minutes, and the chunky bass swirled topwater, gills pulsating, next to our canoe.

Leaning over, Roger grabbed the fish by its lower jaw, then whipped aboard three pounds of squirming bass. I opened a spare clip on our stringer so he could add it to two smaller fish. Then we drifted downstream toward the South Arm of Lake Charlevoix and more action.

Smallmouth bass are an occasional enigma. In some places in Michigan they are sometimes overfished—like Waugoshance Point (25) or the Beaver Island group—but in other spots, especially rivers throughout the state, they are often overlooked.

But why mess with smallmouths anyway? Well, for several reasons. First, smallies are our toughest-fighting warm-water gamefish species. They smash lures and live bait with gusto, spend about half their battle time in midair, and yet still come to the net grudgingly after giving 110 percent. Some anglers say that the smallmouth bass, or "bronzeback" as admirers call him, fights like a steelhead and, ounce for ounce, battles better than a steelhead.

Smallmouth bass are "page one" in my book.

Jack Warner
Genesee

25
WAUGOSHANCE POINT

Some 12,000 years ago, the last of many mile-high walls of ice inched its way from the north. These glaciers were polar ice caps out of control. They ground and gouged their way down through the Great Lakes region, scooping out basins for the five inland seas. Upon retreating, they formed kettle holes which would become inland lakes and left low mountain backbones and ridges of gravel called eskers. In the Great Lakes themselves, these abandonments included islands of rock and drowned reefs, house-size boulders, and points.

You can see the work of the powerful icefields throughout the state, but nowhere is the geologic evidence stronger than in northwest lower Michigan. In the rolling hardwood-hills country of Antrim, Charlevoix and Emmet counties, for example, the deep lakes have a north-to-south orientation. Lying along a similar axis are dozens of drumlins—streamlined hills of glacial till from one- to two-miles long.

Further proof of elemental carving is the Waugoshance Point region of northwest Emmet County. There, a fantastic arrangement of shoal-water reefs forms a bridge from the mainland 30 miles into Lake Michigan to the Beaver Island group. These rocky shoals are a pastureland for smallmouth bass and other fish.

Fishing Schedule

Smallmouth bass attract wading fishermen as well as boat anglers to Waugoshance Point from mid-June until mid-July. Here they find the spawning bronzebacks in water from two to five feet deep.

The fishery, however, has dropped off in recent years; most smallmouths run one to 1-1/2 pounds, and many are sub-legal in size. The main reason is that water temperature (68 degrees F.) and depth must be right for spawning; both can change abruptly in this region, so sometimes the hatch is poor. Too much fishing pressure can also hurt smallmouth bass anywhere in the Great Lakes, and this area has been heavily targeted in the past. But the potential for improved fishing is always there.

Techniques call for casting small spinnerbaits, spinners, Mister Twisters and other jigs, or small surface poppers to smallmouth lairs. Depending upon light availability and water temperature, color may or may not be critical, but good ones to try include black, yellow, white, and chartreuse. The nest-protecting males, in particular, will rush lures. Try casting to the shaded side of rocks, easy enough to see in the clear, shallow water. You may also spot spawning beds—crater-like depressions the size of dinner plates—with females over the nest and males hovering nearby.

Boat anglers can spincast the same lures or flyfish with small poppers, rubber spiders, dry flies or even live bait such as wigglers and mayflies. The shallow waters can be extremely dangerous to the uninitiated boater, however, so it is best to fish this area a time or two with someone experienced and even then to proceed with caution.

The best smallmouth action occurs along the point and around Temperance and Waugoshance islands.

Further out in the freighter channel (marked by buoys) and the Grays Reef, Middle, Vienna and East shoals areas might be good

Smallmouth bass provide early summer sport for anglers at Waugoshance Point.

spots to troll for lake trout and transient salmon in summer. However, until you learn the jagged bottom, you will likely lose some tackle. Strings of cowbells ahead of sewn minnows or small spoons (Andy Reekers, Chargers, No. 88 Sutton Spoons) or plugs (Tiny Tads, Fire Plugs, Wobble-Glos) would be best choices. Also consider chrome dodgers with these same lures or trolling flies (Sparkle Flies, Jon's Flies, Michigan Squids), then stack a couple of lines with spoons for salmon. I know of no one actually trolling the area for trout and salmon, but it could be a sleeper and deserves a second look.

The reefs, along with Sturgeon Bay, produce fair to good yellow-perch fishing. Best bets would be to drift with worms or minnows or anchor and lightly jig minnows, wigglers or small crayfish off bottom. Sporadic action occurs from spring though fall, and there is some opportunity for ice fishermen when Sturgeon Bay freezes over. A few northern pike are also caught year-round, and area streams support occasional runs of smelt.

Preferred Temperatures

Great Lakes fish have preferred temperatures that vary according to the species. Currents, along with wind and wave action and seasonal changes, serve to give temperature a gypsy personality—here today, gone tomorrow, back the next day. While finding key temperatures for the fish you are seeking does not guarantee that you will catch any, it is the place to start looking. Temperature preferences (in degrees F.) for the main Great Lakes species are:

Bluegills—64-70
Brown Trout—65-75
Chinook salmon—50-58
Coho salmon—50-58
Lake Trout—45-55
Largemouth Bass—75-80
Muskellunge—65-75
Northern Pike—65-75
Rock Bass—55-60
Smallmouth Bass—68-70
Steelhead/Rainbows—58-62
Walleyes—65-68
Yellow Perch—66-70

Planting Records

There are no releases of hatchery-reared fish in this area.

Facilities

A boat launch is located at the north end of Sturgeon Bay off Lakeview Road. The only accommodations in the area are at Wilderness State Park (which includes Waugoshance Point). Those entering the park with vehicles must have a valid state parks sticker affixed to the windshield. The state rents several trailside and frontier cabins, and there is camping allowed in the park. For information and cabin-rental reservations, contact the Wilderness State Park Manager, P.O. Box 380, Carp Lake 49718; (616) 456-5381.

Further Information

Chambers of Commerce:

West Michigan Tourist Association, 136 Fulton East, Grand Rapids 49503; (616) 456-8557.

Bait & Tackle Shops:

None known.

Charter Fishing:

None known.

Department of Natural Resources:

Two fisheries biologists work out of District Headquarters at 1732 W. M-32, Gaylord 49735; (517) 732-3541.

Coast Guard:

Charlevoix Station, (616) 547-2541 or 547-2565.

25
WAUGOSHANCE POINT

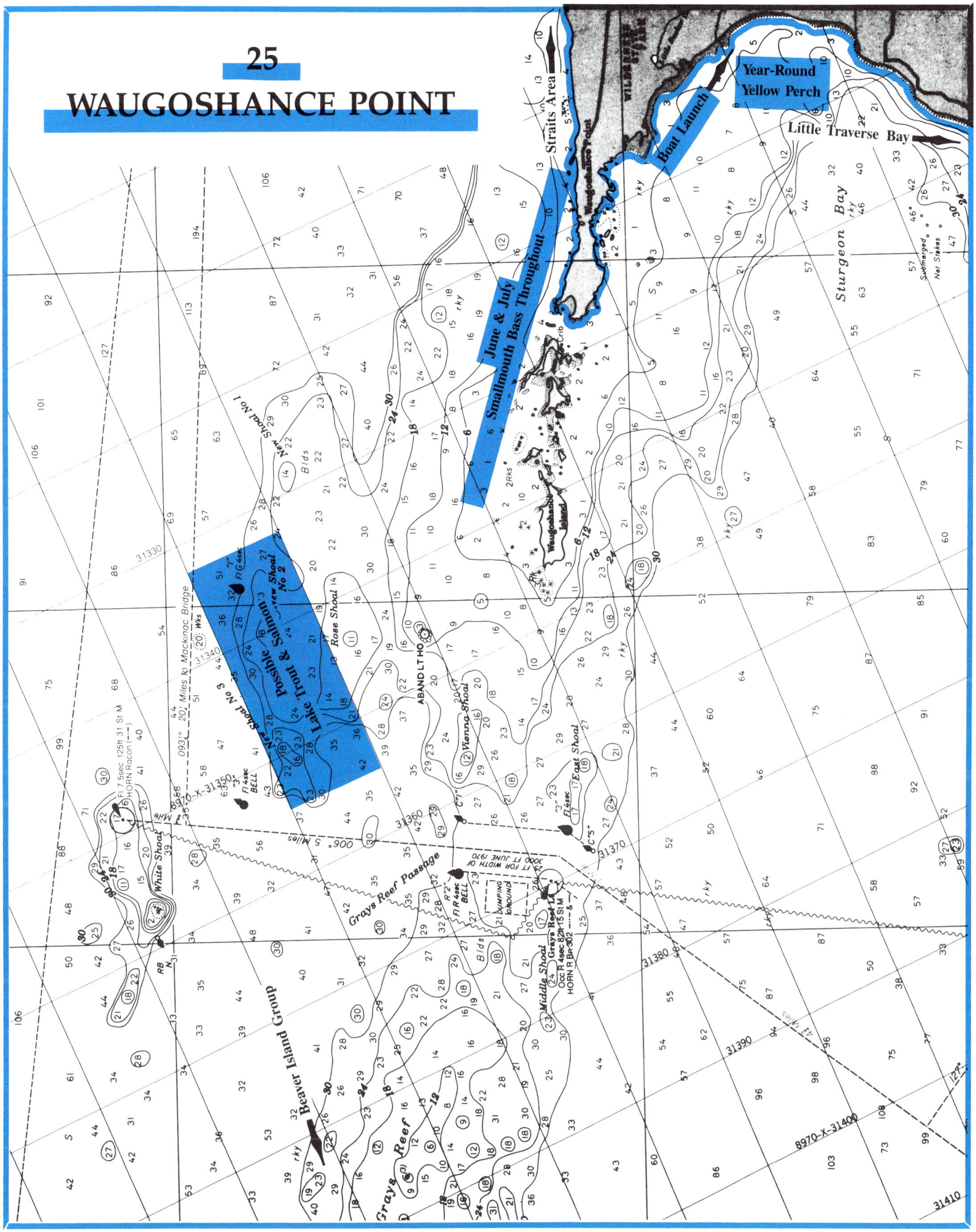

26
STRAITS AREA

"There's an awfully lot of water out here and very few fishermen," says Ross Nave, the only charterboat skipper I know of in the Straits of Mackinac area. It is not uncommon to see more freighters than trolling boats in the area.

There are some reasons for this: (1) Indian gillnetting in the region, which has reduced the populations of some species and caused problems with net tangles, (2) crosswinds that create trouble for small boats caught on the open lake, (3) lack of sport fishermen with enough experience to handle the area's unusual conditions, and (4) general lack of awareness of the abundance of good fishing in this area.

In an effort to promote the area, the first Budweiser Straits of Mackinac Fishing Festival was held September 7-30, 1984. Prizes worth $6,000 were awarded for 11 species of fish.

Rocky reefs; a smattering of islands including Mackinac, Round, and St. Martins; hefty DNR fish plants; and facilities such as launch sites and protected harbors are reasons that fishermen *should* consider the Straits area. One thing is certain—they will experience little competition.

Fishing Schedule

SPRING

Spring action occurs in April and May with an influx of yellow perch off the Mackinaw City and St. Ignace piers. These areas as well as stream mouths along the shores of both peninsulas produce some Chinook salmon, steelhead, brown trout and lake trout for the few that seek them. Surf casters can take these silvery fish on heavy spoons featuring silver with bright colors.

The Brevort River, just west of the Straits, has been stocked with steelheads and should produce good opportunities both in the river and at the mouth. The nearby Cut River hosts some naturally reproduced steelheads.

Smelt dippers also enjoy occasional spring action as the silvery spawners invade small streams. It is not uncommon for smelters to have lonely beach strands to themselves. The Brevort and Cut rivers, again, are good places to try.

A few trollers go after spring trout and salmon in the shallows. Ross Nave works the shoals from Forty Mile Point to Mackinac Island. His spring catch consists of 80 percent lake trout, with the remaining 20 percent made up of a few browns, steelhead and salmon. Nave runs homemade dual planer boards, stacking up to five lines per ski, 20 feet apart, with the help of shower-curtain rings. He uses silver-and-black and gold-and-black Rapalas as well as Stinger spoons in chartreuse or green. Shallow-set downriggers and long-set flatlines also produce.

SUMMER

Lakers go deeper in *summer*, so anglers often have to put lures close to bottom in 75-125 feet of water. Attractors rigged with small spoons or plugs are hot choices, especially in chrome and combinations of blue, green, and chartreuse. Those who stack laker setups with flake-thin spoons can pick up kings and pinks, too.

Nave usually switches over from the lethargic lakers by mid-June, when salmon show up. Besides 10- to 20-pound kings, the northern lake was full of pink salmon during the 1985 trolling season. Chartreuse spoons were hot for kings; chrome got the okay from pinks. Nave mixes in Stingers with Northport Nailers when hunting salmon.

Louis Colegrove, a friend and fellow sport angler from St. Ignace, reports that nearby Moran Bay produces Chinook salmon in summer and fall. Louis advises running lures 50-80 feet behind the boat and trolling at medium speeds through 25-35 feet of water. Hot lures are Nailers in chartreuse, blue stripe on silver, and gold stripe on black. Fall tactics involve casting glow-in-the-dark Ping-A-Ts, luminescent Krocodiles, and 3/4-ounce Little Cleos.

In addition to the salmonids, summer produces a smorgasbord of other fish. Boat anglers catch walleyes, smallmouths, northern pike, whitefish, cisco, menominee, perch and herring. For catching tactics, see 83 (St. Martin Bay).

The annual mayfly hatch—sometimes phenomenal in scope—that comes off over reefs each year from late June through early August is the big reason that herring infest lake shallows. Hatches generally begin in waters of the eastern Upper Peninsula and progress westerly. As I walked the shores of Mackinac Island one summer evening a couple of years ago, I watched thousands of mayflies take to the air. Trout and herring were slurping down as many as they could. Sadly, I had no fishing equipment along.

FALL

Fall sends salmon to the shallows again, and now that the DNR has established annual releases at St. Ignace, look for even better August and September sport to develop there. The pinks, of course, sustain themselves through natural reproduction. Nearly any stream with a decent current and bedding gravel will host the little spawners from mid-September into October. Once in the streams, pinks hit tiny spinners and yarn flies.

WINTER

Winter fishing keys on northern-pike spearing and tip-up fishing in the many bays and coves of the Straits area. Yellow perch are a big draw, too, although some years fishing may be poor, especially for the exciting jumbos. But when the big slabs are in, such as at Epoufette Bay, ice men get fast sport on wigglers pinned to Russian Hooks and to teardrops.

26 STRAITS AREA

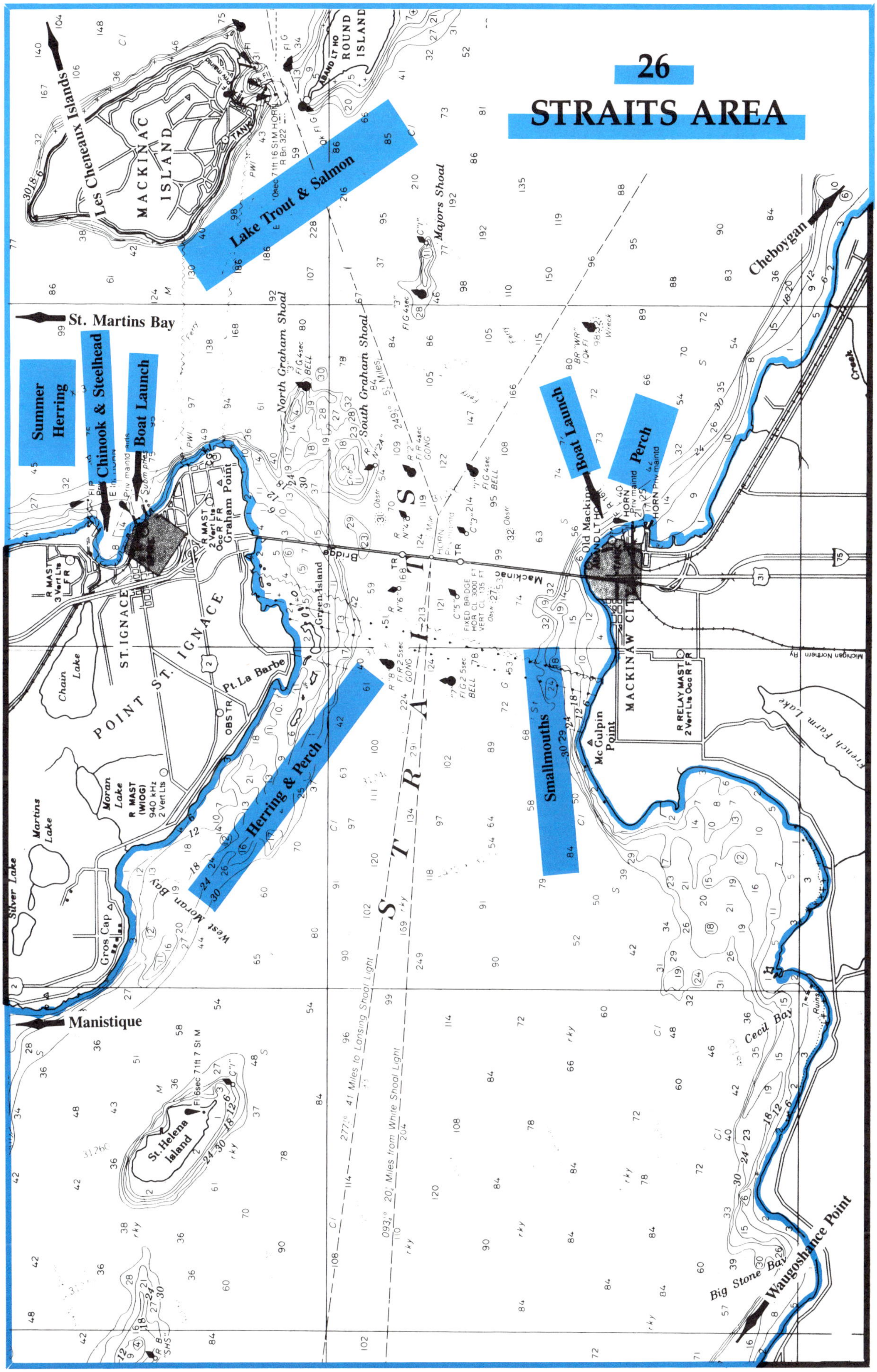

Planting Records

A release of 100,000 Chinook salmon fingerlings was first made at St. Ignace in 1984, and the DNR plans additional annual plants of that size through 1990. Small fish should be available in 1985, with the first returns of mature fish occurring in 1987.

Also at St. Ignace, each year for the next five years the DNR expects to release 30,000 fingerling lake trout. In the future, the DNR plans to target Middle Entrance Reef, along with St. Ignace, for laker releases. Round Island Shoal received 100,000 fall fingerling lake trout in 1981 and 1983.

The Brevort River, just west of the Straits, has been stocked with 10,000 yearling steelheads. Plantings will continue at that rate until 1990.

Facilities

A two-lane city-owned ramp awaits boaters at Mackinaw City, and a DNR two-lane cement ramp is available at St. Ignace.

Three ports of refuge serve the area. At Mackinaw City, transient accommodations, gasoline and diesel fuel, water, electricity, restrooms, shower facilities, sewage pump-out and haul-out facilities, VHF-FM radio and a dock attendant are available services. Call (616) 436-5269 for information.

Across the Straits at St. Ignace, the DNR operates a small harbor with these services: transient accommodations, gasoline, water, electricity, restrooms, shower facilities, dock attendant, holding-tank pump-out and VHF-FM radio. The telephone number is (906) 643-8131.

On Mackinac Island, boaters will find transient accommodations, gasoline and diesel fuel, water, electricity, restrooms, a dock attendant, holding-tank pump-out and VHF-FM radio. For further details call (906) 847-3561. There is room for 100 boats.

Further Information

Chambers of Commerce:

1. Greater Mackinaw City Chamber of Commerce, Box 475, Mackinaw City 49701; (616) 436-5574.
2. St. Ignace Area Chamber of Commerce, South State St., St. Ignace 49781 (906) 643-8317.

Bait & Tackle Shops:

1. Northern Michigan Outdoor Supply, 838 N. State, St. Ignace 49781; (906) 643-7481.
2. Ace Hardware, 7 S. State St., St. Ignace 49781; (906) 643-7721.

Charter Fishing:

Captain Ross Nave, Rt. 2 Milligan Creek Trail, Onaway 49765; (517) 733-8585. 25-foot Imp, *Moonshiner*.

Department of Natural Resources:

A fisheries biologist works out of District Headquarters at 1732 W. M-32, Gaylord 49735; (517) 732-3541. Another works out of the Indian River Field Office, 6984 M-68, Indian River 49749; (616) 238-9313. The St. Ignace area is served by two fisheries biologists from District Headquarters at 309 W. McMillan Ave., Newberry 49868; (906) 293-5131.

Sport trollers in the Straits area generally have the action all to themselves.

Taking Care of Business

Thousands of people visit Mackinac Island every summer, yet very few realize how good the fishing is. The southeast end of the island is only about a half-mile from Round Island. That area is full of shoal water 15 feet or deeper, and Mackinac Island itself is mostly ringed with an irregular bottom featuring huge boulders.

Fish love the structure and that is why I come here. I have taken as many as 10 salmon on a charter, plus lake trout when I decide to fish for them.

One evening in late July, I pulled up to the Mackinac Island harbor and began showing people some of the fish I had caught. They had been told there were no fish around the island, but I guess seeing is believing because soon I had a charter trip arranged on the spot.

We caught salmon, mostly on No. 3 chartreuse J-Plugs while trolling from the Grand Hotel to Arch Rock. Again, the tourists couldn't believe their eyes.

You might say I was "taking care of business."

Captain Ross Nave
Onaway

27 CHEBOYGAN

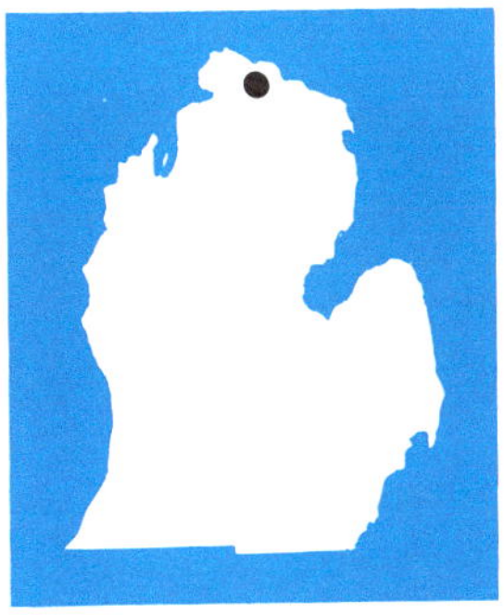

Cheboygan teems with offshore structure which offers some unusual opportunities to northern Lake Huron trollers. Bois Blanc Island looms offshore. It, too, is ringed with structure and features a breakwall on the south end. The region also provides river, surf and pier fishing. A short boat ride up the coast brings one to the Straits of Mackinac and continued good fishing.

Fishing Schedule

SPRING

Spring action begins in April, when perch fishermen line the banks of the Cheboygan River. A large congregation forms at Gordon Turner Park, at the river entrance to Lake Huron. Wigglers, worms, and small minnows produce hits from yellow-bellies. Perch, along with some salmon and lake trout, are also available to boaters who run longlines in the shallows all along the coast and in the shoal waters between the mainland and Bois Blanc Island. Minnow-imitating plugs (Bombers, Rebel Fastracs, Bagley Deep-Diving Bang-O-Lures, Rapalas) and flutter-type spoons (Northport Nailers, Stingers, Evil Eyes, Flutter Chucks) are best. Chrome is always a good color when run alone or matched with hot shades. Perch fishing in May and June is also good along the south shore of the island. Trollers in the channel between the mainland and island pick up some steelhead and brown trout during this period.

The Cheboygan River is also productive for steelhead in spring. Spawn bags and wigglers are good bets. Single salmon eggs will take menominee from the pier at this time.

Key fishing targets, for all species, to the northwest of the rivermouth are Stony Point, Point Au Sable, and Cadottes Point. To the east lies Lighthouse Point, Grass Bay, Cordwood Point and Nine Mile Point. Small streams that gush into Lake Huron along both stretches of shoreline often load up with spawning smelt to provide dipping opportunities. Few anglers, however, take advantage.

But the best spring hotspot for overall action is usually at the Cheboygan River mouth. Charterboat-skipper Ross Nave figures 80 percent of his spring catch there is lake trout. He targets water under 40 feet along shore but sometimes runs in as shallow as six or eight feet. Nave drops cannonballs just under the surface, or he longlines. For depths under 20 feet, Wobble-Glos or Stinger spoons are run clean. From 20-40 feet deep, he will usually mate these and other lures to 0, 00 or even 000 dodgers or willow-leaf cowbells. Chartreuse and dark-green colors account for 90 percent of his spring take.

In early spring, when fish easily spook in the area's clear water, Nave runs planer boards, stacking up to five lines (with the aid of shower-curtain rings) per board. Then he typically adds two downriggers and spots a single flatline. Planer-board-run Rapalas (small size in silver and black or gold and black) and Stingers

In spite of Indian gillnetting in the Cheboygan area, several species of fish, such as this big lake trout I'm doing battle with, can be taken.

(chrome or brown with pearl ladder) interest brown trout the most.

SUMMER

Summer action shifts to smallmouth bass that enter shallow areas of rock structure to spawn. A good spot is inside Zola Reef, along the northwest shore of Bois Blanc. Another good stretch is all along the island's southeast end off Rosie, Nichols, Walkers, and Lafayette points. Duncan Bay, east of the harbor, is yet another steady summer producer of smallmouths along with decent-sized northern pike.

The best smallie fishing occurs in June and July. Boat anglers driftfish Junebug Spinners and nightcrawler harnesses or cast spinnerbaits, spinners, and small spoons. Bass occasionally infest rocky shallows to only two or three feet; therefore, the fun is not limited to just those with boats. Wading anglers with spincasting or flyfishing gear also score.

Mid-June announces the arrival of salmon to the Cheboygan area. In 1985, kings and hordes of pinks contributed to the fun. Stingers and Northport Nailers were rated spoons, with chartreuse the hot color for Chinooks and chrome getting the nod for pinks. With a charter aboard, Nave typically runs up to 13 lines, stacking four downriggers and running planer boards to either side and a flatline down the center.

Summer lake-trout anglers go deep, often to depths of 100 or more feet, which can be found surprisingly close to shore in the Cheboygan area. Another choice laker hangout all year, but especially in summer, is McRae Bay on the northeast side of Bois Blanc. Deep-water trollers use wire line to pound big spoons in and out of lake-bottom mud, or they pull attractors ahead of small Tadpollies, Wobble-Glos, lookalike Soft Touch plugs by Burke, and various flutter-type hardware.

Walleyes move into the river in June to provide good summer fishing through August. The entire lower river for a mile below the dam is productive. Nightcrawlers, trolled, driftfished or spincast, are productive. So are Mister Twisters spincast from shore or boats. The river also serves up channel catfish to 10 pounds each for those who seek them.

Herring, which invade area shallows from their normal deep-water haunts, can be taken on mayfly wigglers and nymphs or adult insects rigged to flyrods or cane poles and fished just under the surface. Best results occur from late June through July when mayflies begin hatching over shallow-water reefs.

FALL

The Cheboygan River does not receive hatchery-reared king salmon, yet *fall*-run spawning brutes arrive at summer's close to provide decent offshore and river sport as late as October. The fish are likely strays from Carp River (St. Martin Bay, 83) or old Ocqueoc River plants. Or they might be fish naturally produced in the Cheboygan River itself. At any rate, trollers nail them on big, wobbling plugs such as Ping-A-Ts, Kwikfish, magnum Tadpollies and Flatfish. Shorebounders spincast 1/2-ounce to one-ounce spoons (Kastmasters, Little Jewels, Cop-E-Cats Imps) or fish bags of spawn on bottom.

Fall can also be a productive time for menominee. Anglers take them from the piers by pinning single salmon eggs to small hooks.

WINTER

Winter sport is pretty much limited to inland-lake fishing on nearby Mullet, Black, and Burt lakes.

Planting Records

The Cheboygan River has historically received between 10,000 and 20,000 yearling steelhead each year. The DNR has pledged to continue releases at the rate of 20,000 fish annually through 1990. Other trout and salmon caught in the area are likely from stockings elsewhere.

Facilities

A county-owned four-lane ramp awaits boaters. In addition, the DNR operates a port of refuge with transient accommodations, gasoline and diesel fuel, pay telephone, water, electricity, restrooms, haul-out facilities and holding-tank pump-out. There is no dock attendant, however.

Across the channel at Bois Blanc Island, transient accommodations, electricity and water await boaters.

Cheboygan, a town of 5,000, abundantly caters to visitors, including fishermen.

Further Information

Chambers of Commerce:

1. Cheboygan Area Chamber of Commerce, Box 69, Cheboygan 49721; (616) 627-2770.
2. East Michigan Tourist Association, One Wenonah Park, Bay City 48706; (517) 895-8823.

Bait & Tackle Shops:

1. Glenn's Bait Supplies, 337 Water St., Cheboygan 49721; (616) 627-5273.

Charter Fishing:

Captain Ross Nave, Rt. 2 Milligan Creek Trail, Onaway 49765; (517) 733-8585. 25-foot Imp, *Moonshiner*.

Department of Natural Resources:

A fisheries biologist works out of District Headquarters at 1732 W. M-32, Gaylord 49735; (517) 732-3541. Another works out of the Indian River Field Office, 6984 M-68, Indian River 49749; (616) 238-9313.

Coast Guard:

St. Ignace Station, (906) 643-9191.

Walleyes a la Carte

A lot of people don't realize that excellent walleye fishing can be had in the Cheboygan River. Fish normally show up there the last week in May or the first week in June and stay into the fall. Big fish average six pounds, but I have weighed them at our store to 13 pounds each.

My 71-year-old father, William, who started our bait shop here 44 years ago, is quite a walleye fisherman himself, but with a twist—he likes to use light line, sometimes as fine as 1/2-pound test. The light line, besides being sporting, makes for a more natural presentation, and one the sharp-eyed fish can't see as easily.

In late August 1985, Dad cast a Mepps spinner into the river across from the bait shop. A big fish hit and gave him quite a fight. Dad had the walleye right alongside the dock when it broke his four-pound-test line. How big was it? Dad had a good look at its scales and figured the fish at 10 pounds. He has taken larger ones from the Cheboygan River.

We expect walleye fishing to get even better because Consumers Power Company has started up its plant here again. Their big turbines stir up bottom and create a current, which is like ringing the dinner bell for Lake Huron walleyes.

Bob Glenn
Glenn's Bait Supplies, Cheboygan

27
CHEBOYGAN

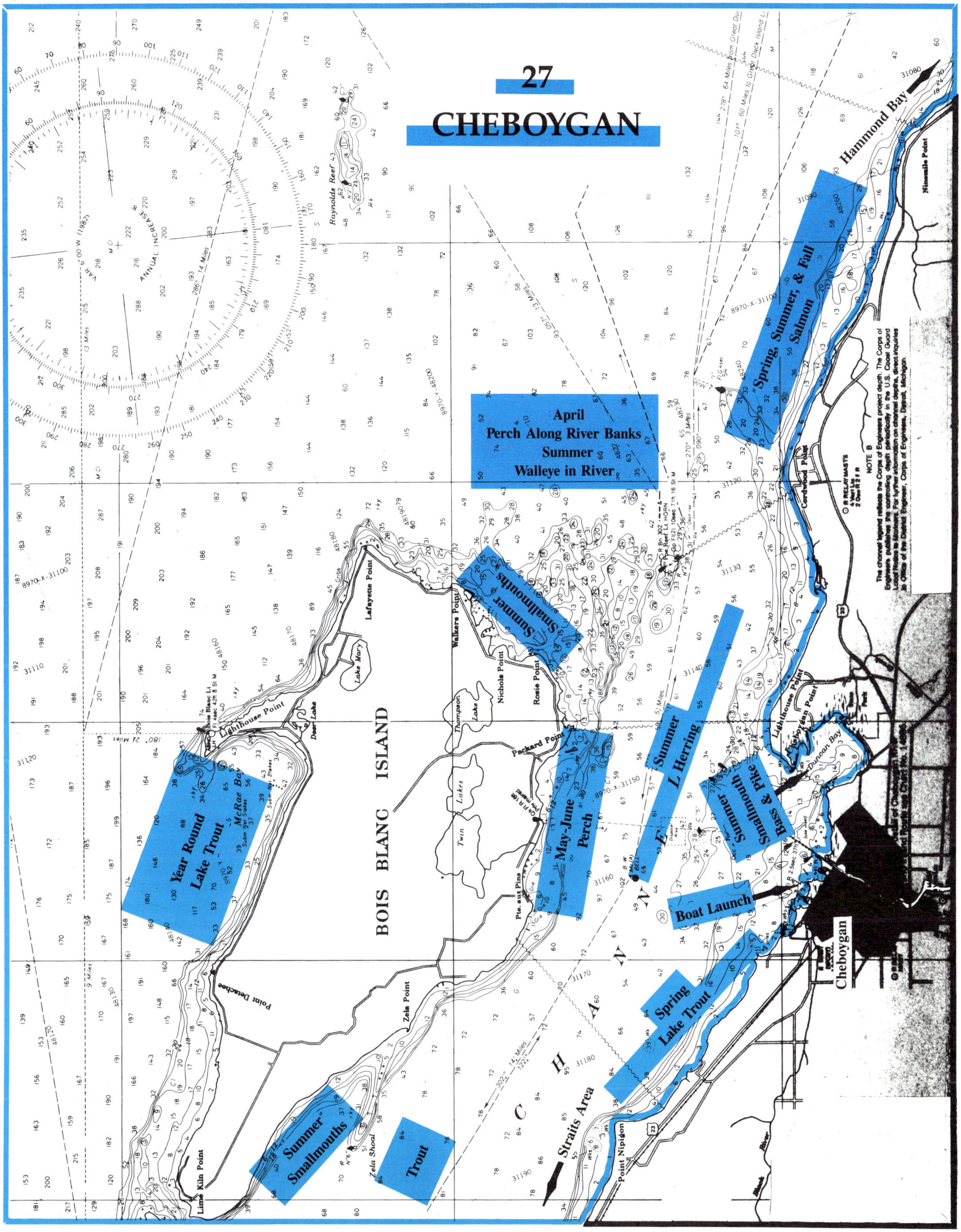

28
HAMMOND BAY

Hammond Bay is a 10-mile-wide indentation of northern Lake Huron between Rogers City and Cheboygan. To date, the bay has not received much pressure from sport anglers, yet it offers fair to good angling opportunities, a modern launch site, and a harbor of refuge formed by two sea breakwalls.

But interest is growing. According to Harold DeHart, harbormaster for the DNR and local charterboat captain, a newly formed sports anglers group, the Hammond Bay Area Anglers Association, has grown to about 140 members.

Fishing Schedule

SPRING

Spring fishing for steelhead in the Ocqueoc River is rated good. The rivermouth produces steelhead and brown trout for surf casters and trollers. Trollers also catch a few steelhead and brown trout in the open bay within a half-mile of shore and lake trout by longlining in the shallows with Krocodiles, Countdown Rapalas, and other small spoons and plugs. The breakwalls serve up some fish to shorebound anglers.

The protected bay is often ideal for spring trolling with planer boards. Anglers who use them report catches of lake trout, brown trout and some steelhead, as well as salmon released elsewhere in Lake Huron but that cruise the Hammond Bay area.

The salmon, which used to show up in midsummer, made an appearance in early June of the 1985 trolling season. Hot lures were chartreuse and dark-green Stinger spoons and Flutter Spoons. In past years, blue-and-chrome Spring Spoons have also rated. Spring trollers run these thin hardware choices clean in shallow water and match them with 0-sized dodgers in deeper water.

Though Hammond Bay continues to serve up excellent overall sport at times, there has been a severe drop in lake-trout catches. One possible reason is that, after annual releases of 75,000-100,000 yearling lakers, the DNR cut back plants to under 35,000. The Hammond Bay Area Anglers Association hopes to convince the DNR to release more lake trout and brown trout.

Another reason for the depleted lake-trout catches in this area, according to DeHart, is Indian gillnetting. "A few years ago, on any given day at any time, a fisherman could go out in Hammond Bay and get his five lake trout," he says. "Today, he might get none." Treaty waters open to Indian gillnetting exist outside of Hammond Bay, and whitefish trap netting by licensed fishermen is allowed in the bay itself.

So sport anglers must exercise caution in the region. Although most nets are well marked, tangles—some potentially serious (See "Mayday on Hammond Bay, page 120)—with a Hammond Bay net, are inevitable.

"The tribes are marking their nets better today," DeHart says, "but sometimes storms can pull anchor leads, and that can make for trouble." DeHart said he recently hooked a gillnet down 50-60 feet over 100 feet of water. The Bureau of Indian Fisheries sent a crew from St. Ignace to lift the net, but it was too heavy. So the DNR dispatched its 50-foot research boat, the *Chinook*, which was able to raise the net. It was about 2,000 feet long. Logs and debris were balled into it, and the stench of rotted fish was unbearable.

These facts are not meant to discourage fishermen from coming here. Action is excellent at times, and overall prospects for the future look good.

SUMMER

Summer sport includes fishing for Chinook salmon, which were planted in the Ocqueoc River years ago and have long since established spawning runs of naturally reproduced fish. The kings normally make their appearance by mid-August. In 1985, trollers also picked up many pink salmon in the Hammond Bay area while fishing for trout and kings.

Good lures for summer salmon include the chartreuse and dark-green Stingers as well as these color combinations: white with blue or green prism, orange with gold-prism ladderback, and black with pearl ladderback. Lake-trout trollers reported catches off cowbells strung ahead of dark-green Wobble-Glos run off bottom in 50-60 feet of water. Few summer anglers venture beyond these depths because concentrations of lakers are hard to find.

Fishing for warm-water species in Hammond Bay is not very productive, although some fishermen report channel catfish to 12 pounds each on downrigger-trolled lures. The Ocqueoc River produces summer smallmouth bass and yellow perch, and there are some walleyes upstream in Ocqueoc Lake.

FALL

Fall yields infrequent Chinooks and some browns off the Ocqueoc River mouth. Stream fishermen are advised that current regulations have closed the river below US-23 from September 10 until October 31. Check a current *Michigan Fishing Guide* for details. The river is also closed to *winter* fishing.

28
HAMMOND BAY

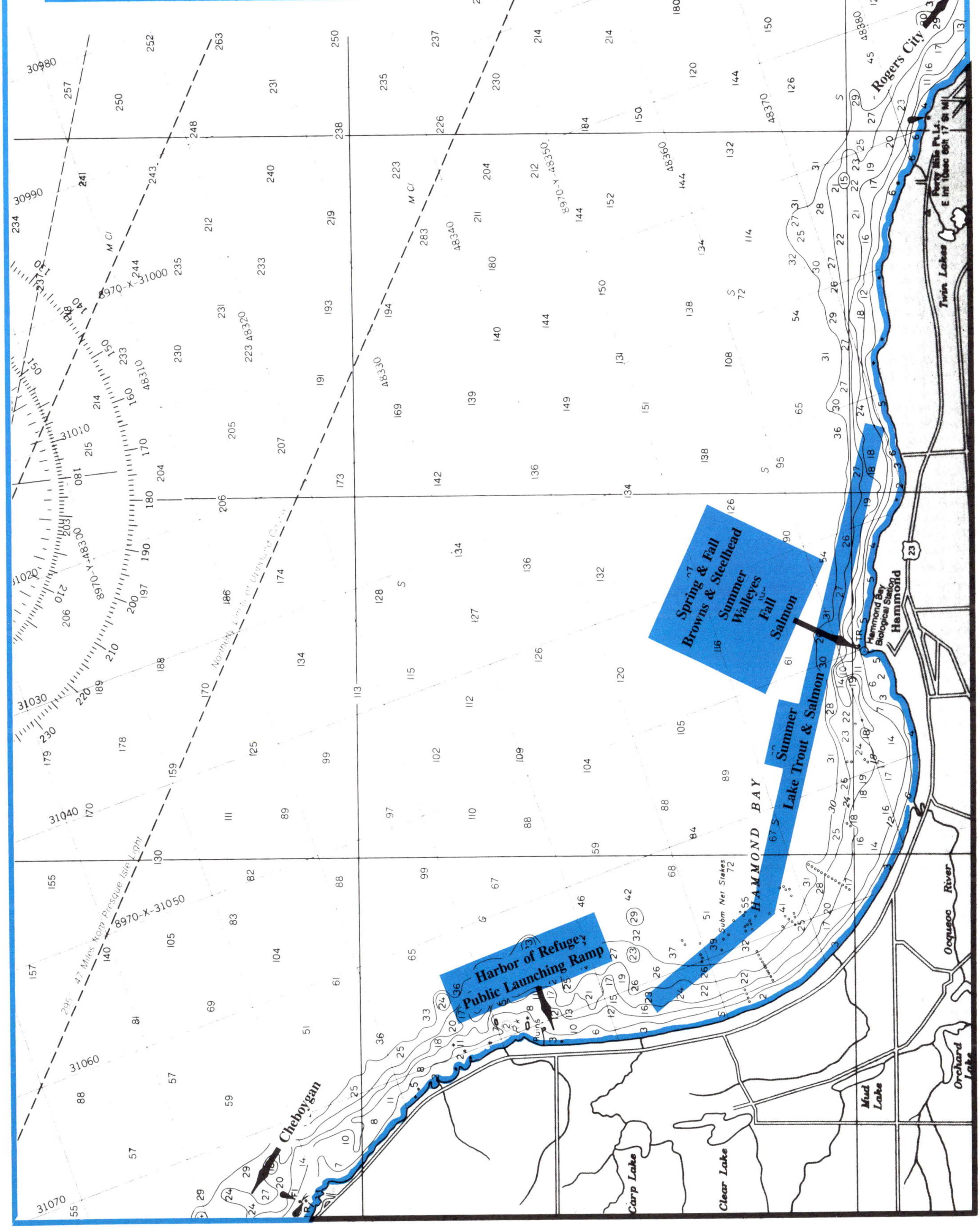

Planting Records

For the next five years, anglers can expect Hammond Bay to receive an average of 34,000 fall fingerling brown trout, 35,000 rainbow yearlings and 20,000 brown-trout yearlings. Fingerling-sized browns were first released in 1983 along with yearling rainbows. These fish have been contributing to steadily improving sport. In addition, the Ocqueoc River has historically received 10,000 steelhead yearlings each year and will continue to get them through 1990.

Facilities

Hammond Bay is served by a paved double ramp that can accommodate all trailerable boats. The DNR also operates a harbor of refuge with gas, water, electricity, restrooms, shower facilities, dock attendant, holding-tank pump-out and VHF-FM radio available. Thirteen slips are also available. Telephone number of the harbormaster is (517) 938-9281.

Rogers City and Cheboygan, to the south and north respectively on US-23, have accommodations for visitors.

Further Information

Chambers of Commerce:

East Michigan Tourist Association, One Wenonah Park, Bay City 48706; (517) 895-8823. See also 29 (Rogers City) and 27 (Cheboygan).

Bait & Tackle Shops:

See 29 (Rogers City) and 27 (Cheboygan).

Charter Fishing:

1. Captain Harold DeHart, Orchard Lake Box 175, Ocqueoc 49759; (517) 733-8569. 26-foot Skiffcraft, *Lady Lizabeth*.
2. Captain Ross Nave, Rt. 2, Milligan Creek Trail, Onaway 49765; (517) 733-8585. 25-foot Imp, *Moonshiner*.

Department of Natural Resources:

Two fisheries biologists work out of District Headquarters at 1732 W. M-32, Gaylord 49735; (517) 732-3541.

King salmon, naturally reproduced, provide offshore action off the mouth of the Ocqueoc River in Hammond Bay.

Coast Guard:

St. Ignace Station (906) 643-9191.

Mayday on Hammond Bay

Waves pushed by a northwest wind were running three to five feet that early May morning about five years ago. But my friend Harry Wheaton, his son Carl, and I decided to venture out into Hammond Bay to go lake-trout fishing. Traveling with the waves, we set downrigger lines at five feet deep over about 40 feet of water.

Suddenly I noticed a flag, apparently the lead marker for a trap net, between us and shore a half-mile away. Commercial fishermen net whitefish in this area, so we sport anglers must keep track of the nets to avoid tangles. But before I could change course, our cannonballs caught the huge net. My boat, a 19-1/2 foot center-console powered by a 115-hp outboard with a six-hp kicker on back, was held fast. Harry ran the small motor in reverse to hold us steady against the waves while I tried to cut us free from the meshes.

But waves cuffed the boat about badly. Soon our propeller was also ensnared, and the net's heavy weight pulled us low enough for waves to start pouring in. Before long the boat was full of water. Wallowing forward through the water, we reached the bow where we tried to raise someone on the C.B. radio. No response. Apparently we were the only fishermen out that day.

Suddenly the boat rolled over, throwing Harry and Carl into the 47-degree-F. water. I managed to keep my balance and stay atop the bellied-up boat. It was too far to swim to shore, especially in that frigid water. That left one thing to do—cut the net free and stay with the overturned boat. After much effort, Harry freed the net, then clambered aboard with me and Carl. Harry was shaking badly, so I took off my down vest and jacket and put the dry garments around him.

I hated thinking about what might happen in the two hours it would take to drift to shore. But, luckily, a boy on shore saw what had happened while playing basketball in his parents' driveway. He ran to a beached dinghy and, with the help of a seven-hp outboard on the little boat, motored out and rescued us.

Harold DeHart
Onaway

29
ROGERS CITY

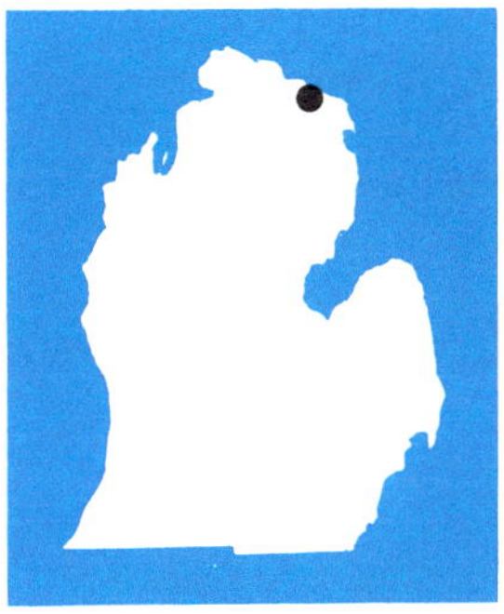

More and more anglers are coming to regard Rogers City as the hub of a steadily improving northern Lake Huron fishery. Adams Point has long received lake-trout releases. Small plants of Chinook salmon at Nagles Creek have been replaced by huge annual releases of coho and Chinooks in Swan Creek. Plus, the area receives brown trout and rainbows. Thanks to these releases, sport trolling keeps getting better, although Indian gillnetting, legal north of Forty Mile Point, has no doubt reduced the number of lake trout in the region.

Rogers City has good facilities for fishermen, including bait and tackle shops, a modern launch ramp, and a protected harbor.

Fishing Schedule

SPRING

Some of the best sport occurs in *spring*, when trollers target Swan Bay for lake trout and brown trout. Lake trout run three to 12 pounds; browns in spring 1985, averaged three to five pounds. This fishery begins in late April (lake trout are currently legal on May 1) and lasts until late June. Tactics include longlining in 20-30 feet of water with small spoons such as Finn Spoons, Krocodiles, and Little Cleos. Some spring (and fall) trollers run planer boards for browns. In addition, many fishermen rely upon Big Jon cowbells (they remove one of the three blades) ahead of P-Nuts or Spin-N-Glos in chartreuse, pink, white or yellow. Typical rigging puts attractors 25 feet behind releases, and an ounce of lead three feet above the hardware.

Spring trolling in the shallows east or west of Rogers City can be productive for salmon, too, with best catches occurring in May and June. Boaters who take a 90-degree-east heading upon leaving Rogers City will cross the U.S. Steel Lighthouse at two miles, then Adams Point at about five miles. Continuing the 90-degree course about 12 miles further, the next landmark is the Presque Isle Lighthouse. To the west of Rogers City lies Seagull Point (one mile), Nagles Creek at P.F. Hoeft State Park (five miles), Forty Mile Point (six miles), and the U.S. Biological Station at the entrance to Hammond Bay (12 miles). Fishing can be good anywhere along this shoreline to depths of 125 feet.

SUMMER

Summer trollers can go after salmon, brown trout and lake trout. Ted Planck, who owns the Driftwood Motel and who charter fishes the region, has success with summer salmon on Finn Spoons, Andy Reekers, Silver Streaks, G.W. Salmon Slammers, or J-Plugs and Northport Nailer Plugs on bottom and stacking with Northport Nailers, Andy Reekers, Stingers or Finn Spoons above. Planck says his best overall color is chartreuse with green tape, but he plays the spectrum of color, too, depending upon light conditions and time of day. Attractor rigs go on out-downs, with stern-end riggers run clean. It is not uncommon for him to pick up lake trout on the attractor set-ups and salmon on the stacked offerings.

Salmon fishing took off in summer 1985 after the 4th of July, with excellent catches of 12- to 15-pound kings coming in 40-60 feet of water from Swan Bay to Presque Isle Harbor. A particular hotspot is a piece of structure that begins one mile east of Adams Point and runs out 1-1/2 miles into the lake. A half-mile from shore, the reef comes up within a few feet of the surface and at its end is about 17-feet deep with 100 feet of water all around it. Charterboat-skipper Phil Petz and others have enjoyed salmon fishing so good that they have skipped seeking lakers altogether.

Petz targets 54-degree-F. water, then sends down Salmon Slammers (fluorescent green with chartreuse ladderback), Northport Nailers (green with black ladderback), various colors of Big Ed Flutter Chucks, and a seven-inch J-Plug imitation called the Gold

Lake Huron

Length in miles from mouth of St. Mary's River to head of St. Clair River—223 miles

Breadth—183 miles

Length of coastline (including Canada and islands)—3,830 miles

Total water surface—23,050 square miles

U.S. water surface—9,150 square miles

Total land drainage basin—51,700 square miles

U.S. drainage—16,200 square miles

Maximum depth—750 feet

Average depth—195 feet

Volume of water - 849 cubic miles

Star (chrome with green ladderback). He runs four Cannon Digi-Troll downriggers with six-foot booms, setting up plugs high on the out-downs and running them back 100 feet. Spoons go 30 feet back of releases, down 25-60 feet, and are typically spotted on inside, corner-set downriggers. Petz sometimes adds Deep Sixes 15 feet deep off outriggers.

Pink salmon also infested the waters of Rogers City during the 1985 trolling season and provided good action from spring through fall. Most catches of the two-pounders came on highlines pulling flutter-type hardware.

Some anglers reported catches of summer steelhead, likely from 1984 Au Sable River releases. The long, slim 10-pounders came from 80- to 90-foot depths off Rogers City and hit spoons or plugs featuring red color.

Brown-trout catches are reported to be fairly good in August, both east and west of the harbor. Try slow trolling up high with small-sized Stingers. Rated color is brown with pearl ladder. Fishing for 21-inch-plus lakers was rated only fair.

During summer 1985, Adams Point served up fair to good catches of four-pound browns, five-pound steelhead (06 Miller Spoons, Northport Nailers, and Stingers) and limit catches of pink salmon.

Some surprising numbers of smallmouth bass are also available throughout the summer. The previously mentioned reef is a good bet; so are micropieces of structure all along the coast. And don't overlook the old Coast Guard pilings at the U.S. Biological Station.

FALL

Fall action is reportedly good for salmon, with most trollers keying again on Swan Bay. Many mature kings, thanks to an abundant forage base, are checking in at 30-34 pounds. In fall the charter skippers and others switch to planer boards and Flatfish or Ping-A-Ts. Spawning kings in the shallows hit these big, wobbling plugs when they are trolled slowly. Transparent-colored Ping-A-Ts (lemon, chartreuse, pink) are usually hot. So are red-and-yellow fluorescent Flatfish.

Cohos prefer orange or red Stingers, Salmon Slammers, and Northport Nailers as well as small plugs (Rapalas, Fat Raps, Hot 'N Tots). Some trollers also take them on bright-colored squids and flies mated to 00 silver dodgers and rigged tightly to cannonballs.

Spawn fishermen and hardware casters are getting good fall catches of salmon, brown trout and menominee in the Rogers City harbor as well as outside the breakwalls. Other west-shore gathering points for landed fishermen include Trout River, Nagles Creek and Schmidt Creek.

WINTER

Winter angling opportunities are limited to the harbor, where shanty fishermen take brown trout and a few perch. In all likelihood, action should improve, at least for browns and probably rainbows.

Planting Records

Rogers City has a long history of salmonid plants, and, from all indications, fishing should improve for several years. Annual releases of yearling lake trout at Adams Point have been as high as 100,000, although recent plants have been in the neighborhood of 60,000-70,000. For the next five years, look for an annual average of 90,000 forktails.

Brown-trout stockings, begun with 20,000 fall fingerlings in 1982, will continue at a rate of 30,000 fish each year. In addition, 30,000 yearling rainbows are targeted, up from the 10,000 first planted in 1984. These fish should be available from spring through fall and will also likely contribute to a winter fishery within the harbor.

But salmon are the big story at Rogers City. A yearly plant of 50,000 king fingerlings at Nagles Creek has given area anglers a taste of big-salmon sport. Now they will be able to contend with returning kings from annual releases of 850,000 fingerlings at Swan Creek. Future releases at Swan Creek will also include 550,000 Chinook fingerlings. The release of 250,000 coho smolts, also at Swan Creek, each of the past two springs constitutes the largst coho release in Lake Huron.

Facilities

A free first-class two-lane paved ramp services boat anglers, and launching is also available at R.C. Marina. The DNR operates a spacious small-boat harbor with the following services: gasoline and diesel fuel, water, electricity, transient accommodations, restrooms, shower facilities, holding-tank pump-out, refuse

Bad Timing

A northwest wind pushed waves to three feet, and from all indications the blow was going to increase. But my two-man charter wanted salmon. So knowing things were safe enough for the time being, we ventured out of the Rogers City marina for a mid-August afternoon of salmon fishing.

I headed northwest, into the waves, toward Nagles Creek until reaching 90 feet of water. I took temperature readings until I found 55-degree-F. water, then began setting lines. Although we marked a few fish, we couldn't get any takers, so we headed toward the creek and shallower water. More check marks showed up on the graph. Soon a rod went off, and one of the customers had his hands full with a 15-pound king.

Meanwhile, the waves had gotten to his partner, who was sick in the cabin. He managed to come out and steer the boat while I began pulling our other three lines. Mature kings are tough enough to handle on calm seas when you have other lines in the water. So I usually pull them when a fish strikes, especially when I know it is going to be a rampaging salmon. Once that 15-pounder hit the deck, we spun the boat around, headed back into the wind, and reset trolling lines.

A savage strike soon popped one of the rods, but this time I was able to get in only one line. A second, then a third release had us into a triple with our hands already full. We got two fish in the box and lost the third. With the waves building higher, my seasick passenger was growing more ill.

Now that we had found the salmon, we decided to make one more pass but only set two lines. The first one went off almost immediately. Then, while turning the boat to run with the wind, the second rod snapped to. We put both of these fish into the cooler, which now held five beautiful kings from 15 to 18 pounds each. Altogether, we had fished only an hour and a half, but, with the waves at four feet and still rising, we headed back to the harbor.

I felt bad for my client's partner. He sure picked the wrong time to be sick.

Captain Ted Planck
Rogers City

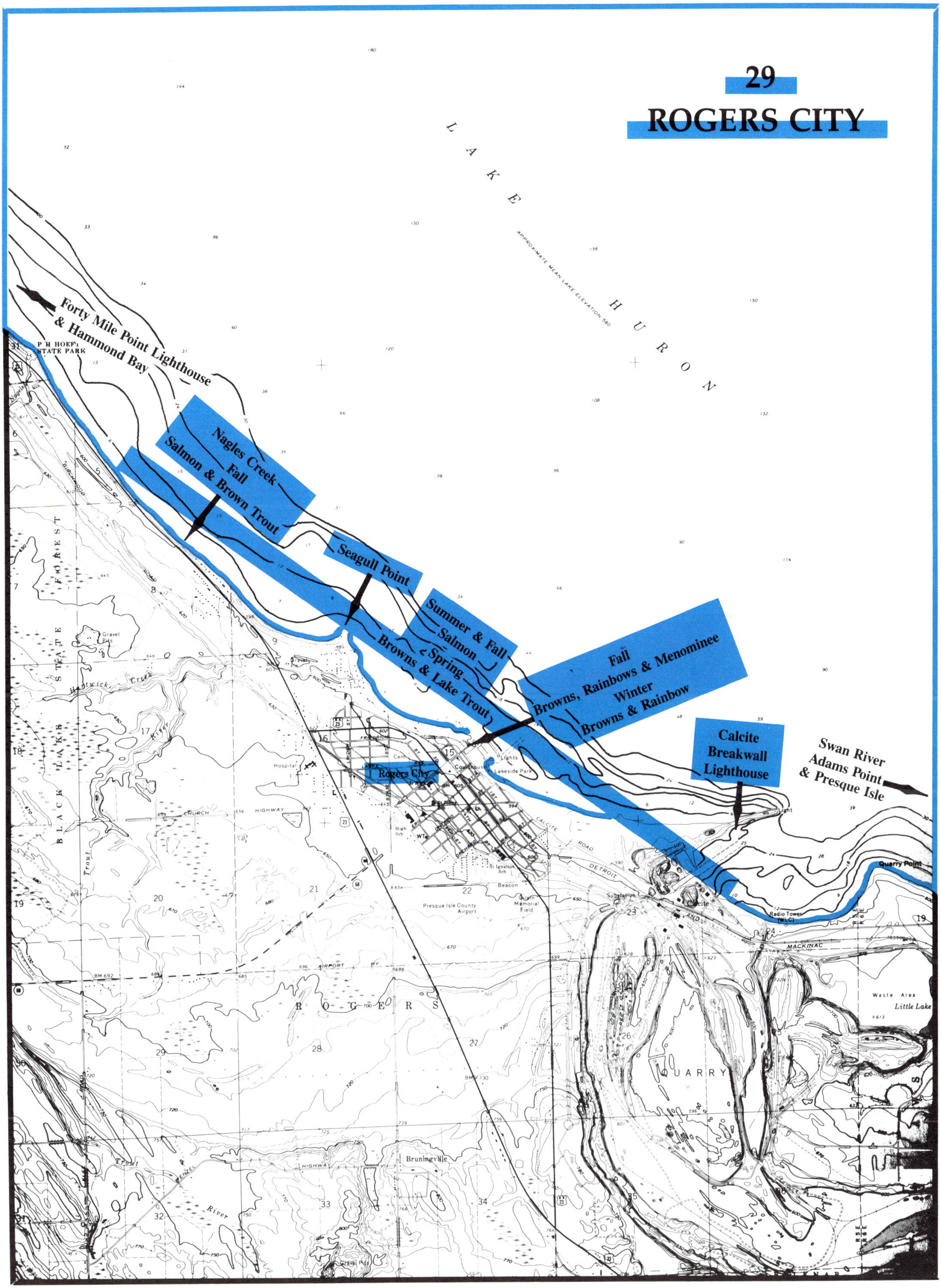
29
ROGERS CITY
LAKE HURON
Forty Mile Point Lighthouse & Hammond Bay
Nagles Creek Fall Salmon & Brown Trout
Seagull Point
Summer & Fall Salmon
Spring Browns & Lake Trout
Fall Browns, Rainbows & Menominee
Winter Browns & Rainbow
Calcite Breakwall Lighthouse
Swan River Adams Point & Presque Isle
Rogers City
P H HOEFT STATE PARK
BLACK LAKE STATE FOREST
QUARRY
Bruningville

facilities, dock attendant and VHF-FM radio. You can reach the harbor master by calling (517) 734-3808.

Rogers City, a community of 4,000, caters to visitors, including fishermen. P.F. Hoeft State Park beckons campers.

Further Information

Chambers of Commerce:

1. Rogers City Chamber of Commerce, P.O. Box 55C, Rogers City 49779; (517) 734-2535.
2. East Michigan Tourist Association, One Wenonah Park, Bay City 48706; (517) 895-8823.

Bait & Tackle Shops:

1. Adrian's Sport Shop, 335 N. Bradley Hwy., Rogers City 49779; (517) 734-2303.
2. Rogers City Boat Harbor, 270 Lake, Rogers City 49779; (517) 734-3808.
3. Driftwood Motel, 540 W. 3rd St., Rogers City 49779; (517) 734-4777.

Charter Fishing:

1. Captain Ted Planck, 540 W. 3rd St., Rogers City 49779; (517) 734-47777. 27-foot Sea Ray Amberjack, *Driftwood II.*
2. Captain Phil Petz, 2353 M-68 Highway, Rogers city 49779; (517) 734-3855. 27-foot Sportcraft Sport Fisherman, *Fish Ahoy II.*

Department of Natural Resources:

Two fisheries biologists work out of District Headquarters at 1732 W. M-32, Gaylord 49735; (517) 732-3541.

Coast Guard:

St. Ignace Station, (906) 643-9191.

Hurondezvous With Salmon

One lazy August evening, fishing-buddy Joe Zikewich and I were trolling the Lake Huron shallows in hopes of boxing a big king salmon or two. Joe wheeled us along the inside edge of a slight hump down 25 feet, trying to prompt a salmon to drill one of four downrigger-trolled lures.

Listening to the Tigers' game on the radio, I was sipping an Old Milwaukee and had my feet propped up on our empty cooler.

Jack Morris was winding up for a one-out, full-count pitch, when the first rod went off as though spring-loaded. I had the bucking pole in my hands about the time the batter fouled off Morris' pitch. With the drag lightly set, the line fairly smoked from the level-wind reel. A tuna-shaped fish of about 20 pounds detonated on the surface of Lake Huron 50 yards behind our boat. Joe whooped his approval while I jammed the rod butt into my belly and tried to stop this king on a one-way scramble to Canada.

That's when a second rod popped. Joe pounced on it like a Vegas crapshooter beating the house. His fish, a carbon copy in size to my king, also spirited up and away. The rod tip pointed like an angry finger and the reel grudgingly gave up line. Forget the Tigers; we had our own version of a twi-night double-header going.

Ten minutes later, twin 18-pound Chinooks break-danced along the bottom of Joe's boat. Besides beer, we now had over 35 pounds of prime salmon in the cooler.

Oh, yeah. Morris struck out the guy, but the Tigers lost the game.

Tom Huggler
Otisville

Swan Creek near Rogers City is northern Lake Huron's biggest magnet for coho and king salmon, such as this big brawler.

30
PRESQUE ISLE HARBOR

"It's the nicest natural harbor in Michigan," says Alpena charterboat-captain Ed Retherford, who has fished all over the state. Besides a picturesque setting (which includes a historical lighthouse), Presque Isle Harbor has some of the cleanest water in the Great Lakes—so clean that freighters used to take on their water supply here.

Appealing to fishermen is the fact that 80- to 120-foot water—ideal for summer salmon and lake trout—is found very close to shore. Plus there are plenty of drowned points, reefs and other food-rich structure to attract and hold predator species.

Because Presque Isle Harbor has a launching facility suitable for small boats only, the area receives light fishing pressure. Fifteen or 20 boats is average, according to Alpena schoolteacher Steve Speaks, who owns a cottage here and fishes the area from spring through fall. Many anglers who come to the harbor troll or run southeast from Rogers City (29), a distance of about 17 miles. Others put in at Rockport (31) 15 miles down the coast.

Fishing Schedule

SPRING

Spring sport begins very close to shore for salmon, lake trout and some brown trout as they invade shallows in search of spawning smelt. North and South Albany points to the southeast are good places to work over. So are Presque Isle Point, North Bay, Black Point, Thompsons Harbor, and Observatory Point to the northwest. For best results in early spring, troll in the upper half of 30-50 feet of water. Body baits such as Rapalas are good in hot colors, singly or in combination with chrome, blue, and green. Small spoons in the same colors are also rated.

Shore fishing action includes dipping for smelt in small streams throughout the area and casting spoons, as well as still fishing spawn bags, in the harbor itself.

SUMMER

When the thermocline develops in *summer* (usually by mid-June), anglers key on 60- to 90-foot depths for salmon and go even deeper for lake trout. Chuck Obeginski, a sport troller from Lachine, has had good success here by fishing around the entrance buoy to Rogers City, where, though only a quarter-mile from shore, water drops off quickly to 90 feet. Obeginski pulls chartreuse or silver-and-green Flutter Spoons clean or chartreuse, light-green, or pearl Wobble-Glos behind three-blade, silver-prism George's Attractors. Another trick he employs is to use Williams Wablers as attractors by removing the hook and dragging the big spoons backwards. This, he claims, imparts a tantalizing action to Northport Nailers.

The deep water lends itself to stacking lines or adding free sliders to lures already in place. Chuck has also had good luck by mating Evil Eye, Silver Streak, and Northport Nailer spoons to deep-running Bombers or Rapalas. Best salmon colors seem to be chartreuse or black with green. Sometimes, even in the heat of summer and certainly again in fall, salmon will stack up along dropoffs and ridges, occasionally in water as shallow as 10 feet.

Charterboat-skippers Ed Retherford and Dale Hallman visit Presque Isle harbor after running up from Rockport (31). J-Plugs and Grizzly Plugs have been hot tickets for the pair, especially choices in silver or green with white or pearl. Best salmon scores occur by working points north of the harbor.

FALL

Fall fishing continues to be good. Steve Speaks likes to fish east and northeast of the old lighthouse in 50-60 feet of water, with the strike zone down 40 feet. Hot lure has been a Northport Nailer, white with orange stripe. I was supposed to fish this port with Speaks over a recent Labor Day weekend but had to cancel. I should have gone fishing. Steve called to tell me that he and another friend had boxed a fine steelhead and a 21-1/2 pound Chinook, plus lost three other fish.

The first catches of 20,000 brook trout planted in spring 1985 are just starting to be reported. Although not yet big (10-12 inches), these exciting fish promise excellent sport in years to come, especially if they continue to stay in the harbor and do not become snacks for foraging salmon.

WINTER

It is also possible that the brookies could serve up some good sport in *winter*.

Planting Records

Trout and salmon caught in the Presque Isle Harbor region are from releases at Rogers City (29), Rockport (31) and elsewhere. The DNR has just begun to stock brook-trout fingerlings in the harbor and will continue to do so at the rate of 20,000 fish each year through at least 1990.

Facilities

Although the state owns land here, it has not yet given the DNR money to construct a new launching facility. Existing launch facilities are inadequate for all but shallow-draft boats, so if you are going to attempt to launch a bigger boat come equipped with a 4WD vehicle.

For accommodations and other facilities, see 29 (Rogers City) and 33 (Alpena).

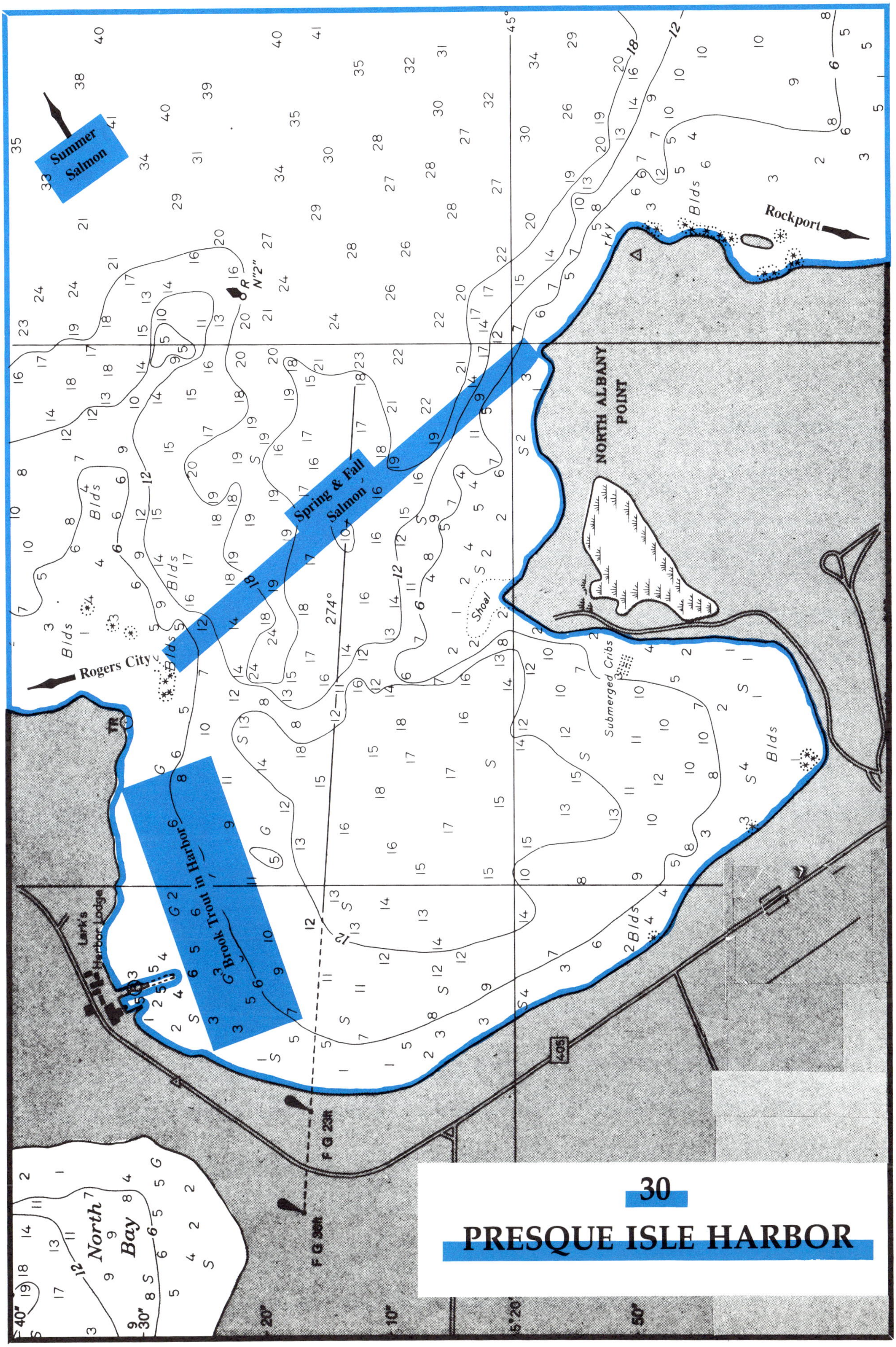

30 PRESQUE ISLE HARBOR

Further Information

Chambers of Commerce:

East Michigan Tourist Association, One Wenonah Park, Bay City 48706; (517) 895-8823.

Bait & Tackle Shops:

See 29 (Rogers City) and 33 (Alpena).

Charter Fishing:

1. Captain Ed Retherford, 220 Richardson, Alpena 49707; (517) 356-9361. 23-foot Starcraft, *Trout Scout III.*
2. Captain Dale Hallman, Fish Trap Charters, 6651 Webb Rd., Hale 48739; (517) 728-2143. 23-foot Starcraft, *Fish Trap*.

Department of Natural Resources:

Two fisheries biologists work out of District Headquarters at 1732 W. M-32, Gaylord 49735; (517) 732-3541.

Coast Guard:

St. Ignace Station, (906) 643-9191.

Think Pink!

I'd heard about the pink salmon invasion in Lake Huron and had even caught a few in Thunder Bay while trolling for brown trout. But nothing prepared me for what happened that mid-June morning.

I, my wife Ann, and our daughters Sarah, age seven, and Heidi, age 12, motored out from our cottage at Presque Isle Harbor to go salmon fishing. I swung around the point and, when I hit 30 feet of water on the west side of the lighthouse, flipped on the graph. We were looking for Chinook salmon. We found pinks instead. The graph was solid with black marks from a huge school of the little salmon.

We set downriggers at 12 feet and added flatlines but couldn't keep them in the water. Black-and-silver Shad Raps did a number on the pinks. Because their mouths are soft, we lost quite a few fish. No matter. Two or three others would strike the plug before we could get it back to the boat.

We caught 19 of the two-pounders in an hour, all within 100-150 feet of shore. I was hoping for bigger salmon, but we simply could not troll out of the school.

I believe we could have filled the boat had we wanted to.

Steve Speaks
Alpena

Thanks to prevailing winds from the west, Lake Huron fishermen often enjoy peaceful fishing trips like this one.

31
ROCKPORT

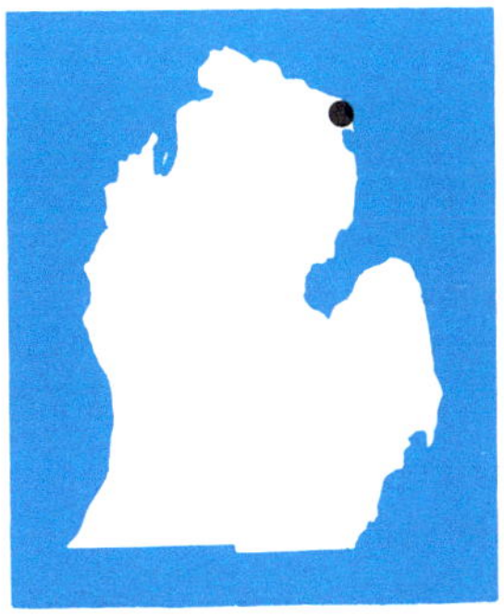

News seldom spreads faster than among the Great Lakes trolling fleet. So when fishermen began making good catches out of Rockport, the little port began getting fast and long-overdue attention. On a mid-August 1985 weekend, for example, one man estimated that 60 boats put in from the state launch. With that fairly new Class 1 ramp (paved and suitable for launching big boats), Rockport offers the only good launch facility between Alpena (33), 17 miles southeast, and Rogers City (29), about 25 miles northwest.

The entire shoreline between Rockport and those cities is studded with drowned points, creek flows, and offshore reefs. Ferron Point, Bolton Point, False Presque Isle, Stoneport, and South and North Albany points lie to the north. To the south are Monaghan Point, Morris Bay and South Nine Mile Point. A fisherman could spend the entire trolling season out of Rockport and still not learn all the intricate structure available.

And deep water close to shore also makes the area a haven (most of the time, anyway) for small-boat anglers. Those without boats can fish within the harbor while casting from shore.

Hefty releases of lake trout and brown trout, plus improving numbers of salmon that cruise the region, are spring, summer and fall calling cards.

Fishing Schedule

Rockport offers a spring, summer and fall fishery for trout and salmon.

SPRING

Spring fishing rates fair to excellent for salmon, brown trout, and lake trout. Alpena sport-angler Loren Urlaub, who, with his sons Mike and David, targets Rockport each spring for king salmon, reports that their overall catch runs about 60 percent salmon, 20 percent brown trout, and 20 percent lake trout. For lures they like Northport Nailers in blue and white and Flutter Spoons in green and white and clown color (yellow with red dots). When salmon fishing, he uses his graph to locate suspended fish, then puts lures on the money. When targeting browns, Loren likes to longline.

In spring, shallows also produce brown trout, as well as menominee and smallmouth bass, and a few salmon and lake trout.

SUMMER

Summer trollers key along 50- to 125-foot depths all along the coast. They also head for the east side of Middle Island, then take a bearing off the Nord Mere Wreck Reef, to the southeast 12 miles away, and troll the 50- to 90-foot depths en route. Reef structure in this area is fish-rich with Chinook, pink and some coho salmon, plus lake trout. It is possible to run steadily in one direction and pass over enough fish to preclude having to turn around and retroll the same water.

Many salmon are taken out of temperature at this port, according to Alpena charterboat-skipper Ed Retherford, who sometimes fishes the area. Action can be tremendous. Ed's notes show 21 lakers for 57 minutes of trolling one summer. The next season on a 2-1/2 hour charter, a party of five coolered 25 salmon. Those are exceptions, of course, but they help underscore the fact that fishing is generally very good at this port.

Many anglers, after both trout and salmon, rig dodgers and

Recently, northern Lake Huron teemed with pink salmon, like these five shown with one Chinook salmon.

flies or small plugs to bottom-running setups, then stack with flutter-light spoons. Both salmon and lake trout will hit Ale-E flies and Sparkle Flies behind silver, key-lime, or yellow/white dodgers.

If you wish to try exclusively for lake trout, run cowbells or dodgers ahead of Wobble-Glos, Wobble Trolls, Spin-N-Glos, L'il Guys, Fire Plugs, No. 88 Flutter Spoons, small Flutter Chucks or Northport Nailers. Chartreuse, green, yellow, blue, and pearl are rated laker colors. Troll slowly, with attractors run close to or on bottom.

FALL

Fall trolling remains good for brown trout, plus pink salmon invade streams, and kings and cohos begin surging to Swan Bay and other northern release sites. Planer boards and longlining in the shallows produce best for browns and also work on salmon when they are there. Try Finn Spoons, McMahon Spoons, Silver Streaks, Cobras, Krocodiles, Mainliners, and other small spoons. Rated brown-trout colors are yellow, brown, dull orange, pearl, and blue or green. Fall browns will also sock J-7 Rapalas and Hot 'N Tots in the same colors.

Shore fishermen catch browns and some fall salmon on gobs of spawn and nightcrawlers. Spincasters flip Rooster Tails, Kastmasters, Little Cleos, and Devle Dogs. No doubt many of the rocky points and reefs would also produce smallmouth bass in fall (and summer), but few anglers try the sport.

WINTER

Unpredictable ice in *winter* makes for unpredictable fishing. When ice men can venture onto the hardwater, best action should be for brown trout.

Planting Records

For many years, Middle Island Reef has received annual releases of yearling and fall fingerling lake trout. The lakers tend to stay in this area because of suitable structure and a solid forage base of smelt, alewives and some lake emerald shiners. Annual plants call for 92,500 forktail yearlings through 1990.

In 1983 the DNR began releasing brown trout at Rockport Harbor with 25,000 yearling fish. They followed up the next year with 20,000 browns and plan to stock 15,000 each year for at least the next five years.

Facilities

A free boat launch with paved double ramp awaits boaters. There are no other facilities, however.

Further Information

Chambers of Commerce:

1. Alpena Area Chamber of Commerce, 133 Johnson St. (P.O. Box 65), Alpena 49707; 1-800-582-1906 or (517) 354-4181.
2. East Michigan Tourist Association, One Wenonah Park, Bay City 48706; (517) 895-8823.

Bait & Tackle Shops:

Refer to 33 (Alpena).

Charter Fishing:

1. Captain Ed Retherford, 220 Richardson, Alpena 49707; (517) 356-9361. 23-foot Starcraft, *Trout Scout III.*
2. Captain Dale Hallman, Fish Trap Charters, 6651 Webb Rd., Hale 48739; (517) 728-2143. 23-foot Starcraft, *Fish Trap*.

Department of Natural Resources:

Two fisheries biologists work out of District Headquarters at 1732 W. M-32, Gaylord 49735; (517) 732-3541.

Coast Guard:

Tawas Station, (517) 362-4428 or St. Ignace Station, (906) 643-9191.

Salmon City

I won't soon forget the fishing trip that began routinely on an early August morning. Five salmon fishermen from Saginaw and I ran from Rockport to the outside of Middle Island. There, we set lines in 41-50 feet of water, then trolled southeast toward the Nord Mere wreck, 12 miles away. We stacked four downriggers and ran a pair of Dipsy-Divers off the boat sides. Most of the lures we put down were Silver Streaks and Finn Spoons.

But it was too nice a day, too bright for good salmon fishing. Or so I thought. Two minutes after we had everything rigged, a fish struck one of the lures. And for the next four hours, that's the way it went: singles and doubles, top lines and deep lines, light color or dark color. The salmon were stacked up and they were hungry.

At noon we counted the damage. In the box were 13 king salmon—most in the seven- to eight-pound class, but one 24-pound brute—two cohos, and nine pink salmon. The pinks were especially rewarding since seven of them weighed between 3-1/2 and 4-1/2 pounds and were big enough for entry in the DNR Master Angler Award Program **(see page 319)****. We lost plenty of salmon, too.**

I told the fishermen, first-time customers of mine, that they couldn't expect action like this all the time. My words have since proved prophetic. Although they've been back since and we've enjoyed some good fishing, nothing can top that day of super salmon.

Captain Dale Hallman
Hale

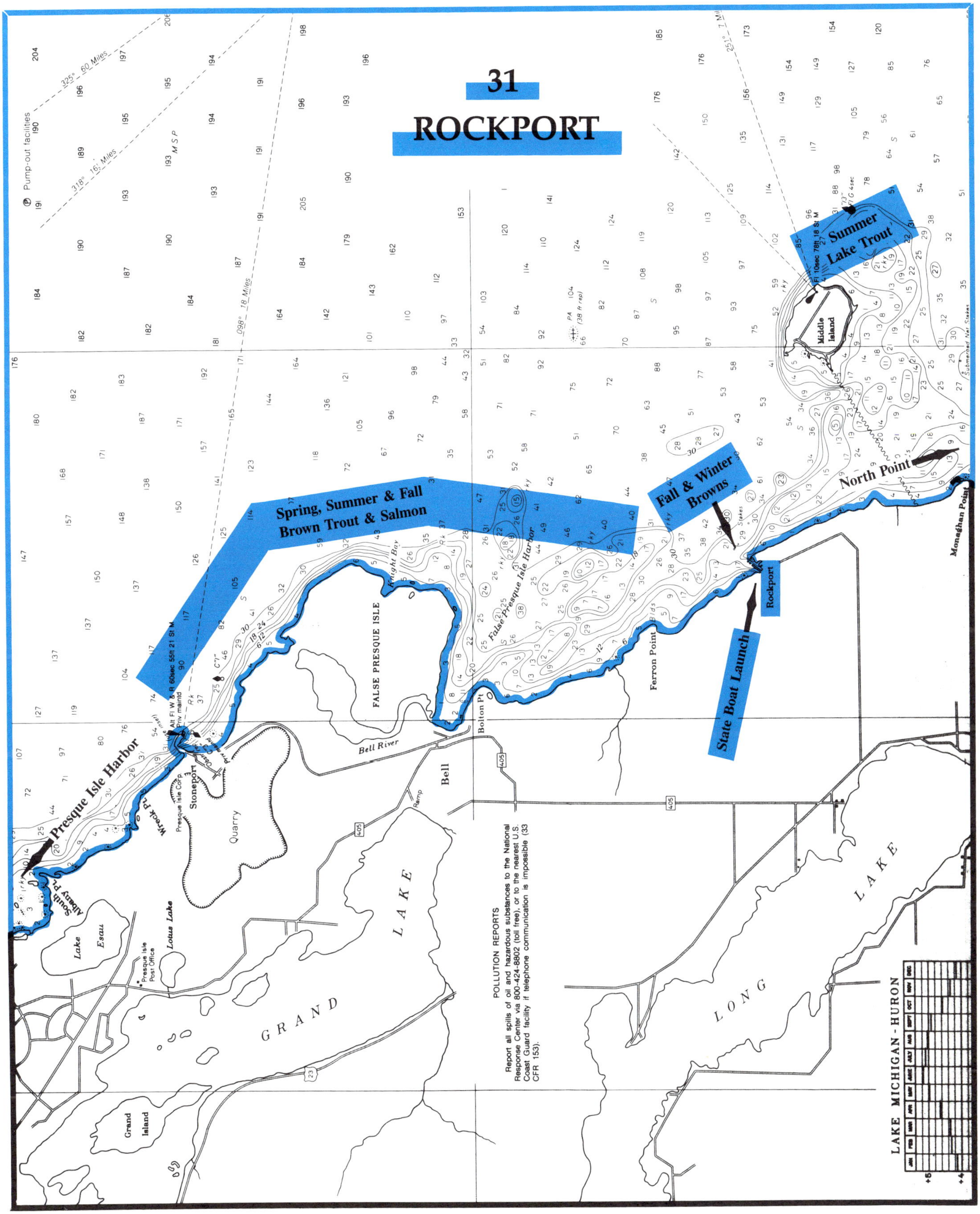
31
ROCKPORT
Spring, Summer & Fall Brown Trout & Salmon
Fall & Winter Browns
Summer Lake Trout
North Point
State Boat Launch
Rockport
Presque Isle Harbor
Middle Island
Monaghan Point
FALSE PRESQUE ISLE
False Presque Isle Harbor
Knight Bay
Bolton Pt
Ferron Point
Bell River
Bell
Stoneport
Presque Isle Corp.
Quarry
Wreck Pt
Albany Pt
South Pt
Lake Esau
Lotus Lake
Presque Isle Post Office
Grand Island
GRAND LAKE
LONG LAKE
Pump-out facilities
325° 60 Miles
318° 15 Miles
098° 18 Miles
251° 7 Miles
Submerged Net Stakes
POLLUTION REPORTS
Report all spills of oil and hazardous substances to the National Response Center via 800-424-8802 (toll free), or to the nearest U.S. Coast Guard facility if telephone communication is impossible (33 CFR 153).
LAKE MICHIGAN - HURON
JAN FEB MAR APR MAY JUNE JULY AUG SEPT OCT NOV DEC

32
NORTH POINT to MIDDLE ISLAND

"I've had a little utopia up here for awhile, but I knew it couldn't last forever." That's what Alpena charterboat-skipper Ed Retherford had to say about the fish-rich coastline from Thunder Bay north to Rockport.

This 12-mile stretch in northern Lake Huron has some of the best structure of any place in the Great Lakes. The water is clean and deep, and a troller can find 100-foot depths within a mile or two of shore. Several small bays and coves punctuate the shoreline, and reefs from two to 100 feet deep shape up everywhere. Prevailing winds are from the west, making for safe boating conditions, even for small craft, most of the time.

A variety of native warm-water species plus hefty plants of salmon and trout make this a troller's paradise. Competition is generally light, and the area could take considerably more angling pressure.

Fishing Schedule

SPRING

Shore anglers in *spring* can catch menominees off Long Lake Creek (also called Turnbull Creek, locally) and other small unnamed streams in this area. Wigglers are hot bait, but single salmon eggs work well, too, if fishermen first chum offshore structure within wading distance with a few handfuls of salmon eggs.

Perch fishing with shiner minnows in five to 20 feet of water is good in spring and peaks in June. And trollers pulling Flatfish, Dardevle Spoons, and Rapalas report good catches of northern pike to a dozen pounds each on the east side of Crooked Island and between Misery Bay and Sugar Island. Also try coves and bays throughout the area. There are plenty of underwater nooks and crannies that attract gamefish all through this region. Boat fishermen who run past any of it could be making a big mistake.

SUMMER

The area also produces top-drawer lake-trout and salmon fishing beginning in spring but coming into its own each *summer*. Lake trout are available in May in water to 50 feet deep, but by June, when the thermocline develops, they often go to depths of 100 or more feet. Kings and cohos released further north often school off deep-water reefs in summer.

One of the best spots for both lakers and salmon is the Nord Mere Wreck reef area, a couple of miles north of Thunder Bay Island. The 22- to 30-foot-deep structure—marked at the southwest end by the superstructure of the sunken German freighter and on the northeast end by a buoy—is surrounded by 45- to 50-foot depths. Another key lake-trout trolling area is the south side of Thunder Bay Island below the old Coast Guard masts.

Plenty of dogleg structure shapes up from Thunder Bay Island north to Middle Island. It is possible to troll between the islands and never have to go back for marked fish. An excellent spot to troll is off Stoneport where the water drops to 100 feet only a mile from shore. Further, many points, such as South Nine Mile Point and Potter Point, are hot for summer lakers and salmon when an east wind blows cold water in to shore.

Catching tactics for lake trout include running attractors and lures, especially 0-sized dodgers and trolling flies or squids. Good attractor colors here are banana (half white/half yellow), key lime (half green/half chartreuse), silver, and white with pink. Run the dodgers ahead of Twinkle Squids, Michigan Squids, and Sparkle Flies in purple with yellow and white, blue and white, green and white, and Christmas-tree patterns.

Most trollers pull the attractors early in the day, then switch to Silver Streaks, Flutter Spoons, Sutton Spoons, and Miller Spoons pulled clean. Those that stack these spoons, as well as Finn Spoons, Chargers, and G.W. Salmon Slammers, often pick up king salmon. No. 3 and No. 4 J-Plugs or Grizzly Plugs take the big kings, too. Productive colors include silver (plain or with ladderback designs), greens, blues, and rainbow trout.

Charterboats, such as the *Fish Trap*, skippered by Dale Hallman, typically host eight trolling rods. Normal rigging includes two inside stern-end dodger/fly setups, two stacked out-downs featuring spoons, and a pair of Dipsy-Divers trailing small spoons. If salmon turn on to dodgers, Hallman replaces the bottom halves of the stacked out-downs with more dodger/fly combinations. If not, he jerks the stern-end pair and switches to spoons.

Besides kings, lakers and cohos, trollers are also apt to pick up pink salmon, as the area has been packed with the little fish. They typically hit highlines and can be sporting fun on light and ultra-light rods.

Waders and boat fishermen take spawning smallmouth bass beginning in June, but a cold east wind can shut action down until the wind stops and/or until the temperature rises. Best success occurs in July along the entire shoreline but especially in Misery, Huron, and Morris bays. Much of the area, however, is accessible

32

NORTH POINT TO MIDDLE ISLAND

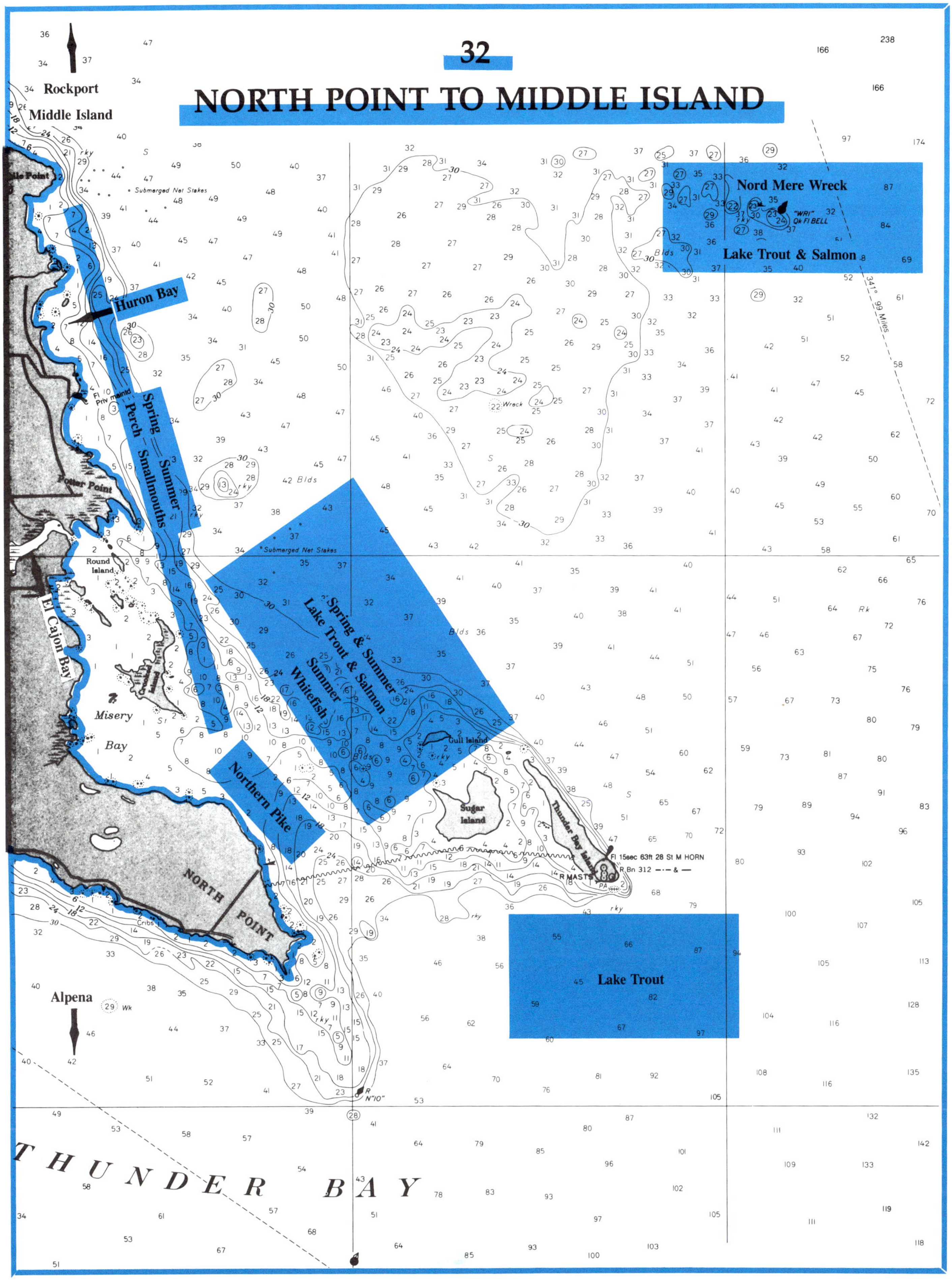

only by boat because of the fact that most of the shoreline is privately owned and therefore not accessible to wading fishermen. (Anglers might want to check out a plat book, as there are small parcels of state land, at El Cajon Bay, for example, fronting the lake at a few spots. The Alpena Area Chamber of Commerce has plat books for sale at $10 each). Small spinners, Mister Twisters, and lead-head jigs tipped with a minnow or crawler piece work well on the two- and three-pound smallmouths. There are also tackle-eaters here to five pounds.

Whitefish are an overlooked summer fishery. The area, in fact, literally teems with whitefish, so much so that a couple of licensed commercial netters usually fill trap-net quotas easily. These trap nets can be found anywhere from Alpena to Rockport, but they are well marked and have posed no problems to date for boat fishermen,.

Because the reef structure serves as hatching grounds for mayflies, wigglers (larvae of the mayfly) or nymphs are good baits. Use a fly rod or cane pole and a tiny split shot to get bait a foot or two under the surface, where whitefish will suck it in. Whitefish will also drill Swedish Pimples tipped with minnows or wigglers and pounded in and out of lake-bottom mud with the help of heavy sinkers. For best results, try 40- to 80-foot depths.

Another overlooked summer sport in this area is bowhunt fishing for carp, which invade shoreline shallows to spawn in June. There is no shortage of 20- to 30-pounders, and anglers wearing polarizing sunglasses can see them among pencil reeds and bulrushes close to shore.

Fall action remains good for pike, smallmouths, perch and whitefish. Most of the salmon, however, have migrated north to natal spawning grounds.

Winter sport is somewhat limited due to unpredictable ice conditions. Where ice forms over protected shallows, such as in the bays and coves, perch fishing and pike spearing is considered good. An overlooked winter burbot fishery exists in this area, as well as in Thunder and Squaw bays further south. Night fishing with dead smelt on bottom is the best tactic.

How to Buy a Boat

Five people—including Bob and Anne Hemeon, who live in Sarasota, Florida, and own a summer home here—boarded my charterboat to try for some salmon on a late-July day a couple of years ago. This area of the Great Lakes is one of the last to be discovered and developed as a trout and salmon fishery. So most trollers to the area, like the Hemeons, are newcomers.

The best opportunities lay along reef structure in the 12-mile run between North Point and Middle Island. So we put in at Rockport, ran to the south side of Middle Island, and set trolling lines. Almost exclusively our lures that day were purple-and-yellow Ale-E flies; red, green, and white Sparkle Flies; and blue-and-white and green-and-white Michigan Squids. We rigged the flies behind 0-sized dodgers in key-lime (yellow and green) and banana (white and yellow) colors.

We got into fish immediately, beautiful king salmon from eight to 26 pounds each. The action was frantic, unheard of at that time. We even had six fish on at once and managed to land four. In just 2-1/2 hours of fishing, we put 25 king salmon on ice. Both live wells were bulging.

Anne and Bob were so impressed that they went right out and bought a 22-foot fishing boat. Already they have traded up to a 24-footer, which they pull to Florida in winter, then trail back here for the summer.

I can't say that anyone has gone so far as to mortgage the house when bitten by the salmon-fishing bug. But other charter skippers tell me the same story: "We had such super fishing that my customers bought their own boat."

How can I blame them? That's why I bought my boat in the first place.

Captain Ed Retherford
Alpena

Planting Records

Middle Island reefs off Rockport and Thunder Bay Island reefs have each received 70,000-90,000 lake trout annually. Similar-sized releases will continue for at least the next five years.

Facilities

Fishermen with big boats launch at either Alpena's Small Boat Harbor and run north or at Rockport and troll south. Those with small aluminum boats or canoes can launch at a privately owned gravel ramp at Misery Bay for $3. There are a few wooden boats for rent there, too, but anglers should bring their own motors.

Further Information

Chambers of Commerce:

1. Alpena Area Chamber of Commerce, 133 Johnson St. (P.O. Box 65), Alpena 49707; 1-800-582-1906 (in Michigan) or (517) 354-4181.
2. East Michigan Tourist Association, One Wenonah Park, Bay City 48706; (517) 895-8823.

Bait & Tackle Shops and Charter Fishing:

See 33 (Alpena and Thunder Bay).

Department of Natural Resources:

Two fisheries biologists work out of District Headquarters at 1732 W. M-32, Gaylord 49735; (517) 732-3541.

Coast Guard:

Tawas Station, (517) 362-4428 or St. Ignace Station, (906) 643-9191.

33

ALPENA and THUNDER BAY

A Warm and Friendly Port is the way the local chamber of commerce describes Alpena and the 100-square-mile greater Thunder Bay area. Fishermen who come here will find good accommodations and a variety of angling opportunities.

Further, they will not have much competition. On a recent midweek trolling trip for brown trout, I counted only 19 other boats. This was in mid-July, just as summer brown-trout fishing was swinging into high gear. Pressure from the trolling fleet could be increased considerably without any adverse effects. In fact, the DNR has long wanted to pull pressure north from Oscoda (38) and Harrisville (37) and to promote tourism in the northern lake.

The area offers unspoiled beauty and untapped fishing potential. Structure, including shipwrecks, islands and drowned reefs, abounds. There have been hefty trout and salmon plants in recent years. Indian gillnetting, although legal above the 45th parallel, just south of the city limits, has not seemed to impact the sport fishery to any extent. Lake Huron from Alpena north is one of the fastest-growing sport fisheries in Michigan.

Fishing Schedule

SPRING

Ice-out in *spring* brings smelt, perch and brown trout into Thunder Bay for close-to-shore action. According to the log books of Alpena resident Omer Turnbull, who has fished the area for 40 years, action can begin as early as late March or as late as mid-April. Small streams, such as the Devil River at Ossineke, get smelt. So does the Thunder Bay River, where dippers net fish off the breakwall at the entrance to Small Boat Harbor and at 9th Street Dam. Steelhead fishing is good in the river from the mouth to the dam. Spawn and nightcrawlers are hot spring baits.

Anglers in small boats or from shore catch perch on wigglers, minnows and worms. They also take brown trout by casting 2/5- to 3/4-ounce spoons (Little Cleos, Mainliners, Krocodiles, etc.). The mouth of the Thunder Bay River is a favorite spot as is the warm-water discharge at the cement plant.

Trollers report spring brown-trout and lake-trout success by pulling body baits (Rapalas, Rebel Fastracs, Bill Norman plugs) or by rigging sewn minnows behind cowbell strings. For best bets, stay within 20-foot-deep water and work the shoals of Sulphur Island and the shoreline area. Action continues well into May, then tapers off until later in the summer.

SUMMER

Summer fishing kicks off with the bass opener (traditionally the Saturday before Memorial Day), with smallmouth anglers targeting Squaw Bay, Whitefish Bay (off Norwegian Creek), Partridge Point (34), and other shallow-water structure. Spinnerbaits, nightcrawler harnesses, and Junebug spinners are favored, and trolling or casting are rated tactics.

Lake-trout fishing is also good at this time in 25- to 40-foot depths about four miles straight out from the harbor. As temperatures warm, laker seekers target 80- to 120-foot depths in two locations: (1) directly south of 9-Mile Can and (2) a deep-water dropoff immediately east of Scarecrow Island.

To catch forktails, run small spoons clean, cowbell/Wobble-Glo combinations, or dodger/Flutter Spoon matches close to bottom when you can find temperatures of 48-52 degrees F. Stacking with slider or add-a-line rigs can help pick up brown trout and salmon in these same locations. Charterboat-captain Denny Huggler reports that, during the May 1-September 15 trolling season, his overall catch shows about 50 percent lake trout, 30 percent salmon and 20 percent brown trout.

Many boat fishermen at Thunder Bay call upon brown trout for first-string summer action and often relegate lakers and salmon to reserve-player status. The "second-string" salmon and lake trout,

I heft a pair of five-pound brown trout. Thunder Bay has long been known as a holding tank for brown trout.

however, have saved many a charterboat from a skunking, because anyone who has targeted brown trout knows how temperamental they can be. Good summer sport for browns kicks off about July 4 and lasts until the end of the month, culminating with the annual Brown Trout Festival. Hotspots include 20- to 30-foot depths over humps between Whitefish and Bare points. Mischley's Hole, in 40-60 feet of water between Whitefish and North points, is also good. A third spot to try is southwest of 9-Mile Can in 45-60 feet of water.

The most successful troller at Alpena is, without question, Captain Ed Retherford. Ed runs double charters, as many as 150 in a trolling season, and his annual catch rate falls between 1,700 and 2,500 fish. Retherford seeks 58-degree-F. temperature in the previously mentioned areas, then sends down small spoons on his four Big Jon downriggers. The out-downs are stacked with add-a-lines, making for a six-rod setup. When I fished with Ed aboard the *Trout Scout III* during the summer of 1985, he ran McMahon Spoons, Finn Spoons, and Cobras in combinations of brass, copper, and silver. Yellow and green are other traditionally good colors for browns. Retherford also believes in plenty of flash. To get it, he dips and rubs lures in metal polish.

Another good brown-trout fisherman is sport-angler Steve Speaks, a native Buckeye who came here nearly 20 years ago to teach high-school math. Over three separate summers, the winning fish in the annual Brown Trout Festival was caught from Speaks' 18-foot Starcraft, *Bi Fish*. Steve says the best brown-trout fishing occurs in mid to late July. Typically, weather patterns (especially storms, which change water clarity and temperature) dictate the best fishing, which generally runs hot or cold in three-day cycles.

Speaks also says that the biggest browns—football-shaped bruisers to 20 pounds—are nearly always caught during a 24-hour period. "When someone gets a big brown, many of us fish round the clock because we know the best chances occur over a short period of time," he says. Another trick Steve employs is to continue working over areas that others vacate. Some anglers think that browns, due to trolling traffic, leave. But instead, says Speaks, "Many times they go deep, so I drop my cannonballs in the mud and go after them."

Summer tactics include longlining (100-150 feet behind releases) and running side planers and outriggers. A zig-zag trolling pattern and occasional bursts of speed often help to trigger strikes. Brown trout live in this area year-round but are sometimes hard to find and equally difficult to get to strike.

By August the browns become lethargic, so anglers turn their attention to salmon. The same lures and rigging tactics that work for browns also take salmon, but many fishermen also mix in J-Plugs and body baits with their lure arsenal.

Landmarks, in addition to 9-Mile Can and various prominent points, include the cement-plant stacks at Alpena and a water tower on the west shore off Devil Lake. Trollers south of Partridge Point (34) normally take compass bearings off the point and Scarecrow Island.

In addition to some cohos and good numbers of Chinooks streaming north to natal spawning sites, the Thunder Bay region during the summer of 1985 also served up plenty of pink salmon. Trollers reported that the little 15- to 20-inch salmon hit high-lines, Dipsy-Divers and stackers. Some even struck flies trolled behind dodgers.

FALL

Fall fishing for brown trout can be exceptional from shore. (See 34, Partridge Point/Squaw Bay for details). In addition, perch make another appearance in shallows throughout Thunder Bay, and Chinook salmon begin stacking up outside the Thunder Bay River mouth. Small-boat anglers can get them via trolling and casting tactics. There is very little room along the breakwall for shorebounders, however.

WINTER

Winter sport is good for perch and brown trout, and there are reports of whitefish being taken through the ice in Thunder Bay. An especially good spot for browns is off the cement plant. In February 1985, a week after a tip-up fisherman had caught a 21-pound brown there, seven of us ventured onto the ice in temperatures that hovered at -25 degrees F. Our party drew a blank, but a father-son team that was there managed to ice an eight-pounder. A couple of other fishermen were casting spoons to open water from the warm-water discharge. Winter anglers here must exercise caution, however, as ice grows thin, even on the most frigid of days.

To catch browns through the ice, pin small smelt or sucker minnows to a tiny treble or No. 2 hook. Use a small steel leader, or a thieving pike may break you off. A little split shot will take the bait to three or four feet off bottom.

The Thunder Bay River serves up solid winter fishing action for shanty and open-air anglers alike. Fishermen working the area off the senior citizens residence downstream from 9th Street Dam take walleyes, perch, northern pike and browns. Upstream from the dam behind the college and behind Cow Island are good spots for perch, crappies, bluegills and some pike.

For additional area catching details see North Point (32), Rockport (31), Presque Isle Bay (30), Rogers City (29), Hammond Bay (28), Cheboygan (27), the Straits area (26), Partridge Point/Squaw Bay (34), and Ossineke (35).

Planting Records

The Alpena region has a long history of receiving hatchery-reared lake trout, brown trout and steelhead. From 50,000-100,000 lake trout have been released each year over reefs at Scarecrow Island. Plants will average 90,000 during each of the next five years. Brown-trout releases at Partridge Point (34) will approximate 100,000 during the same period. Steelhead plants at 9th Street Dam will increase to 30,000 yearly, along with 15,000 rainbows going into Small Boat Harbor. Salmon in the area are from releases to the north and south.

All in all, angling prospects appear to be very good for the future.

Facilities

Minimal but adequate launch facilities include a double ramp at city-owned Small Boat Harbor. Fees are $1 daily or $15 for the season. Facilities include gasoline and diesel fuel, water, electricity, restrooms, showers, haul-out and holding-tank pump-out service. Rental slip space is also available. Telephone number of the dock attendant is (517) 354-5684. A pay launch is also located at a private marina at Partride Point (34).

At Small Boat Harbor there is no pier and, because cement blocks line the river, little breakwall space for shorebound fishermen. Also, a fish-cleaning station is sorely needed.

The city of Alpena (population 15,000) offers a wide variety of restaurants and accommodations for visitors.

Further Information

Chambers of Commerce:

1. Alpena Area Chamber of Commerce, 133 Johnson St. (P.O. Box 65), Alpena 49707; 1-800-582-1906 or (517) 354-4181.

33 ALPENA and THUNDER BAY

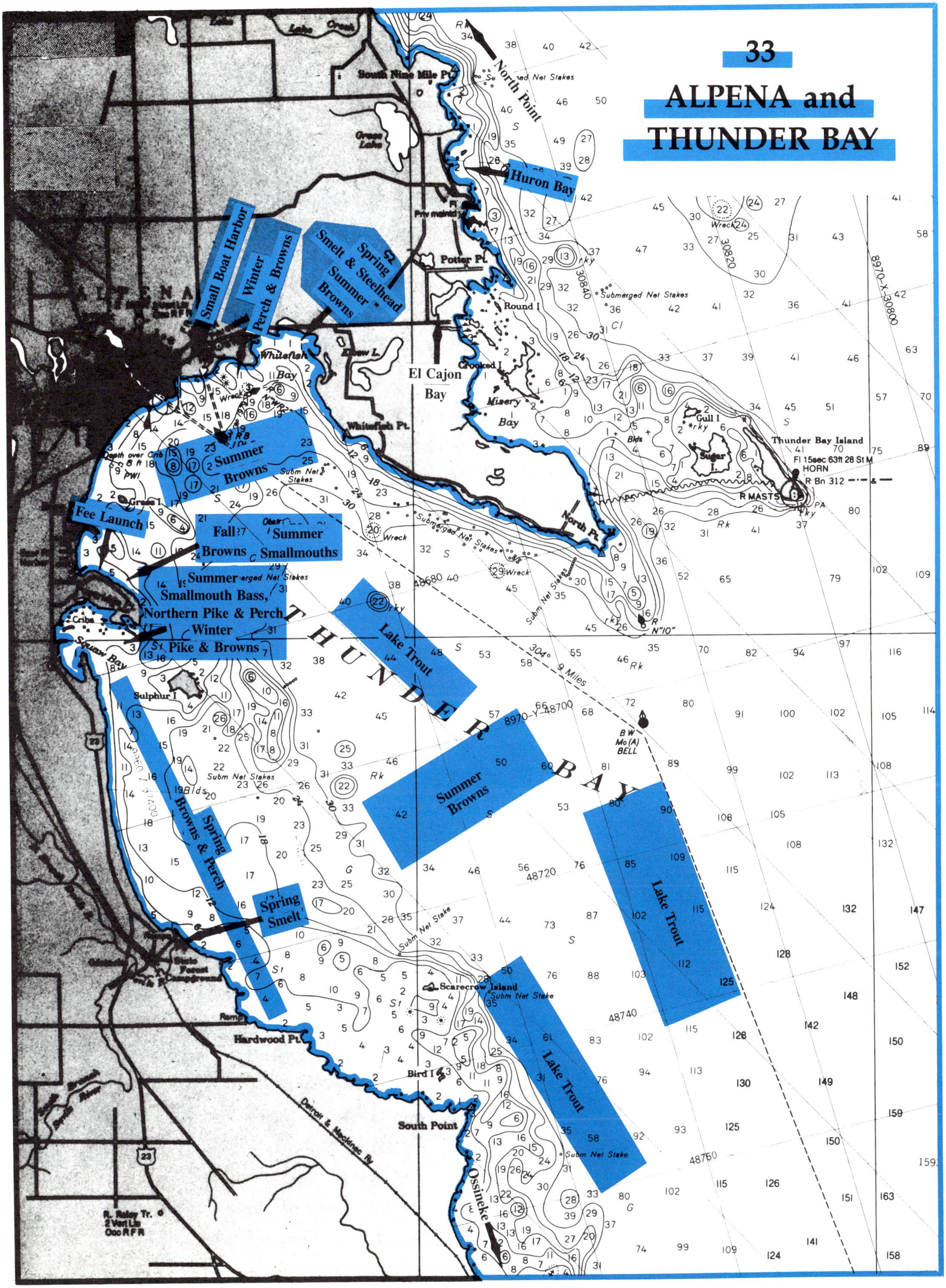

2. East Michigan Tourist Association, One Wenonah Park, Bay City 48706; (517) 895-8823.

Bait & Tackle Shops:

1. Buck's Tackle, 8501 US-23 N., Alpena 49707; (517) 595-2121.
2. Clem's Live Bait & Tackle, 304 N. 9th Ave., Alpena 49707; (517) 354-2070.
3. Arnold's Boat Works, 400 E. Chisholm, Alpena 49707; (517) 356-0551.

Charter Fishing:

1. Captain Ed Retherford, 220 Richardson, Alpena 49707; (517) 356-9361. 23-foot Starcraft, *Trout Scout III*.
2. Captain Dale Hallman, Fish Trap Charters, 6651 Webb Rd., Hale 48739; (517) 728-2143. 23-foot Starcraft, *Fish Trap*.
3. Captain Jerry Kramer, Kramer Charter Service, 8515 US-23 N., Alpena 49707; (517) 595-6165 (evenings). 24-foot Sea Ray, *Why Knot*.
4. Captain Denny Huggler, Denny's Charter Service, 140 Channel Rd. #1, Alpena 49707; (517) 354-8334 (evenings). 31-foot Silverton, *Patti's Den*.

Department of Natural Resources:

Two fisheries biologists work out of District Headquarters at 1732 W. M-32, Gaylord 49735; (517) 732-3541.

Coast Guard:

Tawas Station, (517) 362-4428 or St. Ignace Station, (906) 643-9191.

A Party For Perch

One of the best times to catch yellow perch from Squaw Bay is in the spring. The big jumbos come into the shallows then, and 13-14 inchers are common. The best Squaw Bay perch I ever caught measured exactly 18 inches—the size of a lunker bass.

When the wind is right, we like to drift across the bay with nightcrawler harnesses until we get strikes. Then we anchor and have at 'em.

But early on a June 1983 morning, when my son Scott and I took two friends onto Squaw Bay, there was little wind. So we stopped my boat over a weed bed I had found with a locator. We fished minnows and worms on single hooks, getting them to bottom with the help of bell sinkers.

Soon we had a strike, and a fat 12-inch perch came aboard. Then another and another. Action continued like that for two hours until our party of four filled a five-gallon pail with about 40 perch. The smallest was 10 inches; the biggest, 16 inches.

We don't always get perch action like that, but when we do, it's a real party.

Charles Obeginski
Lachine

Four For Four

At 6:00 p.m. on July 11, my buddy Tom, his Uncle Omer and I climbed aboard the *Trout Scout III*, a charter-boat skippered by Alpena's Ed Retherford. Retherford has quite a reputation among big-lake trollers. He consistently catches brown trout, which, I know from my own experiences, can be mighty moody.

We ran out six miles from Small Boat Harbor on a calm sea. I helped Ed rig four downriggers and two stacker set-ups as Dale Hallman, another captain in this area, cut the boat engine and locked our trolling speed at 3.0-3.5 mph on Ed's EMS Hawk. Then, as the evening breeze hummed through downrigger wires, we sent down McMahon and Finn spoons and a couple of Cobras.

We had washed those baits for nearly three hours without a knock-off, when suddenly Ed yelled, "Fish on!" Tom grabbed that rod and began to duel a small brown trout that wore himself out leaping from the lake again and again. Tom had the fish about 20 feet from the boat when three other rods went off at the same time. Omer, Dale and I each grabbed one while Ed scrambled to handle netting chores and keep a hand on the wheel.

The lines were going everywhere, and I just knew that we would get a tangle or, worse yet, lose one or more of our four fish. Tom swung his brown, a 3-1/2 pounder, aboard. Then he swiped the net from Ed and secured Omer's fish. Ten minutes later, we had four browns to seven pounds each on ice.

The entire evening's action was limited to those 10 minutes of wild sport. I've never experienced four browns at once, but I sure wouldn't pass up the chance to do it again.

Joe Zikewich
Lake Orion

Devil of a Smelt Run

I was born in Alpena 70 years ago and have fished Thunder Bay and the Ossineke area for over 40 years. During the past several, I have kept a diary of my fishing activities, including those on April 14, 1983. That was one of the most memorable days of fishing in my life.

Three friends and I went down to the mouth of the Devil River to see if the smelt might be in. They were—big spawners and more plentiful than I had ever seen in my life.

Taking turns, two of us dipped while the other pair hauled five-gallon pails of smelt a block and a half to our pickup truck. Each swipe of the net brought up nearly a basket full of smelt. In a short time, we had four tubs that each held several five-gallon pails. You might say we filled the pickup. After giving most of the smelt away to friends in Alpena, we went back and filled four more tubs.

It was fun, until it came time to clean them.

Omer Turnbull
Alpena

34
PARTRIDGE POINT and SQUAW BAY

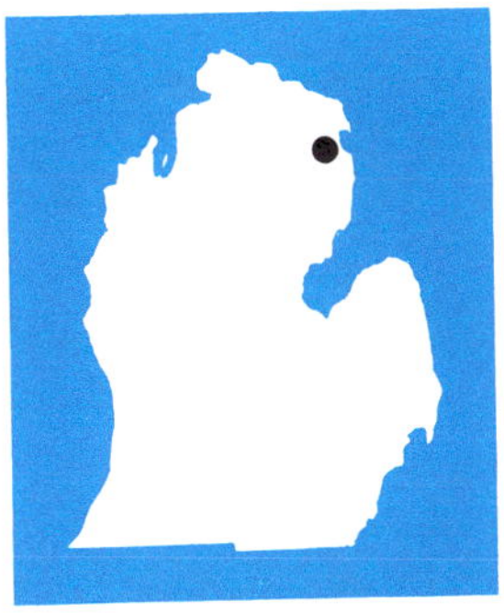

Although they are actually a part of the larger Thunder Bay area (33), Partridge Point and Squaw Bay feature some fishing opportunities not found elsewhere. Therefore, they deserve special mention.

Fishing Schedule

SPRING

Spring activity begins with yellow perch along the shoreline, in Squaw Bay to depths of 15 feet, and throughout the Sulphur Island area. Action begins by late April and generally lasts until late June. Quality varies from day to day and season to season. Wigglers and small minnows are preferred bait when jigged from anchored boats or driftfished. Shorebound fishermen like the easy access to the east of US-23. In the marsh area to the west of the highway, however, perch fishing appears to have fallen off in recent years.

The May 15 northern-pike season opener attracts fishermen, who go after the three- to 15-pound pike between the island and shore in five to 10 feet of water. This area supports good numbers of smelt, perch and shiners, which are the calling cards for northerns. The west and north sides of Sulphur Island are also good bets for pike. Catching tactics include bobber fishing with four- and five-inch minnows over weed beds, spoon and plug casting among bulrushes and pencil reeds, and trolling with wobbling plugs (Pike Minnows, Flatfish, Creek Chubs) or Spoons (Kush Spoons, Eppinger Rok'T-Devlets, Red Eyes).

SUMMER

Summer action continues with yellow perch and pike, plus smallmouth bass. Off Partridge Point Road is plenty of rock structure from three to 15 feet deep. Spawning smallmouths come there about the time of the season opener (traditionally the Saturday before Memorial Day) and provide top sport for wading fishermen who cast and retrieve spinners, spinnerbaits, buzzbaits, jigs, and plastic worms. Perhaps the hottest local lure is a yellow or chartreuse Mister Twister. Trollers also report good catches on Junebug Spinners and nightcrawler harnesses featuring silver blades. Bass average two pounds, with an occasional four- and five-pound fish turning up. Action remains good well into summer.

In addition, Squaw Bay serves up rock bass, crappies, catfish and a few largemouth bass.

FALL

In *fall* these same species are available along with brown trout. The DNR has historically planted Partridge Point with up to 100,000 yearling and/or fall fingerling browns. Trollers begin picking them up betweeen Sulphur Island and Partridge Point on silver-plated spoons (McMahon and Finn spoons, along with Cobras, are excellent choices). Waders fling casting spoons from shore all along the Partridge Point tip. Hot lures in recent years have been 3/8-ounce Krocodiles in chartreuse and silver and chartreuse and gold and 1/3-ounce Little Cleos in white with red tip or blue with glitter tape.

Action varies throughout September into late October, with the browns making periodic runs into rock-strewn shallows. I fished here for two days in September several years ago and couldn't buy a strike. But the following weekend, spincasters really took the browns to task. Rough weather (wind and waves), in particular, gets these magnificent fish to porpoising. Early morning and evening are the best times to catch them.

WINTER

Winter sport keys on yellow perch between Sulphur Island and shore, with ice men pinning waxworms to teardrop spoons or shiner minnows to Russian Hooks. Many, using Swedish Pimples or Jigging Rapalas, jig for brown trout from shanties or on the open ice. Tip-ups featuring two-inch minnows produce browns and northern pike. The best spot for pike, including a sag-belly fish or two over 20 pounds each winter, is on the north side of Squaw Bay.

For additional information and map, see 33 (Alpena and Thunder Bay).

Planting Records

The DNR plans to continue hefty brown-trout releases (about 100,000 on the average each year) through 1990.

Facilities

The only launch ramp is located at a private marina on the north side of Partridge Point. Expect to pay a nominal fee. A cartop boat or canoe can be launched from the US-23 highway.

Further Information

Chambers of Commerce:

1. Alpena Area Chamber of Commerce, 133 Johnson St. (P.O. Box 65), Alpena 49707; 1-800-582-1906 (in Michigan) or (517) 354-4181.

2. East Michigan Tourist Association, One Wenonah Park, Bay City 48706; (517) 895-8823.

Bait & Tackle Shops:

See 33 (Alpena and Thunder Bay).

Charter Fishing:

Chuck Obeginski, Hooker Charters, 13158 Lachine St., Lachine 49753; (517) 379-3080. Perch-fishing charters on Squaw Bay. 19-foot Islander, *Hooker II*.

Department of Natural Resources:

Two fisheries biologists work out of District Headquarters at 1732 W. M-32, Gaylord 49735; (517) 732-3541.

Coast Guard:

Tawas Station, (517) 362-4428 or St. Ignace Station, (906) 643-9191.

These surf fishermen scored in the Lake Huron shallows. Partridge Point is an excellent spot for brown trout in the fall.

35 OSSINEKE

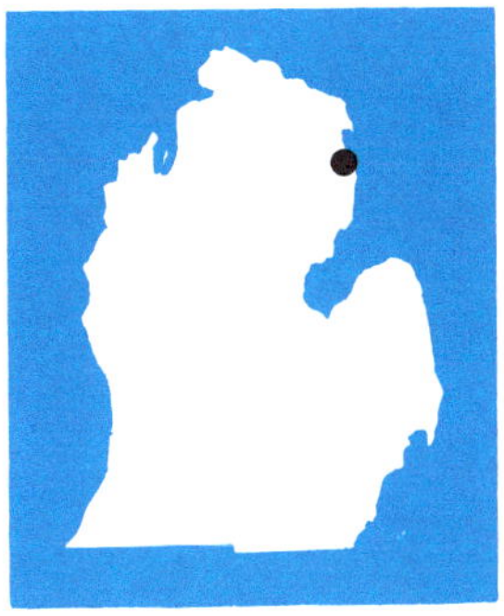

Ossineke, located in the southern portion of Thunder Bay, offers unique angling opportunities and the only decent boat launch between Partridge Point (34) and Black River (36).

The light to moderate winds generally favor the small-boat fisherman. In April, morning winds are often from the northwest but switch to the southwest by afternoon. In May they begin in the southwest, then switch to the southeast. Summer and fall winds have a west/southwest bent.

Fishing Schedule

SPRING

Spring fishing begins soon after ice-out, about mid-April, when runs of perch and smelt, attracted to the Devil River runoff, begin. The area does not get a lot of pressure because spring action is sporadic and unpredictable. Some years, though, it can be exceptional, especially for smelt (see "Devil of a Smelt Run", pg. 138). Smelters work the rivermouth as well as shoreline shallows to the north and south. Most perch fishermen go out in small boats and look for weed beds and structure. Likely spots include near the boat launch at Nicholson Hill Rd., the Devil River to the north, Hardwood Point to the south, and Scarecrow Island, a couple of miles offshore from Hardwood Point.

In early May, trollers can take lake trout, brown trout and a few salmon in the shallows as the predator fish come in to eat spawning smelt. (See 33, Alpena and Thunder Bay for catching details.)

SUMMER

Hot *summer* fishing off Ossineke includes smallmouth bass. From late May well into June, the spawning smallies seek rock structure from five to 12 feet deep in which to lay their eggs. Little patches of such microstructure are scattered throughout the Ossineke area. The water is clear enough to see the bass beds—scooped-out depressions in the rubble about the size of large dinner plates—with the aid of polarizing sunglasses. The territorial smallmouths will hit spinnerbaits, buzzbaits, crankbaits, and fake worms cast near them.

June is also a good month to catch lake trout, which have historically been released over Scarecrow Island reefs. Work the inclines to 120 feet deep on the west and north sides of the island. For best results, keep downrigger weights close to bottom and rig L'il Guys, Wobble-Glos, Clatter Tads or small Fire Plugs behind cowbells or 00 dodgers. Troll on the slow side (2.0 mph or less).

Fishermen who stack spoons (especially Northport Nailers, Flutter Chucks, Finn Spoons, G.W. Salmon Slammers, McMahon Spoons, and Silver Streaks) with slider or add-a-line rigs can often pick up salmon and browns.

Summer fishermen also report catches of rock bass, channel cats and northern pike, especially where pencil reeds and submerged weed beds can be found. In recent years, this has been somewhat difficult to do because of high water. The 60- to 120-foot depths east and south of Scarecrow Island produce salmon for trollers who target them.

FALL

Fall fishing opportunities continue for northern pike and panfish, including perch.

There are no *winter* fishing activities to speak of.

Planting Records

Releases of hatchery-reared fish in this area are limited to lake-trout plants at Scarecrow Island. In recent years, the DNR has released from 50,000-100,000 lakers (both yearlings and fall fingerlings) annually. Over the next five years, the annual goal is 90,000.

Facilities

The DNR operates a free single-ramp boat launch at the end of Nicholson Hill Rd., just south of the Devil River. Since Ossineke is more of a crossroads than a planned community, other facilities are poor. Alpena (33), however, lies only a few miles north.

Further Information

Chambers of Commerce:

1. East Michigan Tourist Association, One Wenonah Park, Bay City 48706; (517) 895-8823.
2. Alpena Area Chamber of Commerce, 133 Johnson St. (P.O. Box 65), Alpena 49707; 1-800-582-1906 (in Michigan) or (517) 354-4181.

Bait & Tackle Shops and Charter Fishing:

Refer to 33 (Alpena and Thunder Bay).

Department of Natural Resources:

Two fisheries biologists work out of District Headquarters at 1732 W. M-32, Gaylord 49735; (517) 732-3541.

Coast Guard:

Tawas Station, (517) 362-4428 or St. Ignace Station, (906) 643-9191.

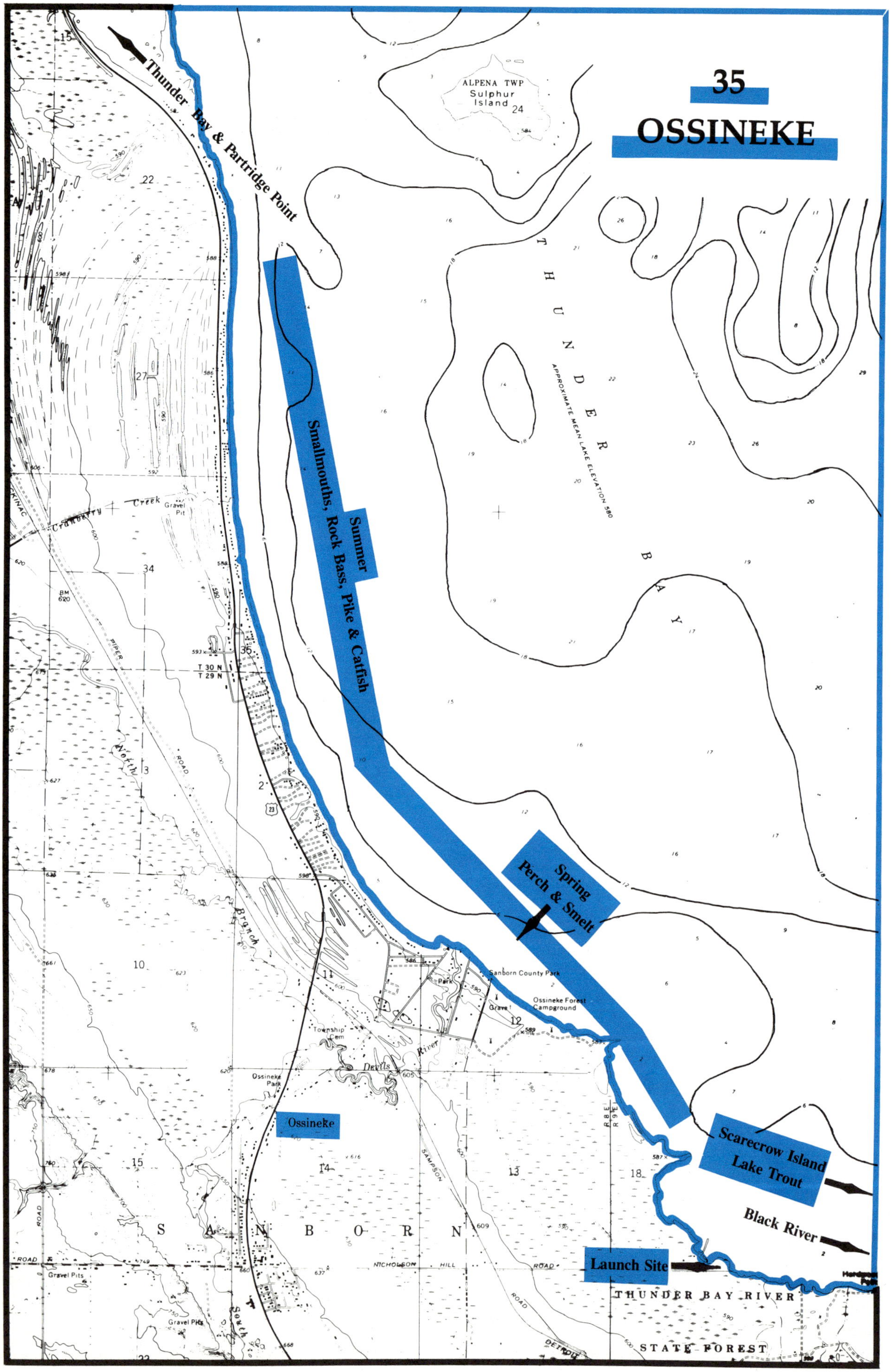
35
OSSINEKE
Thunder Bay & Partridge Point
Summer
Smallmouths, Rock Bass, Pike & Catfish
Spring
Perch & Smelt
Scarecrow Island
Lake Trout
Black River
Launch Site
Ossineke
ALPENA TWP
Sulphur Island
THUNDER BAY
APPROXIMATE MEAN LAKE ELEVATION 580
Sanborn County Park
Ossineke Forest Campground
Township Cem
Ossineke Park
Devils River
Cranberry Creek
North Branch
SANBORN
THUNDER BAY RIVER
STATE FOREST
NICHOLSON HILL ROAD
SAMPSON ROAD
PIPER ROAD
Gravel Pits
T 30 N
T 29 N

36
BLACK RIVER MOUTH

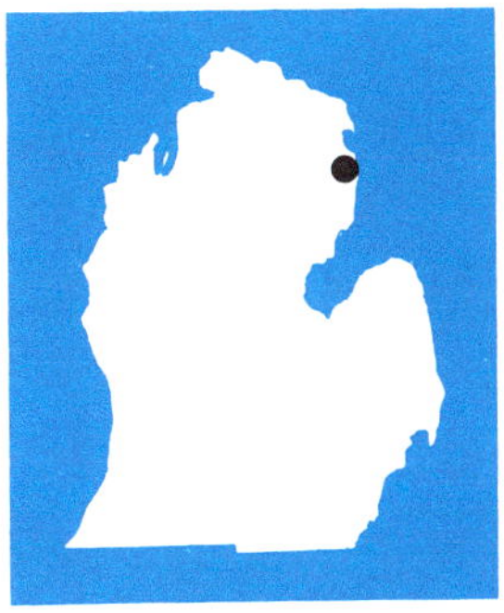

"I rate it as one of the two best steelhead streams on the east side," says outdoor-writer Mike Modrzynski of Oscoda. "The other is the Ocqueoc River (see 28, Hammond Bay).

The Black River yields steelhead in spring and fall; brook trout in early spring, summer and fall; and Chinook salmon in late summer/early fall. Besides river fishing, there are some fair to good angling opportunities offshore for trout, salmon, pike, perch and smallmouths.

Fishing Schedule

SPRING

Since current regulations allow fishing from the junction of the north and south branches of the Black River to its mouth from April 1-December 31, *spring* steelheaders get ice-out action. Modrzynski and friends are there, taking five- to 10-pound fish from the dark water. They rely upon dime-sized bags of fresh steelhead spawn with Fenton Flies (floating bodies with a twist of bright yarn) tied just ahead of the sack. The flies help keep the sack off bottom, plus the yarn makes the offering more visible to steelhead.

Upper reaches of the river, mostly meandering through private property, also contain brook trout. Beginning the last Saturday in April (the traditional season opener), trouters catch the seven- to 12-inch brookies on leaf worms or nightcrawler pieces threaded to small gold spinners or plain hooks in gold. Fly fishing with dries on the narrow stream can be a tough, but rewarding exercise.

Spring fishing activity also includes yellow perch and northern pike, both in the river and south of the mouth, where there are some weed beds.

Tremendous shoal water containing rocky reefs honeycomb the area, making for good smallmouth bass fishing. A top spot is north of the rivermouth. Anglers toss spinnerbaits or straight-line spinners such as Blue Fox Super Vibrax or Mepps Aglia brands. Trollers and drifters pull nightcrawlers pinned to Junebug Spinners or nightcrawler harnesses. A few flip lead-headed jigs with or without meat.

Water in this area is extremely shallow, and boaters should exercise caution. You can almost walk to Black River Island a mile and one-half offshore, according to Conservation Officer Gary Sims.

SUMMER

Summer sport includes fishing for northern pike, smallmouth bass, yellow perch and catfish. Offshore trollers also get into occasional good catches of lake trout, pink salmon and some king salmon. Charterboat-skipper Jerry Kramer runs south with his *Why Knot* from Alpena to troll the south side of Black River Island in 90 feet of water. Catching combination is chartreuse

Many consider the mouth of the Black River to be Lake Huron's top steelhead spot in spring and fall.

Wobble-Glos behind either cowbells or 0-sized Les Davis Herring Dodgers.

Sport-troller Howard Kitter, also of Alpena, targets the 105- to 110-foot water four to five miles offshore from the rivermouth. He and his wife have taken lake trout to 11-1/2 pounds each by pulling Northport Nailers, run clean and close to bottom. Hot color has been silver with black. The Kitters also report success on black-colored Silver Streaks and orange J-Plugs. "You have to find rough bottom," Kitter says. "We look for up-and-down structure, then go to bottom with our lures." Howard and his wife typically set four downriggers off their 18-foot boat.

FALL

In *fall* they fish closer to shore, picking up stray steelhead around the island and salmon in the shoal waters. Labor Day usually marks the time for Chinooks in the river, which then normally hosts its biggest crowds of the year. Those bottomfishing with crawlers and spawn bags pick off some of the big spawners. Spoon tossers report success with silver-and-green and silver-and-blue Little Cleos. Unfortunately, an illegal snag fishery also develops, and this keeps C.O. Sims and other enforcement officers busy writing tickets.

Some steelhead enter the river again in late fall to winter over and spawn the following spring. These are generally darker fish that sport pink racing stripes.

September is also a good time for channel catfish in the river. Nightcrawler gobs or blood baits fished on bottom produce the cats.

WINTER

There are few *winter* fishing opportunities worth reporting. When ice is safe, however, shanty fishermen might try for pike and perch in the weed beds.

Planting Records

Black River Island has traditionally received 50,000-90,000 yearling lake trout. The DNR plans to release 90,000 each year for at least the next five years.

Chinook and steelhead in the Black River are apparently sustaining natural reproduction. There are no releases of hatchery-reared fish.

Facilities

The DNR operates a free shallow-water gravel launch at the rivermouth with ample space for vehicle and trailer parking. Better launches exist at Ossineke (35) to the north and Harrisville (37) to the south. The Fish House, a party store/motel on US-23 at the river, has a launch with cement ribbons. Expect to pay a nominal fee.

Further Information

Chambers of Commerce:

East Michigan Tourist Association, One Wenonah Park, Bay City 48706; (517) 895-8823.

Bait & Tackle Shops:

The Fish House, just west of the Black River Bridge; (517) 471-5090.

Charter Fishing:

Captain Jerry Kramer, Kramer Charter Service, 8515 US-23 N., Alpena 49707; (517) 595-6165 (evenings). 24-foot Sea Ray, *Why Knot*.

Department of Natural Resources:

Two fisheries biologists work out of District Headquarters at 191 S. Mt. Tom Rd., Mio 48647; (517) 826-3211.

Coast Guard:

Tawas Station, (517) 362-4428.

Weigh-In Time

Barbers aren't the only ones who get to hear great fish stories. In fact, owning a bait and tackle shop means a fellow not only gets to hear the stories—he gets to see the fish, too. Like the big Chinook salmon which just last week (early September 1985) came right up on the boat ramp. Maybe he thought it was a spawning bed.

Fishing keeps getting better and better, and one of the best parts about my work is weighing in fish for customers, some of whom have been coming here for many years. I've put salmon on the scales to 25 pounds, steelhead to 15 pounds, and plenty of channel catfish in the five- and six-pound range. And you should hear the stories of the ones that got away!

John Rowell
The Fish House, Black River Bridge
Black River Mouth

36 BLACK RIVER MOUTH

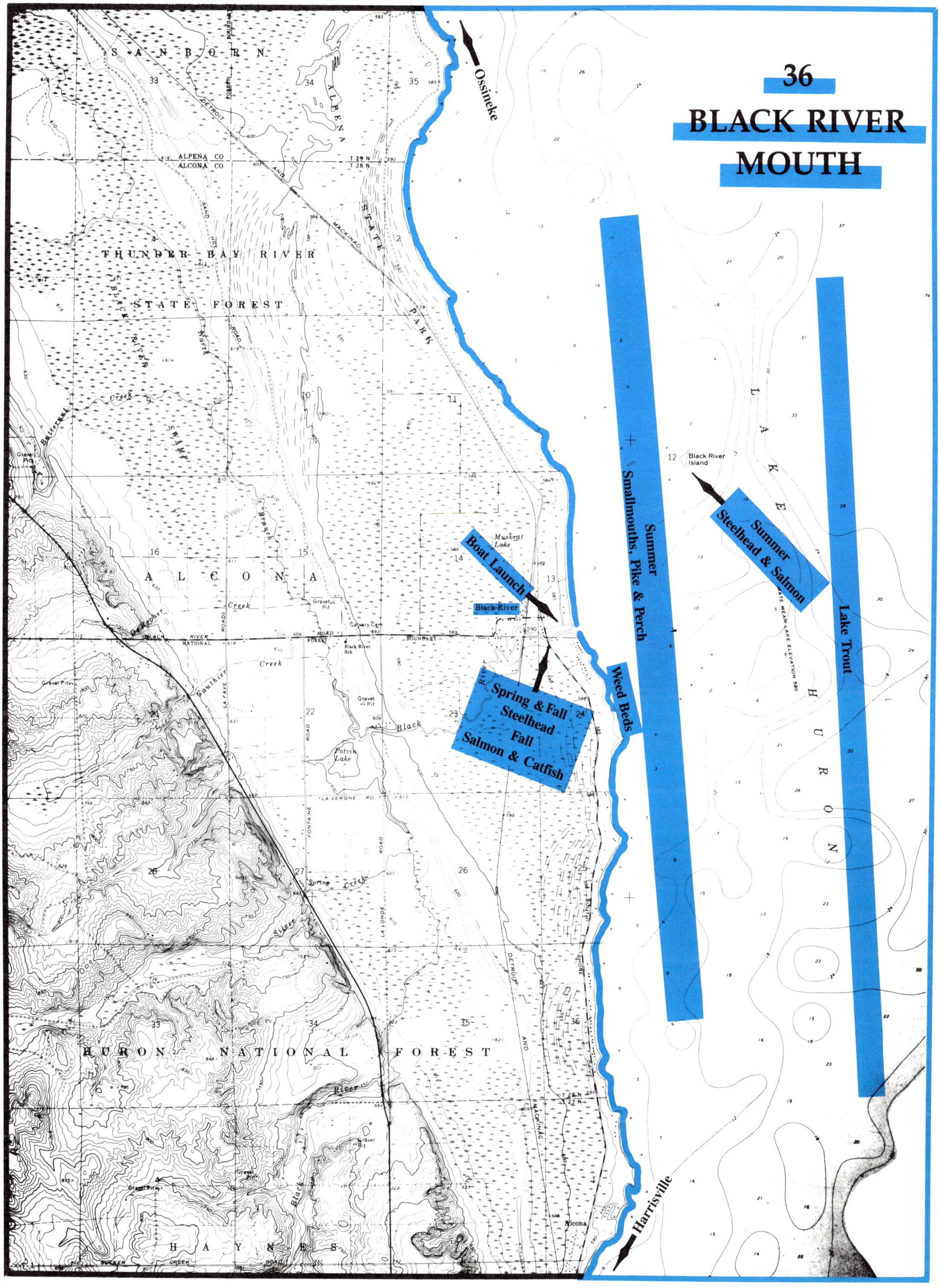

37

HARRISVILLE

Tell someone you're going lake-trout or salmon fishing on Lake Huron, and he'll ask, "Where, Harrisville or Oscoda (38)? In many respects, these are the two most popular ports along the lake. Each was among the earliest Lake Huron release sites to receive salmonids. Fishermen have not been sorry.

Harrisville has been targeted for Chinook salmon for about 15 years. Yet lake trout, because of consistent releases at Sturgeon Point and at Greenbush, about five miles north and south respectively, vie for popularity. The Harrisville Lake Trout Festival, held each year in mid-July, offers several thousand dollars in cash prizes for big lake trout and salmon. Entry fee has been $25.

Brown trout, steelhead and rainbows are newer calling cards at this site.

Fishing Schedule

SPRING

Spring fishing in the shallows rates very good for lake trout and fair to good for salmon. Each spring in the early 1980s, I and Joe Zikewich, my fishing/hunting partner, would trail his Sea Nymph, the *Shelldrake*, to Harrisville and park it near our cabin in the woods. We were here to hunt wild turkeys along the Black River, about seven miles north of Harrisville. Since, in those days, turkey hunting ended daily at noon and there was no closed season on lake trout (currently it begins May 1 and ends August 15), afternoons would find us trolling for spring lakers out of Harrisville.

And most years we enjoyed good fishing. One spring we coolered a half-dozen forktails by trolling six- to nine-foot depths from the south breakwall to the boulders off Harrisville State Park. Small, straight Rapalas in black and silver were the ticket. Another year, in 30 feet of water just off the south breakwall, the lakers pounded our blue-scale Fire Plugs mated to three-blade cowbell strings.

I have never done well on early spring salmon out of Harrisville, but others report that they take a few kings and an occasional brown trout and steelhead with the above-mentioned lures. Better fishing for both trout and salmon occurs in *summer*.

SUMMER

Flint sport-troller Dave Keene regularly keys on Harrisville from June through September. Until the end of July, his overall catch rate runs 90 percent lake trout and 10 percent salmon. In August and September the reverse is true. (Lakers caught after August 15 must be released, however.) Keene claims the best lake-trout fishing occurs when forkies are stacked up in 80-110 feet of water. This normally starts in late June from five to eight miles offshore.

Dave likes to run north to Sturgeon Point where, with the help of landmarks such as the Sturgeon Point Lighthouse and a line of trees immediately to the south, he trolls north and south. Depths of 80-110 feet in this region contain cobblestone, ideal rooting grounds for lake trout looking for sculpin and small crabs to eat. The Harrisville water tower is another useful landmark for offshore trollers. So are the "cans," a half-dozen marker buoys just north of the harbor and a mile offshore. Boulders along shore at the state park are useful landmarks for shallow-water fishermen. Further south, a slot in the treeline denotes Greenbush. Even further down the lake is the Lakewood Shores water tower.

From his fully equipped Thompson, the *Fish'n Machine*, Keene runs cowbells and small lures on bottom or within a couple of feet of it. Hot colors on attractor blades include aluminum, chrome, chartreuse, and green and pearl. Wobble-Glos, Spin-N-Glos, Tiny Tads, and Fire Plugs in chrome, chartreuse and red dots, kelly green, pink, pearl, metallic green, metallic blue, or gold are effective matches. Occasionally Dave will run 0-sized chrome dodgers with blue or green Sparkle Flies.

Best speed for summertime lakers is 1.7-2.1 knots. Keene likes to rig cowbells six to 12 feet behind cannonballs (six or eight feet for Williams Wablers), spotting stacker lines 20-40 feet back. Little tricks, such as popping rods free and letting them flutter to the surface while under power, or putting the boat in neutral and counting to five before slipping it back into gear, will sometimes get lethargic lakers to strike.

Wobble-Glos rigged to either cowbells or dodgers account for probably 75 percent of Harrisville lake-trout catches for most fishermen. I used to fish this port at least once each summer with Terry Walsh, one of the area's original (and, in my opinion, one of Lake Huron's most experienced and capable) charterboat captains. Walsh fishes Lake Huron from his Au Gres home north to Alpena (33), and Harrisville is a regular summertime haunt. If I remember correctly, we never failed to get limits for Terry's customers on morning charters. Later in the afternoon, he and I would go out and catch a few more, plus maybe a salmon or two, for our freezers or for photo sessions. Wobble-Glos always did the damage. Terry would fine-tune his laker-trolling operation by removing one of three blades from Big Jon cowbells, by painting black dots on kelly-green Wobble-Glos, and by eyeballing his graph and trolling speed.

Stacking with Hooksters, Flutter Spoons, Strikers, and Southport Slammers often accounts for both lake trout and king

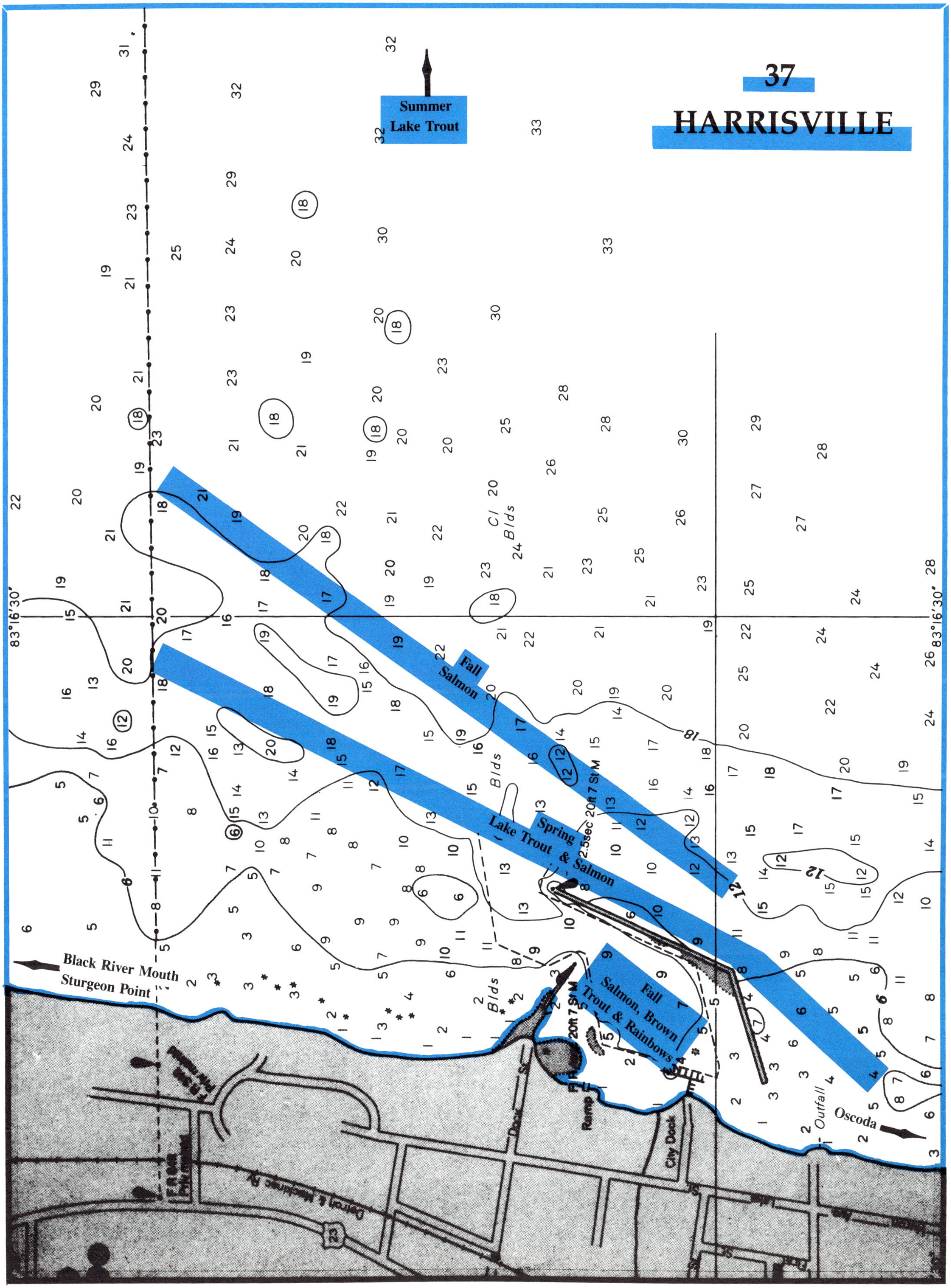
37
HARRISVILLE
Summer Lake Trout
Fall Salmon
Spring Lake Trout & Salmon
Fall Salmon, Brown Trout & Rainbows
Black River Mouth
Sturgeon Point
Oscoda
City Dock
Outfall
83°16'30'

Harrisville Harbor is productive in fall for boat and shore fishermen seeking Chinook salmon. — Michigan Travel Bureau Photo —

HARRISVILLE (cont.)

salmon, the latter as July nears an end. In 1985, Harrisville produced pink salmon all summer long, many of which were caught off stacked spoons. Productive spoon colors for Keene are chrome with blue stripe, chartreuse and green, brass and chrome, black and gold, kelly green with green tape, and chartreuse with red ladderback. Sometimes he will use Williams Wablers as attractors with these and other lures behind.

By August 1, many trollers completely switch over to salmon, and you will see outrigger poles, Dipsy-Divers and planer boards on trolling boats.

FALL

As the big kings crowd the harbor, normally by Labor Day, the *fall* fishing season officially begins. By mid-September most of the action occurs within a half-mile of the harbor. Tiger Plugs, J-Plugs, Grizzly Plugs, Hooksters, Flutter Spoons, Southport Slammers, Flutter Chucks, dodgers and Sparkle Flies, Willy's Worms, Hot 'N Tots, and Ping-A-Ts all make an appearance for salmon. Hot colors are chrome, gold, pearl, green with black skeletal, chartreuse with red, white with pink tape, and black with gold tape.

On one memorable mid-September trip, I, Joe Zikewich and our wives washed lures all day Saturday. We boxed only one king, a 17-pound male, for our efforts, which included burning up two tanks of gasoline. The next day was a repeat, and we were ready to hang it up at noon. But while playing with Joe's marine radio, I heard two fishermen talking on an offbeat channel.

"Get over here now," once voice commanded.

"Why? What's up?"

"Kings. They're everywhere. Sutton Spoons down 20 feet. I can't keep a line in the water."

"Where in hell are you?"

"Same place I was yesterday."

"I'm on my way."

I recognized the fisherman's voice and, with the help of my 400mm camera lens, located his boat near the previously mentioned "cans." I told Joe and the ladies to reef lines, then, while Joe gunned the *Shelldrake*, rummaged through his tackle boxes for Sutton Spoons. I found four and, when Joe shut down to trolling speed in 25 feet of water, began sending them down.

Over the next hour, we put five khaki-colored kings to 24 pounds each in the cooler, lost another at the net, and had two others on. This hot action included a triple, though we farmered one fish.

After the king and pink-salmon runs, look for this port to host steelhead, rainbows and browns. Harbor fishermen catch both trout and salmon in September and October by fishing fresh-cut spawn on No. 8 treble hooks on bottom with the help of pencil bobbers. Silver or hot-colored Little Cleos, Krocodiles, Devle Dogs, Locos, and Kastmasters produce for spincasters.

WINTER

There are no *winter* fishing activities to speak of. However, with the introduction of brown and rainbow trout, it is most likely that ice anglers using tip-ups or jigging with minnows or nightcrawlers will be rewarded. Whole-kernel corn or waxworms are also worth a try.

Planting Records

Annual plants of 300,000 Chinook fingerlings will continue, as they have for several years, through at least 1990. Lake-trout releases at Greenbush and Sturgeon Point have fluctuated between 60,000 and 90,000 and will continue at 100,000 and 120,000 respectively.

Harrisville Harbor first received brown trout and rainbow trout in 1984. A total of 10,000 yearlings each will be stocked annually through at least 1990. Although steelhead releases apparently will not continue, fishermen should, for several years, be able to catch steelies from a 1983 plant of 10,000 yearlings.

Facilities

Harrisville Harbor is serviced by a dock attendant, shower facilities, restrooms, electricity, water, sewage pump-out, VHF-FM radio, transient accommodations, and gasoline and diesel fuel. The telephone number is (517) 724-5242. Six paved DNR boat launches are available.

Though numbering less than 600 permanent residents, Harrisville caters heavily to tourists, and there are plenty of accommodations in this friendly town.

Further Information

Chambers of Commerce:

East Michigan Tourist Association, One Wenonah Park, Bay City 48706; (517) 895-8823.

Bait & Tackle Shops:

Tackle Land, US-23, Harrisville; (517) 724-5524.

Charter Fishing:

1. Captain Terry Walsh, TerMar Charters, 426 Michigan Ave., Au Gres 48703; (517) 876-8318. 26-foot Stamas, *Ter-Mar*.
2. Captain Ron Skiba, Ski-Ba-Doo Sport Fishing Charters, 401 N. Poor Farm Rd., Harrisville 48740; (313) 353-2000. 26-foot Sea Ray, *Ski-Ba-Doo*.
3. About a dozen other professional skippers charter out of Harrisville. Most belong to the Harrisville Charter Boat Association, P.O. Box 601, Harrisville 48740; (517) 724-6516.

Department of Natural Resources:

Two fisheries biologists work out of District Headquarters at 191 Mt. Tom Rd., Mio 48647; (517) 826-3211.

Coast Guard:

Tawas Station, (517) 362-4428.

Harrisville *Fish 'n Machine*

Wind, rain and some fog added up to a miserable day to spend on the lake when my brother Scott and I arrived at Harrisville at 8:30 on a mid-June Saturday morning. We listened to the marine radio for awhile, and, sure enough, there were a few boats out. But they weren't catching anything. We were tempted to forget fishing.

But we had made a long early morning drive from Flint and were expecting three friends on board my boat, the *Fish'n Machine*, the next morning. So we decided to find out where the fish were—or weren't.

We ran out to 45 feet of water and set the first line, a string of aluminum cowbells and a green Wobble-Glo, at 43 feet. I never got the rod in the holder. Bang! A nice strike. Quickly I handed the rod to Scott, and he started battle with the first of 17 lake trout in 2-1/2 hours. Those lakers were really stacked up from 50 feet to bottom, and I could not get more than three rods set at any one time. We kept our limit of six fish and released all others.

Sunday morning looked like an excellent weather day—calm seas, no wind, and partly cloudy. At seven o'clock our friends arrived, and we headed out, full of anticipation that we would find the school of lakers again. But at 50 feet there were no marks on the Vexilar and no takers for our lures.

Figuring maybe the storm had moved the fish to deeper water, we trolled out to a depth of 65 feet. Fish on! Before we could get him into the net, another rod went off, then a third. That's the way it went all morning, with the largest concentration of lake trout right on bottom in 75 feet of water. By 11:30 we had our five-man limit of 15 forktails, including some beautiful 10- to 13-pounders.

In less than seven hours of trolling over two days, we had boated 32 lake trout. Harrisville is all right in my book.

Dave Keene
Flint

This fine lake trout hit an 0-sized white dodger and a Sparkle Fly.

38
OSCODA

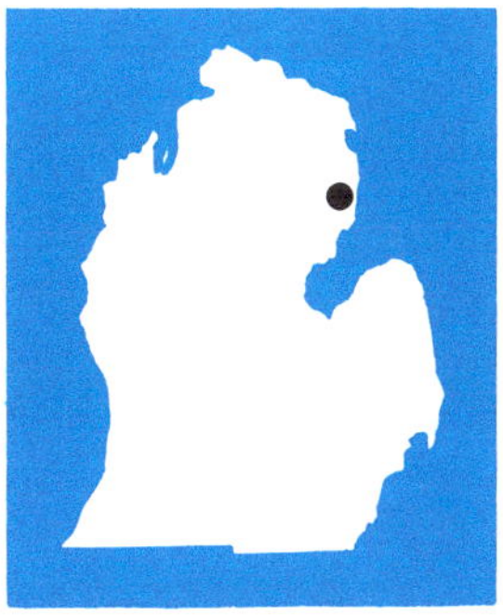

Oscoda is quite likely the busiest port on Lake Huron. The reasons are its good facilities, midlake location, big-money fishing tournament, and tremendous sport fishing. Calling cards at the Au Sable River mouth include large numbers of lake trout and salmon and also steelhead, rainbow, brown trout, walleyes, catfish, perch and menominees. The river itself also yields these species along with northern pike and smallmouth bass.

Fishing Schedule

SPRING

In *spring*, Au Sable River runoff attracts smelt, which in turn draw hungry trout and salmon. Pier anglers and trollers working the color line as it seeps far into the lake can score in April and May. Countdown Rapalas and floating Rapalas pinned to shallow-set downriggers are good lures. Krocodile spoons, Thindevles and Arbogast Doctor Spoons are effective hardware to troll.

In April and early May, best catches come in the upper 20 feet of water between 25 and 50 feet deep. Later in May, the fish move to depths of 50-100 feet and in the summer may be as deep as 150 feet. Besides the color line, spring trollers also seek wave troughs parallel to shore and peck away at the edges of the trolling fleet. The Au Sable rivermouth and Au Sable Point, a couple of miles south, are magnets.

You don't need a boat, though, to catch fish at Oscoda. Smelt dippers line the piers and work shoreline shallows in this area. Fishing for menominees from the piers is also rapidly growing in popularity as a spring (and fall) sport. Most anglers pierce single salmon eggs, wigglers or small worms with a tiny hook, weight it with one or two BB-sized split shot, and work it near bottom along the structures. Menominees have tiny, soft mouths and therefore must be played gingerly. The piers also serve up fair to good perch fishing in spring.

Spawn-bag fishermen also enjoy top sport from Oscoda piers in spring. Fresh steelhead or brown-trout spawn works best when tied into grape-sized bags and weighted to bottom. Hardware throwers report catches of salmon and steelhead plus a few browns, rainbows and lake trout. (Lakers, however, must be released if caught before May 1.) Any spoon in silver or silver with blue, green or hot color and weighing from 2/5 ounce to one ounce will likely produce.

SUMMER

Summer fishing is excellent for lake trout, with salmon-catching opportunities improving as the season wears on. The lakers continue to move out to deeper water in stages as Lake Huron develops a thermocline and as storms come and go throughout the summer. Optimum depths can vary from 30 feet on the May 1 opener to 140 feet by the season's close on August 15. Wobble-Glos in green, pearl, chartreuse or clown color get the nod when rigged 12-16 inches behind dodgers or 18-30 inches behind cowbells. For best success pull them in lake-bottom mud or as close to it as possible.

Stacking with Northport Nailers, Ivanhoe Salmonizers, Hook-sters, G.W. Salmon Slammers, and Silver Streaks will produce king salmon, pink salmon and some cohos. As lake-trout fishing winds down by early August, many trollers, like charterboat-captains Steve Paslaski and Bob Bingle, rely upon plugs to catch salmon. J-Plugs, Gold Stars, and Producer Tigers in blues, chrome, gold, and blacks are especially effecive plugs on August kings.

I have fished with Bingle many times from this port and have always been amazed at how fine-tuning lures can increase catches. For example, Captain Bob will sometimes go through three or four J-Plug changes in an hour. Making it a point to leave the dock before daylight, he typically chooses black or khaki-colored J-Plugs, then gradually changes to lighter colors (blues, greens) as the day brightens, finally settling on pearly white and chrome when the sun clears the eastern horizon.

Jim Beyers of New Baltimore knows all about Oscoda late-summer salmon. Beyers has shown up here each of the past 14 years—same as migrant salmon. Every August for the past seven years he has skippered charters out of Main Pier Marina. Beyers' records show that kings generally approach shore in three stages lasting from one to two weeks each.

Lake-trout trollers begin coolering salmon in late July or early August off bottom from 90-110 feet of water. Salmon are loosely schooled at this time and, once found, are easily induced to snap hardware and plugs. Beyers relies upon Kingfishers, Northport Nailers, Flutter Chucks, and Lucky Lures in silver with combinations of blue, green, orange, and chartreuse. He runs at a medium to fast clip (2.5-4.0 mph), spotting lures at varying depths from 50 feet to bottom.

"After a week or so, the kings move to the next stage—troughs that are 80-90 feet down," Beyers explains. "That's when we go with dodgers and flies."

When the dodger/fly game shuts off, Beyers and others concentrate on the 40- to 60-foot-deep water, where kings are poising for their final assault on the rivermouth. Beyers then breaks out body baits—No. 4 and No. 5 J-Plugs (greens, chrome, pearl, Easter egg, khaki, and black), haze-green Topkats, blue Bang-O-Lures, and clear-lemon Ping-A-Ts. He also spreads outriggers, sets flatlines, and lengthens leads to 20 feet behind cannonballs and to 150 feet for highlines. The reason? Kings are usually spooky in shallow water, and boat traffic and bright sun can combine to scatter fish and send them deep.

Summer pier anglers score on salmon after sundown and in the last hour before dawn. Chinooks in particular will go several degrees out of temperature to make commando-like raids on rivermouths in the dark of night. Spoon tossers can take them by flinging heavy hardware in fluorescent colors or by adding fluorescent tape to their lures. A fast retrieve often produces arm-shocking strikes, not unlike those furious hits you might have read about from striped bass on a topwater bite.

Some of the finest catfish angling in the Great Lakes occurs from Oscoda piers from sundown throughout the night in July and August. You'll see fishermen in lawn chairs, listening to the Tigers game and sipping a brew, while at their feet, tied to a stringer and suspended in the Au Sable River flow, will be a hefty catch of two- to 10-pound cats. Blood baits or nightcrawler gobs strung on sharp treble hooks and fished on bottom are the winning ticket for catfish.

Each summer, big walleyes move into the river from Lake Huron to provide a limited (and whispered) fishery for those in the know. Best catches occur at night with plugs and Mepps Lusox spinners and Syclops spoons. John Hook of Oscoda won the 1985 Mepps Saginaw Bay Walleye Hunt weekly contest five times in a row with Au Sable River entries that weighed up to nearly 12 pounds. And he wasn't the only fisherman to win with river-caught walleyes.

Perch fishing runs hot and cold all summer from the pier and offshore to depths of 50 feet. Shiner minnows are the best bait in summer. Try wigglers in spring.

Various fishing tournaments have been held in Oscoda each summer for several years. One or more generally tie in with the annual Paul Bunyan Festival held each July. Others extend into August. The local chamber of commerce has details (see "Further Information" for address).

FALL

Fall fishing for Chinook salmon improves through August, with a peak occurring from about September 1-15. J-Plugs, Ping-A-Ts, Tadpollies, and Flatfish are rated plugs. The big spawners will also hit Salmonizer spoons and Big Ed Flutter Chucks. Try bright colors and slow retrieves. Outriggers and planer boards, along with longlining off shallow-set downriggers or flatlines, produce. Keep in mind, however, that trolling traffic thickens as salmon concentrate outside the harbor. It is not uncommon to see 200 boats working the shallows from mid-August until the end of September.

Pier fishermen toss Little Cleos and Ping-A-Ts, among other lures. Clear-plastic Ping-A-Ts produce best. Blue and silver or silver and orange are the best colors in spoons.

After the king-salmon assault is over, the rivermouth serves up improving action for steelhead, rainbows and brown trout, and shore fishermen are able to stay with their sport until Thanksgiving. Rated methods include bottomfishing with spawn bags and tossing brightly colored spoons in the chute between pierheads and outside the structures.

WINTER

Winter fishing activities are limited to the river itself for browns, steelhead and rainbows. Fishermen work its length all winter, when ice conditions allow, by either driftboat fishing with crankbaits or wader fishing with spawn, spinners, spoons, and streamers. The current is reasonably slow, and dark-colored water hides holes, logs and fish. The river is open to steelheaders all year from its mouth to Foote Dam.

Planting Records

Oscoda has historically received the largest Chinook releases in Lake Huron, ranging from 475,000-600,000 spring fingerlings each year. The DNR plans to maintain this commitment, with 600,000 fingerlings going into Van Ettan Creek (an Au Sable River tributary) each spring through at least 1990. During this period, releases of yearling steelhead will increase to 120,000, up from 50,000-60,000 for the past several years. Planting of brown-trout and rainbow yearlings, first stocked in the Au Sable in 1983, will continue at 20,000 and 40,000 respectively.

Facilities

The DNR maintains a paved four-lane ramp, with plenty of parking space, at the Au Sable River mouth. There is no small-boat harbor at Oscoda, however.

Oscoda is one of Lake Huron's most popular tourist towns. Visitors will find plenty of attractions and excellent accommodations.

Further Information

Chambers of Commerce:

1. Oscoda-Au Sable Chamber of Commerce, 100 W. Michigan Ave., Oscoda 48750; (517) 739-7322.
2. East Michigan Tourist Association, One Wenonah Park, Bay City 48706; (517) 895-8823.

Bait & Tackle Shops:

1. Main Pier Marina, US-23 at the bridge, Oscoda 48750; (517) 739-8530.
2. Bunyan Town Enterprises, 4494 N. US-23, Oscoda 48750; (517) 739-2371.
3. Harbor Boat & Canoe, 101 Mill, Oscoda 48750; (517) 739-4447.

Charter Fishing:

1. Captain Steve Paslaski, TMB Charter Service, P.O. Box 301, Oscoda 48750; (517) 739-2301. 37-foot Pacemaker, *T.M.B. II*.
2. Captain Jim Beyers, Jim's Sport Fishing Charter Service, 34846 Jerome, New Baltimore 48047; (313) 465-0820. 27-foot Sportcraft, *Fishin Machine*.
3. Captain Bob Bingle, Bob's Charter Service, 8997 Anchor Bay Dr., Fair Haven 48023; (313) 794-3854. 28-foot Inland Seas, *Steelhead*.

Department of Natural Resources:

Two fisheries biologists work out of District Headquarters at 191 S. Mt. Tom Rd., Mio 48647; (517) 826-3211.

Coast Guard:

Tawas Station, (517) 362-4428.

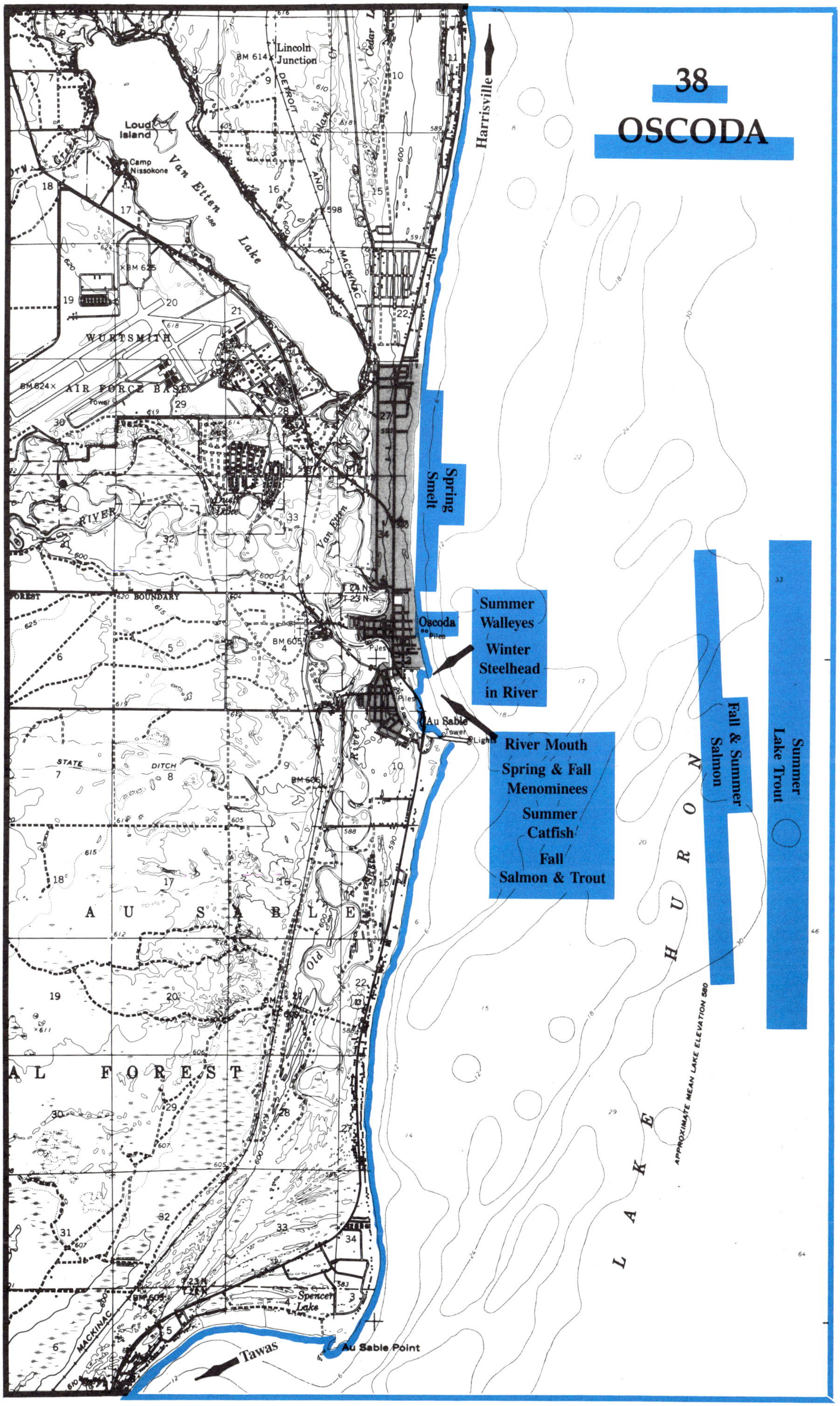
38
OSCODA
Harrisville
Spring Smelt
Summer Walleyes
Winter Steelhead in River
River Mouth
Spring & Fall Menominees
Summer Catfish
Fall Salmon & Trout
Fall & Summer Salmon
Summer Lake Trout
Oscoda
Au Sable
Au Sable Point
Tawas
Lincoln Junction
Loud Island
Camp Nissokone
Van Etten Lake
WURTSMITH AIR FORCE BASE
Spencer Lake
A U S A B L E
F O R E S T
L A K E H U R O N
APPROXIMATE MEAN LAKE ELEVATION 580

These lunker walleyes were weekly winners in the Mepps Saginaw Bay Walleye Hunt. Two of the three were caught in the Au Sable River in mid-June.

Close Encounters at Oscoda

All the conditions—trolling speed, temperature, marks on the graph—were right for an attack from a big king salmon. That's what I and my fishing partner, Alex Joseph, thought as we prowled the 60-foot water-depth about a mile out from the Au Sable River mouth one late-August morning. But after two hours of washing lures, we still hadn't straightened a single rod.

The strike finally came. I hollered, and Alex let go of the wheel and grabbed the rod now throbbing with life. Suddenly he had his hands full of a chunky Chinook that fought like a boxed-in bobcat. I popped the throttle stick into "neutral" and jumped to pull in the other lines.

"Let 'em be," Alex said. "Get the boat back in gear. We've sweated this hard; let's go for a double."

I looked at my partner's rod, the tip of which was flattened out like a cobra's head. I knew on the other end was 20 pounds of fighting-mad king salmon just waiting to do a figure-eight in our still-set lines.

"You sure?" I countered.

"I'm sure."

I slid the gear shift back into "forward" and the boat lurched ahead. Seconds later another rod leaped straight up, and a light-set drag made the reel talk.

"Here we go!" Alex roared, grabbing the second rod, too. For a second he looked like a ballet dancer, pirouetting on tiptoes while trying to keep his balance. I snatched the rod from him just as a hog salmon slashed topwater 75 yards away.

With the boat still in gear, we alternated steering with one hand behind our backs while those feisty kings pulled every trick in the bag to foul lines. Alex's fish suddenly charged at the boat, then sounded at its sight. When my partner nursed it back, the king, with a chrome J-Plug hanging two feet from its lower jaw, threatened to get under our prop. Luckily, my fish kept swapping ends at a safe distance as Alex *S*-weaved his rod in and out of the downriggers and the prop itself. He looked like he was crocheting something with a giant needle.

Eventually he got the king close enough for the net, missed with a not-so-deft stab, then came up with 20 pounds of silver fury. He dumped the break-dancing salmon at my feet.

"Now for your troublemaker," he said, a big grin on his face. This is the kind of excitement my partner lives for. His eyes were lighted up like a kid parked atop a ferris wheel. Two minutes later, my fish, an 18-pounder, slumped in the net in a silvery *U*. Alex reversed the cords and the king thudded to the boat deck where it began to play tag with the other salmon.

Nothing but wave action for two hours, then 15 minutes of unbelievable excitement from 40 pounds of salmon. That's the way trolling out of Oscoda can be.

Eldon Thomas
Flint

39
TAWAS BAY

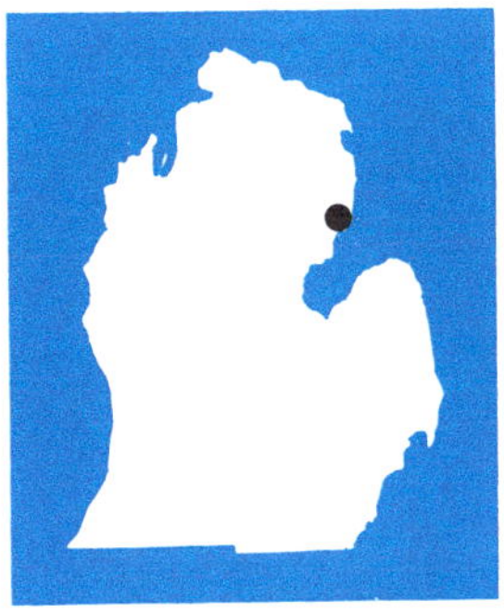

Tawas Bay is popular with an increasing number of Lake Huron fishermen for several reasons. One is the wide variety of trout, salmon and warm-water species available to anglers year-round. Another is that this area and Alpena (33) are two major Lake Huron holding tanks for brown trout. A third is the lack of angling pressure. At Oscoda (38) and Harrisville (37), the next two ports up the lake, shorecasters jockey for real estate, and trollers often wait in long lines to launch their boats.

That is rarely the case at Tawas Bay.

Fishing Schedule

SPRING

Each *spring*, smelt turn on the whole region as they invade shoreline shallows and the Tawas River to spawn. In late April, dippers sweep the water and river current with nets late into the night.

These same smelt also attract predatory packs of hungry brown trout, which provide good fishing from ice-out to about June 1 in depths of 15 feet and less. Some of the best fishing occurs from the rivermouth south to The Tube, the local place-name for the U.S. Gypsum loading dock at Alabaster. Another spring hotspot for browns is between No. 2 and No. 4 buoys in 20 feet of water. A third popular hangout is ledge structure from No. 2 Buoy to Au Sable Point, halfway between Tawas and Oscoda (38).

Rebels in brown-trout color, red-and-silver and black-and-gold Hot 'N Tots, Little Cleos, pink-with-pearl ladderback E.T. Pink Surprises, and Krocodiles are good lures to run in Tawas Bay. Some anglers also report success longlining with Willy's Worms and Countdown Rapalas off flatlines. Shallow-set downriggers account for plenty of browns, too, with Andy Reekers and Krocodiles getting the frequent nod. Chartreuse, yellows, greens, and blues, especially when doctored with light-catching prism tape, are favored. Some brown-trout fishermen rig live smelt to small hooks by running the barbs through the smelts' mouths, then fish the bait near bottom with the aid of an egg-shaped sinker.

Spring also produces lake trout and salmon (both cohos and Chinooks) in the shallows, along with steelhead. But brown trout hold the spring interest of most trollers and some shore fishermen, many attracted to the area by the annual Brown Trout Derby, held each April and May.

SUMMER

During the *summer* many Tawas Bay trollers turn to lake trout. Bill Ray, a local fisherman and lure maker, targets 52- to 55-degree-F. water from June until the August 15 season closure. When water temperature is right, a good place to start looking for lake trout is in 34 feet of water off the Tawas Point Lighthouse near Buoy No. 2. Early action is often keyed to cowbells and six-inch dodgers pulling spoons, small plugs, and trolling flies. Ray relies on willow-leaf cowbells with copper (dark day) or silver (bright day) blades, which he also fine-tunes with prism tape. Early in the season he likes small blades on his homemade 'bells, but as summer progresses he switches to bigger blades to simulate the larger alewives available at this time. Lake trout feed on smelt and small minnows at first, then begin loading up on alewives later in the summer.

Ray watches the winds as clues to lake-trout fishing success. Northeast blows generally bring in cool water, and lakers will therefore be found at shallower depths than previously. A west or southwest wind produces warm inland breezes, which in turn can push forktails out to deeper water. The lakers eventually migrate to one of two 70-foot holes, north and south of Tawas Point. There, they stack up all summer to provide solid sport.

Fire Plugs, P-Nuts, L'il Guys, Wobble Trolls, and Spin-N-Glos are good lures behind attractors. Try chartreuse, pearl, green, clown color, and green and yellow. Bill Ray makes long-haired jigs and single and tandem trolling flies and rigs the Ray's Way Flies, as he calls them, within 18 inches of attractors, preferably various shades of blue.

Another good laker taker in these waters is Grand Blanc sport-troller Jim Smith. Smith catches forktails by bouncing bottom with his cannonballs and running Wobble-Glos clean or with cow-bells. Northport Nailers, especially the white with blue zig-zag (locally called Old Blue), are a hot lure.

Summer perch provide erratic fishing opportunities throughout Tawas Bay. Sometimes, to the delight of pier fishermen, big schools show up near the city dock. The Tube is also a frequent summer producer. Sometimes perch appear over weed beds between Buoy No. 2 and No. 4. (also a good area for northern pike in summer). Sometimes perch don't show up anywhere at all.

Tawas Bay should produce good walleye fishing in the future (see "Planting Records"). Some salmon and trout trollers already are picking up a few, especially on silver-and-blue and gold-and-red Eppinger Devle Dogs. A good place to try is structure from the lighthouse to No. 2 Buoy.

Salmon are an on-again, off-again summer target in Tawas Bay.

The best place to begin looking is in the previously mentioned 70-foot holes. Trollers can find good structure closer to shore by running out a mile from Au Sable Point to Buoy No. 1. The water there is 50 feet deep; another mile east will bring 60- to 80-foot-deep water, and a mile further yet produces depths to 100-120 feet. In spring and fall, look for kings and cohos along structure from the lighthouse north to the orange water tower (halfway between Tawas and Au Sable points). Be advised, however, that this area is often commercially netted.

Dodgers ahead of blue or green squids are a good bet for summer salmon. Chartreuse-and-blue Northport Nailers are effective on bright days and red-and-black Nailers on overcast ones. Chartreuse or blue-prism Lightning Lures are worth a go, too. So are E.T. and Hobo spoons and green-with-black ladderback Willy's Worms.

FALL

As *fall* nears, salmon approach the Tawas River in stages. Chinooks appear first, followed by cohos. Post-Labor Day generally puts fish inside Tawas Bay in 10-30 feet of water. But not always.

How well I remember a mid-September troll here when I figured banging a limit for first-time salmon-anglers Jim and Karen McCracken, friends from Columbus, Ohio, would be duck soup. We rolled out from Collier's Marina aboard the *White Sands*, a 30-foot charterboat skippered by Barry "Jake" Jacobs. He gunned us out 6-1/2 miles off the orange tower to his favorite spot, one of those 70-foot holes I mentioned.

Jacobs' graph scratched out the uneven bottom on paper while Jim and I helped him deep-six four downriggers armed with tantalizing hardware including J-Plugs, Eppinger Sagamore Spoons, and Sutton Spoons. We scattered these at varying depths while we locked in our trolling speed at exactly 3.0 mph. Wind wailed through downrigger wires, and the *White Sands* bobbed from waves cuffing its bow. Soon a huge Chinook would slam a lure, I thought. I had it all planned how Karen, while complaining of aching arms, would freeze a smile on her face while I shot yet another roll of film. It was just a matter of time.

But I didn't realize how much time. We washed every kind of lure that Barry had and still couldn't buy a strike. Yards of graph paper showed a bottom clean of fish. Salmon are like that—here today, gone tommorow, back the next day. I drove home that night feeling bad that my friends had enjoyed a long boat ride and nothing more. The next day the McCrackens nailed a trio of tackle-busting kings that sagged scales to 14, 17, and 20 pounds respectively. Here today, gone tomorrow, back the next day.

When salmon crowd the rivermouth, however, they provide more dependable sport for trollers and shore fishermen. Many anglers fish spawn right in the current itself; others fling Ping-A-Ts in clear-lemon or yellow colors as well as the transparent model. Ping-A-Ts also account for plenty of salmon caught by trollers, who run the wobbling plugs slowly behind shallow-set downriggers. Magnum Tadpollies, giant Fire Plugs, Kwikfish and big Flatfish also produce. So do big spoons.

Cohos are available into October. Then steelhead and brown trout invade the shoreline again, with browns turning up in the Tawas River as late as Thanksgiving some years. An east wind, in particular, can send them upriver in waves. Spawn, nightcrawlers, and heavy hardware, either cast or trolled, yield the best catches.

WINTER

Tawas Bay *winter* fishing currently keys on yellow perch and northern pike. Perchville, U.S.A., a local fishing contest and festival, is held during the first weekend in February. Fishing success depends upon where the perch decide to show up, but generally weed beds are the best producers. Five- to 20-foot depths between Buoy No. 1 and Buoy No. 2 are a good place to start. Pike are available to both spear-tossers and tip-up fishermen until the last day in February.

Winter catches of browns, rainbows, and walleyes should improve dramatically in the future.

Planting Records

The Tawas area has long received healthy stocks of hatchery-reared fish and will continue to get them in the future. Lake-trout releases at Tawas Point, normally about 70,000 yearlings, are scheduled to increase to 100,000 (depending on availability) each year through 1990. Coho salmon first went into the lake here in 1982, when 100,000 smolts were released. Stockings will continue at this rate, and 75,000 Chinook fingerlings will also be released annually. A total of 10,000 brown- and 30,000 rainbow-trout yearlings will find their way into Tawas Bay annually for at least the next five years. Steelhead, last stocked in 1981, are still available, but the DNR does not plan any future releases. Steelhead are available, though, at the East Branch Au Gres River (40) and Oscoda (38).

In addition, Walleyes for Iosco County, Inc. (WIC) has been instrumental in reintroducing walleyes to Tawas Bay, which years ago supported huge populations of the popular gamefish. A total of 363,000 fingerlings were released in 1984, with another 200,000 stocked in 1985 from Cooke Pond. Fishermen interested in further information or joining or supporting WIC ($10 annual dues, $20 annual sponsor, or $100 life member) can write to WIC treasurer Walt Snow, Box 5820, National City 48748.

Facilities

The DNR maintains a paved four-lane ramp at East Tawas. A state harbor of refuge offers transient accommodations, gasoline and diesel fuel, water, electricity, restrooms, shower facilities, dock attendant, holding-tank pump-out and VHF-FM radio. The telephone number is (517) 362-2731.

East Tawas, with 2,500 people, and Tawas City, with 1,900 residents, cater heavily to tourists. Fishermen will find plenty of motels and restaurants. Contact the Tawas Bay Lodging Association, P.O. Box 63, Tawas City 48764-0063, for more information.

Further Information

Chambers of Commerce:

1. Tawas Area Chamber of Commerce, P.O. Box 608, Tawas City 48763; (517) 362-8643.
2. East Michigan Tourist Association, One Wenonah Park, Bay City 48706; (517) 895-8823.

Bait & Tackle Shops:

1. Collier's Marina, 907 Lake St., Tawas City 48706; (517) 362-2002.
2. North Star Motel and Sport Shop, 1119-A South US-23, Tawas City 48763; (517) 362-2255.
3. Log Cabin Bait, 110 Newman, East Tawas 48730; (517) 362-2803.

Charter Fishing:

1. Gary Collier, Collier's Marina, 907 Lake St., Tawas City 48763; (517) 362-2002. 30-foot Sportcraft, *White Sands*.
2. Brown's Landing (twice-daily perch-fishing trips), 1129 Dyer Rd., Tawas City 48763, (517) 362-3737.
3. Tawas Riverside Resort and Charter Fishing, 730 Lake St., Tawas City 48763; (517) 362-5052.
4. Sportsman's Corral Motel Charter Service, 1115 US-23, Tawas City 48763; (517) 362-2442.

39

TAWAS BAY

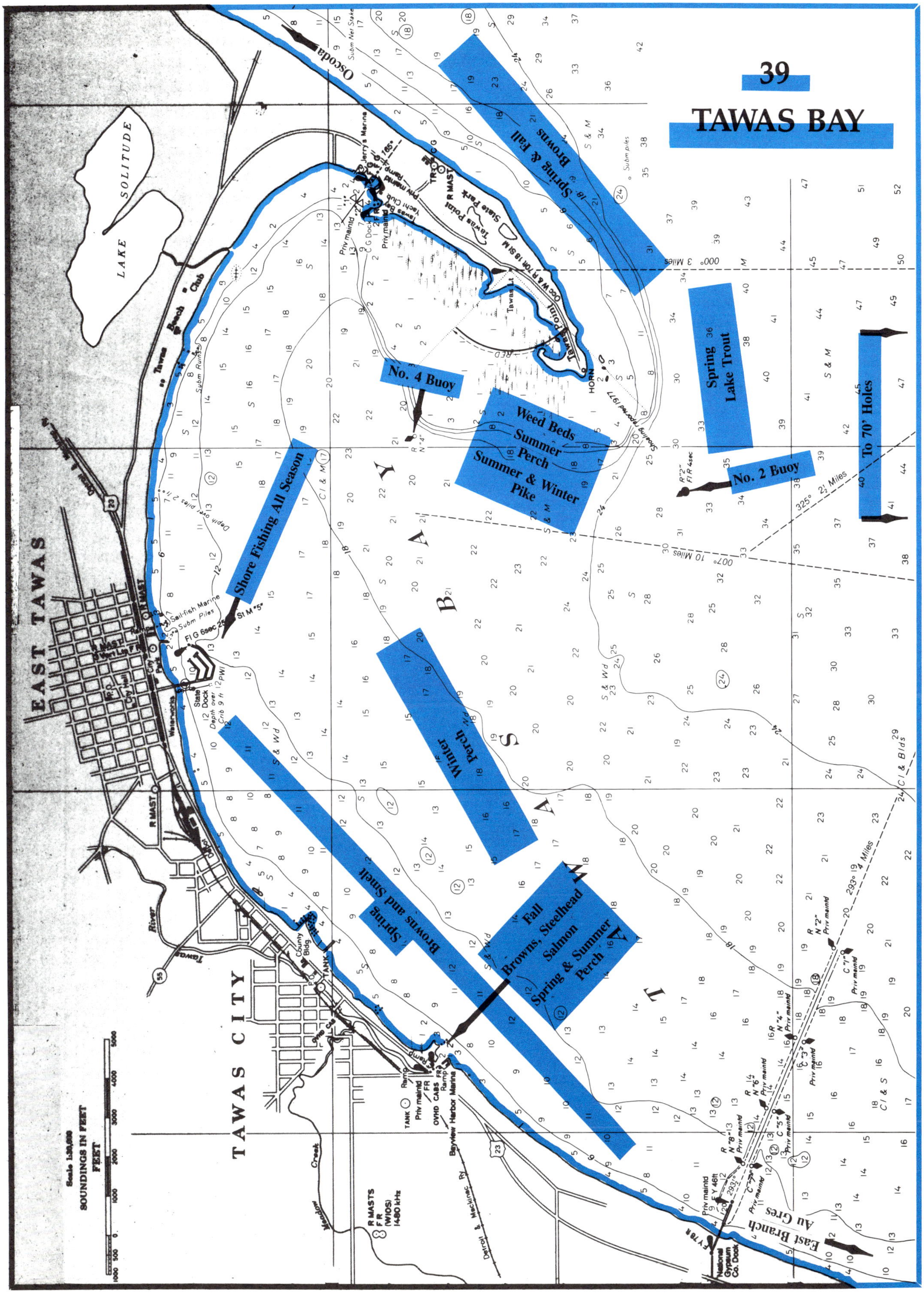

Spring & Fall Browns
Spring Lake Trout
To 70' Holes
No. 4 Buoy
No. 2 Buoy
Weed Beds Summer Perch Summer & Winter Pike
Shore Fishing All Season
Winter Perch
Spring Browns and Smelt
Fall Browns, Steelhead Salmon Spring & Summer Perch
EAST TAWAS
TAWAS CITY
LAKE SOLITUDE
Oscoda
Tawas Point State Park
East Branch Au Gres
TAWAS BAY
SOUNDINGS IN FEET

Department of Natural Resources:
Two fisheries biologists work out of District Headquarters at 191 S. Mt. Tom Rd., Mio 48647; (517) 826-3211.

Coast Guard:
Tawas Station, (517) 362-4428.

One-Eyed Salmon

My wife Liz and I, and Carol and Jim Rutter were running E.T. Spoons and Zipper lures off four downriggers in search of salmon one May Saturday morning. The Rutters, friends from Eaton Rapids, had always wanted to fish the big water but were reluctant to venture too far from shore in their 14-foot boat. So we took them to No. 2 Buoy, only a short distance from shore in about 35 feet of water—no problem for my 18-foot Blue Fin, *White Cloud*.

The one-foot chop on Lake Huron must have been giving our lures the right kind of flash. Soon we had a fish on, then another. But no salmon weighed over five pounds. Yet, oddly, other fishermen in the local fleet of 35-40 boats were netting what appeared to be salmon in the 12- to 16-pound class. We were happy to have action but desperately wanted our friends to catch a big fish. By eleven o'clock we had 12 or 14 salmon in the box, all five pounds and under.

Suddenly Liz jumped for a sprung rod, but when she reefed back, nothing was there. "This is either a small fish or no fish," she announced.

Soon she had our lure, a black E.T. Spoon with green-glitter ladderback, alongside. Imbedded in the barb was the eye of a full-grown salmon. The fish, we figured, must have slashed at the spoon and missed with its mouth. With that, we pulled lines and headed for the dock.

I fish Tawas Bay more than any other Lake Huron port and have been on the lookout for that one-eyed salmon ever since.

Dave Beavers
Flint

Tawas-area trollers get solid action for Chinook and lake trout by keying on two 70-foot-deep holes north and south of Tawas Point.

40
EAST BRANCH AU GRES RIVER

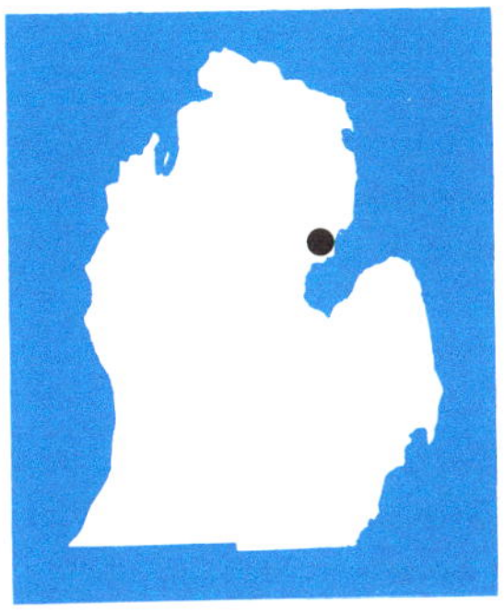

The mouth of the East Branch Au Gres River, also called Whitney Drain and the Singing Bridge, is Michigan's most popular smelt-dipping spot.

Fishing Schedule

SPRING

On a warm *spring* evening in late April, it is not unusual to see several hundred people crowding the rivermouth in hopes of dipping a bucket of tasty smelt. The DNR usually dispatches extra conservation officers to the area in anticipation of crowd-control problems. Few develop, however, especially in recent years since parking facilities (however limited) and fencing have defined public-property boundaries.

Some of the best sport comes in the early hours of the morning after the party crowd has drifted back to their cars and have gone home. Smelt seem to be afraid of too much commotion and will often hang back, even until full daylight at times, before making spawning runs.

But daytime fishermen are just as likely to be after steelhead, which ascend the river in waves to provide good surf-fishing and stream-fishing sport. Waders catch them on spoons, spawn, and flies as far upriver as the M-55 bridge, the upstream limit for the annual April 1 steelhead opener. At the rivermouth, spoon tossers and spawn fishermen work the flow of water that stains the cleaner lake for several hundred yards down the shoreline. Little Cleos, Dazzlers, Little Jewels, and Mepps Syclops Spoons are good choices. Pick lures with flame-orange, hot-yellow, and bright-red colors, with or without silver.

Some fishermen anchor boats just offshore, then flip spoons or bottomfish with spawn. Still others troll up and down the shoreline in five to 25 feet of water.

Action can be slow for hours. Then, suddenly a school of brown trout or steelhead will move in, and fishermen will experience a flurry of excitement for up to a half hour.

SUMMER

Rivermouth fishing begins at ice-out and lasts until early June. You will continue to see fishermen flailing the water with lures and stillfishing with worms and nightcrawlers throughout the *summer*, but they are likely to catch perch, catfish, bullheads and a few northern pike rather than trout. Trollers who venture out to depths of 50 feet or more can sometimes take summertime salmon and even a few lake trout, though none has been planted here.

FALL

Fall brings steelhead and brown trout in close again, with best action occurring at dawn and dusk. Rainy, windy, overcast days, especially when there is an onshore breeze, usually provide day-long sport that is particularly good in late October and well into November. Friends of mine own a cottage just 200 yards upstream. It is not unusual for them and other local homeowners to take 50 or more trout each fall. Some of the cottagers slide rods into offshore sand spikes or plastic PVC pipe attached to the dock, then add big red-and-white pike bobbers so they can watch for strikes from the comfort of their living rooms.

WINTER

Winter fishing is practically non-existent because the rivermouth usually freezes. But whenever die-hard steelheaders can find open water, they'll be there.

Planting Records

In recent years, stockings of hatchery-reared fish have included both steelhead and brown-trout yearlings in numbers ranging from 5,000-15,000. Each year through at least 1990, the DNR plans to release 15,000 steelhead, 15,000 rainbows and 10,000 brown trout.

Facilities

Rental cottages, available along the shoreline, supplement the occasional motels in the area. Taylor's Motel, about three miles south of the rivermouth, is the closest.

At the rivermouth, shore and surf fishing is possible from adjacent state-owned land. Pit toilets and limited parking are available, but there is no boat-launch facility. Some anglers launch car-toppers, but the nearest place to launch a trailerable boat is at Whitney Township Park, about a mile south. A nominal fee may be charged.

Further Information

Chambers of Commerce:

East Michigan Tourist Association, One Wenonah Park, Bay City 48763; (517) 362-8643.

Bait & Tackle Shops:

Singing Bridge Grocery & Restaurant, 1991 N. Huron Rd. (US-23); (517) 362-2828.

Charter Fishing:

None known.

Department of Natural Resources:

Two fisheries biologists work out of District Headquarters at 191 S. Mt. Tom Rd., Mio 48647; (517) 826-3211.

Coast Guard:

Tawas Station, (517) 362-4428.

Michigan Mardi Gras

I arrived at the famed Singing Bridge about midnight that April evening and began looking for my friends. Two or three hundred dippers, looking like a gang of unorganized threshers, swept the shallows of Lake Huron and the final hundred yards of river. Hundreds more crowded the beach. Loud laughter hung on the heavy spring air, which smelled of wood smoke and beer. People were in a party mood, even though the smelt were not cooperating.

I found my friends along the beach. They had been dipping since nine o'clock, yet I could see the metal bottom of their washtub. Wedged inside a truck-tire inner tube, it bobbed with the lake chop. "Slow pickings," Larry said. "Relax. Have a beer."

Their keg was mounted in the sand like some pirate's booty. I filled a mug with beer, then leaned against the keg and watched an ore freighter, lights ablaze, far out in the lake. Nothing happened for an hour. The beer and the long drive were making me sleepy.

"Watch those two guys out there," Darwin, another of my friends, said. "They're picking up a few smelt." My digital watch flashed 1:15 in red numerals. Within a couple of minutes it became obvious that a run was building. We got into the water and right away began scooping up five and six silvery smelt per dip.

"Run's on!" somebody hollered nearby.

A run of smelt at Singing Bridge causes as much excitement—and panic—as a police raid on a blind pig. The beach emptied fast as nearly everyone forgot about their beer and campfires and scurried into the water like a beach full of crabs. One poor sot, in his haste, slipped and went under. His laughing buddies half-dragged him to shore where he lay for a moment like a beached beluga whale. By the time he emptied the water from his waders, the run was over.

Spring smelt dipping is one big carnival. Fishermen, weary from winter, are ready to bust loose, and smelt dipping gives them that opportunity. It happens every April at Singing Bridge.

Eldon Thomas
Flint

Little Dipper with a big spawning smelt at the famed Singing Bridge. Spring smelt dipping is great family sport and a good way to say goodbye to winter.

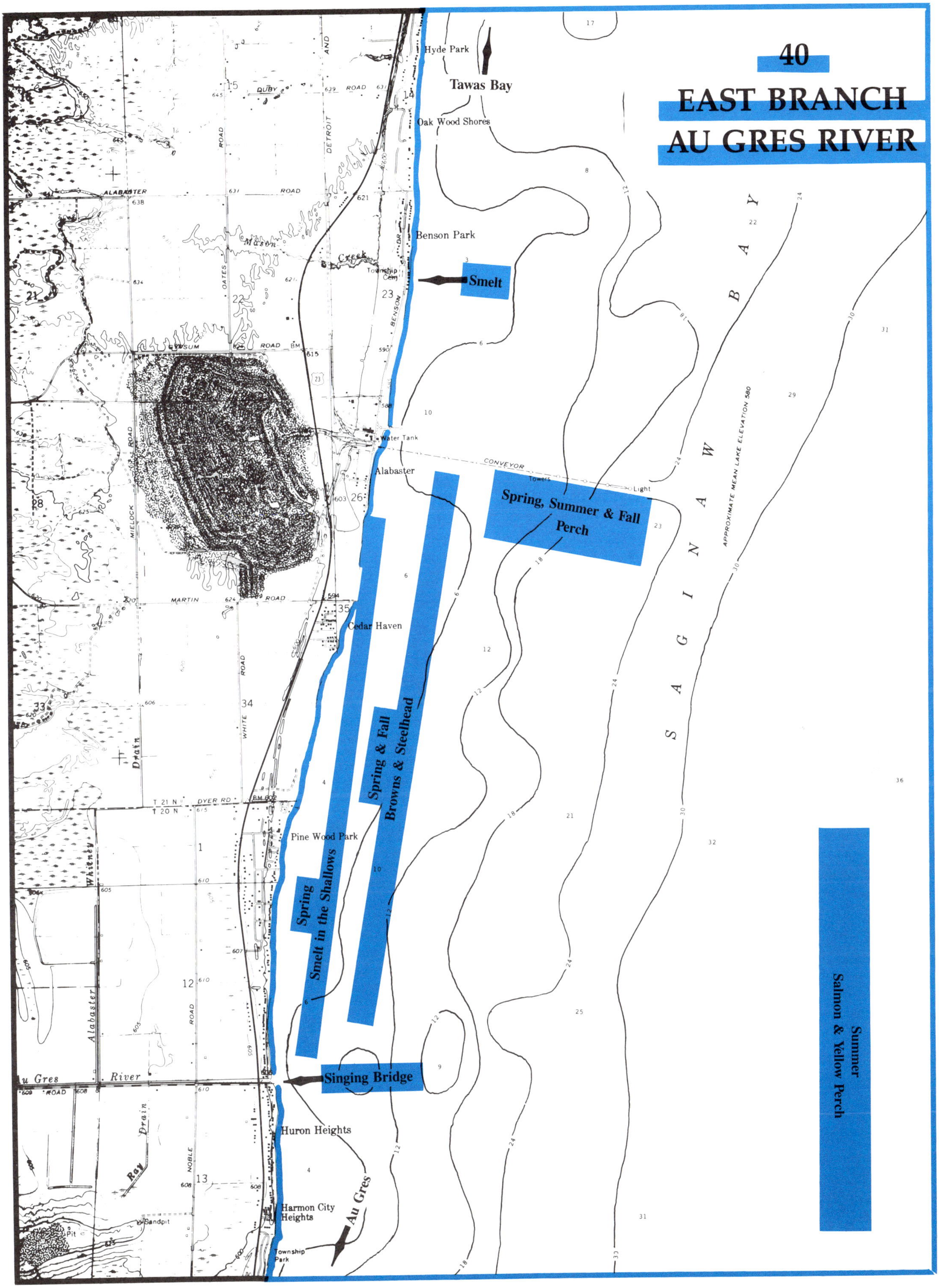

40
EAST BRANCH
AU GRES RIVER
Hyde Park
Tawas Bay
Oak Wood Shores
Benson Park
Smelt
Water Tank
Alabaster
CONVEYOR
Towers
Light
Spring, Summer & Fall
Perch
SAGINAW BAY
APPROXIMATE MEAN LAKE ELEVATION 580
Cedar Haven
Spring & Fall
Browns & Steelhead
Pine Wood Park
Spring
Smelt in the Shallows
Singing Bridge
Huron Heights
Harmon City
Heights
Au Gres
Township
Park
Summer
Salmon & Yellow Perch
Au Gres River
ROAD
Mason Creek
Township Cem
ALABASTER ROAD
GYPSUM ROAD
MARTIN ROAD
DYER RD
T 21 N
T 20 N
BENSON
OATES
DETROIT
WHITE ROAD
MIELOCK
Drain
Whitney
Alabaster
Ray Drain
NOBLE
Sandpit
Pit

41
AU GRES

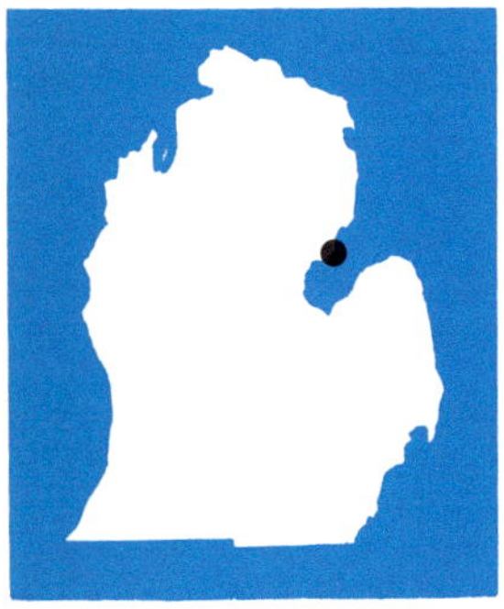

Straddling the Inner and Outer bays of Saginaw Bay, Au Gres' position offers some unique fishing opportunities. The town of 600-700 people bills itself as the Perch Capitol of Michigan, and, indeed, yellow-bellies furnish good sport year-round, with exceptional catches occurring in spring and fall. Walleyes, smallmouth and largemouth bass, northern pike and channel catfish are other warm-water drawing cards.

The Lake Huron shores from Au Gres north also see excellent returns of Chinook salmon. The thuggish kings are available in spring and fall, along with brown trout, steelhead and lake trout. If a fisherman can't find it sport in the Au Gres area, he isn't looking very hard.

Fishing Schedule

SPRING

From ice-out in early *spring* (usually late March) until mid-April, the Au Gres River loads up with yellow perch. Good perching also shapes up in the protected bay area between Point Lookout and Point Au Gres in five to 10 feet of water. The fish enter lake shallows, as well as the river, to spawn. Perch move around in schools according to age class, but in early spring, all sizes from five to 14 inches are available in the river. Stillfishing with wigglers, worms or shiner minnows pinned to two-hook perch spreaders or crappie rigs (one hook about 12 inches above the other) is the rated tactic.

When smelt take over in the river and shoreline shallows, perch tend to move out. But they aren't far away and provide catching opportunities in May and June to depths of 20 feet. As the water warms and the perch move offshore, hardpan-bottom areas produce best. Good locations until summer include Point Au Gres, Point Lookout, and Whitestone Point, as well as micro habitats throughout the bay area. Call or stop at any of the several bait and tackle shops in the area for up-to-the-minute catching reports.

Sucker spawning runs develop along with the perch invasion. One hotbed of excitement is the Rifle River at Michigan's smallest city, Omer, on US-23 a few miles upriver from the rivermouth. The Au Gres River also receives spawning suckers throughout April. Shore anglers can catch them using simple hook-and-line fishing methods with worms as bait. A dipnet fishery also develops.

Spawning smelt also follow the perch in the Au Gres River, where dippers wait for them along its lower stretch. Best action occurs from mid-April until early May. Most years you can time peak runs with the opening of the statewide trout-fishing season, currently the last Saturday in April. Smelt are also available off points of land and at the mouths of small streams that flow into the lake. Even those that contribute just a trickle may produce. Public access to Lake Huron is available at the long Au Gres pier and at the ends of Bessinger and Hammel Beach roads.

About the time that perch and smelt are coming on, the rivermouths and shoreline also host good numbers of steelhead, brown trout, lake trout and some salmon. Each spring, spawning steelhead target the Rifle River, where they were planted. Peak fishing normally occurs when water temperature goes above 45 degrees F., but wading anglers look for action anytime after April 1, the extended season opener. (Devoe Creek outlet dam is the upstream limit for anglers seeking trout during the special early season, and browns may not be taken at all. Check a current copy of *Michigan Fishing Guide* for details.) Sucker and steelhead spawn is the most popular bait, but wigglers and nightcrawlers also produce.

Schoolteacher Terry Walsh, a top-flight charterboat captain from Au Gres, fishes local waters until summer vacation, then targets Harrisville (37) for lake trout and salmon. In April and early May he seeks six to 12 feet of water between Point Lookout and Alabaster, just north of Whitney Drain (E. Branch Au Gres River, 40.) One tactic includes trolling a lazy *S* pattern at variable speeds to impart optimum action to his lures. They are likely to be either body baits (Rapalas, Rebels, and Bombers), 1/3- to 2/5-ounce Little Cleos and Krocodiles, or Flutter Spoons and Northport Nailers. Silver with or without combinations of green, blue, yellow, chartreuse, and orange are good colors to try.

Terry sets downriggers no deeper than three feet and runs his lures back 60-200 feet. Flatlines produce in the spring shallows as do planer boards. Wave troughs and sandbars that develop along shore and off stream mouths make it difficult for wading anglers to present lures on target to hungry fish, but trollers working out of small boats and using planer boards can get to them.

SUMMER

Summer sport goes pretty flat for salmon and trout, the reason being the lack of deep water. (Until you reach the Tawases, and even then, to find 100 feet of water means you must lose sight of land by several miles.)

So summer fishermen in the Au Gres area key on warm-water species. Perch fishing remains good in 20- to 35-foot depths over rocky or otherwise hard-bottom areas. (If you like fishing contests, the Au Gres Area Chamber of Commerce sponsors a summer perch-fishing contest that runs from Memorial Day to Labor Day. Bob's Marina, Lutz's Bait Shop, Point Au Gres Marina, or the Whitestone Trading Post have rules and regulations.) These same locations are also beginning to produce walleyes again, thanks to massive plantings of fingerlings reared in a local pond during recent years. Many anglers with seaworthy boats also flock to the Charity Islands (42) for perch and walleyes. Gravelly Shoals Lighthouse produces on-again, off-again action. (Remember that yellow perch, normally hungry, are constantly on the

41 AU GRES

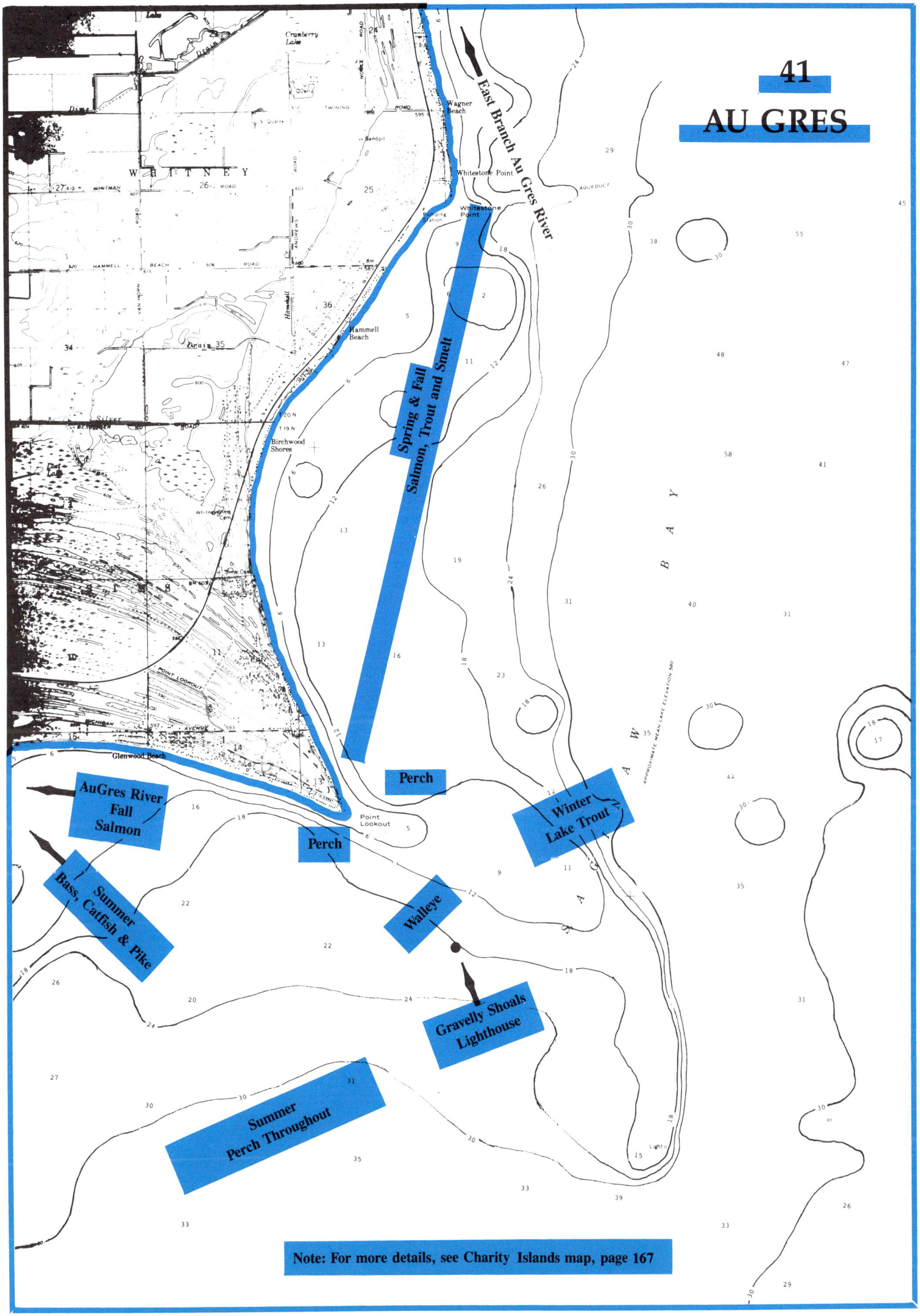
East Branch Au Gres River
Spring & Fall Salmon, Trout and Smelt
AuGres River Fall Salmon
Summer Bass, Catfish & Pike
Perch
Perch
Walleye
Winter Lake Trout
Gravelly Shoals Lighthouse
Summer Perch Throughout
Note: For more details, see Charity Islands map, page 167
Cranberry Lake
Wagner Beach
Whitestone Point
Hammell Beach
Birchwood Shores
Glenwood Beach
Point Lookout
W H I T N E Y
S A G I N A W B A Y

move in search of food.) One July morning there, we caught a wire basket full of nine- and 10-inch perch by fishing the 35- to 40-foot dropoff. Throughout the area, shiner minnows are the preferred summer bait.

Another good bet for summer perch is to fish color lines off the points. This phenomenon occurs when offshore winds and storms pound the area, producing wave action and currents that wash around the points and distribute food.

Bulrushes and scattered cattail pods between Point Au Gres and Point Lookout produce largemouth bass for wading and boating fishermen. Toss crankbaits, surface poppers, or Texas-rigged fake worms.

Live-worm fishermen pick up channel cats throughout the region, but for best action, look to the long pier at sundown. Fish stink baits or worm gobs on bottom in the river because cats often ease into the current at dusk and search for food throughout the night. Most catfish run one to two pounds, but long-whiskered fish to 10 pounds each are taken regularly.

Northern pike are available throughout the area wherever weed beds can be found. High water in recent years has destroyed much of the marsh in this region, though. Smallmouth bass can be taken on spawning beds during June and July wherever structure can be found. Look for concrete slabs, old pilings, and boulder fields near shore. Colorful spinnerbaits, live or plastic worms, and inline spinners produce best.

FALL

Fall fishing begins when salmon and trout return to the shallows. By mid-August, fishermen report Chinooks showing up, although they do not normally enter the Au Gres River, where they were released as fingerlings two and three years before, until after Labor Day. During most falls, anglers can get them well into October. Trollers catch the brawling kings on J-Plugs, Tiger Plugs, Silver Hordes, Tadpollies, and Ping-A-Ts in blue and silver, green, chartreuse, black and silver, and black and green. Spoons such as Northport Nailers, Big Ed Flutter Chucks, and Sutton Spoons also produce. As in the spring, a trolling fishery develops from the Au Gres River north to Whitney Drain. Shore fishermen report success on casting spoons. Try the above-mentioned colors along with fluorescent hardware at dusk or after dark.

Besides the 15- to 30-pound kings, the area serves up improving action for steelhead and brown trout lasting until deer season (November 15-30) and beyond. Browns target the Au Gres River, whereas steelhead migrate to the Rifle, their respective release sites. Both species are also available along the shore. Catching tactics and lures approximate those described for spring sport.

Perch fishing in fall again swings into high gear when feeding yellow-bellies key on the river and 10- to 15-foot depths in the bay. September through October is the catching period.

WINTER

Winter fishing rates fair to good. Early ice and late ice provide twin periods of hot activity for yellow perch off the rivermouth as well as in the river. Some walleyes are also available along with good catches of early ice pike from 10-18 pounds. Try tip-ups off the rivermouth. In late February (the season closes the last day of that month), look to the river itself. An excellent lake-trout fishery off Point Lookout develops in January and goes until breakup. Ice men jig Swedish Pimples, Little Cleos, and Jigging Rapalas, sometimes sweetened with a piece of perch belly. Short, stiff spinning rods with open-face reels or sickle-shaped jigging sticks are preferred. This sport produces lake trout in the 16- to 19-pound class. But be aware that action occurs up to three or more miles offshore, where late-season ice can be honeycombed and dangerous.

Planting Records

For the next five years, annual releases of yearling lake trout off Point Lookout will be reduced from 70,000 to an average of 38,000. The Au Gres River will continue to receive 75,000 Chinook fingerlings and 10,000 brown-trout yearlings during this period. Steelhead, last released in 1983, should contribute to catches for several years yet. But the DNR has switched its steelhead-planting emphasis to the nearby Rifle River, where stockings of 100,000 fall fingerlings are expected each year through 1990. The Rifle River has a native population of brown trout. Hatchery-reared fish were last released in 1980.

Both the Au Gres and Rifle rivermouths have received thousands of pond-reared walleye fingerlings during each of the past several summers. These stockings are expected to continue and should provide good fishing opportunities for many years to come.

Facilities

A paved four-lane ramp and newly built parking area await anglers at the Au Gres River mouth. Expect to pay DNR personnel $1.50 to park or $3 to launch your boat, especially during peak periods of fishing activity. A DNR-maintained harbor of refuge includes restrooms, shower facilities, dock attendant, sewage-tank pump-out and VHF-FM radio. The telephone number is (517) 876-8729.

A large, modern mooring facility, as well as a city park and campground, is located upriver. Several motels and restaurants serve visitors to the Au Gres community.

Further Information

Chambers of Commerce:

1. Au Gres Area Chamber of Commerce, Box 367, Au Gres 48703; (517) 876-8313.
2. East Michigan Tourist Association, One Wenonah Park, Bay City 48706; (517) 895-8823.

Bait & Tackle Shops:

1. Four Seasons Sports, 427 W. Huron, Au Gres 48703; (517) 876-8801.
2. Pt. Au Gres Marina, 2325 Green Dr., Au Gres 48703; (517) 876-7314.
3. Lutz's Bait & Tackle, 415 E. Huron, Au Gres 48703; (517) 876-8313.
4. Bob's Marina, 3712 E. Michigan Ave., Au Gres 48703; (517) 876-8929.
5. Wright's Sport Store, 100 Huron St. (US-23), Au Gres 48703; (517) 876-8720.

Charter Fishing:

1. Captain Terry Walsh, P.O. Box 565, Au Gres 48703; (517) 876-8318. 26-foot Stamas, *TerMar*.
2. Brown's Fishing Trips (perch fishing), Brown's Landing, 1129 Dyer Rd., Tawas City 48763; (517) 362-3737. *Miss Charity Isle.*
3. Joe's Fishing Trips (perch), 2325 Green Dr. (on Pt. Au Gres), Au Gres 48703; (517) 876-7314. *Kathleen.*
4. Rich Seiferlein (walleyes, perch), O.J.'s Motel & Cottages, 500 N. Huron, Au Gres 48703; (517) 876-7512.

Department of Natural Resources:

Two fisheries biologists work out of District Headquarters at 501 Hemlock, Clare 48617; (517) 386-7991.

Coast Guard:

Tawas Station, (517) 386-4428.

42
CHARITY ISLANDS

Big and Little Charity Islands lie just outside Inner Saginaw Bay, about equidistant from Caseville (45) and Au Gres (41). Fishermen in seaworthy boats come from those two ports, plus the Tawases, to the Charities in spring, summer and fall. They usually don't leave disappointed. Good to excellent opportunities exist for smallmouth bass, walleyes, yellow perch, trout and salmon.

The key is intricate reef structure. Structure surrounds the Charities for several miles and supplies predator species with plenty of food—mayflies and other lake-bottom larvae, crayfish and minnows. But boaters must exercise caution—the bottom between the islands comes up to within a foot or two of the surface. "Prop eaters" is one of the nicer terms used to describe the rocky bottom.

Another solid point about fishing at the Charities is that, unlike the Inner Bay, there are virtually no commercial nets in the area.

Fishing Schedule

SPRING

Good *spring* angling prospects begin to shape by early May and improve steadily through July. There are always some yellow perch and walleyes at the Charities, but concentrations of each appear after Memorial Day. Walleyes that have recently spawned in rivers emptying into Saginaw Bay come here to feed as well as to escape warm water in the shallows. Take a water-temperature reading in the vicinity of the islands. If it is approaching 70 degrees F., walleyes won't be far behind. Perch show up even sooner and, in some cases, seem to stay longer.

SUMMER

Summer brings the best sport for both species. By mid-July, the weekend boating fleet may number 200 or more craft. Some walleye anglers driftfish with whole nightcrawlers threaded to drift rigs, crawler harnesses, Erie Dearies, and Crawler Hawlers. Jigging with lead-head jigs and maribou or twister tails works, too. Some fishermen cast off boat corners when a good wind creates a chop and keeps the boat moving. Erie Dearies, Mepps Lusox Spinners, Tom's Lures, and Rooster Eyes are good throwing hardware when carrying whole crawlers.

Trolling is a rated tactic, too, a method I used in July 1985, to catch walleyes to five pounds each while fishing with guide bill Olar between the two islands. Behind Olar's 29-foot pontoon boat, we pulled small Hot 'N Tots, with a green crayfish color the best producer that day. At other times, Olar reports success with black-and-gold, brown crayfish, silver-and-orange, silver-and-green, and silver- and-black colors.

Olar has some interesting theories about how to catch the bigger walleyes here. For one, he trolls or drifts slowly, claiming that bigger fish are lazy and want offerings that are right on target and easy to catch. A second is that he always washes his hands in a neutralizing agent, such as Shaklee Basic H, before handling lures. And he watches his trolling lines carefully. When a walleye bits, Bill drops his rod at him, then sets the hook as line tightens from the fish running off.

Charities fishermen commonly nail walleyes in the six- to nine-pound category, and each summer, fish surpassing 10 pounds are brought into area tackle shops for weighing. The Mepps Company, a tackle manufacturer from Antigo, Wisconsin, sponsors a summer fishing contest in Saginaw Bay for walleyes caught with their lures. Many of the weekly $200 prize winners are fishermen with Charity Islands fish.

The Charities are gaining a reputation not only for big fish, but also for fast action. Captain Steve Fosdick of Caseville, for example, reports a charter that brought aboard 32 walleyes in just two hours off a sunken island northeast of Big Charity. Seven Sebewaing men caught 35 walleyes to eight pounds each during one afternoon in the area. These stories are becoming commonplace.

Incidentally, anglers catching tagged fish are asked to notify

Jud McCarty of Otisville with a dandy six-pound walleye. Up to 200 boats gather off the Charity Islands for walleyes on a summer weekend.

fisheries biologists at DNR District Headquarters, 501 Hemlock, Clare 48617; (517) 386-7991. Metal tags will be located in the upper or lower jaw. In exchange for the tags (or at least the numbers), location and date of catch, and length of the fish, the DNR will notify cooperators when and where their walleyes were tagged.

Yellow perch, too, cluster over the Charities' structures. Try 10-15 feet of water in June. As temperatures increase, go further out to 28 feet or deeper. A clue to good perching is the number of party boats from Au Gres (41) and Tawas City that visit the Charities in June and July. Bay Port sport-fishermen Tom and Bill Ford report excellent catches of large perch in June and July from rocky bottom northeast of Big Charity Island. The men carefully motor to the northeast of Little Charity, then take a sight alignment for locating a long reef that runs for five or more miles northeast of Big Charity. There, the Fords have taken perch in the 14- and 15-inch size class, most of which were crammed with crayfish. Crayfish would be dynamite bait if they were available in shops. In their absence, wigglers and shiner minnows work well.

Perch and walleyes aren't the only calling cards to the Charities. The reefs also produce good smallmouth-bass action from mid-June to early July from spawning fish in the shallows. It is difficult, however, to make a stealthy approach in clear water that is only four or five feet deep. Nightcrawlers, spinners, and small crankbaits and spoons are good offerings to try. Lake trout and salmon also frequent the reefs from May through August, although they are apt to be in water 50 feet or more in depth, at least in midsummer. They are in the region to feed, and trollers can take them with small spoons, dodgers and squids, and cowbells and Wobble-Glos.

FALL

Fall fishing drops off as salmon home in on natal spawning areas, the lake-trout season ends August 15, and perch and walleye leave the area for shoreline shallows.

WINTER

Winter angling opportunities are on-again, off-again for yellow perch. Few anglers try for walleyes this far out from shore, and if they are catching any fish, the word has not yet gotten around. Good lake-trout jigging through the ice off Point Lookout could likely be duplicated over deep-water reefs outside the Charities. It is also likely that jigging fishermen could take whitefish here if they tried.

Planting Records

The Charity Islands do not receive hatchery-reared fish, except for those related elsewhere that migrate there.

Facilities

No one lives on the islands, which are privately owned and off-limits to fishermen. For information about boat launching, chambers of commerce, and bait-and-tackle shops, see 41 (Au Gres), 45 (Caseville), 39 (Tawas Bay), and 43 and 44 (Saginaw Bay).

Further Information

Charter Fishing:

1. Captain Steve Fosdick, Journey Charters, P.O. Box 86, Elkton 48731; (517) 375-4597. 24-foot Wellcraft Airslot Fisherman, *Journey*.
2. Captain Mike Thede, 9035 Port Austin Rd., Bay Port 48720; (517) 656-7174. 24-foot Sea Ray, *Seaducer*.
3. Bill Olar, Olar's Guide Service, 2950 E. Turner Rd., Turner 48765; (517) 876-8454. 29-foot Pontoon boat.
4. Rich Seiferlein, O.J.'s Motel & Cottages, 500 North Huron, Au Gres 48703; (517) 876-7512.

Department of Natural Resources:

Two fisheries biologists work out of District Headquarters at 501 Hemlock, Clare 48617; (517) 386-7991.

Coast Guard:

Tawas Station, (517) 362-4428.

The Crystal-Clear Fog Experience

One spring morning as we cruised just north of Oak Point to 40 feet of water, my charter and I had a feeling that this was going to be a good day. We felt this way in spite of the fact that heavy fog lay over Saginaw Bay and all but one other boat had elected to stay in port. We set salmon-trolling lines identical to those we had used so successfully the week before. The water was just starting to layer for the season. We found our optimum temperature (about 54 degrees F.) at 30 feet deep.

But an hour of working the humps and reefs produced nothing. Over the radio, the other skipper told me he planned to continue down the shore toward Port Austin (*??*). But I figured that the salmon might have dispersed into the lake and could be as far out as the Charity Island reefs. So we roared away in that direction.

Once over the inside reefs, I switched on my King graph. Nothing. To add to our dilemma, my buddy in the other boat announced that he had taken his first laker. It was now 10:00 a.m., the fog was burning off, and we debated whether or not to haul lines and race back to Oak Point.

Suddenly, we passed over a reef, down 30-35 feet and surrounded by water to 50-60 feet deep. The graph said it was loaded with fish. At the same time we noticed a lot of midges or flies on the water and in the boat. We had stumbled into a fly hatch in progress.

What happened over the next three hours is hard to believe—10 kings and five lakers in the box, plus plenty of missed opportunities. Twice we had five fish on at the same time.

Next morning, with the Loran coordinates punched into memory, we repeated our performance. The only difference was that the charter was satisfied with 17 fish and were too tired to catch more. We entered the port by 10:30 a.m.

Sure, the Charity Islands produce good perch and walleye fishing. But, as we proved, they also serve up excellent Chinook and lake-trout fishing.

Captain Steve Fosdick
Caseville

42
CHARITY ISLANDS

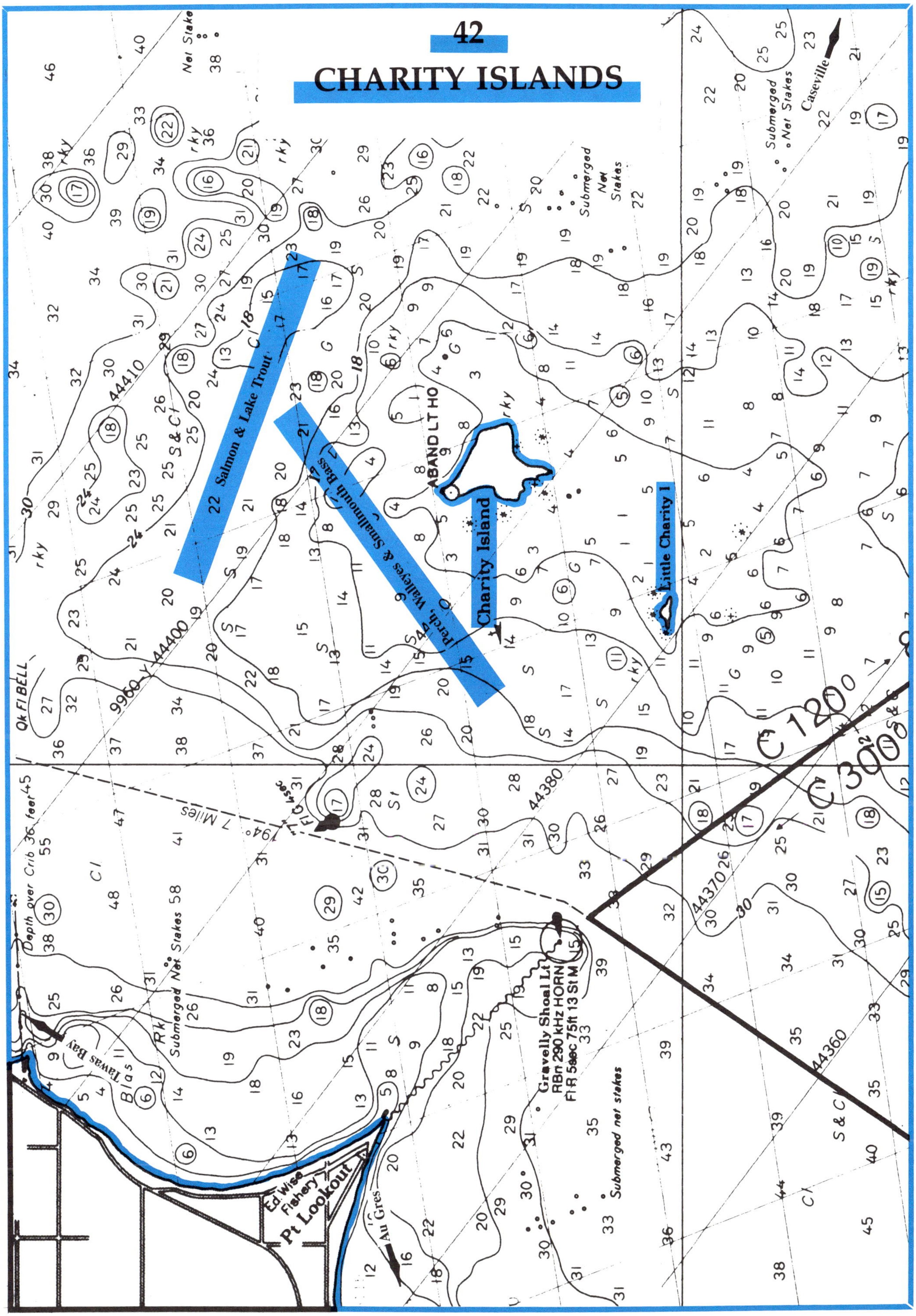

43

SAGINAW BAY (Au Gres to Bay City)

The west shore of Saginaw Bay offers many fishing opportunities. Depending on the time of year, those opportunities range from fair to excellent for largemouth and smallmouth bass, northern pike, yellow perch, carp, panfish, catfish, smelt and walleyes. Pinconning, in particular, has an excellent protected inner bay. Numerous offshore weed beds throughout western Saginaw Bay also make for good fishing.

Fishing Schedule

SPRING

Spring activity kicks off when perch enter the shallows to spawn, with boat and shore anglers scoring evenly in March and April. Any of the dozen rivers and small streams that flow into Saginaw Bay from Point Au Gres to Bay City are fair targets for perch. In particular, the Pine River near Standish, which used to serve up outstanding spring sport, still affords fair to good catching opportunities. Also, from the shallows outside the Pinconning and Saganing bars all the way to Linwood, expect perch to 20-25 feet of water as late as the end of June.

Clusters of fishing boats are always good clues as to where the perchers are and how they're faring. Locate a school of hungry yellow-bellies and you can experience fast action with five- to 14-inch fish. Wigglers, worms, and shiner minnows pinned to two-hook crappie rigs and tightline jigged near bottom produce the best results.

Though better smelt runs develop from Au Gres (41) north, there are some dipping opportunities in Saginaw Bay, too. Mid-April to early May is the best time. Recent-year runs have been considered the best in 20 years. Target stream mouths and nearby shoreline shallows.

Hefty releases of walleye fingerlings in the past several years have beefed up walleye populations. Their spawning runs, previously all but dead in Saginaw Bay for over 40 years, are returning once more.

Walleyes make spawning drives up west-end rivers—the Saginaw and its tributaries (Bad, Shiawassee, Tittabawassee, Chippewa), the Kawkawlin, the Quanicassee, the Au Gres and the Rifle. Spawning walleyes have become so rife in some of these rivers, especially the Kawkawlin, that the DNR has temporarily closed them to all fishing to protect the spawning fish. (The walleye and northern-pike season typically closes on the last day of February and opens again on May 15. Check a current copy of *Michigan Fishing Guide* for details).

The Pinconning area has great potential to become the hub of a good walleye fishery. Releases began in 1978 and have increased in number annually since. Trawl nets run by the DNR in late June 1985, showed good numbers of small walleyes. All of Saginaw Bay is expected to provide better and better walleye fishing. Anglers are just now learning where walleyes go and how to catch them.

After May 15 the stream mouths still produce solid action for both walleyes and northerns. Try casting or trolling spinners and spoons. Northern pike hang out in the shallows all summer long, but walleyes disperse by late May or mid-June. Most apparently migrate up the Slot, a deep-water channel that cuts through the center of the Inner Bay from the Saginaw River mouth to the Charity Islands. Others fan out to the Maisou Island group and stay there all summer. Some go further east to reef structure along the Thumb tip. For complete details, refer to 44 (Saginaw Bay: Bay City to Sand Point), 45 (Caseville), 46 (Port Austin) and 42 (Charity Islands).

Some of the hottest spring walleye fishing occurs at Consumers Power Company's Kern-Weadock hot pond, a mile-long channel at Bay City/Essexville that returns 78-degree-F. water to the Saginaw River. Although Consumers' property is off-limits to the public, anglers can launch at Tacey's Marina, at the end of Jones Road just east of Bay City, and a five-minute boat ride will take them to the hot-pond outflow. On opening day 1983, I checked stringers of fishermen returning to Tacey's and was surprised at the several limit catches of two- to five-pound fish that I saw. Nightcrawlers, fished whole with jigs or harnesses, are hot spring bait.

Don Schafer of Unionville fishes the hot pond after work (Schafer manages the Fish Point Wildlife Area for the DNR) from May 15 until the walleyes disperse. Schafer, a meticulous record keeper, says that walleye dispersal can occur from mid-June through early July. Temperature is the key. When reef-area water warms to 70 degrees F., walleyes flock to it, supposedly to stuff themselves with post-spawn feeding binges.

Schafer relies on three lures which he invented and now manufactures under the trade name Blue Sky Tackle. One, the Crawler Hawler I, is a 1/4- or 1/2-ounce lure with spinner blade and two-hook harness body. The Crawler Hawler II comes in 3/8 ounce and features different colors than the Crawler Hawler I models. The third Schafer lure, the Wall-I Hot Dog, is a 3/8-ounce jig-type lure with propeller blade. All three lures, available in area tackle shops, are proven walleye takers when rigged with live nightcrawlers. Don driftfishes, jigs, and slow retrieves these and other lures off bottom. Color is as important as presentation. No matter whose lures you are using, Schafer suggests changing colors every 15 minutes if you are not getting strikes. Green, yellow, chartreuse, orange, brass, and nickel are all good choices at certain times.

St. Clair River and Wolf River drift rigs are other good systems for fishing whole crawlers. Trolling with weight-forward spinners (Erie Dearies, Mepps Lusox, or Rooster Tails) and nightcrawlers or with small Hot 'N Tots produce throughout Saginaw Bay. Walleyes will also pound jigs tipped with minnows, as well as bare Mister Twisters. White is usually a good spring color.

Besides the hot pond, another good early season hotspot is the broken rocks at the end of Knight Road, a mile east of Tacey's Marina. Driftfishing on evenings with a south or southwest wind to move boats away from the shallow-water rocks is an excellent time to try. And don't overlook the U.S. Army Corps of Engineers landfill north of the Saginaw River mouth about 2-1/2 miles into the bay. Walleyes stack up, temporarily, along the deep-water edges of this 150-acre landfill. Many other smaller areas of structure are waiting for fishermen to discover them.

SUMMER

Summer fishing in western Saginaw Bay rates only fair for perch and walleyes. Perch are generally well scattered (the Charity Islands, 42, serve up top summer sport), and, for the most part, walleyes have left until cooler weather brings fall.

A bow-and-arrow fishery for carp begins in mid-May and lasts throughout June. Archers work shoreline canals and area cattail pods.

Channel catfish and bullheads provide excellent sport beginning in May and lasting throughout July, according to Ray Shepherd, DNR fisheries biologist at Clare. Best fishing is near shore just off the cattails. Fish the bottom with nightcrawlers or blood baits.

Shepherd also says a fishery for largemouth and smallmouth bass is underutilized. Plugs, spinnerbaits, and crawlers fished along and among cattails produce best for largemouths, with August and September (after carp have left the shallows) the best times to go. Smallmouths like structure, so look for areas of hardpan bottom along with dock pilings and rock rubble. There are smallmouths in the Saginaw River that never see a spinnerbait.

FALL

Fall opportunities improve as yellow perch invade cuts, rivers and shoreline areas to feed. Action begins in mid-September and lasts into early winter. The cool weather also sends walleyes back over reefs and hardpan bottom near weed beds. Jigs and spinners dressed with crawlers or minnows are popular lures, but west-end anglers have yet to find fall walleyes in large concentrations.

WINTER

Winter perching rates excellent, especially on early ice, and shantytowns build from one to 10 miles offshore from Pinconning and Linwood. Ice-jigging spoons, fished clean or tipped with shiner minnows, waxworms or mousies, produce best on perch as well as with crappies, bluegills and sunfish. But again, anglers have yet to locate concentrations of offshore walleyes in winter. Many fishermen, however, do exceptionally well in rivers, most notably the Kawkawlin and Tittabawassee. Pike spearers take northerns from five to 15 pounds each from shanties, and tip-up anglers catch them on sucker minnows.

Planting Records

The only plantings being made in western Saginaw Bay at this time are walleye fingerlings that have been reared at ponds located at Fish Point, Kawkawlin, Auburn (two ponds), Au Gres and Tawas. Saginaw Bay releases have been totaling about 600,000 fingerlings each year. (Tawas Bay, 39, receives another 300,000 or so.) From 57,000-159,000 have been released at the mouth of the Pinconning River each of the past three years. At Linwood Road, up to a quarter-million walleyes have been introduced annually, and at the Kawkawlin River mouth, stockings have fluctuated between 30,000 and 150,000 fish.

Facilities

The DNR maintains a gravel-ramp boat-launching site at the end of Coggins Road three miles south of Pinconning, but boaters should watch for nearby submerged pilings. There is no fee to launch either there or at Nayanquing Point, two miles further south. At the mouth of the Pine River, straight east of Standish, is a free shallow-water paved ramp. There is also a launch site at Tacey's Marina, at the end of Jones Rd. east of Bay City, another at Veterans Memorial Park on the Saginaw River (just upstream from the bridge at the end of US-10), and a paved two-lane ramp in Essexville.

From east to west, access is available off Callahan Rd., Hampton-Finn Rd., Knight Harbor on Knight Rd., Jones Rd.,

Channel catfish, such as these, go largely ignored in Saginaw Bay. They are good eating and populations are on the rise.

Essexville, Hoyles Marine on Linwood Rd., Coggins Rd., Bilman's on Newberg Rd., Genow's Marina on Neuman Rd., Pinconning Rd., and the Pine River mouth.

The communities of Standish, Pinconning, Bay City and Essexville cater to visiting fishermen.

Further Information

Chambers of Commerce:

1. Pinconning Area Chamber of Commerce, P.O. Box 856, Pinonning 48650; (517) 879-5888.
2. Standish Chamber of Commerce, P.O. Box 458, Standish 48658; (517) 846-4595.
3. Bay Area Chamber of Commmerce, Box 838, Bay City 48706; (517) 893-4567.
4. East Michigan Tourist Association, One Wenonah Park, Bay City 48706; (517) 895-8823.

Bait & Tackle Shops:

1. Frank's Bait & Tackle, 1206 N. Huron Rd. (US-23), Linwood 48634; (517) 697-4241 or 694-5792.
2. Standish Sporting Goods, 105 N. Main St., Standish 48658; (517) 846-9641.
3. DeKett's Tackle, 2710 State St., Saginaw 48605; (517) 790-0330.
4. Sport 'n' Spirits Bait & Tackle, at the light in Kawkawlin; (517) 686-8400.
5. Dan's Bait & Sport Shop, 510 E. Center Rd., Essexville 48732; (517) 894-5365.
6. Bev's & Jerry Stantz Tackle, 209 Salzburg Ave., Bay City 48706; (517) 892-1351.

Charter Fishing:

Contact the East Michigan Tourist Association, One Wenonah Park, Bay City 48706; (517) 895-8823 for the names of several charterboat fishermen.

Department of Natural Resources:

Two fisheries biologists work out of District Headquarters at 501 Hemlock, Clare 48617; (517) 386-7991.

Coast Guard:

Tawas Station, (517) 362-4428.

Contenders for a Rich Resource

Fishermen coming to Saginaw Bay during the open-water season should be aware that commercial netters legally work the area inside a line from Sand Point to Point Lookout. This 350,000- to 400,000-acre area is known as the Inner Bay. The netters target channel catfish, carp, suckers, rock bass, black crappies and perch. They may not keep walleyes, salmon or trout.

Twenty-eight commercial fishermen (16 north and east of Quanicassee and 12 in the western portion) are currently licensed to net Saginaw Bay. When all of their legally allowed trap nets are in place, the total is 355. Some reach several hundred feet in length. In addition, there are thousands of feet of large mesh gillnets set for carp and thousands of baited hooks for catfish. Special permits, such as whitefish netting and the use of purse seines on an experimental basis, are also issued by the DNR.

The regulations are confusing to the average sport fisherman. Motoring out of Bay Port for some evening catfish angling, he is confronted by a sea of flags. Although nets must be marked, the sport fisherman can't tell what denotes a trap net from a line of hooks. He often becomes entangled in the nets and loses tackle. Trolling, especially with downriggers, is impossible, and he wonders how many walleyes the netters kill, either by keeping the fish illegally or by losing them to incidental mortality. The sport angler is reminded of the rape of Saginaw Bay by greedy profiteers who, at one time, destroyed fishing for both groups.

Some say that commercial fishing is an anachronism, a dinosaur that would become extinct were it not for the DNR propping it up through special allowances. Sportsmen are not happy that this intervention is being paid for by the dollars they spend on sport-fishing licenses. It is a frustrating scenario for the sport fisherman. He wants to know why commercial netters can pay a pittance in license fees, yet glut the bay with nets while insisting upon the right to take even more of the resource.

Commercial netters, on the other hand, say the resource belongs to all the people. Since it is renewable, like timber, why can't they harvest a share, especially when there are increasing numbers of catfish and walleyes, in particular, and sport anglers are making little or no impact on their populations? "Why must we import walleyes from Canada to sell," they ask, "when there is enough in Saginaw Bay for both us and the sport fishermen?"

The commercial interests say they are here to stay and that factors other than netting are to blame for the shabby history of Saginaw Bay. Toxic and sawmill pollution hurt fish stocks more than netting, they claim. "Who stripped walleye eggs and fertilized them to rebuild stocks 40 years and more ago?" they ask. "Commercial fishermen, of course, and out of their own pockets and with their own time." They point to the fact that their group has historically been among the most tightly regulated in Michigan. They argue that commercial fishermen have lived and continue to live in an increasingly vulnerable fish bowl.

The war of words goes on.

Lost in the charges/counter charges is the fact that Saginaw Bay is growing healthy once more. Its waters are cleaner than at any point in memory, its fish populations once more on the rise.

What will become of this resource, growing richer each year? The answer depends largely upon how the interest groups interpret history and whether or not they can find a way to divide the pie into equally acceptable pieces.

Tom Huggler
Otisville

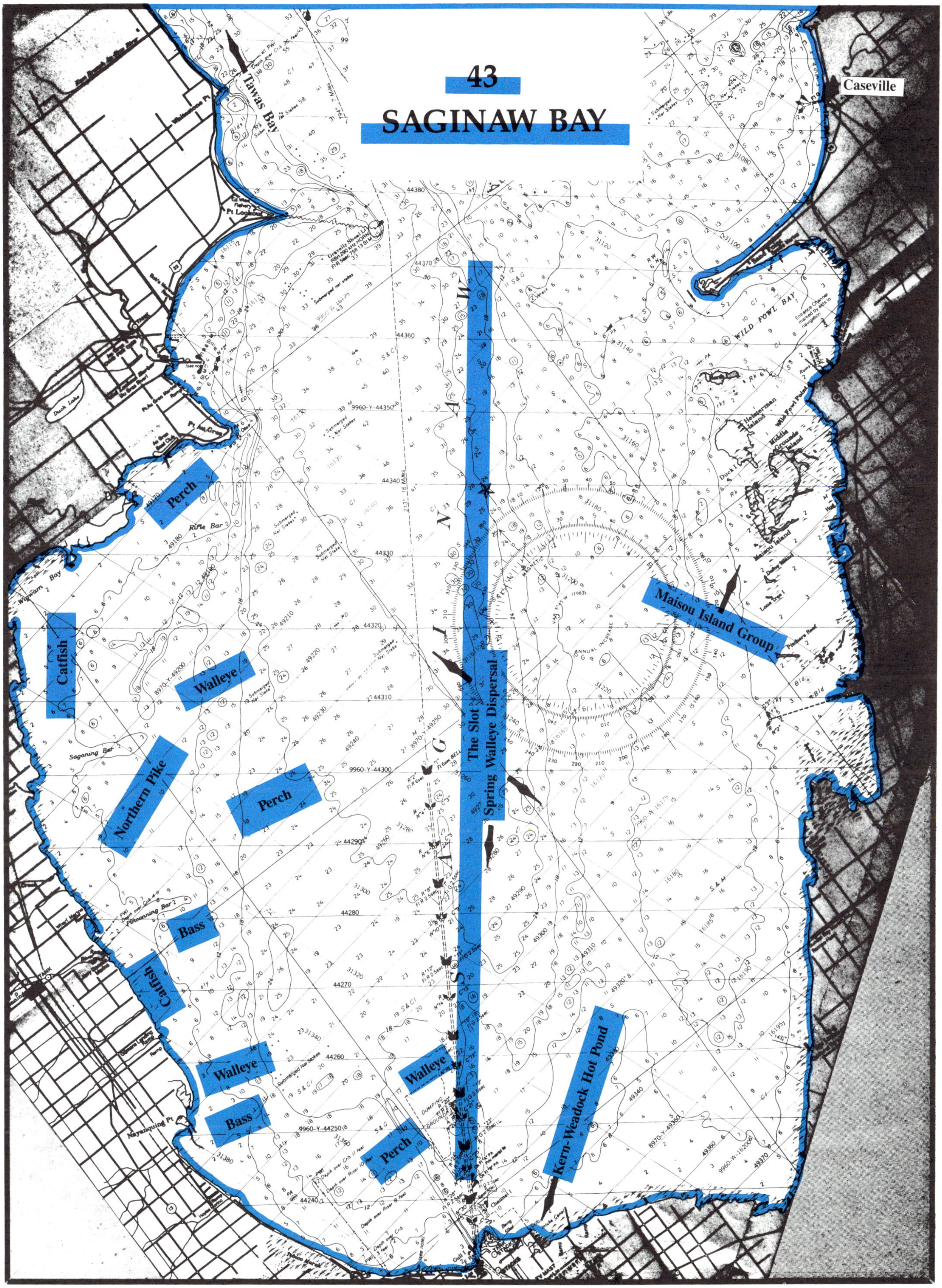
43
SAGINAW BAY
Caseville
Tawas Bay
Pt Lookout
WILD FOWL BAY
Perch
Rifle Bar
Wigwam Bay
Catfish
Walleye
Saganing Bar
Northern Pike
Perch
The Slot
Spring Walleye Dispersal
Maisou Island Group
Bass
Catfish
Walleye
Walleye
Bass
Perch
Kern-Weadock Hot Pond
Nayanquing Pt

44
SAGINAW BAY (Bay City to Sand Point)

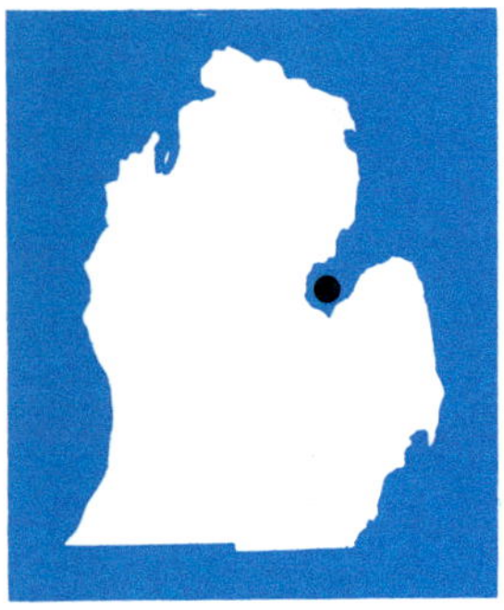

Not long ago, some people referred to the Thumb side of Saginaw Bay as Michigan's biggest carp hole. Dirty water from turbidities and pollution contributed to poor sport-fishing opportunities.

Much has changed in recent years. This region now supports some of the best walleye fishing in eastern Michigan, and there are also improved catches reported of largemouth bass, northern pike, channel catfish, crappies and other panfish, including perch. Quanicassee, Sebewaing, and Bay Port are the centers of this rejuvenated fishing.

Fishing Schedule

SPRING

Ice-out in late March brings yellow perch racing into area cuts and creek mouths to spawn. The Quanicassee and Sebewaing rivers, along with Allen Cut, Thomas Cut, Wiscoggin Drain, and Mud Creek, are good shoreline spots to try. Weed beds and gravel pits close to shore are others. Wigglers are the preferred *spring* bait, but the hungry yellow-bellies also strike worms, nightcrawler pieces, and minnows. Fishing tactics are unelaborate. Simply weight a single hook or crappie spreader with a sinker, bait up, and allow the offering to sit on bottom while you keep a tight line.

Walleye fishing, beginning with the May 15 opener, is good at the mouth of the Quanicassee River. It remains productive until mid or late June when walleyes fan out into the bay. Some shoot up the Slot, a deep-water channel that runs from the Saginaw River mouth to the Charity Islands (see 42 for catching details). Others move to reef structure along the shoreline from Quanicassee to Sand Point, with heavy concentrations outside the Maisou Island group. At this time, walleyes have just finished spawning and are hungry. They hover over sand bars and rocky reefs in five to 15 feet of water in tiny pockets of habitat or long, finger-like bars up to a couple of miles offshore.

SUMMER

As *summer* wears on and water temperatures inch toward 70 degrees F., fishing improves outside the Maisou Islands. Dozens of reefs infest this area from Lone Tree Island to Heisterman Island. Some, like the Hog's Back and Duck Island reefs, have names. Most do not, but if you have a bottom scanner in your boat, they are easy enough to find. Most fishermen carry an empty bleach jug tied to a rope and anchor so that they can mark spots when they begin to get action.

Several year-classes of walleyes are now available throughout Saginaw Bay. Seven- to nine-inch fish are one-year old. Those taping 14-16 inches are two years, 20- to 22-inch fish are three years, 26- to 28-inch walleye are four, and fish 30 inches and up are five years of age.

Fishing for all age classes continues to improve. Patrons of Pop's Place, a Sebewaing-area bar, began tacking walleye heads to a nearby telephone pole a few years ago. Today, there are more heads than ever, and they're bigger than before.

No area angler has been more free with information about catching tactics for walleyes than Don Schafer of Unionville. When walleyes began returning to Saginaw Bay about five years ago—thanks to cleanup efforts and massive stockings from nearby walleye-rearing ponds—Schafer began keeping records. He fishes every chance he gets, and his record book reveals season-long catches from 300-500 fish each year. Don does not weigh his walleyes; instead, he measures them, many of which he tosses back to grow even bigger.

Schafer is a fussy walleye fisherman, as I learned one July evening when we drifted over sand bars just off Fish Point. Don prefers to drift, claiming that outboards spook walleyes in the shallow water. Anchoring and jigging is another productive tactic, yet he claims that few have faith in jigs. "A good jig is one of those tools that catch fish but not fishermen," Schafer wrote in a recent letter to me on the subject. "The biggest mistake that Saginaw Bay walleye fishermen make," he added, "is that they don't keep their bait fresh looking. A second mistake is that they don't experiment with presentation and colors. Walleyes are finicky fish, and you have to give them what they want."

Trollers report fast action at times, for example, with gold-and-black and kelly-green Hot 'N Tots. Others troll or driftfish with nightcrawlers pinned to No. 3 Mepps Comets, Erie Dearies, Mepps Lusox spinners, and Crawler Hawlers. Some jig with Wall-I Hot Dogs, Garland Mini-Jigs, Fuzz-E Grubs, and Mister Twisters. Colors change as fast as (and along with) the weather. Orange, black, green, blue, red, white, yellow, and chartreuse all take fish at one time or another.

Early morning and evening are the best hours for fishing success. Walleyes, however, are taken at all hours during the day, especially if it is overcast and there is a chop on the water. A north wind that roils water and stirs up food on the reefs can also produce fast action for a short period of time.

Bow hunting for spawning carp is an excellent early summer sport along cuts and shoreline marshes. Because there is no limit and carp are so plentiful, some bowmen report arrowing dozens in a single day. Bank fishermen catch the prolific carp, too, along with bullheads, catfish, rock bass, crappies and perch.

Channel catfish from one to 10 pounds appear to be exceptionally plentiful in recent years. Sport-fishermen Tom and Bill Ford of Bay Port report that the east side of Heisterman Island is especially productive for big channel cats from May through September. Prime fishing times are an hour before sunrise and an hour after sunset. Typical rigging involves two No. 4 snelled hooks attached 12 inches apart (one above the other) and weighted with a 1/4-ounce bell-shaped sinker. Nightcrawlers and stink baits draw strikes. Sport-angler Art Perry, who owns a home on the bay at Rowe Rd., says the best shore fishing for catfish occurs in May.

Some fishermen have recently reported incidental catches of white perch. A few commercial netters are also just now beginning to target the ocean invaders, that apparently entered Saginaw Bay by way of Lake Erie. White perch school, much in the manner of silver (white) bass, and could provide fast sport for worm and jig fishermen who want to catch them.

The shallows also produce northern pike from hammer-handle size to eight pounds. In spring, summer and fall, seek them over weed beds and near marshes and either spincast Dardevle-type spoons or bobber fish with live suckers.

Smallmouth bass, though not as plentiful as their largemouth cousins, provide another dimension to sport fishing in this area. Bass anglers can usually locate smallmouths anywhere structure can be found. Some walleye fishermen, drifting with live bait, report incidental catches of the two- to four-pound smallies. Sand Point and the Mud Creek outflow are likely spots to begin looking. Largemouths, on the other hand, are available to both waders and boat fishermen anywhere that cattails or bulrushes are evident. Casting with spinnerbaits, fake crawlers, and crankbaits are productive tactics.

FALL

During September, *fall* fishing improves when most of the walleyes that had moved out to deeper water by the end of July begin drifting back. They can be found in shallows to 10 feet deep when water temperatures cool. Some duck hunters in Saginaw Bay wisely carry fishing gear for those bluebird days when the ducks aren't moving. Also in fall, yellow perch return to cuts and streams to feed. Although fewer and fewer sport anglers venture onto the bay as fall wears on, fishing opportunities exist until freeze-up.

WINTER

Winter fishing rates fair to excellent for northerns, yellow perch and black crappies. Early ice and late ice are twin peaks of activity. Perchers sometimes head out into the bay for miles, but the dead of winter generally serves up basically small fish, five to eight inches each. Phenomenal catches of ruler-length and larger fish, however, are reported on the rotted ice in March each year off Sebewaing and Bay Port. Then, when ice becomes honeycombed, perch concentrate over shallow-water weed beds and

Bulrushes and lily pads are a likely combination for smallmouth and largemouth bass. Although high water has cut back marsh growth, there is still plenty of bass fishing and it is largely underutilized.

gravel bars. But this is dangerous sport, and anglers are best advised to wear waders if fishing the extreme shallows and to drag along a boat if going out deeper. Waxworms, mousies, wigglers, and one-inch shiners are preferred baits when used with teardrop spoons. Others prefer the larger Russian Hooks with or without meat. No matter; when perch can be found, they can usually be induced to hit.

Northern-pike fishing is best in winter, with small shantytowns building off the Sebewaing River at Sebewaing and Sumac Island public access site off Geiger Rd. Tip-up fishermen also score. These pike are not huge—a seven- or eight-pounder is a fine fish—but they are reasonably plentiful.

Crappies When It Rots

From mid-February to mid-March, for some reason, jumbo crappies show up in Saginaw Bay in water from 15 inches to six feet deep. My friends from Fishing Tackle Grab Bag in Davison and I usually make a run or two during that time, and we're liable to show up anywhere on the bay from Fish Point to Sand Point. Sometimes we get skunked.

But sooner or later we know we'll hit those late-ice crappies just right—like on that February morning a couple of years ago that I remember so well. A friend from Flint and I didn't get our first bite until 11:00 a.m . But by noon we had iced a two-man limit of 50 crappies that measured from 12 to 16-1/2 inches each. A couple of these fish, including a two-pound, seven-ounce lunker, won me a DNR Master Angler Award certificate (see page 319.)

You have to take great care to catch these crappies. We prefer overcast days to avoid throwing our shadows on the ice and spooking fish. We look for milky ice to hide our movements and drill several holes at once with a hand auger to hold down the noise. Usually we pack slush in the holes to block light, then poke tiny openings with our ice-rod butts so that we can jig small spoons tipped with waxworms. We use No. 8 Minnesota teardrops, small Russian Hooks, and K & E Big Dipper Spoons. Chartreuse is the best color, although orange and red fluorescent are sometimes good, too. Hook barbs should be covered. Some guys squeeze a waxworm to milk it, then add a second larvae to give the crappies a big offering. Minnows and wigglers sometimes take hard-to-bite fish.

No matter the bait, best success comes when we jig up slowly to the top of the hole and then drop back fast. Use light line down to two-pound test and don't use any split shot at all.

I don't know why these jumbo crappies flock to the shallows during late-ice conditions. But I'm glad they do.

Steve Provost
Davison

Planting Records

Annual stockings of walleye fingerlings are being made at the Quanicassee River mouth, Thomas Cut public access site, Wiscoggin Drain at Fish Point, and Sebewaing VFW. Walleyes have also been released at Sumac Island access site.

Facilities

Moving from west to east, boat launching facilities are available at Quanicassee River (paved two-lane DNR ramp), Allen Cut (gravel two-lane ramp), Thomas Cut (gravel ramp), Sebewaing (city-owned paved two-lane ramp, with site regularly dredged by the Army Corps of Engineers), Bud's Landing at Rose Island (boats to 18 feet), Sumac Island public access site at Geiger Road (car toppers and boats to 16 feet), Winiecki's Marina between Sebewaing and Bay Port, Bay Port (new two-lane paved ramp), Bayshore Marina (any size boat), and Wildfowl Bay Resort (small boats).

The towns of Sebewaing and Bay Port cater to visiting fishermen.

Further Information

Chambers of Commerce:

1. Sebewaing Chamber of Commerce, P.O. Box 622, Sebewaing 48759; (517) 883-3000.
2. East Michigan Tourist Association, One Wenonah Park, Bay City 48706; (517) 895-8823.

Bait & Tackle Shops:

1. Bay House Sports, Box 128, Bay Port 48720; (517) 656-2551.
2. Bayshore Marina, Port Austin Rd. (M-25), Bay Port 48720; (517) 656-7191.
3. Wildfowl Bay Resort, 8592 Port Austin Rd. (M-25), Pigeon 48755; (517) 856-3101.
4. Don's Sport Shop, 8830 Unionville Rd., Sebewaing 48759; (517) 883-3700.
5. Dan's Bait & Sport Shop, 510 E. Center Rd., Essexville 48732; (517) 894-5365.

Charter Fishing:

None known. However, several captains that charter to the Charity Islands are likely candidates. See 42 for names and addresses or contact the East Michigan Tourist Association (address listed above).

Department of Natural Resources:

Two fisheries biologists work out of District Headquarters at 715 S. Cedar St., Imlay City 48444; (313) 724-2015.

Coast Guard:

Tawas Station, (517) 362-4428.

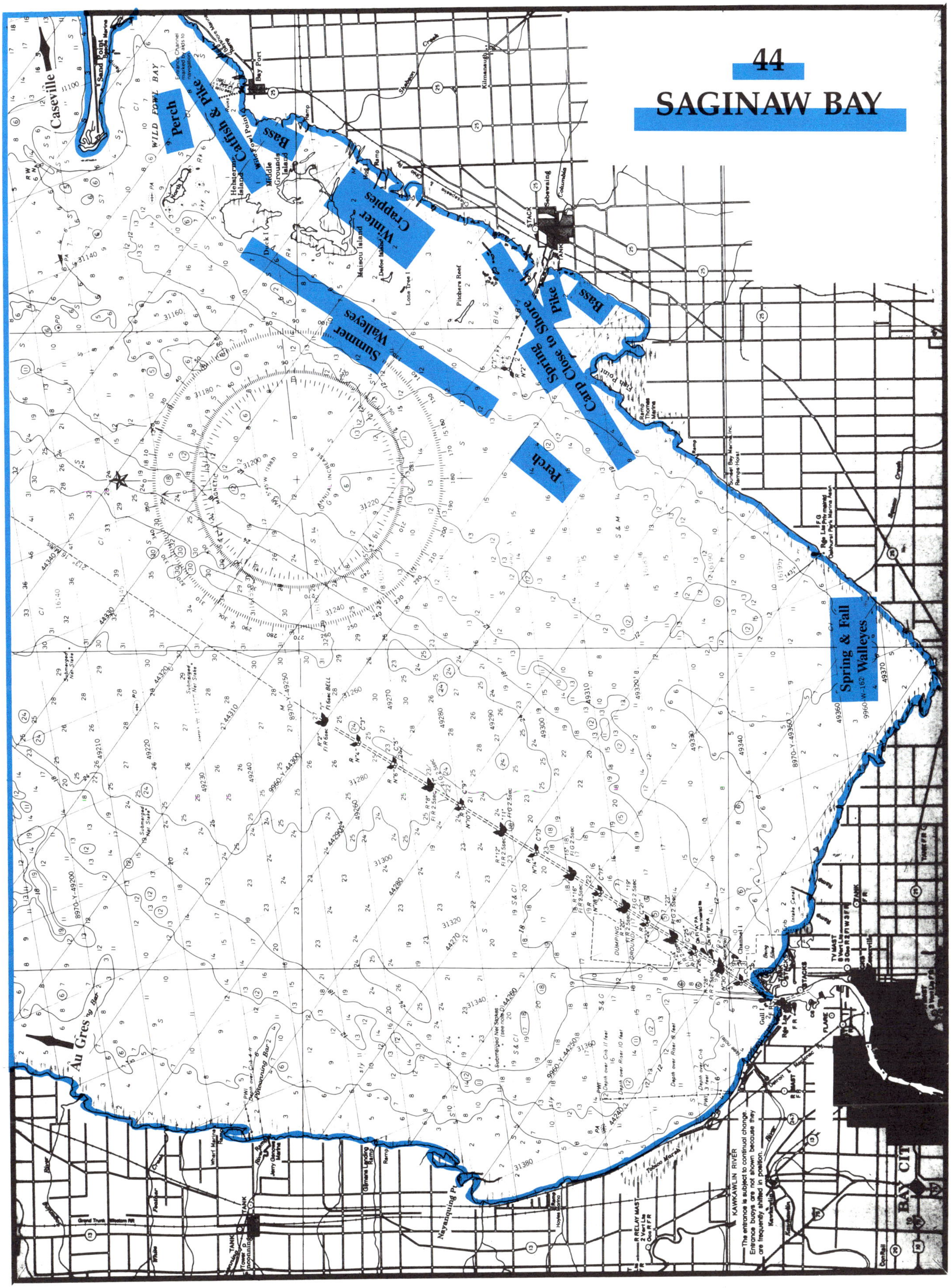
44
SAGINAW BAY
Caseville
Sand Point
Bay Port
WILD FOWL BAY
Perch
Catfish & Pike
Bass
Heisterman Island
Middle Grounds Island
Winter Crappies
Maisou Island
Defoe Island
Duck I
Lone Tree I
Pitchers Reef
Sebewaing
Summer Walleyes
Spring Pike
Carp Close to Shore
Bass
Fish Point
Perch
Spring & Fall Walleyes
Channel I
Gull I
Au Gres
Pinconning Bar
Nayanquing Pt.
KAWKAWLIN RIVER
The entrance is subject to continual change. Entrance buoys are not shown because they are frequently shifted in position.
BAY CITY

45
CASEVILLE

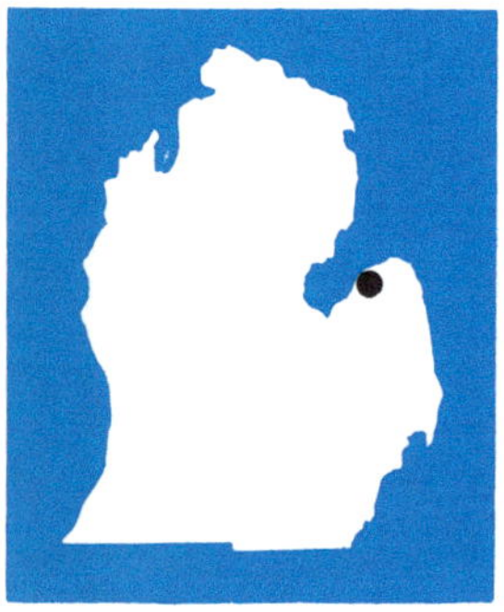

The Lake Huron ports of Caseville and Au Gres (41) lie across from each other, separated by about 25 miles of Saginaw Bay. They have a lot in common, especially their geographic position of straddling the Inner and Outer portions of Saginaw Bay. Both vie for the title, Perch Capitol of Michigan, if not the world. A secret just now unfolding is that each also produces far more than perch for anglers willing to experiment.

The Inner Bay alone contains some 300,000 warm, shallow and sandy acres. Walleyes, crappies, catfish, largemouth bass and carp, as well as yellow perch, love its weedbeds. The Outer Bay, on the other hand, has cold-water depths to 90 feet, undiscovered reefs, and some excellent lake-trout and Chinook salmon fishing—in addition to perch and walleyes.

Four years ago, charterboat-skipper Steve Fosdick began running out of Caseville because he could see the unique opportunities, as well as the excellent facilities, this port offered. Fosdick, who ramrods one of the few boats for hire here, has not been sorry with his decision. Fosdick puts his boat, *Journey*, into the water by mid-April and stores it in late October. During that period in 1985, he averaged six trout/salmon per charter, or a fish every half hour. Fosdick also reports improving success with walleyes and says there are always plenty of yellow perch.

Fishing Schedule

SPRING

Fosdick reports good Chinook and lake-trout action from ice-out to Memorial Day by trolling in the temperature break between the warm water of the Pigeon River (the Thumb's largest stream) and cold bay water. This color line accounts for 50 percent of *spring* fish in *Journey*'s cooler. Fosdick sets up outriggers and planer boards and drops his Riviera downrigger cannonballs (two stern-end and two out-down models with four-foot arms) just under the surface or spots flatlines a long way (100 or more feet) behind the boat. He rigs with 12- to 15-pound-test line and runs most lures clean (no attractors). Choices include Northport Nailers and Dr. Hooks, but as fish move to deeper reef structure, the captain will deep-six 00 dodgers 12-15 inches ahead of Lindy Finsel Flies or Wobble-Glos. Good colors are greens, chartreuse, blues, and silver.

Plenty of tackle-testing yellow perch, from eight to 14 inches, concentrate in April along the breakwall and off the rivermouth access sites. Wigglers, worms, and shiner minnows produce the best catches.

By the May 15 opener, post-spawn walleyes fan out to numerous reefs outside the harbor. (See also the map with 47, Grindstone City, which details the entire Thumb tip.) Caseville-area trollers go after walleyes with Hot 'N Tots and Lindy Shadlings, or they driftfish with crawler harnesses. Fish average two or three pounds, but four- to 10-pounders are not uncommon.

SUMMER

By *summer*, trout and salmon trollers head for the Outer Bay, and since trips may require 10-12 miles of run, safe and durable offshore boats are a necessity. The Outer Bay, where waves can brew to six-footers in just minutes, is no place for 12- to 16-foot boats. Fosdick targets reefs and humps off the Charity Islands (see 42, which contains an overview map). For lake trout he throttles down to 1-1/4 to 1-3/4 knots on his EMS trolling meter while running 00 or 000 dodgers with flies, small plugs, or flake-thin spoons. Sometimes he stacks attractor rigs with clean-running spoons, and the result is often king-salmon strikes.

Fosdick claims that Caseville is Lake Huron's super sleeper port, with undiscovered reefs throughout the Outer Bay awaiting trout and salmon trollers willing to experiment. "We find at least one new reef each season," he told me in a letter on the subject.

The walleye fishery is just coming on, with over ***one million*** fingerlings released over the past five years in Saginaw Bay from five hatchery ponds. The Mepps Company, a tackle manufacturer out of Antigo, Wisconsin, has sponsored a Saginaw Bay walleye fishing tournament for several weeks during each of the past two summers. The contest—with weekly prizes of $200 for the biggest fish—has triggered anglers to experiment with new lures and techniques and to seek hog walleyes in little-known reef areas. Those willing to slow troll or driftfish with Mepps Lusox spinners, Syclops spoons, Lindy Rigs, small crankbaits, or nightcrawler harnesses can get fast action at times. In addition to the Charities, close-to-shore reefs off Oak Point and the Sand Point area also produce.

Perching remains good throughout the summer, too. Green- or red-beaded perch rigs containing small hooks and shiner minnows will do a number on yellow-bellies. Most of the summer boat traffic running out of Caseville Harbor is pleasure craft, a surprising number of which carry perch-fishing gear. One of the best days of perching I ever enjoyed on Saginaw Bay occurred while we cruised out of Caseville on a sailboat. True, the perch were small—six to eight inches. But there were plenty of them and they were exceptionally good eating.

Fall sport includes a hot perch run up Bay-area cuts and the Pigeon River in October. Walleyes are also in offshore shallows, but more fishermen are needed to find the best catching tactics. Because Caseville does not receive plants of trout and salmon, better fishing occurs off Port Austin (46) and Grindstone City

45 CASEVILLE

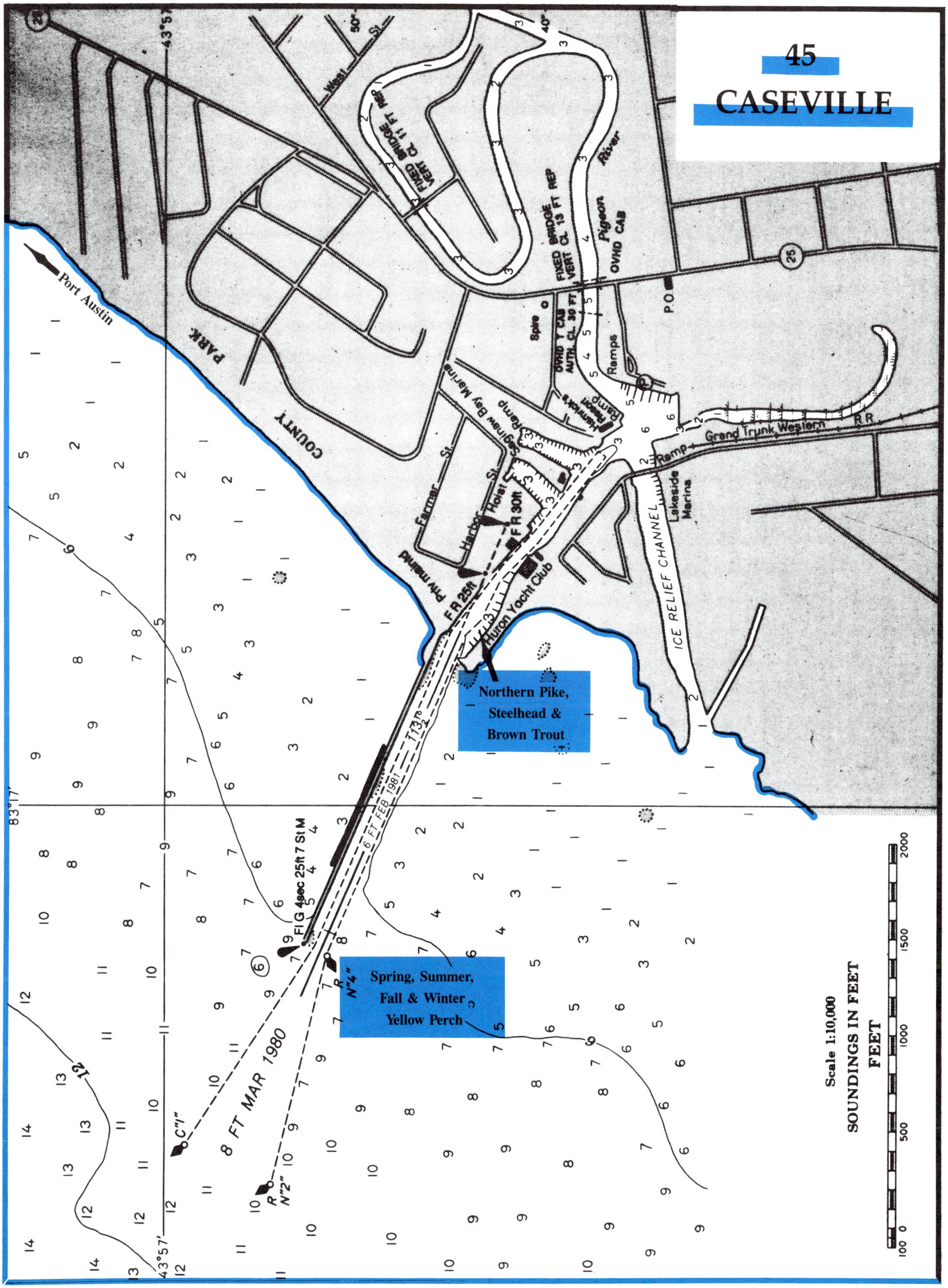

Reefs in the Caseville area and elsewhere throughout Saginaw Bay are serving up fine walleyes like this one.

CASEVILLE (cont.)

(47) to the east and Tawas (39) and Oscoda (38) across the bay to the north. Interesting though, DNR test nets set off Sand Point have produced plenty of fat lake trout during October each of the past two years. The season, however, closes August 15. Below Sand Point in Wildfowl Bay, excellent walleye, perch and catfish angling can be had into the fall. For details see 43 and 44 (Saginaw Bay).

Winter fishing activity at Caseville is rated excellent for yellow perch on Russian Hooks tipped with perch eyes or a couple of waxworms. Northern lovers go after three- to eight-pound pike with tip-up and spear. Walleye fishing is improving and can be exceptional—especially for big pre-spawn females—on February days off the breakwall and rivermouth access sites. The Pigeon River serves up steelhead and a few browns in late fall and early spring for die-hard waders using spawn or streamers.

Planting Records

Annual plants of 15,000 steelhead yearlings by the DNR in the Pigeon River were discontinued in 1984, but are expected to resume for the period 1985-90.

Facilities

A modern harbor of refuge includes pier-fishing opportunities from the breakwall. Boating facilities include gasoline, water, electricity, restrooms, showers and holding-tank pump-out. The telephone number of the dock attendant is (517) 856-4590.

There is a two-lane concrete pay ramp at Beadle Bay Marina on the south side of Sand Point off Crescent Beach Road. Those with small boats can launch them at Oak Beach, between Port Austin (46) and Caseville. Albert Sleeper State Park, with 1,000 acres and 280 campsites but no boat launch, lies three miles to the east of Caseville.

Caseville, a vacation-hosting community of 600, has good motels, restaurants, and stores.

Further Information

Chambers of Commerce:

East Michigan Tourist Association, One Wenonah Park, Bay City 48706; (517) 895-8823.

Bait & Tackle Shops:

1. Lakeside Marina, 6600 River St., Caseville 48725; (517) 856-2274.
2. Beadle Bay Marina, 4375 Lone Eagle Trail, Caseville 48725; (517) 856-4911.

Charter Fishing:

1. Steve Fosdick, Journey Charters, P.O. Box 86, Elkton 48731; (517) 375-4597. 24-foot Wellcraft Airslot Fisherman, *Journey*.
2. Mike Thede, 9035 Port Austin Rd., Bay Port 48720; (517) 656-7174. 24-foot Sea Ray, *Seaducer*.
3. Larry Coder, 5530 N. Garner, Akron 48701; (517) 674-2437. 22-foot Sea Ray, *Sea Gypsy*.

Department of Natural Resources:

Two fisheries biologists work out of District Headquarters at 715 S. Cedar St., Imlay City 48444; (313) 724-2015.

Coast Guard:

East Tawas Station, (517) 362-4428.

The Case For Caseville

Art Perry, who lives near Mud Creek on Saginaw Bay, is the kind of resource a researcher delights in finding. Eighty years old and still active as a sportsman, Art has fished Saginaw Bay, including the Caseville area, for 70 years. A lifetime of fishing at Caseville and throughout Saginaw Bay has given Art Perry some valuable insights. He travels to DNR headquarters in Lansing on occasion, and his counsel is still sought and appreciated by fisheries biologists and other policy makers.

Born and raised in Rochester, he first saw the bay in 1914. His grandmother bought a cabin at Caseville then, and the young adventurer took the Grand Trunk Railroad north from Oxford to visit her.

Plenty has changed in the Thumb over those years. Fishing opportunities in particular come to Art's mind. He remembers May 8, 1930, when he and some friends caught 987 perch in four feet of water off Bay Port. How big? "Well, 900 weighed a pound or more each," Art says. "But perch fishing ain't like that any more," he adds, blaming the demise on too many commercial netters working out of Bay Port.

But not all fishing has gotten poorer. During World War I, young Perry used to catch northern pike from the Pigeon River. He still fishes there and last winter caught a 13-pounder that measured 40 inches long. "And you can get a half-dozen catfish from four to eight pounds in two hours of fishing right in front of my house on any summer evening," he claims. Some opportunities have improved dramatically in recent years, and Perry points to hefty walleye and lake-trout plants as one reason. He also claims the bay is getting cleaner each year and is optimistic that smallmouth bass will return in good numbers.

"Show me another body of water in the world where you can catch Chinook salmon, lake trout, brown trout, steelhead, yellow perch, crappies, walleyes, largemouth and smallmouth bass, catfish and northern pike. Just show me," says Art.

46
PORT AUSTIN

Port Austin, at the tip of the Thumb in Lake Huron, is a good port getting better. Outstanding lake-trout fishing, long the trump card, is being challenged by improved action for Chinook salmon and walleyes. The region also serves up yellow perch, smallmouth bass, and some steelhead-rainbows and brown trout. There is sport aplenty for shorebound and boat anglers alike. Port Austin, with new facilities, excellent accommodations, and a friendly and helpful chamber of commerce, caters to visitors.

What more could a fisherman want?

Fishing Schedule

Lake-trout fishing, Port Austin's drawing card, is so good because plenty of reefs, from 100 feet to several hundred yards in length, lie underwater along a 30-mile strip from Oak Point (near Caseville, 45) to Point aux Barques Lighthouse and beyond to Huron City. These reefs vary from a couple of feet to 50 feet under water. Lake trout move onto them at ice-out to gorge themselves on smelt, which are in the area to spawn. When the smelt leave by late April, they are replaced by alewives and lake emerald shiners, also invading the shallows to spawn. Reef fishing thus begins strong at the May 1 lake-trout opener and remains good throughout the month. Until the end of June, lakers can normally be caught in 40-50 feet of water.

Smelt-imitating plugs (Rebels, Rapalas) are hot in spring. So are small lures such as Tiny Tads, Fire Plugs, and Countdown Rapalas. Planer boards, outriggers, flatlines, and shallow-water downrigger trolling are all used. Some anglers even motor up to the reefs, cut engines, and spincast Little Cleos and Dardevle lures to catch lake trout. A few, such as charterboat-captain Bruce DeShano of Offshore Charters, report success by jigging from anchored boats. But trolling takes far more fish.

SPRING

Typical *spring* rigging on DeShano's *Shadow* calls for four lines off four Invader downriggers (all mounted to the transom with double rod-holders) with dodger/Sparkle Fly combos or cowbell/Wobble-Glo, Wobble Troll or L'il Guy matches getting the inside nod (pearl, lime green, pink, and 50/50 chartreuse and green) and clean-running spoons (Northport Nailers, Flutter Spoons, etc.) going on outside riggers. The object is to bump bottom every few feet with cannonballs so as to stir up things. The resulting commotion of flash and mud swirls trigger bottom-hugging lakers to drill lures. Bruce will also run a couple of Dipsy-Divers off outriggers (mostly for steelhead and browns) and spot a flatline or two down the boat wake. Good outrigger and flatline lures are Fire Plugs, Tiny Tads, Wee Warts, and small Hot 'N Tots. Try chartreuse, yellow, and hot green.

Port Austin catches in May and June usually run about 70 percent lake trout, 25 percent salmon, and five percent browns and steelhead. Popular reefs in spring include Hat Point Reef (locally called the Honey Hole) off Oak Beach, Osceola Reef, McGraw Park Reef, an unnamed reef off the mouth of the Pinnebog River at Port Crescent State Park, and Flat Rock Point Reef (locally called Broken Rocks). These reefs are all located west of Port Austin between Hat Point and Flat Rock Point. At Port Austin itself, sunken Seagull Island, found halfway between shore and the lighthouse, is good. So are the reefs around the lighthouse and the mouth of Bird Creek. Other shallow-water reefs shape up to the east off Point aux Barques, Alaska Bay, and Eagle Bay. (See 47, Grindstone City, for details. Also, that particular map details the entire Thumb Tip.)

SUMMER

An excellent deep-water reef for *summer* fishing is the Junkpile, just northwest of the Port Austin light. In June and July, both lake trout and salmon flock to the 50-foot-deep reef surrounded by 90-foot-deep water. By August the lakers are usually in water as deep as 120 feet, several miles from shore, but kings continue to target the area.

Summer laker lures remain the same as in spring. But because Chinook salmon haunt these same reef areas (though normally suspended and well scattered until late June), many anglers begin to stack or slide No. 88 Sutton Spoons, No. 06 or No. 22 Miller Spoons, No. 171 Clearwater Spoons, magnum Northport Nailers, and Lucky Lures.

When the Chinooks do begin to concentrate, most Port Austin trollers ignore lakers and rig exclusively for the brawling kings. Those "hunting" salmon run J-Plugs and Mac Squids, or spoons tolerant of the fast troll. These include Krocodiles, Cop-E-Cats, and Little Cleos, and they are usually spotted back 50-75 feet behind cannonballs. Once kings are found, many anglers back off to 2.0-3.0 mph and send down dodgers mated with Sparkle Flies, Crinkle Flies, Tiny Tads, or Northport Nailers. Good fall king fishing lasts well into September.

Walleye fishing has just come on at Port Austin reefs in the past couple of years. One theory has it that post-spawn walleyes bust loose from Bay City-area rivers (Saginaw, Quanicassee, Kawkawlin), then fan out along the Saginaw Bay shoreline all the way to the Thumb's tip. Others claim Port Austin-region walleyes are resident, non-migratory fish that spawn off local reefs.

Doesn't matter, really. The fish are here and many are trophy-sized. Try shallows from five to 12 feet deep in spring. An especially good spot at the opener is the mouth of the Pinnebog. Slow troll with Erie Dearies/ nightcrawlers, nightcrawler harnesses, or small Hot 'N Tots in black and gold, silver and blue, silver and green, or orange and gold. Some fishermen anchor and spincast Mepps spinners and small spoons with or without nightcrawler meat. When the wind is right, others drift with whole crawlers pinned to Crawler Hawlers or Lindy Rigs.

Perch fishing in the area is also good in spring, summer and fall. Just about every boat—sailboats and other pleasure craft included—has perch-fishing poles and a minnow bucket of shiners aboard. The yellow-bellies move about the Port Austin area in schools according to age class. Get into a mess of jumbos—off the pier in spring or fall, in water to 50 feet deep in summer—and you will have a new definition of fun.

Shallow-water reefs produce some smallmouth action for wading spincasters in June and early July. The same waters would likely yield bronzebacks in fall, but nobody fishes for them. The mouths of Bird Creek and the Pinnebog River are fair for spring steelhead and fall brown trout.

Ladies' Day

My most memorable day of fishing at Port Austin occurred during a Thumb Chapter Steelheaders powder-puff tournament late July a couple of years ago. My wife Marilyn and I had joined captain Bill Sturm, his wife Margaret and her sister Phyllis Hunt aboard Sturm's *Invader*.

While trolling east of Port Austin along a reef in 50-80 feet of water, we had no more than set lines, when a rod went off from a vicious strike. King salmon, we presumed. The ladies handled that one well and, after a while, muscled a spirited king to the net. As the fish was coming in, another rod bounced straight up. Another big Chinook. Our Salmon Slammer lures in black and gold and gold with hot green were really working. In fact, we were just preparing to switch our inside lines (pulling dodger/ Sparkle Fly rigs) to spoons when both of those setups tripped. You're right if you guessed they were lake trout. (Attractor rigs run on bottom are hot tickets for Thumb-area lakers). One went in the cooler and one went back into Lake Huron to grow up. Meanwhile, our red-hot salmon action continued.

At tourney's end we motored back to port, the girls complaining of sore arms, and eight fish in the box weighing in at about 150 pounds. We just knew we were the winning boat.

No way. The 25 or so other boats entered in the tournament also experienced a super day. Over 200 fish were weighed. Even though we had hooked over 20 trout and salmon and had put eight fish on the scales, we finished a distant fifth.

Captain Bruce DeShano
Port Austin, *Shadow*

Planting Records

Port Austin has a long history of lake-trout and Chinook salmon releases. Annual plants have averaged 60,000 and 100,000 respectively. Look for consistent numbers of lakers and increases to 150,000 kings annually to occur through 1990. Steelhead were last released in 1980, and token browns also went into the lake at sporadic times during the past five years. DNR plans, however, call for 15,000 fall fingerling browns to be released annually through 1990.

Facilities

Port Austin boaters have a new launch site with 72 feet of ramp space, enough to de-trailer four boats at once. In addition, several downstate sport-fishing clubs pooled money to build a modern fish-cleaning station here. Those with small boats can also launch at the shallow-water ramp at Oak Beach, between Port Austin and Caseville (45). If you have a state park sticker, you may use the launch at Port Crescent State Park, five miles west.

A state-run port of refuge has water, electricity, restrooms, shower facilities, haul-out facilities and holding-tank pump-out. The telephone number of the dock attendant is (517) 738-8712. The City of Port Austin recently received a $500,000 government grant to connect the harbor's outer breakwall to shore, thus creating a future extended shore fishery.

Camping is available at Port Crescent State Park and at Albert Sleeper State Park near Caseville (45). The popular parks fill fast, however, so campers are advised to have reservations. Call the DNR in Lansing (517) 373-1270 for reservation forms or contact the state parks for late reservation requests. The number at Albert Sleeper is (517) 856-4411. For Port Crescent call (517) 738-8863.

Restaurants, gas stations, and motels are among accommodations at Port Austin, a community of 900.

Further Information

Chambers of Commerce:

1. Greater Port Austin Area Chamber of Commerce, P.O. Box 274, Port Austin 48467; (517) 738-7600.
2. East Michigan Tourist Association, One Wenonah Park, Bay City 48706; (517) 895-8823.

Bait & Tackle Shops:

1. Offshore Tackle, 27 E. Spring St., Port Austin 48467; (517) 738-8247.
2. Chet's Boat Livery, 113 E. Spring St., Port Austin 48467; (517) 738-8446.

Charter Fishing:

1. Offshore Charters, P.O. Box 88, Port Austin 48467; (517) 728-8247. Bruce DeShano, Larry Hartwick and Bill Sturm, respective captains of the *Shadow, Rod-Bender*, and *Invader*.
2. *Miss Port Austin* (perch fishing), Port Austin State Dock; (517) 738-5271.

Department of Natural Resources:

Two fisheries biologists work out of District Headquarters at 715 S. Cedar St., Imlay City 48444; (313) 724-2015.

Coast Guard:

Harbor Beach Station, (517) 479-3285 or East Tawas Station, (517) 362-4428.

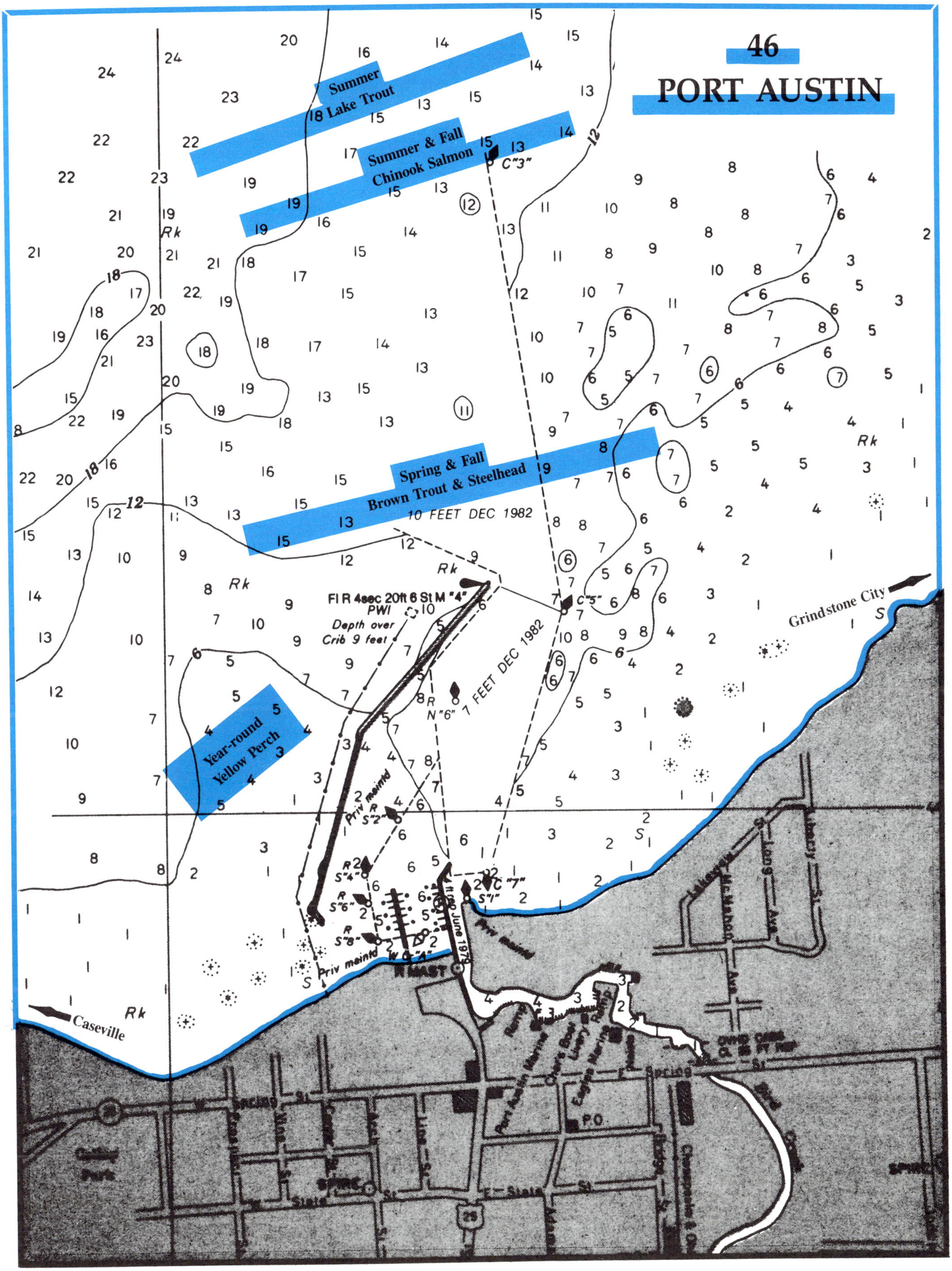
46
PORT AUSTIN
Summer Lake Trout
Summer & Fall Chinook Salmon
Spring & Fall Brown Trout & Steelhead
Year-round Yellow Perch
10 FEET DEC 1982
7 FEET DEC 1982
Fl R 4sec 20ft 6 St M "4"
Depth over Crib 9 feet
Grindstone City
Caseville
MAST
P.O.

47
GRINDSTONE CITY

Punctuating the tip of the Thumb in Lake Huron are over 30 miles of reefs running from Oak Park near Caseville (45) to Point aux Barques Lighthouse and beyond to Huron City. Some are only a few inches underwater; others may be 50 or more feet deep. All provide food and security for a variety of gamefish, namely lake trout, brown trout, steelhead, Chinook salmon, yellow perch, smallmouth bass and walleyes.

Reef-hugging lake trout have long been a main draw at Grindstone City. For the past two years, the lakers have been running large, with eight to 10-pounders the norm. Charterboat-skipper Maurice Mousseau reports that, while fishing from only 9:45 to 11:15 one mid-June 1985 morning, he and three other fishermen took a 12-fish limit of lake trout from 12 to 14-1/2 pounds each. During a powder puff derby held in the area a couple of years ago, every boat had at least eight king salmon. Perch fishing can be phenomenal at times, and walleye fishing is just coming on, too.

Fishing Schedule

SPRING

Spring activity kicks off in the harbor as ice is going out, with shore anglers and a few boaters reporting a few brown trout to 16 pounds and some rainbow-steelhead. Catching tactics involve spincasting heavy spoons such as Little Cleos and Kastmasters. A few fish are taken with spawn fished on bottom. Perch also invade the harbor and can be caught with wigglers, worms or small shiners pinned to Russian Hooks or teardrop spoons.

By May 1, when the lake-trout season opens, lakers have infested structure as shallow as three feet deep. A five- to 25-foot-deep horsehoe-shaped reef in Eagle Bay just west of Grindstone City harbor is a popular spot. Moving west, Eagle Bay shapes into Alaska Bay, which has a shallow-water reef at its east end and plenty of structure throughout. Other excellent reefs and drowned fingers exist north and east of the Grindstone City harbor mouth and run out to seven miles.

Most lakers are taken near bottom, so anglers unfamiliar with reef fishing are going to lose cannonballs and tackle—dues to be paid in exchange for experience. Small Rapalas, Rebels, and crankbaits are good spring lures because they imitate the smelt, alewives and lake emerald shiners that are in the shallows to spawn and which lake trout feed upon. Longline with flatlines or drop cannonballs just under the surface.

Spring fishing peaks from mid to late May, when temperatures force baitfish and lake trout into deeper water.

SUMMER

A second peak usually occurs in early *summer*—mid-June to mid-July. Lakers, then, will be in water from 50-100 feet deep, with some trollers reporting catches as far as 12 miles out in 140 feet of water. Lakers generally prefer 48- to 52-degree-F. temperatures. Find this mark near bottom with structure, and you will box forktails.

Good lures in late spring and summer include 0 or 00 dodgers 12-16 inches ahead of Sparkle Flies, Michigan Squids and other trolling flies, or lightweight hardware such as Flutter spoons, Apex lures, and small Chargers. Try chrome, white, or kelly-green dodgers with green, chartreuse, yellow, and blue colors in lures. Another good match is Whirl-A-Gig or other cowbell strings featuring willow-leaf blades (silver, blue, or green) ahead of Wobble-Glos in pearl, hot green, clown color, or pink.

Many summer trollers stack their laker rigs with lightweight spoons in hopes of tripping up a salmon or two. Typical early summer rigging aboard Captain "Moose" Mousseau's *Yellow Dog* involves eight rods—two Dipsy-Diver rigs with Flutter Spoons off outriggers, two stern-end downriggers with Northport Nailers stacked five feet above with double rods (via Offshore Releases to Flutter Spoons or Lucky Lures), and a pair of out-downs with dodgers and flies below and Flutter Spoons on free-running sliders. Not uncommonly, "Moose's" fish box contains both lakers and kings.

King salmon to 25 pounds are generally scattered well into June but begin schooling late in the month. This schooling phenomenon usually causes salmon fever to catch hold by mid to late July, when many anglers forget about lakers and target the big silvery Chinooks instead.

To target salmon alone, seek 53- to 55-degree-F. water and look for magnum hooks on your graph anywhere from 25 feet down to bottom at 100 feet. Run J-Plugs and heavier hardware that can be trolled fast (three to five mph). Once you find schooling kings, you can opt for attractor rigs and Crinkle Flies, Dazzlers, Sparkle Flies or run flutter-type hardware clean.

Late summer also offers some little-known brown-trout fishing. Find 59- to 62-degree-F. water near structure, then longline Flutter Spoons, Krocodiles, Rattlespoons, Cop-E-Cats, or other spoons in chartreuse, yellow, copper or green—either singly or in combination with silver. One summer, Mousseau took 40 browns with clown-colored No. 44 Flutter Spoons. The trick? He used steel wool to expose the chrome on the inside of his lures. It's worth a try.

Summer perch fishing takes off over reefs to 40 feet deep, where big yellow-bellies move to nail hatching crayfish and mayflies. Wigglers or small craws are top bait. If you can't get them, try shiner minnows.

47
GRINDSTONE CITY
(Thumb Tip)

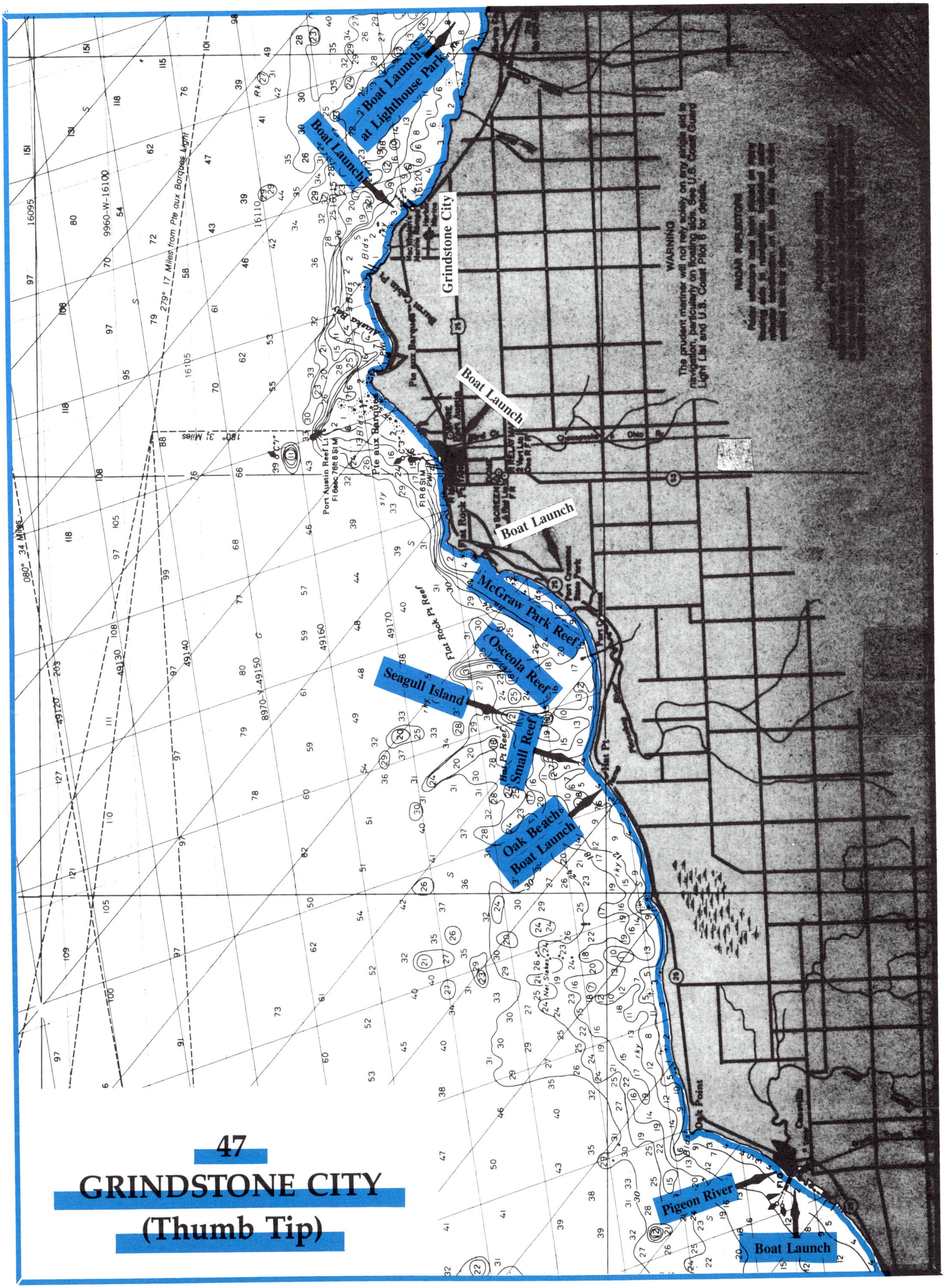

Spring and fall are good times for Grindstone City anglers to catch browns and steelhead from shore. This lunker steelhead fell for a small spoon.

GRINDSTONE CITY (cont.)

Smallmouth bass begin spawning in rocky shallows in June; anglers can catch them by spincasting Mepps spinners, small spinnerbaits, plastic worms, and lead-head jigs. Eagle Bay used to serve up tremendous smallmouth fishing, but opportunities have fallen off in recent years due to angling pressure.

Increasing numbers of walleyes are beginning to infest Thumb-tip reefs. Anglers can catch fish to eight pounds by slow-trolling Hot 'N Tots, Erie Dearies, and Mepps Lusox spinners. Gold, yellow, green, and black are favorite colors.

Fall fishing at Grindstone City remains good for king salmon until mid-September, brown trout and rainbow-steelhead until November, and perch and walleye until freeze-up.

Winter fishing is confined to jigging in the harbor for a few perch and an occasional brown and steelhead.

Note: The map included with this description features the entire Thumb tip, which includes Grindstone City as well as several other excellent major points of entry. For more details see 45 (Caseville), 46 (Port Austin), 48 (Lighthouse Park) and 49 (Port Hope).

Planting Records

Grindstone City has a long history of trout plantings, including an average of 100,000 lake trout each year since 1980. From 10,000-25,000 rainbows and brown trout (mostly fall fingerlings) have also been released annually during this period. DNR plans until 1990 include an average annual stocking of 66,500 lakers, 25,000 rainbows, and 15,000 brown-trout yearlings or 20,000 fingerlings. The DNR also plans to stock 15,000 brook trout in Eagle Bay each year until 1990.

Grindstone City is not a target port for salmon releases. Kings taken here are from plants at Oscoda (38), Port Austin (46) and downlake ports.

Facilities

A DNR-run cement ramp is available at no charge to boaters. Although a harbor light is not available, the channel is marked for safe passage. Pit toilets and picnic tables are also available at the state-owned site. There is also a single cement ramp at Harbor Marine. Expect to pay a fee to launch here. For restaurants and overnight accommodations, refer to 46 (Port Austin).

Further Information

Chambers of Commerce:

1. The Greater Port Austin Chamber of Commerce, Box 274, Port Austin 48467; (517) 738-7600.
2. East Michigan Tourist Association, One Wenonah Park, Bay City 48706; (517) 895-8823.

Bait & Tackle Shops:

1. Harbor Marine, 3379 Pt. Aux Barques Rd. (at launch site), Grindstone City 48467; (517) 738-7558.
2. Offshore Tackle, M-25, Port Austin 48467; (517) 738-8247.

Charter Fishing:

1. Captain Maurice Mousseau, 5121 Kinde St., Kinde 48445; (517) 874-4428. 23-foot Slickcraft, *Yellow Dog*.
2. Bruce DeShano, Bill Sturm and Larry Hartwick, Offshore Charters, P.O. Box 88, Port Austin 48467; (517) 738-8247. 24-foot boats, *Shadow, Invader*, and *Rod-Bender*.

Department of Natural Resources:

Two fisheries biologists work out of District Headquarters at 715 S. Cedar St., Imlay City 48444; (313) 724-2015.

Coast Guard:

Harbor Beach Station, (517) 479-3285 or East Tawas Station, (517) 362-4428.

A 90-Minute Battle

About 10 years ago, Bob Vargo, Chuck Holzworth and I were trolling for lake trout in 110 feet of water directly off Lighthouse Park. Three huge fish that suddenly showed up on bottom left scratch marks an inch long on our graph. Hoping they were monster lake trout, we sent down dodgers and spoons. When that didn't work, we tried other lures. But for two hours the giant fish ignored everything we sent by them. They remained rooted on bottom.

When I rigged a No. 2 Les Davis Herring Dodger ahead of a muskie-sized Rapala, one of the brutes finally struck. Over the next hour and a half, I fought that fish but succeeded in lifting it off bottom only about five feet. Eventually it broke me off.

I figure it had to be a sturgeon. How big? I don't know—maybe a couple hundred pounds.

Captain Larry Hartwick
***Rod-Bender*, Harbor Beach**

Grindstone Grab Bag

My good friend, freelance-writer Gene Kroupa, from Madison, Wisconsin, arrived at my place in early May to stay for a few days while he interviewed Thumb-area farmers for magazine articles. Later, we went lake-trout fishing at Grindstone City with another buddy, Lake Orion native Joe Zikewich.

Gene, who had never fished Lake Huron, finished his interviews in just two days, so Saturday morning found us loading the cooler and trolling rods into Joe's 16-foot boat, the *Shelldrake*. Already that spring, by cautiously probing reef edges and longlining small lures, Joe had cleaned up on Grindstone forktails. I motored the *Shelldrake* out in 20 feet of water on a sea as flat as pear juice on a plate. Backing down the throttle to a gurgle, I turned left, and putted toward Eagle Bay. Meanwhile my partners rigged Joe's favorite lure, clown-colored Flutter Spoons, and dropped cannonballs.

We hadn't gone 200 yards when a downrigger rod broke free, then began jabbing like a scorpion's tail. Gene pounced on the rod and cranked into his first Lake Huron lake trout. Typically, it dug for bottom, sprinted away on a short run or two, then ghosted into view—its creamy belly glowing white—just behind the boat. Gene lifted his rod, and Joe tucked our first laker, a 10-pounder, into net meshes.

After traversing Eagle Bay, we wound in and out of Alaska Bay and picked up a pair of six-pounders. Soon we hit a honey hole—a reef edge six or eight feet down stacked full with lake trout. Pass after pass resulted in one or more strikes. Within an hour, we had a nine-fish limit in the cooler.

We then motored out for deeper water, where we hoped to finish limits with salmon. We did, too, but that's another story.

Tom Huggler
Otisville

Spring trollers in Lake Huron shallows catch salmon or trout by running planer boards, flatlines and shallow-set downriggers. Visitors to Lighthouse Park will also catch walleyes, perch and smallmouth bass.

48
LIGHTHOUSE PARK

Intricate reef structure close to shore and a new double ramp beckon the small-boat angler to Lighthouse Park, located about four miles southeast of Grindstone City.

Anglers who answer the call will not be disappointed. They will catch a mixed bag of gamefish throughout the long fishing season and will experience little competition. Charterboat-skipper Maurice Mousseau of Kinde tells about a friend who trolled this area in early June, running silver-and-blue Hot 'N Tots off Yellow Bird planers in eight to 10 feet of water. His catch? A brown trout, lake trout, several walleyes and 25 yellow perch, some of which were over 15 inches.

Fishing Schedule

SPRING

Spring sport kicks off in April with the appearance of some steelhead off Willow Creek at Huron City and the New River to the north. Surf fishermen can also cast off numerous points and an unnamed stream to the south. Steelhead or salmon spawn, knotted into dime-sized bags and tossed into the surf, are a solid bet. Also fancast 1/4- to 3/4-ounce spoons in plain silver or silver with orange, green, blue, or yellow.

Perch fishermen score among the intricate reefs, as do walleye anglers after the opener. Both gamefish species are here for larvae and other food hatching off the reefs. Jigging with shiner minnows or trolling small plugs and spoons both work.

Lake-trout trollers can also bang forktails to 15 pounds by bumping bottom with downrigger weights and pulling Wobble-Glos or small Chargers and flutter-type spoons behind a string of cowbells or dodger flash. Anglers without downriggers score by working the five- to 15-foot-deep reefs with rubber-core sinkers ahead of small spoons or plugs or by opting for digging crankbaits to get down deep. Until you learn the tricky structures, however, be prepared to lose a little tackle.

A few Chinook and coho salmon are also reported in spring.

SUMMER

Summer lake-trout fishing remains excellent, but the big forktails will have moved to depths of 50-130 feet. This deep water is surprisingly close to shore (see map).

Trollers will also begin picking up a few Chinook salmon. As summer wears on, the big kings gather together in preparation for fall spawning, so you will usually find them suspended in small schools. Target 53- to 55-degree-F. water and run Northport Nailers, Lucky Lures, Flutter Chucks, Salmon Slammers, or similar hardware for best results. J-Plugs produce, too, especially as summer winds down.

An excellent and overlooked summer smallmouth-bass fishery exists in these close-to-shore reefs, too. Smallmouths begin spawning in this region about Memorial Day, but you can get close-to-shore action as late as the 4th of July. Spincast spinners, rubber worms, spinnerbaits, and jigs tipped with minnows over the rocky reefs. Another good smallmouth spot is Whiskey Harbor, halfway between Lighthouse Park and Port Hope (see 49 for details).

Perch and walleye fishing remains good throughout the summer, too.

FALL

Fall fishing opportunities remain solid for perch, smallmouths and walleyes. Pods of salmon, either kings running to Grindstone City (47)/Port Austin (46) or cohos heading for Port Hope (49), continue to appear offshore. Fall is also a good time to pick off a steelhead or brown trout tight to shore. You'll catch spawning lakers, too, except that by law they must be returned after August 15.

Planting Records

Releases by the DNR are traditionally made at Grindstone City (47) and Port Austin (46) to the north and Port Hope (49) to the south.

Facilities

The Huron County Road Commission has installed a new double-ramp boat launch, which can handle boats under 20 feet. The launch and accompanying parking space are free. At the scenic park itself, which contains one of Michigan's oldest lighthouses, pit toilets and picnic tables are available.

The closest gasoline and restaurant facilities are located at Port Hope (49).

Further Information

Chambers of Commerce:

See 46 (Port Austin)

Bait & Tackle Shops:

See 46 (Port Austin), 47 (Grindstone City) or 49 (Port Hope).

Charter Fishing:

Captain Maurice Mousseau, 5121 Kinde St., Kinde 48445; (517) 874-4428. 23-foot Slickcraft, *Yellow Dog*.

Department of Natural Resources:

Two fisheries biologists work out of District Headquarters at 715 South Cedar St., Imlay City 48444; (313) 724-2015.

Coast Guard:

Harbor Beach Station, (517) 479-7255.

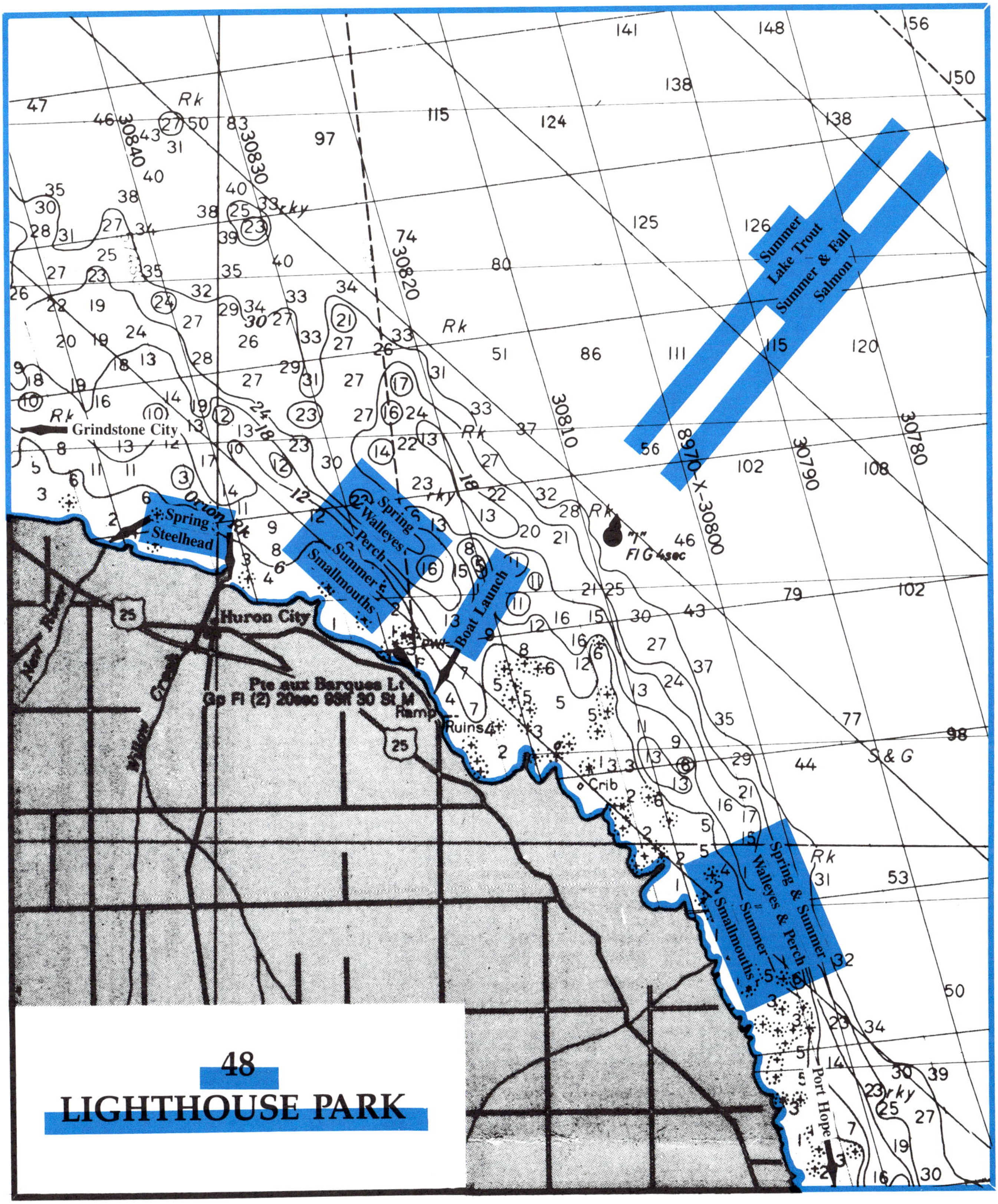

48
LIGHTHOUSE PARK

49
PORT HOPE

Located about midway between Grindstone City (47) and Harbor Beach (50), Port Hope gets a fraction of the pressure that those popular ports receive. Reduced fish plants by the department of natural resources is one reason. Better facilities, at least at Harbor Beach, is another. Lack of publicity might be the biggest of all.

Truth is, Port Hope yields some good to excellent angling opportunities for Chinook salmon, lake trout, rainbows and yellow perch. And a red-hot coho-salmon fishery here, especially in fall, is largely ignored. Too bad, because, with the the exception of Swan Creek in the northern lake, Port Hope is the only place where a consistent Lake Huron coho fishery can be found.

Fishing Schedule

SPRING

Ice-out sometime in April brings smelt and, later, alewives close to shore as they seek stream mouths and shallows in which to spawn. Trout and salmon are close behind. *Spring* catches typically run about 70 percent Chinook salmon, 20 percent steelhead-rainbows, five percent lake trout, and five percent cohos.

Body baits, which resemble forage species, get the nod. Long A Bombers followed by Rebel Spoonbills and Rapalas are best. Port Hope hot colors include spot-tail pattern, fire tiger, and Wonder Bread respectively. A trolling speed of two to three mph will impart correct action to these lures. Until water reaches 45 degrees F., target reefs with depths under 20 feet. By early to mid-May, when temperatures exceed 45 degrees, head for water to 100 feet deep, but wash lures in the upper 25 feet.

When the thermocline develops, usually by early June, seek 53- to 55-degree-F. water at any depth and troll lures through and to either side of that mark.

In May, Captain Maurice Mousseau, like most other area skippers, keys at Harbor Beach (50), seven miles to the south. (June brings him to Grindstone City, 47, until mid-August when he returns to Harbor Beach. In October he targets Port Hope exclusively—more in a moment.) However, many days in May will find him trolling the structure off Port Hope in search of spring kings and lakers. "Moose" typically runs a pair of Big Jon downriggers off the stern of his 23-foot Slickcraft, *Yellow Dog*, and twin Big Jon out-downs with five-foot arms to port and starboard. Sometimes he will run one or more outriggers and/or planer boards. He likes 8-1/2 foot custom-made graphite rods and 47H Daiwa reels.

SUMMER

The intricate reefs along the area, which make for such good spring trout and salmon fishing, also serve up walleyes to *summer* trollers pulling small Hot 'N Tots or jigging with minnows pinned to lead heads. And Whiskey Bay, between Port Hope and Lighthouse Park (48), yields smallmouths to wading anglers using flies, spinners, and rubber worms.

Some of the finest perch fishing in Lake Huron begins over the shallow-water reefs in mid-July and lasts well into October. Some perchers dunk worms and minnows off harbor walls, while others jig from anchored boats. Many of the perch contain crayfish, which hatch in summer off the reefs. The tiny (one to 1-1/2 inches long) "craws" are ideal bait if you can find them. Bait and tackle shops on the state's east side do not carry them, however.

FALL

Fall fishing action begins in mid to late August when coho salmon swarm to their natal release site at Diamond Creek. There, lack of flow stacks up fish in and outside of the harbor. An especially good spot to try for cohos, from about September 15 to as late as November 1, is the five- to 15-foot-deep horseshoe-shaped reef just outside the harbor itself. Captain Larry Hartwick and two friends coolored a 15-fish limit there one morning in October 1984. Hot lures were No. 040 Fire Plugs in red and warm pink, as well as Tiny Tads in bright colors. Chrome dodgers (0-sized) mated to Sparkle Flies in green and blue also produced. Also in fall 1984, another charterboat skipper, Bill Thede of the *Country Bumpkin*, took 25 cohos in the same spot with similar lures. His hot tactic was to troll with planer boards (Thede claims spooky fish in shallow water is the reason he runs boards) and highlines.

Captain "Moose" Mousseau longlines plugs in the shallows over Port Hope area reefs throughout the month of October. He likes 040 and 060 Fire Plugs in pink, orange, red with black spots, and bright red but also scores with X4 and X5 Flatfish in similar colors plus chartreuse. Mousseau typically runs lures back 50-75 feet behind downriggers (just under the surface), 100-125 feet off outrigger poles, and 10-25 feet off planers. Side rigging may be necessary on bright days, when fish sometimes spook from boat shadow.

Mousseau reports that the coho-catching peak falls about October 1 and that the best action occurs within two miles of the harbor launch site. He stresses slow trolling, especially when running Tadpollies or Flatfish.

WINTER

Winter activity centers around jigging for yellow perch and rainbows, plus some browns. Best location is the harbor itself. The sport can be especially exciting late in the day, when anglers jig tight to harbor walls.

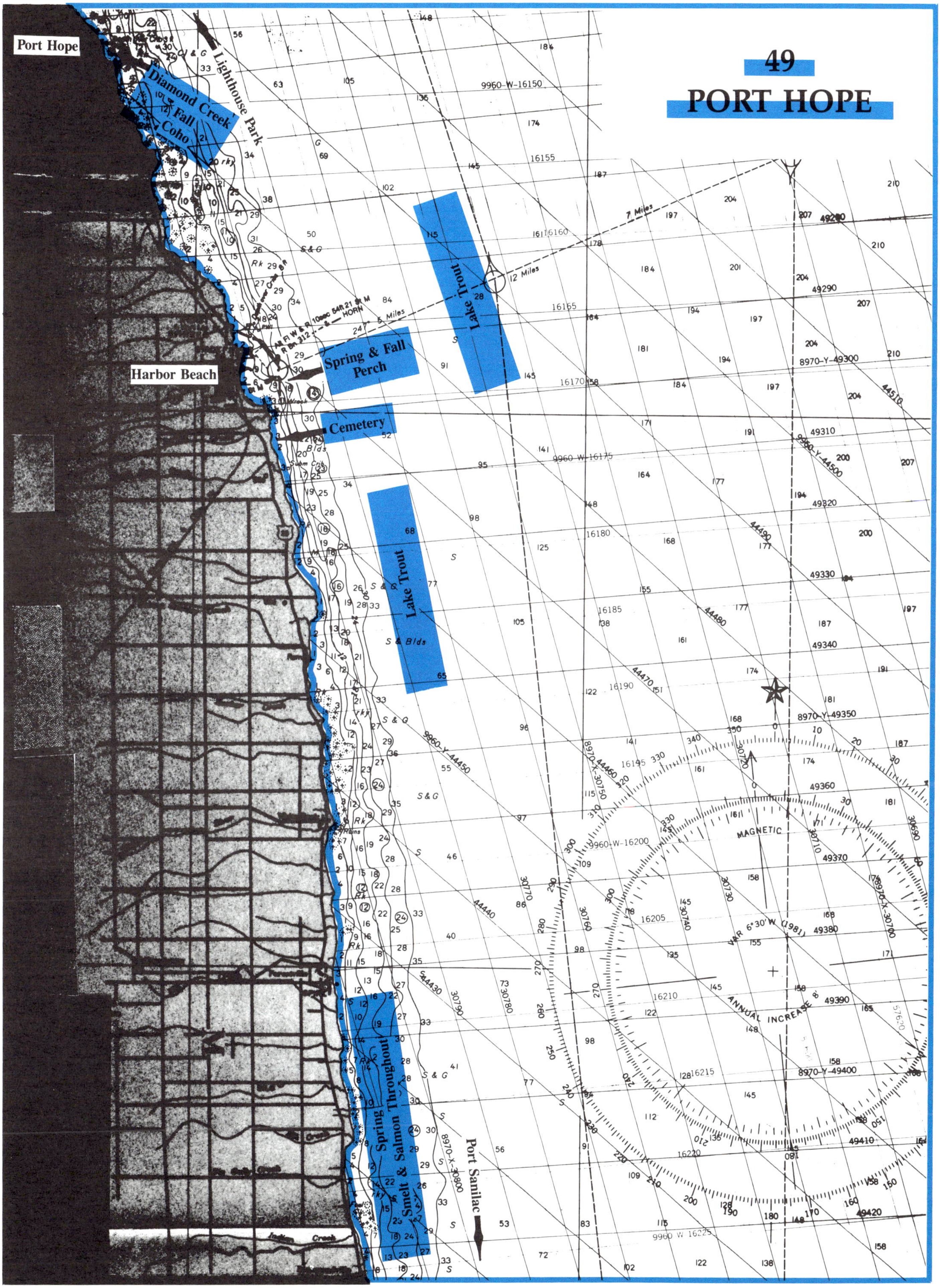

49
PORT HOPE
Port Hope
Diamond Creek
Fall
Coho
Lighthouse Park
Lake Trout
Spring & Fall
Perch
Harbor Beach
Cemetery
Lake Trout
Spring Throughout
Smelt & Salmon
Port Sanilac
MAGNETIC
VAR 6°30'W (1981)
ANNUAL INCREASE 8'
7 Miles
12 Miles
5 Miles

Planting Records

DNR plans call for annual releases of 100,000 cohos, 25,000 rainbow and 15,000 fall fingerling brown trout through 1990. With the exception of the brown-trout addition, these figures are in line with average yearly releases since 1980. Lake trout and Chinook salmon caught in the Port Hope area come from plants elsewhere in Lake Huron, most notably at Harbor Beach (50) and Grindstone City (47).

Facilities

With a population of less than 400, Port Hope offers limited facilities to visiting anglers, though a gasoline station and restaurant are available. Nearby Harbor Beach (50) has a marina and increased facilities. There is no state harbor of refuge at Port Hope. However, a modern two-lane launching ramp—completed just a few years ago—can handle all trailerable boats. There is no fee to launch, and parking space is adequate.

Further Information

Chambers of Commerce:

1. East Michigan Tourist Association, One Wenonah Park, Bay City 48706; (517) 895-8823.
2. The nearest local chambers of commerce are in Harbor Beach and Bad Axe.

Bait & Tackle Shops:

Sport Hope Tackle Company, 4419 Main St., Port Hope 48468; (517) 428-4818.

Charter Fishing:

1. Captain Maurice Mousseau, 5121 Kinde St., Kinde 48445; (517) 874-4428. 23-foot Slickcraft, *Yellow Dog*.
2. Captain Larry Hartwick, Offshore Charters, 7169 Bay City/Forestville Rd., Cass City 48726; (517) 872-3921 or (517) 479-6064. 24-foot boat, *Rod-Bender*.
3. Captain Bill Thede, Thumb Charter Service, 305 E. Main St., Sebewaing 48759; (517) 883-2018. 25-foot Cherokee, *Country Bumpkin*.

Department of Natural Resources:

Two fisheries biologists work out of District Headquarters at 715 S. Cedar St., Imlay City 48444; (313) 724-2015.

Coast Guard:

Harbor Beach Station, (517) 479-3285.

A Carnival for Cohos

Carl, a bartender friend and client of mine from Bloomfield Hills, called the night of September 15 to ask how fishing was. "Lousy," I told him, at least at Harbor Beach where by boat was. "But I've been wanting to try Port Hope for cohos," I added. "I'll check it out and let you know."

The next day I stopped at the harbor and talked to some of the local fishermen. They said coho fishing was great. So I called Carl, but it was two weeks before he could come up.

Carl and a buddy arrived at 6:15 on the morning of September 30. We left the Harbor Beach dock at 6:30, ran seven miles north to Port Hope, and began setting lines off the harbor wall at 7:05. Carl wheeled my boat while I rigged two Flatfish to stern-end downriggers and Fire Plugs to each of the outrigger setups. I locked in trolling speed on my Pelican at 1.5-1.8. Taking over the wheel, I made a wide left turn and edged up to a reef 11 feet down. The sun had yet to make its appearance.

Somebody yelled, "Fish on!" and Carl's friend grabbed the port-side outrigger rod. The salmon was a real scrapper, and after a 15-minute slugfest, Carl's buddy led a 10-pound silvery male to the waiting net.

Then all hell broke loose. A second, then a third rod went off. By 2:00 p.m. we had fought 18 cohos and put 12 fish from eight to 11 pounds each in the box. Beautiful cohos, the males were bright silver and the hens yielded eggs tight to the skein. And hardly anyone else was fishing.

I'll be going back for those Port Hope coho soon—real soon.

Captain Maurice Mousseau
Kinde, *Yellow Dog*

Spring and fall are twin catching times for Port Hope coho salmon.

50
HARBOR BEACH

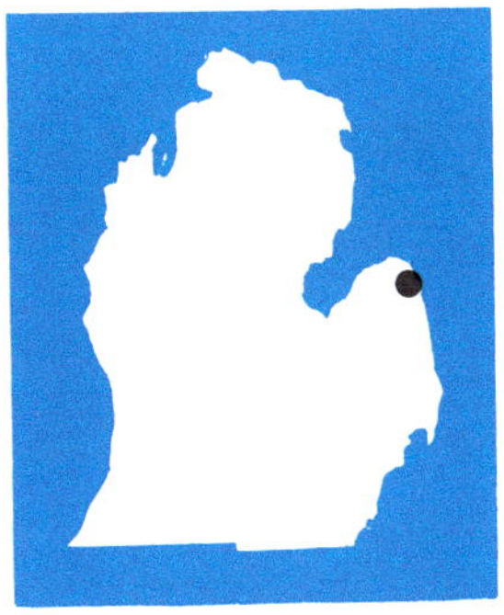

Home of the world's largest freshwater harbor, Harbor Beach may also have the best trout and salmon fishing in lower Lake Huron. Good facilities, plenty of offshore structure, and small streams that throw tastes into the big lake all make for good fishing conditions. Steady, consistent releases of trout and salmon by the DNR ensure it.

Harbor Beach has also turned into a breeding ground for some excellent charterboat skippers. Men like Larry Hartwick and Bill Thede are now registering 700 hours and more on the big lake each trolling season. And, although they work out of several ports, Harbor Beach typically gets most of their attention. There is no better testimony for good fishing.

Fishing Schedule

SPRING

Salmon (mostly kings, although some years cohos show up in good numbers, too) make their appearance in early *spring*, usually by late April. They are here to scarf down spawning smelt off stream mouths and in the shallows. Hot salmon fishing continues throughout the month of May or until alewives finish their reproductive chores. Most trollers start with body baits (Rebels, Bombers, and Rapalas) then work in spoons such as Northport Nailers. Captain Thede keeps daily log books on fishing conditions, hot lures and numbers of fish coolered. Good plug colors for him have been silver and gold, with blacks and whites getting the nod for hardware choices. Planer boards and outriggers account for up to 50 percent of the spring catch. Apex lures, Hot 'N Tots, and Northport Nailers are good lures to try when side rigging. However, as fish go deeper in late May and into June, most trollers put away the boards until fall or the next spring.

Good spring fishing locations south of town include reefs off the hillside cemetery, off Rock Falls Creek, a small creek near Wagner Park, off the Clay Banks at White Rock, and off Sanilac County Park south of Forestville (see 51, Port Sanilac). Turning north, there is *beaucoup* structure from five to 30 feet deep starting at the radio tower north of town and running all the way to Port Hope (49).

Harbor Beach can really serve up some exciting spring fishing action. Like the unforgettable day in 1983 when a friend and I went out with Captain Larry Hartwick and his dad. Late getting on the water, we roared downlake to the Sanilac County Park. There, Bill Thede was already boxing his 12th salmon of the morning when we motored up. Fish were stacked up on the south side of a fish-hook-shaped reef. Larry cannonballed his two favorite lures that spring—a chrome-and-green Deep Diving Rebel (also called a Spoonbill) and an orange-green-and-black fire tiger Long A Bomber.

Those plugs—along with a chrome-and-orange Bomber, a gold-and-green Rebel, a gold-and-orange Rapala, and a chrome Hermans—helped us to a dozen silvery kings. On our first pass, a 12-pound Chinook shot from the water with a fire tiger pasted to its mouth. Five minutes later on our second pass, the senior Hartwick sent home the hooks of a Spoonbill into the lower jaw of a fighting-mad 18-pounder.

Minutes later Bill Thede punched the ticket on a full five-man limit with his 15th fish and, with salmon tails sticking from his magnum cooler, headed for home.

Lakers also infest area shallows in spring but will have to be returned prior to the May 1 season opener. After that time and throughout the month of May, you can catch them with the same lures and in the same areas where salmon are found. As May meets June, begin targeting drop-off areas where preferred temperature (48-52 degrees F.) is near bottom. Then run cowbells or dodgers ahead of Wobble-Glos, Tiny Tads, Fire Plugs, Spin-N-Glos, and other small plugs.

Besides salmon and lake trout, Harbor Beach also yields perch, walleyes, browns and steelhead. Thede's records show that typical spring trolling catches yield 75 percent salmon, 20 percent lake trout, and the balance in perch, walleye, steelhead and browns. Some hot yellow-perch fishing kicks off about May 1 and lasts at least two weeks. Most fishermen stillfish shiner minnows on perch rigs off the north wall, in the harbor itself, and especially in the center gap (for those with a boat) between breakwalls.

A couple of years ago, a scuba diver told me that one summer morning the inside harbor walls at Harbor Beach itself had been loaded with big walleyes, perhaps there to feed off crayfish or some larval form. But above, no one was fishing for them. While trolling Harbor Beach on May 9th one year, I witnessed a nearby fisherman catch three walleyes, from eight to 10 pounds each, off salmon plugs. The fish, no doubt spawning females, were over the same reefs, 10 feet down, that salmon were targeting for baitfish. Although I have never done it, trolling over these reefs with plugs and spoons or jigging with lead-heads after dark should produce walleyes in the latter half of May. Lower Lake Huron could use more experimenting walleye fishermen.

SUMMER

Salmon success falls off in *summer* as kings and cohos scatter north and further into the lake. Lake-trout trolling remains good, however, as does perch fishing for jumbos, especially in midsummer. Good laker grounds in summer include the 80- to 120-foot incline about 3-1/4 miles out on a 247-degree course for a mile south to the Old Dumping Grounds. Other good spots are drowned roller-coaster hills off Rock Falls Creek in 75-100 feet of water, and a fairly dramatic drop from 45 to 100 feet off Helena Road about three miles south of town. To the north, try the deep water off Hardwood Point.

Walleyes should also be available off deep-water reefs for sundown jiggers. Try the 30- to 50-foot dropoff a half-mile out from the harbor.

FALL

Fall marks the return of brawling king salmon. The sport actually begins picking up in late July and runs through Labor Day and beyond. Most trollers start with G & W Salmon Slammers, 06 Millers, Ivanhoe Salmonizers, magnum Northports, Dr. Hook and other big spoons. Best colors are usually green, white, black, and silver. As kings close in on the harbor, many anglers switch to J-Plugs, Mac Squids and other lookalike lures in the above-mentioned colors.

Decent fall perch fishing is also reported along with some brown-trout and rainbow action. Opportunities should improve for these species in the future.

WINTER

Winter sport, limited to the harbor, is underutilized. Some ice men jig for a few perch and improving numbers of brown trout and rainbow-steelhead. A few others spear pike from shanties or catch them on tip-ups.

Planting Records

In the early 1980s, the DNR annually put 100,000 yearling lakers into Lake Huron off Harbor Beach. In 1984, stocks were cut back to 60,000 and will likely remain at that level through 1990. Chinook releases have varied from 100,000-300,000 each year during the period, 1980-84. Look for average annual plantings of 175,000 until at least 1990. For the past couple of years, 15,000-20,000 rainbows have been annually released. This figure will increase to 25,000. Dating from 1980, Harbor Beach has also received token brown-trout releases, and the DNR will attempt to continue plants of 15,000 yearlings for the next several years.

Facilities

The DNR recently completed a new boat-launch facility, which features six ramps and three skid piers, near the waterworks just north of town. State facilities, under construction at this writing, when completed will include the following services: gasoline and diesel fuel, water, electricity, restrooms, showers, holding-tank pump-out and a dock attendant. Boaters can also launch at Offshore Marine, just south of the Edison Plant.

Harbor Beach, a community of over 2,000, has accommodations and restaurants.

Further Information

Chambers of Commerce:

1. Harbor Beach Chamber of Commerce, 132 State St., Harbor Beach 48441; (517) 479-6450.
2. East Michigan Tourist Association, One Wenonah Park, Bay City 48706; (517) 895-8823.

Bait & Tackle Shops:

Offshore Marine, 5 Lytle Ave., Harbor Beach 48441; (517) 479-6064.

Charter Fishing:

1. Captain Larry Hartwick, Offshore Charters, 7169 Bay City/Forestville Rd., Cass City 48726; (517) 872-3921. 24-foot Dolphin, *Rod-Bender*.
2. Captain Bill Thede, Thumb Charter Service, 305 E. Main St., Sebewaing 48759; (517) 883-2018. 25-foot Cherokee, *Country Bumpkin*.
3. Captain Maurice Mousseau, 5121 Kinde St., Kinde 48445; (517) 874-4428. 23-foot Slickcraft, *Yellow Dog*.

Department of Natural Resources:

Two fisheries biologists work out of District Headquarters at 715 S. Cedar St., Imlay City 48444; (313) 724-2015.

Coast Guard:

Harbor Beach Station, (517) 479-3285.

King Salmon City

Conditions at Harbor Beach that mid-August afternoon were anything but ideal. The water was clear enough to see a cannonball at 30 feet, and there wasn't a cloud in the sky. A great afternoon for a boat ride, but not the conditions that salmon dreams are made of.

Two buddies and I worked the 80- to 110-foot dropoff, experimenting with various colors and lures. Our results for three hours of effort were identical to the other boats on the water that day—zip! The fish were there in good numbers, but they wouldn't cooperate—not unusual under bluebird conditions.

About 6:00 p.m. we decided to go for broke. Figuring the kings might turn on just before dark, we rigged all lines for low-light conditions—in other words, black colors. Two Les Davis fluted-chrome dodgers and black Michigan Squids went down, followed by a pair of silver Whirl-A-Gig attractor strings pulling black Ivanhoe Salmonizers 30 inches back. We stacked these two rigs with black Northport Nailers.

We were stitching on and off the dropoff when one of the dodger/squid rods flattened out with a bang. The reel drag squealed as the big Chinook streaked for deeper water. Another rod went off, then a third popped. In less time than it takes to tell about it, hungry kings drilled all six rods. What do you do with six salmon at 15-pounds-plus each and only three people aboard? Simply put, the best you can!

A couple of fish in the box and lines reset, we trolled back over the school of fish and registered six more hits. And if that wasn't enough, we repeated the frantic scene a third time.

The box score? Well, not as high as it should have been, although it took more than one trip to the parking lot to unload our fish.

Over several years and hundreds of hours each season fishing on Lake Huron, I'd have to rate that Harbor Beach experience as one of the best.

Captain Larry Hartwick
Cass City

50 HARBOR BEACH

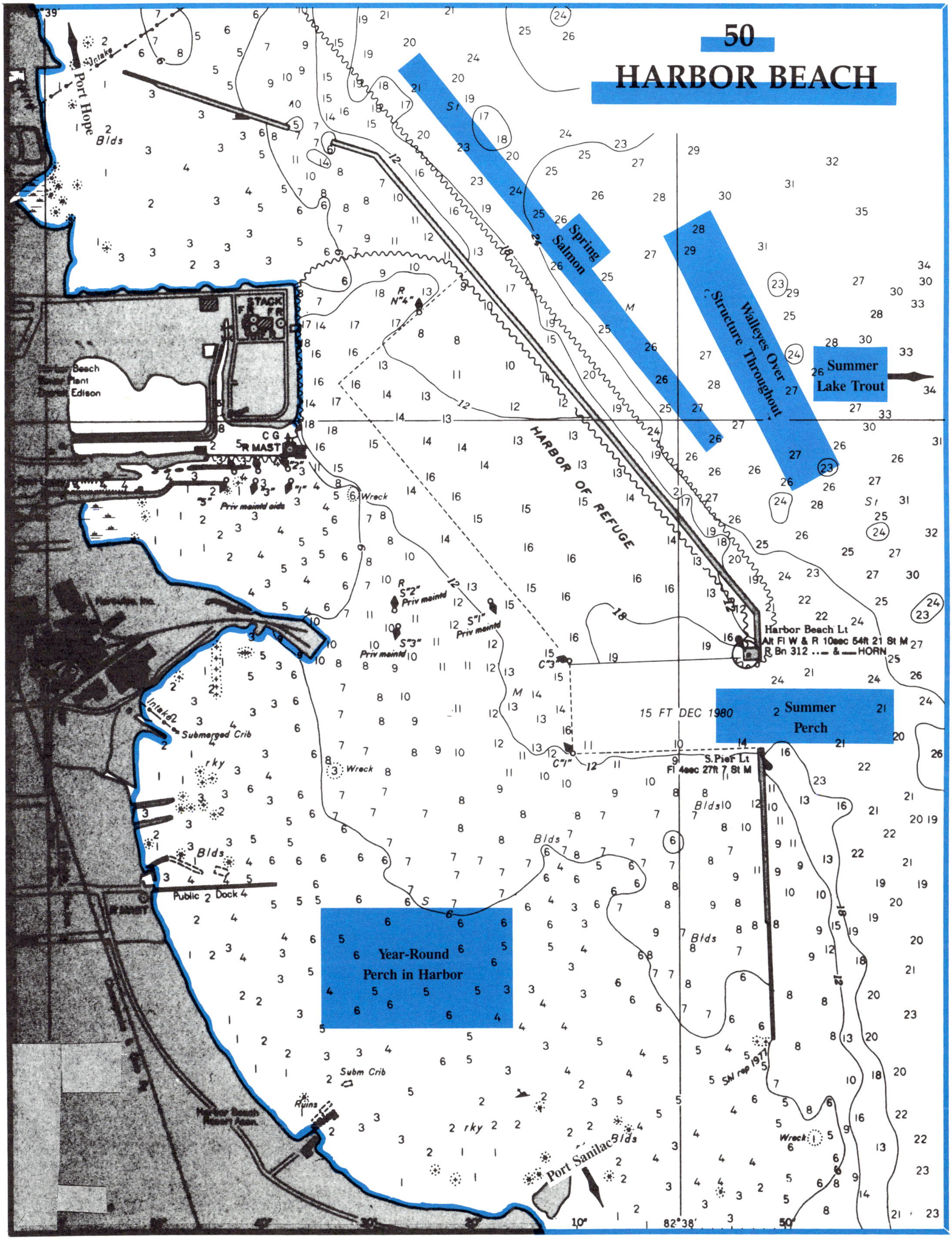

51
PORT SANILAC

Ice-out along Great Lakes shorelines can occur anytime from late March until late April. Eagerly awaiting the thaw are spring salmon fishermen from all over Michigan and elsewhere in the Midwest. They are ready to gun winter preservative from their outboards, cram boats with salmon-trolling gear, and start setting the season's first lines.

I like to keep records, and my files bulge with lots of what some would call "trivia." Included is the Imlay City District DNR *Outdoor Report* for the week of March 27 one year which says: "As ice breaks up outside Port Sanilac, early anglers are getting good action for cohos and browns. Cohos are averaging 1-1/2 pounds, and browns are going to five pounds."

Port Sanilac hosts hot sport for trout and salmon in spring, early summer and again in fall. Browns and rainbows are available in the harbor to ice fishermen. Good perch fishing shapes up off and on, with twin peaks in spring and fall. There is some tremendous potential for walleye fishing here, too, and it is being ignored by most fishermen.

Fishing Schedule

Experts say that salmon, in late fall and throughout the winter, drift back from Lake Huron to winter in Lake St. Clair (55) and the lower St. Clair River (54). Ice-out—helped along by spring rains, factory and power-plant thermal effluent (in the St. Clair River at least), warming sun, and river runoff—triggers a northward migration. As Port Sanilac trollers and breakwall anglers wait impatiently, the salmon, mostly kings along with some cohos, shoot from the St. Clair River into lower Lake Huron. Then they move north in schools.

SPRING

When they arrive, *spring* can be a tremendous time to go salmon fishing at Port Sanilac. Shorebounders nail them on Devle Dogs, Little Cleos, Krocodiles, K.O. Wobblers, and Kastmaster spoons in 2/5-, 1/2-, 5/8-, and 3/4-ounce sizes. Hot colors are silver, blue, green, orange, gold, and combinations of these.

Hot trolling lures are smelt-sized body baits. No. 14 and No. 15 Long A Bombers (chrome or black top/orange bottom or fire tiger), orange broken-back Rapalas in size J-7 or J-9, and chrome-and-green Spoonbill Rebels are all top picks. Captain Al Lesh, who skippers from Port Sanilac in April and May, has had excellent success on Bombers in rainbow-trout (locally called "watermelon") color and clear with black-spot patterns. Most trollers work the 30-foot break that runs north and south within a half-mile of shore. (See 52, Lexington, and 50, Harbor Beach, for shoreline and shallow-water map details.)

By mid-May, trollers switch to Northport Nailers, Sutton Spoons, Lakeview Nailers, Flutter Spoons, and a local lure called the Huron Herring. Chartreuse, chartreuse and red, silver, silver and black, blue, and dark green produce, according to cloud cover and time of day. With plugs or spoons, most anglers drop cannonballs halfway to bottom and longline topside lines in the shallows. Some send out planer boards and/or outriggers. Wee Warts, Hot 'N Tots, Bomber As, and Tadpollies are good side-rigged cranks to run. Try any of the above-mentioned colors.

Catching hotspots north of town include structure off the trailer park, the Flower Hill area, the mouth of Elk Creek, reef structure off Forester, and the southern end of a deep-water reef that begins just south of Sanilac County Park. Running south, try New London Point, the second sand bank, and Camp Cavelle. Numerous streams that empty into Lake Huron from Lexington to Harbor Beach are other likely spots to try for spring trout and salmon. Incidentally, many of these tributaries host runs of spawning smelt.

Spring trollers catch mostly Chinook salmon from five to 20 pounds, although there are plenty of cohos, too, and last summer a pink salmon invasion in southern Lake Huron spiced up catches. A few lake trout contribute to coolers, but returns from several years of releases at Port Sanilac have been disappointing. Incidental catches of rainbows, brown trout and steelhead are also reported.

SUMMER

Summer fishing should be good for lakers, but apparently fishermen have not discovered local laker haunts. When lake trout do return to their natal release site south of the lighthouse, autumn is well in hand and the season is over (currently it ends August 15).

Salmon, however, continue to provide summer big-fish action, but trollers must seek water that is 80-115 feet deep. Not only that, but as tackle-shop owner Denny Schommer says, "Salmon here have two citizenships. A stiff west wind will bring the thermocline into 50-60 feet of water, but a strong east wind will send the fish packing to Canada."

Hotspots developed in June and July 1985 between Port Sanilac up to six miles offshore from Forester. Hot lures that summer were chrome-fluted dodgers attached two feet behind cannonballs and 10 inches ahead of dark-green or dark-blue Jon's Flies, Michigan Squids, and Sparkle Flies.

Yellow-perch fishing rated good to excellent out of Port Sanilac in 1985. Breakwall anglers got their best action from late May until mid-June and again in fall. Schommer said mid-June through August is prime time for boat fishermen, who generally take the best catches in 20-30 feet of water. Fifty to 80, even 100 perch per boat, is a reasonable expectation.

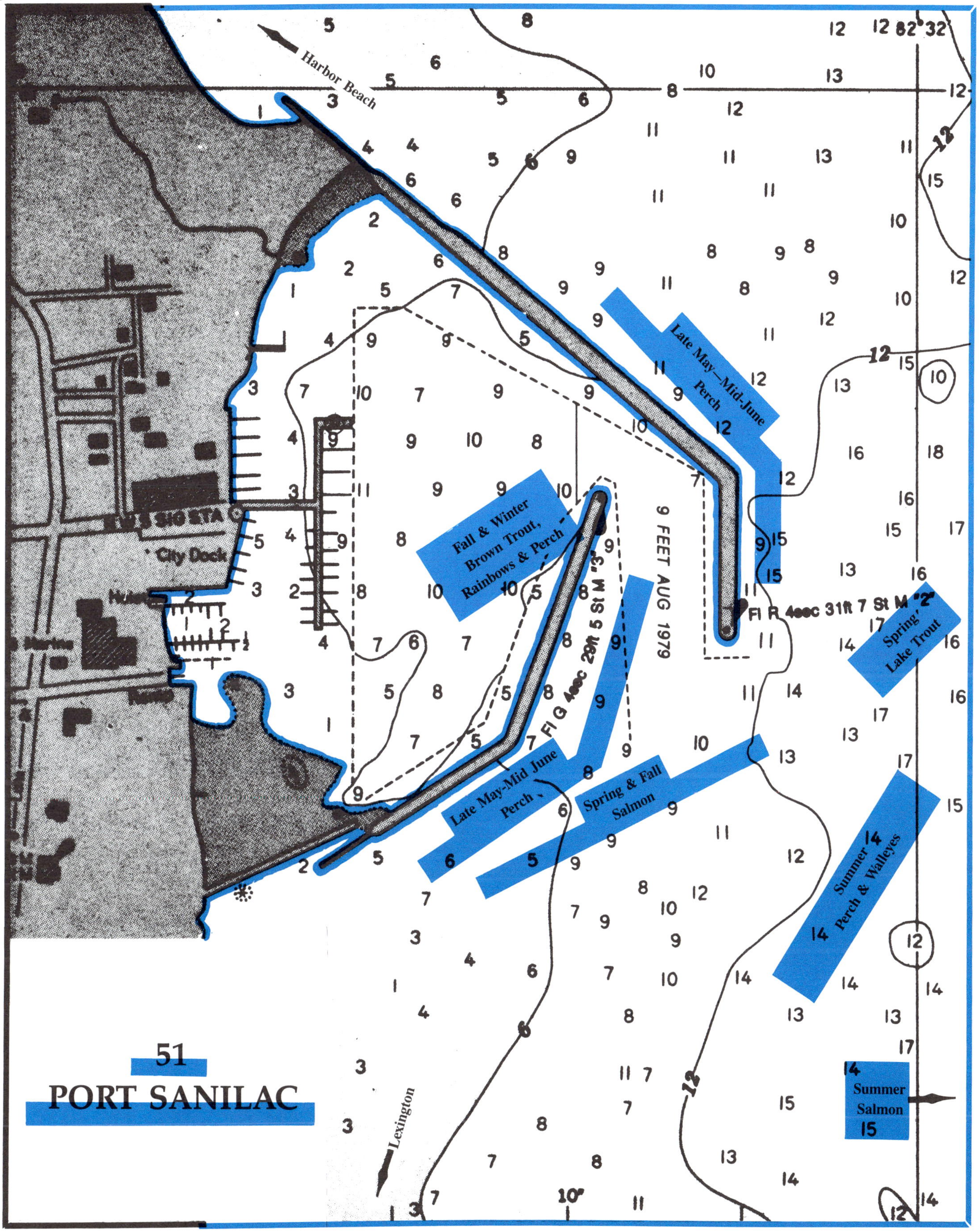
51
PORT SANILAC
Harbor Beach
Lexington
City Dock
Late May–Mid-June Perch
Fall & Winter Brown Trout, Rainbows & Perch
Late May-Mid June Perch
Spring & Fall Salmon
Spring Lake Trout
Summer Perch & Walleyes
Summer Salmon
9 FEET AUG 1979
Fl G 4sec 29ft 5 St M "3"
Fl R 4sec 31ft 7 St M "2"

Summer perch are best sought over hard bottom of cobble or jagged structure. In July and August, these areas produce emerging crayfish, which would be dynamite bait if they were available at tackle shops. Unfortunately, they are not. Fishermen mark a school of yellow-bellies on their graphs, then toss out a marker buoy. Motoring upwind a short distance, they double-anchor their boats, then—using two- or three-inch spot-tail minnows or lake emerald shiners and slide bobbers—drift their minnows over the school. This trick helps to avoid spooking the fish. Traditional methods of anchoring and jigging below the boat seem to produce mostly small perch. Big ones like a large, moving bait, made possible through the slide-bobber technique or merely by drifting a boat with the wind.

Late July and August is also a tremendous time to go for big walleyes, but few fishermen do. The mouth of the harbor produces infrequent walleyes for salmon trollers, but reefs from 30 to 90 or more feet host walleyes, opportunistic predators there to snap up baitfish and crabs. Small Hot 'N Tots in green, brown crayfish, or chrome with orange would be dynamite lures. Nightcrawlers strung to two- and three-hook harnesses, Beetle Spins, or Erie Dearies should produce, too, especially when drift-fished over reefs. Twister Tails and lead-heads sweetened with half-crawlers or minnows and vigorously jigged is a third technique to try.

This walleye action could last well into the *fall*. For the past two Septembers, commercial fishermen targeting whitefish out of Forester report heavy lifts of walleyes (which, by law, they must return). A report out of the Imlay City DNR district revealed that

Stacy Hanson of New Jersey isn't sure she wants to handle her first Great Lakes Chinook salmon. Dave Yeager offers assurance. Port Sanilac delivers solid spring action for salmon.

118 walleyes were netted in 90-foot, 64-degree-F. water off Forester during just one week in September 1985. Where are the sport fishermen?.

Soon-to-spawn salmon stage outside the harbor beginning in early August. By Labor Day or soon thereafter, the big khaki-colored kings begin to enter. Spawn fishermen and those tossing bright-colored hardware catch them. So do shallow-water trollers pulling magnum lures—No. 5 J-Plugs, Dandy-Glos, and Big Ed Flutter Chucks.

Later, browns and rainbows converge on the harbor. And here's a hot tip: Brown-trout fishermen should concentrate at Elk Creek outflow, as 10,000 yearling fish released there in 1984 should serve up sport to both surf fishermen and trollers. Try orange, chartreuse, yellow, or silver Krocodiles and similar hardware, and don't be shy about doctoring spoons with plenty of light-catching prism.

WINTER

Winter sport produces some perch and improving catches of rainbow trout and brown trout in the harbor. The trout fishery is underutilized. For perch, try jigging mousies, waxworms, and shiner minnows stuck to teardrop spoons. Trout will hit these offerings, too, as well as Swedish Pimples, Jigging Rapalas (with or without meat), and whole-kernel corn.

Planting Records

For each of the next five years, the DNR plans to beef up releases of Chinook salmon from 100,000 to 175,000 fingerlings. During this period, an average of 60,000 lake trout, 25,000 rainbows and 15,000 brown trout will be planted at Port Sanilac. These are target figures for yearling fish, if available If not, larger releases of fingerlings are pledged.

Facilities

The community of Port Sanilac recently spent $17,000 to upgrade launch facilities, which include a paved two-lane ramp and off-site public parking. The DNR maintains a harbor of refuge which includes transient accommodations, gasoline and diesel fuel, water, electricity, restrooms, shower facilities, dock attendant, haul-out facilities, holding-tank pump-out, VHF-FM radio and courtesy land transport. The telephone number is (313) 622-8818.

Port Sanilac is a community of 600 people with limited accommodations and service for visiting fishermen.

Further Information

Chambers of Commerce:

1. Southeast Michigan Travel & Tourist Association, P.O., Box 1590, Troy 48099; (313) 585-8220.

Bait & Tackle Shops:

1. Schommer's Sport Shop, Ridge St., Port Sanilac 48469; (313) 622-9936.

Charter Fishing:

1. Captain Al Lesh, 3233 Los Angeles, Warren 48091; (313) 756-3711. 26-foot Stamas, *Albacore*.
2. Captain Bernard A. Falter Sr., Schommer's Sport Shop, Ridge St., Port Sanilac 48469; (313) 622-9936. 28-foot Bertram, *Fish Finder*.

Department of Natural Resources:

Two fisheries biologists work out of District Headquarters at 715 South Cedar St., Imlay City 48444; (313) 724-2015.

Coast Guard:

Harbor Beach Station, (517) 479-3285.

Run-of-the-Mill Salmon

Saturday, April 11, dawned while Henry Mack and I were northbound on M-25 heading for Port Sanilac and what we hoped would be a super day of salmon fishing. The pickup headlights stabbed at a big doe, heavy with fawn, as she scampered across the blacktop in this flat farm country. Dawn was just seeping over Canada, promising high cloud cover and ideal conditions.

We waited in line to launch, then raced a half-mile south in my partner's boat, a 16-foot fiberglass equipped with four downriggers. Henry sliced the throttle, popped the stick into "neutral" and dropped a temperature probe over the side in 25 feet of water. "Forty-four degrees," he announced. "Just what spring kings want." But an hour's worth of washing three changes of baits produced no hits.

Henry suggested we pull lines and go further south to Mill Creek. Once there, we reset our lures. On the first pass off the north end, a rod busted loose from the downrigger. Henry snatched it from the holder just as a five-pound fish jumped from the lake 40 yards behind our boat. I grabbed the wheel while Henry swapped muscle with the spirited salmon. He netted his own fish, a squirming chrome-plated king.

"That green Northport Nailer that was so hot last week," he said, unhooking the fish, "I got another one in the tackle box. Pull that left out-downrigger and we'll switch it."

But the rod released before I could get to it. I cranked up the slack and immediately felt the kind of pressure that only a brutal spring-run Chinook can deliver. This was no five-pound fish. The rod bucked and the reel whined as some 75 yards of line disappeared from the spool in about five seconds. "You got a screamer, for sure!" Henry hollered.

The sound of a running 20-pound salmon has no equal. On a properly set drag it sounds something like *ZZZZZZsssssccccchhh*! In spring, a noise like that can wipe out a cold winter, a long boat ride, and even a busted wallet from buying too many lottery tickets.

Henry cleared lines to make way for my brawler. Good thing he did, too, because the salmon had already raced across two lines, forcing my partner to goose the engine and make a hard inside turn to avoid a tangle. That brought the king out parallel to the boat a good hundred yards away. His dorsal fin creased the still surface like some freshwater shark.

When he squirted away on another power run, I bit down on my lower lip and hung on. When he shook himself like an NFL fullback taking hits, I still hung on. And when I got a good look at him close to the boat—before he sounded for a final time—I was mighty glad those hooks were buried deep in his lower jaw.

Fifteen minutes later, Henry swung him aboard, 21 pounds of slap-happy salmon. Although we caught four others off the mouth of Mill Creek, that bruiser was our best fish of the day.

Al Dowd
Detroit

52 LEXINGTON

About the time winter doldrums makes cabin fever unbearable, many anglers think about Lexington as a cure for their woes. And Lexington, a small, friendly harbor town, usually lives up to its billing as a top springtime fishing port. When ice-out finally occurs on this lower Lake Huron port, fishing action soon follows, and catches here can be phenomenal. Spring brings early returns of salmon migrating to the north, and good fishing lasts into early June.

Summer anglers can take lake trout and perch, and salmon come back as summer slips into fall.

Fishing Schedule

SPRING

Spring action begins after ice-out, with some success starting as early as March. Jack McNulty, a local sport angler, and his young son, Tim, ply Lexington-area waters all season long in their boat, the *Chocalate Chinook*. The McNultys have caught steelhead near harbor walls as early as March 6. As water temperatures warm and fish move northward, king and coho salmon are prime targets. After the May 15 lake-trout opener, fishermen can also catch lakers by trolling off bottom with dodgers or cowbells ahead of P-Nuts or Michigan Squids.

Angling is not limited to just trolling for salmon and trout. Breakwall anglers take the same fish in spring by casting spoons and stillfishing spawn bags. Lexington also sports year-round yellow-perch fishing. Besides the harbor itself, the best perching occurs to depths of 40 feet about nine miles north at the foot of French Line Road. Wigglers and shiner minnows are preferred. And many of the nameless creeks that trickle tastes of warm spring water to Lake Huron also house spawning smelt.

But salmon are the main draw in spring. Three miles north of Lexington is Camp Cavelle, where large Chinook cruise the shallows in spring. You can landmark Camp Cavelle by the large buildings that are close to the beach. Three miles to the south of Lexington, Mill Creek received salmon plants in the early 1970s and is just now getting steelhead releases. Limit catches of salmon are reported there in 21-45 feet of water. Lexington also boasts great spring sport for salmon near the harbor. Many times when fish are difficult to locate, a sweep in front of the harbor may spring rods into action. This tactic has proved successful after high winds have blown inland from the lake and most anglers have concluded that the fish have moved out into deeper water.

Most spring trollers at Lexington use body baits in early morning and late evening, twin key periods of good fishing, largely because of low light conditions at those times. Frank Arleth, a charterboat skipper who normally runs out of Frankfort (16) but sometimes can be found at Lexington in spring, relies on colors in this order: orange, blue, black, and perch. Rapalas, jointed and deep-diving Rebels, Red Fins, and shad-black top with orange-belly Bagleys are good. Other rated colors include metallic-green back (with orange belly) and pearl with orange. Begin trolling in depths from 45-70 feet while running baits in the 15- to 35-foot range. If you don't get strikes, move out to 70-feet-plus and spot lures down from 20-50 feet. For best results, trail body baits about 15-30 feet behind weights. From late morning through the afternoon, if action slows, switch to spoons. Pick similar colors but mix in some chrome and gold choices. And consider white-colored hardware. Jack McNulty rates white spoons as very effective, especially in morning.

Runs of spring fish can drive any angler crazy. With changing water temperatures and the annual migration northward, spotty fishing conditions sometimes occur at Lexington. Salmon seem to squirt out of the St. Clair River at Port Huron, then surge north in waves; so, without warning, action can fall flat as day-old beer, and even experienced anglers may have difficulty marking fish. A stop into a local bait shop can produce valuable information that will help eliminate wasted time on the water. Still, there are days when you must persevere, but that situation, of course, is not limited to Lexington.

SUMMER

Summer catches during the 1985 trolling season included pink salmon, odd-year spawners that appear to be in Lake Huron to stay. Pinks are sporting fun on light line, as they willingly strike lures programmed for bigger salmon. Summer king salmon are available, too, but, for the most part, trollers take them in July and August far from shore.

Also, consider the potentially great walleye fishing found out of Lexington in summer. Excellent structure, including a couple of deep holes where walleyes (and sometimes salmon) suspend, can be found about eight miles south near the junction of Fisher (the county line) and Lakeshore roads. Some of these hog walleyes will plunge a butcher's scale to 12 pounds or more.

One unforgettable summer morning I stopped into a Lexington bakery and, while buying doughnuts, asked how the fishing was. The counter girl motioned me to the back room. There on a butcher block were a pair of walleyes about nine and 11 pounds. "My brother caught them," she said, "about midnight last night while jigging over a reef out in the lake. You should try it."

I've never followed up on her advice but am fully convinced

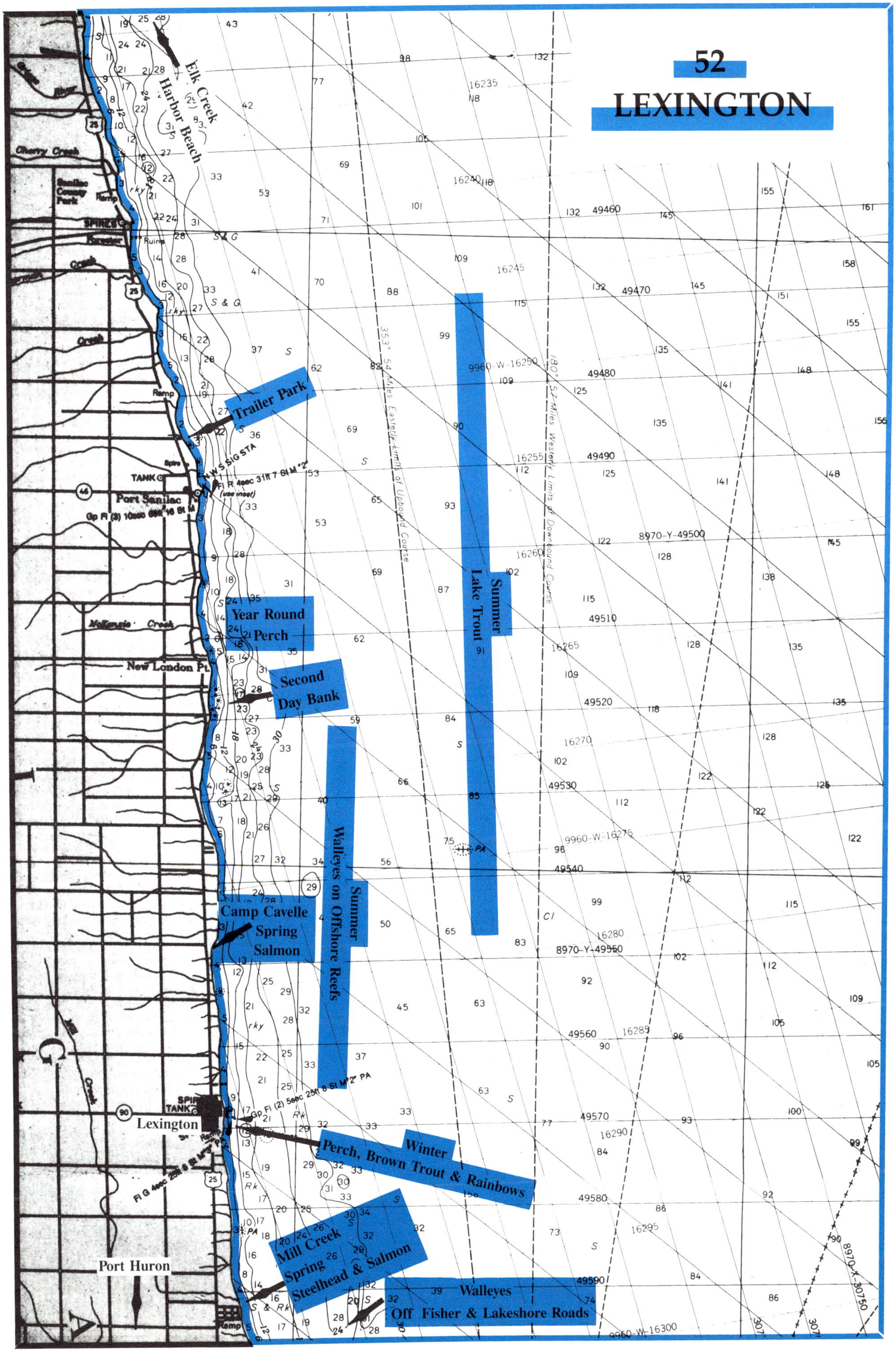

52
LEXINGTON
Elk Creek
Harbor Beach
Cherry Creek
Sanilac County Park
Trailer Park
Port Sanilac
Year Round Perch
New London Pt.
Second Day Bank
Summer Lake Trout
Summer Walleyes on Offshore Reefs
Camp Cavelle Spring Salmon
Lexington
Winter Perch, Brown Trout & Rainbows
Mill Creek Spring Steelhead & Salmon
Walleyes Off Fisher & Lakeshore Roads
Port Huron
353° 54 Miles Easterly Limits of Upbound Course
180° 57 Miles Westerly Limits of Downbound Course

An Old Rule of Thumb

One late April morning, my father, my two sons, friend Terry Walsh and I decided to fish Lexington. Cars were lined up to use the ramps, so we waited until eight o'clock to get onto the water. According to the radio, action sounded slow anyway.

I normally fish out of Frankfort (16), on Lake Michigan, where I have learned to apply certain rules of thumb. One is to troll north when the wind is from the south and vice versa. That day, because we had a north wind, I pointed the *Salley-E* south. When we got away from all the boat traffic, we started rigging lines 12 feet down over 20 feet of water.

Just as I finished setting the third downrigger, the first went off, then the second, and then the third! We had on a triple. Action continued like that all morning until we had a five-man limit of 24 kings and a laker. Another rule of thumb is that light line definitely helps in shallow water in spring. So does tying Rapalas with loop knots, which we also did that day. All the fish came on Rapalas tied to a five-foot leader of eight-pound test and held by a black barrel swivel to 10-pound-test backing.

The next morning our same group went to the same spot and caught 18 kings by midafternoon. The difference that day was that 12 of our fish came off planer boards and the downriggers were almost dead.

Old rules of thumb sure worked for us at Lexington.

Captain Frank Arleth
Roscommon

LEXINGTON (cont.)

there is some super walleye fishing going untouched in the Lexington area. The key, of course, is locating small offshore reefs where walleyes congregate at night to feed.

The French Line Road area serves up yellow perch all summer and into the fall. Lake trout, too, are available. Run small spoons and plugs with attractors close to bottom in depths from 90-120 feet.

FALL WINTER

Fall sport keys on perch again, as well as salmon. Even though the DNR has released hefty numbers of Chinook at Lexington, returns are not as heavy as at other ports further north. Likely, that is because many of the salmon join others in their northerly runs.

The harbor itself serves up some *winter* sport for perch and rainbow and brown-trout fishermen. Wigglers or small minnows are good baits, but some ice men also report success, at least for rainbows, on whole-kernel corn.

Planting Records

Completion of a new launch facility has prompted the DNR to beef up Lexington trout and salmon plants. Chinook fingerling releases have built steadily to 250,000 each spring and will continue at this rate at least through 1990. Lake-trout plants ended with 25,000 yearlings in 1983. However, brown-trout and rainbow stockings will continue at 25,000 and 20,000 respectively each year. Further, Mill Creek is expected to receive about 20,000 steelhead annually for the next five years.

Facilities

Lexington, with Port Huron (53) and the St. Clair River (54) to the south and Port Sanilac (51) to the north, offers a central location and new launching facilities. A $1 million project completed in 1981 includes a six-lane paved ramp, mooring facility, and paved parking lot. Services available include gasoline and diesel fuel, water, electricity, holding-tank pump-out, and transient accommodations. Telephone number of the dock attendant is (313) 359-5600.

Further Information

Chambers of Commerce:

1. Croswell Chamber of Commerce, Box 251, Croswell 48422; (313) 679-3800.
2. Southeast Michigan Travel & Tourist Association, P.O. Box 1590, Troy 48099; (313) 585-8220.

Bait & Tackle Shops:

Water Works Sport Shop, 7318 Huron, Lexington 48450; (313) 359-5451.

Charter Fishing:

1. Captain Howard Mills, 7228 Flamingo Rd., Algonac 48001; (313) 794-9609. 30-foot, *Paramour*.
2. Captain Al Lesh, 3233 Los Angeles, Warren 48091; (313) 756-3711 or (313) 754-7689. 26-foot Stamas, *Albacore*.
3. Captains Carol and Ed Tinsley, 3377 N. Range Rd., Port Huron 48060; (313) 982-2576. 26-foot Stamas, *Wendy K.*

Department of Natural Resources:

Two fisheries biologists work out of District Headquarters at 715 South Cedar St., Imlay City 48444; (313) 724-2015.

Coast Guard:

Harbor Beach Station, (517) 479-3285 or Port Huron Station, (313) 982-2684.

Lexington provides spring action for salmon such as this 12-pound Chinook. Fish are in the shallows seeking smelt.

53
PORT HURON and UPPER ST. CLAIR RIVER

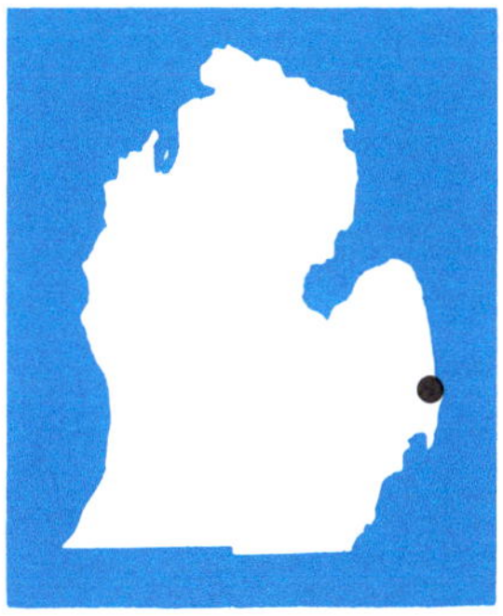

Walleye fishermen in the St. Clair River are taking advantage of liberal regulations that include a six-fish-per-angler limit and a year-round open season. Key catching times are spring and fall, with opportunities fairly steady all summer long.

Besides walleyes, the river hosts fair to good runs of spawning smelt and, depending upon ice conditions in the river, phenomenal spring salmon fishing.

Fishing Schedule

SPRING

Chinook and coho salmon apparently drop back from southern Lake Huron to winter over in Lake St. Clair (55) and the St. Clair (54) and Detroit (56) rivers. But when *spring* approaches and ice floes begin to break up in the river, waves of salmon run back upstream. Southern Lake Huron shallows warm fast, plus the river is fed by spring tributary runoff and warm-water discharge from factories and power plants on both the American and Canadian sides. These conditions attract spawning smelt and hungry salmon who feed on them. In the upper river, the Edison Marysville power plant, for example, is a hotspot.

Fishing derbies held in spring often tally upwards of 1,000 salmon, mostly kings, although cohos and pinks are well represented along with incidental entries of steelhead and brown trout. Most of the fish are caught in southern Lake Huron, but from 25-50 percent are taken in the river when it can be safely fished (besides ice floes, boaters want to keep a wary eye on freighter traffic).

Salmon fishing, however, can be unpredictable. In spring 1985, for example, when the river was jammed with ice, the salmon squirted north without staging as usual. Trollers had to run to Lexington (52) and Port Sanilac (51) to find them. Charterboat-skipper Howard Mills, who used to fish the river regularly for spring salmon, now runs out of Lexington and other ports further north because, he claims, too many boats, especially on weekends, can spook fish badly. This condition further contributes to sporadic success.

But when salmon do show up in the river, they generally provide good action until late April. Husband and wife charterboat-captains Ed and Carol Tinsley of Port Huron drop lures at the mouth of the Black River. Then they troll five miles downstream (in neutral or just faster than the eight-mph current) to the Blue Whale Condominiums by the golf course in Marysville. Other fishermen backtroll as they drift downstream. Still others find a school of fish on sonar, then troll a zig-zag pattern back and forth over them while switching colors and lure types, raising and lowering cannonballs, and goosing the engine a time or two. Spring salmon in the river are hungry; if fish don't hit after trying these tactics, they likely are not salmon.

Hot lures vary each spring. Clatter Tads, Tiny Tads, River Runts, Hot Shots, Countdown Rapalas, Cop-E-Cat Imps, Andy Reekers, and Locos all were solid choices one year in greens, chrome, black, and red. Taking off the following year were the body baits—Rebels in brown-trout color, Husky Rapalas (No. 13) in crawdad or perch color, Long A Bombers in watermelon color. Zippers were the spoon of choice that spring. Then in 1985, red dodgers with black flies were big producers.

If you have a Canadian fishing license, Sarnia Bay is a good place for spring salmon and steelhead. Offshore trollers working the American side from the Bluewater Bridge to Lexington (52) get on-again, off-again action. Try 20-foot depths all along the shore, the mouths of numerous creeks contributing spring runoff, and reef structure off Lakeport State Park. Longlining with crankbaits (Hot Shots, Mann's Razorbacks, Fat Raps) or Rapalas placed four feet under the surface with downriggers are effective in the shallows. Cranks or Countdown Rapalas rigged to planer boards also work. Any of the previously mentioned colors are worth a go.

The upper St. Clair River produces good smelting, which, not surprisingly, coincides with the best salmon time. Dippers with long-poled (to 24 feet) nets work in tandem along area boardwalks and docks. One partner quickly runs the net to bottom while the other holds a rope attached to the hoop. The pair walk quickly downstream for several yards, then the man on the rope hand-over-hands the net back to the surface. I have tried this sport in the lower river, and, believe me, it is tough work. But it can produce good catches of smelt, even under the shadow of the Blue Water Bridge.

Spring walleye fishing in the upper river from dusk until midnight and later yields eight- and 10-pound spawners. Most boat fishermen anchor their craft, then bounce bottom with Pencil

Plugs, a locally made lure. For over 50 years, fishermen used 20-foot bamboo poles with a large reel, plenty of taped-on guides, and a two-ounce sinker with the Pencil Plug attached to the end of a five-foot lead. The bait chugged with the current just below the water surface.

Modern tactics include bottom bouncing—suspending a lead weight of four or more ounces 18 inches below a three-way swivel. Attached to the second swivel loop is a five-foot leader and Rapala or Pencil Plug. In spring and summer, hot colors are black or Wonder Bread (pastel blue and pink). Fall catching colors include bright orange, chrome and blue, and chrome and green. Another method is chugging, which involves the use of six- or eight-ounce sinkers and Pencil Plugs or other body baits with a short, stiff jigging rod or stick. Chuggers troll upstream and pound their lures in and out of bottom weeds and mud.

SUMMER

In *summer* the upper St. Clair River produces smallmouth bass, silver (white) bass, yellow perch, crappies, sunfish, and freshwater drum. But most anglers still target walleyes, and wire-line trollers and drift fishermen now join those using the previously described methods. Catches are split between Pencil Plugs and live crawlers pinned to two-hook drift rigs featuring bright beads and clam-style spinners. Chartreuse, yellow, green, orange, and red and white are good combinations to try. Increasing numbers of shore and anchored-boat fishermen cast Mister Twister jigs—quartering across and upstream—then work the jigs back, as they tumble down the flow, with a jerk-and-retrieve method. White is the best color with purple and yellow the next best respective choices.

Those previously mentioned reefs off Lakeport State Park serve up good to excellent perching in June, July and August, along with walleyes to those who seek them.

FALL

Fall sport continues for large walleyes and occasional salmon.

Winter fishermen go downstream to Lake St. Clair or across the Bluewater Bridge to Sarnia Bay in Canada.

Lowering the Boom

About 6:00 a.m. on a Sunday morning in June, four generations of VanLuvens—I, my son, my seven-year-old grandson, and my father—left our dock on the Black River for some Lake Huron salmon fishing. We headed the *Vantasea*, the 27-foot Sea Ray I have recently worked as a charterboat for hire, out to the St. Clair River, then planned to turn north into the lake.

But to get from the Black River into the St. Clair River, we had to pass beneath the Military Street Bridge in Port Huron. The clearance is only 7-1/2 or eight feet, so most wheelmen have to toot their horn to signal the operator in the bridge house to raise the bridge. We blew the horn and the bridge started up.

But this is an old bridge with a history of problems. It went up well enough, but apparently the operator was distracted or the bridge malfunctioned because, suddenly, it started down again with us underneath. I blew the horn, but the bridge kept falling. It's a weird feeling to know you need another foot of clearance and it just isn't there. I touched the throttle to add a couple of hundred rpms but was afraid to goose it too hard for fear the bow would ride up and smash into the bridge. But, too little, too late. The bridge crunched into my boat, crushing the cloth top, ripping the canvas, and bending the frame—$800 worth of damage. By a stroke of luck, we weren't hurt.

Angry and frightened, I docked the boat at a nearby restaurant and ran to the bridge house. The operator, an older man, was so shook up he couldn't talk. The Port Huron police soon arrived and took the matter into their hands.

Mine isn't the only boat to get hit by the Military Street Bridge. It tore a fly bridge off another boat last year, I understand, and, just this past summer, took out a sailboat mast.

I hope it doesn't lower the boom on me again.

Captain Bill Van Luven
Port Huron

Planting Records

The DNR began releasing brown trout to the St. Clair River and Black River, along with steelhead to the Belle River, several years ago. Those fish are still available, but in the future, stockings will be limited to 20,000 brown-trout yearlings in the upper Black River. The Canadians release several thousand steelhead in Sarnia Bay each year. Salmon taken in the area are from Belle Isle or southern Lake Huron plants.

Facilities

A new city-owned four-lane paved ramp awaits boaters at 12th St. Bridge. The city of Port Huron also maintains a similar facility at the I-94 overpass. Further downstream is a public launch at Marysville. Boats may also be launched at Lakeport State Park and across the river at Sarnia's Centennial Park.

Upstream from 7th St., the DNR maintains a mooring facility which includes transient accommodations, gasoline and diesel fuel, water, electricity, restrooms, shower facilties, dock attendant, holding-tank pump-out, CATV, and VHF-FM radio. Call (313) 985-5676.

Shore anglers have been able to fish the river from several downtown business properties, the most popular probably being the Sears dock. Access is also provided at Lighthouse Park in front of the Coast Guard station. Much of the Canadian shoreline is nationalized and therefore open to the public.

Further Information

Chambers of Commerce:

1. Greater Port Huron—Marysville Chamber of Commerce, 920 Pine Grove Ave., Port Huron 48060; (313) 985-7101.
2. Southeast Michigan Travel & Tourist Association, P.O. Box 1590, Troy 48099; (313) 585-8220.

Bait & Tackle Shops:

1. Military Street Bait & Tackle, 2125 Military, Port Huron 48060; (313) 985-6266.
2. Pro Bait, 4003 24th Avenue (US-25), Port Huron 48060; (313) 385-5474.
3. Park Bait & Tackle, 1425 Pine Grove, Port Huron 48060; (313) 982-8590.

Charter Fishing:

1. Captains Carol and Ed Tinsley, 3377 N. Range Rd., Port Huron 48060; (313) 982-2576. 26-foot Stamas, *Wendy K.*
2. Captain Bill VanLuven, 4316 Old Forge Rd., Port Huron 48060; (313) 987-5893. 27-foot Sea Ray, *Vantasea*.
3. Captain Howard Mills, 7228 Flamingo Rd., Algonac 48001; (313) 794-9609. 30-foot Sea Ray, *Paramour*.

53
PORT HURON and UPPER ST. CLAIR RIVER

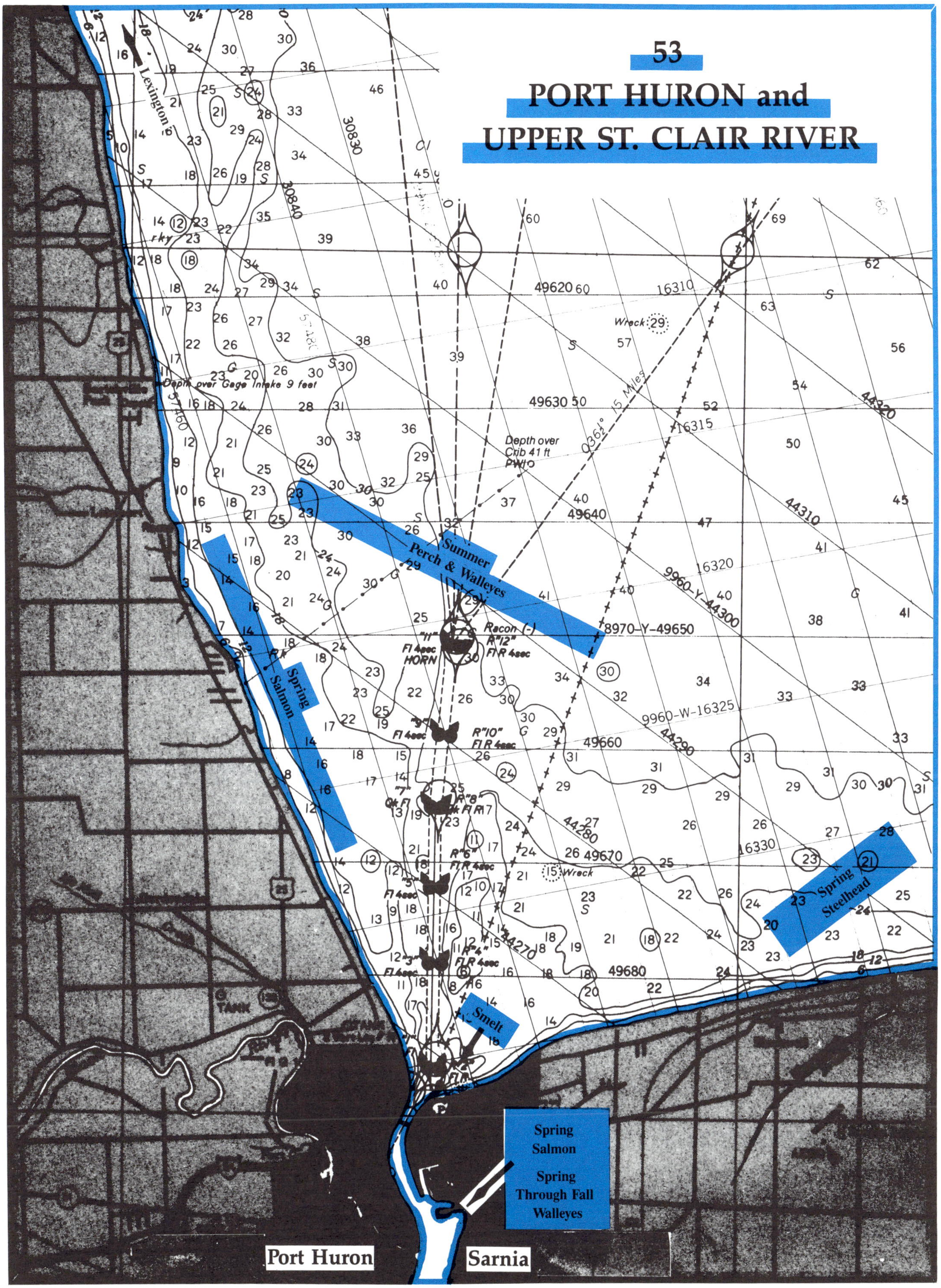

Spring two-day fishing tournaments in southern Lake Huron have produced upwards of a thousand salmon and trout. Many are taken in the St. Clair River.

PORT HURON (cont.)

4. Captain Al Tyrrell, 3065 Laurel, Port Huron 48060; (313) 982-3313. 25-foot Penn Yan, *Tunnel of Love*.

Department of Natural Resources:

Two fisheries biologists work out of District Headquarters at 715 South Cedar St., Imlay City 48444; (313) 724-2015. They are responsible for southern Lake Huron. Two additional fisheries biologists work out of District Headquarters at 2455 N. Williams Lake Rd., Pontiac 48504; (313) 666-1500. They are responsible for the St. Clair River.

Coast Guard:

Port Huron Station, (313) 982-2684.

54
ST CLAIR RIVER (Marysville to Marine City)

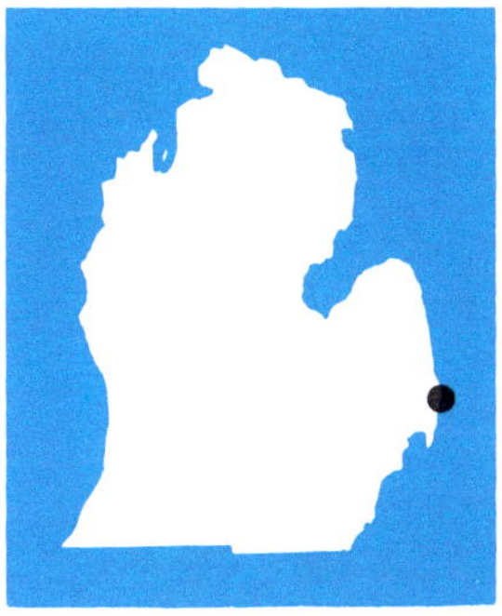

Walleyes are the main calling card in the St. Clair River, with thousands caught every year. But shore and boat anglers can catch just about anything from smelt to sturgeon, mud puppies to muskies.

Boaters should exercise care because of the fast current (six mph and more) and ore-freighter traffic. In spring, large ice floes can be dangerous, too.

Fishing Schedule

SPRING

Spring walleye fishing is good for large, egg-heavy females. Fish come from just about anywhere in the river when anglers can get lures down to a hard bottom. Tactics include chugging and trolling upstream with six-ounce to 1-1/2 pound sinkers, and drifting downstream with bottom bouncers — smaller amounts of lead suspended 18 inches below three-way swivels. Pencil Plugs and Rapalas are preferred lures.

Lure colors vary, but pastel blue, yellow, and pink (locally called Easter egg or Wonder Bread colors) are good choices, with black, green, blue or chrome combinations also productive. Best fishing occurs near dusk and lasts well into the night. Early spring fishermen don't catch lots of walleyes, but the ones they do hook are often lunkers, sometimes 10 pounds or more.

Sporadic spurts of salmon also appear in the river, beginning in late March or early April and lasting until mid-May. Most fish boxes yield about 80 percent kings and 20 percent cohos, with incidental takes of pink salmon, steelhead and brown trout. Catching conditions depend upon ice floes, water clarity and trolling traffic. Action begins in the North Channel, with fish staging below the Lambton Hydro power plant in Canada (Canadian license required to fish these waters, however) and below the Detroit Edison plants at Marine City and St. Clair.

Howard Mills, a veteran salmon man and charterboat captain, says that some muddy conditions are favorable because they tend to keep fish from spooking. One year heavy rains dirtied the river so much that fishing shut off completely. It took a week for the river to clean up. On the third or fourth day of that period, Mills and some friends worked the current downstream from the St. Clair power plant. Their graph showed huge schools of fish stacked up. The salmon, previously unmolested by trollers, pounded nearly every lure the men put down. Two days later, when the river cleared and more trollers began working over the school, it broke up and left for parts unknown.

Mills says further catching keys include avoiding other boats, staying away from weed beds and deep holes (most salmon are taken in the upper 10-20 feet of the river), and watching for structure on the graph. Mills also advises searching for new water, as salmon will suddenly show up in places where they had not been seen before.

When smelt are in the river, minnow-imitating lures are good choices. Howard has scored with Rapalas, Long A Bombers, Bagley Bang-O-Lures, and Rebel Fastracs and Spoonbills. When smelt runs peter out, he switches to Northport Nailers, Krocodiles, and Flukes — a homemade lure that his son Eric perfected years ago. Catching colors in spoons or plugs include blue-and-silver, silver, chartreuse, black, and hot orange-and-green choices.

Mills patterns downriggers to approximate the slope of the river channel (outside lines deeper than inside offerings). He trolls downstream, usually just faster than the current, but sometimes backtrolls to entice lures with action when the current is especially swift. Outriggers sporting large Deep Sixes are sometimes effective. So are the bottom-bouncer setups that I described for walleyes.

Smelt give a fair to excellent accounting of themselves each spring, beginning in mid to late April and lasting about two weeks. Productive areas are just about anywhere you can get to the river and find dipping room. You will need dipnets attached to long poles (to 24 feet) and a partner to pull up the hoop with a rope after you run it to bottom while walking quickly downstream.

SUMMER

Summer action is generally good for two- to four-pound walleyes. Nightcrawlers pinned to drift-river rigs get the nod, along with chugged or drifted Pencil Plugs and Mister Twisters spincast from shore.

Other tactics, 50 or more years old and specific to this area, can also be used to take river walleyes. Driftfishing, for instance, is often done with a board about 18 inches long with a *V*-crotch in each end. Two to six ounces of weight, 12 inches below a three-way swivel, help the fisherman to bang his offering straight up and down off bottom. Chugging anglers often anchor in the river,

Veteran skippers Bob Bingle (left) and Howard Mills discuss trolling strategy for salmon below the Marine City Edison plant. The date is April 3.

then rely on short, stiff rods to pound bait or lures off bottom. Effective baits for either drifting or chugging are pork rind, nightcrawlers, or, even white balloons. Some anglers also wrap live minnows with a rubber band to No. 2 or No. 3 treble hooks.

Old timers often troll with 60-pound-test seven-strand uncoated wire line. They fish nightcrawlers by day and Pencil Plugs by night. A five-foot-long trolling shank (available at area tackle shops) located above sinker weights (which can weigh two pounds each, depending upon the current at the fishing location) allows the angler to fish three leads. Leads are five feet long at bottom, 10 feet long at 10 inches higher, and 40 feet long at another 25 inches higher. Thus, the three leads are 35 inches from bottom, 10 inches from bottom, and on bottom itself. The closer to bottom they appear, the closer they should be to the wire line. As with chugging or drifting, the fisherman slowly jigs up and down as he trolls along.

Walleyers also catch a few smallmouth bass, along with yellow perch, freshwater drum and an occasional crappie, rock bass and channel catfish.

The entire river is productive, although most anglers have special drifts they repeat again and again. A very popular one occurs in midriver from Buoy No. 48 for a mile downstream to the Lambton plant. Another is from north of St. Clair to the Diamond Crystal Company salt piles. A third is from Marysville Park to a mile or two downstream.

Fall sport continues for walleyes, with all of the previously described methods proving effective. Fishermen also pick up salmon and trout that are drifting back to Lake St. Clair.

Winter anglers casting from shore catch a few browns, steelhead and salmon, except when the river freezes solid. Because of tricky currents, it is best to stay off the river in winter.

Planting Records

The St. Clair River no longer receives hatchery-reared fish. The last stocking was 50,000 fall fingerling brown trout by the DNR in 1983. Those fish should be available for several more years, however.

Other species caught are either bred here or released elsewhere.

Facilities

Boaters can launch at Marysville Park, at a DNR site on the Pine River at St. Clair (which includes a mooring facility), and at Marine City. Limited shoreline access is available at Marysville Park, the St. Clair boardwalk, and Marine City, either at the public beach or an area down from the ferry dock.

Services at the St. Clair mooring facility include transient accommodations, gasoline and diesel fuel, water, electricity, restrooms, shower facilities and holding-tank pump-out. A dock attendant oversees the facility. The telephone number is (313) 329-4125.

Further Information

Chambers of Commerce:

1. Port Huron-Marysville Chamber of Commerce, 920 Pine Grove Ave., Port Huron 48060; (313) 985-7101.
2. Marine City Chamber of Commerce, Box 521, Marine City 48039; (313) 765-4501.
3. Southeast Michigan Travel & Tourist Association, P.O. Box 1590, Troy 48099; (313) 585-8820.

Bait and Tackle Shops:

1. Angler Rod Company Factory Outlet, 1420 Oakland, St. Clair 48079; (313) 329-2253.

Charter Fishing:

1. Captain Howard Mills, 7228 Flamingo Rd., Algonac 48001; (313) 794-9609. 30-foot Sea Ray, *Paramour*.
2. Captain Al Tyrrell, 2065 Laurel Lane, Port Huron 48060; (313) 982-3313. 24-foot Penn Yan, *Tunnel 'O Love*.
3. Captain Bob Bingle, Bob's Charter Service, 8997 Anchor Bay Dr., Fair Haven 48023; (313) 794-3854. 28-foot Inland Seas, *Steelhead*.

Department of Natural Resources:

Two fisheries biologists work out of District Headquarters at 2455 N. Williams Lake Rd., Pontiac 48054; (313) 666-1500.

Coast Guard:

Port Huron Station, (313) 982-2684.

Divine Inspiration

You might think that a skipper who has chartered the St. Clair River and Lake St. Clair for over 35 years has seen it all. I've had people from all walks of life aboard my boat. Some are happy whether or not they take fish, and a few tend to grumble if they don't catch lunkers every time out. But each charter provides an opportunity to make new friends and to learn something new.

I've turned a lot of customers into friends over the years, but one group that really stands out in my memory first came aboard in May 1984. On that evening, I took out six men on a four-hour walleye charter. All six men were Church of God ministers. Now there is nothing unusual about that, except when you consider how lucky these fellows have been.

On that initial charter we fished Pencil Plugs at night in the St. Clair River about a half-mile upstream from Marine City. Those ministers took a limit of 36 walleyes, from three to 11 pounds each, and also caught a pair of 18-pound Chinook salmon. They have been out with me four times since and have always enjoyed good fishing. They caught 20 or 21 salmon on another trip.

It makes a fellow wonder if divine inspiration is at work for these fishing clergymen. If so, I guess it is for me, too.

Captain Hank Bradley
Marine City

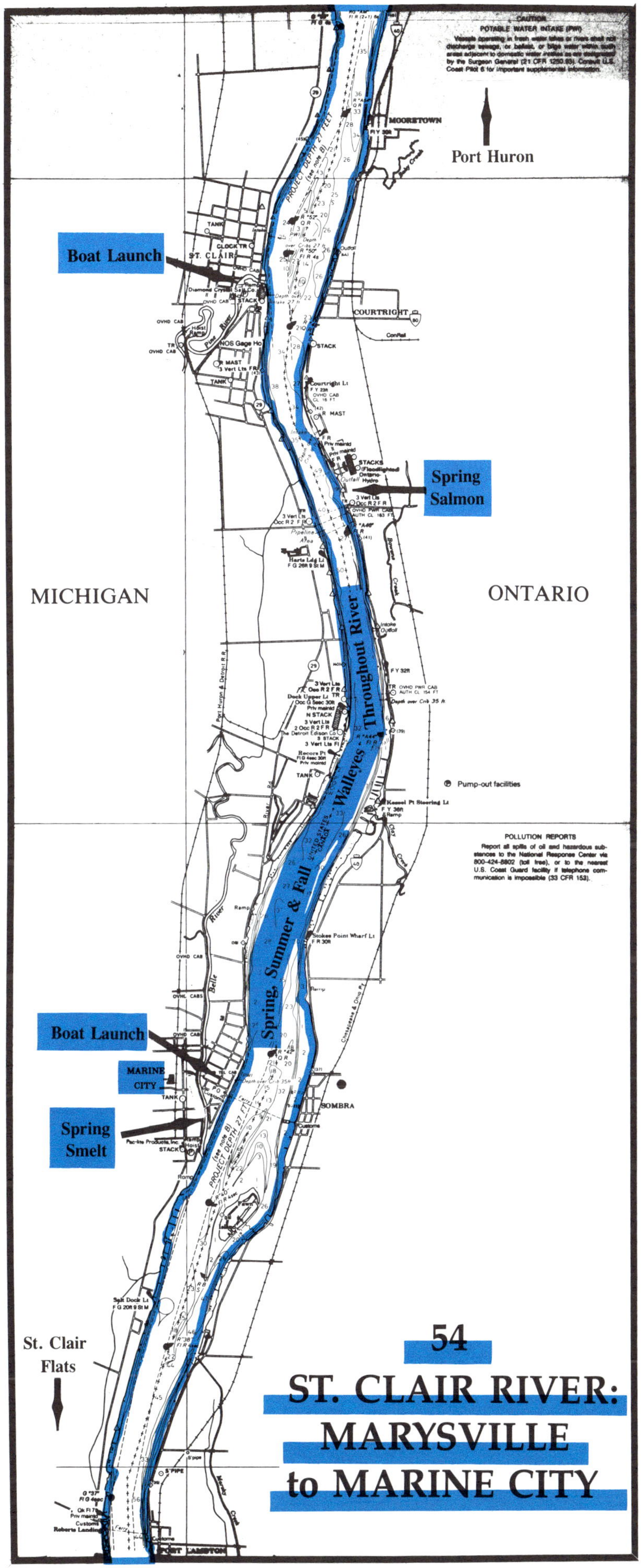
CAUTION
POTABLE WATER INTAKE (PWI)
MOORETOWN
Port Huron
Boat Launch
ST. CLAIR
COURTRIGHT
Spring Salmon
MICHIGAN
ONTARIO
Spring, Summer & Fall Walleyes Throughout River
Pump-out facilities
POLLUTION REPORTS
Report all spills of oil and hazardous substances to the National Response Center via 800-424-8802 (toll free), or to the nearest U.S. Coast Guard facility if telephone communication is impossible (33 CFR 153).
Boat Launch
MARINE CITY
SOMBRA
Spring Smelt
St. Clair Flats
PORT LAMBTON
54
ST. CLAIR RIVER: MARYSVILLE to MARINE CITY

55

LAKE ST. CLAIR

Three words—*something for everyone*—aptly summarize the fishing opportunities in Lake St. Clair. And it isn't just that walleyes, northern pike, muskies, smallmouth and largemouth bass, yellow perch, white bass and other species are merely present in the 450-square-mile mini Great Lake. They are present *in great abundance*. Fishing, at times, can border on the uncanny; it is that good. Further benefits include an abundance of marinas, bait and tackle shops, launching sites, motels, and restaurants which dot the American side. (About one-third of the lake and half of her feeder streams are in the U.S.; the balance are in Canada.)

But, to the newcomer especially, fishing in Lake St. Clair can be a less than perfect experience for several reasons. First, the lake is a sleeping giant that can awaken quickly and without warning. Storms whip together in a hurry, turning calm waters into a wind-lashed monster that threatens sailboaters, water skiers and anglers. The first time I fished here, high waves tossed around our 12-foot boat like a wood chip in a water spout, and for a couple of hours, a friend and I hardly knew where we were. It was a stomach-sinking experience.

Second, the lake's sheer size can be intimidating. Most newcomers, in fact, hire a guide the first couple of times they want to sample her fishing. For good reason. North-end marshes and canals contribute to what some call the Michigan Everglades, a maze of green and blue that looks all the same to the uninitiated. It's not too hard to get lost, either there or on the open lake.

The third reason is also size-related. Gamefish here move around a lot chasing baitfish, so where you catch fish today is not necessarily where you will catch them tomorrow. Small wonder, then, that many of her best fishermen are specialists who target one, or perhaps two, species, then bust chops to keep up with their whereabouts during the long fishing season.

But the advantages of fishing Lake St. Clair far outweigh the problems. One can fish walleyes or bass from the channels for a few hours, then within minutes be in another world casting spoons to the quiet bays within a marsh. On a summer 1985 trip to Walpole Island (see "Walpole Island Smorgasbord," page 217), my friends and I caught largemouth and smallmouth bass, rock bass, white bass, bluegills, walleyes and many many northern pike, though none of the pike was larger than five pounds.

All in all, this shallow, gray-green lake really is one super fishing hole.

Because of its uniqueness, I will detail Lake St. Clair angling opportunities by explaining where and how to catch *individual species* throughout the *entire* lake, rather than keying on individual ports or rivermouths as I have done throughout most of the rest of the book.

Walleyes

Walleyes may very well be Lake St. Clair's biggest trump card. Currently there is no closed season, a minimum size of 13 inches (as compared to 15 inches throughout most of Michigan), and a daily limit of six fish. In the Canadian waters of Lake St. Clair, there is no size limit and no closed season, and each angler may creel six fish. However, you will need a Canadian license to fish there.

Hot walleye action begins in early to mid-May off the Thames River in Canada and in Michigan off the Clinton River mouth and over the Dumping Grounds just outside the Shipping Channel at the lake's lower end. Big spawners—mostly hang-belly females bursting with eggs and that weigh up to 12 pounds each—move into these areas.

Anglers troll or anchor in the rivers themselves and fish with Pencil Plugs or driftfish just outside the flow with nightcrawlers or small minnows. Gail Van Alstine of Drayton Plains has experienced excellent success in the rivers while using two Pencil Plugs at the same time. Tactics include fishing from an anchored boat just before dark or after dark with 25- or 30-pound-test black, braided line and two-ounce sinkers. Van Alstine attaches the sinkers via three-way swivels to a 12-inch dropper line four feet and

Drifting for walleyes is a popular tactic in Lake St. Clair.

eight feet, respectively, ahead of his Pencil Plugs

Other spring, as well as summer and fall, walleye hotspots can shape up nearly anywhere. And big fish are not just caught in spring—they also test tackle in the fall. As a general rule, the rivers and channels produce best in spring, the flats areas in summer, and shoreline shallows in fall. A good region to try at any time is from 11 Mile Road to the Clinton River mouth. Key spots within this stretch and elsewhere—off and on throughout the open-water fishing season—include Metropolitan Beach, Belvidere Bay, Selfridge Air National Guard, Brandenburg Park, behind Bud's Restaurant on Anchor Bay, any of the north-end channels (including the Cutoff Channel and the Sni), Salt River and Stony Creek outflows, Strawberry Island, the Baltimore Channel, and at the mouth of the North Channel between the Black Can (Buoy No. 20) and the Firecracker (red Buoy No. 20).

Trolling or drifting over weed beds are rated tactics in the open lake. Submergent weed beds produce best when nightcrawlers are presented very slowly over them. Most anglers rig 24- to 36-inch two- or three-hook harnesses, each containing beads and a large blade. You can buy them at local tackle shops, although many fishermen prefer to make their own. Water conditions seem to dictate color choice. Hot chartreuse, gold, and orange work best in murky water on overcast days. For clear, bright conditions, go with white or chrome. Red or hot green are good all-around colors.

To rig these offerings, most fishermen drop a two- or four-ounce pencil-shaped sinker 12-18 inches below a three-way swivel. The amount of lead depends upon wind speed and weed depth. One day, for example, a gentle wind promised to push us along at a mile per hour or so. Instead of rigging heavy lead sinkers, we opted for a couple of split shots, which allowed us to walk our nightcrawlers through weed beds only a foot under the surface. The tactic was pure dynamite.

Some fishermen report hot walleye action with small Rapalas and Rebels in gold or silver, either trolled or spincast. Others toss Mister Twisters in purple, white or yellow colors. A few cruise areas of emergent weeds on warm, quiet summer evenings. By making a stealthy approach, they get close enough to flip floating Rapalas to feeding walleyes. Many times you will hear a charging walleye's tail slap just before he busts your plug.

Paul Wargo, a savvy Lake St. Clair fisherman, who visits regularly from his home in Harrison, keys on north-end channels, especially in the Walpole Island area. Walleyes are one of many species he seeks there (see "Walpole Island Smorgasbord," page 217). To catch them, Wargo fishes jigs with four-pound-test monofilament, spooled to a Shimano Bantam 1000 reel, and a homemade seven-foot graphite casting rod. The light equipment allows him to present effectively white or yellow 1/4- and 3/8-ounce bucktail jigs tipped with live minnows or trimmed-down Knight's L'il Fishies.

"Anglers have to *work* the jig and maintain a *feel* through a tight line," Paul advises. "Otherwise, the lure will drag on bottom and the current will force a bow in the line, which will keep the angler out of touch with lure and fish." Wargo trims bucktails right at the collar of the jig so that there is just enough to cover the hook. His fine-tuned methods of fishing the channels generally outscore traditional tactics of dunking nightcrawler harnesses with two- or four-ounce sinkers.

Bass

The many bass-fishing tournaments that are held each summer attest to Lake St. Clair's popularity for these warm-water scrappers. Creel studies show that smallmouths here outnumber largemouths about 15 to one. But there are pockets of shallow water, especially within north-end marsh islands and west-side cuts, that hold good numbers of bigmouths. It is not uncommon to catch both species of bass on a single trip. In summer 1985, for example, three of us fished Walpole Island, and after taking some dandy smallmouths from channels, we chanced upon a honey hole for largemouths.

The bass-fishing season on Lake St. Clair generally begins on the third Saturday in June as compared to the statewide opener on the Saturday before Memorial Day. (Check a current *Michigan Fishing Guide* for details.) This late start gives most bass time to spawn without facing too much fishing pressure. Pencil reeds in backwater bays, which have usually warmed to 60 degrees F. by the opener, are good spots to try. The channels are usually about five degrees cooler at this time. But as summer progresses, they, too, warm to 60 degrees F. or more, causing baitfish to enter them and bass (especially smallmouths) to follow.

The channels remain productive until late October. On warm fall days, bass also show up again in areas containing pencil reeds.

Few anglers know the lake for bass as intimately as bass-pro Kim Stricker of Howell, who has won several fishing tournaments on Lake St. Clair. Stricker recommends these Canadian locations for smallmouths: In June and July, fish near the buoy markers on the west side of Mitchell Bay, the Grassy Ben Islands, between the buoy markers off Mitchell Point, and Dynamite Cut (which links Goose Lake and Johnston Bay. Both are on Walpole Island, where an Indian fishing permit is required. See "Walpole Island Smorgasbord," page 217, for details). From July through October, check out the Chematogan, Bassett, and Johnston channels; the mouths of the South Channel and the St. Clair Cutoff; and look to weedy dropoffs on the outer fringe of Mitchell Bay. The South Channel (the international boundary line) is also good.

In American waters, good early summer locations include pencil reeds outside Little Muscamoot Bay, the mouth of the Sni (at Strawberry Island), the cluster of islands off the north end of Long Point Bay, and the Clinton River mouth. From midsummer through fall, Stricker prefers Big Muscamoot Bay, the mouth of the Middle Channel, and the North Channel just downstream from Decker's Landing and at the entrance to the Baltimore Channel.

Few fishermen have honed their catching tactics as sharply as Stricker. He prefers a 5-1/2 foot graphite baitcasting rod with medium action and a baitcasting reel spooled with 12-pound-test line. He says that the combination allows for pinpoint casting and less hangups on pencil reeds.

In spring and summer, Kim relies heavily upon Big 'Un Spinnerbaits with white or chartreuse heads and purple, white or chartreuse skirts. Tactics include steady retrieves through pencil reeds and over the top of weed beds just under the surface. Just outside the main flow in the channels and along weed-bed edges, he uses a lift-and-drop method. A good lure in fall is a three-inch white grub on a jig head, fished either clean or tipped with a small minnow or piece of nightcrawler. The object is to cast the lure, allow it to drop to bottom, then skip it along bottom. Bass normally sock the offering on the drop. An effective all-around lure throughout the season is the 1/4-ounce Bomber Model A crankbait in crayfish, chrome or perch color. If you are purely a bass fisherman, however, the disadvantage of using crankbaits is that small pike attack them.

No matter what the lure, Stricker knows that smallmouths move around a great deal and that if they aren't hitting his offerings, they usually aren't in the area. In that situation, he will change locations often.

Another savvy Lake St. Clair bass fisherman is Larry Gargus of Lapeer. Besides many of the places previously mentioned, Gargus also fishes cuts, pockets of water within marshes, and culverts from Metropolitan Beach to Fair Haven. Larry believes that most of the bass-fishing pressure on Lake St. Clair occurs on the main channels and that if anglers seek out-of-the-way spots, they can score much better.

Small pools formed from water rushing through road tubes (culverts) are especially productive when anglers "flip" lures to them. Flipping is the practice of tossing artificials, with an underhand motion, short distances to a small area. Hot flipping lures for Gargus include black or brown Pigs 'N Jigs, silver- or fish-finish Rapalas and Bang-O-Lures, and various buzzbaits, fake nightcrawlers or spinnerbaits.

Lake St. Clair

Length—26 miles

Width—24 miles

Length of coastline (including Canada and islands)—257 miles

Total water surface—490 square miles

U.S. water surface—198 square miles

Total land drainage basin—6,930 square miles

U.S. drainage—2,850 square miles

Maximum depth—21 feet

Average depth—10 feet

Volume of water—1 cubic mile

Muskies

The state-record Great Lakes muskie, a 62-1/2 pound submarine that taped an even 59 inches, was caught in Lake St. Clair in 1940. The record will almost certainly never be matched here or elsewhere in the state. In Lake St. Clair, at least, there are few, if any, fish left within 20 pounds of that mark. In fact, it is becoming rare to catch a 30-pounder these days. Besides fewer big fish, the lake is also serving up diminishing numbers of legal-sized (in Michigan waters, currently 38 inches; in Canadian waters, currently 30 inches) muskies. The reason, according to veteran observers, is heavy fishing pressure from anglers who catch—yet do not release—fish in the 20-pound-and-up class.

But any muskie—no matter how big—is a thrill to catch, and for that reason alone, many fishermen continue to seek them in Lake St. Clair.

In June, post-spawn muskies can be caught around weed beds in Anchor Bay. Then, smaller fish to 20 pounds will move around in packs like freshwater wolves. Muskies closer to 30 pounds are typically loners.

As summer wears on and water temperatures warm, many muskies slowly work their way to the lake head where colder Lake Huron water—sluiced through the St. Clair River and its fingering channels—comes surging in. Look for weed beds off the mouths of the South, St. Clair Cutoff, and North channels. Close to shore between Nine Mile Road and Jefferson Beach Marina is a good spot, as is the stretch from Metropolitan Beach to the Clinton River mouth. The Dumping Grounds and the Shipping Channel produce in July and August respectively. L'Anse Creuse Bay is a good spot in September and October.

In Canadian waters in July and August, try weed beds off the mouths of Pike Creek and the Puce, Belle, and Ruscom rivers. Stoney Point and the Thames River mouth are September and October hotspots. Some claim that the Thames River mouth now yields the biggest muskies in the lake.

One of the most respected muskie men on the lake is guide Jim Beyers of New Baltimore. Though June is generally the best time to go after muskies (the season usually ends in early December), Beyers especially likes the fall period after Labor Day. More fish and bigger fish are caught then, and boat traffic and fishing pressure are lighter. In addition, the American side becomes more productive than Canadian waters, which typically hold the upper hand in summer. Further, fishing in U.S. waters eliminates a long boat ride and the need for a Canadian license.

Muskie fishing on Lake St. Clair is highly specialized, and that is why many fishermen hire a guide, at least until they grow familiar with the sport. Consider the basic equipment needed: Beyers, for example, uses rods from five feet to 12 feet in length, each as stiff as a pool cue. Such spiney poles are necessary in order to troll magnum lures at a fast clip and to drive home hooks into the bony mouth of a muskie. Beyers insists on stainless-steel or carbide rod guides, claiming that ceramic or glass guides will self-destruct on the first fishing trip. He buys 40- to 60-pound-test braided Dacron line because most monofilament has too much stretch and can cause a missed strike. On the other hand, you want a little stretch near the lure, and that is why Beyers adds 80-pound-test mono leaders instead of the steel leaders popular with other muskie men. He then attaches 60- or 70-pound-test ball-bearing swivels with coast-lock snaps to his lures. Reels are big level-wind Penn 209s or 309s; rod holders are Salty Big Throat models with dual clamps.

Heavy-duty equipment for heavy-duty fish.

Believers, Swim Whizzes, Top Cat Gold Stars, and Creek Chubs in perch, frog or silver finish are Beyers' choices in plugs. Other fishermen report catches on magnum Rapalas, Rebels, Bagley Diving Bang-O-Lures, Big Macs, Lazy Ikes, and Radjke's Pike Minnows. Good spoons include Spoonplugs, Ivanhoes, Swim Zags, and Eppinger Huskie Devles.

Live-bait fishing and spincasting with bucktails are normally good muskie-fishing tactics, but few use them on Lake St. Clair. Instead, trolling is the rated method. Most burn lures along at a 4.0- to 6.0-mph clip, especially in warm, clear water. When water temperatures are below 60 degrees F. or when the lake is roiled, cut boat speed accordingly. Patterning your troll with sharp turns, making tight figure-eights, and now and then repeating a triangle shape will sometimes provoke the normally moody muskies into belting lures. Most fish strike between 10:00 a.m. and 2:00 p.m. That may be due to daily optimum light or temperature, perhaps both.

Beyers says that trolling lures must be properly tuned so that they wiggle or wobble with maximum action and run straight. Depth, boat speed, the size and shape of the lure, and rod length are major variables that determine just how productive a lure will be. To this end, Beyers cites three reasons for using rods of varying length: (1) to provide spacing between lures, (2) to enable the angler to fish a variety of depths and lure positions, and (3) to allow for lures to run at different speeds.

"You have to have complete confidence that each rod can catch a muskie," is the way Jim explains his system, which includes 10 rods arranged in five sets of pairs (legal, assuming he has five fishermen aboard). All lures are run within 50 feet of the boat.

55 LAKE ST. CLAIR

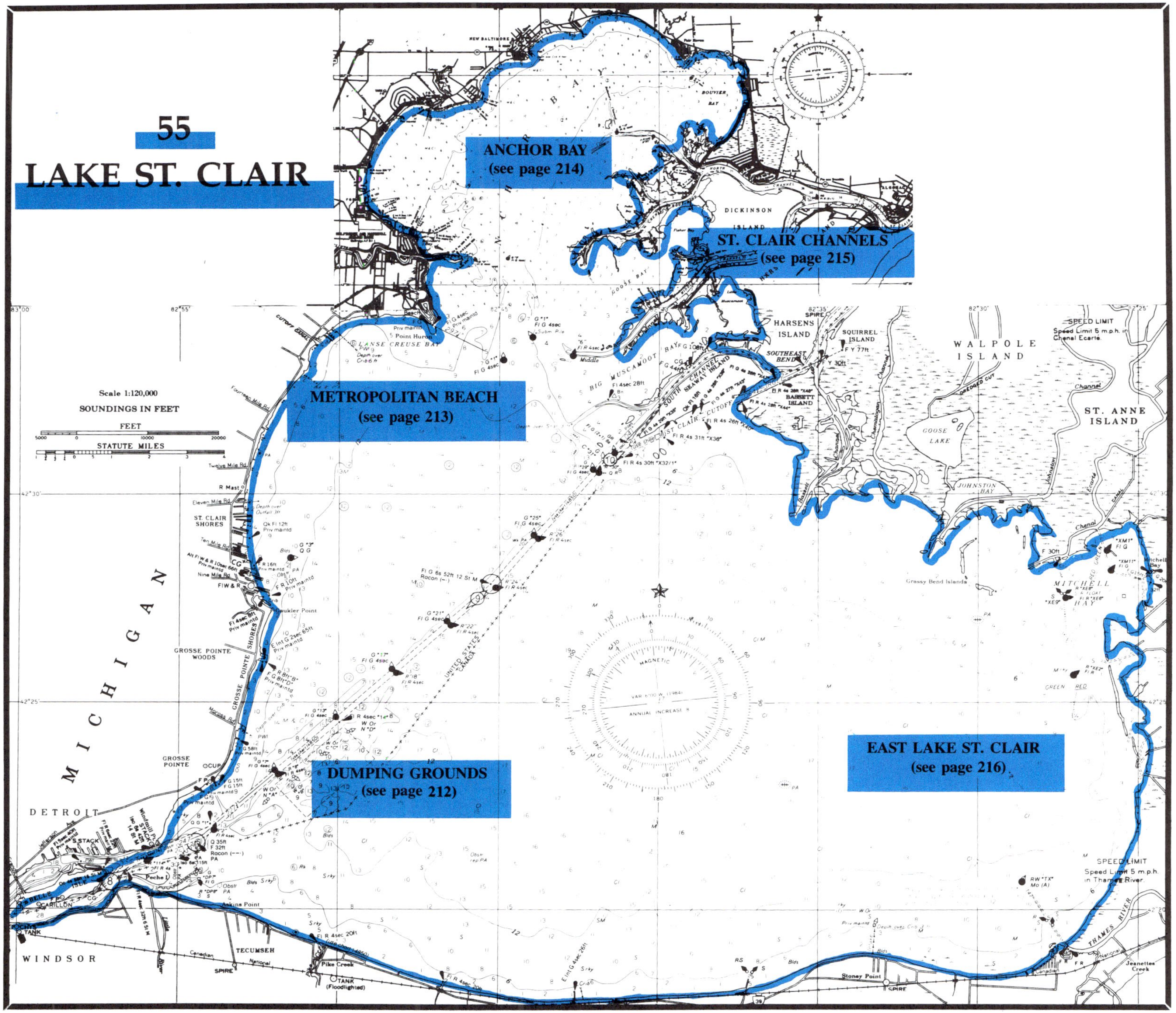

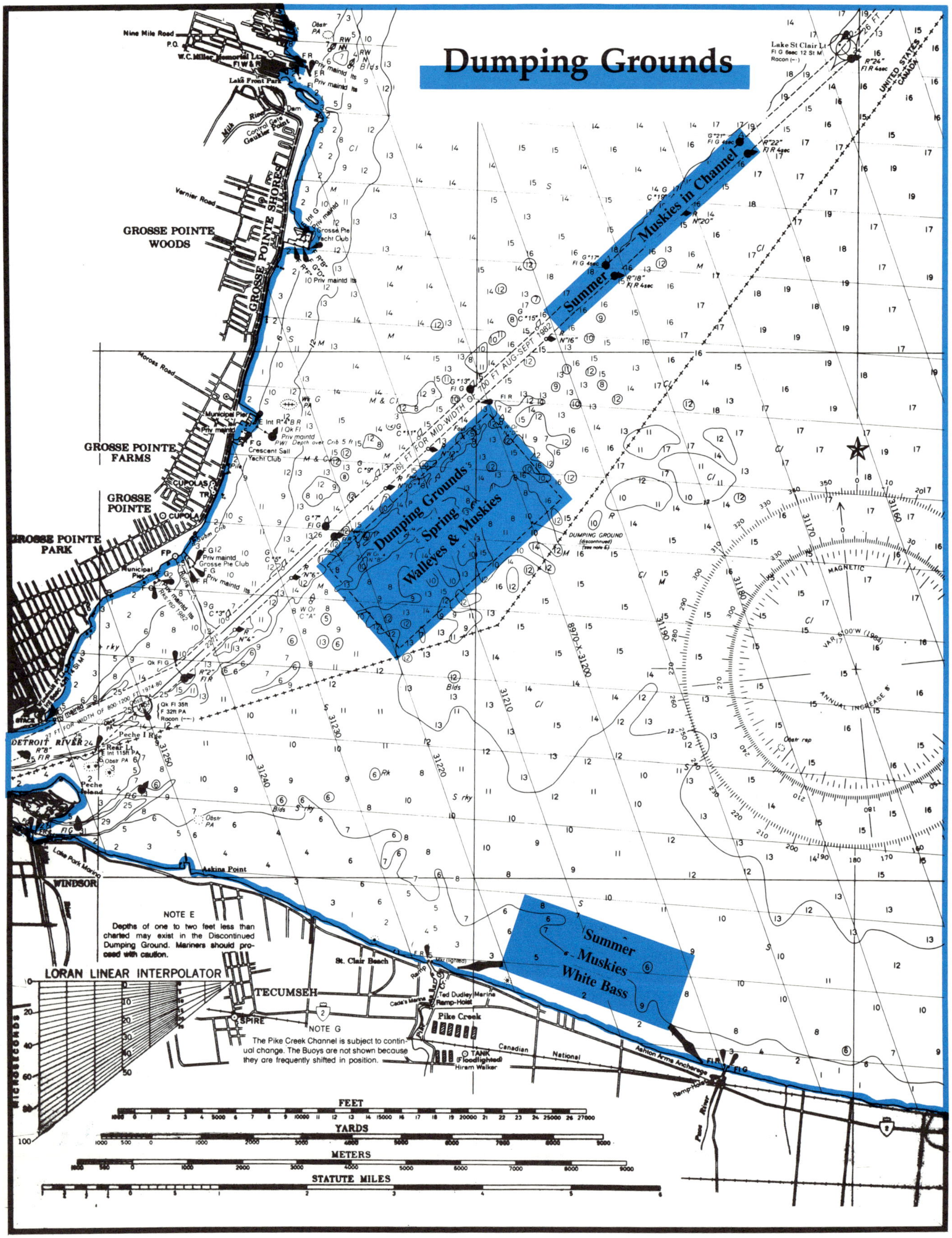
Dumping Grounds
Summer Muskies in Channel
Dumping Grounds Spring Walleyes & Muskies
Summer Muskies White Bass
Nine Mile Road
W.C. Miller Memorial Lt.
Lake Front Park
Gaukler Point
Vernier Road
GROSSE POINTE WOODS
GROSSE POINTE SHORES
Moross Road
Municipal Pier
Crescent Sail Yacht Club
GROSSE POINTE FARMS
GROSSE POINTE
GROSSE POINTE PARK
Grosse Pte Club
Grosse Pte Yacht Club
Lake St Clair Lt
UNITED STATES
CANADA
DUMPING GROUND (discontinued) (see note E)
DETROIT RIVER
Peche Island
Rear Lt
WINDSOR
Askins Point
St. Clair Beach
TECUMSEH
Pike Creek
Ted Dudley Marina Ramp-Hoist
Cade's Marina
TANK (Floodlighted) Hiram Walker
Canadian National
Ashton Arms Anchorage
MAGNETIC
NOTE E
Depths of one to two feet less than charted may exist in the Discontinued Dumping Ground. Mariners should proceed with caution.
NOTE G
The Pike Creek Channel is subject to continual change. The Buoys are not shown because they are frequently shifted in position.
LORAN LINEAR INTERPOLATOR
MICROSECONDS
FEET
YARDS
METERS
STATUTE MILES

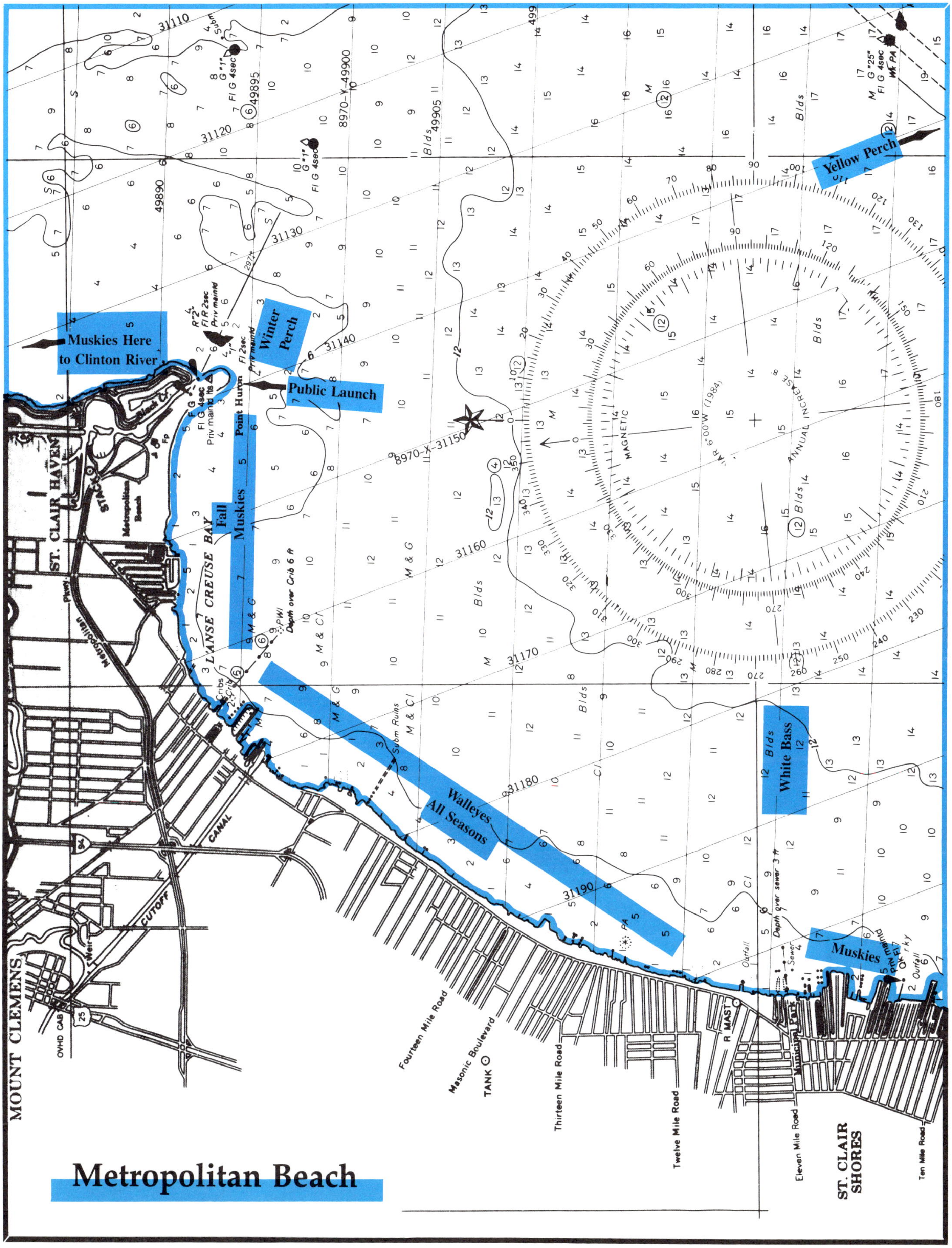

Metropolitan Beach

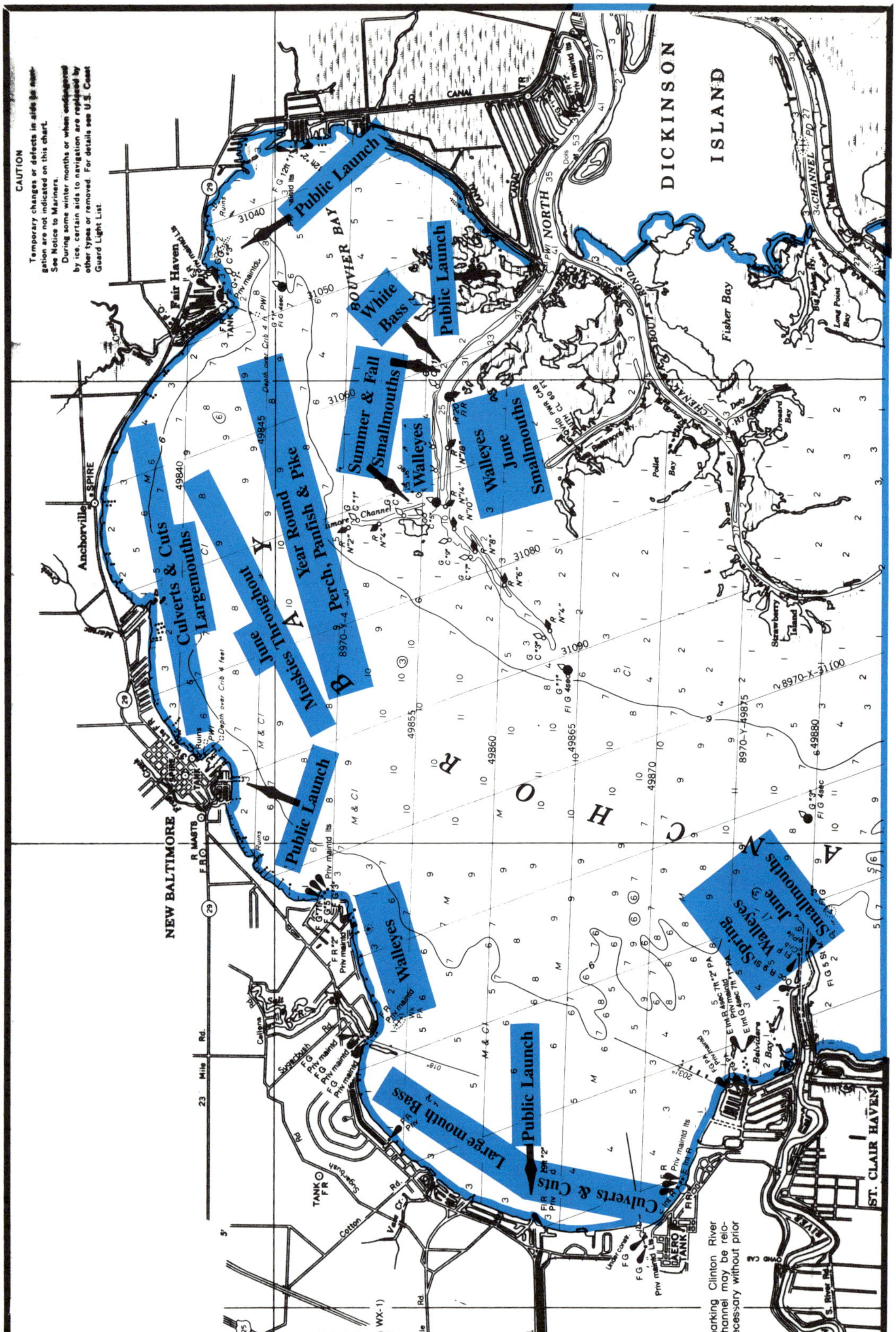
Anchor Bay
Public Launch
Public Launch
Public Launch
Public Launch
White Bass
Summer & Fall Smallmouths
Walleyes
Walleyes June Smallmouths
Culverts & Cuts Largemouths
June Muskies Throughout
Year Round Perch, Panfish & Pike
Walleyes
Large-mouth Bass
Culverts & Cuts
Spring Walleyes June Smallmouths
ANCHOR BAY
BOUVIER BAY
DICKINSON ISLAND
Fisher Bay
NEW BALTIMORE
Anchorville
Fair Haven
ST. CLAIR HAVEN
CAUTION
Temporary changes or defects in aids to navigation are not indicated on this chart. See Notice to Mariners.
During some winter months or when endangered by ice, certain aids to navigation are replaced by other types or removed. For details see U.S. Coast Guard Light List.
NOAA VHF-FM WEATHER BROADCASTS
The National Weather Service station listed below provides continuous marine weather broadcasts. The range of reception is variable, but for most stations is usually 20 to 40 miles from the antenna site.
Detroit, MI. KEC-63 162.550 MHz (Chan WX-1)
Buoys marking Clinton River Entrance Channel may be relocated as necessary without prior notice.

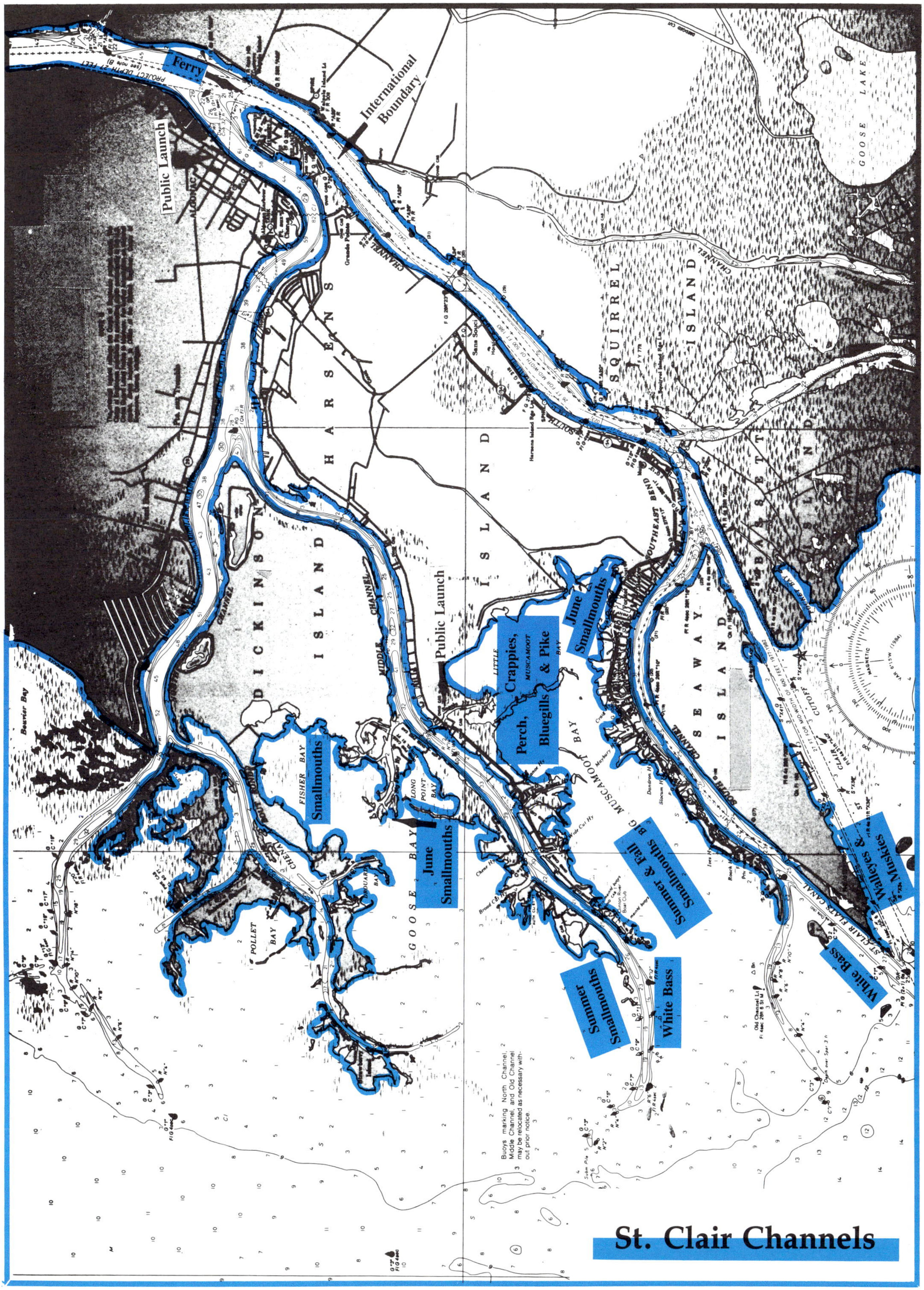

St. Clair Channels

East Lake St. Clair

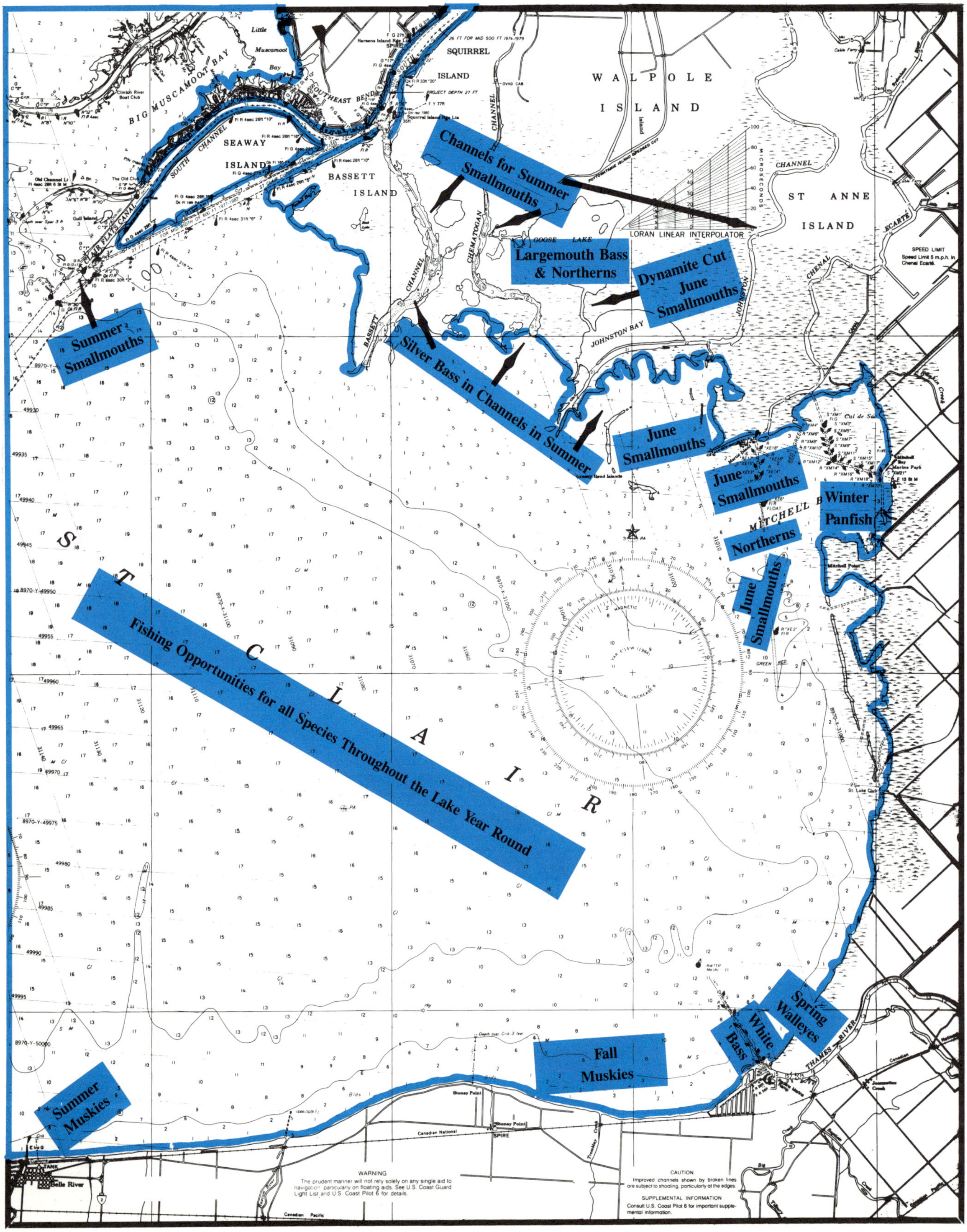

The most productive pair is located halfway between stern and bow, one to a side, and typically feature eight-foot rods, 30 feet of line, and one-to four-ounce sinkers. Ahead (toward the bow) of this duo is a set of 12-foot rods with five feet of line and 10-ounce sinkers. Closest to the bow are two four-foot rods (pointed down) with 10 feet of line and 20-ounce sinkers. Off the boat corners at the stern are two five-foot rods with 15 feet of line and eight- to 14-ounce weights. Across the transom to each side of the engine is a 10-foot rod with 10 feet of line and a six- to eight-ounce sinker. If a sixth angler is aboard, Beyers completes his rigging program with a single surface line down the middle. It is 50 feet long and features a five-foot rod and either no weight or a three-ounce sinker.

All of the weights are cigar-shaped sinkers with steel or heavy brass wire running through them. Beyers does not like to use keel sinkers, as some others do, citing problems with them becoming directional at high trolling speeds.

The veteran Beyers, who has 25 years of Great Lakes fishing experience, offers a final bit of advice for muskie fishermen: "Your hooks must be so sharp that when you look at them, you bleed."

Walpole Island Smorgasbord

One of the most unique places to fish in the Great Lakes is Walpole Island. Owned by Canadian Indians, who have prevented its development, Walpole Island has a wild setting. It is hard to believe that you can see loons and ospreys here within sight of ore freighters on the channel and that, 20 miles away, Detroit skyscrapers appear on the horizon like some giant hunching his shoulders.

However, visiting anglers are cautioned that certain rules and regulations apply. For example, they will need both an Ontario fishing license (currently, the non-resident cost is $10-$30, depending upon the time period for which it is purchased) and an Indian permit (currently $15). Both are usually available from personnel at the ferry that whisks visitors across the river from Algonac or at Lakeside Sport Shop in St. Clair Shores.

One August afternoon in 1984, Rodger Sharp and I drifted for walleyes on the Cutoff Channel where it splits from the South Channel. Within an hour, we each picked up three or four walleyes.

Suddenly, silver bass surfaced in the shallows near shore. We moved up quickly and caught a dozen keepers in just 10 minutes, then quit counting as we caught and released fish after fish until the school moved on. Rather than follow them, we went back to work on the walleyes.

Later, while drifting over a weed bed, we switched to light jigs and quickly caught twin 19-inch smallmouths. By then it was sunset, so we slipped into a shallow bay that fronted the channel and immediately got into a school of crappies, catching 14 in the 12-inch range before dark.

We had the whole bay to ourselves. In fact, during the entire afternoon, we saw more freighters than fishing boats.

Paul Wargo
Harrison

Muskies are Mean

When it comes to muskie stories, I could fill a book. Each muskie hunt I have been on would warrant its own story because muskies—especially the big ones that everyone likes to talk about—are solitary fish with singular personalities.

But muskies share some common characteristics, too. For example, whenever you are checking or changing a lure, be prepared for a strike because it happens often and usually close to the boat. And a muskie's strike is exceptionally violent and lightning fast.

Also remember that a muskie is one Great Lakes fish that can really inflict some damage on you. If you bring a muskie aboard your boat, exercise great care in handling him. He will not only have a big set of hooks in his mouth, but he will also have a big set of teeth. His gill plates are razor sharp, too, and he can slice open a finger faster than it takes to talk about it. Those are reasons why I always wear gloves when handling one of the toothy predators.

And keep this in the back of your mind at all times: A muskie has no fear of you or your damn boat. As a matter of fact, he really doesn't like you at all.

Captain Jim Beyers
New Baltimore

Although muskie size in Lake St. Clair has diminished in recent years, the lake continues to serve up plenty of 20-pounders such as this one.

Northern Pike

Currently, Canadian-caught northern pike have no size limit, no season restriction, and a daily limit of six fish. The Michigan season typically opens May 15, and the limit is five pike which must be 20 inches each or longer. Lake St. Clair produces plenty of three- to eight-pound northerns, with occasional brutes going to 18 or 20 pounds. These are nearly always sag-belly females.

The same places that produce largemouth bass—weed beds, the edges of dropoffs, and shallow areas of bulrushes and cattails—produce northerns. Small pike, often called "hammer handles," are especially plentiful in backwater bays. In midsummer, when water is clear, strikes are often visible.

Mepps Lusox and bucktail spinners, Roostertails, and Luhr Jensen Shysters are good spinners to toss at northerns. Rated spoons include Eppinger Dardevles and Cop-E-Cat Imps, Krocodiles, Kush Spoons, and Johnson Silver Minnows. Paul Wargo of Harrison reports top action on 1/2-ounce Silver Minnnows with a four-inch Mann Strawberry Worm or a Mister Twister tail attached. Besides doctoring Silver Minnows in this manner, Wargo also removes the weedguards to make for a better hook set.

Good plugs for shallow water are body baits (Rapalas and Rebels); for deep water, try crankbaits (Shad Raps, Willy's Worms, and Mann's Hacklebacks.) Surface baits (Jitter Bugs, Hula Poppers) often produce in both shallow and deep water. Colors are hardly important to the opportunistic northern pike, which is always looking for a meal.

Besides casting, some northern-pike fishermen troll, and many more stillfish with bobbers and three- to six-inch sucker or shiner minnows. In winter many fishermen go after pike with tip-up and spear. Little and Big Muscamoot bays, Anchor Bay and Mitchell Bay all sport shantytowns of pike fishermen.

Late Ice is Hot Ice

The two men squatting on the ice on Michigan's Little Muscamoot Bay looked like members of a polar expedition. From where I sat in my truck a quarter-mile away, they seemed frozen, as if they were studying the ice for some scientific experiment.

But when I scoped them through 7X binoculars, I could see they weren't motionless at all. Their movements were deft and quick, and the experiment seemed to be how many slab-sided bluegills they could plop into their five-gallon pails. It seemed strange that others were not on the rotting ice that March day to share the action. It also struck me as strange that the men wore chest waders.

Chest waders for ice fishing? This needed checking, so, grabbing an ice drill, fishing rod and plastic bucket, I headed their way. Fifty yards from the silent pair, one raised a finger to his lips as a sign to be quiet, then unhooked a fat bluegill while my eyes bulged. I began to tip-toe across the pock-marked ice until he stopped me with an open hand. There at my feet was the hole he apparently wanted me to see. I squatted to the ice, opened my Copenhagen tin of fish bait, and stabbed a mealworm with a tiny ice fly.

I began to jig in the three-foot-deep water. Minutes passed but nothing happened. I stole a glance over my shoulder; there were my nameless partners still icing 'gills. It was obvious now that, by hunkering over holes, they were trying to block the light. And I could see that they were using only about 18 inches of line. That was because the water was shallow, which also explained why the men wore chest waders, in case the ice gave way.

I copied their fishing technique and soon saw my line kink—the telltale sign of a hog 'gill sucking in the bait. I set the hook and skittered my first late-ice prize over the ice—a pug-nosed bluegill of nine inches.

Six more joined him on the ice before the school moved to parts unknown.

Eldon Thomas
Flint

Panfish

Panfish angling in Lake St. Clair offers some unsung sport. For example, *white (silver) bass* that migrate from Lake Erie in early summer up the Detroit River mix with Lake St. Clair fish to provide good catching opportunities in the channels. One of the best places is on the South Channel side of Gull Island just below the sand bar. Deep water there holds fish throughout the summer. Other hotspots include between Buoys 19 and 21 in the North Channel, the head of the Baltimore Channel leading into Anchor Bay, a mile out in the lake from 11 Mile Road, and at the end of the Middle Channel by the Clinton River Boat Club. Best Canadian waters are both sides of the Thames River and off PikeCreek.

Fishing for white bass is fast sport that is fun. The fish move around in piranha-like schools looking for baitfish, which literally leap from the water when being chased by these efficient little predators. A school of silvers busting minnows on the surface will quicken the heartbeat of the most sluggish fisherman. Some silver-bass seekers cruise the channels while looking for such feeding activity. In addition to leaping minnows, dive-bombing gulls are another clue that a school of baitfish is nearby.

When fishermen find such a school, they cut the outboard engine and drift or use a whisper-quiet electric motor to sneak within casting range. Small spoons, spinners and jigs tossed into the feeding melee will produce strikes, pronto. Other fishermen keep an ultra-light rod rigged with a small jig or spoon ready at hand while they drift for walleyes. When bass appear, it takes only a moment to switch poles and have at them.

Years ago, area charterboat-captains Bob Bingle and Howard Mills developed a lure and a technique for mopping up on white bass. Dubbed Captain Bob's Meat-Hog Agitator, the lure is a big wooden plug containing two lead-head jigs off foot-long dropper lines. When tossed into the middle of a feeding school of silvers, the plug sometimes produces double catches. You can fill a 25-fish limit mighty fast with this method.

Like walleyes, *yellow perch* are well distributed and easy to catch when you can find them. A cluster of fishing boats is a clue as to their whereabouts. If you are unfamiliar with Lake St. Clair, one good way to find these boats is to motor out four miles east of 9-1/2 Mile Road. This will bring you to the St. Clair Lighthouse in the Shipping Channel, and from that point it is an easy matter to find parties of fishing boats after yellow-bellies (or walleyes).

Currently, there is no closed season and no size limit on Lake St. Clair perch. However, anglers must stop at 50 fish, all you will ever want to clean at one sitting. Steady producers in midsummer include the water around Strawberry Island and in the North Channel, where anglers rely on perch spreaders and double hooks containing spot-tail or shiner minnows, worms or small crayfish. During winter, perch fishermen congregate off Metropolitan Beach and in Anchor and Big and Little Muscamoot bays.

They use Russian Hooks or teardrop spoons, tipping both with waxworms, spikes or small minnows.

Crappies, bluegills, and *sunfish* provide good sport in spring and winter and off-and-on action in summer and fall. April through mid-June finds these species spawning in shallow-water areas featuring hard bottom and pencil reeds.

During conditions of early and late ice, Mitchell Bay in Canada and portions of Anchor, Big Muscamoot, and Snyder bays in American waters serve up solid sport. The fish apparently move in and out of these shallow bays in search of food, and sometimes ice men pick them off in water that is only two feet deep. For safety's sake, Joe Zikewich, a panfishing ace from Lake Orion, wears waders when he visits Little and Big Muscamoot bays during such thin-ice conditions.

Zikewich chooses a patch of milky ice to conceal his movements, then drills enough fishing holes to last the day so he doesn't disturb fish later. If the day is bright, Joe will fill his fishing hole with slush and ice chips to block the light, which may frighten fish away. Spring bobbers or sensitive graphite rods and one- or two-pound-test line are needed to detect the soft tap of a feeding bluegill or sunfish sucking in the bait, usually a mousie, waxworm or corn borer. Crappies typically sock lures with more gusto.

Zikewich adds the larvae to tiny ice flies or small teardrop spoons in chartreuse with black dot, orange, hot green or yellow. It is important to keep bait fresh and to cover the barb completely. Ever-so-careful jigging—a few inches at a time—is the fine-tuned presentation that produces hits.

Something for everyone. That's Lake St. Clair.

The lake supports good populations of panfish, including bluegills like this slab. Ice-fishing sport is equally popular with those who fish the open water. —Michigan DNR photo—

Planting Records

Each year several thousand walleye fingerlings, raised in a pond at Selfridge Air National Guard, are released in the Clinton River. These stockings have helped to restore an anadromous run of walleyes to the river from Lake St. Clair.

All other fish in Lake St. Clair are either reproduced naturally or migrate here.

Facilities

Public launch sites are located at Metropolitan Beach, in Selfridge Park at Hall Road, at M-29 in New Baltimore, at Fair Haven off M-19, at the end of Anchor Bay Drive, at Middle Channel Drive and at Algonac. Many marinas that dot the American side of Lake St. Clair also have launch slips.

The DNR maintains a harbor of refuge at Metro Beach Metropark, a short distance up Black Creek at Point Huron. Services include water, electricity, restrooms, shower facilities, and holding-tank pump-out. The telephone number of the dock attendant is (313) 463-4581.

Restaurants and some motels are located all along the American side. The Canadian side of Lake St. Clair is largely undeveloped, and most Americans that fish there cross Lake St. Clair in their boats.

Further Information

Chambers of Commerce:

1. Our Chamber of Commerce, 27602 Jefferson, St. Clair Shores 48081; (313) 777-2741.
2. Central Macomb County Chamber of Commerce, 10 North Avenue, Mt. Clemens 48043; (313) 462-1528.
3. Southeast Michigan Travel & Tourist Associaton, P.O. Box 1590, Troy 48099; (313) 585-8220.

Bait & Tackle Shops:

There are dozens all along the American side. Two of the better equipped and best known are in St. Clair Shores:

1. Lakeview Tackle, 24317 E. Jefferson; (313) 772-5340.
2. Lakeside Tackle, 25110 E. Jefferson; (313) 777-7004.

Both dispense solid fishing news and information.

Charter Fishing:

About three dozen charterboat captains have boats for hire on Lake St. Clair and its connecting rivers. Here are four good ones:

1. Captain Jim Beyers, (muskies) 34846 Jerome, New Baltimore 48047; (313) 725-4020. 27-foot Sportcraft, *Fishin Machine*.
2. Captain Hank Bradley (walleyes, perch, smallmouth bass, pike and muskies), 576 S. Main, Marine City 48039; (313) 765-3353. 27-foot Sportcraft, *American Sportsman*.
3. Captain Bob Bingle, (muskies, walleyes, perch), 8997 Anchor Bay Dr., Fair Haven 48023; (313) 794-3854. 28-foot Inland Seas, *Steelhead*.
4. Captain Al Lesh (muskies, walleyes, bass), 3233 Los Angeles, Warren 48091; (313) 754-7689 or 756-3711. 26-foot Stamas, *Albacore*.

Department of Natural Resources:

Two fisheries biologists work out of District Headquarters at 2455 N. Williams Lake Rd., Pontiac 48054; (313) 666-1500. Also, a DNR biologist works at the Lake St. Clair Fisheries Station, 33135 South River Rd., Mt. Clemens 48045; (313) 465-4771.

Coast Guard:

St. Clair Shores Station, (313) 778-0590.

The Riddle of Lake St. Clair

On the American side of Lake St. Clair throbs a pulsating population of over two million people. There is industrial and residential pressure, marsh draining and filling, Great Lakes ship traffic, channel dredging, and constant pressure from ice-boaters, anglers, sailboaters, duck hunters and trappers. Yet fishing action in the area continues to be some of the hottest in the Great Lakes.

How come?

There are several reasons. One is the geography of this area. Fed by cold Lake Huron via the slick-running St. Clair River, Lake St. Clair remains relatively cool and clean all summer. At the north end, the St. Clair River splits into three main channels and numerous canals that produce dense marshes like those found in southern states. These marshes help to filter the water naturally as it enters the lake. They also provide refuge for young fish.

Also, the lake is shallow, averaging only 12 feet in depth with holes to 20 feet deep. This feature encourages a broad distribution of gamefish as well as excellent food production. This shallow depth and the lake's many tributaries make for successful spawning sites for the variety of gamefish found here.

Other reasons for the sport-fishing surge are cleanup efforts undertaken by industries around the lake and a restocking program of walleyes by a local sportsman's group. Fifteen years ago, for example, high mercury levels caused a ban on walleye fishing, but today the fish are toxin-free and good to eat. (On the other hand, an eating advisory remains in effect for muskies, which are long-lived and which may still contain contaminants.)

Limits on commercial fishing and the lack of an active Indian fishery also contribute to good sport fishing. And natural reproduction is so high that hatchery stocks are not needed.

In fact, fishing is so good that you can't just say to someone, "I'm going fishing on Lake St. Clair." You have to say, "I'm going fishing for walleyes . . . or muskies . . . or perch . . . or crappies . . . or bluegills . . . or northern pike . . . or smallmouth, largemouth or white bass."

Then don't be surprised if you catch some of each.

Tom Huggler
Otisville

Kim Stricker of Howell lands a scrappy smallmouth for Joe Zikewich of Lake Orion. Action occurred in July on Walpole Island.

56
DETROIT RIVER

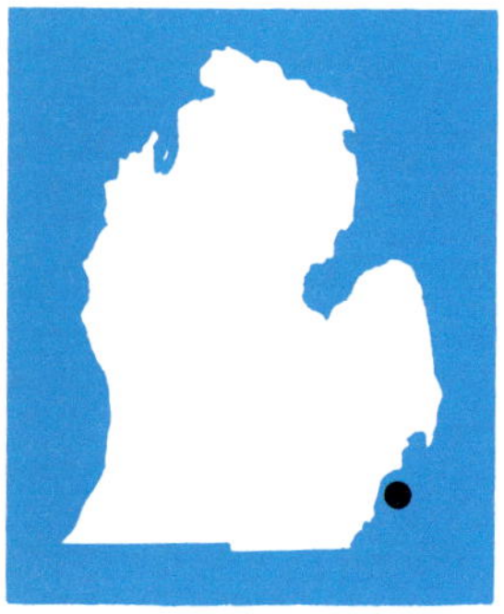

The 1969 mercury contaminant scare that hit Lake St. Clair and its connecting tributaries—the inflowing St. Clair River and the outflowing Detroit River—produced both good news and bad news. The bad news was that both commercial and sport fishermen were barred from catching walleyes. When the river cleaned up, thanks to the enforcement of tough anti-pollution standards, the ban was lifted for sport fishermen. Walleyes are still off-limits to commercial netters, however, and that's the good news.

The Detroit River is once again a good place to fish, and there are plenty of fish for the taking. Detroit River creel census results by the DNR for the period October 1983 through September 1984 showed that anglers caught nearly 200,000 walleyes. They also caught yellow perch (63,000), rock bass (49,000), freshwater drum (87,000), and a huge number of white bass (586,000).

Fishing Schedule

It's hard to believe that in the shadow of Detroit's Ren Cen and other downtown skyscrapers anglers tear up walleyes.

SPRING

Some of the best fishing occurs in *spring* near the head of the river in the Peche Island area and in the nearby Sturgeon Hole on the Canadian side. Big spawning walleyes from six to 12 pounds each are the calling card here. This activity occurs in March and April, and by early May the post-spawn fish drop back downstream to provide good fishing until July.

There is also some spring start-up fishing for big spawners in the Trenton Channel from Elizabeth Park north, at the southern end of Grosse Ile in the Sugar Island region, and in the Livingstone Channel near Bois Blanc Island in Canada.

After the spawning period is over, fishing actually improves, although the walleyes are smaller, averaging perhaps two to 3-1/2 pounds. In late May and early June, when water temperatures rise to between 65 and 70 degrees F., walleyes become active feeders. Best time to fish during this post-spawn period is late afternoon and very early evening when daily highest water temperature is reached.

Good spots include in front of the Ren Cen itself, the horseshoe-shaped cove at the north end of Bois Blanc Island, Pickerel Alley (downbound freighter channel south of Buoy No. 19 in the Livingstone Channel), and the upbound Amherstburg Channel between markers No. 63 and 61.

By early to mid-June, schools of white bass, migrating north from Lake Erie, shut down the walleye action, causing dedicated walleye fishermen to try upriver, where they seek river-channel inclines. Good ones are the Sugar Island and Livingstone channels, the No. 8 Buoy at Peche Island, and in the Garwood Mansion area from the northwest tip of Belle Isle to the mouth.

SUMMER

Good fishing lasts during the heat of *summer*, usually from four to six weeks, or until the walleyes leave the river. Some of the most determined fishermen, dubbed "river rats," follow the 'eyes right into Lake St. Clair, where they catch them from mid to late summer in the vicinity of the Dumping Grounds. Good river fishing returns in September and lasts until nearly Christmas.

First-timers to the Detroit River should bear in mind that the river moves along at a seven-mph clip and that freighter traffic can make for close fishing quarters, especially if you plan to target the channels. Uninitiated anglers, therefore, might want to hire a guide for their first trip or two or until they gain a familiarity with the area.

A guide will also teach them the specialized tactics developed by the river rats and now in vogue among most fishermen. One such expert is Walter Herac, who has been hunting Detroit River walleyes for 25 years. A charterboat captain, Herac pilots his *Mesick Two* nearly every day from April through November. His favorite walleye fishing technique is handlining—trolling with wire line.

This tactic involves the use of automatic trolling reels mounted on boat gunwales near the stern. Seven-strand uncoated 60-pound-test wire line is used along with weights from one to five pounds each. Three lines are attached to a 3-1/2 foot-long steel leader, called a "trolling shank." Size 7 or 9 floating Rapalas, brass-headed locally made wooden plugs called Wobblers, locally made spoons, Pencil Plugs, or minnows are the rated lures and bait.

Handlining with weights of a pound or more is sport? Apparently so, according to Herac. "Strikes feel just like a telegraph wire," he said, "and doubles are not uncommon. You'd be surprised how much fun it is. I've tried all the methods, and, believe me, this one is the best."

Night-time chuggers (using wooden sticks about 18 inches long for rods) pound Pencil Plugs in and out of the bottom with the aid of 50-pound-test cat-gut and pencil-shaped sinkers with pre-drilled holes. At night, when fish may be either high or low, Pencil Plugs are used exclusively. A full-moon, clear-night situation calls for bright colors such as Easter-egg white with blue-and-red spots or bright blue with red spots. Dark nights get darker plugs.

Besides trolling and chugging, driftfishing is also popular with Detroit River walleye anglers. Best conditions occur when the wind blows downstream. (In fact, when the wind blows upstream, it is impossible, at times, to maintain a tight line.) One technique calls for drifting a floating Rapala two to 10 feet below the surface after weighting the plug with an ounce of lead on a dropper line.

For the most part, walleyes are bottom-feeding fish, so most drift fishermen use Junebug Spinners containing about 24 inches of heavy mono with a No. 4 hook and nightcrawler at one end and a clam-shaped blade and several bright beads at the other. A 1/2- to two-ounce sinker is attached via a dropper line from a three-way swivel. The object is to skip the weight along bottom during the drift. Yellow, white, red, green, and gold—alone or in combinations—are the best lure colors.

Bill Deephouse, a DNR fisheries biologist and sport angler from Imlay City, driftfishes for river walleyes with 36-inch leaders and a nightcrawler harness rigged to two gold hooks. Half-ounce bell sinkers dropped a foot below three-way swivels take both bait and lure deep. "Lure colors change daily," Deephouse reports. "Our technique is to start at daybreak, with each angler in the boat using a different color lure until we find the day's pattern." In general, though, fluorescent lures are usually best on cloudy days, bright lures on clear days.

Shore-fishing tactics include tossing X-4, X-5 or F-7 Flatfish weighted with six or seven ounces of lead. Sometimes the lure will skip slowly downstream. Other times the weight will hold it just off bottom, where it will shimmy to attract strikers. Best colors are orange with a black stripe or yellow with a black stripe.

Another good shore-fishing tip is to night-cast lead-headed jigs, such as Mister Twisters, in white, yellow, purple or black color. The few anglers that use this method rely on nine-foot rods and four-pound test to sling lures upstream. Then they retrieve them just off bottom as the lures tumble downstream.

Walleyes, though the main calling card, aren't the only sport in the Detroit River. White bass also provide red-hot action, especially in May and June. The fish enter the Detroit River from Lake Erie, then run its length en route to Lake St. Clair. "We are wall-to-wall with silver (white) bass in May," says Colleen Tennant, who, along with husband Jim, runs the Horse Island Boat Basin in Gibraltar. "We track the fish coming in. Generally, smelt come in April and walleyes by early May. Then white bass are right behind."

Horse Island, the southeast end of Celeron Island, Calf Island, Hickory Island and Sugar Island all experience fantastic white-bass fishing. In fact, the whole southern end of Grosse Ile is good, according to Mrs. Tennant.

"The hottest action lasts about a month," Colleen says. "It's one of our biggest seasons. Fishermen get them off docks or by anchoring their boats just a few feet into the river. Some boats fill a pair of five-gallon buckets by midmorning." (The limit is 25 fish per angler.)

Best fishing is from 6:00 a.m. to 10:00 a.m. Anglers either spincast silver-colored jigs or small spoons or bottomfish shiner minnows on crappie spreaders. Mrs. Tennant advises fishing the four- to five-foot shallows first and then, if fishermen don't register strikes, moving out into 10- to 12-foot depths. She says that the white bass are generally up high and that anglers should fish the edge of the river channel whenever possible.

Most of the other warm-water species in the Detroit River—yellow perch, rock bass, freshwater drum (sheepshead) and smallmouth bass—are incidental catches by walleye and white-bass fishermen using the above lures and tactics.

Some excellent dipnetting for spawning smelt in spring goes largely unnoticed in the Detroit River. Dipping in the shallows offshore from the islands or from docks all along shore produces best from mid-April through mid-May.

The Detroit River hosts Michigan's finest white-bass fishing. This fisherman caught several in early June while fishing from a dock.

The DNR has planted coho salmon for several years in the vicinity of Belle Isle, but to date, fishing success has been marginal. There are several reasons. One is that young salmon released in spring swim downstream to Lake Erie and, en route, must run the gamut of hordes of hungry walleyes that are surging upstream. Due to heavy mortality by these walleyes and other predators, returns of adult salmon from plants in Lake Erie run a disappointing two to five percent. Canadian commercial netters, no doubt, take a toll of the salmon, too.

Another reason for poor returns is due to chemical imprinting problems with young cohos. Currently, the DNR is experimenting with coho releases in the inland waterway on Belle Isle rather than in the river itself. The young salmon are then flushed through the

Whiskey Fishing

When, in 1920, prohibition became national, illicit liquor operators turned to Canada for supplies. Liquor flowed freely across the Detroit River, and Detroit quickly became the funnel through which millions of gallons of bootlegged booze flowed to the Midwest.

As one truck, loaded with illegal whiskey, attempted to cross the frozen Livingstone Channel from Canada in March 1920, it fell through the ice and sank.

When federal agents investigated, they discovered an underwater "graveyard" of many missing cargoes of Canadian liquor. Word of the discovery leaked, and area residents flocked to the site to "angle" through the ice for the liquor. Federal agents had to issue a special order forbidding people from "whiskey fishing."

Detroit River

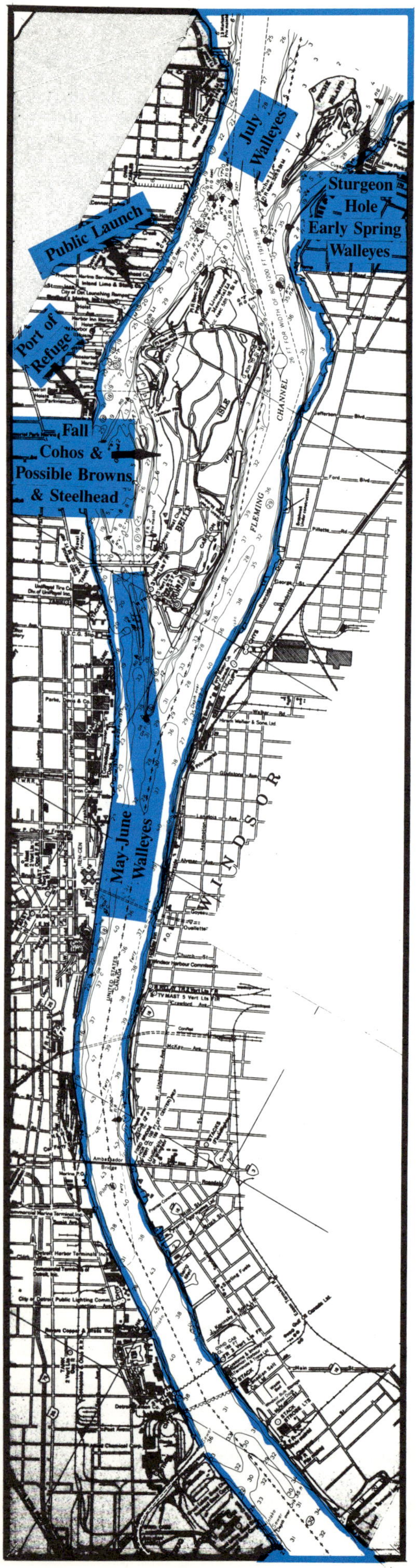

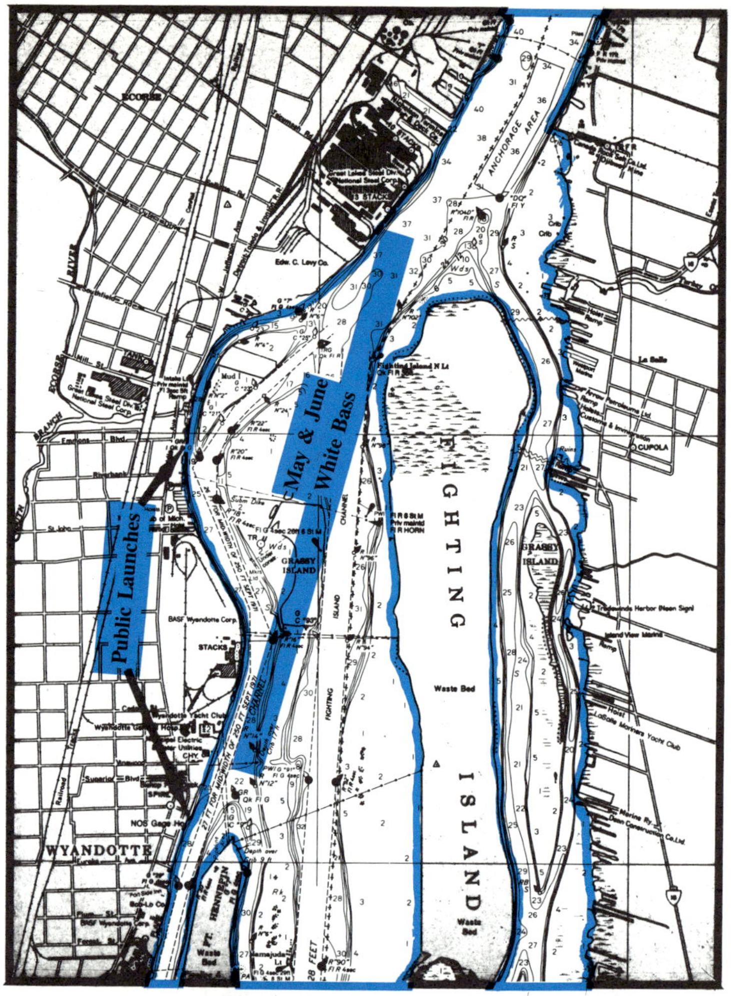

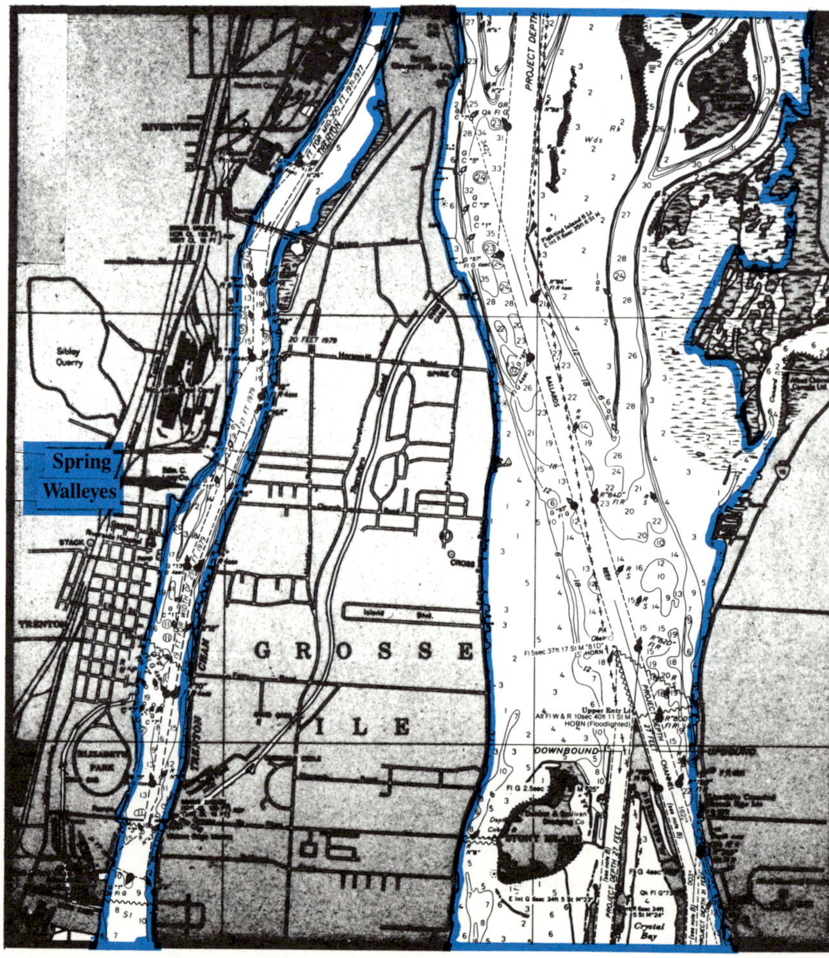

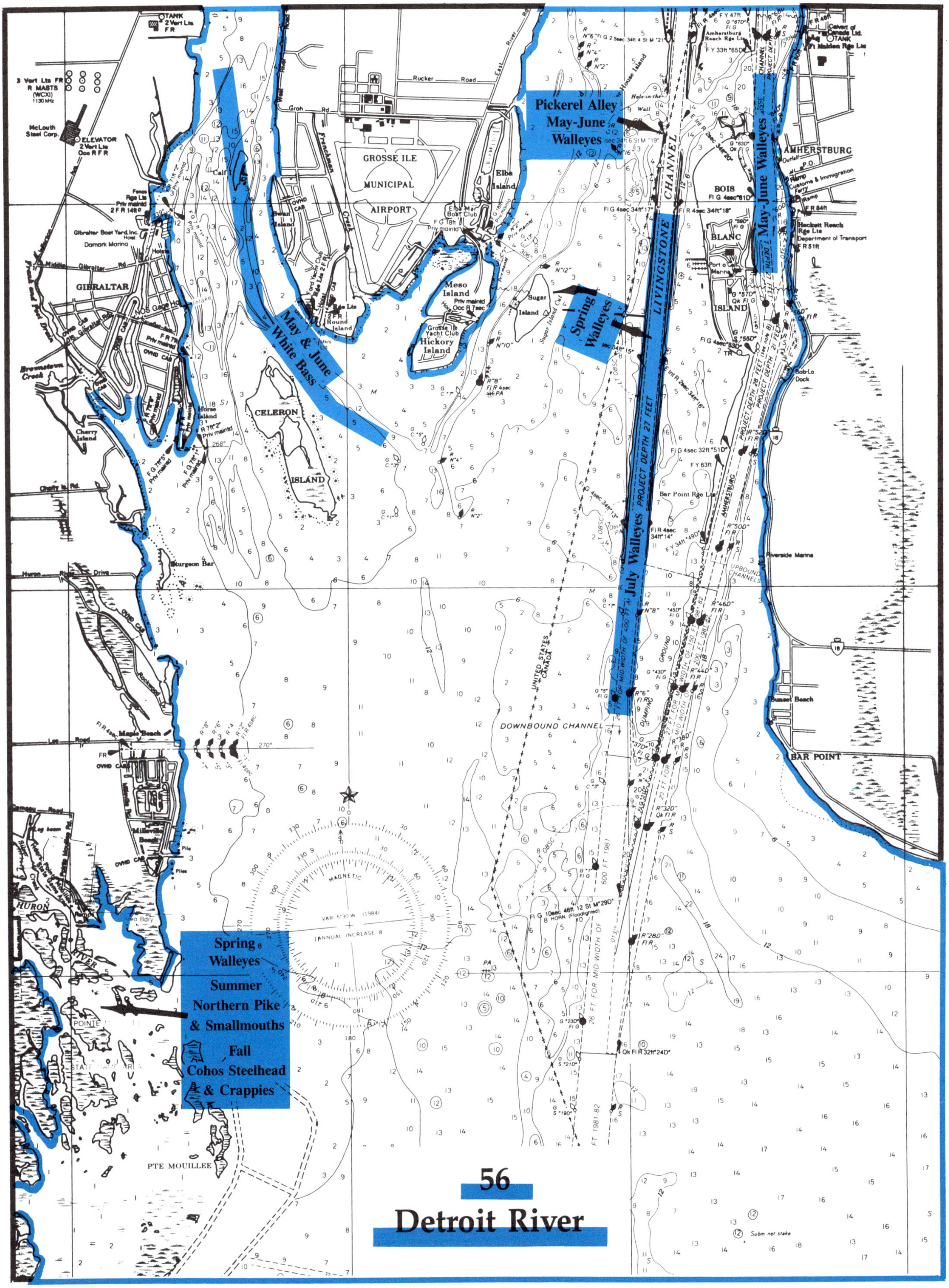
Pickerel Alley
May-June
Walleyes
May & June
White Bass
Spring
Walleyes
July Walleyes
May-June Walleyes
Spring
Walleyes
Summer
Northern Pike
& Smallmouths
Fall
Cohos Steelhead
& Crappies
GROSSE ILE
MUNICIPAL
AIRPORT
GIBRALTAR
CELERON
ISLAND
Sugar
Island
Elba
Island
Meso
Island
Hickory
Island
AMHERSTBURG
BOIS
BLANC
ISLAND
LIVINGSTONE
CHANNEL
DOWNBOUND CHANNEL
UNITED STATES
CANADA
BAR POINT
Sturgeon Bar
PTE MOUILLEE
Brownstown Creek
Cherry Island
Horse Island
Calf I
Swan Island
Maple Beach
Milleville Beach
Riverside Marina
Sunset Beach
Bob-Lo Dock
McLouth Steel Corp.
MAGNETIC
VAR 5°30'W (1984)
ANNUAL INCREASE 8'
56
Detroit River

waterway to the Detroit River with water pumped from the river itself.

To date, a widespread trolling fishery for salmon has not materialized. That is due both to the need for experimentation by fishermen and with releases and to the fact that vegetative debris in the river in fall fouls downrigger lines. Shore fishermen, however, have had the best overall success by casting spoons and stillfishing spawn on the American side of Belle Isle. There is a quarter-mile of public access there that is relatively snag-free. The Belle Isle inland waterway is another good spot, with fishermen reporting coho catches in *fall* and even through the ice in winter. Jigging with spoons or single salmon eggs works best.

There is no bona fide brown- and rainbow-trout fishery in the Detroit River at this time, but Ron Spitler, DNR fisheries biologist for the Pontiac District, is expecting one to develop, especially in the vicinity of Belle Isle. A second place where anglers might look for browns and steelhead—as well as cohos—is the mouth of the Huron River where it flows into Lake Erie near Flat Rock (where the Detroit River also discharges into Lake Erie).

A consistent fall steelhead run lasts into winter and even spring in the Huron River, with fishing opportunities to Flat Rock Dam (a fish ladder will open up a new 14-mile stretch upriver in the future). Cohos show up in fall along with a few naturally produced Chinooks (from releases of hatchery-reared fish years ago). Further, the Huron River hosts good numbers of smallmouth bass, northern pike, black crappies and an anadromous run of walleyes from Lake Erie.

Two Fisherman Types

While traveling through northern Michigan one day, I noticed a church sign with this announcement: *To Find Out What a Man Is Really Like, Watch What He Does on Vacation.* I got to wondering if that's true.

In the case of Great Lakes trout and salmon trollers, I'll bet it is.

You can tell plenty about how a fellow lives and how his mind grinds by noting how he handles tackle and by watching the trolling tactics he puts together.

Two types have evolved on the big lakes. The first is likely to say, "I know that green J-Plug just has to be in this box of junk somewhere." Spoons, plugs, spare cannonballs and assorted gear are scattered helter-skelter, making his boat look like Sanford and Son's backyard. He sends down whatever catches his eye, and there is plenty of stuff to catch his eye. He doesn't care much if his lures run in harness, he rarely jerks them to change offerings, and he spends more time sorting out fouled lines than he does netting fish.

The other type has a mind like a file cabinet and the pick-up habits of an operating-room nurse. There is no chance of stepping on a stray hook or stumbling over a gas can on his boat. Everything is shipshape and he is in control. He is pickier than the Hills Brothers coffee-bean buyer about his trolling speed. For every running lure, he knows what color, what depth, what wobble. He always tows an experimental line, pays close attention to radio traffic, and pops rods to change lures when they don't produce.

The Sanfords and Sons get the odd knock-off and maybe a fish or two for their box. But the Hills Brothers ice limits.

Tom Huggler
Otisville

Planting Records

The jury is out on whether or not the DNR will continue releases of trout and salmon in the Detroit River. If returns improve from current disappointing levels, look for about 200,000 coho smolts and 50,000 rainbow- and brown-trout yearlings to go in the Belle Isle waterway or nearby in the Detroit River each year. The Huron River is slated for 200,000 cohos and 15,000 steelhead yearlings each year through at least 1990.

Warm-water species are naturally reproduced.

Facilities

Public launch sites are located below Windmill Pointe, at the South Branch of the Ecorse River, off Eureka Avenue in Wyandotte, and at the Pointe Mouillee State Game Area. For boaters, Memorial Park Marina, on E. Jefferson Avenue across from Belle Isle, has transient accommodations, water, electricity, restrooms, shower facilities, laundry and a holding-tank pump-out station. Telephone number of the dock attendant is (313) 267-7143.

The Lake Erie Metropark, on Lee Rd. in Rockwood, features transient accommodations, water, electricity, restrooms, a pump-out service and a dock attendant. The telephone number is (313) 379-9351.

Further Information

Chambers of Commerce:

1. Greater Detroit Chamber of Commerce, 150 Michigan Ave., Detroit 48226; (313) 964-4000.
2. Southeast Michigan Travel & Tourist Association, P.O. Box 1590, Troy 48099; (313) 585-8220.

Bait & Tackle Shops:

1. Frypan Bait & Tackle, 4464 W. Jefferson, Ecorse 48229; (313) 383-3011.
2. Zubok's Tackle Shack & Ski Shop, 22985 VanBorn Rd., Taylor 48180; (313) 295-2230.
3. Huron River Sport Center, 26425 Atwater, Flat Rock 48134; (313) 782-3633.
4. Horse Island Boat Basin, 30305 Island Dr., Gibralter 48173; (313) 676-9504.

Charter Fishing:

1. Captain Walter Herac, Fish-N-Fun Charter Service, P.O. Box 15028, Detroit 48215; (313) 882-3018. 26-foot Penn Yan, *Mesick II*.
2. Captain Ed Snella, 19901 E. Ten Mile Rd., St. Clair Shores 48081; (313) 886-8181. 30-foot Trojan, *Knot Judy*.
3. Captain Al Lesh, 3233 Los Angeles, Warren 48091; (313) 754-7689 or 756-3711. 26-foot Stamas, *Albacore*.
4. Captain Joe Bodrie, 18660 Valade St., Riverview 48192; (313) 283-1843. 39-foot boat, *The Clipper*.

Department of Natural Resources:

Two fisheries biologists work out of District Headquarters at 2455 N. Williams Lake Rd., Pontiac 48054; (313) 666-1500.

Coast Guard:

Belle Isle Station, (313) 331-3110.

57 WESTERN LAKE ERIE

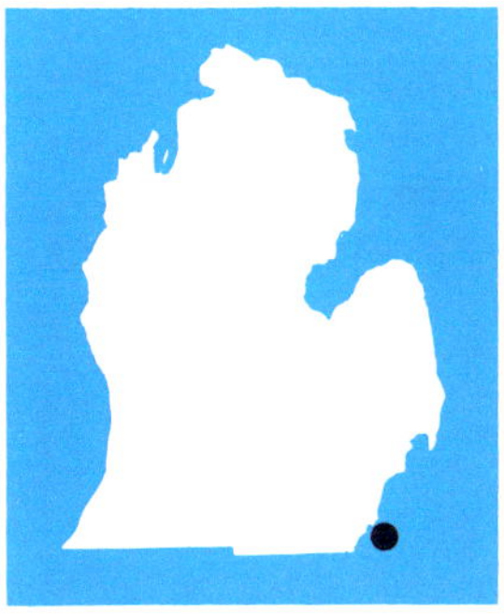

If you fish, especially for walleyes, you have likely heard about Lake Erie's rebirth. But if you have never fished here, you will probably scoff at the fishing tales. Good fishing, sure, but action so fast that your arms tire and your wrists ache from cranking up fish? Walleyes so plentiful that anglers toss back anything under two pounds? Fish so hungry that a gang of eight anglers with 20-dozen nightcrawlers have been known to run out of bait in a single outing?

Come on now.

How can a body of water, written off 10 years ago as the American Dead Sea, produce fishing so fantastic? Here is a lake where raw sewage from Cleveland, Toledo, Detroit, Windsor and other cities ran unchecked for decades. For years, factories vomited mercury and other poisons, most of which settled out as sludge to upset the food chain. Farmers applied heavy doses of fertilizer to their land and unwittingly added dangerous levels of phosphates via runoff to the lake.

These combined burdens caused Erie's base water temperature to rise 2.0 degrees F. between 1920 and 1970. A seemingly permanent 800-square-mile patch of algae formed in the Western Basin. People joked about lighting fires on the scum-slick surface. Beaches were closed. Michigan, Ohio and Ontario banned sport and commercial fishing for walleyes, which were laced with mercury beyond tolerance levels.

Former Secretary of the Interior Stewart Udall best summed up the catastrophe when he said that Lake Erie was a "patient assassin, which chokes its victims ever so slowly and silently."

Then, tough state and federal anti-pollution laws and expensive sewage-treatment plants provided a turning point. Some incredible walleye hatches soon followed. Bans on commercial netting in Ohio and Michigan, put into effect 15 years ago, are on the books yet today. In a modern-day miracle, Lake Erie has come back from the dead, and some believe the best fishing is yet to come.

Fishing Schedule

SPRING

Although good fishing occurs year-round in several locations, the best walleye action comes in the Western Basin (west of an imaginary line from Sandusky, Ohio, to Point Pelee, Ontario) in Ohio and Michigan waters in *spring*. Spawning occurs there in April, with an estimated 10 percent of the adult fish entering either the Maumee or Sandusky River. Most fish, however, spawn offshore in the rock and rubble of shallow-water reefs.

Post-spawn walleyes generally move slowly in a clockwise direction. Many Maumee River fish surge into Michigan waters along the beach to the Detroit River. Large numbers are likely to continue up to Lake St. Clair, through the St. Clair River, and even into lower Saginaw Bay. Other masses migrate to the West Sister Island area (in Ohio waters) and eventually move on to Pelee and the Hen and Chicken islands (in Ontario waters).

Tagging research has shown, however, that Western Basin walleyes mix freely. For example, many Ontario fall-caught fish are Sandusky River, Ohio, post-spawn walleyes that moved north through Kelleys Island, the Bass Islands, Gull Island Shoal and Middle Island. Hotspots develop throughout Ohio and Michigan waters of the Western Basin.

Usually the best fishing occurs in late May and throughout June. Then, Michigan anglers (who are currently allowed to keep 10 walleyes each, provided they are each 13 inches or longer) key at the stone pile off Point Mouillee, near Toledo Beach, off Stony Point on the north end of Brest Bay, off the cooling towers of the Fermi nuclear generating plant, near the No. 1 Buoy off River Raisin, and four miles east of the Consumers Power Company stacks to the old Dumping Grounds.

Ohio anglers cluster between Buoys 5 and 6 in the Toledo Shipping Channel, near the Toledo water-intake station (locally called the Crib), a half-mile north and a half-mile southwest of West Sister Island, at Niagara and Crane reefs, in shoal waters of the South Passage off Catawba Point, off Marblehead Peninsula, off Port Clinton, and off Camp Perry a bit west of Sandusky.

Top fishing occurs where the water temperature is at or near 60 degrees F. By late June, the spring thermocline usually dissolves,

Lake Erie

Length—241 miles

Width—57 miles

Length of coastline (including Canada and islands)—871 miles

Total water surface—9,910 square miles

U.S. water surface—4,980 square miles

Total land drainage basin—22,700 square miles

U.S. drainage—18,000 square miles

Maximum depth—210 feet

Average depth—62 feet

Volume of water—116 cubic miles

Captain Clay Garrett shows nice-sized walleye he caught off Bolles Harbor on a downrigger.

and water temperature then will be the same, top to bottom. Anglers can still take limit catches at 70 and 75 degrees F., especially both early and late in the day, but when temperatures crowd 80 degrees, fishing typically falls off.

If you are unfamiliar with Lake Erie, be aware that the lake is shallow (deepest spots in the Western Basin are 35 feet) and therefore subject to big waves that can develop quickly when the wind shifts direction and blows hard. Unless you have a large, seaworthy boat, fish close to shore or hire a guide.

Many fishermen, especially the charterboat captains, move with the walleyes north and east as *summer* progresses. But warm-weather fish can still be found in the places that were so productive in spring. One good place to look for is a hard-bottomed reef. Reefs not only produce emerging insects and zooplankton—forage for gizzard shad and lake emerald shiners, upon which walleyes thrive—but they also help to produce more oxygen than mud bottoms. Another productive warm-weather site is rocky shoreline, such as in Ohio's Locust Point area. Summer wave action aerates the water at such locations, and it is believed walleyes then move into the shallows for the increased oxygen.

Anglers can get a clue to bottom composition in Lake Erie by dragging a heavy sinker or spoon along the bottom, by using sensitive sonar graphs, or by looking at the walleyes they catch. Bronze-sided fish are most often taken over hard bottoms. Blue/gray fish that appear somewhat washed-out are usually caught over mud or clay bottoms.

After a two- to four-week slack period in July, action usually picks up again by mid-August, when cool nights drive down water temperatures. Late in the *fall* (October and November), anglers that tough it can catch some big fish, and walleyes are available to ice anglers whenever *winter* fishing conditions are safe.

Most of the walleyes caught during the open-water season are either sub-legal or barely legal in size, and therefore anglers will have to sort fish to build a respectable catch of two- to eight-pounders. Clay Garrett, a charterboat captain running out of Bolles Harbor, keeps records of the number of walleyes he coolers. Over a recent three-year period, 34 trips the first year yielded 919 keeper fish, 42 trips the next season produced 1,188 fish, and in the following year, 45 outings netted 1,216 fish. Plus, Garrett and his customers threw back literally thousands. So do the other guides and most of the sport fishermen who know how to catch walleyes.

As plentiful as Lake Erie walleyes are, anglers must use proved methods to take them. In March they toss spinners and spinner/bead combinations tipped with nightcrawlers or minnows to river-spawning walleyes. In spring on the open lake, anglers bottomfish with drifter rigs and two-inch shiners. White jigs sweetened with minnows or a piece of crawler are hot combinations, too.

From May through November, anglers choose from among three tactics. The most popular is the "count-down" method, which was originated and perfected by Lake Erie fishermen. The theory behind counting down is this: Off-feed fish lie inactive along bottom, but feeding walleyes suspend at varying depths, according to the locations of gizzard shad, spot-tails and lake emerald shiners, on which they feed.

Downriggers for Walleyes?

Captain Clay Garrett was busy freeing my daughter Jenny's two-pound walleye from the net when the fourth rod released. He frantically looked around for someone to grab it, but partner Ken Foyder and I were already hooked into small scrappers. Jenny's friend Lesa was the only angler left with empty hands. She quickly grabbed the fishing rod, pulled it clear of its holder, and laced into a walleye that had every intention of heading for Ontario. The drag on Lesa's baitcasting reel started talking back, and the fish rooted deep.

"That's a good fish," Garrett said, noting the bend in the seven-foot rod. "Four, maybe five pounds."

Foyder and I easily swung our slim walleyes aboard without the net. They were only the size of jumbo perch—14 inches or so—and were quickly returned. Then we watched Captain Garrett swipe his net into Lake Erie and come up with a prize four-pound walleye for Lesa.

But there was no time to admire her fish, the best of the trip so far. Clay's wife, Lucille, who was steering the boat, suddenly announced a topside walleye on rod No. 9. Foyder sprang for it while I began helping our overworked skipper reset the four spent rods and two downrigger hookups.

***Downriggers* for *walleyes*? That sounds about as an unlikely a combination as peanut butter and pickles on whole-wheat toast. Sooner or later, though, it had to happen: Those Great Lakes trolling tactics, so incredibly successful on trout and salmon, just had to be used on other species.**

And the reason that downriggers work so well in western Lake Erie is because walleyes, when feeding on baitfish, suspend between top and bottom. So the depth where they are found, hour to hour and day to day, depends upon where the baitfish are.

Downriggers allow controlled-depth fishing and—along with another tactic called "counting down" (see above)—account for probably 90 percent of the walleyes caught here.

Tom Huggler
Otisville

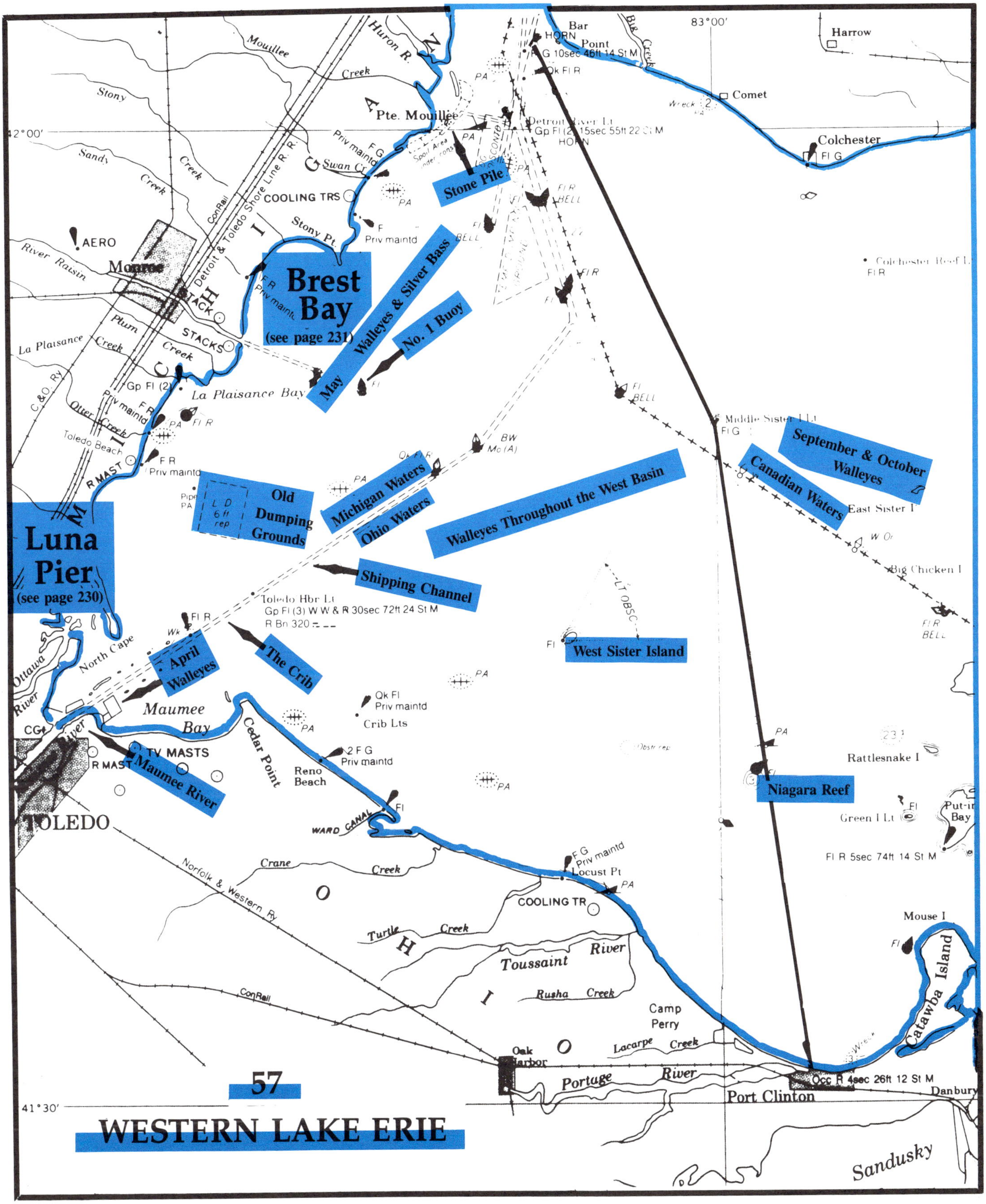

57
WESTERN LAKE ERIE

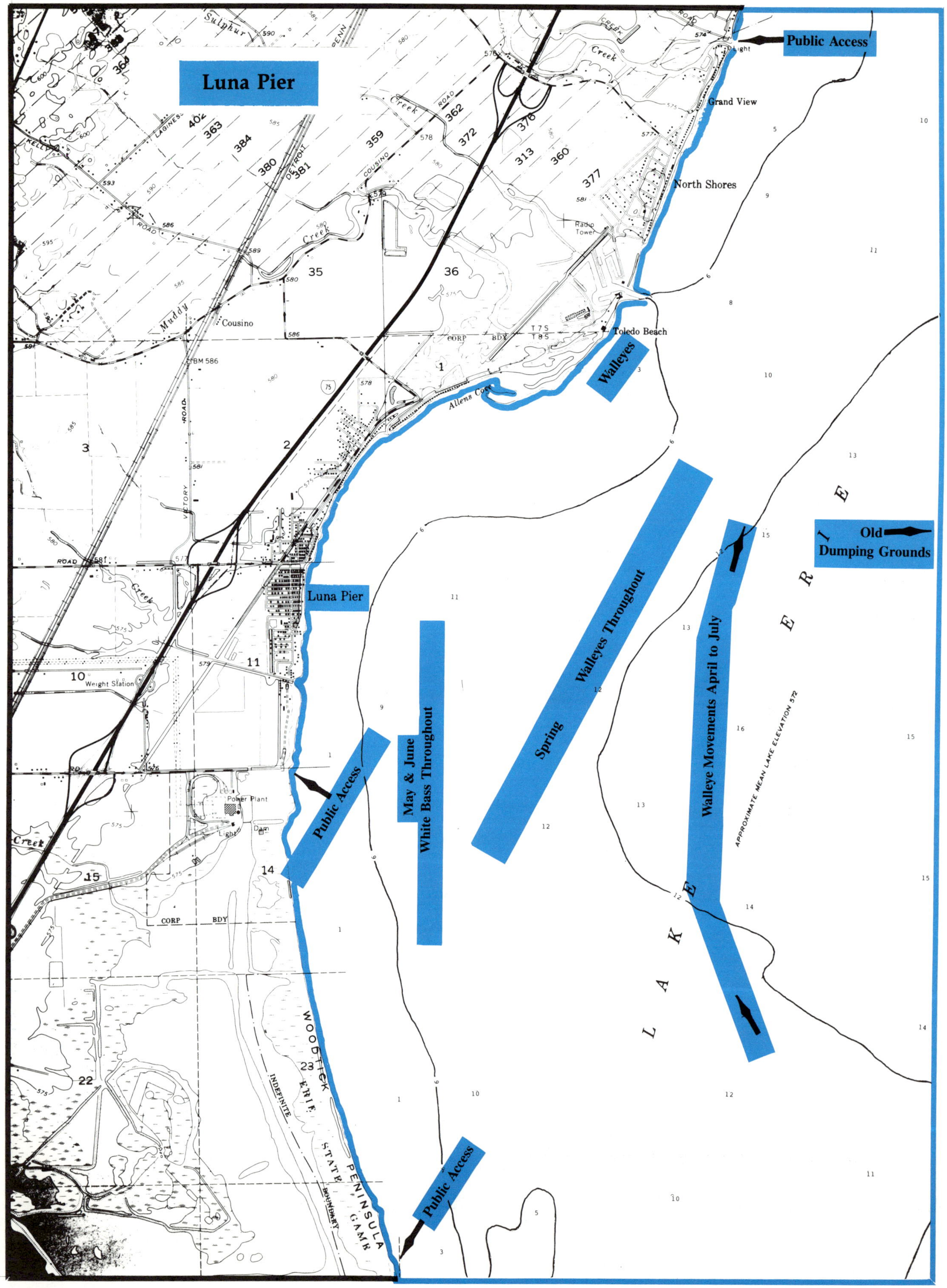

Luna Pier
Public Access
Grand View
North Shores
Radio Tower
Toledo Beach
Walleyes
Allens Cove
Cousino
Luna Pier
Weight Station
Power Plant
Dam
Light
Public Access
May & June White Bass Throughout
Spring Walleyes Throughout
Walleye Movements April to July
Old Dumping Grounds
LAKE ERIE
APPROXIMATE MEAN LAKE ELEVATION 572
WOODTICK PENINSULA
ERIE STATE GAME
INDEFINITE BOUNDARY
Public Access

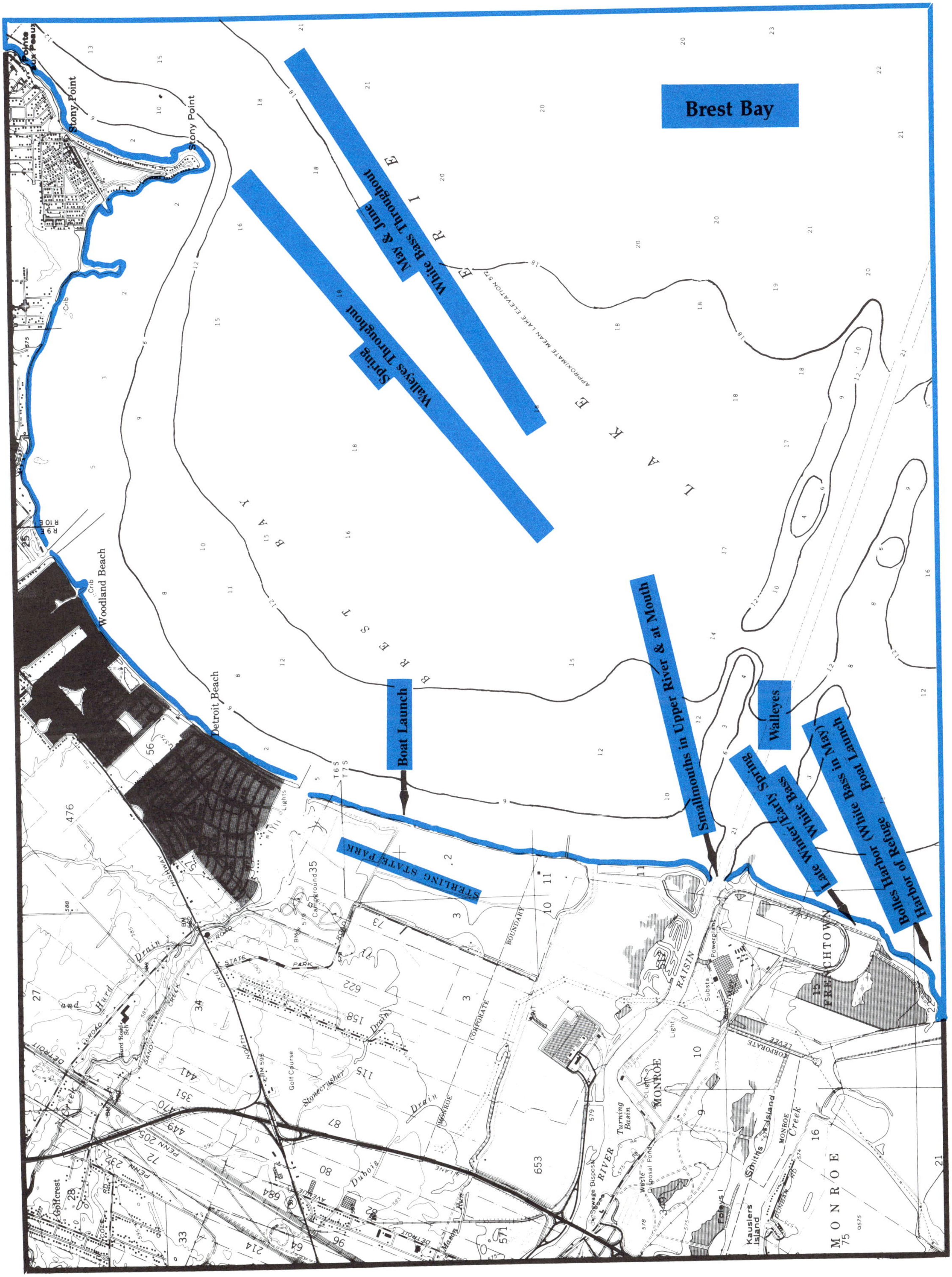
Brest Bay
White Bass Throughout
May & June
Walleyes Throughout
Spring
Boat Launch
Smallmouths in Upper River & at Mouth
Walleyes
Late Winter/Early Spring
White Bass
Bolles Harbor (White Bass in May)
Boat Launch
Harbor of Refuge
STERLING STATE PARK
L A K E E R I E
B R E S T B A Y
Stony Point
Woodland Beach
Detroit Beach
RAISIN RIVER
MONROE
FRENCHTOWN

Western Lake Erie serves up fast action for white bass in May and June.

LAKE ERIE (cont.)

The object, then, is to find the feeding walleyes. Count-down anglers thread the ends of whole nightcrawlers on the hooks of 1/2- or 5/8-ounce weight-forward spinners such as Erie Dearies, Gold Nuggets, Silver Nuggets, Paul Bunyans, Walleye Skids, Lindy's Tom's Lures, West Sister Twisters, Parrish Lures, and Mepps Lusox. Rated colors include silver, gold, chartreuse, red and white, hot green, and yellow. The lure is cast and allowed to sink on a slack line. To locate the depths of feeding walleyes, the fisherman counts *1001, 1002, 1003*, and so forth, or watches the second hand sweep on a wristwatch. You can figure about one foot of drop per second. Counting down requires concentration—you must *feel* the soft strike and gentle lift of a feeding walleye, especially as the line straightens on a wind-pushed sweep. Pointing the rod at a missed strike often results in a hooked walleye, as fish will sock lures a second and even a third time. Replace all nipped nightcrawlers with fresh ones. And remember the depth at which each of the strikes occurs.

In the fall, due to shallow-water conditions, count-down anglers switch to lighter lines (down to two-pound test) and 3/8-ounce lures. Fall walleyes often come off reefs only three or four feet below the surface. Parrish Lures and Walleye Skids in chartreuse, and Gold or Silver Nuggets are hot lures then.

Driftfishing or slow trolling with big-lipped crankbaits or bottom-bouncing with crawler or minnow rigs are other top Lake Erie tactics. Lindy Rigs and homemade nightcrawler harnesses with double-hooked bead/blade combinations are popular. A Bait-Walker or one- or two-ounce pencil sinker on a dropper line below a three-way swivel will keep bait just off bottom. Good colors include orange, green, chartreuse, red, and yellow. Some drift fishermen, like Gail Van Alstine of Drayton Plains, like to pull lures and crawlers along bottom. A hot Lake Erie combination for Gail has been homemade nightcrawler harnesses featuring Colorado blades painted white with a pink dot in the middle.

Trout and salmon trolling tactics using downriggers and planer boards are another method for taking Lake Erie walleyes. Anglers run up to 15 lines, at varying depths, at 2.0-2.5 mph. Best plug choices include Hot 'N Tots, Mann Razorbacks, Willy's Worms, Wee Warts, Hot Shots, Natural Ikes, Bug Plugs and Countdown Rapalas. Good spoons are Evil Eyes, Chargers, Northport Nailers, Krocodiles, and Flutter Chucks. Smaller lures work best.

Captain Garrett rigs trolling lines aboard his charterboat, the *Lucy J*, this way: two stern-end downriggers that are stacked (four rods), two out-downs, two outriggers, and two planer boards that are triple-stacked (six rods), for a total of 14 rods. The arrangement is legal if he has seven fishermen aboard.

Garrett uses a long ski-shaped planer board made by the Wille Company. Multiple coilspring-shaped releases that slide up and down the tether rope allow up to four stacked lines per board. He sets his first line close to the board and at a distance of 40 feet behind it. The second line is spotted 10 feet closer to the boat and run back about 25 feet. The third rig is 10 feet closer again and trails by about 15 feet. Pressure against the trolled lures and the amounts of line released dictate how far down the tether rope the release rings will slide. About half of Garrett's catch comes off these planer boards.

Depending upon lure action, depth, and whether or not walleyes are short-striking (slapping at lures without getting hooked), Garrett will spot his downrigger-trolled lures 10-40 feet behind the cannonballs. He uses adjustable Walker Releases and sets his lures lightly because many of the smaller walleyes have a problem tripping tightly set releases. In fact, that is the biggest criticism of this sport, and there is some justification to it. Thin rubber bands secured with a half hitch to downrigger cable and monofilament may produce quicker releases, too.

Garrett experiments a great deal with lure colors, discarding unproductive choices every half-hour or so. He first tests all hardware alongside the boat to see if they work in sync with those already set.

Besides walleyes, white (silver) bass provide plenty of fast action for Western Basin anglers. The silvers spawn in the rivers during the month of May and, by early June, are usually prowling western Lake Erie reefs in schools. Many apparently leave Lake Erie to run up the Detroit River **(56)** as far as Lake St. Clair **(55)**, where they spend the summer.

Michigan action gears up in late winter off the warm-water discharge from the Edison plant in Monroe. White bass there average one to 1-1/2 pounds. Russ Matthews, who runs a bait shop at nearby Bolles Harbor, says hardy anglers have good success casting and retrieving small spoons or weighted flies at this time. Make a fast retrieve close to the surface for slashing strikes, he advises. Small Frizz Lures (silver spoons tipped with white feathers), silver-colored Shad King spoons, and chartreuse or white Doll Flies are rated hardware to try.

Matthews says the bass come into Bolles Harbor to spawn from about May 9 until Memorial Day. "Anglers use the same cast-and-retrieve method," Matthews says. "Gull activity (birds diving for fish) are a real giveaway to white-bass whereabouts at this time."

Fishing is excellent from Woodtick Peninsula north to Stony Point. White bass are available there all summer long, but anglers then must stillfish deep with minnows pinned to No. 2 or No. 4 hooks and crappie spreaders.

Throughout the long open-water season, fishermen catch a few smallmouth bass (the River Raisin, incidentally, produces good fishing) and plenty of yellow perch, white perch, and freshwater drum (sheepshead). In spring they also catch a few steelhead and jack cohos. Winter fishing activities are mostly for yellow perch and walleyes.

In fall, the Huron River hosts a run of coho salmon, plus steelhead show up in fall, winter and spring. The Huron also contains smallmouths, northern pike, crappies and walleyes. **(See 56, Detroit River, for additional maps and details)**

Planting Records

Warm-water species in Lake Erie are all naturally reproduced. The Huron River, at Flat Rock, has received annual stockings of cohos and steelhead for many years and is slated to get 200,000 coho smolts and 15,000 steelhead yearlings each spring through 1990.

Facilities

The state of Michigan maintains boat launches at Bolles Harbor on La Plaisance Road, Sterling State Park at Monroe, and the Pointe Mouillee State Game Area south of Rockwood. Public access is also provided at Otter Creek (a half-mile south of the state rest stop between Bolles Harbor and Toledo Beach), at the end of Erie Road, and in the Erie State Game Area.

State-run mooring facilities for boaters are located at Bolles Harbor. Services include gasoline, pay telephone, water, electricity, restrooms and haul-out facilities. Transient accommodations are available at nearby commercial marinas. Lake Erie Metropark Marina at Rockwood also has transient accommodations plus water, electricity, restrooms, pump-out service and a dock attendant. The telephone number is (313) 379-9351.

Further Information

Chambers of Commerce:

1. Monroe County Chamber of Commerce, 22 W. Second St., Monroe 48161; (313) 242-3366.
2. Southeast Michigan Travel & Tourist Association, P.O. Box 1590, Troy 48099; (313) 585-8220.

Bait & Tackle Shops:

1. Lake Erie Tackle Shop, 1816 N. Dixie Hwy., Monroe 48161; (313) 289-2750.
2. Matthews Bait, 6955 La Plaisance Rd. (Bolles Harbor), Monroe 48161; (313) 242-0666.
3. Mariner's Market, 1509 E. Front, Monroe 48161; (313) 241-3792.
4. Brest Bay Marina, 4088 Brest Rd., Newport 48166; (313) 289-1234.
5. Fox's Sporting Goods, 4990 N. Dixie Hwy., Newport 48166; (313) 289-1389.

Charter Fishing:

About 50 guides work out of Lake Erie's Western Basin in Michigan waters alone. Here are several excellent choices:

1. Captain Clay Garrett, 4410 Simpson Rd., Owosso 48867; (517) 723-6071. 25-foot Tiara, *Lucy J.*.
2. Captain George Satterfield, 2048 E. Hurd, Monroe 48161; (313) 289-1505. 25-foot Wellcraft, *Miss Val Holly*.
3. Captain Jim Beyers, 34846 Jerome, New Baltimore 48047; (313) 725-4020. 27-foot Sportcraft, *Fishin Machine*.
4. Captain John King, 17181 Beech-Daly, Redford 48240; (313) 255-7877. 22-foot Bayliner, *King Fish*.
5. Captain Jon Nissen (Ohio waters only), E-Z Ketch Charter Service, 113 Amherst Dr., Toledo OH 43614; (419) 836-7931. 27-foot Sportcraft, *E-Z Ketch*.

Department of Natural Resources:

Western Lake Erie sport fisheries are supervised by Michigan DNR biologists from the Jackson and Pontiac district offices. The addresses and phone numbers are: Jackson DNR District Office, 3335 Lansing Ave., Jackson 49202 (517-784-3188) and Pontiac District Office, 2455 N. Williams Lake Rd., Pontiac 48504 (313-666-1500).

Coast Guard:

Toledo Station at Bayview Park, Ohio, (419) 259-6447 or 259-6448.

World's Best Walleye Fishing?

I had hit upon one of those funny dry spells. You know the type—everybody is catching fish but you. I had been getting socked on the average of every third cast but now had somehow lost the "touch." Fifteen, 20, 30 minutes of arm-waving and cranking. Nothing. I must have had the cleanest nightcrawler in western Lake Erie.

So I did what other walleye anglers do when they lose the touch. I began to watch my partners on Captain Jon Nissen's 27-foot charterboat. No problem with their luck. George Richey was unhooking a three-pounder for his son, Casey. Butch Van Amburg's rod was bowed into a scrapper. Larry Winans was rebaiting while first-mate Mike Moriarty washed the rubber net that Butch was hollering for.

The only other guy who wasn't into walleye-catching action was Eldon Thomas. I watched as he cast hard across the corner of the boat. A muggy breeze put a light chop across Erie's gray face on this stormy day and pushed us leisurely along. Eldon's weight-forward spinner, with a nightcrawler sailing behind, arched high. It disappeared with a "plop" 40 yards away, and Eldon closed the bail on his open-face reel but did not spool in the slack. Instead, he let the drifting boat draw tight the bow in his line.

Pointing his rod at the straightening mono, like a worm bass fisherman does, Eldon suddenly set the hook.

"Bingo!" he shouted. "Here's a good one."

"What count?" Captain Jon asked.

"Dunno," Eldon answered. "Didn't count, but I'd say a five."

While his four-pound 'eye thrashed topwater, Eldon explained how the walleyes now seemed to be just a half-dozen feet below the surface.

"Cast off the boat corner and follow your line as it sweeps straight," he suggested. "You'll get a hit every time."

He was right, as I discovered on my second or third cast. I refound my "touch" just in time, too, because 20 minutes later Nissen punched No. 48 on his fish counter and announced, "That's it, boys. Six limits in the box. Any more, no matter how big, go back in the lake."

Forty-eight walleyes to six pounds each in two hours of fishing. Such was my introduction to Lake Erie fishing a couple of years ago. I had heard all the hype about how the Western Basin (in Michigan and Ohio waters) alone is home to over 25 million legal-sized walleyes. I even read somewhere that Lake Erie now has the best walleye fishing in the world.

You want to know the truth? I believe it.

Scott Kincaid
Flint

—Photo by Steve Griffin—

UPPER PENINSULA

Note: Maps included with each chapter are not to be used for navigational purposes.

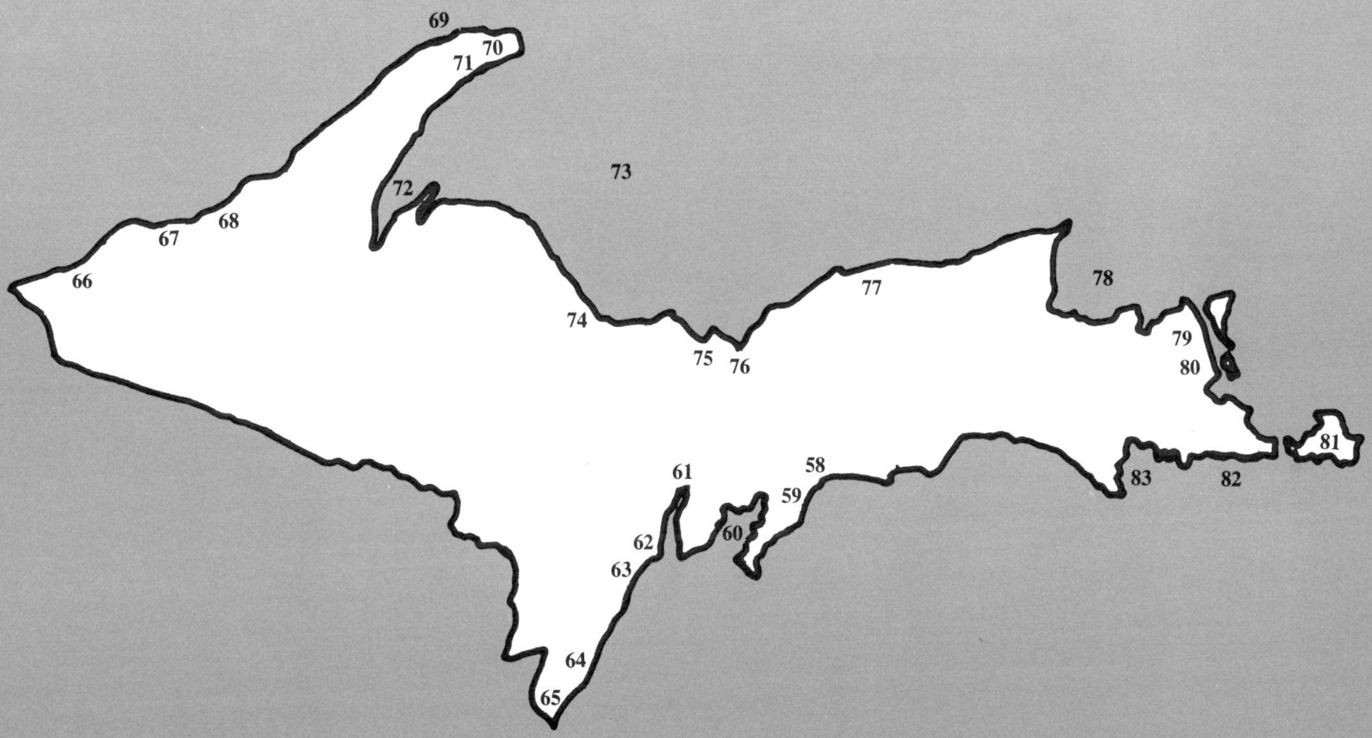

58
MANISTIQUE

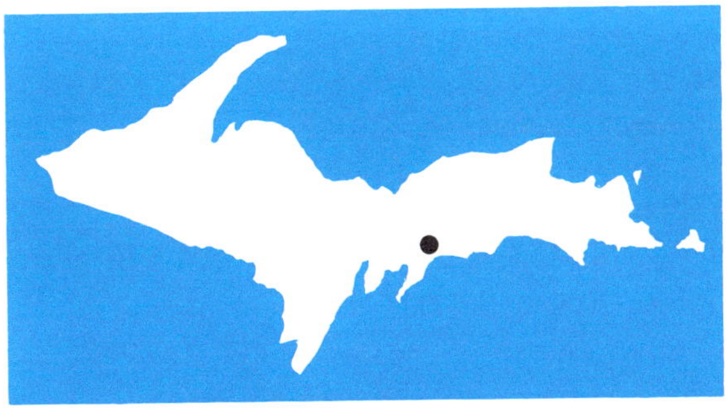

Manistique, a small city of about 4,500 people, has the only decent harbor, boat launch, and visitors' accommodations in a 140-mile stretch along the top of Lake Michigan between St. Ignace and Escanaba (62). The Manistique area offers fair to excellent sport for trout, salmon and a variety of warm-water species to trollers, pier or shore surf fishermen, and river anglers. Another attraction is the lack of competition from other anglers, especially in fall.

Fishing Schedule

SPRING

Spring fishing activity begins at ice-out in the Manistique River for steelhead, both state-planted and naturally reproduced fish. Steelheaders key along gravel runs at the paper-company flume, where they fish yarn flies in the fast water. Chartreuse, yellow, and red are hot colors. Wigglers, fresh steelhead spawn, single salmon eggs, and nightcrawlers are other productive baits. Yarn flies and bright-colored river flies are good artificials.

Pier fishermen catch a few steelies, too, along with an occasional brown trout and Chinook salmon. Besides the natural baits mentioned, spoons or spinners cast into the river or lake then briskly retrieved are also reported to be productive lures.

SUMMER

Walleyes also use the river in spring and can be caught from the May 15 opener well into *summer* by stillfishing or driftfishing nightcrawlers in the Black Bass Hole below the US-2 Bridge. Another good spot is in the fast water where channels come together to form the main river.

Summer angling prospects include smallmouth bass, northern pike and brown trout, all of which move in and out of the river from Lake Michigan. For smallmouths and browns, target the previously mentioned fast water and spincast small Mepps spinners or flip nightcrawlers pinned to small jigs (yellow, white or black). Northerns will hit any color of spoon or spinnerbait run through the holes. Manistique Harbor pike fishermen, who either troll spoons or bobber-fish with five-inch minnows, report catching northerns to 10 pounds each.

There are some summer yellow-perch fishing opportunities from the pier and from boats in the harbor area. Worms or minnows are preferred baits, although success is usually spotty, which may be due to Indian gillnetting in the region.

A few offshore salmon trollers target the 80- to 90-foot bank about three miles out from the harbor. There, they seek 54- to 58-degree-F. water close to bottom. There are no special lures or downrigger trolling tactics to report at this writing, as this is a developing fishery.

Thermal upwellings, caused by high winds and storms that run over the lake, sometimes bring colder water close to shore. Trout and salmon follow, and pier fishermen get fast action for a day or two. For example, in mid-July, 1985, a large school of kings suddenly showed up at Manistique. Pier anglers, standing shoulder to shoulder, caught about 200 fish by casting spoons and plugs.

FALL

Fall fishing is the best season of all for several reasons. There is an excellent run of channel catfish to eight pounds each, both in the Manistique River and the Millecoquins River further east. Some anglers add a river chain to their small boats or canoes, then driftfish whole nightcrawlers along bottom. Fishing for northerns and smallmouths remains steady, plus in October many

Summer runs of Chinook salmon occur at Manistique when thermal upwellings bring cold water to shore.

walleyes drop back from Indian Lake into the lower river and Lake Michigan. Hordes of pink salmon show up from early to late September, especially in odd-numbered years (1987, 1989, etc.) and can be caught on small spinners or yarn flies. Chinooks enter the river from late August until late September, and brown trout and steelhead follow the salmon to provide spincasting sport until freeze-up.

Winter fishermen catch a few trout, northern pike and yellow perch in the harbor area.

Planting Records

The DNR plans to release 50,000 Chinook salmon fingerlings and 10,000 steelhead yearlings each year through at least 1990. Nearby Thompson Creek (59) is receiving 10,000 rainbows, 10,000 brown trout, and 100,000 cohos during this period.

Facilities

The DNR maintains a harbor of refuge with the following services: transient accommodations, gasoline, water, electricity, restrooms, shower facilities, holding-tank pump-out and VHF-FM and CB radio. The telephone number of the dock attendant is (906) 341-6841.

Further Information

Chambers of Commerce:

1. Schoolcraft County Chamber of Commerce, County Courthouse Building, Room 207, Manistique 49854; (906) 341-5010.
2. Upper Peninsula Travel and Recreatioin Association, P.O. Box 400, Iron Mountain 49801; (906) 774-5480.

Bait & Tackle Shops:

Top of the Lake Sport Shop, 206 S. Cedar St., Manistique 49854; (906) 341-5241.

Charter Fishing:

None known.

Department of Natural Resources:

Two fisheries biologists work out of District Headquarters at 309 W. McMillan Ave., Newberry 49868; (906) 293-5131.

Coast Guard:

St. Ignace Station, (906) 643-9192.

Michigan's Catfish Holes

Channel and flathead catfish and their smaller cousins, the black, brown and yellow bullhead, are all underfished in Michigan waters of the Great Lakes. Channel catfish, in particular, are fairly well distributed, sporting fun to catch and outstanding to eat.

Catfish live in shallow bays and rivers emptying into Lakes Michigan, Huron, Erie and St. Clair. In rivers, cats prefer wide-running sections that meander to form oxbows and that feature quiet water and bayous. In bays and harbors, they can be caught from pier, breakwall, dock or shore, as well as from anchored boats. Good rivers and harbors on Lake Michigan include the St. Joseph, Grand, Muskegon (9), Whitehall/Montague (10), Manistee (13), Manistique (58), Escanaba (62), Cedar (64) and Menominee (65). On Lake Huron try the Cheboygan (27), Black (36), Au Sable, Tawas, Au Gres (41) and Saginaw (and its upstream tributaries. Catfish are available throughout Lake St. Clair (55) and the western shore of Lake Erie (57).

Probably more catfish, though, are caught in Saginaw Bay (43 and 44), by sport and commercial fishermen alike, than anywhere else in Michigan. Shorebound anglers take them from cuts all along the bay and from piers at Caseville (45) and Au Gres (41). Boat anglers key in the Maisou Island group in the Bay Port/ Sebewaing area, although catfish can be taken just about anywhere offshore in Saginaw Bay.

Channel cats can grow to whopper size. The state record is a 47-pound, eight-ounce monster caught in the Maple River in 1937, one of the oldest marks still on the books. Minimum entry weight in the DNR Master Angler Award Contest (see page 319) is eight pounds, up from the old qualifying mark of six pounds. Seems that too many people were catching six-pound cats, evidence that these sporting fish are doing well and that more Michigan anglers are seeking them. Even so, they remain one of our most underharvested fish.

Try a Michigan catfish hole this summer.

Tom Huggler
Otisville

58 MANISTIQUE

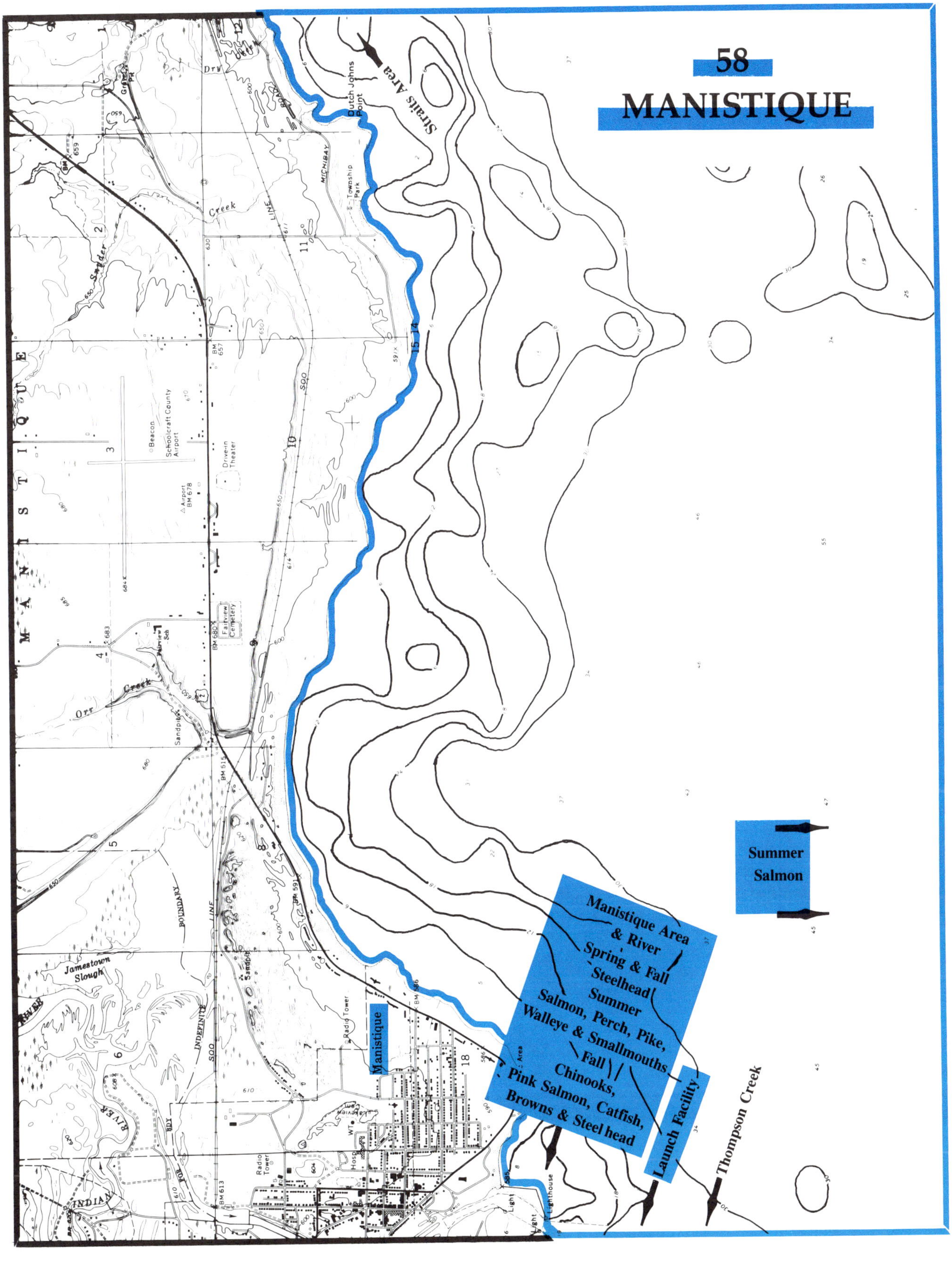

59
THOMPSON CREEK

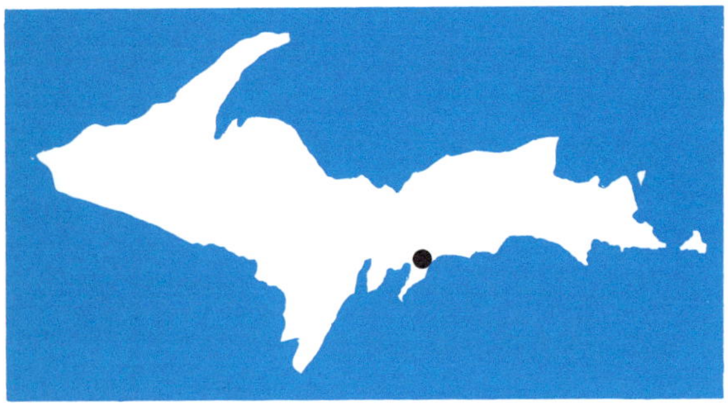

The Thompson Creek mouth area, between Point Aux Barques and Manistique (58), has historically received solid plantings of hatchery-reared fish. Together with Manistique, this wide bay in northern Lake Michigan is now being stocked with cohos, Chinooks, brown trout, steelhead and rainbows.

According to DNR district fisheries biologist John Schrouder, the area is underfished, especially in fall. Many of the anglers who do visit Thompson Creek mouth are from Minnesota and Wisconsin. Their annual pilgrimage is strong evidence that Michigan fishermen could be missing a good bet.

Fishing Schedule

SPRING

Besides rainbows that are planted here, there is some natural reproduction, and from ice-out until mid-June, *spring* steelheaders can expect good fishing. Most wade into the surf and either toss Little Cleos and other spoons or spot spawn bags on bottom, then slide their long, whippy rods into sand spikes or forked branches shoved into beach sand. Trollers can work the 12- to 15-foot-deep contour breaks up to a mile offshore. Good lures are small, hot-colored cranks (Thin Fins, Hot Shots, Fire Plugs, Wee Warts) or No. 7 or No. 9 Rapalas in fluorescent orange, silver and black, or silver and blue. Most trollers drop cannonballs just under the surface and/or flatline one or two lures. Side rigging with planer boards would be a good tactic to try, too.

SUMMER

In spring these same methods also produce a few young cohos and fairly good numbers of brown trout from two to 11 pounds each. The browns are available throughout the *summer*, too, at all depths, depending upon water temperature. Most area trollers head for the 80- to 90-foot bank that lies about three miles offshore. There, they find Chinooks, cohos, browns, a few steelhead/rainbows, and an occasional lake trout.

Tactics involve downrigger fishing in the thermocline (which, at least in midsummer, usually forms near the bank early or late in the day) with a variety of spoons and plugs. Be sure to run a highline or two, as steelhead and browns cruise the upper-lake reaches in summer. Brown trout, in particular, can sometimes be seen porpoising on the surface when the air is calm and the day is bright and warm.

Thermal upwellings in summer from strong winds with a southern bent can turn over the water rather quickly, sending both cold water and trout and salmon in close to land. When this happens, shore and pier fishermen at both Thompson Creek and Manistique (58) have a heyday, if only for a brief period.

FALL

Coho spawning runs in *fall* have been exceptional since the DNR began imprinting smolts in 1983 in the Williams Creek raceway, a tributary to Thompson Creek. Fish now can leave the stream and enter Lake Michigan whenever they want, and the longer they remain in the stream, the stronger their homing instincts become. Trollers begin picking up cohos to nine pounds each by mid-August, using the same rigging tactics and lures as in spring. Surf casters catch them with spoons or egg sacks. Runs peak between Labor Day and early October.

Recent years have also seen heavy returns of pink salmon to Thompson Creek. The natural-spawning pinks usually enter the creek from September 10-30 and are followed by shoreward onslaughts from brown trout and steelhead/rainbows.

WINTER

There is a *winter* fishery for these trout, with anglers braving wind, waves and cold weather to fish the surf. A few who venture onto shelf ice as it forms in Lake Michigan either drill holes in the ice or fish the edges. Adding minnows, small pieces of cut bait, or nightcrawlers to Jigging Rapalas or Swedish Pimples, then jigging vigorously, is the productive tactic.

Planting Records

Consistent annual releases of 100,000 coho smolts and 10,000 yearlings each of rainbows and brown trout are planned for Thompson Creek through at least 1990. Only a few miles away, the Manistique River receives 50,000 Chinooks and 10,000 steelhead yearlings each year, and these fish no doubt contribute to catches in the Thompson Creek area.

Facilities

The closest DNR harbor of refuge is at Manistique (58). Anglers with big boats should also consider putting in at Manistique as the boat-launch facility at Thompson Creek is poor and can accommodate only small boats.

Further Information

Chambers of Commerce:

1. Schoolcraft County Chamber of Commerce, County Courthouse Building, Room 207, Manistique 49854; (906) 341-5010.

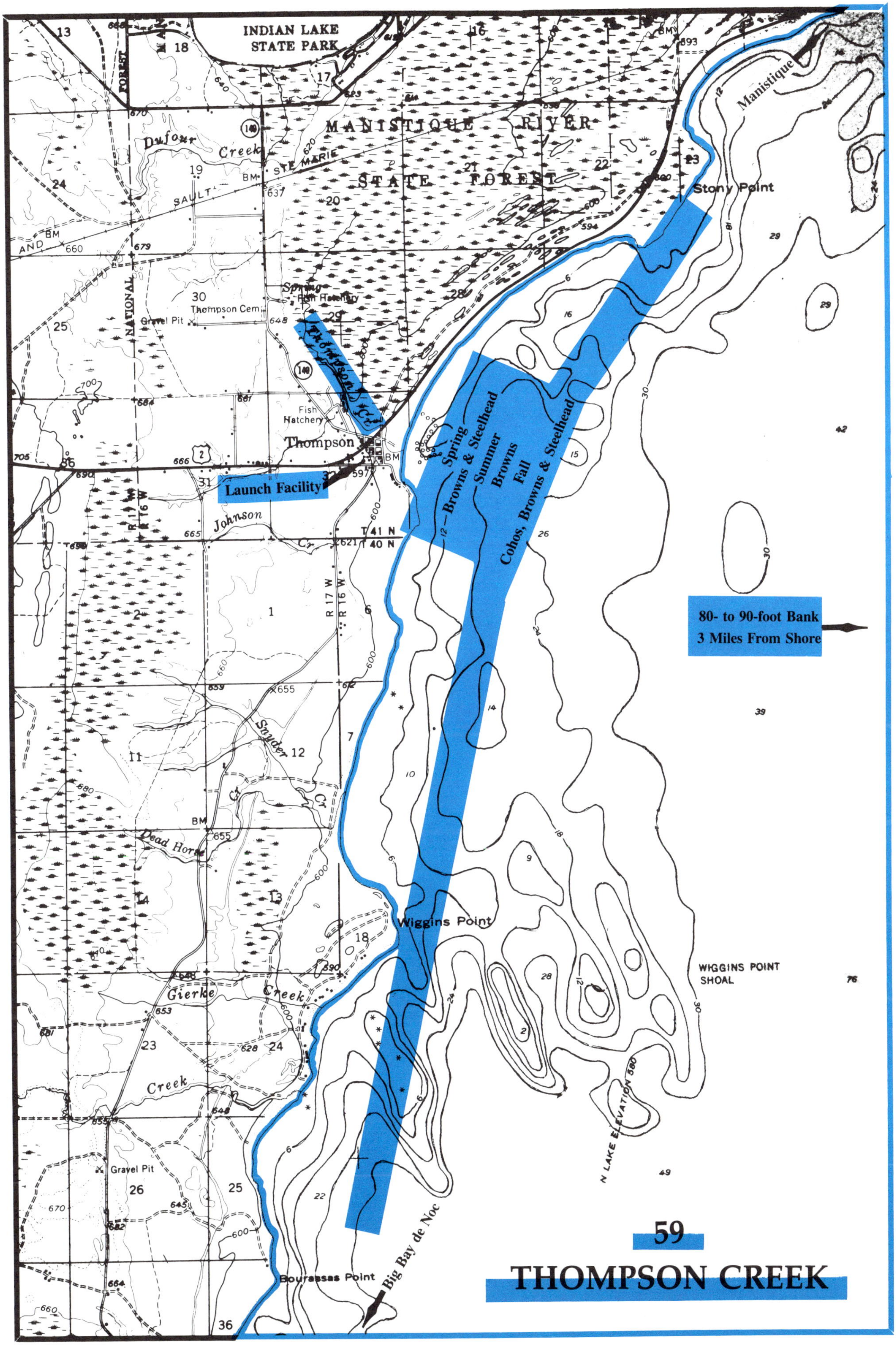

INDIAN LAKE STATE PARK
MANISTIQUE RIVER STATE FOREST
Manistique
Stony Point
Thompson Cr.
Fish Hatchery
Thompson
Launch Facility
Spring Browns & Steelhead
Summer Browns
Fall Cohos, Browns & Steelhead
80- to 90-foot Bank
3 Miles From Shore
Wiggins Point
WIGGINS POINT SHOAL
Bourassas Point
Big Bay de Noc
59
THOMPSON CREEK

Surf fishermen at Thompson Creek can catch returning cohos, steelhead and brown trout as well as Chinooks, like this fine 14-pounder. Chinooks have been planted at nearby Manistique.

2. Upper Peninsula Travel and Recreation Association, P.O. Box 400, Iron Mountain 49801; (906) 774-5480.

Bait & Tackle Shops:

Refer to Manistique (58).

Charter Fishing:

None known.

Department of Natural Resources:

Two fisheries biologists work out of District Headquarters at 309 W. McMillan Ave., Newberry 49868; (906) 293-5131.

Coast Guard:

St. Ignace Station, (906) 643-9192.

Spring Salmon Fever

Signs vary with the individual. One guy repacks wheel bearings on the boat trailer outside while snowflakes form a spring storm dance around his head. Another's wife serves supper on TV snack trays because the dining table is littered with every type of Great Lakes trolling lure known to man. A third, dreaming that a downrigger rod has popped, kicks his wife awake in the mad dash to be first to the pole.

Call it salmon fever, Chinook mania, the coho crazies or what you will. In the end, it gets just about everyone who has ever pinched release pads while setting lines for spring salmon. The outdoor shows with all their hoopla and hype are over; the time for action is *now*.

Salmon are never easier to catch than in spring. Warming water temperatures trigger a brain fold somewhere that tells these fish to gobble like market-bound hogs. After a dormant winter spent mostly in southern shallows, salmon are ready to go (just like fishermen!). Those 18-month-old cohos, averaging three to five pounds, will double weights by late August. Kings, too, will pack on the girth, especially 3-1/2 year-old females destined to spawn and die in the fall. The feeding binge that begins shortly after ice-out in spring and lasts all summer is nature's way of ensuring a tough, spirited spawner that is ready for fall river challenges.

You can catch salmon fever all season long, but one thing is certain: There is no time more exciting than in spring.

Eldon Thomas
Flint

60

BIG BAY DE NOC

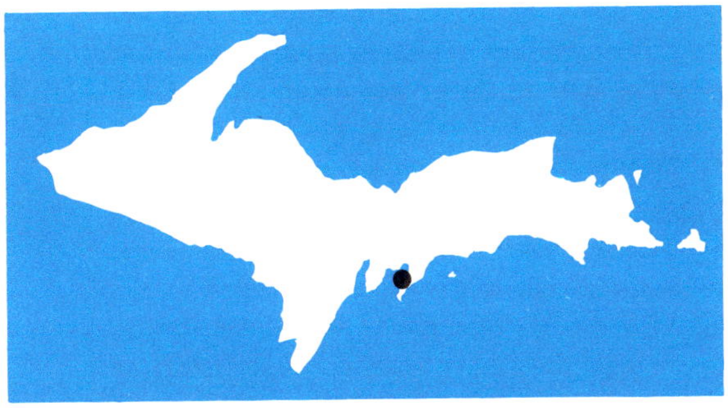

Big Bay de Noc could stand more sport-fishing pressure, especially now that this region along the Garden Peninsula of northern Lake Michigan has been designated a restoration area and, as such, will remain closed to Indian netting activities until at least the year 2000. There are, however, several white commercial netters targeting whitefish with impoundment gear. But those fishermen generally concentrate efforts in deeper water of the bay, while sport anglers mostly stay within the many coves that indent the shoreline.

Many small streams and the Fishdam, Sturgeon and Ogontz rivers flow into Big Bay de Noc, one of the most picturesque areas in northern Michigan. The rugged, barren eastern shore is especially scenic, with its high limestone bluffs, Snail Shell Harbor (site of a reconstructed ghost town and a state park), and Indian paintings and caves among the cliffs along Burnt Bluff.

The Garden Peninsula is aptly named.

Fishing Schedule

Spring action kicks off at ice-out in the upper reaches of the bay, usually off tributary mouths. Many streams support good to excellent smelt dipping, which begins most years by early or mid-April. Hottest action usually occurs in Valentine Creek and the Fishdam River.

Yellow perch invade the rivermouths and shallow-water areas about the same time or just a little later. Perching in Big Bay de Noc can border on the phenomenal some years, with steady action until mid-June in some places. Most anglers fish wigglers or small minnows on either slip sinkers or perch spreaders sent to bottom with bell sinkers.

Best spots in spring, moving clockwise from the Stonington Peninsula, are Wilsey Bay area, St. Vital Island, in Ogontz Bay off the boat launch, Kates Bay, Ansels Point, Garden Bay (especially off Hermes Cabins and the boat ramp on the opposite shore), outside the J-hook of Snail Shell Harbor, and off the boat ramp in Sand Bay.

An excellent fishery for northern pike and big walleyes begins off the Fishdam River mouth at the mid-May statewide opener and lasts about a month, most years. The walleyes, in particular, could use more angling pressure. Best results come from drifting and trolling either nightcrawler harnesses, Junebug Spinners or small Rapalas. Pike anglers who troll contour breaks near weed beds can score on three- to 12-pound pike. Best lures are red-and-white Dardevle spoons or large Rapalas.

Besides the mouth of the Fishdam, good pike-fishing spots (moving counterclockwise from the river) include Porcupine Point, Ogontz Bay (between Indian Point and the cabins a few hundred yards up the bay), Martin Bay, and in an unnamed bay immediately west of Ripley Shoal (try the fast dropoff here in particular).

Yellow perch, northerns and walleyes can be caught all *summer* from these same areas, but the best fishing occurs in spring. An exception is Ogontz Bay, which consistently produces northerns until freeze-up.

Soon after the statewide bass opener (usually the Saturday before Memorial Day), Big Bay de Noc produces nice stringers of smallmouths, with action lasting all summer and well into the *fall*. Again moving clockwise from Stonington Peninsula, hot-spots are east side of Peninsula Point, Wilsey Bay Point, contour breaks a quarter-mile southeast of St. Vital Island, seven- to 12-foot depths off the Ogontz River, Indian Point, off the Nahma stacks at Stony Point, Poplar Point, the long contour from Poplar Point to Porcupine Point, South River Bay, Middle Bluff above Fayette State Park, the boat launch below the park, and Sand Bay below Burnt Bluff.

Wading fishermen using wigglers and surface poppers or dry flies with flyrods score. So do spincasters who toss spinnerbaits, crankbaits, jigs, Mister Twisters or small in-line spinners from boat or shore.

Winter fishing remains good for yellow perch and fair to good for northern pike and walleyes at the locations previously stated for those fish.

Planting Records

There are no releases of hatchery-reared fish being made in Big Bay de Noc at this time nor are any planned in the immediate future. All species are naturally reproduced.

Facilities

Several boat launches and access sites await fishermen. They include the west side of Ogontz Bay, the Fishdam River, Vans Harbor in Garden Bay, the south shore of Garden Bay, and Sand Bay below Fayette State Park. Small boats can also be launched from shore in Wilsey Bay, but there is no ramp.

Further Information

Chambers of Commerce:

1. Delta County Area Chamber of Commerce, 230 Ludington St., Escanaba 49829; (906) 786-2192.

2. Upper Peninsula Travel and Recreation Association, P.O. Box 400, Iron Mountain 49801; (906) 774-5480.

Bait & Tackle Shops:

The Ogontz Store, Bait & Restaurant just west of the Ogontz River Bridge on US-2, (906) 474-9900.

Charter Fishing:

None known.

Department of Natural Resources:

Two fisheries biologists work out of District Headquarters at 6833 US-2, Escanaba 49829; (906) 786-2351.

Coast Guard:

Sturgeon Bay, Wisconsin, Station (414) 743-3366 or 743-3367.

Big Bay de Noc serves up excellent spring perch-fishing action most years from ice-out until early summer.

—Michigan DNR photo—

Ice Fishing With a Portable Fish Finder

Serious wintertime fishermen (are there any ice anglers who aren't serious about their sport?) can increase their catches with the use of a good portable depth sounder. Old standby flashers and the new liquid-crystal units, such as Humminbird's LCR Portable, help fishermen to locate bottom, structure, weed beds and—most importantly—fish.

But through the ice?

Right. Through the ice. Here's how it works: Find a suitable fishing area, one that has fresh, solid ice which is void of air pockets. Clear the snow away and add a small puddle of liquid (water or anti-freeze) to the ice. Then, place the transducer on the wet surface and turn the unit on. On the LCR Portable, the automatic sensitivity feature will find the bottom and set the proper depth range. Once the fisherman is satisfied that he is in the right area, he can then drill his holes.

The LCR unit should be positioned where the fisherman can constantly monitor the readout, because fish moving within the transducer cone angle will be recorded on the display. Some LCR models even have a fish-alarm feature which audibly signals the angler. This is a handy feature for fishermen who like to work two rods.

Larry Colombo
Humminbird Company

Unique Lighthouses

The Fort Gratiot Lighthouse, just north of the Blue Water Bridge at Port Huron (53), is the oldest of Michigan's 50-plus lighthouses. The original lighthouse was built during the late 1820s then replaced in 1861 with the present tower. The structure is also the first object in Michigan to be touched by the rays of the morning sun.

Grey's Reef Lighthouse, 32 miles off Charlevoix (22), was the last manned offshore Great Lakes lighthouse. The lighthouse, which had housed a crew since 1891, became fully automated in October 1976.

The Little Sable Lighthouse, south of Pentwater (11), was the last kerosene-powered light on the Great Lakes, not being electrified until 1954.

The Livingston Memorial Lighthouse, built in the Detroit River (56) on the eastern tip of Belle Isle in 1930, is the only marble lighthouse in the country.

Point Betsie Lighthouse, near Frankfort (16), was the last manned lighthouse on mainland Michigan. The lighthouse, which had been operated manually since 1858, became fully automated in April 1983.

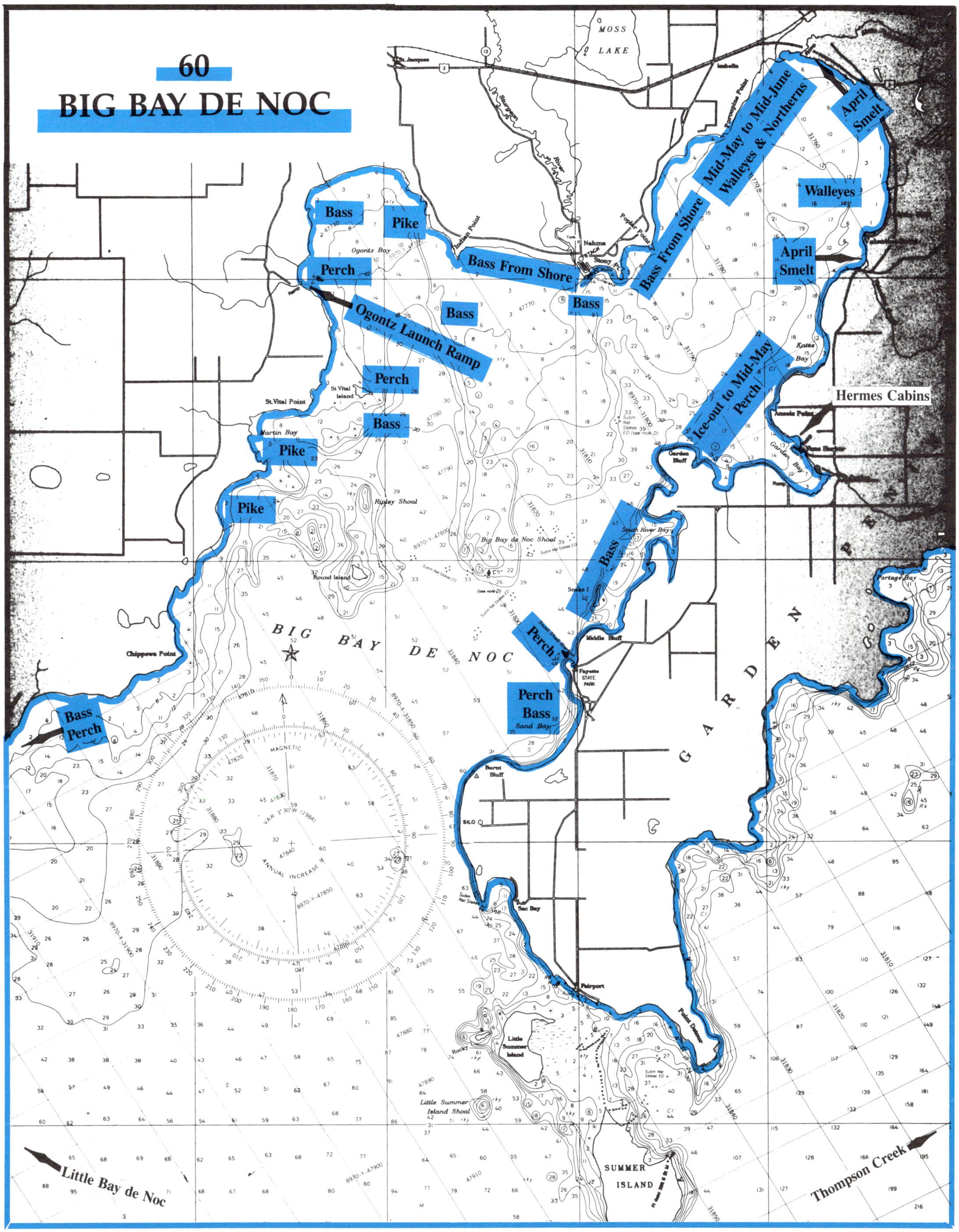
60
BIG BAY DE NOC
MOSS LAKE
Bass
Pike
Perch
Ogontz Bay
Ogontz Launch Ramp
Bass From Shore
Bass
Bass
Mid-May to Mid-June Walleyes & Northerns
April Smelt
Walleyes
Bass From Shore
April Smelt
Ice-out to Mid-May Perch
Hermes Cabins
Perch
St Vital Point
Bass
Martin Bay
Pike
Pike
Ripley Shoal
Big Bay de Noc Shoal
Round Island
South River Bay
Bass
Snake I
Chippewa Point
BIG BAY DE NOC
Perch
Perch
Bass
Sand Bay
Bass
Perch
GARDEN
MAGNETIC
Sac Bay
Fairport
Little Summer Island
SUMMER ISLAND
Little Summer Island Shoal
Little Bay de Noc
Thompson Creek

61
LITTLE BAY DE NOC

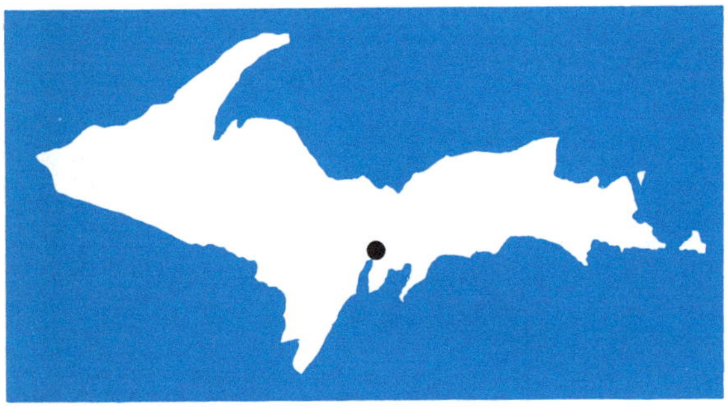

Rx for a bored fisherman: Load a 75-square-mile Lake Michigan bay with a dozen gamefish species including Chinook salmon, steelhead and brown trout, walleyes, smallmouth bass, northern pike and yellow perch. Provide launch facilities, restaurants, motels and bait and tackle shops. Then declare a 15-year moratorium on all Indian gillnetting. Locate it near Escanaba in Michigan's Upper Peninsula.

Call it *Little Bay de Noc*.

"Fishing is so good for so many different kinds of fish that people sometimes don't know what to try for," says Don Ronn, owner of Bay Shore Resort, Bait and Tackle just outside Gladstone on the west side of the bay. "But that's a healthy problem, isn't it? Especially when you consider that there are opportunities for both bank and boat anglers."

Little Bay de Noc's future looks good. As part of a recent settlement between the State of Michigan and Indian fishermen (for details, see page 294), the bay has been designated as a restoration area and will remain closed to netting for 15 years. Natural reproduction of both gamefish and baitfish is good, plus gamefish populations are being augmented by hefty DNR releases of hatchery-reared fish.

Four rivers—the Days, Tacoosh, Whitefish and Rapid—enter Little Bay de Noc near its head at Rapid River. Dropoffs, points and reefs punctuate much of the bay to provide good structure. Sand bars and weed beds dominate shallow coves, and these areas serve up fair to excellent angling in spring, summer and fall. Every winter, clusters of pike-spearers' shacks develop along the south side of Garth Point and offshore from the fuel tanks at Kipling. On January 30, 1985, Dick Stafford, a charterboat captain from Escanaba (62), counted 857 shanties on the ice in the Gladstone area.

And every year Little Bay de Noc offers at least one bonus, in addition to the usual smorgasbord. Some years it is jumbo yellow perch to two-pounds-plus. Two springs ago (1984), it was exciting catches of brook trout at the mouth of the Days River. (The Wisconsin DNR had released the brookies into Lake Michigan in an effort to build a coaster brook-trout fishery.) Then last spring and summer (1985), walleyes took center stage to provide anglers with their best sport in 20 years and stringers of 3-1/2 to nine-pound fish. That fall, Chinook salmon made their maiden return to Butlers Island shoal just outside Gladstone. When I drove by in early October, people battled salmon while leaning against their parked cars.

Ronn predicts that big northern pike will be the next trump card in Little Bay de Noc's deck. Why? "They're no longer getting pressure, now that people are targeting walleyes and perch," he said. "We always see a 20-pound pike in the winter, but I'm expecting someone to take a 25- or even a 30-pound fish."

Fishing Schedule

By species, here are the best times and places to go:

Yellow Perch—At ice-out (normally April 12-20) try three to 10 feet of water between the public access site at Rapid River and the mouth of the Days River. As ice moves out down the bay, action for five- to 10-inch perch follows. Perch are available all year to anglers using wigglers, worms, and small minnows for bait. A summer hotspot is the Black Bottom area south of a line between the Gladstone Yacht Club and Squaw Point Light.

Smelt—Try the north shore of the Days River between the old highway and the rivermouth on land the DNR has leased. Many anglers (some from as far away as St. Louis, Missouri) fish perch by day and smelt by night.

Walleyes—Most catches at the May 15 opener occur above a line from the Days River to a mile south of Garth Point. Throughout the summer, try the 10- and 20-foot reefs north of the shipping channel (marked by buoys) at Kipling. Another good spot is reef structure in the center of the bay between the Days River and Vagabond Resort. Small black-and-silver Rapalas, blue-and-silver Little Cleos, and F4 or F6 Flatfish in silver, silver and pink dots, and red fluorescent are good lures. Nightcrawlers pinned to harnesses with red, fluorescent orange, or chartreuse blades and red or pearl beads are effective when drifted or trolled.

Bass—The statewide bass opener (usually the Saturday before Memorial Day) finds smallmouth anglers tossing No. 7 Rapalas, 1/8-ounce Mister Twisters in yellow or white, and Mepps spinners. Gravel shoals off the rivermouths are good spots for early season spawners. In summer turn to weed beds off Hunters Point and rock structure near the No. 11 Buoy in the Saunders Point area. After Labor Day, smallmouth anglers switch to small suckers hooked through the head to No. 2 Aberdeen hooks, then

61
LITTLE BAY DE NOC

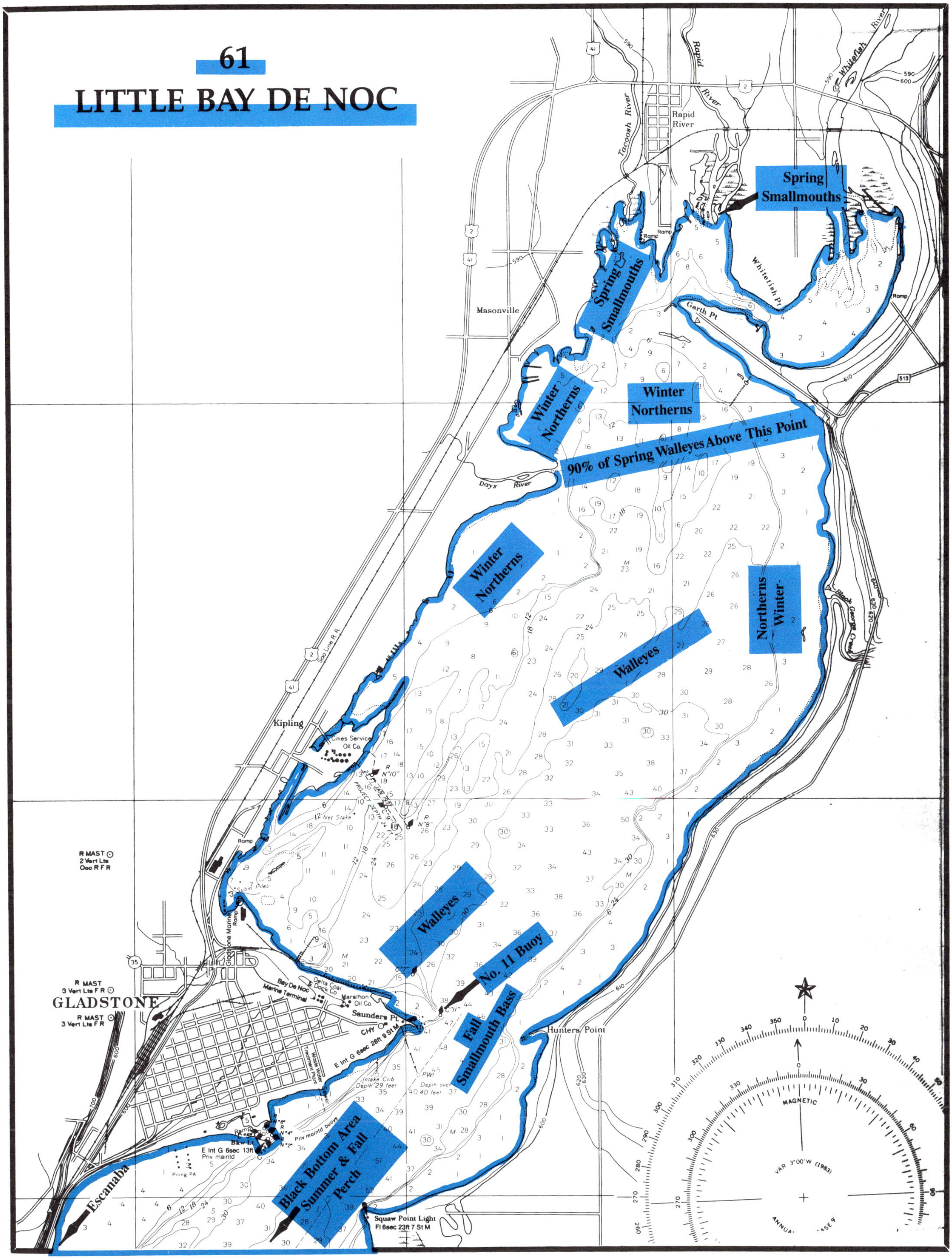

Little Bay de Noc has recently been serving up some fine walleyes, like this tip-up-caught five-pounder.

driftfish off bottom with the help of small split shots. Best place to catch a largemouth bass is around Butlers Island.

Northern Pike—On the May 15 opener and throughout the summer, seek eight- to 12-foot dropoffs featuring structure or weeds. No. 9 straight and No. 11 jointed Rapalas in blue and silver and black and silver are rated plugs. Spincasting with Kush Spoons and Mepps Musky Killers is effective. So is stillfishing with bobbers and five- to nine-inch suckers. Post Labor Day is an excellent time for big northerns. Using a zig-zag technique, trollers pull red-and-white Dardevle spoons and magnum Rapalas and Rebel Spoonbills in gold-and-black, silver-and-black, and perch colors. Hotspots include ledges south of the Beach House to the Escanaba River and south of Escanaba from the Yacht Harbor to the tip of Portage Point. Winter fishing shapes up at the same two spots.

Trout and Salmon—For fair to excellent ice-out action for browns, try longlining in three to 10 feet of water at the river-mouths with Litle Cleos, Krocodiles and Rapalas. Combinations of silver, blue, green, and chartreuse are the best colors. Later in the summer, use the same tactics and lures in deeper water of the bay. The Whitefish River hosts a steelhead run in spring. Sporadic catches of lake trout are reported in the summer throughout Little Bay de Noc. In fall the lakers concentrate at Saunders Point, where they were released, but the season is closed. Expect Chinook salmon to appear in the Escanaba area in August, and by Labor Day they can be caught off Saunders Point and between shore and Butlers Island in 14-18 feet of water. J-Plugs, Rapalas and Little Cleos are hot lures.

Planting Records

Annual DNR stockings of 100,000 Chinook fingerlings, 15,000 steelhead yearlings, 10,000 brown-trout yearlings and upwards of 250,000 walleye fingerlings will continue through at least 1990. Natural reproduction is also very good for pike, perch, bass, panfish and catfish.

Facilities

The DNR maintains a harbor of refuge at Gladstone with the following services: transient accommodations, gasoline, water, electricity, restrooms, shower facilities, holding-tank pump-out and VHF-FM radio. The telephone number of the dock attendant is (906) 428-4915.

Anglers can launch boats at Escanaba (62), Gladstone (the public launch site is off US-2 next to Bay Shore Resort, Bait and Tackle), and Rapid River.

Further Information

Chambers of Commerce:

1. Delta County Area Chamber of Commerce, 230 Ludington St., Escanaba 49829; (906) 786-2192.
2. Upper Peninsula Travel and Recreation Association, P.O. Box 400, Iron Mountain 49801; (906) 774-5480.

Bait & Tackle Shops:

Bay Shore Resort, Bait and Tackle, US-2 & 41, Gladstone 49837; (906) 428-9687.

Charter Fishing:

1. Captain Dick Stafford (trout, salmon, walleyes), 7262 US-2 & 41/M-35, Escanaba 49829;(906) 789-0110. 22-foot Starcraft Mariner, *Take Five*.
2. Jim Murray (walleyes, perch, northern pike, smallmouth bass), Bay Shore Resort, Bait and Tackle, US-2 & 41, Gladstone 49837; (906) 428-9687.

Department of Natural Resources:

Two fisheries biologists work out of District Headquarters at 6833 US-2, Gladstone 49837; (906) 786-2351.

Coast Guard:

Sturgeon Bay, Wisconsin, Station (414) 743-3366 or 743-3367.

The Pike Ferret of Little Bay de Noc

Northern pike in Little Bay de Noc run from 2-1/2 pound keepers to 19-pound lunkers. When I used to live in Plymouth, Michigan, I often made the long drive here to fish for these fascinating predators. Tactics included trolling Rapalas, casting Mepps spinners, or stillfishing sucker minnows—the latter especially during the dog days of summer.

But my favorite method was to cast and retrieve homemade long-haired jigs that I make and label as Ray's Way Jigs. Contrary to most other northern-pike fishermen, I like to fish with light rods that I make myself and light line of four- or six-pound test. Instead of metal, I rely on 20- or 30-pound-test monofilament for leader material.

Northern pike are found throughout Little Bay de Noc, but I have had the best success by trolling dropoffs (see map) and keying on shallow-water bays near structure (rock piles and old pilings), dropoffs and weeds.

One of the best fishing days I ever experienced here occurred soon after the May 15 opener one year. My partners were Bob Hume and outdoor-writer Gordie Charles of Traverse City. It was a warm, cloudy morning, and we were working our way toward the pilings off the Gladstone coal docks. My friends weren't having much luck tossing a variety of lures, so once we anchored off the pilings, I suggested they try some Ray's Way Jigs. We dressed the jigs with frozen smelt and soon had three limits of northerns (15 fish) from three to six pounds each.

Gordie's article that appeared later in the *Traverse City Record-Eagle* stated that there must have been 100 pike in that hole. He was telling the truth.

Besides keying on such structure and dropoffs throughout the bay, consider fishing extremely shallow water in early morning before the sun is up. At times, I have caught northerns in only two or three feet of water before they moved to the shelter of weed beds after full daylight. When they do cruise from the shallows, simply move along with them, changing to lighter-colored lures as daylight increases.

I don't get up to Little Bay de Noc as much as I used to, now that I am living in East Tawas and have some excellent Great Lakes fishing opportunities in my back yard (see 39).

But if you like catching northern pike, consider this beautiful bay in northern Lake Michigan.

Bill Ray
East Tawas

62
ESCANABA

Escanaba is a key fishing port for both Little Bay de Noc and northern Green Bay anglers. Besides trolling and ice fishing on the bays, there are also some fair to good river- and pier-fishing opportunities. Support facilities and services for local and visiting fishermen, alike, are excellent in this city of 15,000 people.

Fishing Schedule

SPRING

Spring sport close to the city is limited to ice-out perch fishing for yellow-bellies that have lingered at the Yacht Harbor in town, the coal docks just north of the Yacht Harbor, and south of Escanaba halfway to Portage Point. Some of these yellow-bellies weigh a pound or more.

In mid to late May, the coal docks produce excellent fishing for spawning black crappies to 15 and 16 inches each. The lower Escanaba River also furnishes spring crappie action. Minnows pinned to small jigs that are skipped along bottom or lifted and dropped just under the ice halfway to bottom are the rated angling tactics. Most crappies hit on the drop.

SUMMER

Summer fishing is generally poor in the immediate Escanaba area, but an exception is the lower Escanaba River for one-half mile to the Mead Paper Company dam. Bridge-timber and logging-dock remains punctuate the bottom there and provide holding cover for post-spawn walleyes and crappies. Small spinners and jig/minnow offerings take crappies, whereas walleyes to nine pounds hit nightcrawler harnesses or Rapalas trolled near bottom.

Besides walleyes, the river hosts a resident population of saugers, a close cousin to the walleye. The only other place in Michigan where a decent population of saugers is found is in the Portage Lake Canal (see Keweenaw Bay, 72, for details).

Also in summer, deep-water trolling to the south off the Ford River (63) and around Wisconsin's Washington Island area is productive for king salmon and lake trout. Escanaba charterboat-captain Dick Stafford reports excellent fishing along the 30- to 118-foot dropoff four miles out from the Ford River in an area known locally as the Ford River Can (a navigational buoy). Tactics involve trolling back and forth along the dropoff and keying in 70 feet of water when temperatures (55-60 degrees F.) are right.

Stafford runs Northport Nailer spoons in chartreuse, blue-and-silver, white-and-orange, chartreuse-and-pink, and white-and-green colors along with blue-scale Flutter Spoons. These lures are generally stacked via Big Jon Add-On Releases above bottom-running No. 11 black-and-silver Countdown Rapalas or Northport Nailer Plugs in yellow with orange dots or white with black dots. Lower lures have the potential of attracting reef-hugging lakers, while high-running hardware interests suspended kings.

While trolling for brown trout along the shoreline shallows of Green Bay, John Lievense caught this three-pound coaster brook trout on a spoon.

62
ESCANABA

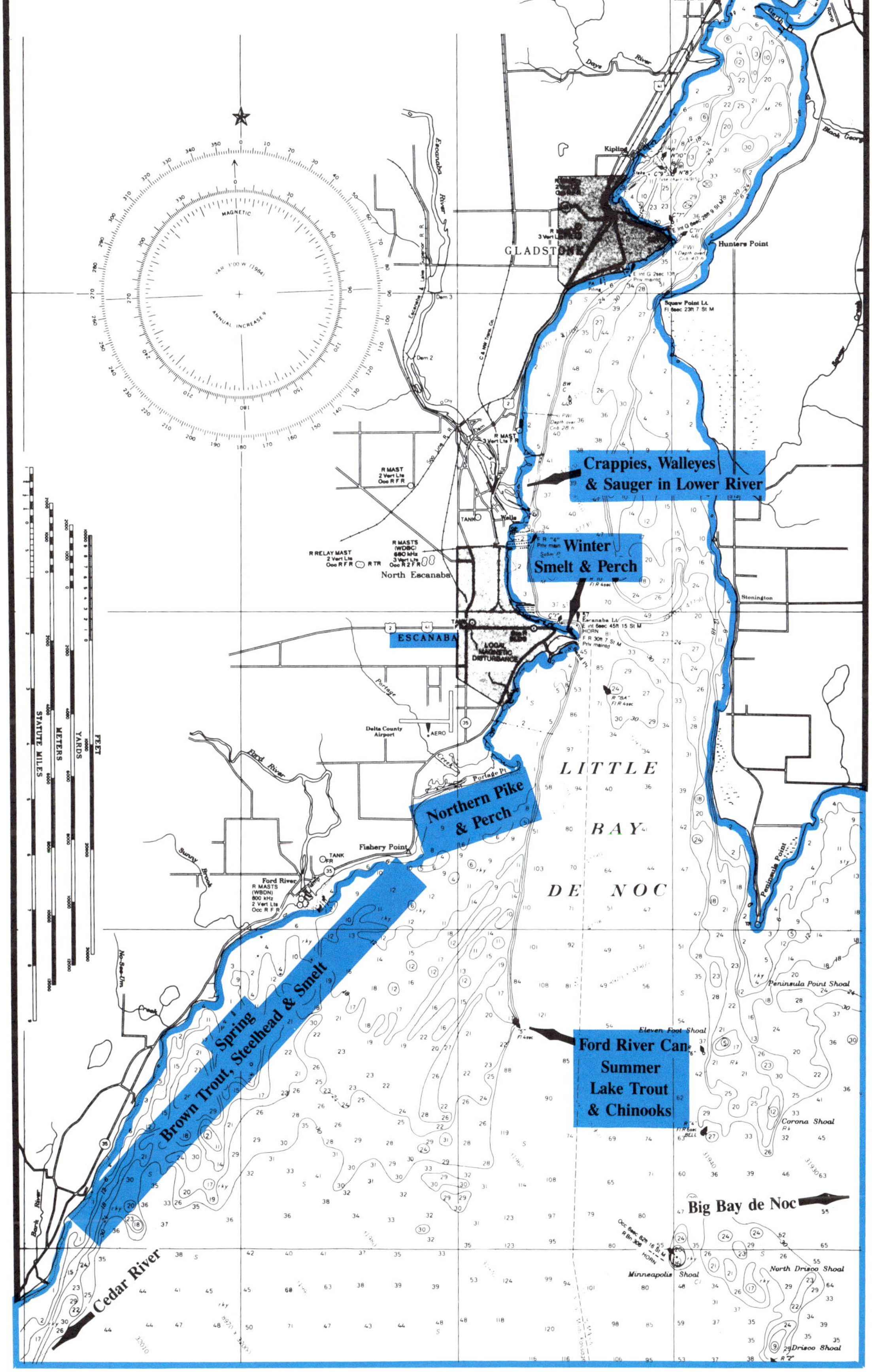

Rapid River
Masonville
Days River
Kipling
Gladstone
Hunters Point
Squaw Point Lt.
Escanaba River
North Escanaba
ESCANABA
Stonington
Delta County Airport
Portage Pt.
Fishery Point
Ford River
Bark River
Cedar River
LITTLE BAY DE NOC
Peninsula Point
Peninsula Point Shoal
Eleven Foot Shoal
Corona Shoal
Minneapolis Shoal
North Drisco Shoal
Drisco Shoal
Crappies, Walleyes & Sauger in Lower River
Winter Smelt & Perch
Northern Pike & Perch
Brown Trout, Spring Steelhead & Smelt
Ford River Can
Summer Lake Trout & Chinooks
Big Bay de Noc
FEET
YARDS
METERS
STATUTE MILES

Fishing can be exceptional. In mid-August of 1984, for example, four charters produced 125 Chinooks, 10 browns and six cohos for Stafford.

FALL

As *fall* approaches, salmon—along with brown trout and steelhead—become increasingly available to Escanaba fishermen. There is also a good pike fishery halfway between the city and Portage Point for those trolling drops and weeds with Rapalas or spoons. Although fish were larger in the past, the area continues to yield northerns to 10-pounds plus.

WINTER

But the best fishing opportunities at Escanaba occur in *winter* for yellow perch, smelt and northern pike. Ice at the Yacht Harbor alone often supports 100 or more ice shacks of perch fishermen, and another shantytown builds at the nearby coal docks. Perchers pin small minnows or wigglers to bare hooks or spoons, then jig the offerings along dropoffs near weed beds. Halfway between Escanaba and Portage Point, they seek larger perch and, to get them, usually jig Swedish Pimples with or without minnows. Quality, not quantity, is the password here, with some fishermen coming ashore with—not 50 yellow-bellies—but rather a couple-dozen fish that may collectively weigh 20-25 pounds.

Just north of the Escanaba River is an improving fishery for smelt, taken through the ice with small minnows on bare hooks.

For full details on fishing opportunities in this area, also see Little Bay de Noc (61).

Planting Records

Releases of hatchery-reared fish were discontinued in 1983 when Chinook stockings were moved to Gladstone, where the DNR expected young salmon to be better imprinted. For area-wide stocking information refer to Little Bay de Noc (61), Ford River (63), Cedar River (64) and Menominee (65).

Facilities

The DNR maintains a harbor of refuge at Escanaba with the following services: transient accommodations, gasoline and diesel fuel, water, electricity, restrooms, shower facilities, holding-tank pump-out, haul-out facilities and VHF-FM radio. The telephone number of the dock attendant is (906) 786-9614.

Further Information

Chambers of Commerce:

1. Delta County Area Chamber of Commerce, 230 Ludington St., Escanaba 49829; (906) 786-2192.
2. Upper Peninsula Travel and Recreation Association, P.O. Box 400, Iron Mountain 49801; (906) 774-5480.

Bait & Tackle Shops:

Ludington Bait & Sporting Goods, 411 S. Ludington, Escanaba 49829; (906) 786-2798.

Charter Fishing:

Captain Dick Stafford, 7262 US-2 and 41/M-35 Escanaba 49829; (906) 789-0110.

Department of Natural Resources:

Two fisheries biologists work out of District Headquarters at 6833 US-2, Gladstone 49837; (906) 786-2351.

Coast Guard:

Sturgeon Bay, Wisconsin, Station, (414) 743-3366 or 743-3367.

Fishing With Graphs

Chart recorders and Great Lakes salmon trolling are as inseparable as Wrigley's Doublemint twins. When the rebirth of Great Lakes fishing, the world's greatest fishing story—next to the parable of the loaves and fishes, of course—was just beginning to unfold 20 years ago, depth finders and other basic electronics were already part of the plot.

I'll never forget one of the first times I fished the big water from a trolling boat with its aft end bristling with downriggers. Captain Emil Dean wheeled the *Mary-E*, his 32-foot Luhrs, on a rough Lake Michigan out of South Haven (5) that May afternoon. We were hoping to target a school of lake trout or maybe a Chinook salmon pack. The wind sang through the downrigger wires, and Dean's sonar graph drew out the slowly falling bottom 120 feet below. I was intrigued by both the sound of that graph and the little "blips" of structure and the occasional fish that shaped up on its small screen.

Suddenly, a half-dozen dark pencil marks like inverted *Vs* appeared 20 feet off bottom. I casually asked Captain Dean what they were, and he bent over for a look. "Magnum hooks!" Dean shouted in my ear. "Hog Chinooks! That's what they are. Watch those rods!"

"Fish on! someone yelped from the back of the boat.

One already-jumping rod was yanked from its holder and shoved into my hands. Another rod popped straight up, someone else grabbed it, then speed-cranked into a muscle-bound Chinook. Meanwhile, my fish rapidly ripped off 50 yards of line. With Dean hollering instructions to clear the other six lines, confusion reigned supreme. My king salmon slashed the surface half a football field away. A kiss of sun glinted briefly off its side, bright as new auto-bumper chrome, as he sped away like an out-of-control submarine.

"Keep your rod up," Captain Dean said over my shoulder, "and don't horse him. He's a good fish—15 pounds plus." I did as my host told me. Twenty minutes later, my stomach was sore from the rod butt shoved into it, and my arms felt ready to give out.

Just then, the fish, big as a Louisville Slugger, suddenly appeared 20 feet away off the port side. Dean guided him into his waiting net and dumped 16 pounds of kicking-mad Chinook aboard. The buck salmon thrashed about the floor of the *Mary-E* until someone thumped him on the head. He joined the other half of our double-header, a 10-pound hen, in the cooler.

Then we trimmed our trolling lines, pointed the snout of the *Mary-E* into the hull-high rollers, and tried to relocate the rest of the salmon school. With the help of the graph we found it.

Tom Huggler
Otisville

63
FORD RIVER

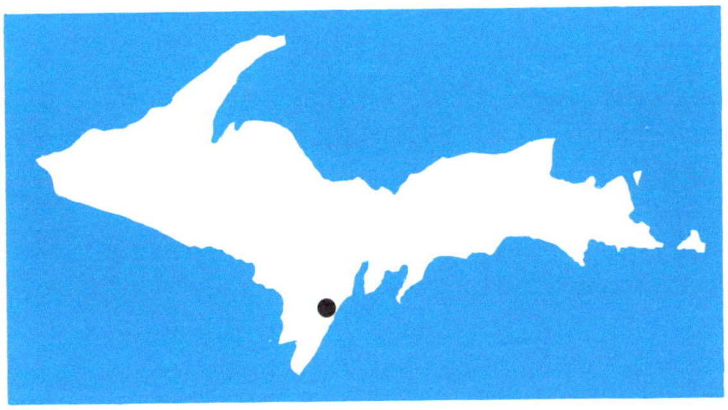

The Ford River, located between Escanaba (62) and the Cedar River (64) on the north end of Green Bay, features the only developed boat-launching site between those two locations. As such, it is a major departure point for fishing trout and salmon further into the bay. It also serves up close-to-shore angling opportunities.

Ice-out is one of the best times of year to go steelheading at rivermouths and in the Great Lakes surf.

Fishing Schedule

The lower Ford River is most noted for its outstanding smallmouth-bass fishery, the only good river fishery—according to DNR district fisheries biologist Bill Bullen—in Menominee County. Fishing is even as good as that at Big Bay de Noc (60). Best catches are made in the lowermost mile of the river in *spring*, from opening day (usually the Saturday preceding Memorial Day) through June, but fishing remains good near the mouth throughout the summer.

SPRING

Boat fishermen can navigate the lower river, and wading anglers can fish the holes between the rapids above the boatable waters. Much angling effort occurs right off the bank at the DNR public-access site adjacent to M-35. Soft-shelled crayfish are by far the best bait, but nightcrawlers and Rapalas also are used.

Brown-trout fishermen do quite well off the rivermouth in shoreline shallows each spring when smelt flock here to spawn. There are also a few steelhead/rainbows available. Better fishing, however, for these species occurs to the south at the Cedar River (64). Spincasters toss Little Cleos, Krocodiles, and K.O. Wobblers or bottomfish with spawn. Trollers rely on Rapalas and small spoons, either flatlined or run behind shallow-set downriggers. Best lure colors are silver, pearl, chartreuse, yellow, green, and various combinations thereof.

Smelt dipping is usually good to excellent in the lower Ford River, even during daylight hours. Sucker netting is also a big springtime activity, especially in the vicinity of Jaeger Rapids, about four miles upriver from the mouth.

As with many Great Lakes tributaries, a sand bar that forms right at the rivermouth causes some problems for boat launchers during low flows, but boats can usually navigate the channel with only minor difficulty.

SUMMER

In recent years, good *summer* Chinook fishing has been found near what is referred to locally as the Ford River Can, a navigational buoy located about four miles east and a little south of the rivermouth, right along a ledge where water drops off from 70 to 118 feet. Good fishing for kings and lake trout begins there in June and continues through late August, when the salmon start moving north toward the planting site near Gladstone in Little Bay de Noc (61).

Best depths for summer salmon are 60-90 feet, with the usual assortment of plugs and spoons producing for trollers. There are no local lures, special colors or unusual tactics to report.

FALL

Lake-trout fishermen also key on this area and troll toward Escanaba (62) during the *fall*. Further, they use the Ford River access to shorten the boat trip out to Wisconsin's Washington Island area for midsummer lake-trout and salmon fishing, which has been reported to be excellent.

Fish the Thermal Bars in Spring

When portions of the big lakes freeze in winter, the densest (39-degree-F.) water sinks to the bottom. Then, spring runoff and the sun's higher rays from the approaching summer solstice combine to warm lake shallows. Eventually, inshore water temperatures higher than 39 degrees meet offshore temperatures less than 39 degrees. When this occurs, a vertical wall of water called an "interface or "thermal bar" results.

This interface moves slowly offshore until sometime in June when the water completely turns over—flattens out so to speak—and a "thermocline" (a horizontal band of water that fluctuates in size and that is a different temperature than water both above and below) takes over. Both temperature layers—the vertical interface and the horizontal thermocline—are important to fishermen.

But the interface is especially important to spring trollers because it creates an "edge" that is attractive to both baitfish and salmonids. Just as deer, grouse, rabbits and other game animals seek the edges of upland- and lowland-cover types, so, too, fish migrate to spring temperature differences in their home turf. Some researchers discuss this phenomenon as the creation of a "reef," since the interface is so attractive to fish. The interface also acts as a type of "corral," since fish often stack up inside.

How can you locate these interfaces? Here are five tips:

1. Look for color changes from greenish (inshore and warm) water to various shades of blue (offshore and cold) water.

2. Keep an eye out for current swirls.

3. Take note of gulls dive-bombing baitfish or baitfish leaping from the water when pursued by trout and salmon.

4. Search for flotsam and debris, which tends to parallel the temperature change.

5. Constantly monitor surface temperatures with a thermometer.

Tom Huggler
Otisville

Planting Records

The only release of hatchery-reared fish in the Ford River area are 30,000 fall fingerling lake trout being planted annually over the Minneapolis Shoal several miles offshore. Refer to Cedar River (64), Menominee (65), Escanaba (62) and Little Bay de Noc (61) for more area planting information.

Facilities

The DNR maintains a harbor of refuge at Escanaba (62) with the following services: transient accommodations, gasoline and diesel fuel, water, electricity, restrooms, shower facilities, holding-tank pump-out, haul-out facilities and VHF-FM radio. The telephone number of the dock attendant is (906) 786-9614.

Further Information

Chambers of Commerce:

1. Delta County Area Chamber of Commerce, 230 Ludington St., Escanaba 49829; (906) 786-2192.
2. Upper Peninsula Travel and Recreation Association, P.O. Box 400, Iron Mountain 49801; (906) 774-5480.

Bait & Tackle Shops:

Refer to Escanaba (62).

Charter Fishing:

Refer to Escanaba (62).

Department of Natural Resources:

Two fisheries biologists work out of District Headquarters at 6833 US-2, Gladstone 49837; (906) 786-2351.

Coast Guard:

Sturgeon Bay, Wisconsin, Station, (414) 743-3366 or 743-3367.

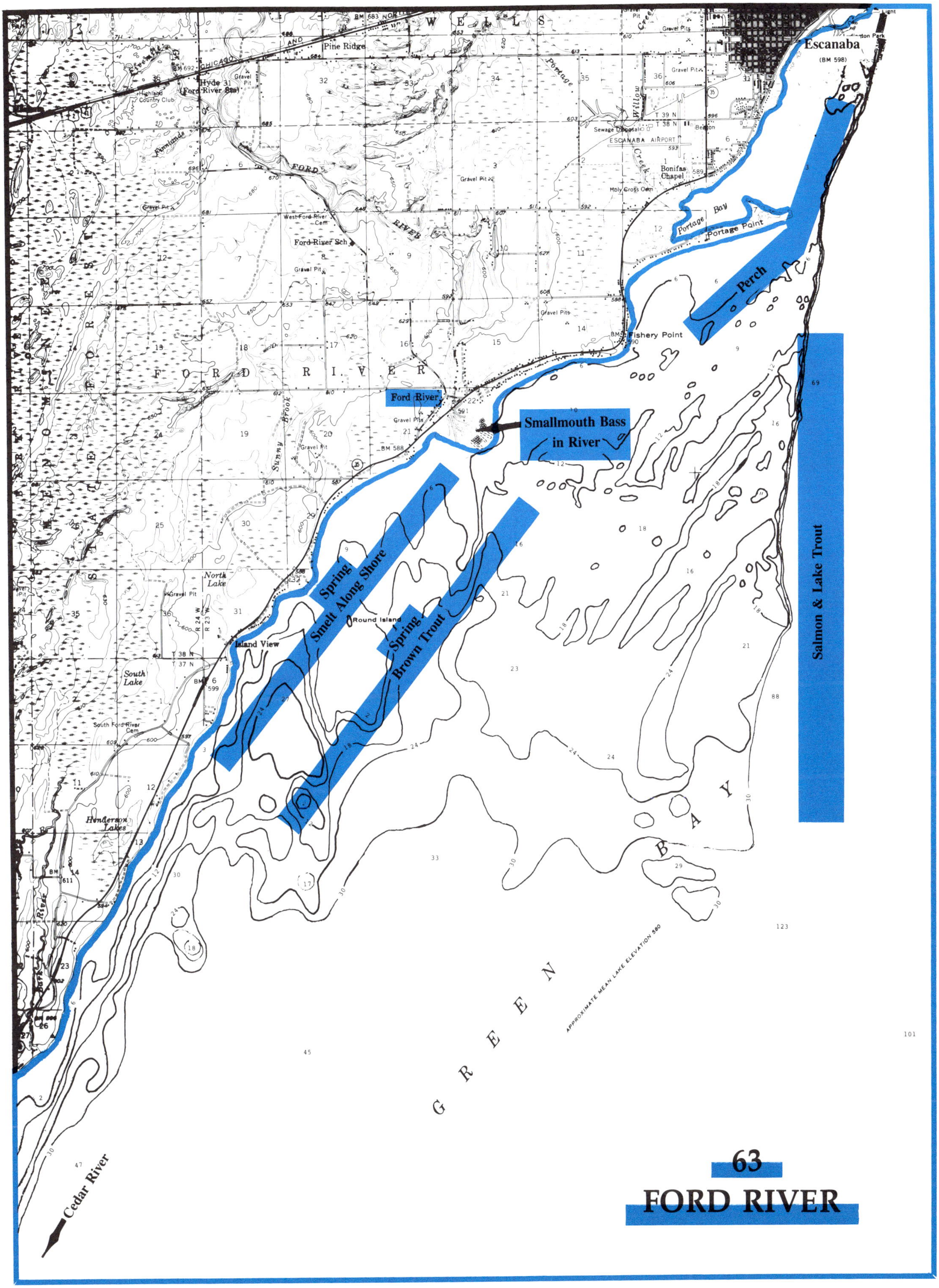

63
FORD RIVER

64
CEDAR RIVER

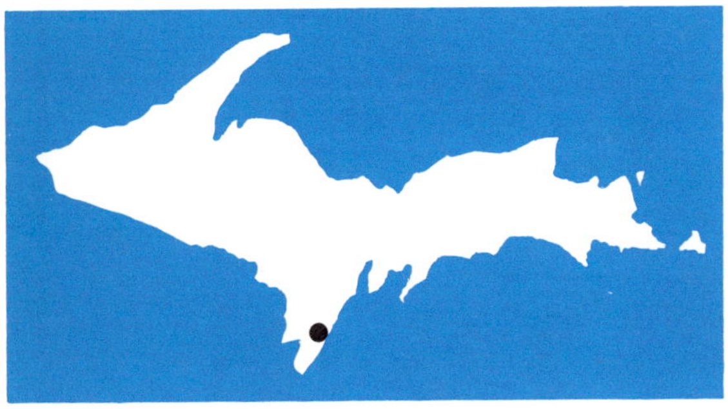

A well-kept fishing secret is the 24 miles of Lake Michigan shoreline from the Cedar River mouth to the Menominee River on the Wisconsin/Michigan boundary. One reason for the quiet is the lack of public boat-launching facilities between these points. Another is that many fishermen key on the more popular areas, such as the Menominee River, to the south and the Escanaba River, to the north.

But they might want to take a second look at the Cedar River region. There are some excellent fishing opportunities available.

Fishing Schedule

SPRING

Spring action begins at ice-out when smelt move into shoreline shallows to spawn, with hungry brown trout just behind. The browns in this area are from releases at Wells State Park, just below the Cedar River in Michigan waters, and in Wisconsin waters of Green Bay, including the Marinette/Menominee area (65). Wind in late March and April along this west shore can move ice in and out, making for hit-and-miss fishing opportunities. When trollers can get out, they stay within 20 feet of water and concentrate at bits of structure and off stream mouths.

I fished this region in early May 1985, and already Stoney Point motel-owner Emil Wright, who is an all-out brown-trout fisherman in this area, had been trolling for a month in his 14-foot Starcraft boat pushed by a 10-hp outboard. Brown-trout catches to that date by Emil and his motel customers had totaled 105 fish from two to 12 pounds each.

Wright says that fishing remains good from ice-out until the smelt start running full tilt. His theory is that the predatory browns have too much to eat then to be interested in lures. When smelt leave the shallows, fishing picks up again. I believe the theory because our group of a dozen fishermen drew mostly blanks, and the smelt were running hard during our two-day stay. The only fisherman in our party that scored consistently was General Motors retiree John Golomb of Saginaw, and he was trolling small emerald shiners that he had sewn to small treble hooks with a surgical needle. He rigged the bait 12 inches or so behind small strings of homemade cowbells.

Hot lures for Emil Wright have been No. 9 jointed or straight floating Rapalas in blue and silver or gold and black. Emil's technique is to slow troll ("I firmly believe in a trolling-speed indicator.") with flatlines, adding perhaps a split shot or two well ahead of the lure so as not to impede action. Contrary to many other brown-trout fishing experts, Wright trolls a straight course, rather than a zig-zag pattern. It is likely that light flutter-type spoons in silver alone or in combination with other colors would take browns, too, especially if the rigging involved long leads (15-50 feet) and shallow-set downriggers (two to five feet deep).

Landmarks south of Wright's Motel include DNR-installed riprap along shore near Stoney Point (1/2 mile south). There, a six-foot-deep reef runs a quarter-mile offshore and features 12 feet of water to either side. Other landmarks include the North Shore Golf Course clubhouse and a large TV tower. Five or six miles further south, smokestacks from Menominee's industry are evident. Landmarks to the north include Beatty's Point, at 1-1/2 miles, and an old green building that used to be Engleson's Fish House.

Besides brown trout, spring fishermen catch occasional rainbow trout, lake trout, coaster brook trout and salmon. Of more significance is an excellent run of perch off Stoney Point immediately following the demise of smelt spawning activity. Weed beds off the riprap to 15 or 20 feet of water produce the best action. Emil likes to tell the story of the June day he came back to his dock with five football-shaped brown trout. "Look at these," he said to some motel guests waiting on shore.

"Oh yeah? Look at these!" they answered, and proceeded to cover the top of a picnic table with jumbo yellow-bellies. Three perch laid end to end nicely fit across the three-foot-wide table.

SUMMER

Summer fishing for perch remains good off rock beds in deeper water and for brown trout near the surface in water to 50 feet deep. Trolling for Chinooks and cohos is good to depths of 65 feet when preferred water temperatures of 56-58 degrees F. can be found. Hot salmon lures are Northport Nailers in silver and blue and white with blue prism. When Wright wants salmon, he typically runs for 20 minutes in a northeasterly direction, stopping to check water temperatures four or five times, until he finds the magic mark.

Summer also produces some lake trout in 50-90 feet of water, with best catches coming off silver spoons pulled clean off downriggers or slammed in and out of the lake bottom with wire line.

FALL

Fall fishing continues to be good for brown trout and perch in the shallows along with incidental catches of rainbows, lakers and salmon.

There are no *winter* fishing activities to report.

The angling opportunities detailed above occur sporadically

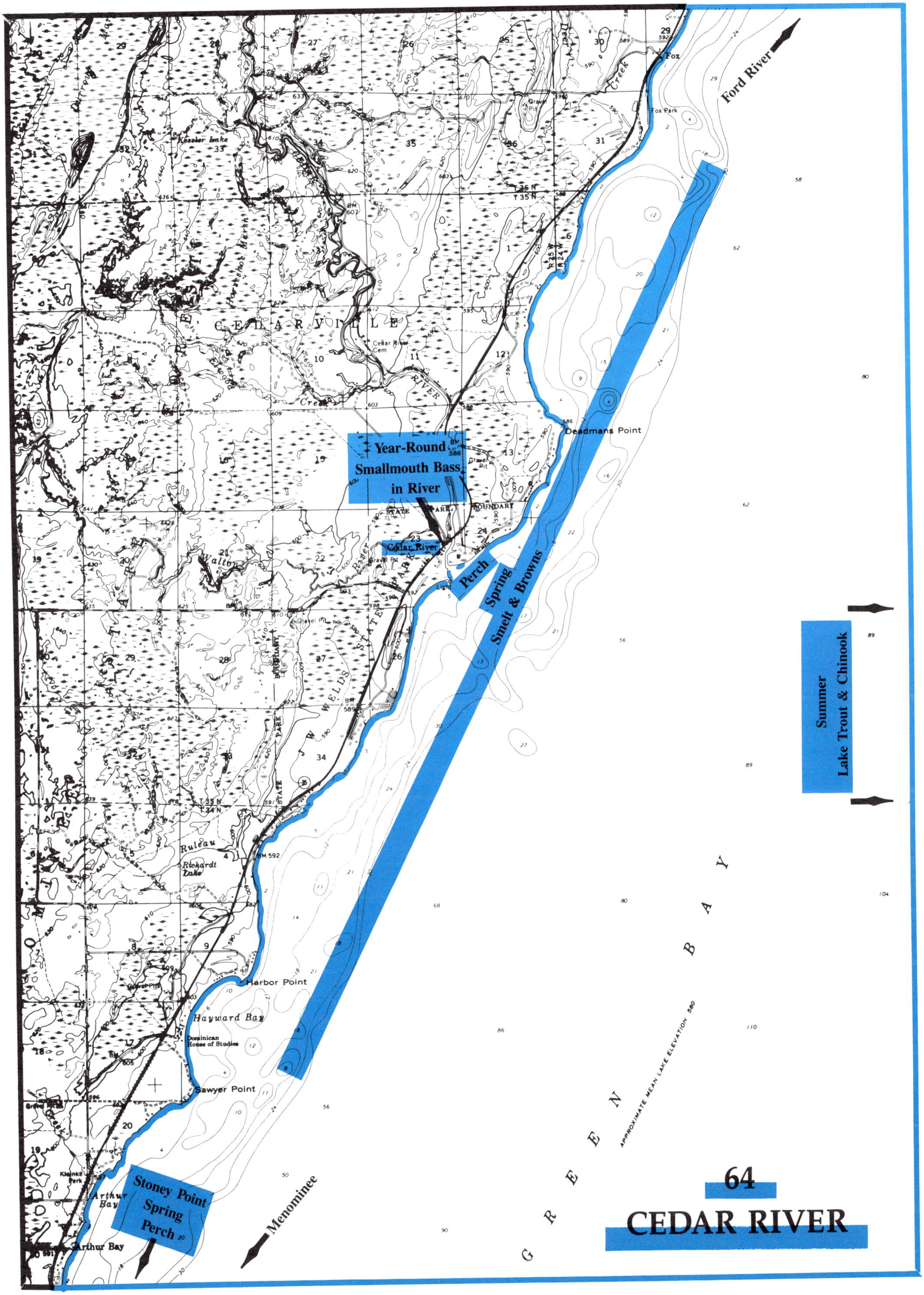
64
CEDAR RIVER
Year-Round
Smallmouth Bass
in River
Cedar River
Perch
Spring
Smelt & Browns
Summer
Lake Trout & Chinook
Stoney Point
Spring
Perch
Ford River
Menominee
GREEN BAY
Deadmans Point
Harbor Point
Sawyer Point
Hayward Bay
Arthur Bay
Fox Park
CEDARVILLE
Dominican
House of Studies
Richardt
Lake
Ruleau
Walton
J W WELLS STATE PARK
STATE PARK BOUNDARY
APPROXIMATE MEAN LAKE ELEVATION 580

What Was It?

It was May 6, 1985, and Roy Olk of Traverse City and I were finishing lunch·and shooting the breeze with Jim Nash. Nash owns a restaurant/bar at the Cedar River mouth and is an area fishing guide. Stan Lievense and John Spencer, also of Traverse City, had already eaten and had walked to the rivermouth to check out fishing conditions. Stan, one of Michigan's best-known anglers, can't stand still for long, especially if a fishing rod is nearby.

Suddenly John burst into the restaurant. "Stan's fighting a huge fish I hooked. Bring your cameras. Hurry!"

But my cameras were at Wright's Motel, 17 miles south at Birch Creek Road. So Roy and I rushed to the motel in Roy's truck while Spencer went back to help Stan.

When we returned about a half-hour later, we found those two, along with Jim Nash, in a small boat. It seems that right after we had left the restaurant, Nash had decided to take a look himself. Stan, wearing waders (which is why John had given the rod to him), was in the bow, his rod bent into a tight *C*, his line disappearing in the brown water just a few yards from the front of the boat.

"It surfaced once," he shouted. "Then it sounded again. I don't know what it is, but it's one helluva fish!"

With the help of hip boots, I was able to wade to within 30 yards and had my camera ready to record the action. Ten mintes passed. Then 10 more. All the while, the trio followed their quarry as it slowly swam up and down the river. I slogged through the shallows, staying as close as possible. Had the water been clearer, I might have seen what was towing their boat.

Suddenly the fish moved under what must have been a log, and Stan's eight-pound-test line snapped like kite string. A roar of disappointment, interjected by profanity, went up from the five of us. Stan's one-hour-and-five-minute battle was over.

What was it?

"I don't know," Lievense confessed, "but it felt like it weighed a hundred pounds."

Sturgeon maybe?

"Sturgeon don't strike lures, and this fish hit my spinner hard," Spencer said.

Huge catfish? Monster brown trout?

"We'll never know," Stan said. "It's enough to make a grown man cry."

Tom Huggler
Otisville

Stan Lievense (in bow of boat) fights mystery fish at the mouth of the Cedar River. John Spencer (on the oars) and local charterboat-captain Jim Nash give him all the help they can.

along the entire shoreline, with other hotspots developing off Wells State Park and especially at the mouth of the Cedar River.

Charterboat-captain Jim Nash, who owns a restaurant at the Cedar River, reported an average of just over nine fish per trip for 35 charters in 1985. Nash says that April and May are best for brown trout, July and August for Chinooks, July for yellow perch, and that lake trout are available all season long. Hot spoon for browns has been blue-and-silver Flutter Spoons, longlined (200-300 feet) at a slow trolling speed behind downrigger weights. King salmon have found silver-and-blue J-Plugs and green Northport Nailers tasty when the lures are set 10-50 feet behind releases and when boat speed is kicked up to 3.0 mph or more. Midsummer hunting tactics for trout and salmon take Nash from seven to 20 miles away from home.

Commercial fishermen, using trap nets off the Cedar River mouth, have proved there is an untapped sport fishery for whitefish in 50-125 feet of water during June and July. Further, the mouth of the Cedar River produces northern pike, smallmouth bass, catfish and all the cold-water species previously mentioned. The river itself hosts some outstanding smallmouth-bass fishing for spincast and live-bait fishermen in summer and fall.

Planting Records

Each spring through at least 1990, the Cedar River will receive 20,000 steelhead, and Wells State Park will get 10,000 rainbows and 15,000 browns. In addition to these traditional releases of yearling-age trout, Henes Park and Rochereau Point are each slated for 25,000 fall fingerling browns during this period.

Facilities

The DNR does not maintain a harbor of refuge in this area. There is one at nearby Menominee (65) with the following services: transient accommodations, gasoline and diesel fuel, water, electricity, restrooms, shower facilities, holding-tank pump-out and VHF-FM radio. The telephone number of the dock attendant is (906) 863-8498. There is some protection for small boats at the entrance to the Cedar River.

Launching sites are located at the rivermouth and at Wells State Park. At this writing, the DNR is constructing a new launch facility next to Wright's Motel, just north of Stoney Point.

Further Information

Chambers of Commerce:

1. Menominee Area Chamber of Commerce, 1005 10th Ave., Menominee 49858; (906) 863-2679.
2. Upper Peninsula Travel and Recreation Association, P.O. Box 400, Iron Mountain 49801; (906) 774-5480.

Bait & Tackle Shops:

None in the immediate area. Refer to Menominee (65) or Escanaba (62).

Charter Fishing:

Captain Jim Nash, Box 2B, Cedar River 49813; (906) 863-9277.

Department of Natural Resources:

Two fisheries biologists work out of District Headquarters at US-2 West, Crystal Falls 49920; (906) 875-6622.

Coast Guard:

Sturgeon Bay, Wisconsin, Station (414) 743-3366 or 743-3367.

65
MENOMINEE

M & M fishing action is the way the local chamber of commerce describes angling opportunities from the sister ports of Menominee, Michigan, and Marinette, Wisconsin. This portion of Green Bay in Lake Michigan serves up solid sport from spring through fall for a variety of gamefish species. Because the Menominee River falls into boundary waters of Michigan and Wisconsin, northern pike, walleyes and bass can be caught anytime. However, as these regulations are subject to change, anglers should carefully read their *Michigan Fishing Guide*.

Fishing Schedule

SPRING

Brown trout are the mainstay of the *spring* fishery at Menominee/Marinette. Action kicks off at ice-out in March or April and lasts through November. This early fishery involves shallow-water trolling (five to 15 feet deep) with 1/4- to 1/2-ounce Little Cleos, small Rebels and Rapalas, Rattlesnake Spoons, No. 44 Flutter Spoons, and small Fire Plugs. Hot colors are silver, silver and blue, silver and orange, chartreuse, and yellow and red. A few trollers pull silver- or copper-bladed cowbells ahead of sewn smelt or sucker minnows. Shallow-set downriggers and planer boards are the local tactics that produce the two- to 10-pound spring browns. Pier fishermen score by spincasting heavy-metal spoons in the above colors or by stillfishing spawn bags or cut bait on bottom.

These brown trout are available close to shore and off stream mouths from the Cedar River (64), north of the twin cities, to the Peshtigo River, south of them.

Spring steelhead/rainbows show up in the Menominee, Little Cedar and Peshtigo rivers and can be caught on fresh spawn, small spinners and spoons. According to local charterboat-captain Rick Estebo, spring trollers and pier anglers also pick up Chinook salmon, which are drawn to these same locations by smelt and other baitfish that gather here in the warmest water available.

Walleye fishing at ice-out is usually excellent in and around the Menominee River, especially at Lighthouse and Government piers (located at the rivermouth). Boat and shore fishermen, alike, work the river from this point upstream one mile to Scott Dam. Black-and-silver and blue-and-silver Rapalas and Rebels are the hot lures when cast or trolled. Nightcrawlers are also effective.

Spring yellow-perch fishing can be phenomenal at times, beginning at ice-out and lasting until June. Besides the Menominee River, best spots are Red Arrow Park, Menominee Marina, Stoney Point and weeded areas along the Green Bay shoreline. Most perchers bait up with minnows, wigglers or worms.

Also in early spring, northern pike fishing is good in the river above Scott Dam, especially on topwater lures worked over weed beds. Spinnerbaits, digging plugs, and surface lures also produce in various colors, as pike are none too picky about slamming what they think is a free meal. Most fishermen spincast or troll these lures, both in the river or on the open bay.

SUMMER

Summer sport continues for brown trout from June through August, but trollers now begin to target 55- to 60-degree-F. water that is 20 to 90 feet deep. Wind direction often dictates where and how deep the thermocline is found in this area. A west wind, for example, blows warm water out into the bay, but an east wind

Brown trout are one of many calling cards at Menominee. This 10-pounder was caught while casting spoons from the pier.

tends to pile up cold water closer to shore. Downriggers and trip-divers, such as Dipsy-Divers and Deep Sixes, help get lures to the depths where browns are holding. Rattlesnake Spoons and Flutter Spoons continue to produce, along with Northport Nailers, Andy Reekers, and Salmon Seekers. Spring colors are equally productive in summer.

Summertime king salmon are generally found in deeper water than browns. Look for 53- to 56-degree-F. water from 40-110 feet. The same lures just mentioned will score with kings, but also plan to run a few J-Plugs or lookalike lures, such as Lucky Louies and Grizzlies, especially if you are "hunting" salmon and stacking lines (plugs on bottom, spoons on top). Silver, alone or in combinations with other colors, is the experts' choice. By mid-August, soon-to-spawn kings will be schooled off the Menominee, Little and Peshtigo rivers. Pier and shore anglers take them then on spoons and spawn, while shallow-water trollers score with big wobbling plugs (J-Plugs, Flatfish, Tadpollies) and any large spoon. Hot-fluorescent colors work best.

Brook trout are available in the Little River to worm, spawn, and spincast fishermen. Boat and pier anglers catch them in all seasons, incidental to other fish.

An excellent smallmouth-bass fishery occurs in June, July, August and September in the Menominee River. Good spots are below Scott Dam in the Train Bridge Island area and above the dam near Cox Boat Landing (which also yields largemouth bass). Nightcrawlers and minnows fished along bottom in the current are good baits. Rated lures are Rooster Tail spinners, Rebels, and Rapalas.

Walleye action continues all summer at the Hattie Street Bridge and the railway bridge while using nightcrawlers fished from shore or boat. Trollers also pull Rebels and Rapalas both above and below Scott Dam.

Perch fishing is a hit-or-miss affair throughout the summer. Clusters of fishing boats mean anglers have found a wandering school of yellow-bellies and are likely catching some.

FALL

Fall fishing remains good for brown trout in the shallows, Chinooks in the rivers, and rainbows near rivermouths. There is a fall run of large northern pike near the Lighthouse Pier and Menominee Marina. Spinnerbaits and spoons produce for spincasters, and dead smelt fished on bottom or live minnows fished halfway to bottom below bobbers rate high among bait fishermen.

In addition, the Menominee River hosts a run of sturgeon in fall, with the area at McAllister Bridge the most popular spot. Best times are early morning, late afternoon or throughout the night. Huge nightcrawler gobs threaded to big treble hooks and fished on the bottom is the rated tactic. Heavy-duty rods and reels and Dacron line in 60- or 80-pound test are necessary to land one of these prehistoric brutes.

WINTER

Fall fishing continues to be good for perch, walleyes and brook trout.

Winter activity is generally good for yellow perch, and tip-up fishermen and spearers score on northern pike.

Planting Records

The Michigan DNR has reduced Menominee-area stockings to just rainbow trout and plans to stock 10,000 yearling fish each spring through at least 1990. However, fish mix freely here and include Chinooks, brown trout and steelhead/rainbow from other Michigan releases. In addition, the Wisconsin DNR annually targets this area of Green Bay for hefty salmonid stockings. In recent years, these include yearly plants of brook trout in the Peshtigo River (to 85,000 fish) and these species at Marinette: 15,000 brook trout, 25,000-50,000 rainbows, 60,000-90,000 brown trout and 200,000-420,000 Chinooks.

Collectively, these liberal stockings should continue to make the *M & M* sister ports a good place to fish for many years.

Facilities

The DNR maintains a harbor of refuge with the following services: transient accommodations, gasoline and diesel fuel, water, electricity, restrooms, shower facilities, holding-tank pump-out and VHF-FM radio. The telephone number of the dock attendant is (906) 863-8498.

There is also a launch facility at the harbor. Other boat launches are located in Michigan at the Cedar River (64) and Stoney Point. Wisconsin launch sites are found at the Little River, Peshtigo River, Cox Boat Landing (one mile northwest of Marinette on Hwy. 180) on the Menominee River, and Red Arrow Park on Leonard Street in Marinette.

Further Information

Chambers of Commerce:

1. Menominee Area Chamber of Commerce, 1005 10th Ave., Menominee 49858; (906) 863-2679.
2. Upper Peninsula Travel and Recreation Association, P.O. Box 400, Iron Mountain 49801; (906) 774-5480.

Bait & Tackle Shops:

Pete's Sport Shop, 2005 10th Ave., Menominee 49858; (906) 863-4673.

Charter Fishing:

Captain Rick Estebo, 1613 15th Ave., Menominee 49858; (906) 863-6502. 17-foot Yar-Craft, *Bald Eagle.*

Department of Natural Resources:

Two fisheries biologists work out of District Headquarters at US-2 West, Crystal Falls 49920; (906) 875-6622.

Coast Guard:

Sturgeon Bay, Wisconsin, Station, (414) 743-3366 or 743-3367.

How to Catch a Trophy Northern

How do you catch a trophy pike? According to Dan Mauser, a pike ferret from Cleveland, Ohio, live bait fished with bobbers produces the biggest fish. Giant pike didn't grow big by being dumb, so fishermen need to be extremely crafty to catch them, according to Mauser, who has caught them from the Great Lakes, Canada and Europe. Here are his suggestions:

1. Be absolutely still, keep your voice down, and do not bang the boat sides or bottom.

2. When your bobber runs in circles, chances are a big northern is playing cat and mouse with the minnow. Twitch the bobber to trigger a strike.

3. If the bobber is running away fast, a pike is in the area. Toss a handful of gravel just ahead of the bobber, again, to trigger a strike.

4. To move a stagnant baitfish along or to free it from the weeds, try using a small balloon as a bobber.

5. Consider painting the bottom half of your bobbers an aqua color to avoid detection by trophy pike.

6. When fishing islands and wind and rain hit, motor to the lee side and resume fishing. Forage fish will flock to the protected side and draw big northerns.

65 MENOMINEE

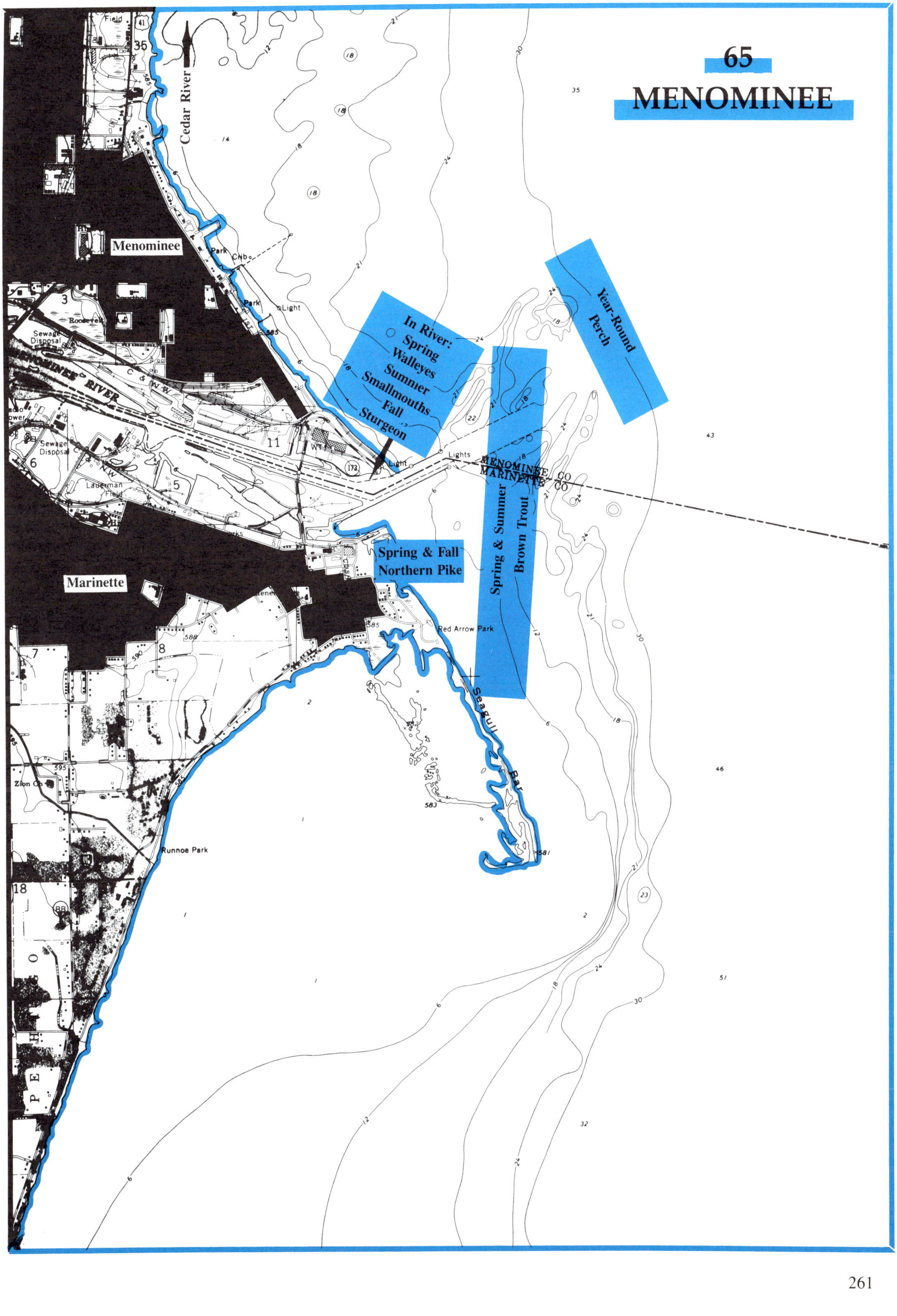

66
BLACK RIVER HARBOR

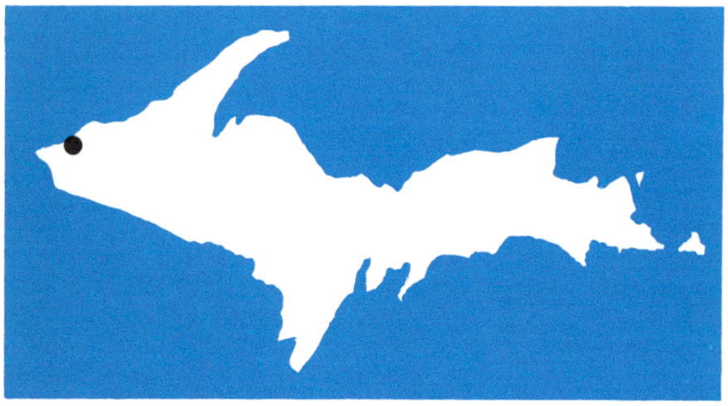

Black River Harbor and the Lake Superior shoreline are favorite spots for trout and salmon fishermen in the western Upper Peninsula. Though the region also serves up brown trout, steelhead, and coho and Chinook salmon, 80 percent of the fishing effort is aimed at lake trout. The Black River Harbor area is one of the few places in Lake Superior which has a population of Siscowet lake trout, locally referred to as "fats." These are barrel-bellied forktails to 20 pounds each or more, not easy to catch, perhaps, but certainly available. It is every lake-trout fisherman's dream to bring one to net.

Fishing Schedule

SPRING

In May, *spring* action kicks off for salmon and lake trout just outside the harbor, with most trollers keying in 50-100 feet of water. Action—consistent whether trollers head west toward Saxon Harbor or east toward Ontonagon Harbor (68)—lasts until October.

Most serious trollers in western Lake Superior rely on planer boards (skis), outriggers and sometimes downriggers to run a wide spread of lures. And because of light pressure from other fishermen, they can often troll close to shore with these specialized tactics. One of the best-known fishermen out of Black River Harbor and Ontonagon (68) is Captain Gary Eskola of Ironwood. Eskola is an innovative angler, and his experimentations with trolling tactics have resulted in the Sparky Ski, a five-foot-long planer board that is the mainstay of his rigging arsenal. (See 68, Ontonagon Harbor, for details.)

Eskola and others take lake trout averaging eight to 10 pounds, cohos in the four-pound class, and kings that run six to 12 pounds, depending upon how they rig. ("If we want to fish strictly for salmon," Gary says, "we raise lines." An average catch of salmon is 15 fish; most local fishermen, however, target lake trout.) They also hook occasional steelhead to 15 pounds each and brown trout to 10 pounds each. Besides looking for 50-100 feet of water, they seek stream mouths, especially for early season action.

Hot lures for Eskola have been three-inch Andy Reeker spoons in silver and green, silver, white with red dots, and red and yellow with black dots. He said that 80 percent of his 1985 catch came off those lures. Other proven fish-getters have been No. 2 and No. 3 Finn Spoons in silver (Eskola scratches the bright-silver spoons to dull them) and gold (he adds red tape and a silver dot); Milje Spoons in yellow with red dots, fluorescent orange, brass, and a new gold color; No. 3 Mepps spoons; and yellow-green or silver Flutter Chucks.

SUMMER

In June most *summer* trollers head for deeper water but key on the thermocline and generally run lures from about 45 feet deep to bottom. Claiming that trolling speed is now critical, Eskola keeps it at 3.2 knots on his SiTex Loran C. In July and August, he generally deepens dropper lines off his skis from 60-80 feet deep and bounces one or more downrigger balls off bottom.

FALL

In *fall*, when lake trout and salmon return to the harbor area to spawn, good lures are No. 3 white or silver J-Plugs, white or chartreuse Mac Squids, and Andy Reeker spoons in chartreuse and silver or white with red dots. Lake trout seem to hit all day, but the best time for salmon is from about 3:30 p.m. until dark or early in the morning before sunup. Although dodgers and flies are a hot coho combination in the Ontonagon Harbor area (68), they have not caught on with Black River Harbor fishermen.

Chinook salmon begin showing up in early August, with peak activity usually occurring around Labor Day. Coho salmon follow and then are replaced by lake trout later in September and October. Steelhead appear later in the fall and in spring. (The Montreal River, near Saxon Harbor on the Wisconsin/Michigan border, offers fair to good spring sport for naturally reproduced steelhead.) All these species are available to breakwall fishermen and those with small boats who ply the harbor or fish just outside the breakwalls. Little Girls Point produces brown-trout and salmon fishing for both boat and shore anglers.

WINTER

Winter fishing activities are fair to good in the harbor for lake trout and occasional browns, salmon and steelhead. When ice forms on Lake Superior, lake-trout success while jigging with cut bait can be exceptional.

Planting Records

The Black River Harbor area has a long history of consistent trout and salmon releases. The Black River itself receives 75,000 each of cohos and kings every spring along with 15,000 steelhead. Reefs in the area are stocked with 60,000 lake trout each year, and the Presque Isle River in Porcupine Mountains State Park (about 25 miles to the northeast) receives 15,000 steelhead each spring. Little Girls Point, about 20 miles to the west, got 15,000 brown trout in 1985. Plantings at these rates will continue

66 BLACK RIVER HARBOR

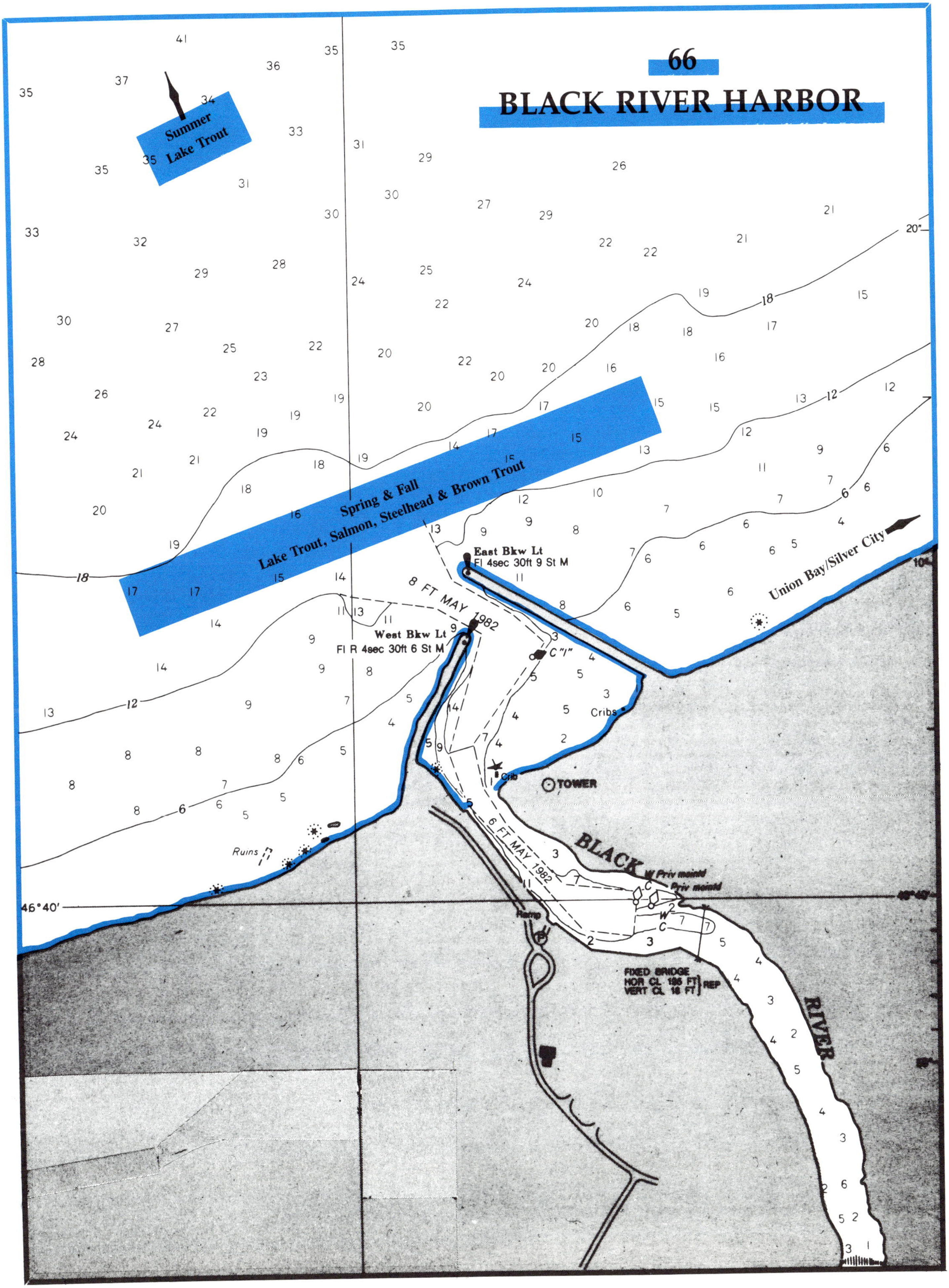

annually through at least 1990.

Facilities

The DNR maintains a harbor of refuge at Black River with gasoline, water and restrooms the only available services. There is also a state-maintained boat launch there.

Further Information

Chambers of Commerce:

1. Ironwood Chamber of Commerce, 100 East Aurora St., Ironwood 49938; (906) 932-1122.
2. Upper Peninsula Travel and Recreation Association, P.O. Box 400, Iron Mountain 49801; (906) 774-5480.

Bait & Tackle Shops:

1. Larry's Bait Shop, US-2 & E. Cloverland Dr., Ironwood 49938; (906) 932-1720.
2. Black Bear Sporting Goods, 101 W. Cloverland Dr., Ironwood 49938; (906) 932-5253.

Charter Fishing:

1. Captain Gary Eskola, E. 5061 Jackson Rd., Ironwood 49938; (906) 932-2478. 31-foot Trojan Sportfisherman, *Sparky*.
2. Captain Jim Johnson, Route 1 Box 357, Ironwood 49938; (906) 932-5196. 32-foot boat, *Jolly Roger V*.

Department of Natural Resources:

Two fisheries biologists work out of District Headquarters at US-41 North, Baraga; (906) 353-6651.

Coast Guard:

Portage Station in Hancock, (906) 482-1520 or 482-3253.

Downriggers for Ice Fishing?

It's funny how new angling techniques originate. I was talking with an old fellow from LaCrosse, Wisconsin, one summer day, and he wondered why I hadn't tried ice fishing with downriggers.

"Because it will never work," I told him.

"How do you know until you try it?" he asked.

I got to thinking about what he said. Then one December day before Christmas, when the snow was already three feet deep, I thought why not? So I and Skip Wich, a retired friend, hauled a small generator and a couple of electric Walker downriggers onto the ice off Washburn near the Onion River.

We plopped our gear onto the ice between the old coal pile and the lighthouse a half-mile from shore over about 100 feet of water. Skip cut holes with a power auger, then we used an old ice-block saw to square them up. Each of our downriggers was mounted to a 2 x 8. These we lay across the holes, then weighted each end of each board with a pile of snow. We hooked dead smelt or chunks of sucker meat to our hooks, added a couple of split shots two feet above (The split shots help the bait to flutter away from the weight.), then—with the help of four-pound cannonballs—sent the bait down. After letting out about 15 feet of line, we pinched the monofilament to our Walker releases (mounted just above the cannonballs), then lowered the rig electrically until the bait was halfway to bottom. We quickly learned that we were able to jig electrically by hitting the switch on our downriggers.

Pretty soon we had a strike, which popped the downrigger rod free of the downrigger (just like trolling), and we fought a six-pound lake trout to the hole. It took only a couple of hours to ice a two-man limit (10 fish) of lake trout and splake from three to 11 pounds each.

The other fishermen on the ice that day seemed to focus a lot of attention on what we were doing. I guess they didn't believe that you can catch trout by ice fishing with downriggers. But that old fellow from LaCrosse was right. You can.

Gary Eskola
Ironwood

These lake-trout trollers team up to land a small forktail from Lake Superior. Although salmon are available to Black River Harbor fishermen, most seek lake trout.

67 UNION BAY and SILVER CITY

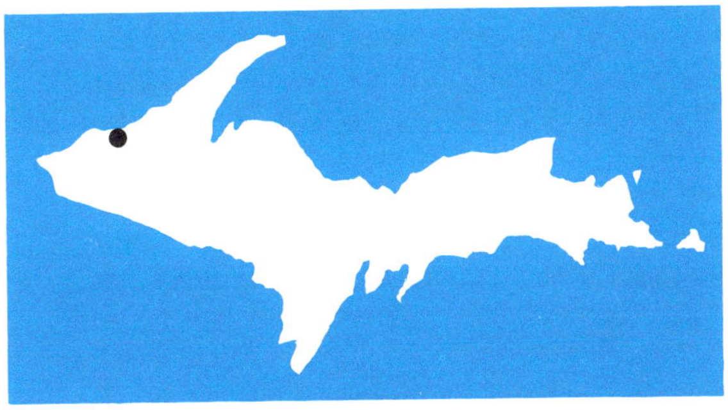

Some 50 miles of Lake Superior lap Ontonagon County shores, and dozens of rivers and creeks race down small mountains or meander through conifer forests into the big lake. Good to excellent fishing opportunities and little competition exist throughout this desolate country. Facilities, however, are very limited.

In addition to Union Bay and Silver City, trolling boats and shore fishermen key at Ontonagon Harbor (68) and Black River Harbor (66).

Fishing Schedule

Probably 90 percent of the fishing activity at Silver City and Union Bay occurs from Memorial Day to Labor Day. Cold water makes fishing success unpredictable earlier than late May, and strong winds can force blow days at summer's end. Further, when Superior feels troublesome, there are no islands or peninsulas in the area to break its wrath. An 18-mph wind from the west or southwest will produce waves to three or four feet, maximum safe height for all but the largest boats.

From Silver City 112 miles east to Ontonagon, the lake does not drop off very rapidly. In fact, five miles from shore the water is only about 130 feet deep. This relatively shallow area is first to warm, a condition that attracts lake trout and salmon in *spring*. The fish are also here because 13 rivers empty warm water and food into Lake Superior in this stretch.

SPRING

Much of Ontonagon County is clay-soiled; therefore, many of her rivers, such as the Ontonagon, are roiled. But trout rivers, like the Big Iron, and many smaller streams often host spawning smelt, which attract lakers. Lake trout, in fact, usually hang out in 60-100 feet of water long after the smelt have left.

So most area trollers head for this region until early or mid-July when temperatures grow too warm for lake trout (they prefer 48-52 degrees F.) Then, the fish move to the west, where a completely different type of habitat exists and where the water is then warming to their liking. As one might expect, dropoffs from the Porcupine Mountains near Union Bay plunge as deep as 130 feet only a few hundred yards offshore. Further, the only substantial stream in the 12- to 15-mile stretch is the Union River, which empties into Union Bay.

Fishing in the two areas, then, is distinctly different and amounts to a game of watching water temperatures. Charterboat-skipper Elton Polecheck of Silver City takes water temperatures constantly, especially after a hard northwest blow or following several days of hot, muggy weather. "It is not an easy area to troll," he says, "because it is large and you have to know the habits of the fish."

That is partly why Polecheck and other all-out fishermen key on lake trout and largely ignore some fine salmon-fishing opportunities here. Because salmon are not the target species, most that are caught are "volunteer" fish. A second reason why Elton and others bypass salmon is because the lake-trout rigging system that they employ is complicated and time-consuming to set up and take down. And thirdly, most of the fishermen in this area have lake trout in their back pockets, so to speak, and can therefore produce more fish for less effort.

Average catches for Elton in 1985 were 10-15 lake trout for a five-hour dock-to-dock charter (about 3-1/2 hours of actual trolling time). Average weight of the lakers was seven or eight pounds, but Polecheck and others reported plenty of 10- to 15-pounders, too. Elton's best catch was a 23-1/2 pound fish, a Siscowet-strain lake trout, locally called a "fat." (See "Lake Superior Lakers," page 266, for an explanation.)

Rigging consists of two handlines (another term for wire-line trolling), two outriggers, and up to six skis (three to a side) that are each five feet long. Each ski can carry up to four dropper

Lake Superior

Length—350 miles

Breadth—160 miles

Length of coastline (including Canada and islands)—2,730 miles

Total water surface—31,700 square miles

U.S. water surface—20,600 square miles

Total land drainage basin—49,300 square miles

U.S. drainage—16,900 square miles

Maximum depth—1,333 feet

Average depth—489 feet

Volume of water—2,935 cubic miles

lines. (For an in-depth explanation of the multi-ski rigging system see "Skiing for Lake Trout," page 270.) This multi-ski system is very successful because lures can be run at varying depths between 20 and 80 feet, the favorite limits throughout the trolling season.

For wire-line trolling, muskie rods, thick as pool cues, are mated to Pfleuger direct-action reels that are spooled with seven-strand 90-pound-test wire line. Special cowbells that are 6-1/2 feet long and that contain three big blades and four smaller ones are rigged 12-14 inches ahead of a marshmallow-sized piece of cut sucker, which itself is attached to a large treble hook. Lead weights of three to four pounds spear the cowbell/cut bait near bottom.

Productive lures include light three- to four-inch-long (less hooks) silver spoons (the make is not important) and Eppinger Dardevle spoons in red and white and jack of diamonds (yellow with red diamonds).

Typical *summer* fishing tactics call for Polecheck to troll out from shore until he finds optimum temperature (48-52 degrees F.) from 50-90 feet down. That is where he will set lines.

Besides lake trout, summer produces good catches of brown trout following several days of hot, still weather. Browns go on feeding binges under those conditions and are then caught near the surface. In addition to browns and occasional salmon, trollers also pick up stray steelhead, again off the highlines.

Some good *fall* salmon-fishing opportunities are going largely unnoticed at this writing. A DNR Baraga District report for September 3, 1985, for example, stated: "King salmon fishing in the Big Iron River is good to excellent, although there have been few reports of anyone getting their limit. The fish are running 13 to 19 pounds and are being found in shallow water—20 feet or less." These fish are available to both shore and shallow-water fishermen. Best tactics would be to slow troll with big wobbling plugs (J-Plugs, Flatfish, Kwikfish, Tadpollies) in bright colors.

There are no *winter* fishing activities to report since ice that does form on Lake Superior in this region is usually unsafe.

SUMMER

FALL

Lake Superior Lakers

According to Jim Peck, a fisheries biologist with the Michigan DNR, there are three races of Lake Superior lake trout: leans, humpers and Siscowet. Leans are being planted by Michigan, Wisconsin and Minnesota departments of natural resources and by the U.S. Fish & Wildlife Service. Leans also reproduce naturally in some offshore areas, such as Stannard Rock (40 miles north of Marquette), 74, and around Isle Royale. Well distributed throughout the lake, they can grow to huge proportions, but most enter coolers as three- to 15-pound statistics. Leans are the best-eating lakers in Superior.

Humpers are a dwarf variety (10 to 15 inches) that don't figure much in the sport catch. Many spawn naturally in the Caribou Island grounds north of Grand Marais, Michigan.

Siscowet are widely distributed throughout deep-water reef areas, sometimes as far down as 300-350 feet. Known locally as "fats," they frequently show up in shallow areas, such as the Black River Harbor region, to feed.

"They're a disagreeable fish," says Elton Polecheck, a charterboat captain from Silver City. "They are oily with jellied layers of fat between the skin and flesh. They are also a slimy fish, and you will have to wash your net after catching one. They're horrible to eat. If you put them in your garden for fertilizer, nothing will grow."

Then why catch them?

"They grow so big," Peck said. "I have seen many of these fish in the 30-pound bracket, and I even saw a commercial catch once of a 40-pounder."

Polecheck says there is at least one other kind of lake trout in Lake Superior. "We call it a "50-50" or a "mooneye," and we think it is a cross between a Siscowet and a lean Mackinaw (lake trout). They're a nice-looking fish with soft, pink meat. A few moments after you bring one aboard, though, their eyes bulge and they turn gold like a goldfish." Polecheck said he catches many of the mooneyes each summer aboard his charters and that a reef on the northeast end of Isle Royale is a breeding ground for the so-called cross-bred lake trout.

Jim Peck, Marquette
Elton Polecheck, Silver City

Planting Records

The Big Iron River at Silver City has been planted with spring fingerling Chinook salmon for many years, and plans call for the DNR to continue releasing 75,000 annually through at least 1990. Union Bay lake-trout stockings have been bumped to 92,500 each year (up from 50,000) during this period. Brown-trout releases of 20,000 fall fingerlings will continue, and a program to introduce rainbows that began in 1985 with 15,000 yearlings is expected to continue at that rate.

Facilities

The DNR maintains a boat-launching ramp on the east bank of the Big Iron River at Silver City. There is also a public launch site in the Porcupine Mountains State Park, but local fishermen rate it only fair and you must have a valid state parks sticker affixed to your vehicle windshield to enter the park. There is no boat launch in Union Bay, nor are there any between Silver City and Ontonagon.

Further Information

Chambers of Commerce:

1. Ontonagon County Chamber of Commerce, Box 266, Ontonagon 49953; (906) 884-4735.
2. Upper Peninsula Travel and Recreation Association, P.O. Box 400, Iron Mountain 49801; (906) 774-5480.

Bait & Tackle Shops:

None known.

Charter Fishing:

Captain Elton Polecheck, P.O. Box 313, White Pine 49971; (906) 885-5435. 36-foot twin-engine Penn Yan, *Mary-El.*

Department of Natural Resources:

Two fisheries biologists work out of District Headquarters at US-41 North, Baraga; (906) 353-6651.

Coast Guard:

Portage Station in Hancock, (906) 482-1520 or 482-3253.

67 UNION BAY and SILVER CITY

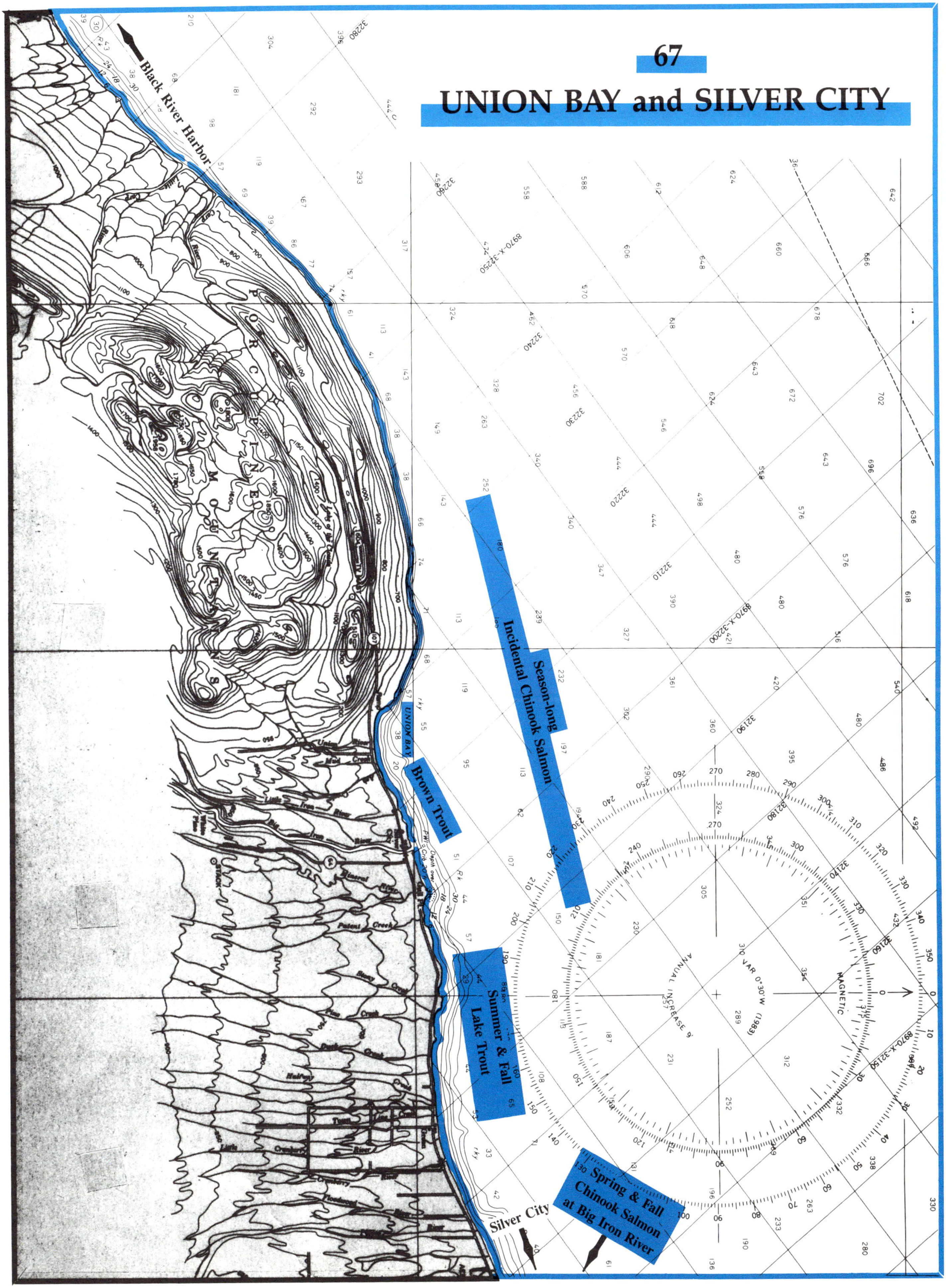

68

ONTONAGON HARBOR

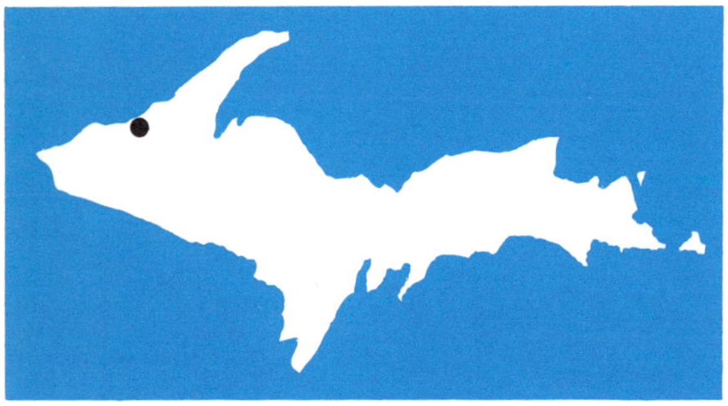

Ontonagon Harbor is located at the base of the Keweenaw Peninsula in western Lake Superior. Most trollers stay within a mile or two of the breakwall for a simple reason: That's where the fish are throughout the early May to October fishing season. The water gradually drops here so that even two miles from shore it is only 80 feet deep.

When I asked a charterboat skipper for an unusual story from this port, he said, "Unusual story? Tell your readers it would be unusual if they didn't fill up. That's how good the fishing is here."

Fishing Schedule

"You can catch just about anything you want here in Ontonagon if you decide to fish for it," says charterboat-skipper Al Pletzke. But lake trout are the target of most trollers and contribute perhaps 80 percent toward daily catches all season long. They average five or six pounds, but forktails to 18 and 20 pounds are not uncommon.

SPRING

In *spring*, trollers work off the mouth of the Ontonagon River, where fish are attracted by warm water and the influx of food entering Lake Superior. Typical rigging on the bigger boats calls for skis with dropper lines and outriggers in the upper 50-60 feet of water. Finn Spoons are preferred, with gold color getting the go-ahead on dark days or when the water is murky, and silver getting the nod on sunny or clear-water days.

SUMMER

Most fishermen regularly take water temperatures, then troll areas of 45-55 degrees F. when they can find this mark. In May, that is likely to be off the rivermouth, but as *summer* progresses and the thermocline develops, it may be a couple of miles from shore.

Cohos and Chinooks, most likely from releases in the Big Iron and Black rivers, further down the lake, show up in the Ontonagon area off and on throughout the trolling season. Pletzke says that if his clients want salmon, it is easy enough to take a dozen fish on an outing. "But most trollers are after lake trout, and because we run skis, it is too much trouble to switch over to highlines and downriggers for salmon," he explains. "Still we catch a few salmon off the skis, too." Best opportunities for salmon begin in late July and last throughout August. Because some of the fish have established runs in the Ontonagon River, they are also available to small-boat and shore fishermen.

Besides lakers and salmon, the region serves up spring smelt-dipping opportunities in small, clear streams emptying into Lake Superior. There are also rainbows in the harbor in spring and fall, plus the Ontonagon River hosts a run of walleyes in June and early July, with fish up to 10 pounds reported. Boat fishermen troll small spoons or nightcrawler harnesses in the harbor, and bank fishermen cast spoons and spinners or fish nightcrawlers on bottom. The Ontonagon River also hosts a run of naturally reproduced brown trout, with fish available to trollers during the hot period of summer and to river fishermen in fall. Pletzke said he and his customers boxed nine browns one summer day in 1985, including a fine 14-pound fish.

FALL

There are some fishing opportunities from the harbor breakwall from spring through *fall*, but great care should be exercised, especially when waves are pounding the structure.

There are no *winter* fishing opportunities to report.

Planting Records

Lake-trout releases over reefs have been the only stockings of hatchery-reared fish in the Ontonagon area. Annual plants have fluctuated between 25,000 and 50,000 fish but are expected to increase to an average of 92,500 through at least 1990.

Facilities

The DNR maintains a boat-launching site and harbor of refuge with the following services: transient accommodations, gasoline, pay telephone, water, electricity, restrooms, shower facilities, haul-out facilities, holding-tank pump-out and dock attendant.

Further Information

Chambers of Commerce:

1. Ontonagon County Chamber of Commerce, Box 266, Ontonagon 49953; (906) 884-4735.
2. Upper Peninsula Travel and Recreation Association, P.O. Box 400, Iron Mountain 49801; (906) 774-5480.

Bait & Tackle Shops:

None known.

Charter Fishing:

1. Captain Al Pletzke, P.O. Box 231, Bruce Crossing 49912; (906) 827-3466. 28-foot boat, *Voyager*.
2. Captain Gary Eskola, P.O. Box 11-V, Ironwood 49938; (906) 932-2478. 31-foot Trojan Sportfisherman, *Sparky*.

68 ONTONAGON HARBOR

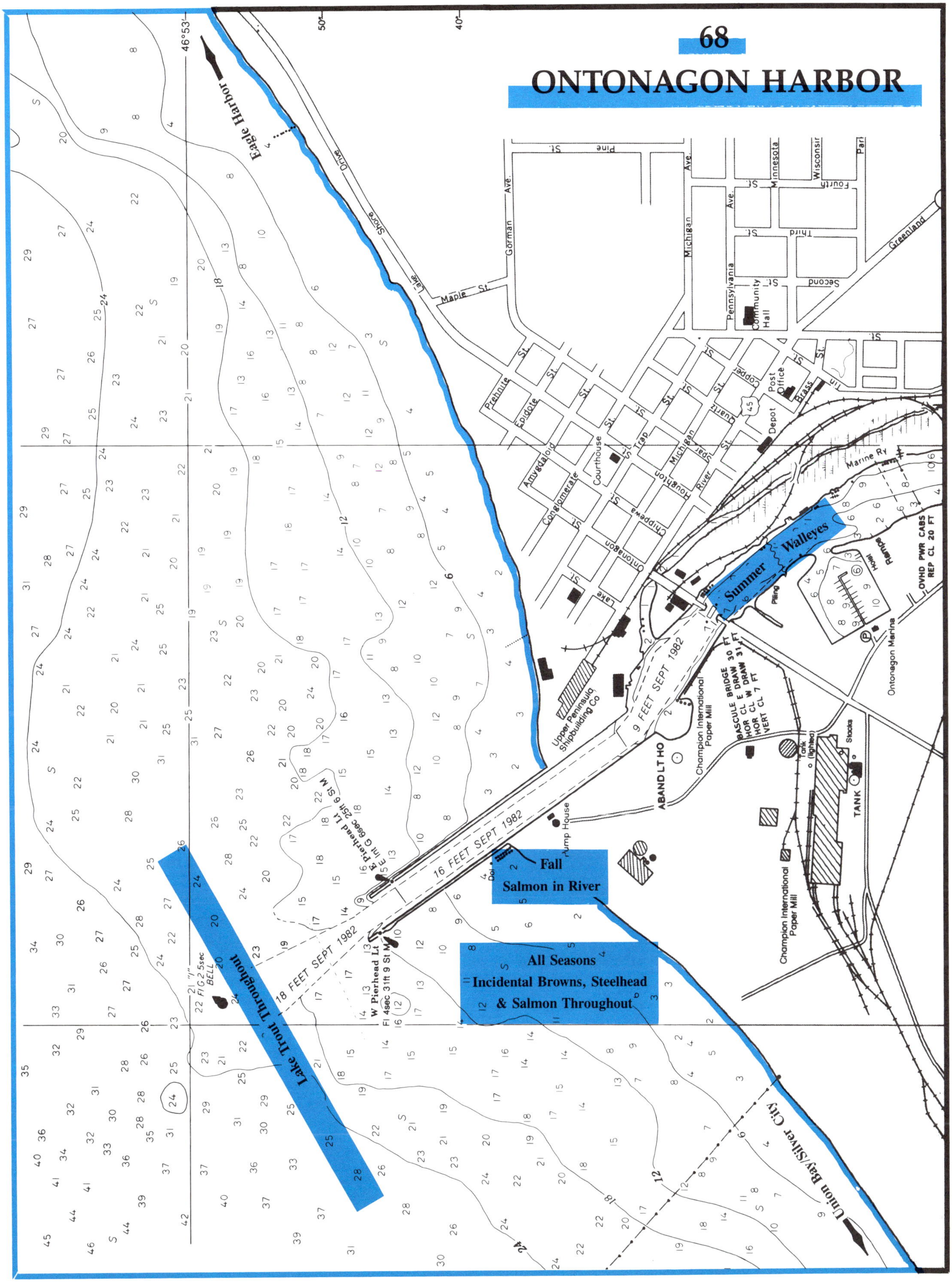

Department of Natural Resources:

Two fisheries biologists work out of District Headquarters at US-41 North, Baraga; (906) 353-6651.

Coast Guard:

Portage Station in Hancock, (906) 482-1520 or 482-3253.

This Lake Superior lake trout hit a dodger and Wobble-Glo.

Skiing for Lake Trout

You would expect trolling tactics for lake trout to be a big production on the biggest of our Great Lakes, and it is. Although many of us use downriggers and wire line, the biggest trolling aid is the "ski," also known downstate as the "planer board." I make and sell my own, which I call Sparky Skis. They are four feet long, and they enable me to troll a swath of water nearly a hundred yards wide to each side of my 31-foot boat.

Here's how they work: Using bolts and brackets, I secure a mast of two inches by four inches by 16 feet to each side of the boat cabin. Four braided-nylon tethers are attached, one above the other, to each mast by means of a 30-inch stretch cord. Each line is then secured to a single ski for a total of four skis per side. The top-set tether is 290 feet long, the distance that the farthest ski will cut away from the boat when the board is dropped into the lake. Lines gradually shorten—from 230 feet to 120 feet to 60 feet—as they come down the mast. A strike on any one ski will ring a bell attached to the mast.

The second half of our unique system is the ski itself. Made of wood with an aluminum keel, each ski features an adjustable spring-loaded release so that when tripped by a strike, the board falls neatly behind the boat. Attached to the center of each ski is a trolling shank of wire line in 20-foot sections up to 100 feet long. A two-pound weight is attached to the lower end, and up to four lures with 18-foot monofilament leaders trail off at 20-foot intervals. Sleeves on the trolling shank stop leaders from sliding, and since each is only 18 feet long, a hooked fish cannot tangle with lines above or below.

We do get an occasional foul-up with this system, but we are also fine-tuning it all the time. For instance, lately I have sent the corner skis further out and replaced one set of skis with downriggers. This helps us to set up faster, too. The biggest problem occurs when a school of Chinook salmon decide to hit the lures. Chinooks can give you fits because they do pretty much what they want.

When a tripped ski swings in behind the boat, my first mate hauls in the tether line through the use of a big stern-mounted reel. As the lures surface, one by one, he wraps them out of the way and, when the fish shows, he unhooks it from the trolling shank then attaches it—by way of a special fitting—to a rod. The fisherman then plays his catch the final few yards on a free line.

You need a lot of room to roam with such a trolling system, and that is why it wouldn't work well, for example, on Lake Michigan. But here in Superior country, where we count on it to produce most of our fish, we are seldom disappointed.

Captain Gary Eskola
Ironwood

69
EAGLE HARBOR

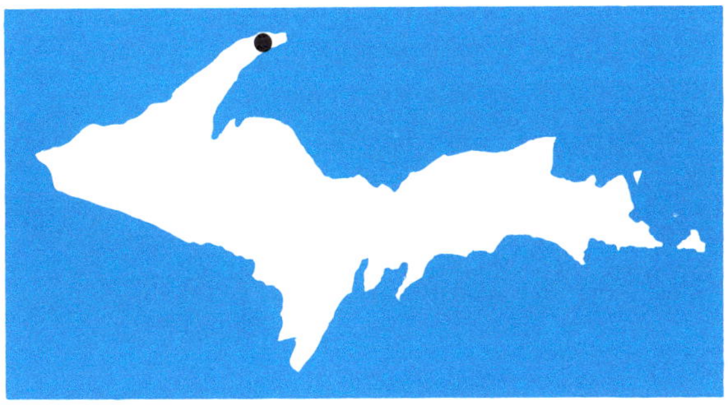

Eagle Harbor lies about 30 miles west of Copper Harbor along the tip of the Keweenaw Peninsula, the most northerly real estate in Michigan. This is an area of rugged scenery including boulder-strewn beaches, coves and natural harbors; cobalt-blue Lake Superior; and vast tracts of northern woods. Agate hunters walk the primeval shoreline past some fairly good fishing opportunities that are going unnoticed.

Fishing Schedule

Lake trout, available from May through October, are the main drawing card at Eagle Harbor, where anglers seek them within a mile or two of shore. Drowned rocks the size of cars and houses litter the Lake Superior bottom from Eagle Harbor to Copper Harbor (70), and lake trout love to spend their lives around such structure. Reefs near the harbormouth hold lakers in spring and fall, and it is likely that spawning fish enter the harbor in fall, although no one really fishes for them to find out.

You can fish the Eagle Harbor area in a small boat if you watch weather conditions. Outside the harbor's protection, Lake Superior can quickly brew up danger from north and northwest winds. Although lake trout are there, few trollers—even in big boats—venture out too far because of the potential of storms and because of Indian gillnetting by the Bayview Wisconsin tribe to the east and west of Eagle Harbor.

Trolling tactics usually call for wire line, one- or two-pound weights, and spoons or flies attached with three-way swivels from 18-inch dropper lines. For best results, troll near bottom in 50-150 feet of water, or find the thermocline and run lures through it and to either side.

Besides lake trout, there are some spring smelt-dipping opportunities in area streams such as Eliza Creek. A DNR brown-trout planting program, begun in 1984, has yet to bear fruit. Thus far, the browns have not stayed in the harbor, and more fishermen are needed to find them.

There is no *winter* fishing to speak of, although lake trout are likely available to those who would seek them through the ice.

There are limited fishing opportunities from Eagle Harbor to Ontonagon (68). Many of the smaller, clearer streams host sporadic runs of spawning smelt, and there are occasional steelhead, brown trout, lake trout and Chinook salmon caught off rivermouths and in shoreline shallows. Fishing for these species, along with trolling for lakers over structure further into Lake Superior, could withstand considerable extra pressure.

There is a good run of lake perch into the Portage Canal near F.J. McLain State Park, usually in midsummer when warming

This fisherman holds a bobbing stick used for jigging for lake trout with cut bait pinned to small spoons or jigs. Bobbing is used throughout Lake Superior while fishing from anchored boats or through the ice.

water temperatures in Lake Superior bring them to shore. However, the exact time varies from year to year and is difficult to predict. For more details on fishing the canal, as well as Portage Lake, see Keweenaw Bay (72).

Planting Records

The DNR stocked 15,000 brown trout in Eagle Harbor in 1984 and followed up with 5,000 fish in 1985. A release of about 5,000 browns, planned for 1986, will be repeated annually through at least 1990 if the fish remain in the area to provide angling opportunities from small-boat fishermen.

Facilities

Lack of facilities along this long, lonely stretch of Lake Superior discourages many from fishing here. Outside of a DNR boat launch on Misery Bay, the only other facility is a boat launch and harbor of refuge at Houghton-Hancock. There, services for boaters include transient accommodations, gasoline and diesel fuel, water, electricity, restrooms, shower facilities, haul-out facilities, holding-tank pump-out and VHF-FM radio. The telephone number of the dock attendant is (906) 482-6010.

Further Information

Chambers of Commerce:

Upper Peninsula Travel and Recreation Association, P.O. Box 400, Iron Mountain 49801; (906) 774-5480.

Bait & Tackle Shops:

None. Refer to Copper Harbor (71) or Keweenaw Bay (72).

Charter Fishing:

None. Refer to Copper Harbor (71).

Department of Natural Resources:

Two fisheries biologists work out of District Headquarters at US-41 North, Baraga; (906) 353-6651.

Coast Guard:

Portage Station in Hancock, (906) 482-1520 or 482-3253.

Return of the Lake Trout

I was born and raised in Copper Harbor and have fished Lake Superior most of my 72 years. My father was a commercial fisherman, a gillnetter, and I helped him lift the nets many times as a young man. Lake trout were then—as they are now—an important part of our lives in this north country.

After returning fom WWII, I made a boat and began a charter service. The best lake trout I ever caught was a 25-pounder in 1947, but a client once brought a laker aboard that weighed 37 pounds. I quit guiding in 1960 because lampreys had decimated the lake-trout population.

But now I'm happy to report that the lake trout have returned and I'm back fishing. The lake trout aren't as big as they used to be, but they are here and fishing continues to improve. I'm concerned, though, about Indian gillnetting in the area. And, last summer, we caught a laker with a lamprey attached, a reminder that this problem could return at any time.

Not long ago, when I knew I would have to retire, I began building a new boat, the *Rose of Sharon*. She's a beauty—26 feet long and made of a white-oak frame and cedar planking that I strip-nailed. I installed a two-cylinder diesel engine in her, and sometimes to slow her down enough to troll, I have to drag a bucket.

I'd say that 80 percent of the fish we catch are fin-clipped, but the number of naturally reproduced lake trout seems to increase each year. Some of these lakers are red-fleshed and, to my taste, they eat better than the paler fish.

It's good to have lake trout back. This time I hope they stay.

Howard Bergh
Copper Harbor

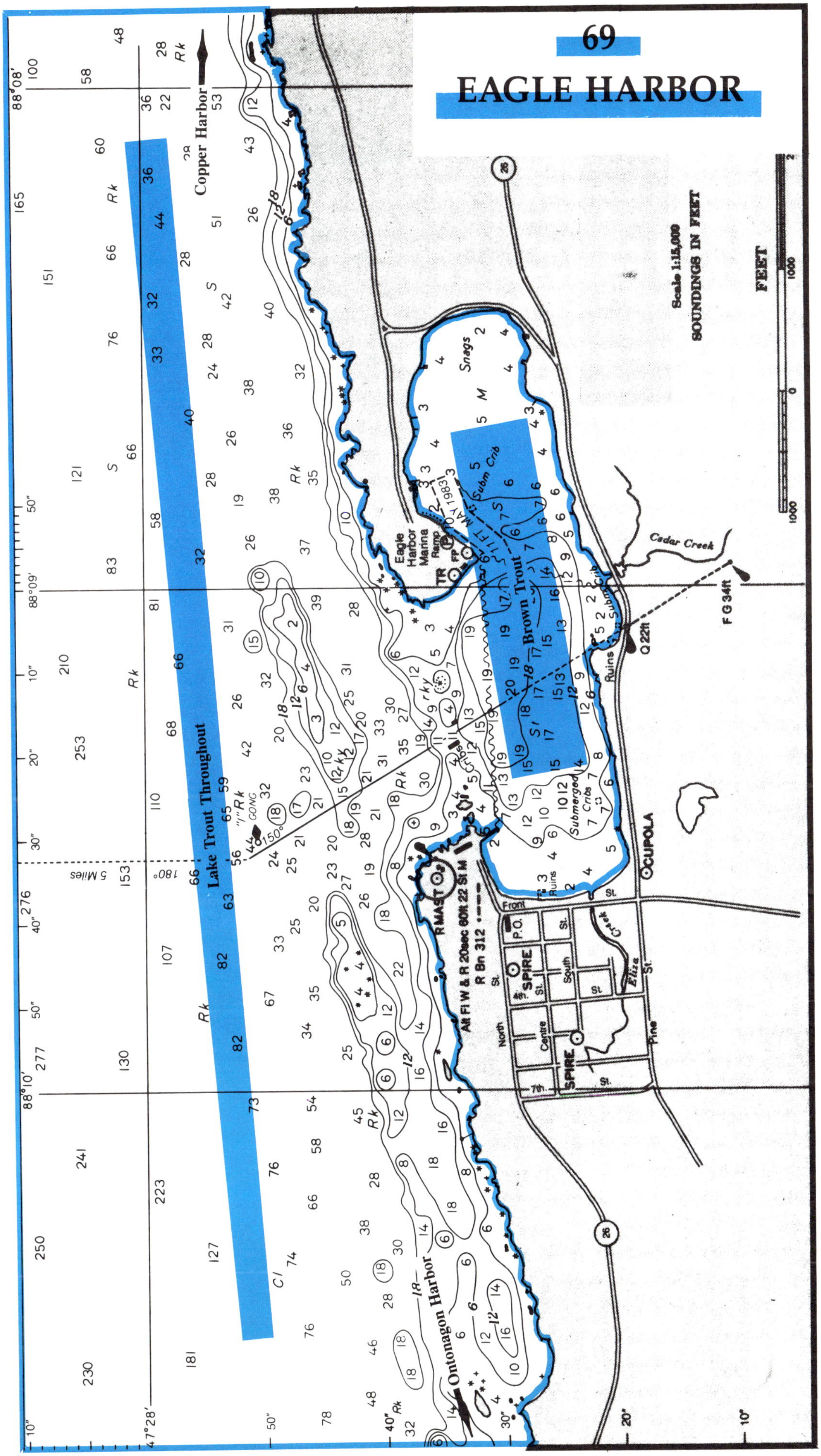
69
EAGLE HARBOR
Lake Trout Throughout
Brown Trout
Copper Harbor
Ontonagon Harbor
Eagle Harbor Marina Ramp
Snags
Subm Crib
Submerged Cribs
Ruins
Cedar Creek
CUPOLA
SPIRE
RMAST
Alt Fl W & R 20sec 60ft 22 St M
R Bn 312
F G 34ft
Q 22ft
GONG
5 Miles
Front St.
Centre St.
South St.
North St.
Pine St.
Eliza St.
4th St.
7th St.
P.O.
Scale 1:15,000
SOUNDINGS IN FEET
FEET

70
COPPER HARBOR

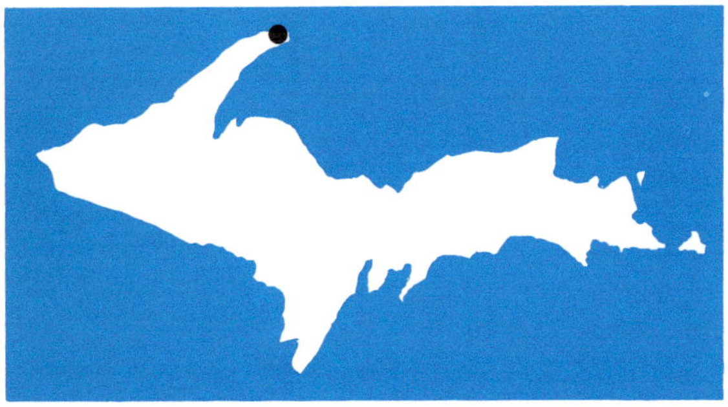

Some of the most remote—and prettiest—real estate in Michigan is found at Copper Harbor. Tourists come to the area from throughout the state and around the country. Here, at the tip of the Keweenaw Peninsula, they find Ft. Wilkins State Park, quaint fishing villages, and miles of boulder-strewn beach, where they can search for agates.

Some pack fishing rods and for good reason. Copper Harbor and its Lake Superior shoreline to the east and west host fishing sport for lake trout in summer and other angling opportunities in spring and fall.

Fishing Schedule

According to DNR biologist Ray Juettan, who oversees Keweenaw-area fisheries from his district office at Baraga, Copper Harbor is home to an exciting fishery for Assinica-strain brook trout. In 1985, the year following the release of these fast-growing fish, anglers caught them to 16 inches each on worms or small spinners in May and June (and into July if they keyed on the deep end of the harbor) and again in fall. In late summer, try casting small spoons and spinners over drowned boulders just outside the harbor.

It is too early at this writing to tell if the brook trout will develop into "coasters"—that is, enter Lake Superior, where they will wax fat, then return to the harbor and neighboring creeks in fall to spawn. When brookies were released here in the 1960s, they confined themselves to the harbor, but no one knows what the Assinica-strain fish will do.

SPRING

Other *spring* sport includes small runs of smelt at Fanny Hooe Creek and the nearby Silver River. The Copper Harbor area also hosts some transient browns and steelhead. The Silver River, in particular, receives a fair run of steelies. Spawn bags or spoons and spinners worked along the rivermouth produce steelhead to eight pounds each.

SUMMER

Summer anglers key on lake trout, which average six to 10 pounds, although 20-pounders are available. Juettan said that recently a friend and his wife caught a six-fish limit of forktails, none of which was under 10 pounds. Howard Bergh, a long-time resident and sport fisherman in the area, catches lake trout outside Copper Harbor, in depths from 80-170 feet, from May until October.

"You don't have to go very far—a half-mile or less—because the bottom drops off rapidly," Bergh says. Only five miles from shore the water is 100 fathoms (600 feet) deep.

Howard reports that best laker catches usually occur in late June and early July, when the thermocline forms and lake trout suspend within 50-80 feet of the surface. "When flies and bugs are on the surface, the trout will rise to feed on them," he says. "Of course, there are always some fish deep, too."

Rated trolling tactic is to use 30-pound-test wire line and 1-3/4 pound lead weights to get lures to whatever depth at which the lakers are holding. An 18-inch dropper line, secured to the wire line with a large three-way swivel, allows the weight to skip along bottom without fouling lures. Bergh likes to run North Star yellow-and-white trolling flies, white Spin-N-Glos, or small Flutter Spoons in various colors, spotting the lures behind eight-inch chrome or brass-and-silver flashers. Short, stiff rods and Pflueger Pakron reels are used with the multi-strand wire line. Along with his system of pulling wire, Bergh usually runs one downrigger.

In addition to lake trout, Bergh catches cohos and occasional brown trout and steelhead while trolling. And he says there are a few pink salmon in the area, too.

FALL

In *fall*, when lake trout move into shoal water and the harbor itself to spawn, local anglers get them by casting 2/5- to one-ounce spoons. Color is usually unimportant.

WINTER

Winter fishing used to be good for hatchery-reared splake, but the planting program for the lake-trout/brook-trout hybrid was discontinued a few years ago. Juettan hopes to target splake releases here once again, as soon as stocks become available in state hatcheries.

The only ice-fishing sport today is cut-bait jigging with Swedish Pimples and Jigging Rapalas for lakers in the harbor. The harbor freezes over, but the wind-swept shore of Lake Superior does not, except for an unsafe area to a few hundred yards offshore.

Planting Records

The DNR has planted lake trout in the Copper Harbor region for many years and plans to continue releasing 30,000 yearlings each year through at least 1990. During this period, 25,000 Assinica-strain brook trout will be stocked annually. Brown trout in the area are from former releases in Lake Fanny Hooe or stray fish from Eagle Harbor (69) plants. Steelhead, apparently, are naturally reproduced.

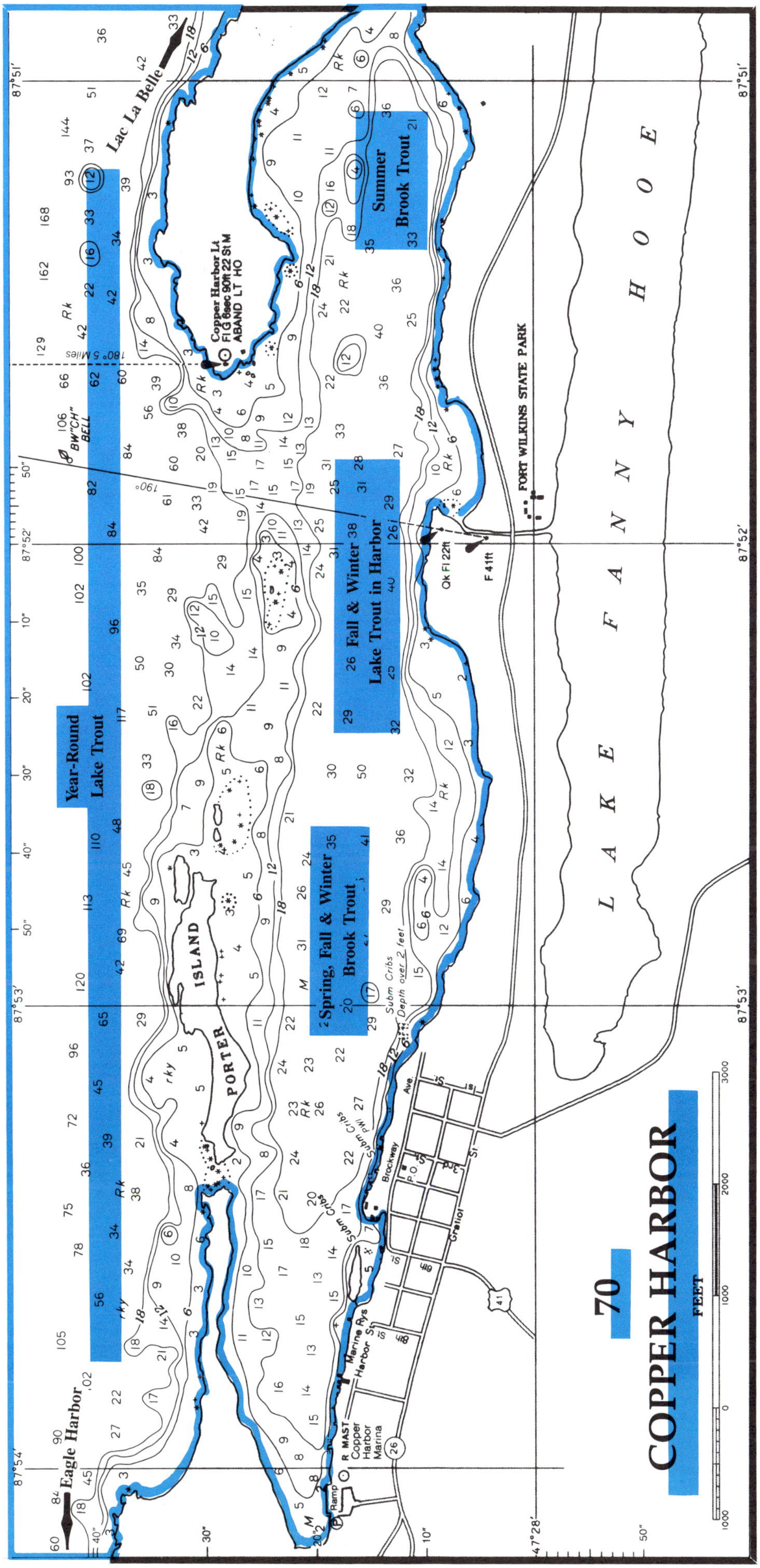
70
COPPER HARBOR
FEET
Year-Round Lake Trout
Summer Brook Trout
Fall & Winter Lake Trout in Harbor
Spring, Fall & Winter Brook Trout
Lac La Belle
Eagle Harbor
LAKE FANNY HOOE
FORT WILKINS STATE PARK
PORTER ISLAND
Copper Harbor Lt
FlG 6sec 90ft 22 St M
ABAND LT HO
180° 5 Miles
BW"CH" BELL
Qk Fl 22ft
F 41ft
Subm Cribs
Depth over 2 feet
R MAST
Copper Harbor Marina
Ramp
Marine Rys
Harbor St
Brockway Ave
Gratiot St
P.O.

Spoon-tossers in spring and fall can get nice-sized lake trout while casting from shore in the Copper Harbor region.

The Lure of Isle Royale

Isle Royale is a striking combination of dense wilderness and clear, blue waters. The entire 45-mile-long island, lying about 40 miles north of Copper Harbor in Lake Superior, is a national park. The island contains 50 inland lakes and teems with wildlife, including moose and wolves. A ferry, the *Isle Royale Queen II*, services the island from Copper Harbor, beginning in mid-May and running through Labor Day.

The shoal waters around Isle Royale host excellent fishing for big lake trout. A Minnesota man caught a 47-pound lake trout near the island in the summer of 1984. Captain Randal D. Houchin runs fishing charters to Isle Royale from June through September. For information, contact the National Park Concessions, P.O. Box 405, Isle Royale National Park, Houghton 49931; (906) 337-4993.

The Northern is No Piker

Northern pike scare the heck out of me. Look a pike in the eye as it slowly gills just before you close a net over its savage, snakelike head, and you can almost read the murderous mind. A friend who once came too near needed 19 stitches to close a nasty bite on his hand. I keep waiting for some Japanese film maker to produce a movie about *The Giant Pike That Ate Tokyo*.

I don't really get nervous—just incredibly alert—around pike, especially when removing a lure half-way down the toothy gullet of one of these Great Lakes alligators. At 12 inches or 12 pounds, the northern is one mean customer, saving most of his fight until you try to get him into your boat. Give him legs and lungs and he could win a Tough Man Contest.

That's the bad news. The good news is that pike are fairly easy and sporting fun to catch. And they are quite plentiful in certain waters of the Great Lakes, namely warm-water bays that contain weeds and plenty of other fish to eat.

Anything that moves and that will fit into their mouths—even objects that won't fit into their mouths—are fair game. Years ago, as Explorer Scouts on a Canadian camping trip, we boys had a contest to see who could catch the biggest fish on the weirdest homemade lure. Northerns were the mainstay, mugging everything from pieces of aluminum pop cans to a red toothbrush with a gang hook trailing behind.

Pike are great fish of the Great Lakes. Just be careful of those teeth. And remember—the northern is no piker.

Eldon Thomas
Flint

Facilities

The DNR maintains a boat-launching facility and a harbor of refuge at Copper Harbor with the following services: transient accommodations, gasoline, water, electricity, restrooms, shower facilities, VHF-FM radio, holding-tank pump-out and a dock attendant. The telephone number is (906) 289-4410.

Further Information

Chambers of Commerce:

Upper Peninsula Travel and Recreation Association, P.O. Box 400, Iron Mountain 49801; (906) 774-5480.

Bait & Tackle Shops:

1. Lake Fanny Hooe Resort, west end of Copper Harbor off M-26; (906) 289-4451.
2. Fanny Hooe Market & Deli, US-41 in Copper Harbor; (906) 289-4811.
3. Gaslight, US-41 in Copper Harbor; (906) 289-4652.

Charter Fishing:

1. Captain Charles Robertson, P.O. Box 87, Copper Harbor 49918; (906) 289-4573. 28-foot twin-engine Omega, *Dreamboat III*.
2. Captain Gordon C. Roberts, P.O. Box 467, Calumet 49913; (906) 337-3127. 30-foot boat, *Teachers Pet II*.
3. Captain Jeff Meilahn, Fanny Hooe Resort, P.O. Box 116, Copper Harbor 49918; (906) 289-4451. 29-foot boat, *Lt. Daniel Ruggles*.

Department of Natural Resources:

Two fisheries biologists work out of District Headquarters at US-31 North, Baraga 49908; (906) 353-6651.

Coast Guard:

Portage Station in Hancock, (906) 482-1520 or 482-3253.

Lac La Belle affords good fishing opportunities for both warm-water and cold-water species. These young fishermen show off a nice stringer of yellow perch and rock bass.

71
LAC LA BELLE

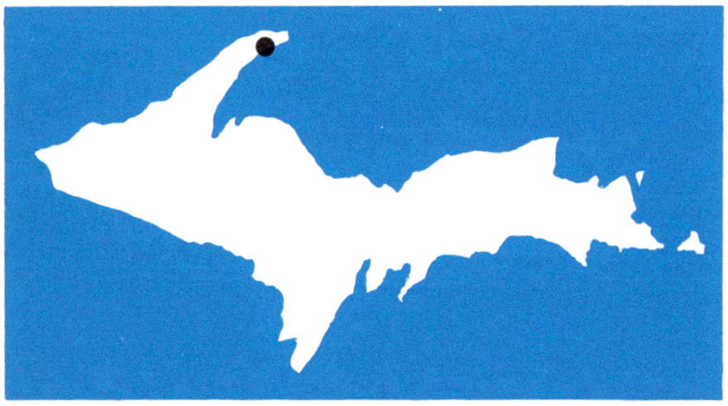

Lac La Belle is both an inland lake and—due to the channel that connects it to Bete Grise Bay on the Keweenaw Peninsula—a natural harbor to Lake Superior. At 1,146 acres, Lac La Belle affords good fishing opportunities for both salmonids and warm-water species.

Fishing Schedule

The Gratiot River, which feeds Lac La Belle, receives a run of steelhead and smelt each *spring*. Besides keying on the river, steelhead anglers also try for three- to 10-pound fish in the channel by drifting spawn bags or casting spoons.

Most local fishermen, however, concentrate on lake trout in Lake Superior, beginning in May and lasting until October. Spring and fall lakers will be found near shore in Bete Grise Bay, but in *summer*, trollers will have to seek them further out in Lake Superior itself. Key places include Point Isabelle and Big and Little Traverse bays, but the entire shoreline from Keweenaw Point to the Portage Lake Channel can be productive.

This is wire-line country for lake trout, although downriggers also produce for those who rely on them. Tactics with either system involve fishing the thermocline when it is available or running lures close to bottom. There is nothing fancy about trolling methods in this area; local fishermen mostly rely on big flashy spoons to which they add a piece of sucker meat or other cut bait.

In *fall*, when spawning lakers seek rocky bottom near shore, spincasters catch the forktails on spoons tossed from the rock-filled breakwall or in the 14- to 16-foot-deep channel. Most lakers run four to eight pounds, but fish to 20 pounds each are available.

Because it is connected to Lake Superior, Lac La Belle itself is fairly cold. And it is easy to fish because of a long sandy shoal that extends to perhaps 100 feet from shore and because an extensive weedbed surrounds much of the lake.

There is a good population of 12- to 24-pound northern pike in Lac La Belle. Most fishermen seek them during the open-water season and, for some reason, neglect what could be some good ice-angling opportunities. A release of about 500 tiger muskies here a few years ago has resulted in the availability of a few 14- to 15-pound fish. Muskie and pike fishermen target the inside and outside edges of the weed belt and either troll with large Rapala or lookalike lures or bobber fish with frozen smelt.

The lake serves up black crappies to those who fish weighted jigs, with or without minnows, along weed-bed edges and over old pilings throughout the shallows. Best times are June and again in fall.

Smallmouth bass to five pounds each have been taken from Lac La Belle while driftfishing nightcrawlers or minnows. Flyrod and spincast fishermen might also try tossing poppers or spinnerbaits just outside the channel in Bete Grise Bay. According to Uno Isaacson, who runs Lac La Belle Resort, scuba divers in the area have reported seeing plenty of big bronzebacks. Within Lac La Belle, a good spot for smallmouths is along the dropoff just before the channel on the south side.

Spring walleye fishing and fall perch fishing for 1-1/2 to two-pound jumbo yellow-bellies have fallen off in recent years, although there are still plenty of smaller perch available. Most fishermen today sort about half their catch to find enough eaters.

Planting Records

Lac La Belle does not receive stockings of hatchery-reared fish. Point Isabella and Big and Little Traverse Bay reefs have traditionally been planted with lake trout. Plans through at least 1990 call for 50,000 lakers annually to be released at Point Isabella and Big Traverse Bay Reef, with Little Traverse Bay Reef targeted for 90,000 lake trout each year during this period.

Facilities

The DNR maintains a harbor of refuge at Lac La Belle with transient accommodations and gasoline. There is also a state boat-launching site.

Further Information

Chambers of Commerce:

Upper Peninsula Travel and Recreation Association, P.O. Box 400, Iron Mountain 49801; (906) 774-5480.

Bait & Tackle Shops:

Lac La Belle Resort, US-41 in Mohawk, (906) 289-4293.

Charter Fishing:

None known. Refer to Copper Harbor (70).

Department of Natural Resources:

Two fisheries biologists work out of District Headquarters at US-41 North, Baraga; (906) 353-6651.

Coast Guard:

Portage Station in Hancock, (906) 482-1520 or 482-3253.

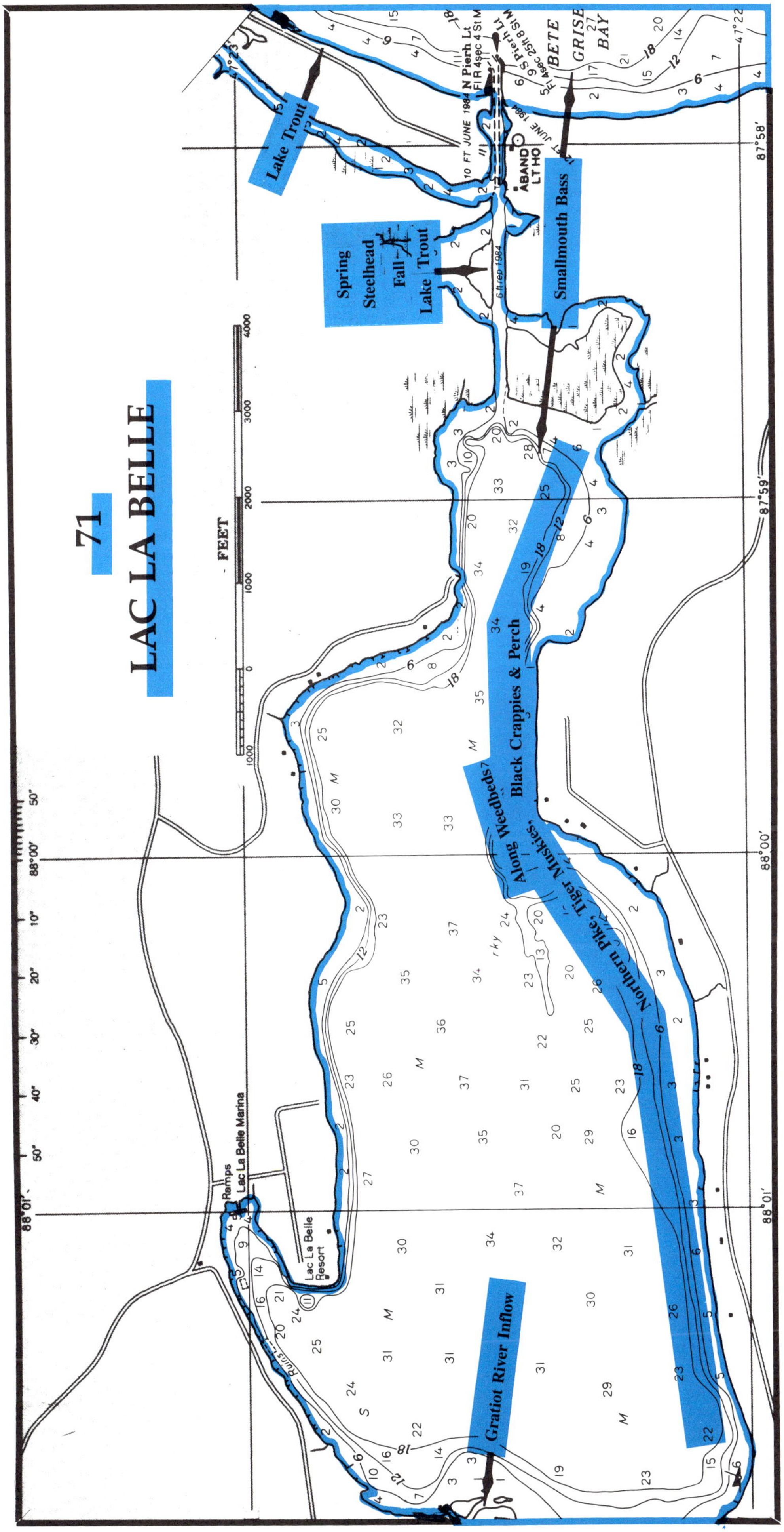
71
LAC LA BELLE
FEET
Lake Trout
Spring Steelhead
Fall Lake Trout
Smallmouth Bass
Black Crappies & Perch
Along Weedbeds
Northern Pike, Tiger Muskies,
Gratiot River Inflow
Ramps
Lac La Belle Marina
Lac La Belle Resort
ABAND LT HO
BETE GRISE BAY

72
KEWEENAW BAY and PORTAGE LAKE

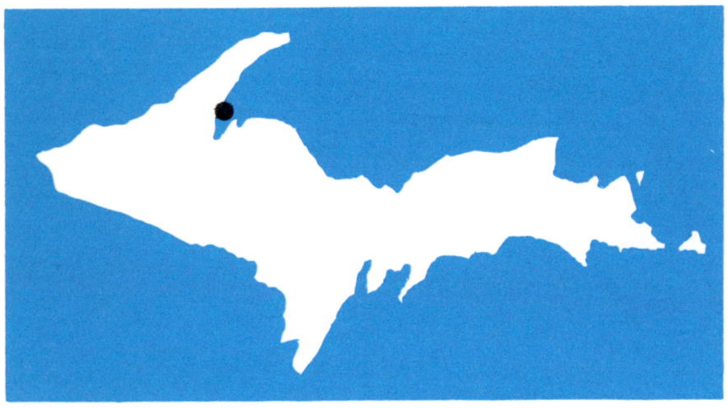

Keweenaw Bay is not the best place on Lake Superior to go sport fishing because, since 1972, Indian gillnetting has taken its toll on whitefish and lake trout. On the other hand, nearby Portage Lake and the Portage Canal and Huron Bay have not been impacted by native fishermen and afford some unique angling opportunities.

Keweenaw Bay and western Lake Superior (from Marquette west) fall into waters covered by the Treaty of 1842 between 13 bands of Chippewa Indians—from Michigan, Wisconsin and Minnesota—and the federal government. At this writing, three Chippewa bands are netting in the Keweenaw Bay area. They include the Keweenaw Bay Tribal Community (from Michigan) and the Bayfield and Red Cliff bands from Wisconsin. An agreement announced by the State of Michigan and several Indian tribes early in 1985 involved the Treaty of 1836 dispute and, as such, affected fishing in Lake Superior east of Marquette. For details on the history and provisions of these treaties and agreements, see 76 (Munising).

There are some sport-fishing opportunities available in Keweenaw Bay, but until a settlement is reached, prospects are not the best.

Fishing Schedule

Keweenaw Bay yields lake trout, coho salmon, whitefish and steelhead throughout the long fishing season, which begins in May and lasts until October. The best places to go for lake trout are near the reefs (see map) and along the 180-foot contour throughout the bay. Most trollers pull cowbells baited with small whole smelt or cut sucker meat.

Fishing for cohos and steelhead begins close to shore in L'Anse Bay at ice-out and lasts until late May. Trollers pull Little Cleos and fluorescent-orange Rapalas, and shorecasters toss these same lures in the shallows. Best spots are near the mouth of the Falls River and off the Celotex dock at L'Anse. Dock fishermen catch steelhead by stillfishing spawn bags on bottom. Beginning in late September and lasting into October, action repeats itself when the salmon return to spawn. Then, the same tactics and lures are used.

Whitefish anglers score from anchored boats, beginning in late April and lasting through the first week in June, by jigging Swedish Pimples (with or without cut bait) in 50- to 70-foot depths offshore from Baraga Marina.

In *Huron Bay* two types of habitat are found. The southern end furnishes good fishing for warm-water species, including big northern pike along with smallmouth bass and yellow perch. The water is very clear, however, so bass anglers will want to use light line and keep a low profile, whether drifting nightcrawler harnesses or Junebug Spinners from a boat or casting poppers and small spinners from shore. The clear waters produce plenty of follows from northern pike, but getting strikes—especially from the biggest fish—can be frustrating. Anglers might have better luck by stillfishing dead smelt on bottom. Perch, on the other hand, readily hit, if you can find a school.

Further into the bay, whitefish and lake-trout jig fishermen report fast action for a short time in spring as well as all winter long. Bobbing with cut bait pinned to jigging spoons, jigging with Swedish Pimples clean, or fishing whole dead smelt on bottom produces best. Many of the several rivers (Slate, Ravine, Silver and Huron) that empty into Huron Bay host fall runs of spawning pink salmon, along with both hatchery-reared and naturally reproduced steelhead. Small spoons, spinners, and brightly colored flies work best for trout and salmon in the rivers when cast across spawning beds or into holding water. Tumbling chunks of spawn or spawn bags into these areas is also effective.

Across Keweenaw Bay, *Portage Lake* and *Portage Canal* offer some excellent year-round sport fishing. Ice-out action for large black crappies (to two pounds each) gears up each spring in the Pike Bay region for small-jig fishermen, who pin clear-plastic bobbers three feet above their lures. Peak fishing lasts only two weeks, however.

At the state-wide pike and walleye opener on May 15, fishing for hefty northerns takes off in Pike Bay and in Oscar Bay up the canal from Houghton/Hancock. By late May/early June, northerns can be caught throughout the Portage Canal near emerging weed beds along any good dropoff. The north end of Torch Bay is a good pike producer as is the west shore of Portage Lake from Chassell to Pilgrim Point. Twenty-pound fish are not uncommon, and in 1982 a 30-pound brute, caught by a Wisconsin angler, won the annual fishing contest sponsored by Dick's Favorite Sports of Houghton.

Trollers rely upon Rapalas and other minnow-imitating lures along with Dardevle-type spoons. Pike also will hit live suckers fished halfway to bottom below large bobbers, as well as whole dead smelt fished on bottom. Tip-up fishermen catch pike in January and February by keying on weed beds and dropoffs in Pike Bay.

Smallmouth bass to five and six pounds each are especially underfished. Hotspots include the southeast shore of Torch Bay, below Dollar Bay on the east shore of the canal, and in the southern end of Torch Lake. Shad Raps and No. 7 Countdown Rapalas are hot lures when cast, but leeches and live minnows, either driftfished or slow-trolled, also produce.

Perch fishing is fair throughout the Portage waterway, with both ends of the canal becoming hotspots for lake-run yellowbellies. When these lake perch enter the waterway—any time in summer that water temperatures are warm enough to attract them—fishermen can get fast action with live minnows. The lake-run perch average 10 or 11 inches in size but include some to 15 inches.

The Sturgeon River, which flows out of Pike Bay, hosts a spring run of spawning walleyes. Fish seem to disappear by late May, then show up off dropoffs throughout Portage Lake in July and August. Slow trolling early and late in the day with nightcrawler harnesses featuring various colors of beads and blades produce best. A decent catch will contain several five- and six-pound fish, but walleyes to nine and even 10 pounds are taken each year. Be advised, however, that due to contamination from mining operations in this area, walleyes and saugers (a cousin to the walleye) are not recommended for human consumption.

Planting Records

Lake-trout stockings in the following locations are being made each year through at least 1990: 50,000 at Big Traverse Bay Reef, 90,000 at Little Traverse Bay Reef, 60,000 at Pequaming Point, 50,000 at Point Abbaye, and 90,000 at Kelsey Creek.

The Portage Canal, at Lily Pond Harbor, is receiving 50,000 coho smolts each spring, and these are no doubt the fish that anglers take in L'Anse Bay in spring and fall. Each year until at least 1990, the Big Huron River is slated to receive 15,000 steelhead, and the Little Huron River will get 25,000 brook trout. Steelhead stockings in the Ravine River were discontinued in 1984.

Facilities

Public boat launches are located at the villages of Baraga and L'Anse, at Baraga State Park, at Arvon Township Park (on the east side of Huron Bay), just upriver from the Coast Guard station at the entrance to the Portage Canal, off the shoreline drive on the east side of Portage Lake, and across the lake below Pilgrim Point.

Three DNR-maintained harbors of refuge await boaters. Limited facilities at Baraga Harbor include transient accommodations and gasoline. Call (906) 353-6237 for more information. At Houghton/Hancock, a more-developed facility with these services is found: transient accommodations, gasoline and diesel fuel, water, electricity, restrooms, shower facilities, dock attendant, haul-out facilities, holding-tank pump-out and VHF-FM radio. Call (906) 482-6010 for more information. Grand Traverse Bay has transient accommodations but limited facilities, with the nearest store seven miles away by road.

Further Information

Chambers of Commerce:

1. Copper Country Chamber of Commerce, Box 336, Houghton 49931; (906) 482-5240.
2. Torch Lake Chamber of Commerce, Box 55, Lake Linden 49945; (906) 296-0948.
3. Upper Peninsula Travel and Recreation Association, P.O. Box 400, Iron Mountain 49801; (906) 774-5480.

Bait & Tackle Shops:

1. Dick's Favorite Sports, 700 Sheldon Ave., Houghton 49931; (906) 482-0412.
2. Wilkinson's in Baraga, (906) 353-6257.
3. Indian Country Sports in L'Anse, (906) 524-6518.

Charter Fishing:

Captain Paul Lucas, 2001 Huntington, Marquette 49855; (906) 228-8199. 26-foot boat, *Ribar*.

Department of Natural Resources:

Two fisheries biologists work out of District Headquarters at US-41 North, Baraga; (906) 353-6651.

Coast Guard:

Portage Station in Hancock, (906) 482-1520 or 482-3253.

More Than He Bobbed For

Here on Lake Superior, we Finlanders have a special method called "bobbing" for catching lake trout. The technique involves the use of jigs with cut bait and nylon-coated wire line spooled on a special jigging or bobbing stick. This stick is an oblong-shaped piece of wood or plastic that is about 15 inches long. In spring, fishermen anchor or slowly drift on a calm day over 100-200 feet of water. After adding a 20-foot leader of 12- or 15-pound-test monofilament, they bob (jig) their lures within six inches of bottom, set the hook fast on a strike, then hand-over-hand their catch to the surface.

Finlanders have an old saying about this fast sport: "Don't tell your partner you have a bite. Tell him you have a fish. Otherwise, you will be too late in setting the hook." Bobbing is also productive through the ice, especially on Keweenaw Bay, where I grew up.

One year, a couple of fellows I knew were bobbing off the smokestacks at Pequaming, just north of L'Anse One man hooked a good fish, which proceeded to give him the fight of his life. He figured that, for sure, a Lake Superior record lake trout was on the end of his line.

His bobbing stick held 300 feet of line. On two or three occasions, the fish, as it struggled and tried to run off, stripped that line to within a couple of wraps of the bare spool. The partner pulled up their ice tent so they would have room to outmaneuver this monster lake trout.

But the record lake trout turned out to be a sturgeon. And they had to spud a larger hole in order to get it through the ice. If I remember right, that fish was over five feet long and weighed 50 pounds on a bathroom scale.

Every winter, it seems, someone hooks a sturgeon while bobbing in Keweenaw Bay. And every time it happens, the fisherman thinks he has a new Lake Superior record lake trout.

Jim Maki
Marquette

72
KEWEENAW BAY and PORTAGE LAKE

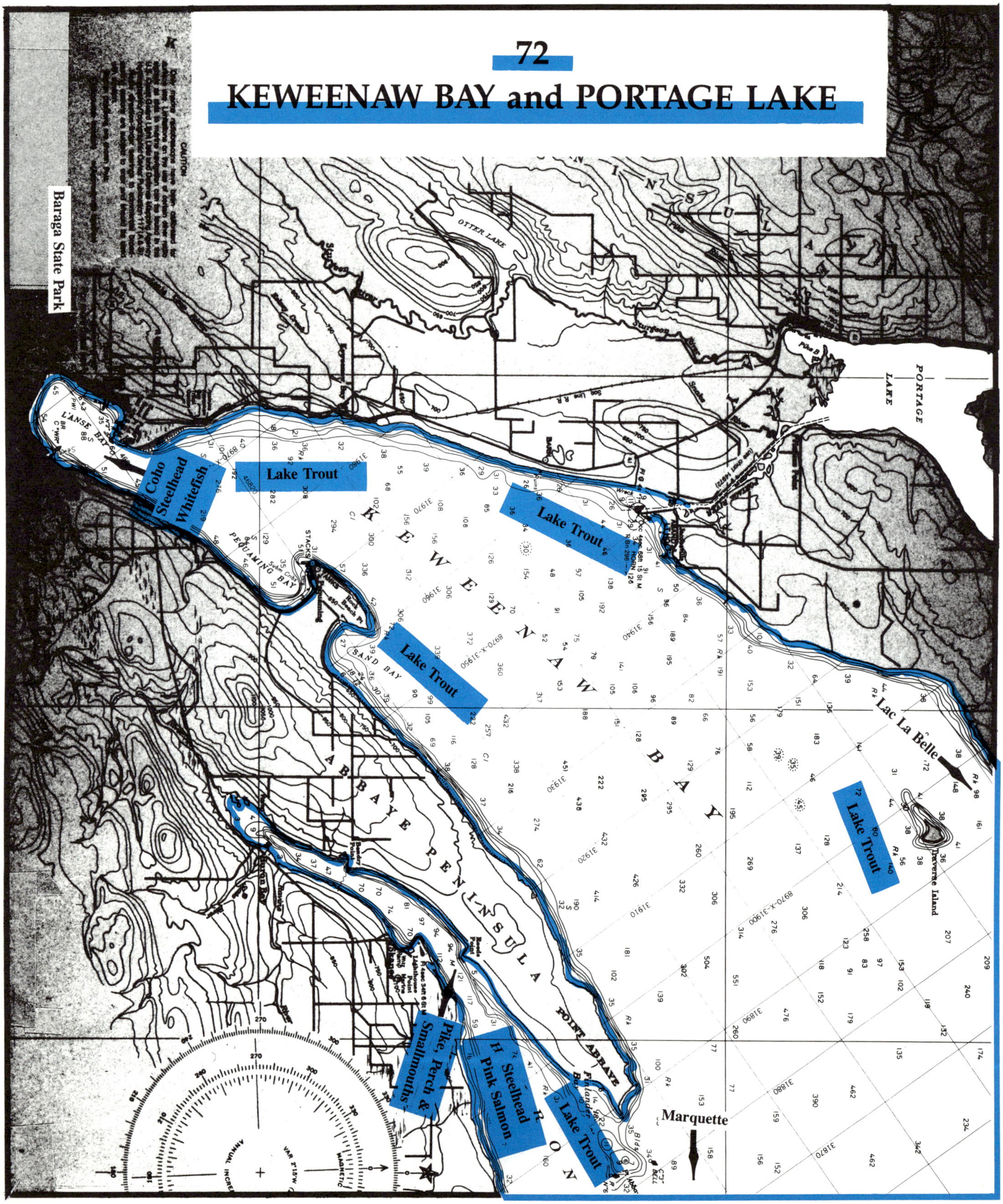

Sometimes huge sturgeon, like this prehistoric giant caught years ago, are iced in Keweenaw Bay by lake-trout and whitefish anglers.
— Michigan DNR photo—

73
STANNARD ROCK

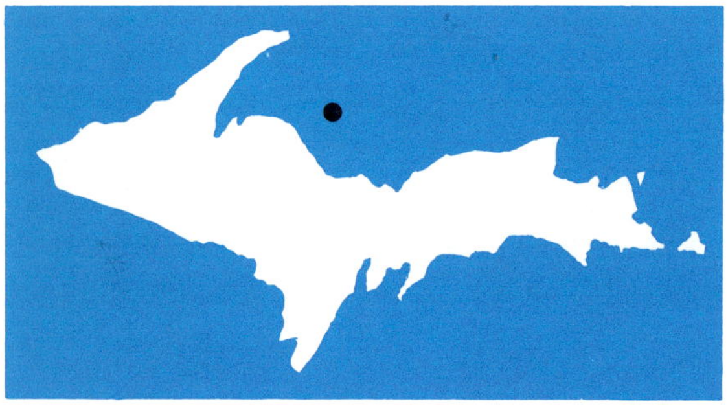

Forty-two miles due north from Marquette Harbor (74) lies Stannard Rock, a large shoal and long-time hazard for Lake Superior ships. A functional, unmanned lighthouse—farther from shore than any other American lighthouse on the Great Lakes—sits atop that portion of the reef that protrudes from the lake. Like an iceberg, much more of the one- by five-mile reef lies 10-50 feet under the surface.

Phenomenal lake-trout fishing is the magnet that attracts fishermen to Stannard Rock.

Fishing Schedule

The area is off limits to all but the largest trolling boats. And even if you own such a seaworthy craft—equipped with modern electronics, such as ship-to-shore radio and Loran C—it is advised that you travel in pairs with other experienced boaters. You can leave Marquette on a beautiful summer morning only to experience a London-type fog 20 miles from shore.

The best fishing begins in late June and lasts until mid-August. July, with its calm seas and nice days, is the best month to go. Lake trout are over the shoals then, and it is not uncommon to catch dozens in a single trip. By mid-August, the lakers, presumably seeking deeper water, are harder to find.

Charterboat-captain Jim Maki of Marquette made eight or nine trips to Stannard Rock during the summer of 1985. Better days yielded 100 lakers for the six fishermen he usually takes out. (Most charters are full since the round-trip run consumes about 50 gallons of fuel.) Top day last season was limit catches of 10-1/2 to 20-pound fish, though some days produced only three- to five-pounders. Typically, someone aboard the dozen or so boats that come to Stannard Rock each day will catch a 20-pounder. A few coho are also caught.

Tactics call for casting spoons such as Cleos, Krocodiles, Locos, and K.O. Wobblers. Some spincasters like to flip heavier hardware like Eppinger Huskie Devles and Kush Spoons. Silver in combination with orange, yellow, blue or green produces best. Some fishermen pin cut bait to their trebles, especially if fishing is slow. Jigging with white lead-head jigs from 1/4 ounce to one ounce has been especially productive for Maki.

Charterboat-skipper Dave Kimar made the 50-mile one-way trip to Stannard Rock from Shelter Bay a total of 27 times in 1985. He and his customers limited (three lakers per angler allowed) on 25 of those trips. Kimar prefers light line of six- to 10-pound test, claiming that it is best for lure presentation and for fight. Dave's best fish last year was a 33-pounder, which gave quite an accounting of itself on 10-pound-test line. Top lures have been silver-and-blue, silver-and-green, and gold-and-green Little Cleos and white or yellow jigs—either tipped with sucker meat or dressed with a twister tail. Kimar usually establishes the day's catching pattern by asking half his customers to cast jigs and the other half to toss spoons. Drifting with the wind and casting, or anchoring and casting are equally productive.

Some fishermen also troll the Stannard Rock area, but they generally donate lots of hardware to the tricky reef. According to Jim Maki, a troller "could empty out a tackle box in a single day there."

Facilities

See 74 (Marquette).

Planting Records

All fish are naturally reproduced.

Further Information

Charter Fishing:

1. Captain Jim Maki, P.O. Box 397, Marquette 49855; (906) 228-9848. 24-foot Crestliner, *Catch-A-Finn*.
2. Captain Dave Kimar, P.O. Box 144, Au Train 49806; (906) 892-8277. 30-foot T-Craft, *Anne K. III*.
3. Wiltze's Marina on Huron Bay.

Department of Natural Resources and Coast Guard:

See 74 (Marquette).

Mackinaw Trout

A long time ago, a native fisherman lay on his side along a rocky ledge worn smooth by eons of pounding waves from *Gitchegumme*, what the white man would some day call Lake Superior. But there were no waves on this golden afternoon in late October. The western giants had finally wrestled the sun below the horizon, and this last blaze of light and hush of wind combined to lend the world a dreamlike quality.

And the Indian dreamed. The igneous slab upon which he rested had retained the sun's heat, and since he had nothing to do but wait, the waiting—even for him—had become intolerable. So he slept . . . and dreamed.

He dreamed that he saw the first assault of mackinaw, the huge fork-tailed fish that one day would be called "lake trout," cruise into the shoals below him. Each year during the Time of the Burning Leaves, they were here among the drowned boulders to spawn, these mackinaw, and the native fishermen came here to spear them.

When he opened his eyes, he knew that the vision had become truth once again. Yes, there they were! In the afternoon glow, he could see shadows moving over rocks just below his spearing perch. One shadow was especially large, and when it rolled on its side for a moment, he saw the wormlike pattern of the trout's upper back and its belly the color of dull birch bark.

The native raised himself to his knees, poised his spear, then hurled the weapon with all his strength. His aim was true, and a 50-pound mackinaw—perhaps older than the spear-thrower's grandfather—thrashed the shallows to a crimson froth.

Lake trout from Lake Superior continue to feed fishermen, as they have done for centuries.

Tom Huggler
Otisville

Stannard Rock yields hefty lake trout, like this 20-pounder, to spincast and jig fishermen.

74 MARQUETTE

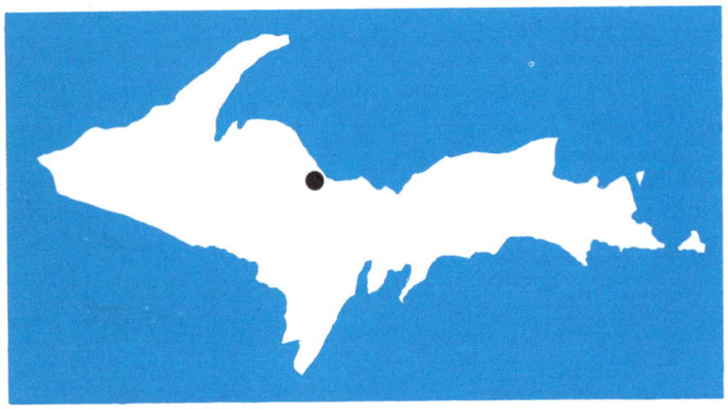

Marquette Harbor is the focus of a growing interest in Lake Superior sport fishing. Good facilities, improving levels of trout and salmon stockings, and an active local sportfishing group are reasons that fishing is good and will likely get better.

Marquette, with her twin harbors, already produces a wide variety of gamefish species. In a recent fishing tournament, for example, 842 anglers (a three-fold increase from the previous year) caught a total of 1,215 fish. Lake trout—which averaged only 20.8 inches in length and three pounds, four ounces in weight—made up 75 percent of the catch. A total of 166 Chinooks averaged 28.3 inches and 12-1/2 pounds. One hundred thirty cohos and seven steelhead/rainbows averaged the same weight and length as the lakers. Charterboat-captain Jim Maki's 1985 catch of 650 fish, including an 18-pound Chinook and a 22-1/2 pound lake trout, is further proof that the Marquette area is productive.

Those weight-and-length averages prove that Lake Superior trout and salmon do not grow as rapidly as those elsewhere in the Great Lakes, where the water is warmer and food more readily available. But, though there may be few 25-pound king salmon in the Marquette area, there are some 25-pound northern pike and 25-pound lake trout.

Fishing Schedule

SPRING

In *spring*, anglers begin showing up at the Upper Peninsula Power Company's Presque Isle Plant in the Upper Harbor. By late March or early April, warm-water discharge from the coal-fired plant mixes with Dead River outflow to weaken ice and attract fish. The same scenario develops in the Lower Harbor, thanks to Carp River discharge and warm-water effluent from the city power house. As ice breaks up, fishermen line the pier and take to small boats at both locations. Their target is 15- to 21-inch coho salmon, and it is not uncommon for anglers to box five-fish limits in 45 minutes. They do this by jigging 1/4- to one-ounce Doll Flies and lookalike homemade lead-heads with hair bodies. White is a hot spring color, with yellow, pink, and orange also productive. Most fishermen tip their jigs with cut bait, that is, small chunks of sucker or other fish.

Besides cohos, jig fishermen in both harbors also take king salmon. In fact, during some springs, the three- to 10-pound Chinooks dominate catches. Steelhead, along with some lakers and browns, are other targets. The city of Marquette owns much of the shoreline in the Lower Harbor area, which gives shorebound fishermen plenty of opportunity.

Spring smelt-fishing success varies from year to year. Harlowe Creek and the Dead, Chocolay, Carp, and Little Garlic rivers are good places to try.

These same tributaries produce rainbows for surf and boat fishermen in spring, as well as some brown trout, salmon and lake trout. (The only boat-launching facilities, however, are in the Upper and Lower harbors.) Any casting spoon in silver, with or without green, blue, orange or chartreuse, is usually productive. Many pier fishermen use spawn; others flip Rapalas and Flatfish after adding a rubber-core sinker a couple of feet above the lure.

By May 1, when most of the ice has left the harbor, charterboat-captain Jim Maki and other fishermen launch their boats for the long trolling season. The twin harbor mouths are popular spring fishing grounds, but the entire Marquette Bay region west and north to Big Bay and east to Shelter Bay is good trolling water. Planer boards, outriggers, downriggers, and flatlines all produce. Most trollers target depths from 100-200 feet because, for one reason, these depths are found close to shore.

Anglers pulling surface lines often pick up steelhead, which cruise the area in loose schools until a thermocline develops by midsummer.

SUMMER

A popular spring and *summer* fishing spot is the 90- to 150-foot-deep Sand Hole between the Lower Harbor lighthouse and Shot Point. Maki likes to troll reef structure, what he calls "banks," between points and area islands. In such areas, he claims, lake trout like to move up and down the inclines, according to temperature and food availability. One such 75- to 180-foot bank lies between the Upper Harbor pier and White Rocks to the northeast. Another 100- to 200-foot-deep ridge provides an underwater link between Partridge Islands and Granite Island. To find this structure, Maki relies upon Loran C coordinates. Fishermen without such electronics can also locate the ridge by trolling straight for Partridge Islands from White Rocks. When they see daylight between the power company smokestacks they will be just entering the ridge. Another good spot, at least one afternoon last fall when I fished it with Maki and his friend, Clarence Sarasien, is a trough between White Rocks and Presque Isle.

Many fishermen in the Marquette area pull wire line for lake trout, to depths of 300 feet. The tactic calls for short, stiff rods and large reels spooled with seven-strand stainless-steel wire. Sinkers, weighing from 12 ounces to one pound, spear cowbells and dodgers with small plugs and spoons to bottom. Here, fishermen chug them in and out of lake-bottom mud. Again, most trollers tip lures with cut bait. Another trick unusual to the area is to run cowbells with dodgers. Innovative anglers like Maki make their own four- or five-blade strings of 'bells, then add an 0-sized Herring Dodger about 24 inches back.

Local lures for lake trout and salmon include Dr. Hook spoons and Northport Nailers in combinations of silver, green, chartreuse, yellow, and orange. Wobble-Glos are preferred behind attractors.

Downriggers are often second-choice rigging for lake trout, although some use them exclusively for fish down to 150 feet. Maki and several other fishermen rely upon pinch-pad Offshore Releases, or what they refer to as "quick releases." Flatfish and Rapalas are good for slower speeds. For higher speeds, rely upon J-Plugs or the previously mentioned spoons run clean. These upper-set lines also produce Chinooks, which usually fight too aggressively for wire-line rigs.

Some trollers practice what is called "meat fishing." Two feet above cannonballs they add a three-way swivel and a cowbell/dodger/lure to one loop of the swivel. This makes for a permanent rig (there is no release), so when a fish strikes, the angler cranks up his prize, downrigger weights and all. It isn't an exciting method, but it is productive, especially for deep-water lakers. Most meat fishermen attach a small piece of surgical tubing between the three-way swivel and the attractor string to take the shock of a fighting laker and also to help prevent his getting off. Sometimes Maki will meat fish with bottom rigs, then stack Northports or J-Plugs (by way of quick releases) 15 feet above and 100-125 feet back. The tactic allows for two lures to be run on or close to bottom.

Anglers in small boats won't want to wander too far out into Lake Superior. Depths to 200 feet can be found within a half-mile of shore.

Black Rocks, located at the tip of Presque Isle, is popular with spincasters. Besides trout and salmon, Black Rocks (and the piers) serves up yellow perch (somewhat rare for Lake Superior), menominees and whitefish. Old pilings in the Lower Harbor have produced northern pike to 25 pounds, but few people fish for them.

FALL

Fall fishing opportunities are rated good to excellent for offshore lake trout, as well as pink, coho and Chinook salmon in area rivers. In particular, key on the Dead River for salmon. Brown trout and steelhead are also available.

WINTER

Winter spincasters catch trout and salmon at the ore docks in the Upper Harbor. The Marquette area also yields fair to good ice action for whitefish, rainbows, browns and lakers. Bobbing, an old Finnish method of catching lake trout, involves jigging with cut bait through the ice (or from an anchored boat). The bobbing stick, an oblong-shaped piece of wood or plastic, holds up to 100 yards of wire line. Old-time fishermen used to carry lures and bobbing sticks in a packbasket, then venture onto thin early season ice with the aid of long cross-country skis. According to Maki, whose eyes twinkle when he tells it, there is an old Finnish saying that, "If two seagulls could land on the ice, then it is strong enough for one Finlander on skis."

A revived winter splake fishery should also develop in the near future.

Planting Records

Marquette Bay and the surrounding area have had a long history of trout and salmon plantings. Lake-trout stockings have increased from 25,000-50,000 fish at Partridge Island, Loma Farms, Big Bay and Laughing Fish Point to 90,000-120,000 each year and will continue at this higher rate through at least 1990. Since 1984 the DNR has moved its Dead River laker releases to Presque Isle Harbor (the Upper Harbor), where 60,000 are targeted for each of the next five years.

Salmon plantings in the Dead River have stabilized at 150,000 cohos and 200,000 king fingerlings each year. The Chocolay River has traditionally received steelhead and will continue to get them at the rate of 20,000 yearlings annually. Steelheaders should also watch for a 1984 release of 20,000 Siletz River (summer-run) fish in Cherry Creek to mature in the next couple of years.

The Chocolay River last received brown trout in 1983. Again, the DNR has switched its release site to Presque Isle Harbor where 20,000 yearlings will be stocked each year. It is possible, however, that brown-trout releases will alternate between Upper

Joe Bolt caught this 25-pound northern pike from Marquette County waters while bottomfishing a dead smelt in August.
—Photo by Richard Smith—

and Lower harbor locations.

After a four-year moratorium on splake stockings, Marquette Bay is again receiving from 10,000-20,000 each year.

Facilities

Presque Isle Harbor, maintained by the DNR, has transient accommodations, gasoline and diesel fuel, water, electricity, restrooms, shower facilities, dock attendant, holding-tank pump-out, VHF-FM radio and courtesy car. The telephone number is (906) 228-9866. For a nominal fee, boaters may launch at a four-lane paved ramp at the harbor.

The Lower Harbor features a city-owned two-lane concrete ramp. Again, a small fee is charged to launch.

Further Information

Chambers of Commerce:

1. Marquette Area Chamber of Commerce, 501 S. Front St., Marquette 49855; (906) 226-6591.
2. Upper Peninsula Travel & Recreation Association, P.O. Box 400, Iron Mountain 49801; (906) 774-5480.

Bait & Tackle Shops:

1. Lindquist's Outdoor Sports, 131 W. Washington, Marquette 49855; (906) 228-6380.
2. Richard's Sport Shop, 143 W. Washington, Marquette 49855; (906) 226-6071.
3. Johnson's Sport Shop, 114 Washington, Marquette 49855; (906) 226-8521.

Charter Fishing:

1. Captain Jim Maki, P.O. Box 397, Marquette 49855; (906) 228-9848. 24-foot Crestliner, *Catch-A-Finn*.
2. Captain Don Knight, P.O. Box 66, Marquette 49855; (906) 475-5129. 30-foot *Barbara J.*
3. Lindquist's Outdoor Sports, 131 W. Washington, Marquette 49855; (906) 228-6380. 26-foot Stamas, *Lucky Link*.

Department of Natural Resources:

Two fisheries biologists work out of District Headquarters at 1126 N. Lincoln Rd., Escanaba 49829; (906) 789-2351. Their supervisor, also a fisheries biologist, works out of Regional Headquarters at 1990 US-41 South, Marquette 49855; (906) 228-6561.

Coast Guard:

Marquette Station, (906) 226-3312.

A Seagull Story

In late July 1981, I and my friend, Clarence Sarasien, were trolling for lakers and king salmon in about a hundred feet of water off Little Presque Isle. Meanwhile, my six-year-old son Jeffry and my eight-year-old daughter Stacy amused themselves by tossing cheese curls to seagulls. As the gulls tried to pick up the finger-food snacks, they kept darting in and out of our trolling lines. I wondered what would happen if one got caught in a line.

Then, as though on cue, it happened. The bird panicked, which only served to entangle it further. The whole business was annoying to me, as we were just entering some structure that could be productive. In fact, Clarence, who was at the wheel, said my graph showed the bottom coming up a little. So I raised the cannonballs about 10 feet before tending to the seagull.

I had the frantic gull reeled halfway in when one of the rods went off. I raced to it in time to feel a couple of solid pulls from a heavy salmon before the fish got off.

I reset the line, then returned to the seagull problem. I got the bird into the boat, but when I tried to unwrap the monofilament from his body, he bit me. Then, as the kids grew more wide-eyed, he relieved himself all over my shirt and pants. Some gratitude.

And that's exactly when another rod went off. Only this time, before I could free it from the holder, a big king—I'm sure larger than the other—surfaced once before breaking off. He took my rod with him, snapping it at the foregrip.

By now my kids were in the cabin, and though I couldn't then, I can laugh today when I remember my son, cautiously peering out and saying, "Daddy, are you mad?"

Captain Jim Maki
Marquette

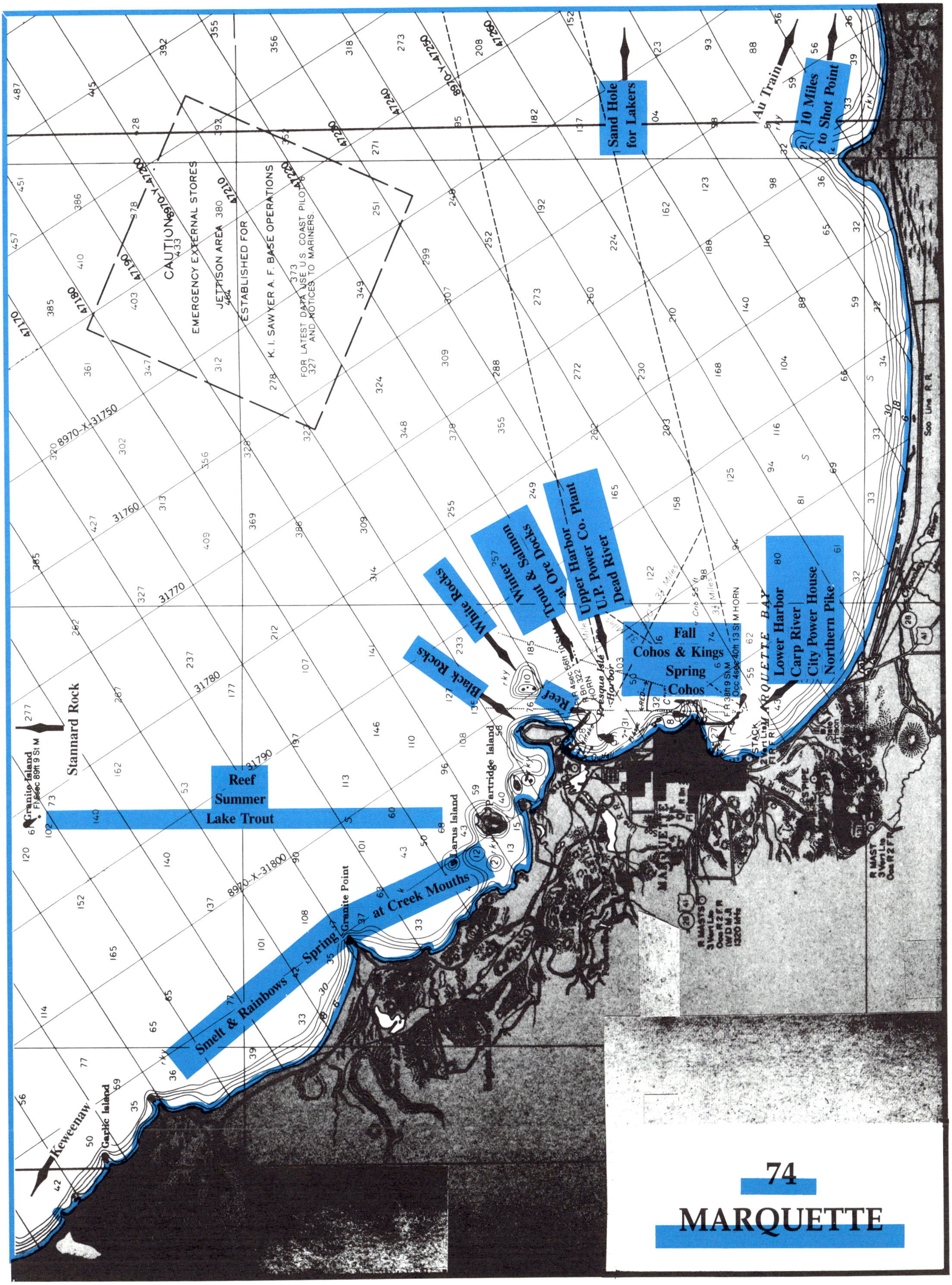

Sand Hole for Lakers
Au Train
10 Miles to Shot Point
CAUTION
EMERGENCY EXTERNAL STORES
JETTISON AREA
ESTABLISHED FOR
K. I. SAWYER A. F. BASE OPERATIONS
FOR LATEST DATA USE U.S. COAST PILOT AND NOTICES TO MARINERS.
Upper Harbor U.P. Power Co. Plant Dead River
Winter Salmon Trout & at Ore Docks
White Rocks
Black Rocks
Reef
Fall Cohos & Kings Spring Cohos
Lower Harbor Carp River City Power House Northern Pike
Presque Isle Harbor
MARQUETTE BAY
Stannard Rock
Granite Island
Reef Summer Lake Trout
Partridge Island
Larus Island
Smelt & Rainbows Spring at Creek Mouths
Granite Point
Keweenaw
Garlic Island
Soo Line R R
74
MARQUETTE

75
AU TRAIN BAY

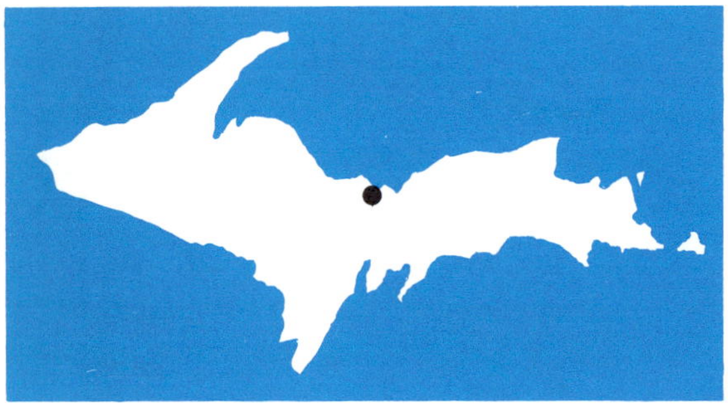

The entire shoreline from Marquette (74) to Munising (76) is often productive in spring for coho and Chinook salmon, along with steelhead, lake trout and some brown trout. In the center of this activity is Au Train Bay, as well as several small bays, inlets and rivermouths. Offshore trollers target lake trout. Smelt dipping, although sporadic in recent years, centers at the Au Train, Laughing Whitefish, and Rock rivers.

Although Indian gillnetting has apparently hurt fishing overall, good catching opportunities remain.

Fishing Schedule

SPRING

Spring activity begins in March at the mouth of the Au Train River, where anglers cast and troll among icebergs in hopes of hooking a scrappy king or coho salmon. Pink Rooster Tails and silver-and-blue or gold-and-red Little Cleos are rated lures. Trolling action sometimes occurs in water as shallow as six feet. Some fishermen rely on bow-mount electric motors, normally used for bass fishing, to make a quiet approach so that they might cast to schooling two- and three-pounders.

According to Dave Kimar, who runs a charterboat service from his cabin-rental business at Shelter Bay, "Some of these spring coho fishermen clean house." Kimar, an 18-year Lake Superior skipper, launches his 30-foot charterboat, the *Anne K. III*, by May 1, then spends much of the May-through-October trolling season about two miles out of Shelter Bay, north of Au Train Island. There, 90- to 200-foot-deep water features structure with a sandy bottom.

Kimar is looking for lake trout. Catches average three to eight pounds, although an occasional fish will top the 20-pound mark. About half of the several hundred lakers that he creels each season are native fish (as evidenced by the lack of fin clips).

Typical rigging includes two or three downriggers, two or three wire-line poles, and a couple of surface lines—either flatlines, planer boards or outriggers. Surface lines usually receive jointed or straight orange Rapalas, silver Rebels or Flatfish, red-and-gold or silver-and-blue Little Cleos, and small Johnson Spoons or Canadian Wonder Spoons in brass-and-silver combinations.

Downrigger setups get cowbells with 0 or 00 dodgers, mated together but with a twist. Cowbells are permanently attached to cannonball weights with a quick release affixed to the dodger. This innovative tactic provides less drag when fighting a hooked lake trout. Hot lures include Wobble Glos, locally made trolling flies featuring bucktails or polar-bear hair, and small plugs such as Flatfish.

Wire-line fishing entails the use of 500 feet of single-strand wire; short, stiff rods and big-spooled reels; and 3/4- to one-pound weights. The object is to chug silver-colored hardware, such as Johnson Spoons, in and out of the bottom. Sometimes Kimar and other trollers will stack wire-line rigs with dodgers and small plugs or spoons, such as Northport Nailers, pulled clean. In that case, Offshore Stacker Releases are preferred.

FALL

Close-to-shore action picks up again in *fall* on a hit-or-miss basis. Some streams in the area host spawning pink salmon, which can be fun to catch on small spinners or bright yarn flies. Other anglers catch steelhead, along with a few lake trout and salmon.

There are no *winter* fishing opportunities worth reporting.

Planting Records

Shelter Bay has historically received from 25,000-50,000 lake-trout fingerlings each year. At least until 1990, however, annual stockings will increase to 60,000 yearlings. During this same period, Au Train Island Reef will receive 92,500 yearling lakers.

Facilities

The DNR maintains a free public launch at Au Train Bay, two miles east of Au Train. The Shelter Bay Grocery, on M-28, has launch facilities, too.

Further Information

Chambers of Commerce:

1. Delta County Area Chamber of Commerce, 230 Ludington St., Escanaba 49829; (906) 786-2192.
2. Upper Peninsula Travel & Recreation Association, P.O. Box 400, Iron Mountain 49801; (906) 774-5480.

Bait & Tackle Shops:

Shelter Bay Grocery, on M-28, sells some tackle but has no live bait. See 76 (Munising) or 74 (Marquette).

75 AU TRAIN BAY

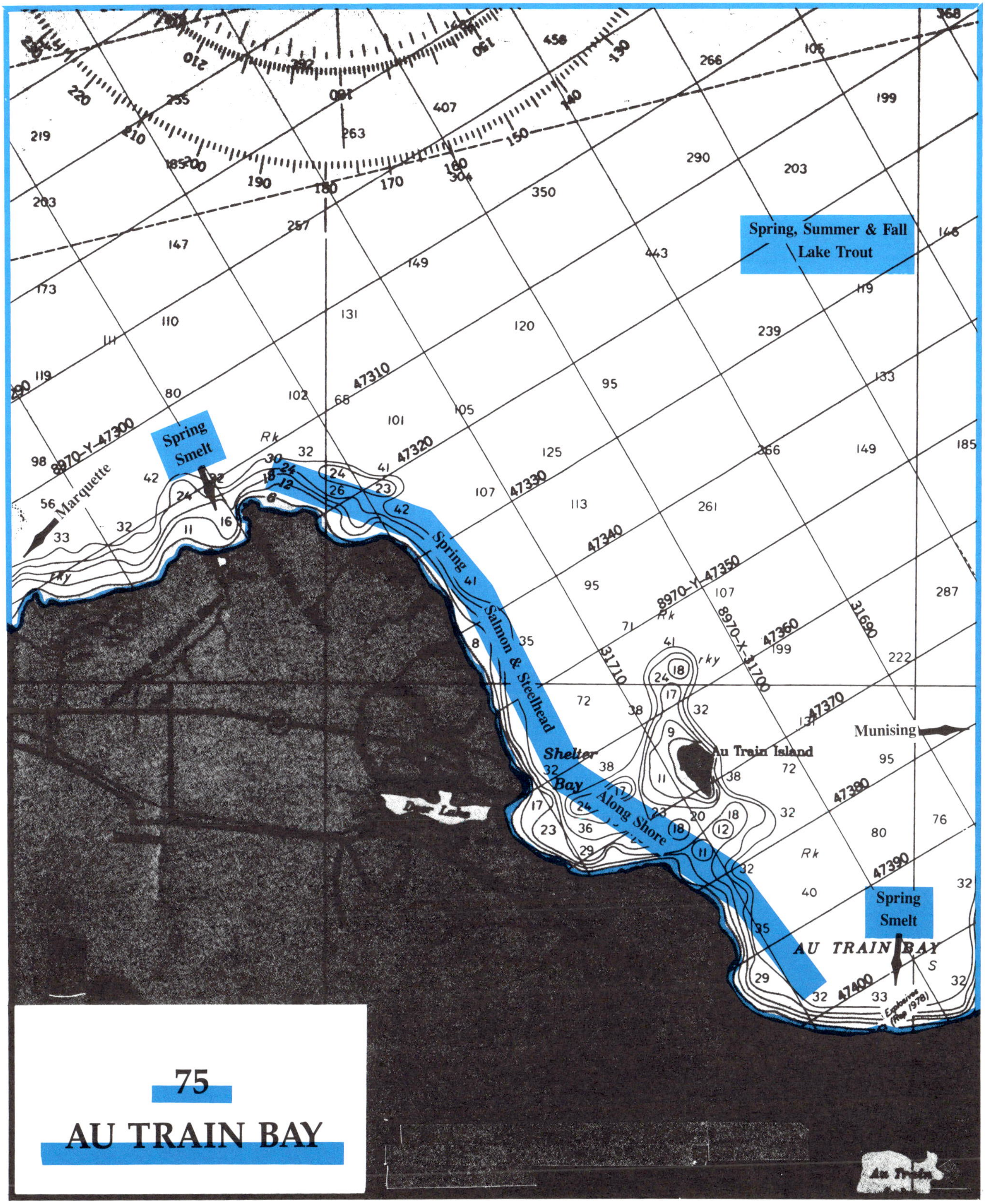

Charter Fishing:

Captain Dave Kimar, P.O. Box 144, Au Train 49806; (906) 892-8277. 30-foot T-Craft, *Anne K. III.*

Department of Natural Resources:

Two fisheries biologists work out of District Headquarters at 1126 N. Lincoln Rd., Escanaba 49829; (906) 786-2351. Their supervisor, also a fisheries biologist, works out of Regional Headquarters at 1990 US-41 South, Marquette 49855; (906) 228-6561.

Coast Guard:

Marquette Station, (906) 226-3312.

Rubber-Band Releases

Ever have trout and salmon slap at your lures without becoming hooked? Only running out of fuel or breaking a $500 graph can be more frustrating. Tightening releases or shortening the distance from cannonball to lure may help a little, but salmon and trout that get slap-happy seem to stay that way, sometimes for days on end. What can a troller do?

Well, if you have rubber bands aboard, you might just give them a try for your release system.

"They sure saved the day for me and my son Bill one day," said Joe Zikewich of Lake Orion. "We must have had 20 knock-offs from lake trout and kings. We tried everything. Finally, I found some old rubber bands in a tackle box and used half-hitches to secure them between our fishing lines and downrigger cables. After that we caught eight fish out of 10 hits."

At today's inflated prices, a fisherman with a week's pay in his pocket can walk into a tackle shop to buy lures and other trolling equipment and leave with hardly enough left over for a Coke and fries. *Inexpensive* is another reason why rubber-band releases make sense.

Emil Dean, the legendary charterboat skipper from Manistee (13), was an early pioneer of rubber-band releases and has been using them exclusively aboard his boat, the *Mary E.*, for some 10 years. His reason is simple: "I haven't had a broken line since switching to them."

Others cite ease in pulling lines and hooking up and sensitivity—even to depths beyond 100 feet—as other reasons for using rubber bands. They are also versatile and can be used with outriggers and planer boards, plus they allow for no-hassles stacking with downriggers.

I can't understand now why more anglers don't use them.

Tom Huggler
Otisville

This is the type of lake-trout fishing action that Lake Superior is capable of producing.

76
MUNISING

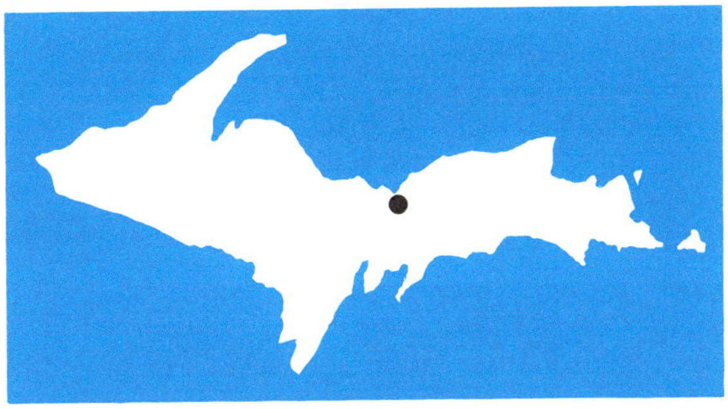

Nobody can hold onto a secret—especially a fishing secret—for long. When charterboat-skipper Pete Lindquist of Munising began pulling monster lake trout from his cooler, people wanted to know where he was getting them. It is Pete's business to be known as a good fisherman, so he is pretty free with information. The hotspot, he revealed, is a three-mile-wide by six-mile-long reef that lies about 20 miles north of Grand Island in Munising Bay. The reef comes up to within 65 feet of the surface, yet less than three miles away are Lake Superior's deepest waters at 1,330 feet.

How big are the lakers that Lindquist has been bringing ashore? Pretty big. Pete and his brothers have caught at least one of Michigan's five biggest forktails in each of the past three years. In 1982, one fat lake trout of 27 pounds, six ounces and another at 27-pounds-even placed fourth and fifth. A 25-pound, 10-ounce laker that was second in 1983 was only one pound off the state's largest fish that year. In 1984, a 26-pound, nine-ounce lake trout placed fifth, and a 31-pound, seven-ounce fish caught here by another Munising fisherman won third place. Lindquist's best laker in 1985 was only a 20-pounder.

"The fish averaged only eight pounds, smaller than usual that year," he said. "I think the reef is getting too popular with local fishermen."

Fishing Schedule

SPRING

Most of these lake trout are caught from mid-June through early August, although trolling begins off Munising earlier in the *spring* (by mid-May) and lasts until mid-September. Most fishermen pull wire, about half also add downriggers, and a few rig big planer boards or skis. Lindquist's set-up includes two downriggers, two pump poles with wire line, and two highlines (flatlines). Highlines get large silver Flatfish, while silver Flutter Spoons (run clean) or attractors with homemade yellow, blue or green trolling flies go on deeper-set offerings. Attractors are usually a combination of a dodger rigged 12 inches ahead of a cowbell string in order to provide plenty of flash in Superior's depths.

SUMMER

From midmorning until midafternoon produces the best *summer* trolling action, with high noon a prime time to have lures down. Lindquist believes that maximum light penetration is likely the reason. One of his best outings in recent years was on a dead calm summer day that produced 10 fish with a total weight of 150 pounds.

FALL

Lake-trout trollers also pick up cohos, and later in the *fall*, salmon catches improve throughout Munising Bay. Over the long trolling season, Pete figures that lakers constitute about 60 percent of his catch, with cohos and Chinooks contributing perhaps 30 percent and 10 percent respectively.

Munising Bay and the mouth of the Anna River produce salmon, brown trout and rainbow trout in spring and fall for both spoon tossers and spawn-bag fishermen. Those who pin single salmon eggs to small hooks and fish bottom with a slip sinker also catch menominees in spring and fall.

WINTER

Winter brings lake whitefish into Munising Bay. Ice fishermen catch the two- to three-pound whitefish (along with an occasional coho) by jigging with bobbing sticks. Tactics call for chumming the holes with whole-kernel corn, then fishing single salmon eggs or corn near bottom in 30-120 feet of water. Shanty towns indicate local hotspots. Some whitefish are available in summer, too, although fishermen then rely on wigglers or mayflies.

Planting Records

Munising Bay receives hatchery-reared lake trout, brown trout, splake, cohos and rainbows. Splake were first stocked in 1982. Releases were then discontinued for a couple of years but have now been resumed through at least 1990, with 20,000 yearlings scheduled for annual plant-out. Cohos were introduced in 1984, when 25,000 smolts were released, and plans call for 50,000 smolts to be stocked annually through at least 1990. During this period, the Munising Bay city dock site will also receive 10,000 yearling browns as well as up to 13,000 rainbows if stocks are available. The Grand Island ferry dock will get 60,000 lake-trout yearlings.

Facilities

The DNR maintains a small-boat harbor with transient accommodations, electricity, restrooms and holding-tank pump-out. Anglers can launch boats at public sites both east and west of town.

Further Information

Chambers of Commerce:

1. Alger County Chamber of Commerce, Box 405, Munising

49862; (906) 387-2138.

2. Upper Peninsula Travel and Recreation Association, P.O. Box 400, Iron Mountain 49801; (906) 774-5480.

Bait & Tackle Shops:

Jernigan's Sport Shop, 212 E. Superior, Munising 49862; (906) 387-2822.

Charter Fishing:

1. Captain Pete Lindquist, 120 Superior St., Munising 49862; (906) 387-2262. 24-foot Chris-Craft, *Venturer*.

2. Captain Thomas Boyak, 310 Cherry St., Munising 49862; (906) 387-2354. 22-foot boat, *Peggy Ann*.

Department of Natural Resources:

Two fisheries biologists work out of District Headquarters at 6833 US-2, Gladstone 49837; (906) 786-2351.

Coast Guard:

Munising Station, (906) 387-2041.

The Lure of Hard-Water Sport

Few outdoor sports have changed as much as ice fishing in recent years. Those scratchy wool Union suits have been replaced with lightweight cold-weather garb that can turn back the most frigid blast. Catalytic heaters in insulated shanties are now the norm instead of charcoal buckets in tarpaper shacks. Although you'll still see old-timers wearing mickey-mouse boots, most ice anglers now opt for comfortable felt-lined pac-style footwear.

The equipment is different, too. Graphite ice rods and light line are making their way onto the ice. So are through-the-ice depth-finders and plenty of new jigs and other lures. Veteran ice anglers' talk is now spiked with comments about late ice, early ice, fish metabolsim and structure fishing.

And ice anglers are fine-tuning tactics. Some doctor lures with splinters of prism tape. Others cut styrofoam bobbers, then reverse them to set hooks on a bobber riding up—indicating a bluegill or crappie venting its gills—rather than waiting for it to be sucked under.

Those reasons—along with media hype, increased focus on ice fishing as a family sport, and new fishing contests from growing winter festivals around the state—are why more and more people are pulling away from winter Sunday afternoon television shows.

If you've strayed from the sport of ice fishing in recent years or have yet to give it a go, the time was never better. Thanks to plenty of catching opportunities around the Great Lakes, the good old days are now.

Tom Huggler
Otisville

Forktails Fight Back

Even the world's largest freshwater lake can get into a jam. First, 30 years ago, lampreys all but closed the door on outstanding lake-trout fishing in the Chippewa Indians' ***Gitchegumme,*** **better known as Lake Superior. Then, just when things were turning around—the lamprey problem under control and massive infusions of hatchery-reared lake trout going into the cold, deep lake—a new problem cropped up: Indian fishermen with pickup trucks full of lethal gill nets and a federal-court order in the glove box.**

For 12 years, negotiators for the Indians and the State of Michigan worked on a settlement. Complicating the issue were two separate treaties signed in 1836 and 1842 that halved Lake Superior and involved different bands of the Chippewa tribe. On March 28, 1985 (149 years to the day from the date of the original treaty in 1836), a settlement was reached with three of the Michigan tribes.

Treaty waters of that settlement include these areas: Lake Michigan—Grand Haven north, Lake Superior—mouth of the Chocolay River (near Marquette) east to Sault Ste. Marie, and Lake Huron—Alpena north.

Each of the three lakes is now being managed according to four zones, with key values assigned to each. These include (1) areas of off-limits to commercial Indian netting, (2) rehabilitation areas, where Indians will fish exclusively under strict rules, (3) areas where Indians may gillnet for up to five years before switching to impoundment gear, and (4) refuges where trap nets only are allowed as long as lake trout caught are released alive. The Indians have permission to target whitefish in treaty waters but are supposed to haul nets if the incidental laker catch—dead or alive—reaches 20 percent.

An important part of the settlement is that sportsmen may fish throughout all four zones. At this writing, negotiations continue with 13 bands of Chippewa Indians from western Michigan, Wisconsin and Minnesota in Lake Superior treaty waters west of Marquette.

Also what the settlement means to sport fishermen is that lake trout in the waters covered by the treaty are now protected in some areas, and the DNR can continue efforts to bring back good fishing through natural reproduction. This is occurring with varying degrees of success throughout Lake Superior. For example, in 1973, DNR test nets on two small reefs in the Marquette area revealed 25 percent and 45 percent native fish respectively (stocked fish are finclipped; native fish are not). Now those rates have soared to 80 percent for each reef, and throughout Lake Superior, sport fishermen report catching increasing numbers of unclipped fish.

Forktails are fighting back in Lake Superior.

Tom Huggler
Otisville

76 MUNISING

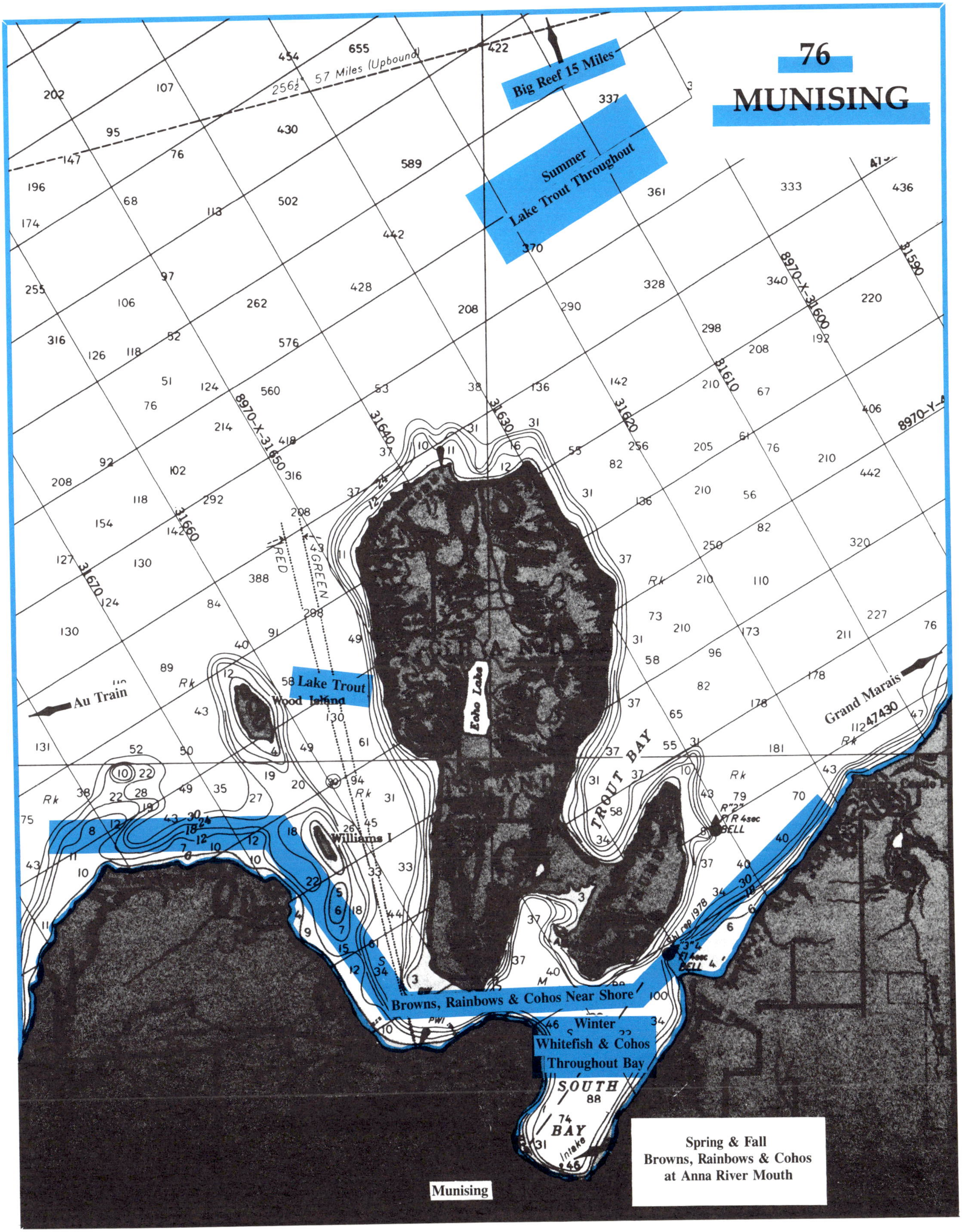
Big Reef 15 Miles
57 Miles (Upbound)
Summer
Lake Trout Throughout
Lake Trout
Wood Island
Au Train
Williams I
Echo Lake
TROUT BAY
Grand Marais
Browns, Rainbows & Cohos Near Shore
Winter
Whitefish & Cohos
Throughout Bay
SOUTH
BAY
Spring & Fall
Browns, Rainbows & Cohos
at Anna River Mouth
Munising

77
GRAND MARAIS

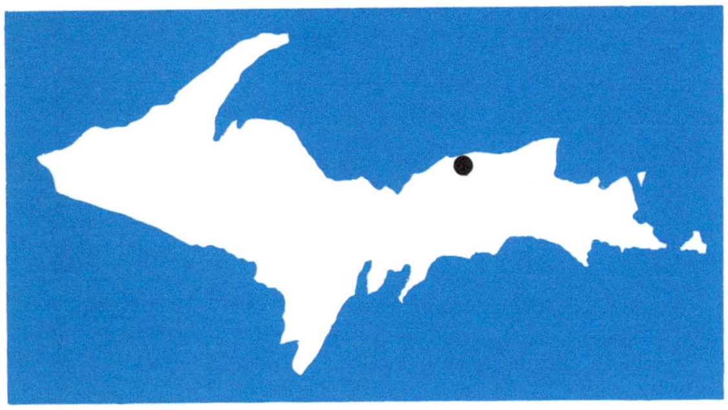

Grand Marais is a small village located on Lake Superior in the eastern Upper Peninsula. Although the area falls within Indian gillnetting treaty waters, there are some good fishing opportunities for several species off the piers, in the West and East bays of the harbor, and in shoal waters of Lake Superior.

Fishing Schedule

Spring sport begins as early as April, when the pier serves up menominees to fishermen using single salmon eggs. Rigging tactics include light line, buggy-whip rods, and either a small slip sinker or a couple of small split shots. Technique calls for slow jigging near bottom along the pier, and the best fishing typically occurs a day or two after a strong northwest blow.

Gail Van Alstine of Drayton Plains has had good menominee fishing—here and at the mouth of the nearby Two Hearted River—by slightly varying the above method. Gail pierces a single salmon egg to each of two No. 10 hooks rigged 18 inches apart on a monofilament dropper line. Three feet up the leader is a swivel and, above that, a small slip sinker. When the soft-striking menominees are hitting, it is not uncommon to catch two at a time.

Beginning about Memorial Day and lasting well into *summer* (usually through July), the smaller menominees are eventually replaced by lake whitefish to 4-1/2 pounds each. Fishermen rely on the same tactics as for menominees, plus they get occasional success using waxworms—fished under a light bobber—as well as dunking small flies and retrieving tiny spinners near bottom. The west pier is especially productive if you fish on the lake side of it.

Sporadic plants of steelhead/rainbows and Chinook and coho salmon have been made in the Grand Marais area from 1968 through 1984. Spring catching success is heavily dependant upon water clarity and wave conditions. Strong winds roil the water here and all but ruin fishing, but when the lake settles down, spoon casters and bait fishermen along the piers score, as do trollers off the rivermouth and in East Bay. In spring and fall, steelhead fishermen roll spawn along bottom or spincast small spinners and spoons at the mouths of the Sucker and Two Hearted rivers.

There are sporadic smelt-dipping opportunities in spring at these and smaller tributaries all along the Alger County shoreline.

Lake-trout fishing begins in early May off rivermouths and in shallows when fish are in close to feed. Small spoons and plugs in silver—with or without blue, green, yellow, orange, and chartreuse colors—work best. Summer laker seekers must head for 100-foot-plus water, where attractors and small spoons or flies (sometimes with cut bait added) produce best. Again in *fall*, the forktails return to shoal waters to spawn. Then, trollers take them while flatlining small spoons and plugs or while casting lures from the pier or even in West Bay itself.

Winter fishing is severely limited due to unsafe ice conditions on Lake Superior. Whitefish Bay (78), to the east, forms safer ice and produces some excellent sport for whitefish.

Planting Records

Annual lake-trout releases off Grand Marais will continue at 30,000 fish at least through 1990. Coho stockings were discontinued in 1984, but it is likely that a few fish will be available through natural reproduction. At least through 1990, the Sucker River will receive annual plants of 10,000 steelhead and 15,000 rainbows, and the Two Hearted River will get 15,000 steelhead. These river stockings are of yearling fish.

Facilities

The DNR maintains a harbor of refuge at Grand Marais with the following services: transient accommodations, gasoline and diesel fuel, water, electricity, holding-tank pump-out and a dock attendant. There is no telephone. A boat ramp is located at the west end of West Bay.

Further Information

Chambers of Commerce:

1. Alger County Chamber of Commerce, Box 405, Munising 49862; (906) 387-2138.
2. Upper Peninsula Travel and Recreation Association, P.O. Box 400, Iron Mountain 49801; (906) 774-5480.

Bait & Tackle Shops:

None known

Charter Fishing:

None known.

Department of Natural Resources:

Two fisheries biologists work out of District Headquarters at 309 W. McMillan Ave., Newberry 49868; (906) 293-5131.

Coast Guard:

Grand Marais Station, (906) 494-2551.

77
GRAND MARAIS

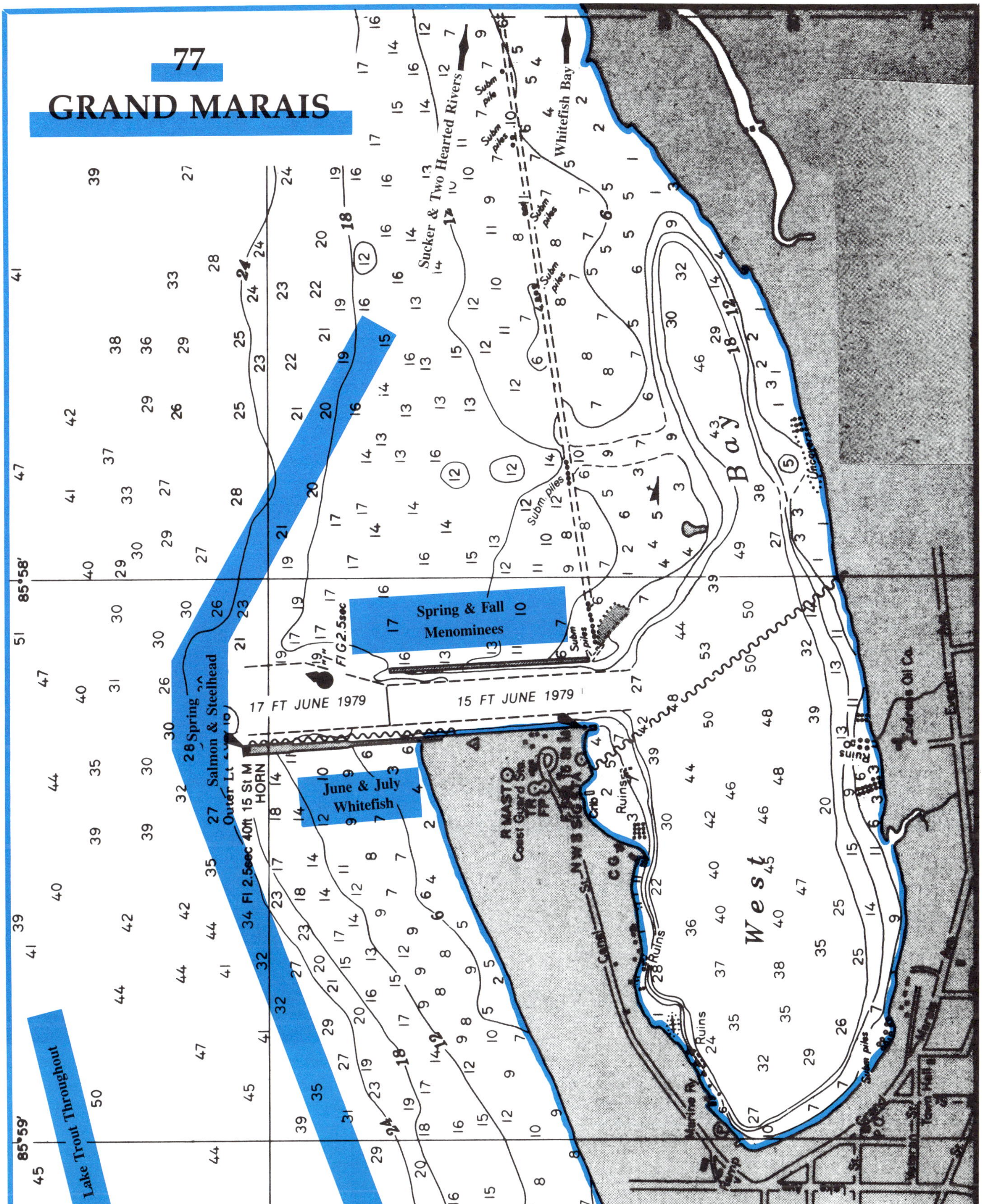

78
WHITEFISH BAY

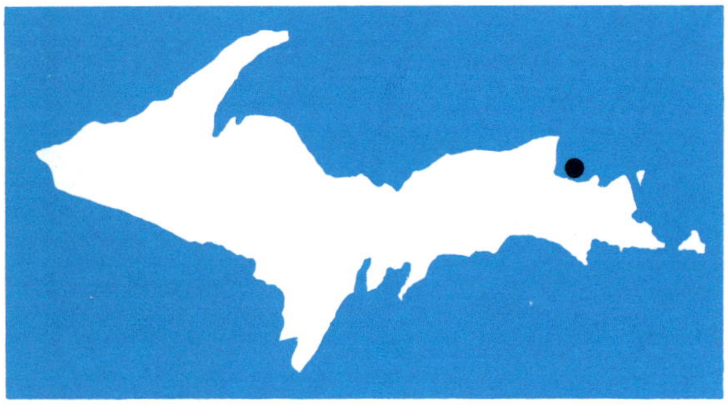

In spite of aggressive Indian gillnetting activities, huge Whitefish Bay, at the northeast corner of Lake Superior, offers fair to good fishing opportunities for a variety of species. And, all in all, these opportunities go largely underused by sport fishermen. Numerous bays, coves and streams punctuate the bay's shoreline. Islands dot the upper St. Mary's River as it flows from the bay toward Sault Ste. Marie, Michigan's oldest settlement.

Thus, the area offers fishing opportunities for trollers as well as stream and shore anglers. Boaters, however, should exercise caution, as storm-lashed waves can build to dangerous levels quickly, as dramatically evidenced by the sinking of the *Edmund Fitzgerald* in Whitefish Bay in 1975.

Fishing Schedule

SPRING

Spring activity kicks off in Waiska Bay west of Brimley, with jumbo perch the calling card. Another hotspot for yellow-bellies occurs over a sand bar between the mouth of the Tahquamenon River and Emerson, near the site of an old lumber camp. Wigglers, worms, and minnows are good baits.

Spring is also a key time to try any of the several rivermouths along southern Whitefish Bay for spawning steelhead. Anglers can troll across rivermouths with Rapalas and silver-plated spoons or can flip spawn bags or river flies into the flows themselves. Another reason that steelhead swarm to rivermouths is to pick off smelt.

Although smelt runs are down overall throughout Lake Superior, there are still enough of the silvery delights to go netting for them. Mother's Day is traditionally the best time.

In early May, whitefish come into the upper St. Mary's River from Lake Superior to seek the 35-foot-deep waters of the shipping channel. Bottom jigging with worms, chunks of pork, single salmon eggs, and partially cooked macaroni is the rated method.

SUMMER

Summer finds large concentrations of whitefish between the St. Mary's Rapids and the Sault Ste. Marie Edison power-plant runoff. The two-mile-long channel, 300 feet wide and 20 feet deep, transports large numbers of mayflies and Canadian soldiers, prime food for whitefish in late June and July. Fishermen report catches to six pounds by using streamers floated just under the surface.

June sees a good run of smallmouth bass in the Tahquamenon River below the lower falls. These are Whitefish Bay smallmouths that run the river—perhaps because they have no reef staging area in the open bay. Try spincasting spinners and small spoons as well as jigs.

The Tahquamenon River mouth is also a good spot to try for a tiger muskie, as occasionally these big fish work their way downstream from inland lakes where they were planted. In the river itself, the stretch between Dollarville Dam and the mouth of the Sage River yields both tigers and purebred (northern) muskies to 30 pounds. Trolling or spincasting big spoons, Believer plugs or bucktail spinners are surefire tactics and lures.

The lower Waiska River serves up walleyes in spring and summer, and anglers can also catch a few off the mouth of the Tahquamenon. Gillnetting activities, however, have cut deeply into the walleye take by sport fishermen. Whitefish Point itself produces intermittent catches of yellow perch off the breakwall there. For fishing opportunities west of Whitefish Point, see 77, (Grand Marais).

FALL

Fall fishing for brown trout is good to excellent in Ashmun Bay just upstream from Sault Ste. Marie. Recent test nettings by the DNR showed surprising numbers of browns. Troll U-20 or X-5 Flatfish in pearl, white or silver. Sugar Spoons, Rattlespoons, and Krocodiles are also good lures in those colors plus yellow, copper, and green. The upper river also gets a run of Chinook salmon in fall. Troll between the power plant and Six-Mile Point, but be on the lookout for ore freighters that ply the waterway. J-Plugs are good lures to put down.

Shore anglers might want to keep Pendills Creek mouth in mind for coho salmon. Pendills Creek was among the first Michigan streams to receive cohos 20 years ago, and although releases were discontinued long ago, natural reproduction occurs.

Many of the Whitefish Bay tributaries receive fall runs of pink or hump-backed salmon. Although the one- to four-pound pinks normally spawn in odd-numbered years, even-year runs of fish maturing in their third year of life are also becoming established. For best results, find bedded fish over gravel just upstream from river mouths. Then use No. 0 or No. 1 Mepps spinners or toss small streamers in bright colors.

WINTER

Winter fishing is good for whitefish in only five to six feet of water off the Emerson Bar, where a shantytown of 15-20 darkhouses normally builds each winter. Ice anglers chum with salmon eggs or canned corn, then pin wigglers to teardrop spoons and hope for a school of whitefish to come through. Success has picked up in recent years, and ice men can expect to take good numbers of three- to four-pound whitefish.

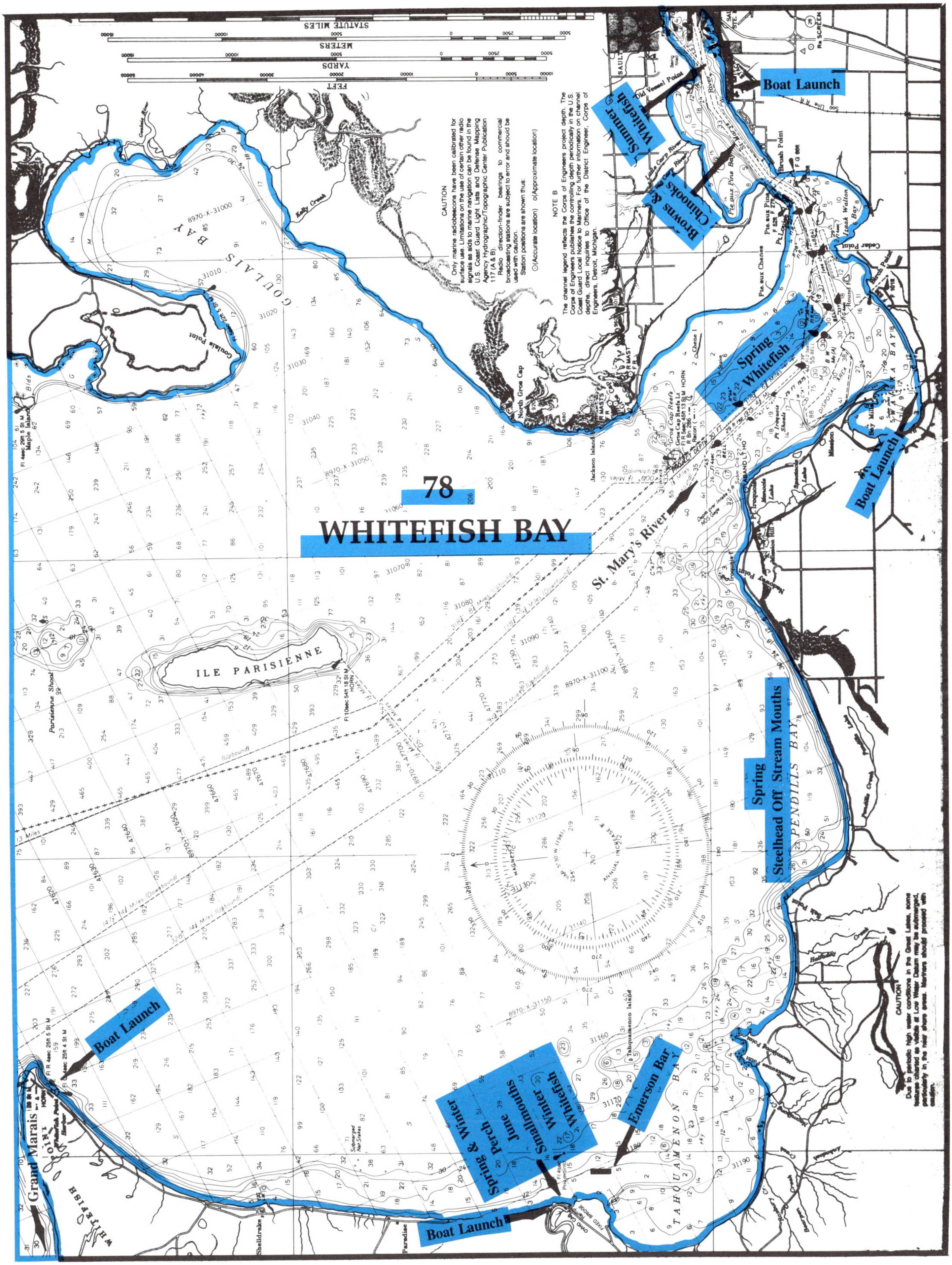
78
WHITEFISH BAY
Boat Launch
Summer Whitefish
Browns & Chinooks
Spring Whitefish
Boat Launch
St. Mary's River
ILE PARISIENNE
GOULAIS BAY
Spring Steelhead Off Stream Mouths
PENDILLS BAY
Boat Launch
Spring & Winter Perch
June Smallmouths
Winter Whitefish
Emerson Bar
TAHQUAMENON BAY
Boat Launch
Grand Marais

Whitefish Bay produces excellent catches of whitefish through the ice. —Photo by Steve Griffin—

WHITEFISH BAY (cont.)

Anglers can also jig for cohos and rainbows off rivermouths, with late ice in April considered to be the optimum time.

Planting Records

The DNR currently releases both Chinook salmon and brown trout in the upper St. Mary's River each year and hopes to introduce Atlantic salmon by 1990. According to DNR biologist John Schrouder, who supplied many of the details for this chapter, researchers are also experimenting with developing a Chinook strain that will spend its life in the upper river.

Annual releases of 100,000-150,000 fall fingerling lake trout over reefs near Tahquamenon Island were discontinued in 1984. The DNR has resumed them and will continue the releases until at least until 1990. Because of intensive native netting, however, few lake trout live to maturity in this region. Sport fishermen are advised to seek lakers elsewhere.

Facilities

Accommodations and facilities for fishermen are good in the region. Boaters with daily or seasonal use stickers affixed to their windshields may use launch facilities at Brimley and Tahquamenon Falls state parks. The city of Sault Ste. Marie maintains a free double ramp at Ashmun Bay. A harbor of refuge at Whitefish Point has a launch facility that offers gasoline, water and restrooms. A harbor and another boat launch at Sault Ste. Marie is located below the city and opposite Sugar Island. (For details, see 79, Upper St. Mary's River.)

The Sault area has a total of 900 rooms spread among 38 motels and hotels. Restaurants and other accommodations also abound. Further west, facilities dwindle, although there are plenty of camping opportunities. Primitive sites in the Hiawatha National Forest are supplemented by the two state parks.

Further Information

Chambers of Commerce:

Sault Area Chamber of Commerce, 2581 I-75 Business Spur, Sault Ste. Marie 49783; (906) 632-3301.

Bait & Tackle Shops:

Hank's Sport Shop, 119 Maple, Sault Ste. Marie 49783; (906) 632-8741.

Charter Fishing:

Dennis Dougherty, 1931 Riverside Dr., Sault Ste. Marie 49783; (906) 632-6490.

Department of Natural Resources:

Two fisheries biologists work out of District Headquarters at 309 W. McMillan Ave., Newberry 49868; (906) 293-5131.

Coast Guard:

Sault Ste. Marie Station, (906) 632-7880.

Emerson Bar(gain)

My son Eric and I often come to the Emerson Bar on Whitefish Bay to try for whitefish through the ice. About half the time we get skunked. But we don't mind, because it's cheap sport and, at times, we have also caught many limits of three- and four-pound fish.

One winter evening a couple of years ago, after firing up our lantern and cutting holes, we threaded waxworms and wigglers to our tiny teardrop spoons, then dropped them 10 feet to bottom. Knowing we'd take suckers off the bottom itself, we cranked up our baits a few inches. We have also learned to use light line (six-pound test) and to quickly set our hooks at the first nibble.

Eric, who was 11 at the time, did this and soon had a big whitefish flopping on the ice. Then it was my turn. Between us we were getting all the action we could handle. As Eric cranked up one scrapper, his other rod suddenly speared into the hole and disappeared! He tried to grab it but it was too late.

We finished with 19 whitefish from 19 to 24 inches long. Five more would have given us a two-man limit. At least that many broke us off during our evening of fishing fun.

Dan Farnsworth
Newberry

79

UPPER ST. MARY'S RIVER

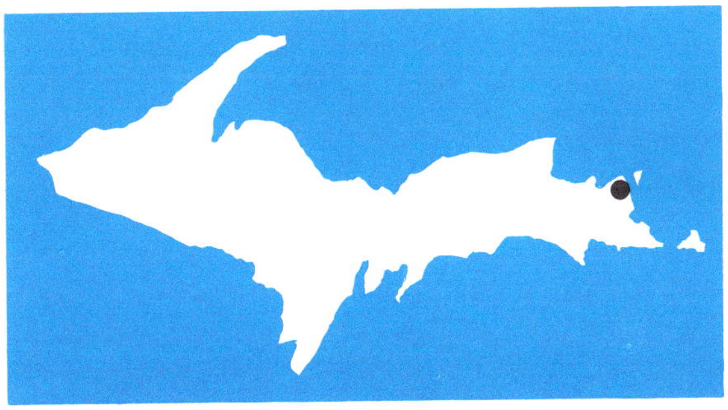

The St. Mary's River has it all—13 species of game fish, including Chinook salmon, steelhead, brown trout, northern pike, Great Lakes muskellunge, walleyes, yellow perch and smallmouth bass. There is something to catch here throughout the year.

Because of the number and variety of fishing opportunities in the river, plus its 63-mile length, I have divided it into two descriptions: (1) *Lower* (80), which includes the stretch from Neebish Island south to DeTour Village, where the river flows into northern Lake Huron, and (2) *Upper*, from Sault Ste. Marie downstream to Neebish Island. (See also 78, Whitefish Bay, and 81, Drummond Island, for additional details about the river.)

Fishing Schedule

SPRING

Ice-out on the St. Mary's normally comes sometime in April. By early May, whitefish work their way from Lake Superior into the upper river. In particular, they infest the 35-foot-deep shipping channel and weed beds along it to provide top-notch sport for winter-weary fishermen. In *spring*, best bait is small chunks of pork, partially cooked macaroni, or worms wrapped around small hooks and fished on bottom. Whitefish have a soft mouth, and, therefore, many are lost before coming to net.

Also in spring, perch fishing kicks off in shallow bays along the river. One of the better places to try is Baie de Wasai, on the northwest side of Sugar Island.

The northern-pike and walleye opener on May 15 finds anglers fishing weedbeds, flats and bulrushes in these same areas. Both American and Canadian waters of Lake George afford good northern action for spooncasters and trollers using Flatfish, Rapalas, and heavy spoons (Kush Spoons, Eppinger Trolldevles). Also, try the Shallows area just west of the Sault Ste. Marie city limits for pike. Six- and eight-pounders are fairly common here, with some lunkers scaling 15-20 pounds.

SUMMER

Summer brings catches of yellow perch, walleyes and smallmouths in the river channel. Brown trout, steelhead and salmon (both kings and pinks) show up in the river in force as summer wears on. From mid-August to mid-September, salmon infest the river from Mission Point to the St. Mary's Rapids. Fish stack up at the rapids and at the Edison Sault power-plant runoff, which is fed by a two-mile-long, hundred-yard-wide, 20-foot-deep canal. A salmon fishing derby, held in August and September, draws 100 or more boats on the river each day. By Labor Day, many king salmon in the 25-pound class have come to net. In addition, in 1985 the river was loaded with pink salmon and will likely be in the future.

Silver and green J-Plugs are rated salmon lures. Others to try include magnum Tadpollies, big Rapalas, Spoonbill Rebels and Bang-O-Lures. Any of the digging crankbaits (Hot 'N Tots, Fat Raps, Shadlings, Ugly Bugs) will work, too, but you'd better replace bass hooks with heavy-duty trebles if you don't want expensive lures torn apart. In addition, both kings and pinks will hit Little Cleos, Krocodiles and Kastmaster spoons. Silver, with or without hot colors, is the best choice. Troll upstream or down (just faster than the current), and vary depths from five feet down to within five feet of bottom.

July is an excellent time to get four- to six-pound whitefish in the Edison power-plant area, where the fish nail emerging hatches of mayflies and Canadian soldiers. Stab whole adult insects to small hooks or teardrop spoons, or drop wet flies three to four feet under the surface. The entire fishery is keyed to the life cycle of the insects, which, according to research a few years ago by the Great Lakes Fishery Laboratory in Ann Arbor, are being threatened by oil pollution. Researchers tested bottom samples in the Lake Nicolet and Lake George channels, which carry the St. Mary's River flow around Sugar Island. They found oil deposits and few *Hexagenia* (mayfly) nymphs in some 30 kilometers of the Lake George Channel from Sault Ste. Marie, Ontario (where a steel mill was the supposed polluter) to the north end of the lake.

FALL

All summer long and well into the *fall*, the Edison power-plant area, in addition to whitefish, also yields steelhead, brown trout and walleyes to trollers relying upon small silver-and-black or gold-and-black Rapalas.

September and October are choice times to take yellow perch from the upper river, too, with perch to two pounds each being served up from Labor Day on. Small minnows and worms work best when driftfished or jigged from an anchored boat.

In fall, speed trolling in the river channel and off adjacent flats from five to 20 feet deep can produce lunker-sized muskies, such as the 25-1/2 pound dandy that troller William Reiss of Auburn boated in the river in late August 1985. Giant spoons and plugs rate best. Try perch and crayfish colors first, then black alone or with orange, yellow or green.

WINTER

Winter fishing activities occur in shallow bays out of the river flow. Perch, walleyes, northern pike and whitefish are the target species.

The upper St. Mary's River yields big, brawling Chinook salmon, like this 22-pounder, every summer and fall.

Planting Records

The Soo Rapids area has traditionally received annual plants of Chinook salmon and steelhead. In recent years, brown trout have also been introduced. All three species, along with rainbow trout, will continue to be released at least through 1990. Spring fingerling Chinook plants will be maintained at 100,000 and steelhead yearlings at 15,000. Stockings of yearling brown trout, first released in 1984, will remain a steady 15,000. The DNR plans to add 20,000 yearling rainbows.

Facilities

A one-lane gravel ramp is located east of the Edison Sault power plant, and another launch site is available at city dock at the end of City Limits Road. There are also ramps on Sugar and Neebish islands. Sault Ste. Marie, Michigan's oldest settlement, offers plenty of accommodations for tourists and fishermen.

Further Information

Chambers of Commerce:

Sault Ste. Marie Chamber of Commerce, 2581 I-75 Business Spur, Sault Ste. Marie 49783; (906) 632-3301.

Bait & Tackle Shops:

1. R & R Marine Supply, 550 E. Portage, Sault Ste. Marie 49783; (906) 632-8934.
2. Riverview Sports & Marina, 3231 Riverside Dr., Sault Ste. Marie 49783; (906) 635-5795.

Charter Fishing:

Dennis Daugherty, 1931 Riverside Dr., Sault Ste. Marie 49783; (906) 632-6490.

Department of Natural Resources:

Two fisheries biologists work out of District Headquarters at 309 W. McMillan Ave., Newberry 49868; (906) 293-5131.

Coast Guard:

Sault Ste. Marie Station, (906) 632-7880.

Freshwater Wolves

About 25 years ago, when I was in high school, I made an unusual resolution: Never go swimming in the St. Mary's River. I had never been to the St. Mary's River, and, actually, I don't think I even knew where the St. Mary's River was.

But I did know that Lyle Reeser, a janitor and bus driver at our school, had caught a monster muskie there. Lyle and his family used to spend summer vacations on Neebish Island. He liked to fish for walleyes, and, if I remember right, had never before caught a Great Lakes muskie, although he had lost what he figured were big fish.

But not this big. I'm going on memory here, but I believe Lyle's lunker was either 51 pounds or 51 inches—maybe both. The state record, a Lake St. Clair monster, caught in 1940 by veteran muskie-man Percy Haver, weighed 62-1/2 pounds and taped 59 inches. One inch usually equals one pound with predators this size. Lyle fought the brute for an hour and a half, and more than once thought about cutting his line. But he finally tired the muskie out and somehow got it into the boat and back to the dock.

Even then I was thinking about being an outdoor writer, so when Lyle brought the fish back home, I asked him if I could take its picture. We went to the corner grocery/liquor store where he had taken the fish to be frozen, and I snapped a few shots with my Kodak Brownie camera. They turned out, too, and right now I would give up pork for a week if I could find them. Or Lyle. He disappeared, and I haven't seen or heard of him in nearly 20 years.

Catching a fish like that certainly rated big in the eyes of us boys, who were happy with five-pound pike. I don't think anyone threw a spitball on Mr. Reeser's bus for the rest of the semester.

I don't know about the others, but that muskie, with a head the size of a garden spade and a mouth full of wicked-looking teeth, made me think of a freshwater wolf.

I never have gone swimming in the St. Mary's River.

Tom Huggler
Otisville

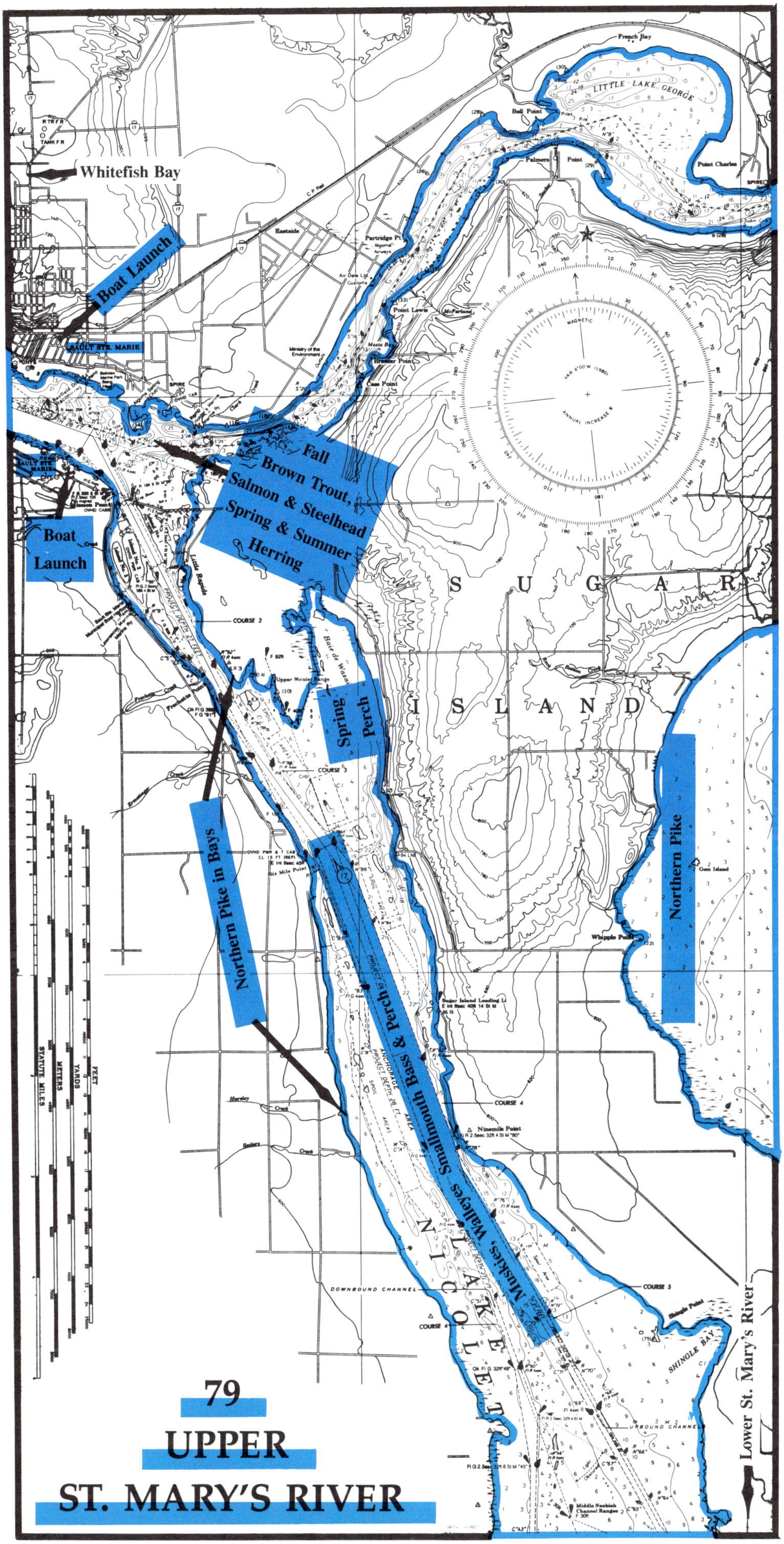
Whitefish Bay
Boat Launch
Boat Launch
Fall Brown Trout, Salmon & Steelhead Spring & Summer Herring
Spring Perch
Northern Pike in Bays
Smallmouth Bass & Perch
Muskies, Walleyes
Northern Pike
SUGAR ISLAND
LAKE NICOLET
LITTLE LAKE GEORGE
Lower St. Mary's River
SAULT STE. MARIE
STATUTE MILES
METERS
YARDS
FEET
79
UPPER
ST. MARY'S RIVER

80
LOWER ST. MARY'S RIVER

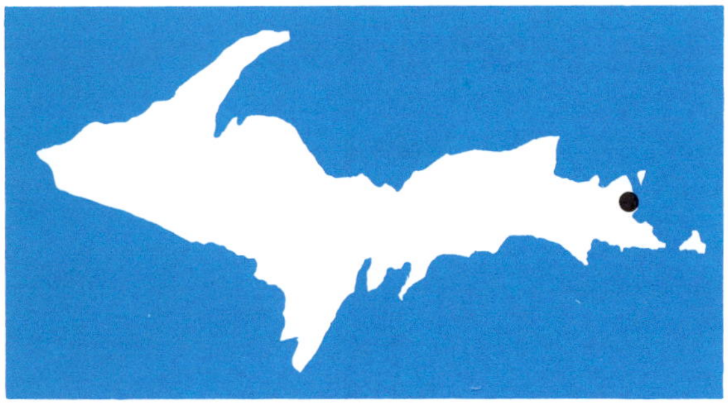

The St. Mary's River is one of the Upper Peninsula's, indeed the state's, finest fishing rivers. There are plenty of fish here, from two-pound perch to 25-pound muskies, three-pound bass to 30-pound king salmon.

This is big, fast water. Hard to believe that a river this short rates number eight among U.S. rivers for rate of flow.

Because of the number and variety of fishing opportunities in the river, plus its 63-mile length, I have divided it into two descriptions: (1) *Lower*, which includes the stretch from Neebish Island south to DeTour Village, where the river flows into northern Lake Huron, and (2) *Upper* (79), from Sault Ste. Marie downstream to Neebish Island. (See also 78, Whitefish Bay, and 81, Drummond Island, for additional details about the river.)

Fishing Schedule

SPRING

Walleyes are one of the biggest *spring* drawing cards. Anglers seek them in shallow Raber and Munuscong bays from the May 15 opener until mid-June, when the fish return to the river channel and deeper (30-35 feet) water. Water in the six- to eight-foot-deep bays is usually stained, plus it can grow riled quickly when thrashed by wind and storms.

Peak action can vary by two weeks or more, depending on weather conditions. One spring about 20 years ago, for example, a friend of mine came to Munuscong Bay for the opener. He hit the walleyes just right by drifting with nightcrawlers. For a year that was all I heard about. Next May 15, I went with him and, you guessed it, we got skunked—not even a nibble for three days of fishing. But when walleyes are in, catching can be phenomenal. So, many people make a mission of coming here each year.

Mike Modrzynski of Oscoda makes the trek, sometimes two and three times each year. He hooks whole crawlers, live minnows or leeches to 1/4-ounce lead-head jigs, then drifts with the wind or current while his bait taps along bottom a mere 10 feet away. Good jig colors are yellow, flame orange, and black. June-bug Spinners and nightcrawler harnesses take plenty of walleyes each spring, too. Another hot lure in 1985, when trolled, was the Hot 'N Tot in green-crayfish color with a fluorescent-orange stripe on the belly.

Perch fishing in spring is often outstanding in the Lower St. Mary's River, with action beginning soon after ice-out in April. A school of ruler-long perch can be just as exciting as a pack of small walleyes. Anglers get the spawning jumbo yellow-bellies by hooking wigglers or small minnows to jigs, teardrop spoons, and perch spreaders, then drifting across the bays and coves while keeping a tight line.

Northern-pike fishing also kicks off with walleyes on May 15. Both Raber and Munuscong Bay, as well as coves and bays on the Canadian side, have plenty of four-pound-average pike, but there are lunkers here, too. Modrzynski said that, just before his arrival in June, a Detroit angler boated a 25-pounder.

SUMMER

Summer fishing, in some respects, is even better. Joe Barden, a farmer from my home town, and his friends (all of whom carry both Canadian and American licenses) have come to Raber Bay for 38 consecutive years. Joe (who times his trips after the corn is cultivated and there isn't much else to do in mid-July but fish) has kept records of their catches. I wrote a magazine article that highlighted their 1982 trip, at that time their best ever. Of the 37 northerns they caught, 28 weighed over 10 pounds each, including a 17-pound 41-incher caught by Barden's 15-year-old cousin, Ross Millsaps. The Tennessee lad also caught the surprise of the trip, a 24-pound 43-inch muskie.

After I wrote that story, Joe had an even better trip—at least for lunkers. In 1983 he boated 17-, 19-, and 20-1/2 pound northerns—his lifetime best. On that same trip, a member of his party caught a 26-pound muskie.

The St. Mary's River channel also serves up Great Lakes muskellunge. Most are barely legal, but every now and then someone hooks into a lunker of 20-pounds-plus. Speed trolling Hot 'N Tots or big wobbling plugs trigger strikes from the toothy monsters. Exercise great care, however, when fishing in the channel, since huge freighters ply the river.

Some fishermen, like Barden, cast bucktail spinners (Buchertails, Mepps Musky Killers, Blue Fox Super Vibrax), heavy spoons (Eppinger Husky Devles, Rok't Spoons, Bearcats), and old wooden plugs (Suick Plugs, Pike Minnows, Creek Chubs). They drift along in 10 feet of water with the current or use an electric trolling motor to ease within tossing range of bulrushes.

Summer also brings outstanding herring fishing to the lower St. Mary's River. Top sport centers in the Lime Island area outside Raber Bay, as early as late June and lasting until late July some years. Since the herring are after mayflies hatching in the region, anglers catch the fish on small hooks baited with the insect.

Summer perch fishing remains good, and there are smallmouth bass in the river along with walleyes, channel catfish, rock bass and bullheads. King salmon, which begin ascending the river in July and August, can be taken with Rapalas, J-Plugs, and flutter-

80

LOWER ST. MARY'S RIVER

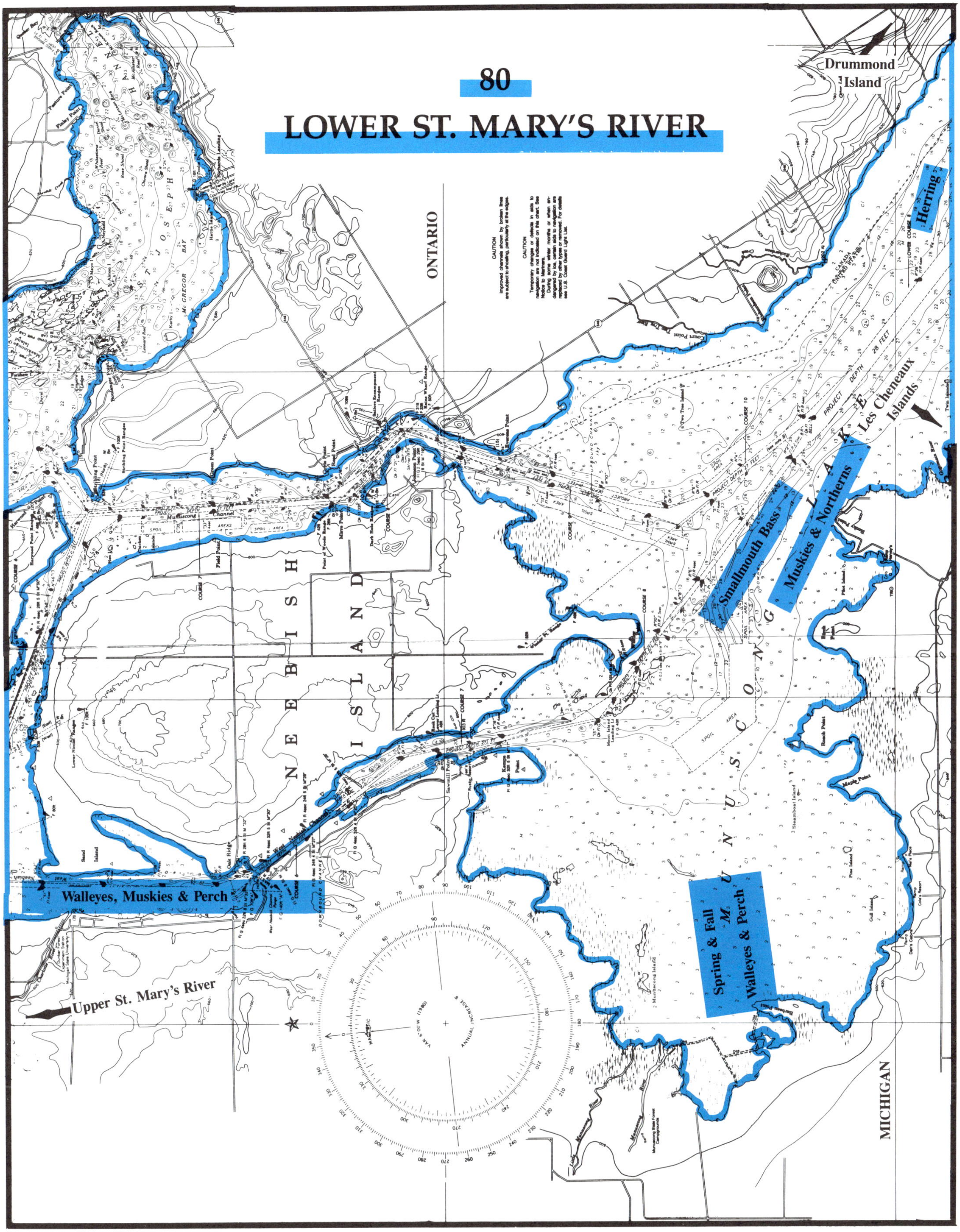

Both the American and Canadian sides of the St. Mary's River provide steady action for a variety of gamefish, including big muskies.
—Ontario MNR photo—

type spoons along the channel. In 1985 the river was loaded with pink salmon, too, which hit the smaller lures. Further, there are brown trout, lake trout and steelhead here.

FALL

Fall anglers gear up for yellow perch, pike, muskies, smallmouth bass, browns, steelhead and salmon. Early last September, DeTour Passage, between DeTour Village and Drummond Island, was jammed with pink salmon that were striking nearly any lure of any color. The better king salmon and trout fishing, however, will be further upriver. As temperatures cool, perch and walleyes again invade Raber and Munuscong bays to provide solid sport.

WINTER

Winter fishermen key on northerns, walleyes and yellow perch, with the bays, again, getting the most attention. There should be some decent lake-trout fishing, too, off DeTour Village, provided the ice is safe. Pike come via the spear and tip-up, walleyes and perch by jigging spoons sweetened with a slice of fish belly, a minnow or a waxworm.

Walleyes move across Munuscong Bay in schools, sometimes in water only a couple of feet deep. Anglers must sit quietly in order to catch them. Average size is two pounds, but fish to nine pounds are not a rarity. Late ice and early ice are usually the best times. Dave Taylor, another local friend of mine, fishes for walleyes each winter out of Johnston's Resort on Munuscong Bay. He and his buddies pinch minnow heads to big jack hooks or small spoons in yellow (especially if water is stained), red-and-white, and black-and-white colors.

Planting Records

The DeTour Village area began receiving lake-trout yearlings several years ago. In 1982, two million eyed eggs were released there, and the following year 25,000 fall fingerlings. The DNR does not plan to continue these releases, at least through 1990, but instead plans to release 75,000 Chinook fingerlings at the DeTour Ferry Dock each spring for the next five years. The DNR will, however, make annual stockings of 60,000 fall fingerling lakers at Trout Island Shoal in nearby Potagannissing Bay and 119,000 yearling lakers at other Drummond Island reefs. According to terms of the Indian netting agreement (see page 294) the DNR will also stock nearby Seymour Creek with 500,000 Chinook fingerlings each year through the year 2000.

King salmon, brown trout and steelhead taken in the lower river are likely from plants at Soo Rapids. For figures, see 79 (Upper St. Mary's River).

Facilities

DeTour Village, with a population of only about 500 permanent residents, does have accommodations for fishermen. Also, Goetzville and Pickford are not far away, and there are probably a dozen resorts on Munuscong Bay and several on Raber Bay. Most have launch sites at no charge to customers or for a nominal fee of a dollar or two for non-guests.

The DNR maintains paved ramps at DeTour Village and Raber Bay and a gravel launch site at Munuscong Bay. No fee is charged. The DNR has just completed a harbor of refuge at DeTour Village which includes transient accommodations, gasoline and diesel fuel, water, electricity, restrooms, shower facilities, a dock attendant, sewage pump-out and VHF-FM radio. The telephone number is (906) 297-2581

Further Information

Chambers of Commerce:

No local chambers serve the area. Contact the Upper Peninsula Travel and Recreation Association, P.O. Box 400, Iron Mountain 49801; (906) 774-5480.

Bait & Tackle Shops:

Most resorts carry live bait and some have fishing tackle.

Charter Fishing:

None known.

Department of Natural Resources:

Two DNR fisheries biologists work out of District Headquarters at 309 W. McMillan Ave., Newberry 49868; (906) 293-5131.

Coast Guard:

St. Ignace Station, (906) 643-9191, or Sault Ste. Marie Station, (906) 632-7880.

Fishing Secrets

When you fish an area for 38 straight years, you get to know it and its people pretty well. And usually, but in my case not always, you get to learn their fishing secrets, too.

One of the most interesting and knowledgeable fellows it has been my pleasure to know was Jack Fehner of Raber Bay. From the early days, when we fished from a small plywood boat pushed by a three-hp motor and pitched a tent in an orchard near the cabins that Fehner rented, I listened in fascination to his stories. Jack, a tall, raw-boned man who appeared to be of Scandinavian descent, told me how his parents had come from Canada to homestead here. And he spent hours telling me about the farming life they had lived and of the good fishing he had enjoyed.

Jack, who lived into his 80s, knew this region of the St. Mary's River better than anybody else. But he was one of the hardest fellows to get next to—at least as far as fishing secrets go—that I ever experienced. For years I tried to pry fishing secrets from Jack, but he was about as tight-jawed as a beagle with a hambone.

One time, he took my friend's young son with him across the river to Canada to go pike fishing. The stringer of pike they returned with would pop your eyes. Yet, nary a word from Jack about what technique they used or exactly where they fished. "Over there," he'd say as he waved his arm somewhere in the general direction of Ontario.

Through the years, though, the better we got to know him, the more talkative he became. And he did have some good fishing secrets. For example, he nearly always caught lake trout through the ice on his winter trips up to Lake Superior. But, for years, we never knew how. With eggshells, that's how. Catching was easy if you had eggshells, he finally told us. He would take along as many eggshells as he could find, then throw them into the hole so they would flutter to bottom and attract the trout.

Jack died not long ago and we sure miss him. Going to Raber Bay is not the same.

Joe Barden
Otisville

81
DRUMMOND ISLAND

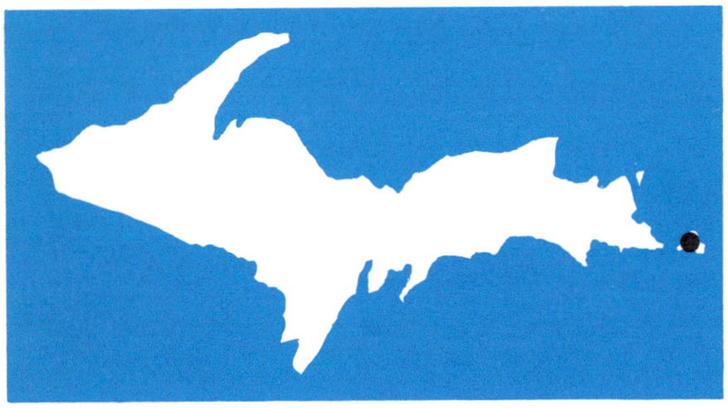

Gem of the Huron says the welcome sign greeting ferry passengers as they come ashore on 12- by 22-mile Drummond Island, at the far eastern tip of the Upper Peninsula. Drummond Island and its 136 square miles is aptly named. Its resorts beckon vacationers and sportsmen alike, and fishing opportunities abound.

A ferry whisks passengers and their vehicles across the mile-wide St. Mary's River between DeTour Village and Drummond Island every half hour around the clock. On the island itself, there are plenty of accommodations, including private and public campgrounds.

Fishing Opportunities

SPRING

In early *spring* (usually by late April), several little streams that flow into the island's coves and small bays host spawning runs of smelt and suckers.

Perch fishing kicks off about the same time or just as ice is leaving. Island-studded Potagannissing Bay is a fisherman's mecca for yellow perch (also walleyes and northern pike), and it is not uncommon to see up to 100 boats on the bay. Most perchers drift across the bay until they feel the familiar *tap, tap, tap* of a striking yellow-belly. Then they drop anchor until the school moves on. Sometimes fish will also be found immediately off stream mouths, including the outflow of the Potagannissing River, and other times they show up around the Maxton Bay islands and in Scott Bay.

Cane poles, bobbers, telescoping rods and spinning tackle are just a few of the myriad of equipment you might see. Steve Gilbert of Four Seasons Resort reports good catches on big-bladed (red- or green-flourescent) perch rigs and No. 4 hooks with minnows or wigglers. But there is simply no one best method for taking spring perch.

The prospect of bountiful yellow perch has brought Flint native Ray Ross, 73, here every spring for the past 23 years. A phone call to Lakeview Resort, where Ross and his friends stay, tells him whether or not the ice is gone and the perch are in to spawn. In Ross's experience, the earliest date was April 11; the latest, May 6. In spring 1985, Ray's party, using shiner minnows and snelled hooks attached to perch spreaders, caught 150 perch averaging nine inches. Ross has done better.

The best day of fishing Ross ever enjoyed occurred a few years ago, he says, when he and three friends began by drifting at Peck Island toward Scott Bay. But it was a slow fishing day, and, as shore approached, the two-boat party thought about starting engines and trying somewhere else. Suddenly, Ross nailed a 10-inch perch. Then his partner's rod began dancing with a twin fish. When their friends motored up in the other boat, the four men really took the yellow-bellies to task, boating 125 over the next couple of hours. Next day they stringered 100 more, all nine inches or better.

Wigglers (larvae of the mayfly) pinned to small hooks and slowly lifted off bottom will get strikes not only from perch, but also from ciscoes (lake herring) in the spring shallows. This fishery lasts throughout the eastern Upper Peninsula until mid-July.

Walleyes are another spring target after the May 15 statewide opener. Spawners show up off rivermouths in late May and early June. The average date for top fishing is June 6-7, but fishermen coming long distances would be wise to call first, as action is short-lived. Nightcrawler harnesses with split-shot sinkers pinched three feet above swivels do a number on walleyes when wind-drifted or slowly trolled around island structure and rivermouths. Other tactics include slow-trolling small Flatfish, Rebels, and crankbaits.

SUMMER

Summer fishing switches to northern pike and smallmouth bass. The entire Potagannissing Bay hosts plenty of weed beds, where northerns love to lie in wait to ambush prey. I recently photographed the five-fish limit catch of eight- to 12-pound pike caught by a Kentucky retiree who has fished here for years. Anglers like him come here from all over just for northerns, which average three pounds, with lunkers to 20 pounds.

Tactics include bobber fishing with chubs or suckers; trolling with Kush Spoons, Cop-E-Cats, Red Eyes, and Dardevles or old stand-by plugs such as Flatfish, Pike Minnows and Creek Chubs; or spincasting heavy spoons, Mepps bucktail spinners and floating plugs like Heddon Meadow Mice and Plunkers.

The north end of Drummond Island, accessible by durable 16-foot boat and 25-hp motor, features good smallmouth-bass fishing in rocky shallows when the fish come in to spawn in late June and early July. Spincasters report fun sport by tossing twister-tail jigs, spinnerbaits, small buzzbaits, straight spinners, and plastic worms, either from anchored boats or while wading from shore. Average size is 12-15 inches.

FALL

As summer merges into *fall*, bass anglers can still get smallmouths if they work gravel-bottom water off points and drop offs to 10 feet deep. Pike fishermen pick up trophy-sized fish,

81

DRUMMOND ISLAND

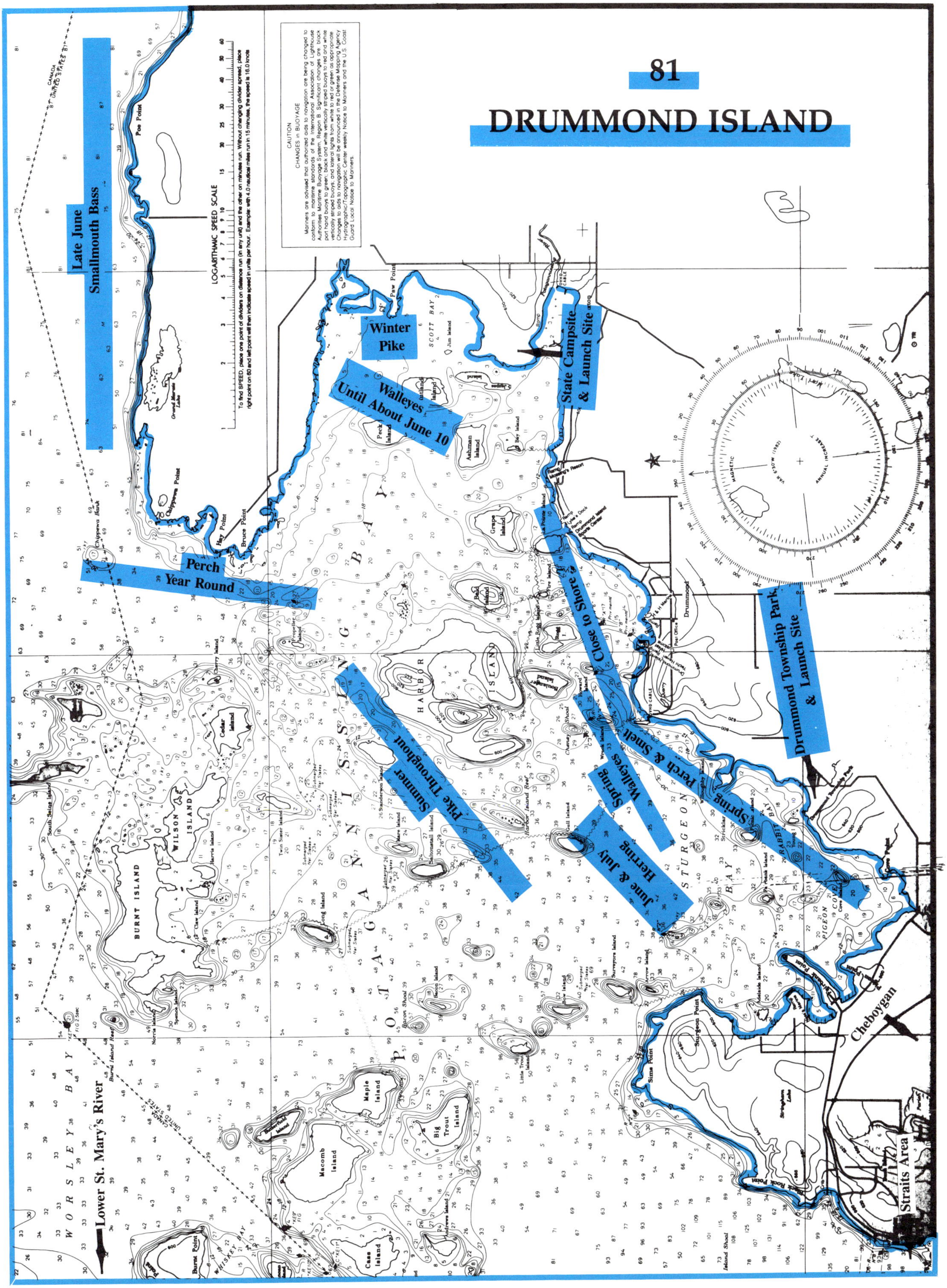

Scott Bay on Drummond Island is home to big northern pike like this 12-pounder. Ice fishermen use tip-ups or spears.

DRUMMOND ISLAND (cont.)

perch come back with another assault on shoreline shallows, and walleye fishing improves as waters cool. Some anglers report good herring catches as late as mid-October. Straying Chinook salmon from St. Mary's River and northern Lake Huron releases show up off stream mouths and in coves throughout the north and west shore.

WINTER

Winter pike fishing, with an occasional northern sagging scales to 20 pounds, is good for spear-throwers and tip-up fishermen in Scott Bay. Perch fishing remains steady through the ice off stream mouths and over weed beds. Late-ice conditions in April is an especially productive time for perch.

Planting Records

Each year through 1990, the DNR plans to release 60,000 fall fingerling lake trout at Trout Island Shoal in Potagannissing Bay. Other reefs in the Drummond Island area will receive a total of 119,000 yearling lakers annually during this period.

Facilities

Drummond Island has plenty of resort facilities, including cabin and cottage rental, housekeeping units, and campgrounds. For more details on these and other accommodations, contact the chamber of commerce (address listed below). Most resorts have boats and motors for rent and bait for sale, and some include them with the price of the cottage or cabin.

Many of the resorts have their own launch facilities, plus there is a free ramp at the state-run campground on Maxton Bay and at Drummond Township Park on Rabbit Bay.

Further Information

Chambers of Commerce:

Drummond Island Chamber of Commerce, Box 200, Drummond Island 49726; (906) 493-5245.

Bait & Tackle Shops:

1. Martin's Sportsman, 103 Ontario, DeTour Village 49725; (906) 297-6461.
2. Drummond Island Sport Center and Motel, Drummond Island 49726; (906) 493-5270.
3. Kelly's Sport Shop, Box 268, Drummond Island 49726; (906) 493-5509.

Charter Fishing:

Anglers may be able to make special arrangements with local resorts.

Department of Natural Resources:

Two fisheries biologists work out of District Headquarters at 309 W. McMillan Ave., Newberry 49868; (906) 293-5131.

Coast Guard:

Sault Ste. Marie Station, (906) 632-7880 or St. Ignace Station, (906) 643-9191.

A Picnic for Northern Pike

A night-falling rain had stopped when I awoke to a scarlet wash bleeding the eastern sky. A quick breakfast of oatmeal and warmed-over walleye fillets steadied my two partners and me for a morning's pike fishing off Drummond Island among the islands of Potagannissing Bay. By the time the sun popped, we were motoring our way toward Burnt Island in a 14-foot aluminum boat pushed by a 10-hp outboard.

Jerry Morris cut the throttle to a whisper as we passed Long Island, and I sent a gray/black straight Rapala with two pea-sized split shot ahead of it over the side. Jack Bellamy tested a frog-colored Flatfish in the water, then let it go until it was 30 yards behind our boat. It bobbed in our boat wake until Jack thumbed his spool and the lure slurped from sight.

Morris was rigging a nightcrawler harness when a savage strike nearly tore the rod from my hand. Rearing back, I felt the raw power of a fighting-mad pike on the other end. The fish boiled to the surface 20 yards away, then charged deep, as big pike do.

Bellamy burned his Flatfish back to the boat, then grabbed our net while I fingered my star-drag to remove a little tension. A moment later, 11 pounds of kicking-mad pike beat a tattoo into our boat bottom.

This was our first fish in a super day of pike trolling. Morris was next to drive home the hooks into a sag-belly fish that weighed 9-1/2 pounds and taped an even 34 inches. Our third fish drilled a red-and-white Dardevle that Jack had chosen to replace his Flatfish. By 11 o'clock, with the sun burning down on us relentlessly, we headed in. Seven clips on the metal stringer claimed seven northerns weighing from seven to 11 pounds each.

As often happens, the biggest fish got away. Bellamy had nursed one brute, which looked to be as long as a fence post, to the boat after a 20-minute struggle. But while diving under the boat, that pike, which we figured at 18-20 pounds, cracked Jack's rod on the gunwale and broke his 15-pound-test line.

Tom Huggler
Otisville

82

LES CHENEAUX ISLANDS

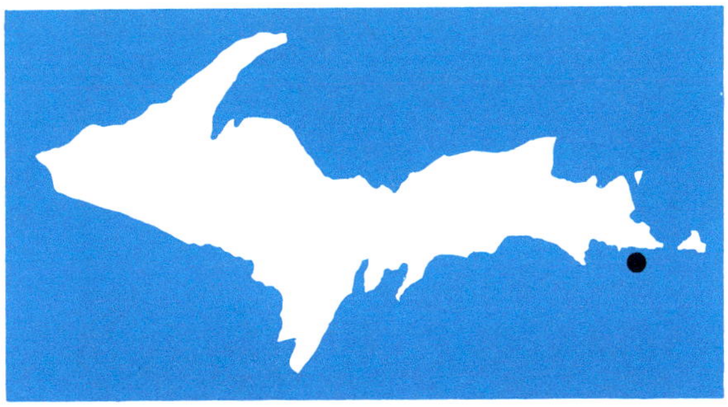

The 36 islands in the Les Cheneaux group make up some of the most beautiful and unique real estate in the Great Lakes area. The marl-bottomed reefs; dozens of coves, bays and channels; and plenty of bulrushes and weed beds also contribute to excellent habitat for fish. Three hundred years ago, French *voyageurs* traveled the Les Cheneaux going to and from Mackinac Island. Today, the still-beautiful islands attract sailboaters and anglers.

Yellow perch, northern pike and herring are the main species sought. As the Les Cheneaux waters deepen into northern Lake Huron, opportunities improve for Chinook and pink salmon and lake trout. Closer to shore, brown-trout fishing is expected to improve.

Fishing Schedule

SPRING

Spring fishing kicks off when yellow perch invade the channels and shallows to spawn. Wigglers and worms are good bait, along with minnows as summer advances. Smelt are available from creeks that pass under M-143.

The northern-pike opener on May 15 attracts spincasters, who flip spoons and crankbaits into bulrushes near shore and around the several islands. Plenty of small pike infest the shallows then, with an occasional 10- to 15-pounder showing up. Later in spring and throughout the summer, trollers pulling red-and-white spoons and bait fishermen using suckers and bobbers can also score on pike.

In May, spoons and small plugs run clean are productive for lake trout. Middle Entrance Reef, where hatchery-reared fish have been released, is the best place to try.

SUMMER

As spring swings into *summer*, trollers working the 50-foot-plus depths can box forktails by runnning attractors (chrome dodgers or cowbells) ahead of Andy Reeker spoons, Wobble-Glos or small Fire Plugs. Lures in various combinations of green, yellow, and chartreuse produce best. By stacking the attractor rigs with flutter-type spoons (Northport Nailers, Salmon Slammers, Flutter Devles), trollers will pick up occasional Chinook salmon and often plenty of pinks.

Perch fishing has been spotty throughout recent summers. Because perch generally travel in age-class schools, a good fishing year depends upon a successful year's hatch, with good recruitment for the next two years.

The Les Cheneaux also produce smallmouth bass for drift fishermen using Junebug Spinners or nightcrawler harnesses.

Herring fishing picks up by late June or early July and can provide some excellent sport for two or three weeks. The herring move throughout the Les Cheneaux in schools. Top bait is adult mayflies or waxworms threaded to small hooks or teardrop spoons. (For catching details, see "Here's to Herring," page 316.)

FALL

Fall fishing continues for northern pike, smallmouths and yellow perch.

WINTER

Winter sport keys on pike spearing from shanties, plus tip-up fishing. Perchers get action on Russian Hooks, teardrops, and size 4 and 6 Mitzi Ditzi Spoons in white and chartreuse. Early ice and late ice are twin key periods for pike and perch. Muscallonge Bay used to host up to 100 ice shacks in winter, but interest has dropped somewhat in recent years. Today, a shantytown of 20-30 structures normally builds by midwinter.

Moving west to east throughout the islands, the best fishing locations are: Search Bay—west side of Brule Point for herring; West Entrance—Brule Point for brown trout, south and north of Horse Rock Point for herring, Misner Bay for pike, north of Long Island and Hessel Bay for perch; Hessel Point area, Mackinac Bay and Snows Channel—for northern pike; Muscallonge Bay—for perch, pike and herring; Cedarville Bay northwest of Island No. 8—for herring; Government Bay—for perch and herring; southeast Moscow Channel—for perch and brown trout, McKay Bay—for herring; Prentiss Bay—for northern pike and herring.

Planting Records

Middle Entrance Reef off Marquette Island received 75,000-100,000 yearling and fall fingerling lake trout annually in the early 1980s. No releases were made in 1984; the DNR, however, planted 30,000 fall fingerlings in 1985 and will continue to do so at that rate each year through 1990.

In the Hessel-Cedarville area, 10,000 and 15,000 fall fingerling brown trout were stocked respectively in 1980 and 1982. In 1983, 20,000 yearling browns went into the Les Cheneaux here. The following year the DNR began planting Brule Point with a release of 15,000 yearling browns and plans to continue that annual commitment at least through 1990. Lakeside Road Access north of Hill Island will receive an equal number during that period. This should result in a good spring, fall, and possibly winter fishery.

Facilities

The DNR operates free two-lane paved launches at Hessel and Cedarville. In addition, many of the resorts that service the Les Cheneaux have launch facilities for their guests or for a nominal fee to non-guests. Many of the resorts also have boats and motors for rent.

Further Information

Chambers of Commerce:

Les Cheneaux Chamber of Commerce, Cedarville 49719; (906) 484-3935.

Bait & Tackle Shops:

Most of the resorts in this area have live bait and some have tackle for sale. Here are names and telephone numbers (all area code 906) of several:

1. Paul's Waterfront Cottages on Cedarville Bay, 484-2868.
2. Loreli Lodges and Marina in Hessel, 484-2636.
3. Les Cheneaux Park Cottages on Snows Channel, 484-2419.
4. Irene's Antique Shop on McKay's Bay, 484-2288.
5. Spring Lodge & Cottages at Cedarville, 484-2282.
6. Barefoots Resort on Hill Island Rd., 484-2270.
7. Hills Point Resort on Hill Island Rd., 484-2876.
8. Torsky's Resort on Snows Channel, 484-3342.

Tackle and bait are also available at:

9. Gambles Store in Cedarville, 484-3339.
10. Hill's Marina in Hessel, 484-2640.
11. Bob's Bait and Tackle in Cedarville, 484-3037.

Charter Fishing:

None known. Check with resorts for guide availability.

Department of Natural Resources:

Two fisheries biologists work out of District Headquarters at 309 W. McMillan Ave., Newberry 49868; (906) 293-5131.

Coast Guard:

St. Ignace Station, (906) 643-9191.

Spring smelt are just one of several reasons many anglers look to the Les Cheneaux Islands. —Michigan DNR photo—

A Game of 20-20

I have fished the eastern Upper Peninsula for some 35 years for a variety of gamefish species. Pike spearing and tip-up fishing through the ice grew to be an early love. And one of my favorite places to go is in the Les Cheneaux Islands.

The object is to find a reef or dropoff in six to 10 feet of water where northerns are likely to cruise in search of food. Good fishing times are early and late ice, although I prefer the early season because late ice can be unpredictable and dangerous.

Spearing from an ice shack, where you patiently watch the gloomily lighted hole while surrounded by pitch blackness, is a silent, solitary sport. You spend a lot of time thinking and waiting for what, to me, is the sportsman's greatest thrill—watching a lunker pike suddenly appear in the spearing hole. Then your heart will pound as though a 10-point buck is creeping by your stand.

Like big bucks, big pike come from nowhere. They are so beautiful and so fast. Make any noise at all—like bumping the shack—and they are gone like magic. Snowmobiles, passing jets, or even road traffic can spook them.

At Les Cheneaux one December morning in 1978, I sat with spear poised over the hole and watched my 10-inch sucker decoy become very nervous. He had good reason: a huge northern suddenly appeared. I flung my heavy, sharp spear at him, aiming behind the head where his neck would be, if pike had a neck.

My aim was true, and, after quite a struggle, I got the sag-belly fish through the door of my spearing shack and onto the ice. Years before I had speared a pike weighing in the teens. This one looked bigger.

It was, and my biggest pike ever, a 43-incher, now graces our living room wall. When I counted back to my first experience with Les Cheneaux northerns, I realized it had taken me exactly 20 years to get this trophy. How much did he weigh? Twenty pounds, right on the mark.

Louis Colegrove
St. Ignace

82

LES CHENEAUX ISLANDS

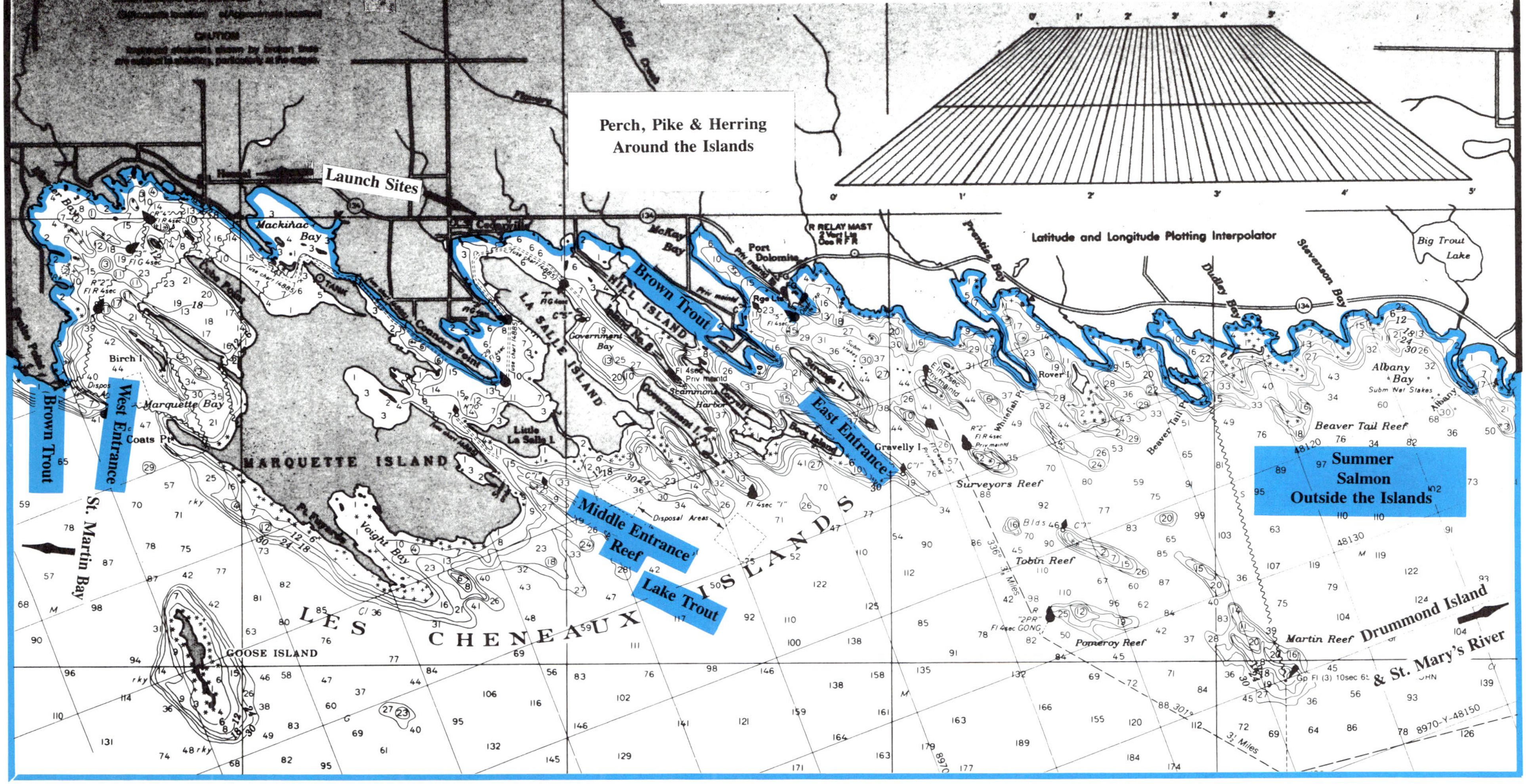

83
ST. MARTIN BAY

St. Martin Bay, located around the corner from St. Ignace in northern Lake Huron, affords unique structure and fishing opportunities. Further, it has become the target of stepped-up trout and salmon releases by the DNR.

Most years, fishing is good, and St. Martin Bay is popular with both Upper Peninsula and downstate fishermen.

Fishing Schedule

SPRING

In *spring*, yellow perch show up in the Pine River, but access can be difficult since most of the land is privately owned. The Carp River, on the west side of the bay, also receives perch in spring. Public land is found there, along with a boat launch. Other good spring perching grounds lie off Redman's Park, and yellow-bellies can be caught off and on throughout the bay. Wigglers are a choice spring bait.

Spoon tossers and spawn fishermen work the Carp River mouth in spring for brown trout and steelhead. The Carp itself is a decent steelhead river and is becoming more popular with spring fishermen each year. It currently opens April 1 and closes December 31, with Mud Lake outlet being the upstream limit.

About the time of the general trout opener (last Saturday in April), the Carp River also receives a run of smelt.

SUMMER

Summer anglers catch a few lake trout around St. Martin and Big St. Martin islands, but for the most part lakers are not taken in St. Martin Bay. Chinook and pink salmon, as well as brown trout, are. Late summer is especially good, as the kings and browns, along with steelhead, home in on the Carp River, where they were released. Pink salmon also appear in the Carp and Pine rivers, but they sustain themselves through natural reproduction.

Trollers and shore anglers eagerly await the return of these fish, but catching success varies from year to year. St. Ignace sport-angler Louis Colegrove said brown-trout fishing, in particular, was exceptional three or four years ago, and now that the DNR has pledged to continue annual releases of yearling browns he looks for excellent fishing to return. The overall 1985 fishing season, however, was poor throughout the Straits area, according to Colegrove. High water and winds were likely to blame, as were odd weather patterns which brought a late summer, including stifling heat after Labor Day.

Slow trolling with U20 Flatfish in orange, silver or pearl is the rated tactic for browns. J-Plugs, Northport Nailers, and Ping-A-Ts do a number on the big king salmon here to spawn. Pink salmon nail nearly any small spoon offered.

Carp River mouth anglers toss Krocodiles, Little Jewels, and Dardevle Rok-t spoons. They are opportunistic, hoping to catch any of the species mentioned. Silver, with or without a hot color, seems to produce best. And don't overlook spawn, especially fresh steelhead or brown-trout roe. When knotted into marble-sized bags and tossed into the current, the spawn is productive for salmon, steelhead, and browns, which enter the river in that order. Action for the trout species lasts until Thanksgiving some years. Veterans like Colegrove, who has fished the eastern Upper Peninsula for 35 years, look for a nasty east wind and a rainy day. "Those are the best conditions for brown trout," he says.

A few nice-sized smallmouth bass are caught in the bay each summer, along with northern pike to 12 pounds. Channel catfish also appear to be coming back, with the Pine River being the best place to try.

Herring are a tremendous draw each summer, beginning about July 4, when the tasty deep-water fish invade St. Martin Bay to gobble hordes of mayflies hatching off the reefs. Action normally lasts two or three weeks, but it can begin as early as late June and continue into August. Anglers catch the one- to two-pound fish, along with an occasional whopper crowding three pounds, on mayflies and long poles. (See "Here's to Herring, page 316.)

FALL

Fall action centers mainly on trout and salmon as mentioned, plus perch are available.

WINTER

Winter fishermen key on perch and northern pike, although interest (as determined by the number of ice shacks) appears to be flagging in recent years.

Planting Records

Plantings of trout and salmon in the Carp River go back many years. Coho releases were last made in 1980, but Chinook stockings of 50,000-100,000 spring fingerlings have continued steadily since. The DNR plans to maintain a release of 100,000 kings each year through 1990.

Annual plantings of 10,000 steelhead yearlings will increase to 15,000 for the next five years. An equal number of brown-trout yearlings, first stocked in 1983, will continue as well. And in summer 1985, as part of an Indian gillnetting settlement, the DNR released 55,000 walleye fingerlings in St. Martin Bay. These fish should reach catchable size by 1987.

83

ST. MARTIN BAY

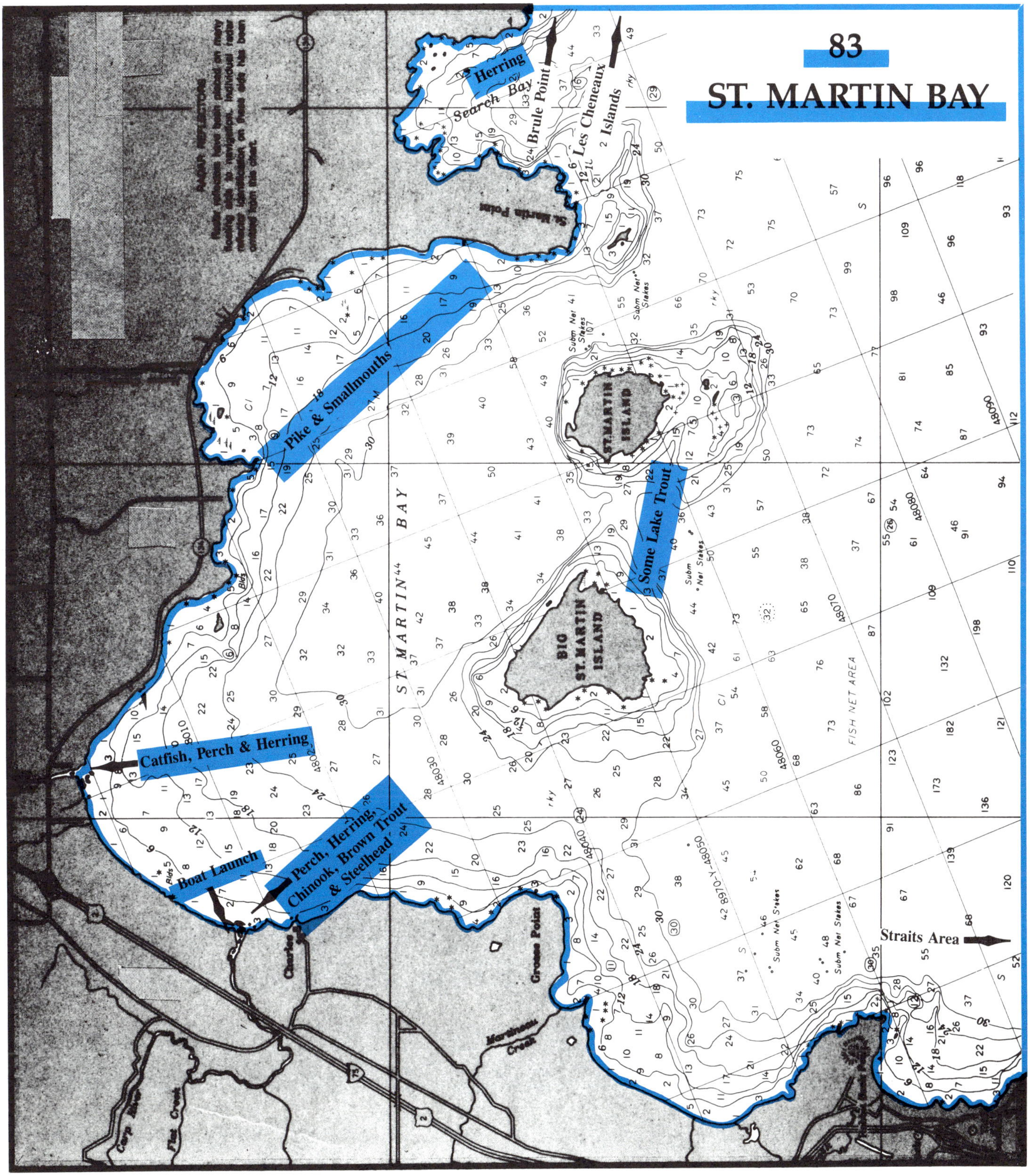

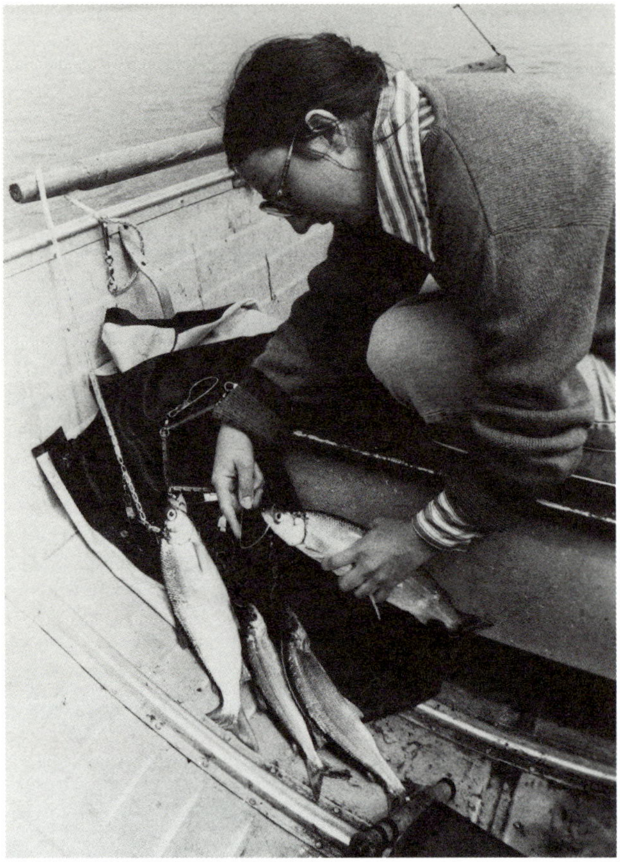

Lucy Smith of Marquette, Michigan, adds another northern Lake Huron herring to the stringer. —Photo by Richard Smith—

ST. MARTIN BAY (cont.)

Facilities

The DNR operates a free paved boat launch at the mouth of the Carp River. Small boats can also be launched at the end of Gorman Road. The nearest town is St. Ignace (population, 2,600), which caters to tourists, including fishermen.

Further Information

Chambers of Commerce:

St. Ignace Area Chamber of Commerce, South State St., St. Ignace 49781; (906) 643-8317.

Bait & Tackle Shops:

1. Northern Michigan Outdoor Supply, 838 N. State, St. Ignace 49781; (906) 643-7481.
2. Ace Hardware, 7 S. State, St. Ignace 49781; (906) 643-7721.

Charter Fishing:

None known.

Department of Natural Resources:

Two DNR fisheries biologists work out of District Headquarters at 309 W. McMillan Ave., Newberry 49868; (906) 293-5131.

Coast Guard:

St. Ignace Station, (906) 643-9191.

Here's To Herring

Each summer beginning about the Fourth of July, we eastern Upper Peninsula sportsmen get a taste of fishing unheard of elsewhere in Michigan. Midsummer, you see, is the time of the herring invasion to marl-bottomed reefs of northern Lake Huron. We eagerly anticipate their return. And when they do, we enjoy two or three weeks of some of the year's best sport.

Herring fishing is keyed to the hatching of millions of mayflies. Larvae of the mayfly (*Hexigenia*), known as *wigglers*, live in lake-bottom mud for several years, then swim to the surface on a warm midsummer night and emerge as mayflies. Herring (and other fish) snatch them up, both as nymphs and as adult insects. The mayfly hatch begins off reefs in the Drummond Island area and works its way west.

Mayflies are literally everywhere when a big hatch is in progress. When herring enter St. Martin Bay in early July, we fishermen pick up mayflies under street lights and use them for bait. We pin teardrop spoons (red or white are very productive) or small hooks under the backplate between wings and bring the barb out the head. This gives the bait a natural look. Then, with the help of 12- to 16-foot cane poles and a tiny split shot one foot above the bait, we swing the offering from the boat and allow it to sink slowly. Sometimes the herring hit it just under the surface. Other times the bait must sink to bottom 15-20 feet down.

Herring travel in schools throughout St. Martin Bay. But you can always tell where they are. Fleets of 50 or more boats will be clustered over them. Best spots for me over the years have been the mouths of the Carp and Pine rivers. Also, the west shore of Brule Point is good, as is the Green Island area at the Straits of Mackinac.

How many herring can you catch? Well, there is no limit in size or creel. When our party of three fishermen have about 80 on the stringer, we call it quits.

Louis Colegrove
St. Ignace

HOW TO RECORD YOUR TROPHY CATCH

Many fishermen realize too late that the fish they have released or eaten could have been a record. There are three repositories to consider for entering your trophy Great Lakes catch.

National Fresh Water Fishing Hall of Fame

The National Fresh Water Fishing Hall of Fame, P.O. Box 33, Hall of Fame Drive, Hayward, Wisconsin 54843 (715-634-4440) has U.S. sport-caught records for over 125 fish species in all-tackle all-line classes. Annual membership is $12, but you do not have to be a member to enter your catch. There are some stringent rules and regulations, however, that apply. They include:

1. Making certain that you are the only person to touch the line and tackle during your encounter with "the big one."

2. Getting the fish weighed on a scale that bears a number, inspector and date of check.

3. Weighing your fish *ONLY ONCE* and in the presence of two disinterested witnesses, whose full names and addresses you should record. Also be sure to measure girth, fork length and total length of the fish.

4. Having your fish identified as to species by a professional fisheries person or taxonomist. Get the identifier's full name, address and place of employment.

5. Taking photos (color is best) of the fish broadside for further positive identification purposes. A black-and-white photo is also useful for future press reprint purposes. Use a good camera, take well-lighted, clear, sharp close-up photos. For small fish close-ups, waist shots are best.

6. Saving the first 25 feet or more of line next to the hook/bait for laboratory line-test purposes. Wind the line on a notched piece of cardboard to avoid kinks or tangles and send it with your application. For flyfishing records, save 15 inches or more of the tippet used, leaving the fly/hook attached. For rod/line/no reel or ice-fishing records, only the heaviest of species is recognized, so a line sample need not be submitted.

The International Game Fish Association

The International Game Fish Association maintains all-tackle, line-class and tippet-class categories for over 150 freshwater and saltwater fishes. Rules and regulations are exacting. For information on them, copies of entry forms, and ordering details for the latest edition of their 300-plus page record book, write to The International Game Fish Association, 3000 E. Las Olas Blvd., Fort Lauderdale, Florida 33316-1616.

The Michigan DNR Master Angler Awards Program

Each year 600-700 anglers enter their trophy Michigan-caught fish in the DNR Master Angler Awards program.

Arm patches are awarded to all entries meeting established minimum weights, except that no more than one patch per species is awarded to each angler per year. Master Angler Certificates are awarded to anglers who catch State Record fish or one of the top five fish of each species entered during the calendar year.

Rules are simple:

1. Fish must be taken by legal Michigan sportfishing methods in public waters of Michigan.

2. Weigh fish on inspected scales (grocery stores, meat markets, etc.) and record scales' inspection date and, if possible, inspector's name. (Scales' owner should have a record slip of inspection date and inspector's name if same cannot be located on the scales.) Record catch location and date of catch.

3. Obtain signature of two witnesses verifying weight of the catch.

4. If the catch exceeds the listed current State Record (see following chart), you must contact a DNR Fisheries biologist for positive identification and verification. To be certified as a state record, the fish must be fresh or fresh frozen. Mounted fish will not be considered for the record.

5. A clear, closeup side-view photo of the entire fish, for identification purposes (color photo preferred), must be submitted if the entry has not been identified by a Department fisheries biologist. Please try to show the fins and tail in a spread-out position, if possible.

6. Submit entry and photo to DNR, Fisheries Division, Box 30028, Lansing, Michigan 48909. Forms and assistance are also available from DNR District and Regional Offices (see listings in the text of this book or *Michigan Fishing Guide* for office locations.)

7. Entries for the previous calendar year must be received in the Fisheries Division Office by January 10th.

8. Fisheries Division reserves the right to reject an application if the entry does not meet the established criteria. *NOTE*: Master Angler entries should be kept frozen at least two weeks past submission of application form in case further identification is required.

Minimum Entry Weights and Current State Records

Species	Min. Ent. Wt.	Current State Record	Species	Min. Ent. Wt.	Current State Record	Species	Min. Ent. Wt.	Current State Record
Lake Sturgeon	70-0	193-0	Burbot	5-0	18-4	C. Catfish	8-0	47-8
Atlantic Salmon	12-0	32-10	Walleye	9-0	17-3	F. Catfish	10-0	38-2
Chinook Salmon	30-0	46-1	Sauger	5-0	6-9	Brown Bullhead	2-0	3-1
Coho Salmon	12-0	30-9	Perch	1-12	3-12	Black Bullhead	1-8	2-0
Pink Salmon	3-0	6-2	LM Bass	6-0	11-15	Yel. Bullhead	1-8	3-7¼
Kokanee Salmon	1-0	1-15½	SM Bass	5-0	9-4	Bowfin (Dogfish)	7-0	14-9
Rainbow Trout			White Bass	2-0	3-3	Redhorse Sucker	4-0	9-0
(Steelhead)	16-0	26-8	Rock Bass	1-8	3-10	White Sucker	2-8	7-3
Brown Trout	16-0	34-6	Warmouth Bass	1-0	——	Longnose Sucker	2-0	6-9
Brook Trout	2-0	6-2	Green Sunfish	0-12	——	Hog Sucker	1-8	1-13
Lake Trout	18-0	53-0	Bluegill	1-0	2-12	Carpsucker	3-0	4-3
Splake	14-0	16-4	Pumpkinseed	0-12	1-0	Carp	20-0	61-8
Gt. Lks. Musky	20-0	62-8	Redear Sunfish	1-4	1-9	Freshwater Drum	7-0	26-0
Northern Musky	20-0	45-0	White Crappie	1-12	2-10	Lk. Whitefish	6-0	12-14
Tiger Musky	20-0	51-3	Black Crappie	1-12	4-2	Men. Whitefish	1-0	3-12
Northern Pike	18-0	39-0	Gar	5-0	15-0	Lk. Herring (Cisco)	2-8	4-15½
						Mooneye	0-12	1-2

How to Pick a Charterboat Captain

The ability to catch fish is not usually the first requirement that fishermen shopping for a charter consider. In fact, it isn't even the second or third criterion. According to preliminary results of an in-depth study of 80 Great Lakes captains in Michigan and about 450 of their customers who returned questionnaires, MSU researchers found some interesting reasons as to how potential customers choose a boat for hire.

The captain's ability to *locate* fish was the number one priority. His hospitality was second, and the safety provisions of the charter service was third. Ranking fourth in importance was the captain's ability to *catch* fish in the area. Next considerations were the species of fish available in the area and the comfort and other amenities (fish cleaning, guaranteed catch or no pay, etc.) offered.

The findings parallel those of another recent study conducted at Texas A & M University, which also indicated that catching fish was not the most important factor in a satisfying fishing trip.

The charterboat captains listed in this book are, to the best of our knowledge, the finest guides available. Either the author has fished with them or they have been highly recommended by trustworthy and discriminating anglers. However, there are, undoubtedly, many good ones that we have overlooked. For that reason and because many of the captains change ports and fishing operations as opportunities change, readers might want to pick up a free copy of *Michigan Fishing and Specialty Charters* from the Travel Bureau, Michigan Department of Commerce, P.O. Box 30226, Lansing 48909.

If you have never fished aboard a boat for hire, consider bringing along soft-soled shoes, sunglasses, a hat or cap, sunscreen lotion, rain slicker and jacket. In spring and fall, dress as though it is 25 degrees colder because on the lake it probably will be. Bring plenty of eats and beverages (check with the captain to see if alcoholic beverages are allowed) in an ample cooler.

Why ample? Hopefully, to hold all the fish you'll get to take home!

PLACE NAME INDEX

THE AUTHOR

Tom Huggler lives on a small farm in Otisville, Michigan. Besides writing articles on hunting and fishing, he pens fiction pieces and stories on farming, history, travel and biography.

Huggler is a full-time freelancer whose writings appear regularly in many of the nation's finest outdoor magazines. He is a regular monthly contributor to *Great Lakes Fisherman*, *Lakeland Boating*, and *Michigan Out-of-Doors* and is Michigan Editor of *Outdoor Life*.

Huggler brings many years of fishing expertise throughout the Great Lakes to this book.

Fish Michigan—Great Lakes is Huggler's fifth book. His other works include:

Trout Streams of Michigan, Vol. I; editor (1977)
Westwind Woods (1978)
Midwest Meanders (1984)
Hunt Michigan! How To, When To, Where To (1985)

--Photo by Randy Carrels--

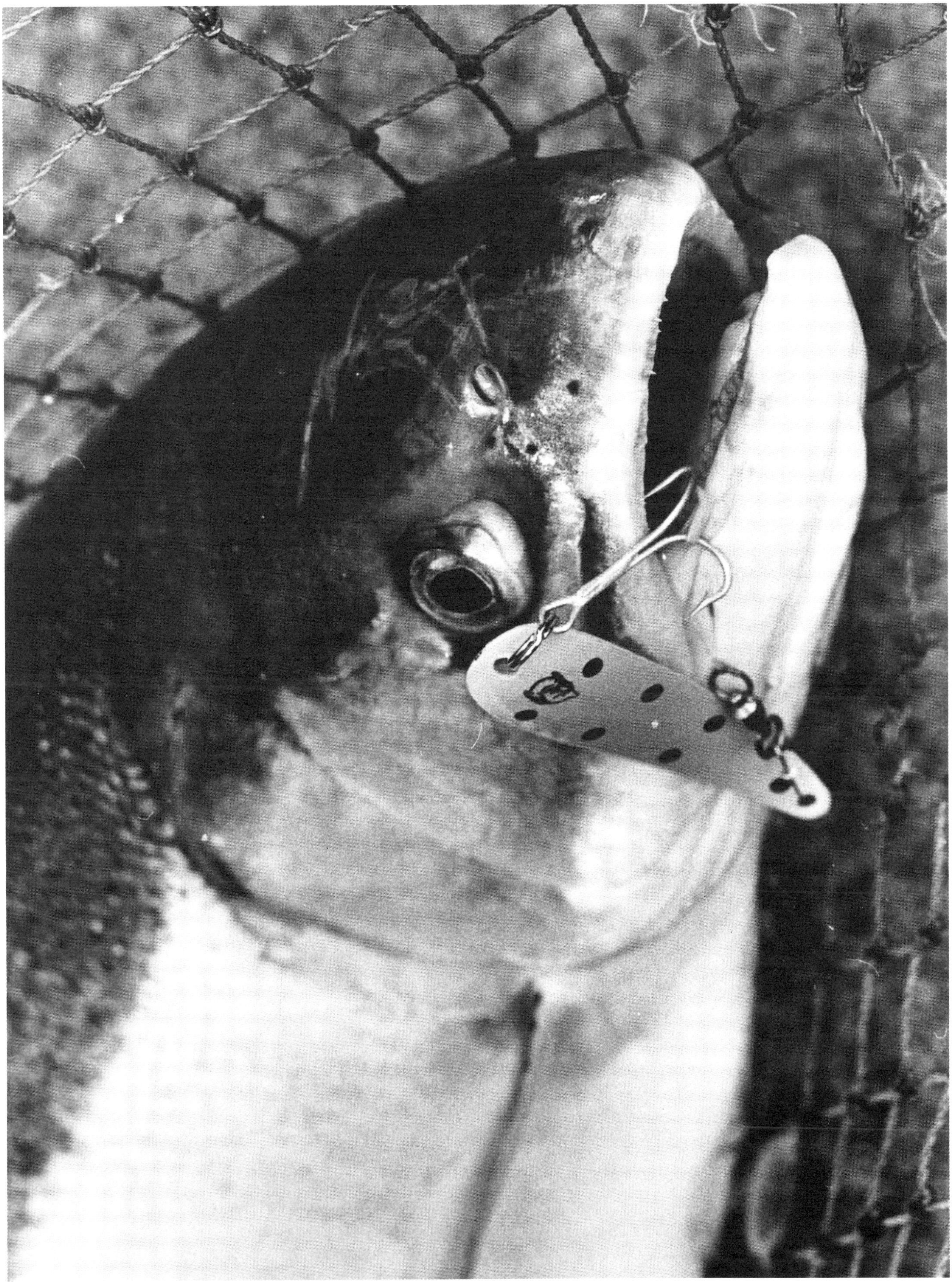